THE POLITICAL ECONOMY OF HUNGER

SCHOOL OF ORIENTAL AND AFRICAN STUDIES

University of London

Please return or renew by the last date stamped below.
A fine will be charged for late return.
Application for renewal should be made on or befo
by post or by e-mail
LIBRENEWALS@SOAS.AC.U

6/11/01

SOAS LIBRARY
WITHDRAWN

D1321535

WIDER

Studies in Development Economics embody the output of the research programmes of the World Institute for Development Economics Research (WIDER), which was established by the United Nations University as its first research and training centre in 1984 and started work in Helsinki in 1985. The principal purpose of the Institute is to help identify and meet the need for policy-oriented socio-economic research on pressing global and development problems, as well as common domestic problems and their interrelationships.

The Political Economy of Hunger

Selected Essays

Edited by

JEAN DRÈZE, AMARTYA SEN
AND ATHAR HUSSAIN

CLARENDON PRESS · OXFORD

Oxford University Press, Great Clarendon Street, Oxford OX2 6DP

Oxford New York
Athens Auckland Bangkok Bogota Bombay
Buenos Aires Calcutta Cape Town Dar es Salaam
Delhi Florence Hong Kong Istanbul Karachi
Kuala Lumpur Madras Madrid Melbourne
Mexico City Nairobi Paris Singapore
Taipei Tokyo Toronto Warsaw

and associated companies in
Berlin Ibadan

Oxford is a trade mark of Oxford University Press

Published in the United States by
Oxford University Press Inc., New York

© The United Nations University, 1995
WIDER: World Institute for Development Economics
Research (WIDER)—Katajanokanlaituri 6B,
00160 Helsinki, Finland

First published 1995
Reprinted 1997

All rights reserved. No part of this publication may be reproduced,
stored in a retrieval system, or transmitted, in any form or by any means,
without the prior permission in writing of Oxford University Press.
Within the UK, exceptions are allowed in respect of any fair dealing for the
purpose of research or private study, or criticism or review, as permitted
under the Copyright, Designs and Patents Act, 1988, or in the case of
reprographic reproduction in accordance with the terms of the licences
issued by the Copyright Licensing Agency. Enquiries concerning
reproduction outside these terms and in other countries should be
sent to the Rights Department, Oxford University Press,
at the address above

British Library Cataloguing in Publication Data
Data available

Library of Congress Cataloging in Publication Data
The political economy of hunger : selected essays / edited by Jean Drèze,
Amartya Sen, and Athar Hussain.
p. cm.—(WIDER studies in development economics)
Includes bibliographical references.
1. Nutrition policy—Developing countries. 2. Food supply—
Developing countries. I. Drèze, Jean. II. Sen, Amartya Kumar.
III. Series: Studies in development economics.
TX360.5.P65 1994 363.8'09172'4—dc20 94-31709
ISBN 0-19-828883-2 (Pbk.)

3 5 7 9 10 8 6 4 2

Printed in Great Britain
on acid-free paper by
Bookcraft (Bath) Ltd., Midsomer Norton, Avon

SOAS LIBRARY

FOREWORD

Poverty is not only a condition that prevents underprivileged individuals and families from satisfying their basic needs or participating fully in society. It is a socio-economic phenomenon, which on a large scale has wide-ranging effects on society as a whole: the growth and composition of the population; its health and level of culture; patterns of settlement and migration; economic development; political stability; and environmental issues. Poverty is a plague affecting all parts of the world in the 1990s and it has many faces and dimensions. Empirical studies on the nature, causes, and consequences of poverty have revealed its characteristics in both urban and rural environments, in developing and industrialized countries. The political, social, economic, and cultural dimensions of poverty all have their own roots. There are differences between countries regarding the factors that cause poverty and deprivation: the stagnation and decline of economic growth; low productivity; a poor level of public services; marginalization of sectors of society because of limited access to information and education; gross inequalities in income distribution; exclusion from gainful employment because of discrimination, etc. One of the most important and most common manifestations of poverty is the denial of access to the basic necessities of human existence.

The UNU/WIDER research programme 'Hunger and Poverty: The Poorest Billion', from which the papers in this volume were selected was concluded at the end of 1993. It was a comprehensive, multi-dimensional, policy-orientated project that ran over several years, with the participation of almost one hundred experts. Various books and pamphlets have been published as country monographs and comparative, issue-orientated studies, which have revealed the global dimensions of hunger and poverty. In the early 1990s the number of poor people included close to 30 per cent of the population of the developing world. The number of undernourished people was estimated at between 730 and 780 million—about 20 per cent of the population of the developing world, and about half of these people were suffering from chronic malnutrition. Asia is still home to most of these people, despite the fact that the numbers of malnourished have been in decline for some time. However, in sub-Saharan Africa and Latin America poverty and hunger have been on the increase since the 1980s.

Using an entitlement approach, the research team analyses factors such as land tenure, agricultural technology, price fluctuations, under- and unemployment, and age and gender discrimination. Analysis led to proposals for suitable public policies for the reduction or elimination of widespread hunger, and these recommendations have received special attention from governments and international organizations.

The feasability of the various projects depends on the capability of governments and local authorities to implement them on different levels. The next UNU/WIDER programme for 1994–5, 'The Human Dimension of Global Economic Development', will build on the foundations laid down in the Hunger and Poverty programme.

As the Director of UNU/WIDER, I am especially happy to present this book to readers. The world will have to deal with the social aspects of development in a much more efficient way than in the past. The improvement of the human condition is more than just a humanitarian proposition for the coming decades; it is a necessity for survival. No stable political order can be built on the foundations of societies in turmoil because of extreme poverty. This volume may serve as a source of inspiration and ideas for achieving that aim.

Mihaly Simai
Helsinki, 24 March 1994   Director of UNU/WIDER

CONTENTS

LIST OF CONTRIBUTORS

SUDHIR ANAND is University Lecturer in Quantitative Economic Analysis at the University of Oxford, and Fellow and Tutor at St Catherine's College.

KAUSHIK BASU is Professor of Economics at the Delhi School of Economics.

JEAN DRÈZE, is Fellow of the Centre of Development Economics at the Delhi School of Economics.

BARBARA HARRISS is University Lecturer in Agricultural Economics at Queen Elizabeth House, University of Oxford, and Fellow of Wolfson College.

ATHAR HUSSAIN is Director of Development Economics Research Programme at the Suntory–Toyota International Centre for Economics and Related Disciplines, and Director of Centre for Asian Economy, Politics and Society at the London School of Economics.

S. M. RAVI KANBUR, formerly Professor of Economics at the University of Warwick, is Head of the World Bank Resident Mission in Ghana.

S. R. OSMANI is Professor of Economics at the University of Ulster, Jordanstown.

JEAN-PHILIPPE PLATTEAU is Professor of Economics at the Facultés Universitaires, Namur, Belgium.

N. RAM is Associate Editor of the *Hindu*, a leading national daily newspaper, based in Madras.

CARL RISKIN is Professor of Economics at Queens College, City University of New York, and Senior Research Scholar at the East Asian Institute, Columbia University.

AMARTYA SEN is Lamont University Professor at Harvard University.

LIST OF TABLES

LIST OF FIGURES

LIST OF MAPS

INTRODUCTION

Athar Hussain

This volume consists of ten out of twenty-six papers and the general introduction to the three-volume *The Political Economy of Hunger* (ed. Drèze and Sen) arising from an 'investigation of the causal antecedents, characteristic features, and policy demands of hunger in the modern world' initiated by WIDER in 1985. The purpose of this volume is to make available a selection of them to a wider readership and which is also suitable for university courses. It neither supersedes the original volumes nor does it reflect on the merit of original papers. We therefore include the Table of Contents of the parent volumes to encourage readers to refer to them. Its geographical focus is Asia and Sub-Saharan Africa. For reasons of space we have had to omit some case studies of these regions and also of Latin America. It also excludes papers which are relatively technical and of interest to a specialist audience. The term 'political economy' appearing in the title was commonly used in the eighteenth and nineteenth centuries to refer to what would later come to be known as economics. However, the coverage of treatises on political economy was different from that of the present-day economics, and the term has in recent years been resuscitated to refer to analyses of issues that cut across disciplines, in particular economics and politics. Its use here emphasizes that the choice of issues and methods of analysis is not bound by economics narrowly defined.

Borrowing a medical term, hunger is a 'syndrome': a combination of symptoms which are found in varying degrees in particular cases. There is no unique set of characteristics of general endemic hunger nor of its extreme form, famine. There are clear instances to which the term 'famine' has undisputed application, such as the situations in some sub-Saharan African countries in recent years. But there are also others which partake some central features of undisputed instances, such as a sharp rise in the death rate from the usual, but lack others. For example, Sen refers to 'boom famines', when economic activity is buoyant and the average income comparatively high, and 'slump famines', when economic activity and the average income are both lower than usual. In particular, 'endemic hunger' covers a broad spectrum and may continue to exist without attracting attention even though over time it may claim a heavier death toll than famines.

Traditionally, undernourishment has been analysed in terms of actual food intake compared to the required level. As is well recognized, the 'required level' varies widely with age, sex, physical activity, and climate. Moreover, there may be significant inter-individual differences in the utilization of food intake. Some have taken this variation a stage further to argue that the body adapts (autoregulates) itself to large fluctuations in food intake through a compensating variation in storage and the metabolic rate without any adverse physiological effects. Thus, the argument goes, the measurement of undernutrition on the basis of food intake exaggerates the incidence of hunger. The main contribution of this literature is more to emphasize wide inter-individual variation in calorie and nutrient requirement consistent with 'normal' functioning of the body than to establish 'autoregulation' or adaptation. It rightly cautions care in measuring undernutrition. The dividing line between 'adaptation' and 'symptom' of hunger is not pre-given. Low weight, short height, and a slow metabolic rate may be regarded either as adaptation to undernutrition or its symptoms. The distinction between the two involves the judgement of what requires intervention and what is to be left as is, which is based not only on physiological factors but also on social and economic norms of physical capabilities. The literature on nutrition is large and is reviewed in various contexts by Harriss in this selection, and Dasgupta and Ray (1990), Osmani (1990), and Svedberg (1990) in the original volumes.

As shown by case studies, famines and hunger take a variety of forms; although they share overlapping similarities, each has some unique features to it. Moreover their causes may be different. The diversity of forms and causes suggests that explanations of famines and hunger in terms of a single factor or a general law are bound to be deficient and even misleading. Typically such explanations equate famines with 'food shortage' and rely on some version of the Malthusian world view. As an explanatory factor 'food shortage' begs a number of questions, such as, 'what is the geographical frame of reference?', 'is the reference to production or consumption?', and 'if to the former, what is being assumed about market exchange in food nationally and internationally?'. Sen (1981), Drèze and Sen (1989), and Drèze in the two papers in this selection draw on a wide range of cases to show convincingly that in the twentieth century famines have happened even when the overall supply of food was higher than average and improving. No less important, in numerous instances public action has succeeded in averting famines in cases of a serious shortfall in the food supply. Malthusianism in its explicit form would seem to be discredited but it resurfaces in various guises in the analyses of hunger as 'too many people and not enough food'. In a very trivial sense it is true in that if those starving did not exist then there would be no famine. For the 'population pressure' to have any explanatory power it has to be defined in terms of factors other than the incidence of hunger and famine, which it is supposed to explain. Historically, famines or hunger have occurred in both sparsely and densely populated areas. Whereas most of the sub-Saharan African countries which in recent years have suffered from famines are sparsely populated by international standards, the successful economic performers in Asia, for example, the four tigers, are all densely populated. The thrust of these criticisms is, however, not to deny the importance of food production, the 'supply side factors' or of the population and its growth. Rather it is to emphasize that there is no unique link between food production or natural disasters and hunger, thereby clearing the ground for its analysis in terms of diverse factors.

Many of the papers in this selection and the parent volumes rely on the notion of 'entitlement', which for the present purposes may be defined as 'the set of alternative commodity bundles which a person can command' (Sen, 1981: 46). It directs attention to the constellation of economic, political, social, and cultural relations determining the 'acquirement of food by individuals'. These relations may be market exchange and the terms of trade, those within the family or a community and those between the government and citizens. In many cases entitlement may be taken to depend on 'income' but there are also various instances where it cannot be. In every economy there are many who do not have an income in the usual sense, and their food consumption depends on factors such as the pattern of allocation within the household, the treatment of males and females and social provision. Sen's paper in this selection discusses the salient features of the approach in terms of entitlement. The term has gained in currency and also come in for criticisms from various quarters. It is open-ended in the same way as, for example, the notions of rights and social welfare are. The entitlement of an individual or a group can only be discovered through an analysis of specific situations as relations constitutive of it may differ from one society to another and amongst individuals within the same society. It does not supply a menu of causes of famines or hunger; if this is taken to be the criterion of a 'theory' then it is not a theory. Nor does the qualification of famine as 'entitlement failure' constitute a discriminatory explanation. Rather its importance lies in providing a perspective for the analysis of deprivation, including famines, which emphasizes that individuals who starve or go hungry are not simply receptacles of food but have distinct social and economic identities and also a gender. More important, these have a bearing on the causes of their starvation or undernutrition. Finally, entitlement is not an alternative term for the distribution of income or food. Rather its emphasis is on factors or relations which underlie particular outcomes such as particular groups of individuals lacking enough command over food.

The other side of entitlement, which is less abstract and more immediate, is the notion of 'vulnerable group' sharing some common features which make them susceptible to deprivation. For example, as pointed out by Drèze in this selection (Chapter 3), historically in India landless labourers and rural artisans have been a group particularly vulnerable to famines or hunger. Elsewhere these may be different, such as small farmers specializing in the production of cash crops susceptible to relatively large changes in the terms of trade with respect to staple food. Platteau (Chapter 10) points out that famine victims in sub-Saharan African countries have mostly been small farmers reliant on own-produced food.

As exemplified by Sen (1981) and Drèze and Sen (1989) and a number of papers in this selection, a fruitful starting point for an analysis of famine and hunger is a salient observation calling for an explanation. To mention three examples from this selection, the first, which motivates Drèze's paper on India, is a significant reduction in the incidence of famines in India in the twentieth century, in particular in the period since independence in 1947. The second is the oft-cited observation that Sri Lanka, despite being a low-income economy and the one with a lack-lustre growth performance, has managed to achieve a high life expectancy at birth and a low infant mortality rate. This is scrutinized by Anand and Kanbur in their paper on Sri Lanka (Chapter 6), and also discussed in the wider South-Asian context by Basu (Chapter 8). The third is that Bangladesh, although precariously balanced between mild to severe hunger, has managed to avoid famines since 1974 notwithstanding the recurring cycle of floods and other natural disasters. This forms the starting point of the analysis of hunger and famine in Bangladesh by Osmani (Chapter 7).

Given that famines and hunger vary in symptoms and etiology, case studies would appear to be the appropriate approach to their analysis. Such studies, however, need analytical tools. There is a wide range on offer in economics and other social sciences, though in some cases they need to be adapted to the task. Papers in this selection and in the original volumes provide example of how economics may be used for the analysis of hunger (see Basu (Chapter 8) and Ravallion, 1987 and 1990). There is also room for general analytical studies focusing on special aspects. These include measures of undernourishment and their physical impact (see Dasgupta and Ray, 1990 and Osmani, 1990), indicators of the living standard in low-income economies and their use for analysis and policy (see Anand and Harris, 1990) and the design of early warning systems for famines (Desai, 1990).

But for Sen's explanatory paper, the rest in this selection are case studies or surveys of such studies, mostly of South Asia. There are two reasons for this concentration: first, South Asia is varied and provides striking examples of both successes and failures in preventing famines and hunger. Second, there are ample data and background literature for case studies on the region, which also account for the uneven coverage of case studies on South Asia. For example, those on Nepal and Pakistan tend to be few. Although these countries have not suffered from famine in recent history, they are still far from having banished hunger and their record in terms of indices of human welfare, such as life expectancy, infant mortality, and literacy, is very poor (see for example WDR 1993, or HDR 1993). Since the mid-1970s famines seem to have been largely confined to sub-Saharan Africa, the Bangladesh famine of 1974 being an exception. Nevertheless, undernutrition is still widespread and claims a heavy toll in terms of lives in South Asia. There are two studies of sub-Saharan Africa in this selection (those by Platteau (Chapter 10) and Drèze (Chapter 11)), and also a number of others in the parent volumes. There is a need for both more studies relating to sub-Saharan Africa and to guard against the danger of generalization on the basis of the South-Asian experience, which arguably has some particular features.

Turning to case studies in this selection, Drèze's paper examines India's achievement in cutting short the ominous chain from droughts, floods, and other natural disasters to famines or hunger. This examination is structured around the historical question: why did the frequency of famines decline in the twentieth century and especially since independence in 1947? As he demonstrates, the answer does not lie in increasing availability of food. The production of food per capita fell more or less steadily until 1947, and the increase since has been relatively modest. Moreover, natural disasters, floods, and droughts have continued to recur. The post-independence India has had to face a number of major national food crises in the wake of natural disasters such as those in 1966–7 and numerous local ones such as that in Maharashtara in 1970–3. Yet none of them led to a famine. For an answer to the question, Drèze suggests, one should look to the history of public policy towards famine relief. A major historical landmark was the drawing up of the 'famine codes' in the 1880s, which consisted of instructions for identifying emergencies and measures to be taken in such events. These included providing wage employment of public works, which later would become the mainstay of famine relief, and unconditional provision of food (cooked or uncooked) for those unable to work. These codes took some time to be put in operation and the policy up to the independence of India, although fairly successful in reducing the risk of famines, suffered from some disastrous lapses, the most notable being the Bengal famine of 1943. The unfolding catastrophe failed to be recognized by the authorities until it was too late. It was not even officially declared to be a famine. With the independence of India, public action to prevent famines became more systematic and the range of government intervention broader. For example, the government began to involve itself in food storage and price stabilization which it did not in the pre-independence period, because of *laissez-faire*. More importantly, parliamentary democracy and an independent press contributed to increasing responsiveness to impending famines, an issue which we discuss later.

The provision of employment for cash or food on local public works, discussed by Drèze (Chapter 3), Basu (Chapter 8), and Ravallion (1990), has been a central technique of famine prevention and poverty alleviation in India and a number of other countries. It raises three sets of issues: first, how it operates to relieve famine or hunger; secondly, its coverage of those needing relief (the security motive); thirdly, wastage and its effect on economic incentives (the targeting motive). Where employment is for cash, as in Maharashtra in 1970–3, the key mechanism is the replacement of lost income, as with social security benefits. This is likely to be associated with two types of effects: a rise in the food price and, perhaps, also an increase in the local food supply through an increased inflow from other regions. The rise in the food price will reduce food consumption by those not employed on public works, through the usual 'income effect' (a reduction in real income) and perhaps also the 'substitution effect' (an increase in the price of food relative to other commodities). The rise in price is equivalent to a tax on food and has an adverse effect on those not employed on public works. It may also help attract food from other regions, benefiting both the vulnerable and the non-vulnerable groups. The exact effects of public works depend on conditions in both the market for food and the local labour market, and their possible range is wide. As emphasized in Ravallion in the parent volumes, the analysis of public employment should take into account effects on both those who are assisted and those who are not, and the net result may turn out to be very different from what is intended. However, as long as food deficit is not large and there is no speculative hoarding of food on a large scale, public works will succeed in protecting a large percentage of the vulnerable population from famine by evening out reduction in food consumption.

The coverage of public works is limited to those who are able to work and those residing within travelling distance of projects. For a comprehensive coverage of those in need, these have to be complemented by other forms of relief designed for those falling outside the net, such as unconditional provision of cash or food. Public works are automatically targeted to those who are willing to work at the offered wage, and a percentage of these may not be threatened with hunger. If the objective is to confine relief only to those threatened with hunger, then this percentage is the measure of wastage, and its magnitude would depend crucially on the wage rate. This has to be set with reference to two objectives simultaneously: it should be high enough to avert hunger and low enough to reduce the wastage of funds on the 'non-needy' and preserve economic incentives to seek alternative employment. In general, the determination of the wage rate would involve a trade-off between the two motives as there may not be a unique wage rate which would both ensure a high coverage of the needy and avoid a wastage of funds on the 'non-needy'. The relative importance to be attached to the two objectives depends crucially on the situation. The issues of targeting and wage determination are discussed by Basu (Chapter 8) and Ravallion (1987, 1990).

On balance, as pointed out in Drèze in this selection (Chapter 3), Drèze and Sen (1989), and Solow (1991), public works come out well as a technique or protection from famine and hunger. However, they suffer from some limitations. They presuppose a certain level of public administration, which cannot be taken for granted in all situations, in particular in the case of a civil war. The consensus in favour of public works for developing economies raises a general issue. The technique is not new, the provision of relief conditional on work was common in Victorian England but declined in importance over time and currently plays a minor role in Welfare States. The question is, what are the considerations which commend public works for developing economies but not for developed economies? A major one would be that not much capital is required to employ a person in a developing economy, which makes the organization of public works simpler and also keeps the risk of the wastage of capital low. The other is that targeting through the requirement to perform labour offers special advantages in developing economies because of certain conditions which may not apply to a developed economy. These include lack of reliable information on income, including food available for consumption, which makes targeting through a direct assessment of need especially error

prone. Moreover, corruption in local public administration may make targeting dependent on administrative discretion undesirable. In such cases an
unconditional offer of employment on public works, relying on 'self selection'
for assistance by the population ensures a wider coverage than administrative
selection and avoids a wastage of resources on the non-needy.

Sri Lanka has been the subject of special attention in the literature because
of its exceptional achievement in terms of the indicators of human development. With life expectancy at birth of around 70, an infant mortality rate of less
than 40 per 1,000 live births and the adult literacy rate of around 80 per cent,
Sri Lanka is comparable to upper-middle or developed economies in terms of
most human welfare indicators. Yet in terms of per capita income it is a low-
income economy, and one which has not performed particularly well in terms
of growth. China and Kerala in India present a similar combination of a low
rank in terms of per capita income but a high rank in terms of welfare
indicators. There are also economies with a high rank in terms of per capita
income and/or economic growth but a low rank in terms of welfare indicators.
Such experiences raise two sets of questions: first, are they statistically
significant, given that what looks anomalous to naked eyes may turn out to be
no more than a result of the conjunction of small random influences. Secondly,
what accounts for these experiences and what policy conclusions may be drawn
from them? The first has been a subject of much econometric attention with
respect to Sri Lanka and is discussed in Anand (Chapter 6) and Kanbur and
Basu (Chapter 8). Taking them to be statistically significant, these experiences
undermine the assumption of a simple relation between per capita income and
indicators of human development. They also suggest that an attack on hunger
and deprivation does not have to wait until per capita income has attained a
particular level. Conversely, growth in per capita income on its own may do
little to reduce deprivation. These observations lead on to an issue which
recurs in various papers in this selection and the original volumes: i.e. the role
of public action and government policy in reducing deprivation.

Turning to the role of public policy, it very much seems that exceptional
achievements in reducing deprivation can be traced to a particular set of public
policies and the stance of the government. For example, Anand and Kanbur
(Chapter 6) analyse the role of government policy in Sri Lanka's achievements
through a historical survey of preventive and curative health care, education,
and food subsidies in the form of low-price rations, which were phased out in
the 1980s. Using econometric techniques, they establish that government
interventions played an important role in the improvement of the health and
educational level of the population and that economic growth alone could not
have achieved these improvements. It is important to emphasize that successes
in reducing the incidence of deprivation are not confined to a particular type of
political system. The examples of notable successes include democracies such
as Sri Lanka, Jamaica, and Costa Rica, and also autocratic regimes such as
Pinochet's Chile, China, and Taiwan (Drèze and Sen, 1989). Moreover,

although not exactly the same, there are some similarities in policies responsible for reducing deprivation across widely different countries. These include the provision of agricultural land, employment creation, public provision of health care and education, and price subsidies on necessities. Notwithstanding the questions about the merits of some of these policies in terms of coverage and cost, a general conclusion is that there is an important role for the government in reducing deprivation regardless of the political system and that there are policy lessons to be learned from the experience of other countries, even when political systems are different and policies are not directly transferable.

The above discussion raises the question of the relationship between democracy and the incidence of deprivation. Although democracy can be associated with a variety of outcomes in terms of deprivation, as evidenced by Indian states, it is hard to find cases where democracy, in particular universal suffrage and periodic elections, has over time failed to have a significant impact on deprivation. One problem in establishing a definite relation between the reduction of deprivation and democracy is simply that there are yet few cases of democracies with a relatively long history amongst developing economies. India is a notable exception in this regard. Sen (1982) has laid special emphasis on the role of 'adversarial politics' and a free press in influencing the Indian government's policies towards famine and, to a lesser extent, endemic hunger.

Sen's observation prompts Ram's analysis in this selection of press reporting of emergencies and endemic deprivation, both pre- and post-independence. As compared to other developing economies, the press in India is extensive, multilingual and pluralistic, and is unique in this respect. One may distinguish two possible roles of an independent press: first, providing multiple channels of information and the absence of monopoly control, and, secondly, acting as a watchdog and bringing to surface deprivation and the shortcomings of the government and its policies. Both these roles can also be played by the international press and media, which they did in bringing the African famines of recent years to the world's attention. However, the international press cannot substitute for the domestic one. It usually reaches only a small section of the population, and besides it is bound to be highly selective in what it reports and its attention span is limited. The importance of an independent press has been emphasized in the context of the contrast between China and India by Drèze and Sen (1989). Notwithstanding the natural disasters and the disruptive effects of the break with the Soviet Union, the distortion of information played a central role in the famine of 1959–61 in China, which claimed millions of lives. There is little doubt that the Chinese leadership, fed on exaggerated information, was very slow in realizing the unfolding catastrophe, and whatever opposition there was to the disastrous policies of the Great Leap Forward remained private and was easily silenced. Important though the Indian press has been in putting deprivation on the political agenda, especially in the post-independence period, Ram cautions, one should be careful about not exaggerating its influence. Because of the low level of literacy in the country, newspapers reach a comparatively small proportion of the population. Further, by its very nature the press focuses on 'news'. Endemic deprivation woven into the fabric of everyday life does not make news and has not attracted the same attention by the Indian press as emergencies.

Aside from the role of an independent press, the other neglected factor with a bearing on hunger is gender. Hunger is not uniformly distributed across groups, and there are systematic differences between command over resources and commodities that men and women enjoy. Thus aside from usual social and economic factors, gender can be an important determinant of entitlement. Moreover, the pattern and the impact of gender discrimination differ across countries. A well-established demographic fact is that given the same nutrition and medical attention, women are less susceptible to disease and death. In developed countries, compared to men, women have lower age-specific mortality rates across the whole age range, thus higher life expectancy, and constitute a higher proportion of the population. These demographic patterns can serve as a bench-mark for assessing the impact of discrimination. For example, West Asia, South Asia, and China depart from the pattern and have a higher ratio of men to women, though with large intra- and inter-country differences. This suggests the presence of some 'social and economic disadvantages' offsetting the 'biological advantage' women enjoy, a quantitative indicator of which is the difference between the existing number of women and what it would be had the demographic pattern been the same as in developed economies, or in some developing economies. The difference, termed 'the number of missing women', can be large. But it is important to emphasize that this number depends crucially on the comparison bench-mark and it is due not to one but a large number of factors.

Harriss's paper in the selection is a careful and wide-ranging survey of evidence on intra-family inequality in food intake in India and Bangladesh. She draws on an extensive range of data and case studies. The evidence she finds, although it corroborates intra-family inequality, is mixed. Discrimination against women varies with age, social class, and also region. Cultural factors play a crucial role. The implication is that gender is relevant to deprivation, but discrimination against women is modulated by class, age, and region and thus cannot be encapsulated in the form of a generalization applying to the whole country. Aside from food intake, gender inequality surfaces in other fields such as health care, education, and economic opportunities, which are related in various ways to inequality in food intake.

Turning to the case studies of Bangladesh and China, Osmani (Chapter 7) provides a well-documented and careful analysis of undernourishment and famines in Bangladesh, which can claim considerable success in increasing food production and averting famines. However, he concludes, the country remains highly vulnerable to famines. This is not only due to recurrent natural disasters and the high population pressure but also to policy mistakes.

Compared to South Asia China has been less studied because of the paucity of information in the past. This began to change from the early 1980s when the Chinese government released a vast amount of statistical data and organized a population census (the first since the one in 1964), the results of which were not released. Riskin's paper (Chapter 9) pieces together a detailed picture since 1952 of food availability per capita, the system of food distribution at various levels, and the number of deaths in the famine of 1959–61. The number of excess deaths from the famine, he points out, varies greatly depending on the method of calcualation. Whatever it may be it is huge and the responsibility for most of the deaths lies with the Great Leap Forward policy and the delayed response of the leadership to the crisis.

Sub-Saharan Africa has in recent decades been particularly prone to famines and severe endemic hunger, and policies of African governments have attracted much of the blame. This raises the simple question of why sub-Saharan Africa is prone to such policy mistakes. Moreover, the types of policy mistakes identified in Africa such as discrimination against agriculture in pricing and taxation are not particular to African economies. They are also found in other parts of the world. Platteau in this selection argues that something deeper than a catalogue of policy failures is called for, and goes on to provide a wide-ranging analysis of factors underlying hunger and famine in Sub-Saharan Africa. An important feature of many African countries, Platteau points out, is that the bulk of food output is produced by small family-operated farms, and the rural population without land is still comparatively low. Thus the victims of famines and hunger in many African countries are smallholders producing food for their own consumption. According to Platteau, far more serious than policy mistakes are a number of structural factors impeding agricultural growth in African countries. These include the dispersed rural population, which makes the provision of infrastructure costly, the tradition of extensive rather than intensive farming, the land tenure, lack of technical breakthroughs in root crops staple in rural Africa, and a high degree of political instability. Although land per person is high in Africa, it is typically not of high quality except in certain regions.

In Chapter 11 Drèze examines recent cases of averted famines in Botswana, Cape Verde, Kenya, and Zimbabwe. These success stories provide a useful balance to the harrowing accounts of famines in sub-Saharan Africa. Drèze attributes these successes to public support for vulnerable groups, mostly, initiated and implemented by local and national institutions. He concludes the case studies with a discussion of possible measures to prevent hunger, including the institution of early warning systems, public food distribution, cash support, the development of markets, and of diversification of agriculture.

This selection is intended both to report on the on-going work on hunger and to encourage further work. Banishing hunger and famines is primarily a question of economic policy and political action. We hope that studies presented in this selection will contribute a little towards an adequate informational and analytical basis for the required action.

References

(References to papers in *The Political Economy of Hunger* are given in an abbreviated form as follows: *PEH Vol. I, II, or III.*)

ANAND, S. and HARRIS, C. (1990), 'Food and Standard of Living: An Analysis Based on Sri Lankan Data', *PEH Vol. I.*

DASGUPTA, P. and RAY, D. (1990), 'Adapting to Undernourishment: The Biological Evidence and Its Implications', *PEH Vol. I.*

DESAI, M. (1990), 'Modelling An Early Warning System for Famines', *PEH Vol. II.*

DRÉZE, J. and SEN, A. K. (1989), *Hunger and Public Action* (Oxford: Oxford University Press).

HDR (1993): *Human Development Report 1993*, New York: United Nations Development Programme.

OSMANI, S. R. (1990), 'Nutrition and Economics of Food', *PEH Vol. I.*

RAVALLION, M. (1987), *Markets and Famines* (Oxford: Clarendon Press).

——(1990), 'Market Response to Anti-Hunger Policy,' *PEH Vol. II.*

SEN, A. K. (1981), *Poverty and Famines* (Oxford, Oxford University Press).

——(1982), 'Food Battles: Conflict in Access to Food', *Coromandel Lectures*, Delhi: repr. in *Food and Nutrition*, 10 (1984).

SOLOW, R. M. (1991), 'How to Stop Hunger', *New York Review of Books*, 5 December.

SVEDBERG, P. (1990), 'Undernutrition in Sub-Saharan Africa: A Critical Assessment of the Evidence', *PEH Vol. II.*

WDR (1993): *World Development Report 1993* (Washington D.C: World Bank).

1

Introduction

Jean Drèze and Amartya Sen

The facts are stark enough. Despite the widespread opulence and the unprecedentedly high real income per head in the world, millions of people die prematurely and abruptly from intermittent famines, and a great many million more die every year from endemic undernourishment and deprivation across the globe. Further, hundreds of millions lead lives of persistent insecurity and want.

While all this is quite obvious, many things are unclear about the characteristics, causation, and possible remedies of hunger in the modern world. A great deal of probing investigation—analytical as well as empirical—is needed as background to public policy and action for eradicating famines and eliminating endemic undernutrition. In this collection of twenty-six papers in three volumes, serious attempts have been made to address many of these momentous issues.

1.1. *Organization and structure*

These studies were initiated in 1985 when the World Institute for Development Economics Research (WIDER) was established in Helsinki. First versions of most of the papers were presented at a conference on 'food strategies' held at WIDER in July 1986. In that meeting there were extensive discussions of the analyses presented in the various papers, and some of the debates continued well beyond the conference. The papers have been revised in the light of these exchanges, and further discussions among the authors and the editors. A few new studies were also undertaken during 1986–8 to fill some identified gaps. This book of three volumes represents the fruits of these efforts. It is meant to be a wide-ranging investigation of the causal antecedents, characteristic features, and policy demands of hunger in the modern world. The focus is primarily on sub-Saharan Africa and South Asia, but the experiences of several other countries—from China to Brazil—have also been examined.

Though three of our own essays are included in these volumes, our role has been primarily organizational and editorial. We have, however, also written a monograph of our own, *Hunger and Public Action*,[1] which deals with related

This chapter originally appeared as the introduction to volume 1 of *The Political Economy of Hunger*. All cross-references apply to the original 3-volume edition.

[1] Also published by Oxford University Press in the series of WIDER Studies in Development Economics: Drèze and Sen (1989a).

issues, and there is a clear connection between the two works. The planning and the design of these three volumes of essays, *The Political Economy of Hunger*, have been closely related to the approach explored and developed in *Hunger and Public Action*, and in turn, in that book, we have drawn on the results of the studies presented in these three volumes.

We should, however, emphasize the obvious. We, as editors, must not be identified with all the views that have been expressed in these essays. These three volumes of essays, which are mainly revised conference papers, present investigations and conclusions that deserve, in our view, serious consideration. But although we have been involved at every stage of these studies, and have also presented our critical comments on the various versions, it was not our aim to soldier on with requests for revision until we all agreed. The analyses and the views are those of the respective authors.

1.2. *Political economy*

The essays in the first volume deal with 'general matters'—including the nature and diversity of the problem of world hunger. They set the background for the analysis of government policy and public action. The second volume includes studies of famines and of anti-famine strategies, and altogether there is an attempt here to identify what is needed for the eradication of famines. The third volume takes up endemic deprivation and undernourishment, discusses successes and failures of different lines of action, and investigates the lessons for public policy aimed at eliminating persistent hunger. The different volumes, thus, deal with distinct but interrelated aspects of what we have called 'the political economy of hunger'.

The meaning of the expression 'political economy' is not altogether un-ambiguous. To some it simply means economics. It is indeed the old name of the discipline, common in the nineteenth century, and now rather archaic. To others, political economy is economics seen in a perspective that is a great deal broader than is common in the mainstream of the modern tradition. In this view, the influences of political and social institutions and ideas are taken to be particularly important for economic analysis and must not be pushed to the background with some stylized assumptions of heroic simplicity. Political economy thus interpreted cannot but appear to be rather 'interdisciplinary' as the disciplines are not standardly viewed.

Even though the two interpretations are quite distinct, there is a clear connection between them in the sense that the dominant tradition of economics is much narrower now than it was in the classical political economy of Adam Smith, Robert Malthus, David Ricardo, Karl Marx, John Stuart Mill, and others.[2] Thus the old and archaic term for economics as such is also a reminder

---

[2] On this issue, see Sen (1984, 1989a).

of the breadth of the earlier tradition of the subject. Many of the analyses of the kind that are now seen as interdisciplinary would have appeared to Smith or Mill or Marx as belonging solidly to the discipline of political economy as a subject.

It does not, of course, really matter whether political, social, and cultural influences on economic matters are counted inside or outside the discipline of economics, but it can be tremendously important not to lose sight of these influences in analysing many profoundly important economic problems. This is particularly the case with the problem of hunger. The title of the book, *The Political Economy of Hunger*, is meant to be an explicit reminder of the need to adopt a broad perspective to understand better the causation of hunger and the remedial actions that are needed.

1.3. *Entitlements and political economy*

As was mentioned earlier, the essays included in the first volume of this book deal with rather general matters that serve as background to policy analysis. The topics covered include the characteristics and causal antecedents of famines and endemic deprivation, the interconnections between economic and political factors, the role of social relations and the family, the special problems of women's deprivation, the connection between food consumption and other aspects of living standards, and the medical aspects of undernourishment and its consequences. Several contributions also address the political background of public policy, in particular the connection between the government and the public, including the role of newspapers and the media, and the part played by political commitment and by adversarial politics and pressures.[3]

Chapter 2, 'Food, Economics, and Entitlements' by Amartya Sen, is concerned with some very elementary issues. It points to the need for focusing on the 'acquirement' of food by the respective households and individuals, and the fact that the overall production or availability of food may be a bad predictor of what the vulnerable groups in the population can actually acquire. The 'entitlement approach', already presented elsewhere (see Sen 1977, 1981), concentrates instead on the forces that determine the bundles of commodities over which a family or an individual can establish command. A person can be reduced to starvation if some economic change makes it no longer possible for him or her to acquire any commodity bundle with enough food. This can happen either because of a fall in endowment (e.g. alienation of land, or loss of labour power due to ill health), or because of an unfavourable shift in the conditions of exchange (e.g. loss of employment, fall in wages, rise in food prices, drop in the price of goods or services sold by the person, reduction of social security provisions).

---

[3] On these questions see also Drèze and Sen (1989a).

The chapter then proceeds to use the entitlement perspective to analyse a number of specific policy issues: famine anticipation and warning; famine relief (particularly the use of employment and payment of cash wages to regenerate lost entitlements); the use of food imports; the role of public distribution (of food and other necessities including health care); and the need for diversification in the production structure (particularly in the context of encountering African famines and hunger). Many of these issues are further investigated in other contributions in these volumes.

1.4. *Food commands of countries and regions*

Ravi Kanbur in Chapter 3 examines the regional pattern of food commands in the world. By extending entitlement analysis from the level of individuals and households to nation states and regions, the global position of food production and needs is supplemented by the analysis of each nation's and region's ability to command food. Kanbur also examines the problems of data availability underlying the corresponding estimations.

Not only does this 'intermediate' level of disaggregation provide a different perspective on the trends of food balances in the world, it also directs attention to crucial variables that influence a country's ability to command enough food, e.g. international prices of non-food exports, the possibility of substitution between commodities in production and consumption.

The analysis of hunger has to be, ultimately, thoroughly disaggregative, and the food entitlements of regions and countries cannot by themselves tell us whether many people will go hungry and who they will be. But between the extreme aggregation of global food analysis (popular in some economic as well as journalistic traditions) and the totally disaggregated picture of the entitlements of families and individuals, there is an important intermediate focal point of regional and country-specific food entitlements. Kanbur's investigation concerns that intermediate stage, and he points to the connection between that stage and the ultimate concern with the deprivation of families and persons. In this context, Kanbur also argues for the possibility of making good use of nutrition-based poverty measures supplemented by sensitivity analysis of different cut-off levels of nutritional norms.

1.5. *Politics and the state*

In Chapter 4 Rehman Sobhan extends entitlement analysis in a different —more political—direction. Although he is generally concerned with the diverse political factors—national and international—that govern the entitlements of households, he concentrates specifically on the determination of the entitlements against the state that particular households may have.

Indeed, the state is, to a great extent, a direct instrument for providing entitlements through such mechanisms as public distribution of food and health care, the generation of public employment, the provision of relief in distress situations, the offer of subsidies on particular productive inputs and consumption goods. Sobhan provides a broad-ranging analysis of the political forces that determine the public provision of these entitlements, thereby supplementing the usual concentration in the literature on entitlement analysis in the market economy.[4] He also presents an analysis of the politics of food aid—drawing partly on the experience of Bangladesh.

Sobhan's paper brings out *inter alia* the need for many governments to propitiate influential interest groups and the important effects that this can have on entitlements.[5] The analysis can be extended in other directions as well. The provisions made by the state respond not only to pressures of vested interests, but also to general political pressures. There is some evidence that organized political opposition can be quite effective in influencing state policy even in rather authoritarian states. For example, hard-to-suppress opposition groups may have made quite a substantial contribution to the populist (and, to some extent, welfare-oriented) policies in South Korea and in post-Allende Chile.[6] In general, the positive role of 'adversarial' politics deserves clearer recognition than it tends to get in the literature on world hunger. The tradition of thinking about public action only in terms of policy choice by the government (e.g. in the literature on 'optimal' policy decisions) needs to be supplemented by bringing in the action of the public itself. Public action is action not only *for* the public but also—in an important sense—*by* the public.[7]

1.6. *International policies of the rich countries*

While Sobhan's political analysis draws attention *inter alia* to one aspect of international relations (connected with aid, leverage, and 'food politics'), Kirit Parikh in Chapter 5 examines the influence of the protectionist economic policies of the rich countries on hunger in the Third World. This is done with the help of an 'applied general equilibrium' model, based on explicitly stated—if somewhat exacting—assumptions.[8]

One of the results of his model is that the poor are forced into the role of being 'the adjustors', in the sense that fluctuations of supply—whether in the developed or developing countries—have to be absorbed by the poor (through

[4] In this sense the issues taken up by Sobhan can be seen as complementary to those—related to the functioning of markets—investigated effectively by Ravallion (1987a).

[5] On the need to consider the influence of vested interest groups in the context of the analysis of the Indian economy, see also Jha (1980) and Bardhan (1984).

[6] On this see Drèze and Sen (1989a: ch. 10, 12).

[7] These and related issues have been discussed in Drèze and Sen (1989a, 1989b).

[8] The models used have been more extensively presented and discussed in Parikh and Rabar (1981).

adjustments of their consumption). The intuition behind the result may be explainable by noting the likelihood that the richer people will be able to keep up their consumption of as vital a commodity as food even when things are generally short, so that the losers would have to be those who are overwhelmed in the competition of the market.[9]

Another result concerns the interesting—and rather comforting—conclusion that the protection of agricultural producers in the rich countries on the whole reduces hunger in the poorer countries. Parikh also shows how the protection of the labour market in the richer countries through immigration control has—of all the international policies considered—the largest adverse effect on world hunger. That conclusion is not counter-intuitive, but the political possibility of a real change in this respect is bound to be extremely slim in the near future.

1.7. *The role of the press and the media*

The role of the news media—the press in particular—in the prevention of famines and hunger is examined by the distinguished journalist and editor N. Ram in Chapter 6. Ram's analysis importantly expands our understanding of one of the most neglected aspects of the prevention of hunger—an aspect that has only recently begun to receive attention. By providing information on likely famine threats and pressuring the government to act without delay, an active newspaper system can lead to early and effective intervention by the government. One of the roles of the press is to make it 'too expensive' in political terms for the government to be callous and lethargic, and this can be decisive since famines are extremely easy to prevent by early intervention. Indeed, it appears that no country with a free press *and* scope for oppositional politics has ever experienced a major famine.

The contrast is especially striking in comparing the experience of China and India. The particular fact that China, despite its much greater achievements in reducing endemic deprivation, experienced a gigantic famine during 1958–61 (a famine in which, it is now estimated, 23 to 30 million people died) had a good deal to do with the lack of press freedom and the absence of political opposition.[10] The disastrous policies that had paved the way to the famine were not changed for three years as the famine raged on, and this was made possible by the near-total suppression of news about the famine and the total absence of

---

[9] Determined public action can, in some circumstances, succeed in shifting a substantial part of the burden of downward adjustment from the poor to the relatively prosperous classes (see Jean Drèze's chapter 'Famine Prevention in India' in vol. 2). But this may call for far-reaching measures of protection of the entitlements of the vulnerable groups, and such measures do not belong to Parikh's model. See also ch. 9 in this volume, on the observed priority that consumers evidently give to maintaining food expenditure.

[10] On this see Sen (1983), Ashton *et al.* (1984), Peng (1987). See also Carl Riskin's chapter ('Feeding China') in vol. 3 of this book.

media criticism of what was then happening in China. It is also arguable that the persistence of famines in sub-Saharan Africa has much to do with the absence of media freedom and the suppression of oppositional politics in many countries in that subcontinent. In fact, the differences between the experiences of various African countries—some with more open press and politics than others—also bring out the important role that the media and oppositional politics can play in preventing famines.[11]

However, it appears that even an active press, as in India, can be less than effective in moving governments to act decisively against endemic under-nutrition and deprivation—as opposed to dramatically visible famines. The quiet persistence of 'regular hunger' kills millions in a slow and non-dramatic way, and this phenomenon has not been much affected, it appears, by media critiques. There is need for an analysis here of what explains the difference.

While Ram begins his investigation by referring to international coverage of famines and distress, the focus of his paper is on the role of the national media. Ram distinguishes between the 'credible-informational' role of the press (including the fact that an active and efficient press can be an excellent early warning system against famines) and its 'adversarial' or 'destabilizing' role (in putting pressure on the government to act rapidly to combat famines and persistent undernutrition). Both can be extremely important in famine prevention and *potentially* also in combating endemic undernutrition.

Ram's empirical illustrations come mostly from the history of the Indian press. He shows that the Indian press—by informing the public and by pressuring the government—has indeed been able to play quite a positive part in the prevention of some types of hunger (e.g. open starvation and famines). On the other hand, it has been less successful in dealing with the type of deprivation that requires deeper economic, social, and medical analysis (e.g. endemic deprivation). Ram identifies the problems arising from 'a tendency to dramatize and sensationalize the coverage of poverty and hunger on a mass scale while missing out deeper structural features and processes' (pp. 188). Imprecision, oversimplification, and dilettantism also take their tolls.

If the explanation, as Ram argues, of the ineffectiveness of the Indian press in combating endemic undernutrition (as opposed to famines) lies in the more complicated nature of the phenomenon, the remedy sought would have to go beyond guarding the freedom of the press (important though it is) into ways of improving the quality of news analysis and journalism. Ram's essay suggests some crucial directions in which effective improvements can be made (including greater interaction between academic research and journalism). These particular pointers as well as Ram's general analysis deserve serious attention, given the potential importance of the role of the news media in combating world hunger.

---

[11] On this and related matters, see Drèze and Sen (1989a: chs. 5, 8, 11, 13), and also Jean Drèze's chapter 'Famine Prevention in India' in vol. 2 of this collection.

1.8. *Nutrition, adjustment, and adaptation*

The complexity of the phenomenon of undernourishment is not only a difficulty for good journalistic coverage of endemic deprivation, it can also create problems for the professional literature on hunger and nutrition. Indeed, there have been several protracted—and heated—debates among nutritionists on the criteria for undernourishment. The traditional 'intake norms' approach involves the specification of certain nutritional norms of 'required intakes', and a diagnosis of 'undernourishment' if the actual intakes of people fall below these norms. This approach has been subjected to a good deal of criticism in recent years.[12] The need for some types of nutrients (e.g. the 'protein requirements' of adults) has been shown to be exaggerated in the usual specification of nutritional standards. Even for 'calorie requirements', grave doubts have been raised about the scientific basis and practical usefulness of comparison with prespecified intake norms.

Some reasons for doubting the wisdom of mechanical use of the 'intake norm' approach are clear enough. First, there is much evidence of *inter-individual* variations in metabolic rates and other factors influencing calorie needs. Any statistical analysis of intake observations must take note not only of such variations, but also of the possibility that some of the people with low nutritional needs may in fact *choose* low-intake diets.

Second, there is often a good deal of *intertemporal* variations in intakes, with low calorie consumption in some periods being balanced by higher consumption in others. Thus, the observation of low intake in a given period is no proof of undernourishment.

Third, there is considerable evidence that nutritional differences bring about adjustments of some kinds, e.g. children being shorter and lightly built. What is not clear is how these adjustments impair well-being and working ability (if at all). This has been a field of much debate—with positions taken varying from uncritical acceptance of the contribution of anthropometric factors to good living (e.g. the common presumption that 'taller is better') to attaching no importance at all to those factors (e.g. the general acceptance of the plausibility of being 'small but healthy').

Fourth, some nutritionists have argued that the body can in fact 'adapt' to low intakes by cutting down the nutritional needs without any effect on body size and other physical features and without any impairment of bodily functionings. If the thesis of costless adaptation is biologically sound and widespread in its application, the 'intake-norm' approach would be thoroughly undermined. The adaptationist thesis would also suggest a redirection of policy priorities towards concentrating only on severely deficient intakes —beyond the scope for adaptation—with no need for worrying about those

---

[12] See in particular Sukhatme (1977, 1982*a*, 1982*b*).

with smaller shortfalls who are automatically protected by adaptation. The 'adaptationists' have tended to argue that the magnitudes of nutritional deprivation are much exaggerated in standard estimates.

It should be obvious from this quick summary that the more serious points of medical argumentation are likely to be the last two, and in particular adaptation as a phenomenon would be immensely important if it were widely applicable and quantitatively significant. In Chapter 7, Partha Dasgupta and Debraj Ray argue, on the basis of reviewing the relevant medical literature, that the biological evidence does not favour the thesis of costless adaptation. Both interpersonal differences in nutritional requirements and intertemporal variations in intakes are accepted as real possibilites (though it is also pointed out that because of the 'waste' involved in storage, a fluctuating intake pattern tends to raise the average requirement). But the possibility of costless adaptation is strongly disputed on empirical grounds.

Dasgupta and Ray then go on to investigate the implications of undernourishment for labour markets, including the effects of inadequate nutrition on low work capacity, unemployment, and continuing poverty. They discuss how a 'poverty trap' can operate, with undernourished people finding it hard to get employment because they are weak and remaining weak because they are unemployed.[13] The role of anti-hunger policy, thus, extends well beyond that of preventing escapable mortality or morbidity into achieving a major economic transformation.

Siddiq Osmani in Chapter 8 provides a wide-ranging assessment of the nutritional literature on food intakes and health, and it complements Dasgupta and Ray's analysis of biological evidence. On the specific subject of adaptation, Osmani's conclusions are sceptical, though less critical and decisively dismissive than those of Dasgupta and Ray ('the hypothesis of intraindividual adaptation in requirement is not yet substantiated by scientific evidence, although the possibility cannot be ruled out').

Osmani also investigates the detrimental effects of adjustment to lower nutritional intakes, and finds some 'association' between low intake and impairment (though here too his conclusions are more conditional and cautious than those of Dasgupta and Ray). He also goes into a number of other—related—issues, e.g. the importance of health planning and hygiene in food policy (particularly since food requirements *and* the ability to absorb food depend on a person's health), and the relevance of the nutritional debates for the measurement of poverty (especially for poverty defined as the failure of basic nutritional capabilities).[14] Osmani argues that some of the debates on nutritional economics do not quite have the policy relevance that has been

---

[13] On this see also Dasgupta and Ray (1986, 1987).

[14] A number of papers on these and related themes were presented at a Conference on 'Nutrition and Poverty' at the World Institute for Development Economics Research in July 1987, and these papers were published in a volume edited by Siddiq Osmani: Osmani (1993).

claimed, but he separates out those parts of the debate that are really central to policy choice.

Those who have argued for taking note of the possibility of adaptation and other forms of costless adjustment have often emphasized the case for concentrating on really serious nutritional deprivation as opposed to relatively minor shortfalls that may come out in the wash. It is indeed possible to argue that an exaggeration of the number of the undernourished may distract attention from the urgent need to concentrate on remedying the conditions of those who are tremendously deprived. That point remains relevant even if costless adaptation or adjustment is absent (or possible but uncommon). The actual harm that nutritional shortfall does can rise at an increasing rate, *whether or not* there is costless adaptation. That is a different issue and should be seen as such.

1.9.   *Food and living standard*

The analyses presented by Dasgupta and Ray, and by Osmani, push us in the direction of paying greater attention to the problem of nutritional deprivation, and its manifold medical, economic, and social effects.[15] One of the recurrent themes in the studies included in these three volumes concerns the *interconnections* between the problem of hunger and the broader economic and social concerns.

These connections can work in different directions. The need to link hunger to the failure of economic entitlements indicates one connection—economic penury has to be seen as a major predictor of hunger. For much the same reason, the observation of hunger can also be seen as an indicator of a family's general poverty. Indeed, since there are good reasons to believe that the family would typically give priority to food in its consumption allocation, the expenditure on food may be a better guide to the family's overall economic solvency and opulence than more variable indicators, such as total income or even total expenditure.

In an innovative model, Sudhir Anand and Christopher Harris have analysed in Chapter 9 the way food expenditure can be used as an indicator of the general living standard of a family. If a family's income fluctuates over time, the observation of its income at any point of time may be a very misleading basis for judging its ordinary level of opulence. For reasons that have been discussed by Milton Friedman, among others, there may be more stability in the family's total consumption expenditure, which may be based on long-term average income (the so-called 'permanent income'). But a family may not give equal priority to preserving all types of expenditure, and given the importance of food, it is not unreasonable to expect that it would attach the highest priority to preserving the expenditure on food.

---

[15] See also the papers presented at the Conference on 'Nutrition and Poverty': Osmani (1993).

Equipped with this insight, Anand and Harris present both an analytical model to investigate these connections and also an empirical study of Sri Lankan data. It is shown that if the economic opulence of the family is judged not by the observation of its short-run income, but by the size of food expenditure per capita, the behaviour of consumers becomes much easier to explain (including the observed chronic 'dissaving' of the poorest sections of the people classified in terms of per capita income or per capita total expenditure).

Of the four possible indicators of living standard that Anand and Harris consider (namely income per capita, total expenditure per capita, food expenditure per capita, and the share of food in total expenditure), food expenditure per head seems to give the best guidance to the family's economic opulence. The finding has implications for economic policy—including subsidies and taxation—and it can be seen as an important aid in using short-run data for informed analysis of the economic condition of the people. Observing a family's food expenditure tends to tell more about its general economic conditions than we can find out by observing its short-run income, or total expenditure.[16] Anand and Harris comment on some of the far-reaching implications of the relations analysed.[17] The perspective of food is important not only for the analysis of nutrition, but also for an understanding of general economic conditions and for interpersonal comparisons of the economic state of different families. This broader consideration extends the scope and use of the political economy of hunger.

1.10. *Women's deprivation and intrafamily distribution*

In the analysis of hunger, the divisions of classes and occupation groups are obviously important, and their roles have been recognized for a long time. The fact that gender can also be a crucial variable had not received due acknowledgement until fairly recently. There can be systematic differences between the command over resources and commodities that men and women respectively enjoy. The differences can show up in the levels of undernourishment, morbidity, and mortality respectively experienced by women and men.

There are, in fact, very asymmetrical survival patterns of men and women in different parts of the world. There is fairly strong evidence that if women and men receive similar nutritional and medical attention, women tend to live significantly longer than men. Women seem to be more resistant to disease and more able to deal with hardship, and the survival advantages are particularly

[16] Anand and Harris also consider the proportionate share of food in total expenditure as a basis of classification and find that it is a less useful indicator of living standard than total food expenditure per head. A family would try to preserve its total command over food, but need not particularly worry about maintaining the same ratio of food expenditure to other expenditure.

[17] The authors have explored the implications more extensively in a monograph; see Anand and Harris (forthcoming).

significant for advanced age and also at the other end, especially in the neo-natal period (and even *in utero*).[18] It is, therefore, not surprising that, in Europe and North America, women have a much higher life expectancy at birth than men, and that—because of the greater survival rates of women—the female–male ratio in the total population is around 1.05 or so on the average.[19]

However, the female–male ratio is significantly lower than unity in many parts of the world. The ratio is around 0.93 or 0.94 in South Asia, West Asia, and China.[20] It is also lower than unity—though not by much—in Latin America, and quite a bit less in North Africa. Given the natural, i.e. biological, advantages of women *vis-à-vis* men (when they receive the same nutritional and medical attention), this shortfall of women would tend to indicate a really sharp difference in social treatment (i.e. in the division of necessities of life such as food and medical attention). The shortfalls amount to millions of 'missing women' in Asia and North Africa compared with what would be expected on the basis of the European or North American female–male ratio, and even on the basis of the ratio for sub-Saharan Africa.[21] If India had the female–male ratio that obtains in sub-Saharan Africa (around 1.02), then—given the number of Indian males—there would have been 37 million more women in India in the mid-1980s. The number of 'missing women' in China, similarly calculated, is 44 million.[22] There is need for an explanation as to why women's survival pattern has been so adverse in these countries.[23]

The motivation behind Barbara Harriss's investigation in Chapter 10 can be understood in this context. How much evidence is there of intrafamily inequality in hunger in South Asia, in particular India and Bangladesh? She examines a variety of empirical information, including anthropometric comparisons of women and men, but concentrates on the actual nutrient intakes of different members of a family in relation to the respective nutritional 'norms'. She also investigates the intrafamily distribution according to age, especially the shares of the very old and the very young. As background to these empirical studies, Harriss examines the methodological problems that make such comparisons so difficult. She also throws light on the material and cultural factors

---

[18] See Waldron (1983).

[19] This despite the fact that the 'sex ratio' at birth goes the other way, namely, 105 or 106 male children are born per 100 female children, more or less everywhere in the world.

[20] While Pakistan seems to have the lowest female–male ratio (around 0.90) among all the sizeable countries in the world, there are states in India which have still lower female–male ratios. Uttar Pradesh and Haryana have ratios around 0.88, while in the Indian state of Kerala the ratio is higher than 1.03 (and thus quite close to the female–male ratio in Europe and North America).

[21] See Sen (1988a).

[22] See Drèze and Sen (1989a: ch. 4).

[23] See also Harriss and Watson (1987). There are also 'subtler' patterns of anti-female differences related to such factors as birth order. For example, Monica Das Gupta (1987) has found, with data from Punjab, that while the bias against the first daughter seems to be little, the discrimination becomes quite sharp as later birth-order girls are considered.

that may influence the intrafamily distribution of food, and their relevance for public action.

Barbara Harriss finds rather mixed evidence of intrafamily discrimination in the intakes of nutrients. The inequalities have some regional pattern.[24] There are strong interconnections between differences related to age and gender. Inequalities also differ with socio-economic class. Harriss's conclusions, based on what is probably the most extensive empirical investigation of the available data on food intakes related to gender and age, cover a wide range of questions. In general, however, they indicate that it would be a mistake to diagnose a general pattern of anti-female bias in the intrafamily distribution of nutrients in India, though there are some specific differences connected with age, class, and region.

Given the absence of a general diagnosis of intrafamily inequality of nutrient intake, the question may be asked why there is such a strong pattern of excess female mortality in India for most age groups until the age of the late thirties.[25] In answering this question, two issues have to be borne in mind. First, morbidity and mortality are affected not only by food intake, but also by health care and parental attention. There is some direct evidence of anti-female discrimination in these respects in much of South Asia, both for women *vis-à-vis* men, and for girls *vis-à-vis* boys.[26] As Barbara Harriss notes, intrafamily inequalities in health care, medicine, and general attention can yield, on their own, excess female mortality rates.

Second, one can go further and question whether we really learn enough about gender discrimination in nutrition by concentrating on nutrient intakes. Ultimately, nutritional well-being is concerned with the ability to achieve certain 'functionings', and depends on a variety of factors (including personal characteristics, activity levels, epidemiological environment, access to health care, etc.) of which nutrient intake is only one.[27] Gender bias in this context would take the form of different levels of accepted debilitation for the respective sexes (e.g. tolerating more health dysfunctioning in the case of girls compared with boys). Whether this is occurring or not cannot be deduced simply by comparing actual intakes with a set of intake 'norms' that cannot

[24] Regional contrasts within India of anti-female discrimination have been discussed by Boserup (1970), Bardhan (1974, 1987), Miller (1981, 1989), among others.

[25] The overall life expectancy at birth of women has, it appears, caught up at last with that of men in India (though it remains lower in Pakistan and Bangladesh). But this aggregate index is much influenced by the higher age-specific mortality rates of Indian men beyond the age of 40 (this is in line with the situation in most countries). Below that age, for many of the age-groups, women still have a higher age-specific mortality rate in India. Oddly, there is some evidence that in China, where women's life expectancy had become larger than men's, there has been a movement in the opposite direction since the economic and social changes of 1979. Female life expectancy in China has again fallen below that of the male in the early 1980s (on this see Banister 1987: table 4.12).

[26] See e.g. Chen *et al.* (1981), Kynch and Sen (1983), Sen (1984), Das Gupta (1987).

[27] On this see Sen (1984, 1985), and Drèze and Sen (1989a: chs. 1–4). See also chs. 7 and 8 vol. 1.)

allow for possible variations in the other influences relevant to nutritional well-being. We would need other data that take direct account of the *effects* of differences in intakes, such as clinical signs of undernourishment and morbidity rates.[28]

This observation is not meant as a criticism of Harriss's paper, since her investigation concentrates quite explicitly on nutrient intake patterns rather than on the broader question of gender discrimination in nutritional well-being. But we do need to note that the latter question cannot be adequately addressed without going into the functioning space at some stage of the exercise. The important questions that motivate Barbara Harriss's study can be properly answered only by broadening the informational base.

1.11. *Food production and African women*

In contrast with South Asia, West Asia, North Africa, and China, where women are vastly outnumbered by men, in sub-Saharan Africa there are many more women than men. In terms of survival rates, sub-Saharan African women do better than men (even though the absolute levels of life expectancy of both males and females are often quite low in Africa). Also, sub-Saharan African women have a much bigger role in the production process and in work outside the household than women in the bulk of Asia and North Africa. There has been some discussion as to whether these two facts are related, and whether the larger economic role and the correspondingly greater independence of women in sub-Saharan Africa help to give them a better deal in the intrafamily divisions of commodities and privileges.[29] While that particular hypothesis would demand more examination and scrutiny, the general picture of African women's work and economic role has been far from clear. The need for a better understanding of that picture has become particularly important in the context of assessing the relation of African food problems with the nature of work that African women perform. The links involved include not only the question of gender discrimination (discussed in the preceding section), but also the general relevance of women's work for food strategies and in particular for food production.

Ann Whitehead in Chapter 11 examines this issue with empirical information and conceptual analysis. Whitehead argues that many of the common beliefs about African women's role in food production (e.g. that African agriculture can be neatly divided into a 'female/subsistence' sector and a 'male/commercial' sector) are myths. A substantial part of her paper is devoted to debunking some common myths, and disputing generalizations that have been taken for granted.

[28] On this see Chen *et al.* (1981) and Kynch and Sen (1983).

[29] On this see Boserup (1970), Kandiyoti (1988), Sen (1988*a*, 1989*b*), Drèze and Sen (1989*a*: ch. 4).

A second objective of Whitehead's paper is to assess the effect of development of projects on women in sub-Saharan Africa, and this is supplemented by her analysis of the roles that women can play in expanding African agricultural output. Among other issues, she discusses the assumption of an 'unproblematic unity of interests of household members' on which development strategies have frequently relied. The modelling underlying the development projects has tended to ignore the 'dual' role of African women in production, i.e. women's independent farming as well as women's recruitment as household labour (including 'peasant wives' family labour'). It is the latter that has received priority in the development projects, thereby making it harder for African women to preserve and expand their role as independent producers.

While there are many variations in that general theme (and Whitehead goes into several related issues in her extensive investigation), the nature of the main policy mistake is, in her view, clear enough. The neglect of women's role as independent producers worsens the relative position of women (as Whitehead puts it, 'development planners, perhaps unwittingly, are making it very hard for women' (vol. 1, p. 460)), and it may also be counterproductive for raising agricultural output generally. There is scope for expansion based on a greater use of women's role as independent producers. Whitehead ends her paper with a discussion of policies for the future in line with her diagnostic analysis. Problems of production incentives and ways of removing constraints are assessed in that light.

1.12. Famines and famine prevention

The ten chapters in the first volume cover general grounds on the economic, political, and social background to hunger and deprivation. They are not meant, of course, as exhaustive studies of all the relevant issues. They are purposeful investigations of some specific problems that have to be addressed for a better understanding of hunger and related deprivations in the modern world. The two volumes that follow are more directly concerned with public policy and action.

The six chapters in volume 2 deal primarily with starvation and famines (problems of endemic undernutrition are taken up in volume 3). Sub-Saharan Africa receives much of the attention, since it is there that famines have persistently continued to occur. But there is discussion also of famines and famine prevention in South Asia.

1.13. The Indian experience

Jean Drèze's chapter, 'Famine Prevention in India', scrutinizes India's achievement in preventing droughts, floods, and other natural disasters from developing into famines as they used to in the past. A major step was taken in that direction in the 1880s when the 'Famine Codes' were formulated. These codes included instructions for recreating lost incomes through wages to be paid in public works programmes, supplemented by some unconditional relief for those who could not be employed. Food trade was left almost entirely to private traders throughout the pre-independence period.

The Famine Codes, though clear-headed in analysis, were only a partial success in practice. Sometimes the relief offered was too little and too late, and in one notorious occasion—the Bengal Famine of 1943—the Famine Codes were not even invoked (the famine was simply 'not declared'). In post-independence India the relief system has become more systematic and extensive, but no less importantly, the governments—pressured by the news media and opposition parties—do not any longer have the option of ignoring famine threats. The last major famine in India occurred in 1943, preceding independence in 1947.

Drèze presents a discussion of the rationale of the Famine Codes (and other insights of the Famine Commission Reports), and he also investigates the changes that have been brought about since independence. Aside from a major political transformation, the latter include a considerable increase in the real resources devoted to famine relief, a broadening of the range of support measures, direct state involvement in food trade without eliminating private traders, and the maintenance of a substantial volume of food in public stock. Food management in India seems to have produced a large measure of food price stability, but India's success in famine prevention is still thoroughly dependent on the recreation of lost entitlements through wage-based employment, supplemented by unconditional relief.[30]

Jean Drèze provides two specific case-studies, namely the food crisis of 1966–7 in Bihar and the non-famine of 1970–3 in Maharashtra despite a disastrous drought. Finally, he examines the lessons that can be derived from the Indian experience for famine prevention elsewhere.[31]

1.14. *African successes in famine prevention*

India's success in the eradication of famines is fairly widely acknowledged, even though the reasons for this success are often misunderstood.[32] In

[30] There are few empirical studies of the role played in practice by unconditional relief measures. The interregional contrasts within India in this respect are important. For further discussion and some empirical material relating to the 1987 drought in Gujarat, see Drèze (1988).

[31] Drèze also points to the limitations of the Indian anti-hunger policy, which eliminates famines but tolerates massive endemic undernutrition. See also Drèze (1988).

[32] It is often presumed that famines have been eliminated in independent India through a revolutionary increase in food production. There certainly has been some rise in food production per capita since independence (and the 'green revolution' has been effective in the production of wheat in particular), but the increase in food production per head has not been very large. Indeed, the average per capita food availability in India today is not substantially greater than in the late

contrast, the experiences of successful famine prevention in sub-Saharan Africa are often unacknowledged and ignored. The harrowing tales of unprevented famines in that subcontinent seem to dominate the international perception of what has been happening in Africa.

In his second chapter in volume 2 ('Famine Prevention in Africa: Some Experiences and Lessons'), Jean Drèze concentrates specifically on recent success stories in sub-Saharan Africa, and examines the lessons that can be drawn from them. The case-studies include experiences of averted famines in Botswana, Cape Verde, Kenya, and Zimbabwe. At a very general level, these experiences confirm that public policy for recreating lost entitlements provides a major clue to success in famine prevention. Neither rapid economic growth (as in Botswana), nor rapid growth of agriculture (as in Kenya), nor even rapid growth in food production (as in post-independence Zimbabwe), are by themselves an adequate safeguard against famines. The distinguishing achievements of these countries (as well as of Cape Verde) really lie in their having provided direct public support to their populations in times of crisis.

Aside from this general observation, there are many other lessons to learn from the experiences examined by Drèze. The lessons are partly concerned with the strategy of entitlement protection, and partly with the politics of early action.[33] Regarding the former, Drèze discusses a range of policy issues including the role of food supply management in famine prevention, the question of early warning, the case for greater use of cash support and employment provision, the interconnections between private trade and public distribution, and the long-run importance of economic diversification. As far as early action is concerned, the case-studies presented in the chapter confirm that, in Africa no less than in India, the response of governments has been more a question of political incentives to intervene against a famine than one of ability to rely on formal 'early warning techniques' to anticipate a crisis. There is some diversity in the precise nature of political incentives that have prompted the governments of these African countries to counter resolutely the threat of famine. But one of the features that does emerge again in this context is the importance of public accountability in making it hard for a government to allow a famine to develop.

19th century (a decline over the first half of this century having been balanced by an increase after independence). The causes of success of Indian famine prevention policy have to be sought elsewhere—in the process of entitlement protection through various measures of income generation and price stability, and the compulsion generated by adversarial politics that ensures early public intervention. On this last see ch. 6, vol. 1.

[33] See also Drèze and Sen (1989a: chs. 5–8).

1.15.   Famines in Ethiopia

The success stories from Botswana, Cape Verde, etc. have to be contrasted with failures in famine prevention elsewhere. The case of Ethiopia is often cited in this context. In the third chapter of volume 2 ('Ethiopian Famines 1973–1985: A Case-Study'), B. G. Kumar examines the famines in Ethiopia during 1973–5 and 1982–5. The former set of famines began during Haile Selassie's rule and, in fact, he was deposed during those famines. But the government that followed has not been able to eliminate famines from Ethiopia.

Kumar explains the occurrence of famines and the composition of destitutes by examining the collapse of entitlements to food of different occupation groups. He also argues, however, that there were substantial declines in food availability in each of the famines, and these declines were among the factors that had a major influence on the entitlements of different groups.[34] Kumar also investigates the demographic and social impacts of the Ethiopian famines.

On matters of policy, Kumar's analysis underlines the usefulness of employment creation and the use of cash wages. He also emphasizes the importance of an early response. In this respect Kumar attaches some importance to bettering formal 'early warning' systems, but argues that the main delays in responding have been caused by political factors rather than by technical inadequacies. These lessons have clear affinity with those emerging on the 'other' side, from case-studies of success in India and in sub-Saharan Africa.

1.16.   Early warning systems

There is general agreement on the need to act quickly to defeat threatening famines. 'Early warning systems' are aimed at making it possible to act without

---

[34] As far as the 1973 famine is concerned, earlier discussed in Sen (1981), Kumar disputes Sen's view that the famine was not caused by any significant decline in food availability. Sen's diagnosis referred to food availability in Ethiopia as a whole, whereas Kumar's point is about a decline in food availability specifically in the famine province of Wollo (this was, in fact, noted and discussed by Sen, pp. 88–96). Since there was no ban on food movement between the different provinces during the famine of 1973, the question as to whether Wollo's low food supply should be treated as an endogenous variable governed by local food production in Wollo (as Kumar suggests), *or* as being governed by the low purchasing power of the Wollo population connected with the local agricultural decline (as Sen suggests), turns on the physical possibility of transporting food across the boundaries of Wollo with the rest of Ethiopia. In this context, the undisputed existence of a major highway linking Dessie (the capital of Wollo) to Addis Ababa and Asmera (the highway was in fact used for moving some food *out of* Wollo to elsewhere, on which see Sen 1981: 94), *is* crucial to the point at issue. Further, the fact that food prices in Dessie did not rise and remained roughly similar to those in Addis Ababa and Asmera (Sen 1981: 95–6), despite the famine conditions in and around Dessie, would seem to support the view that the food available in the rest of Ethiopia could not be pulled into Wollo because of the lack of purchasing power of the Wollo population (not because of any assumed transport bottleneck).

delay by making policy makers aware of famine threats. Unfortunately, there is also some agreement that the existing formal systems of early warning are seriously defective.

From here we can go in one of two different directions. One is to abandon the search for an adequate 'early warning' model, and to concentrate on getting the necessary warnings in other ways, e.g. through an active news media reporting early cases of hardship and worsening hunger.[35] The other way is to try to improve the models that have been so far devised. Meghnad Desai takes the second route in his chapter ('Modelling an Early Warning System For Famines'), and suggests ways in which the exercise of early warning can be much improved. He also goes into the use of such systems in determining the timing of policies.

One of the reasons why formal analysis of early warning is difficult is the fact that a famine can develop from a variety of causes. The initiating factor can be a natural phenomenon (e.g. a drought), or an economic one (e.g. widespread loss of employment and income), or a socio-political event (e.g. a civil war). Desai discusses how these processes can respectively—in different ways—affect the economic system and lead to the collapse of entitlements of vulnerable groups.

Desai's analysis throws much light on the requirements of a good early warning system.[36] There may be some scope for doubt as to whether these requirements can be typically fully met given the complexities of the relations involved and the need for speed in data gathering and analysis. That question remains somewhat open at this stage. But even if a fully adequate system of early warning were not to emerge rapidly, the connections that Desai explores can be of a great deal of use in devising anti-famine policies. An analytical system of early warning, of the kind that Desai has explored, relies on unpacking the different components involved in the collapse of entitlements, and those components have to be clearly understood for the formulation of effective policies of entitlement protection and famine prevention. Thus, the scope of Desai's chapter is considerably broader than the title suggests.

1.17. *Anti-hunger policy and market responses*

In the fifth chapter in volume 2 ('Market Responses to Anti-hunger Policies: Effects on Wages, Prices, and Employment'), Martin Ravallion takes up the complex issue of how market responses affect the effectiveness of various public measures to combat hunger of particular groups. This investigation draws on general-equilibrium analysis of the kind that Ravallion has already

---

[35] On this see chs. 2 and 6 vol. 1 and the chapters by Drèze in vol. 2. See also Drèze and Sen (1989a).

[36] See also Desai (1988), and the chapter by d'Souza (1988) in the same volume.

used very successfully in his previous studies of famines (particularly in his book *Markets and Famines*, Ravallion 1987a).

Ravallion considers the major types of measures that have been used in this field, including pure transfer payments, wages for relief work, public grain storage, food price policies, foreign trade, and public information and famine forecasting. In each case, he investigates the ways in which the markets may respond, and their implications for public policy. For example, the overall transfer benefits (inclusive of 'multiplier effects') of public employment programmes will be larger when the wage elasticity of demand for labour is small, and this provides one argument for providing such employment at times when it competes with other employment, rather than just in lean seasons. Of course, these particular considerations have to be integrated with other elements of a full assessment of alternatives, including in this case the 'stabilization benefits' that may be associated with income generation in lean seasons (when incomes are scarce) particularly if opportunities for borrowing are restricted.

Ravallion puts particular emphasis on the less obvious elements of anti-hunger policy. In contrast with the much-discussed cases of relief work and pure transfers, he also investigates the considerable benefits for the poor and the hungry that may result from price stabilization policies, improvement of rural credit, etc. The relative effectiveness of these different lines of action has to be assessed in the light of their respective market responses. Altogether Ravallion has provided an important exploration of alternative anti-hunger policies, the effects they may have (operating *inter alia* through the market), and how their effectiveness may be respectively assessed. The lessons have relevance in combating endemic hunger as well as in devising policies of famine prevention.

1.18.   *Policy variables and structural constraints*

One of the issues facing public policy analysis to combat famines and hunger in sub-Saharan African concerns the assignment of responsibility for its present predicament. Policy mistakes in the past have often been identified as the major offenders in bringing Africa to its present plight. For example, African governments typically have much control—direct and indirect—over prices of agricultural goods in general and food prices in particular, and it has been frequently argued that it is the tendency to keep these prices artificially low that has been a major cause of low food production in Africa.[37]

In so far as the problems of sub-Saharan Africa are seen as arising primarily or largely from policy mistakes, there may be some reason to hope that a

---

[37] This position has been forcefully presented in several contributions by the World Bank and its policy analysts; see e.g. World Bank (1986), Ray (1988).

solution of these problems may be readily available in the form of reversing these policy mistakes. For example, 'getting prices right' has appealed to many as an obvious and sure-fire way of liberating Africa from its present predicament.

While there is clearly some truth in the diagnosis of policy errors, and while price incentives can indeed be important, it is not easy to see a ready salvation for Africa through a simple 'policy reversal'. For one thing, each of these policies has many aspects. For example, high food prices may give more production incentives, but they also make it harder for the poor to acquire food, and a substantial proportion of the African poor have to rely on the market—rather than on home production—for getting the food they eat. For another, the remedy of African poverty calls for a rapid increase in production and incomes in general, and the demands of this have to be distinguished from the policy imperatives of maximizing food production as such. Even though there have undoubtedly been policy mistakes that have contributed to Africa's present problems, straightforward remedies, such as raising food prices, may not be as promising and unproblematic as they have been made to look.[38]

What is at issue is not merely the effectiveness of changes in prices and of other policy variables that the governments can easily control, but also the need to address the harder and less easily influenceable features of the economy and the society. Platteau's chapter ('The Food Crisis in Africa: A Comparative Structural Analysis') discusses many of the structural features that have had a profound bearing on famines and hunger in Africa, particularly through influencing food production. The domain of Platteau's investigation is wide, and he identifies the important influences exercised by land tenure and other institutions, technological constraints, political limitations, and even cultural obstacles. His analysis of Africa's predicament draws on a long-ranging study of history, and he argues strongly in favour of taking fuller note of structural parameters and constraints in understanding African hunger and in seeking effective and lasting remedies.

Platteau's institutional analysis importantly supplements the concentration on easily influenceable policy variables in many other studies. The recurrence of famines in Africa has many aspects and it relates to different antecedent circumstances. The demands of rapidity and durability in remedying the situation include the need for attention being paid to policy issues of widely different kinds.

The chapters in volume 2, taken together, provide a fairly comprehensive investigation of the underlying issues and the different considerations that have to be taken into account in eradicating famines from Africa. While there is scope for much optimism, especially in view of the successes already achieved

---

[38] We have gone into these issues in Drèze and Sen (1989a), particularly in chs. 2, 9, and 13. There is an extensive literature on this; see e.g. Lipton (1987), Streeten (1987), Pinstrup-Andersen (1989).

in some parts of sub-Saharan Africa and elsewhere, the need for deep-rooted, constructive changes cannot be overemphasized.[39] The call for rapidity should not be confused with a search for the 'quick fix'.

1.19. *Endemic undernourishment and deprivation*

While the focus of volume 2 is primarily on eliminating famines, the third volume deals with the challenge of combating persistent want and hunger. Two cases of notable success—China and Sri Lanka—are discussed in some detail. In both these cases a major reduction of deprivation and expansion of life expectancy and related indicators have been achieved despite very low gross national product per capita.

In another book (Drèze and Sen 1989*a*), we have compared and contrasted two different—though not unrelated—general strategies for eliminating endemic undernourishment and deprivation. The approach of 'growth-mediated security' involves rapid economic expansion, including that of GNP per head, and the use of this achievement to eradicate regular hunger and privation. In this general strategy, the fruits of growth are widely shared partly through a participatory growth process (involving, in particular, a rapid and sustained expansion of remunerative and worthwhile employment), but also through the use of the resources generated by economic growth to expand public support of health, nutrition, education, and economic security for the more deprived and vulnerable. In contrast, the approach of 'support-led security' involves going in for public support measures without waiting for the country to become rich through economic growth. Examples of support-led security include, in addition to China and Sri Lanka, such countries as Costa Rica, Cuba, Chile, Jamaica, and the State of Kerala in India.

There is a real contrast between these two strategies, but it is important to recognize that the extensive use of public support measures plays a crucial role in both. While public support is the primary and immediate instrument of action in the strategy of support-led security, it is also an important ingredient of the success of growth-mediated security. Indeed, in the absence of public involvement to guarantee that the fruits of growth are widely shared, rapid economic growth can have a disappointingly poor impact on living conditions.[40] The distinctiveness of the strategy of support-led security is not the *use* of public support to improve living conditions, but the *temporal priority* that is attached to this instrument of action even when the country in question is still quite poor.

It may be asked how poor countries can afford to have extensive public

[39] The positive opportunities that can be effectively used have also been discussed in Drèze and Sen (1989*a*: chs. 5–8).

[40] On the role of public support measures in the recent experiences of growth-mediated security, see Drèze and Sen (1989*a*: ch. 10).

support systems. Part of the answer lies in the labour intensive nature of many of these measures of public delivery—particularly in health care and education —making them cheaper in poorer economies. But some of the explanation also relates to the scope for reorienting the focus of delivery away from providing an enormous lot—expensive and advanced services—to a few (the relatively affluent) to securing minimal basic services for all (including the worst off).[41] Indeed, the fractions of their relatively low GNP per head devoted to public programmes of health care and education in China, Sri Lanka, Kerala, Cuba, and other adopters of the general strategy of support-led security have not been remarkably higher than in countries that have treated education and medicine as the entitlement of the rich and the privileged.

1.20. China's record

Carl Riskin's chapter ('Feeding China: The Experience since 1949') is an illuminating account of China's experience in combating hunger since the revolution.[42] While a problem of undernourishment in many rural areas continues to exist, China has been in general remarkably successful in reducing the reach and magnitude of undernourishment across the country. Food production has generally grown faster than population over these years, but between the 1950s and the reforms of 1979, not by very much.[43] China's success in reducing deprivation is particularly connected with public policies involving relatively egalitarian distribution and widespread public support of health and nutrition. Riskin also discusses in some detail the mechanisms of food distribution in China—between the provinces, between the urban and rural areas, and between different families and persons.

One terrible blot in China's otherwise impressive record is the occurrence of a large famine during 1959–61, in the wake of the failure of the so-called Great Leap Forward. Riskin discusses the factors that contributed to this calamity, including the limited information that the central government had about food production and consumption in the provinces. In the comparison between China and India, on which we commented earlier in this Introduction, it would appear that India has done much worse than China in the reduction of

---

[41] There are many other factors involved in this complex question. On this and related matters (including the considerations involved in the choice between the two general strategies), see Drèze and Sen (1989a: chs. 10–12).

[42] See also Riskin (1987).

[43] Oddly, in the post-reform period, between 1979 and the mid-1980s, while agricultural and food production per head have rapidly increased, the mortality rate has also gone up and there has been a considerable reduction in life expectancy (on this see Banister 1987). These changes are not yet fully studied, but among the factors implicated are general financial stringency and some withdrawal of wide-coverage rural health services, and the introduction of compulsory birth control measures, leading to a neglect (if not worse) of female children. These matters have been discussed in Sen (1988b) and Drèze and Sen (1989a: ch. 11).

endemic undernourishment, but has been more successful in eradicating famines.

The fact that China could have such a famine despite its excellent general record in the reduction of endemic deprivation and normal mortality underlines the need to see the battle against hunger as one with many facets. It also indicates that the eradication of hunger benefits not only from having a dedicated and determined government committed to that objective, but also from having a system that permits participatory and adversarial involvement of the general public.[44] Given the recent developments in China, the relevance of these considerations may extend well beyond the limited field of anti-hunger policy.

1.21. *Public support in Sri Lanka*

Sri Lanka's achievements in raising life expectancy and the quality of life have been the subject of much attention among economists (even though these achievements are in some danger of being overshadowed by the violence and strife into which Sri Lanka has recently been plunged). A life expectancy of 70 years for a country with the low GNP per head that Sri Lanka has is no mean feat. Indeed, its life expectancy is still marginally *higher* than that of South Korea despite the latter's remarkable economic expansion leading to a GNP per capita many times that of Sri Lanka.

Sri Lanka's use of public support measures goes back a long way. Expansion of primary education took place early in the century. A rapid expansion of health services occurred in the mid-1940s. Sri Lanka moved to a system of free or subsidized distribution of rice in 1942. Between 1940 and 1960, its crude death rate fell from above 20 per thousand to around 8 per thousand.

Sri Lanka's radical and innovative public support measures have played a substantial part in its achievements.[45] In their chapter ('Public Policy and Basic Needs Provision: Intervention and Achievement in Sri Lanka'), Sudhir Anand and Ravi Kanbur have provided a probing and far-reaching account of that connection. By using time-series data pertaining to the relevant variables, they have indicated how and when direct public intervention has contributed to reducing deprivation and to enhancing the quality of life in Sri Lanka. These

[44] On this see also Drèze and Sen (1989a). Also ch. 6 vol. 1 and the chapters by Drèze in vol. 2.

[45] Some observers (e.g. Bhalla and Glewwe 1986, Bhalla 1988) have argued that Sri Lanka's high level of life expectancy and other achievements may not have been related to its public support measures and in support of this view they have pointed to its unexceptional expansion of life expectancy and other indicators in the period *since 1960* (compared with other countries). Aside from some methodological problems in the analysis (on which see Isenman 1987, Pyatt 1987, Ravallion 1987b, among others), this line of argument overlooks the fact that the expansion of public support measures in Sri Lanka substantially predates 1960, and that in the period of rapid expansion of public support (particularly from the mid-1940s) Sri Lanka's death rate did fall quite fast. On this and related matters, see Drèze and Sen (1989a: ch. 12).

lessons have considerable bearing on future policy as well, since public support measures have been under severe scrutiny in Sri Lanka—as elsewhere—on the grounds of their being expensive, and there has been some withdrawal (also analysed by Anand and Kanbur) from an interventionist strategy in recent years.

Anand and Kanbur's econometric analysis suggests that the expansion of health services has been rather more effective than food subsidies in bringing about mortality decline in Sri Lanka. The policy issues to be faced in Sri Lanka—and elsewhere—not only concern the recognition of the role of public support measures in general, but also call for a discriminating assessment of the choices to be faced *within* a general strategy of public intervention. Anand and Kanbur have provided a far-reaching account of the diagnostic and policy issues concerning one of the most interesting experiences of combating hunger and deprivation in a poor country.

1.22. *Brazil and unaimed opulence*

While Sri Lanka provides an example of what can be achieved even with a low real income per head and moderate economic growth, Brazil provides an illustration of how little can happen in removing poverty and deprivation even with remarkably rapid growth of GNP per head. In his chapter 'Growth and Poverty: Some Lessons from Brazil', Ignacy Sachs provides a lucid account of this contrary experience.

Brazil's economic growth has not only been fast, it has also been sustained and technologically rich (with widespread use of modern technology). Brazil has also emerged as one of the largest exporters of industrial products in the world, and the incomes generated in production for domestic and foreign markets have raised the level of average income in the country to levels that are very much higher than obtained a few decades ago. And yet there is a good deal of endemic undernutrition in Brazil and there is persistent poverty affecting a substantial section of the population. Sachs discusses how and why rapid economic growth has failed to improve the lives of so many million Brazilians, and why their entitlements have been so little influenced by the newly generated incomes. Identifying inequality as the major villain in all this, Sachs has also briefly explored the scope for 'growth with redistribution' in Brazil.

As we discussed earlier in this Introduction (and more fully in Drèze and Sen 1989a), growth of GNP *can be* a major contributor to removing undernourishment and deprivation, and the strategy of 'growth-mediated security' specifically focuses on this connection. But that recognition should not be confused with the claim that growth of GNP per head must invariably and automatically bring about removal of deprivation across the board. What is at issue is not merely the quality of growth—in particular its participatory nature—but also the willingness of the government to use the fruits of growth to provide public support with comprehensive coverage—guaranteeing basic health services, education, and other basic amenities to all sections of the population, including the most vulnerable and deprived groups. In both these respects the experience of growth-mediated security in, say, South Korea contrasts sharply with the 'unaimed opulence' of Brazil.[46]

1.23. *Latin American poverty and undernourishment*

While Sachs concentrates on Brazil, Ravi Kanbur's chapter 'Malnutrition and Poverty in Latin America' has a much wider coverage. Kanbur identifies the extent of undernourishment in Latin America, which is obviously much less severe than in South Asia or sub-Saharan Africa, but which is far from negligible in magnitude.[47]

Kanbur goes on to discuss the extent to which economic growth on its own can be expected to eliminate undernourishment in the Latin American countries. Here Kanbur's broader analysis supplements the more concentrated study of Brazil by Sachs. Kanbur shows that the 'crossover time' (i.e. the number of years required for the average poor person to cross the poverty line if his or her income grows at the average rate of growth of per capita GNP of the past twenty years) tends to be remarkably high. This takes Kanbur to the question of the *aiming* of economic expansion and the *targeting* of the increase of incomes and consumptions. He outlines some necessary characteristics of a well-targeted policy for alleviating poverty and undernourishment.

Crucial to Kanbur's analysis is his identification of the contrasts between socio-economic groups in terms of vulnerability to deprivation. Throughout Latin America, the incidence of poverty is much higher in the rural areas than in the urban (though the urban slum dwellers form one of the more deprived groups). Within the rural areas, the landless workers and those with tiny holdings are most prone to suffer. Kanbur finds the size of the family to be an important parameter as well, indicating the relevance of population policy. His analysis of targeting in removing undernourishment draws on the results of these diagnostic analyses. The important issue is to replace 'unaimed opulence' by using growth as a mediator of security.

1.24. *The extent of undernourishment in sub-Saharan Africa*

Peter Svedberg's chapter 'Undernutrition in Sub-Saharan Africa: A Critical Assessment of the Evidence' is concerned with the diagnostic question as to

---

[46] The contrast between 'growth-mediated security' and 'unaimed opulence' is discussed in Drèze and Sen (1989a: ch. 10).

[47] While the proportion of people in poverty in Latin America is comparable to that in East Asia in terms of income deprivation, Latin America's record is much worse than that of East Asia in terms of living conditions, including expectation of life.

how much undernourishment exists in sub-Saharan Africa. Svedberg deals with both methodological and substantive issues. He argues that the methodologies used to measure the extent of undernourishment in sub-Saharan Africa have frequently been faulty and have involved the use of unreliable data. He also indicates that the extent of undernourishment has been very often exaggerated.

Svedberg makes extensive use—*inter alia*—of anthropometric evidence to establish his substantive conclusions. There are interpretational problems here too, but Svedberg's critical assessment of the unreliability of the usual high estimates is certainly quite robust. It is important not to read his conclusions as grounds for smugness, since even his own estimates indicate a substantial problem of deprivation and undernourishment in sub-Saharan Africa.

Svedberg's chapter can be seen as an argument for not exaggerating what is in any case quite a momentous problem. It can be added that, by exaggerating the extent of the problem, well-meaning scholars have sometimes inadvertently encouraged a sense of hopelessness and fatalism about hunger in sub-Saharan Africa. This can be changed by a more realistic assessment of the extent of the challenge, followed by a determination to deal with it effectively. Svedberg's essay serves this dialectic purpose in addition to the methodological and diagnostic functions on which he himself concentrates.

1.25. *Institutions and policies for sub-Saharan Africa*

In removing the true—unexaggerated—prevalence of endemic undernourishment in sub-Saharan Africa, the expansion of its agriculture will undoubtedly play an important part. This is not merely because food comes primarily from agriculture, but also because the entitlements of the majority of Africans depend—directly or indirectly—on the functioning of the agricultural sector, and this situation can change only relatively slowly. Despite the importance of distinguishing between the problems of food entitlement and those of food production as such, the crucial contributory role of food production in particular and agricultural production in general can scarcely be denied.

In his chapter 'Policy Options for African Agriculture', Francis Idachaba has provided a broad-ranging analysis of ailments of sub-Saharan agriculture and the policy options that exist. Rather than concentrating on some simple 'remedies', Idachaba surveys the whole gamut of specific issues—social institutions, technological research, rural infrastructure, agricultural prices. It is in this wide setting that he assesses what the governments can do and what policies seem most promising.[48] Idachaba also considers the role of external

---

[48] There is a discussion in Drèze and Sen (1989a: ch. 9) of these issues, including the importance of diversification and the balance of food production *vis-à-vis* the production of cash crops and industrial goods.

assistance and the parts—negative as well as positive—played by international institutions such as the World Bank.

1.26. *Kenyan agriculture and food deprivation*

While Idachaba takes on the whole of sub-Saharan Africa as his field of investigation, Judith Heyer looks specifically at smallholder agriculture in Kenya ('Poverty and Food Deprivation in Kenya's Smallholder Agricultural Areas'). The incidence of poverty among people engaged in smallholder agriculture in Kenya is, of course, very high, and Heyer considers the ways in which this situation can be changed.

Although Heyer examines various internal reforms within smallholder agriculture, she comes to the conclusion that, in bringing about a major change, an important part will have to be played by developments *outside* the sector—in non-agricultural activities and in large-scale farming. Heyer identifies intersectoral interconnections that are important, but which are frequently overlooked in viewing smallholder agriculture on its own. Her argument for a broader economic analysis with an eye to social consequences can be seen as a corrective to some of the prevailing preconceptions in this field.

1.27. *The industrial connection*

Samuel Wangwe's chapter ('The Contribution of Industry to Solving the Food Problem in Africa') has close links with Judith Heyer's broad-based approach. Wangwe looks specifically at the contribution of industry to combating hunger (in this his concentration is rather narrower than that of Heyer), but he does not confine his analysis to any particular country (his focus is, in that respect, broader than that of Heyer).

Given the importance of employment in securing entitlements, Wangwe devotes a good deal of attention to the need for generating opportunities of employment—in off-farm activities and in industry in addition to farm employment. Another industrial connection that receives much attention in Wangwe's paper is the part played by the production, acquisition, and use of agricultural equipment. He also goes on to discuss the role of industry in agricultural processing.

The contributions of Heyer and Wangwe supplement the analysis presented by Idachaba, and help to underline the important fact that the solution of the so-called 'food problem' in sub-Saharan Africa will require a good deal more than a concentration on the internal problems of the food-producing sector. The persistence of endemic undernourishment in sub-Saharan Africa calls for a wide range of remedial actions involving institutional changes and economic reforms both within the food sector and outside it.[49]

[49] See also Mellor *et al.* (1987), Lipton (1987), Eicher (1988), Pinstrup-Andersen (1989). See also Drèze and Sen (1989*a*).

1.28. *Hunger in Bangladesh*

Sub-Saharan Africa is not only plagued by endemic deprivation, it also suffers from the persistence of recurrent famines. In this respect the situation in South Asia is rather less desperate in that famines have rarely occurred in recent years in any of the South Asian economies. The one exception is Bangladesh which experienced a major famine in 1974.[50] But despite this relative absence of famines, the extent of regular undernourishment seems to be, if anything, *larger*—even in proportion to its population—in South Asia than in sub-Saharan Africa.[51]

Among the major countries in South Asia, Bangladesh is not only the poorest, it also has the largest proportion of hungry and undernourished people according to most estimates. In his chapter 'The Food Problems of Bangladesh', Siddiq Osmani has provided a helpful and authoritative account of the problems of undernourishment and famines in Bangladesh. Despite the international perception of the enormous and seemingly incurable nature of Bangladesh's problems (it has frequently been referred to as 'a basket case'), Bangladesh's achievements are far from negligible. It has achieved a growth rate of per capita income of about 2 per cent per year over the fourteen years or so since the famine of 1974,[52] and it has successfully avoided famines despite natural calamities of rather larger dimension than in 1974 (including the widespread and severe flooding of 1988). Osmani discusses the changes that have taken place and the major tasks that remain.

Osmani comes to the conclusion that, despite actually avoiding famines since 1974, Bangladesh's vulnerability to them remains. There is a lack of system in famine prevention and too much reliance on muddling through.[53] As far as endemic hunger is concerned, Osmani also argues that current food policies have the effect of accentuating rather than relieving this problem. The relatively successful overall economic growth has not been adequate in eliminating regular undernourishment.[54]

It is interesting that despite a much faster overall growth of aggregate real income compared with the growth of food production and consumption

---

[50] On this see Alamgir (1980) and Sen (1981: ch. 9).

[51] This is so even according to standard estimates (see Kanbur's chapter 'Malnutrition and Poverty in Latin America' for some comparative figures). Svedberg's criticisms have the effect of indicating that the actual extent of undernourishment is less in sub-Saharan Africa than these estimates suggest.

[52] On this see also Osmani (1989).

[53] It is also possible to argue that the more restricted nature of adversarial politics in Bangladesh compared with India is a factor that keeps the former country more vulnerable to famines arising from the lack of alertness and speed in anti-famine public policy.

[54] There has, however, been a considerable reduction in mortality, morbidity, and clinically diagnosed undernourishment in Bangladesh, connected with better delivery of health services.

(nutritional intake per head has not materially increased over the last two decades), food prices have not risen relative to other prices (in fact, the contrary has happened[55]). This is one result of the fact that Bangladesh's continuing problems have much to do with the persistence—even accentuation—of inequality, and the distribution of ownership and power that lead to unequal results. Osmani discusses the lines of reform that would be needed to meet the major challenge of continuing hunger in Bangladesh.

1.29. *Public support and South Asia*

While Osmani's chapter concentrates on Bangladesh, the chapter by Kaushik Basu ('The Elimination of Endemic Hunger in South Asia: Some Policy Options') considers the problems of South Asia as a whole. The inadequacy of relying only on overall economic growth resurfaces here again in this context. Basu outlines the need for—and the actual possibility of—effective policies of 'direct action' to remove poverty and regular deprivation.

Basu illustrates his arguments with empirical illustrations from the experiences of Sri Lanka, India, and Bangladesh. He also provides a probing scrutiny of various 'poverty alleviation programmes' in use in South Asia, including 'food-for-work' schemes. While many of these programmes have failed in diverse ways, Basu outlines the promising nature of some of these policies if they are effectively planned and implemented.

The 'direct action' programmes take the form of economic action, but their success depends greatly on their political background—in particular the ability to remove the political constraints that often make them ineffective or degenerate. In addition to providing economic analysis of poverty removal, Basu's paper goes into the political requirements of entitlement protection and promotion. Both Osmani and Basu go explicitly into the political factors on which the effectiveness and success of economic policies significantly depend.[56] Here again political economy, in the broader sense outlined earlier, becomes the crucial analytical apparatus.

1.30. *A concluding remark*

This collection of twenty-six papers has ranged over many different aspects of the battle against famines and endemic deprivation. While the responsibility for the views and analyses presented in them is ultimately that of the respective authors, it should be clear even from this Introduction that there are many interlinkages in the arguments and approaches contained in these papers. The challenge of hunger in the modern world calls for close scrutiny of many different issues in the political economy of hunger. These papers constitute elements of such a scrutiny.

[55] On this see Osmani (1989).

[56] On this see also Drèze and Sen (1989a: esp. ch. 13).

References

ALAMGIR, M. (1980), *Famine in South Asia* (Cambridge, Mass.: Oelgeschlager, Gunn & Hain).

ANAND, S., and HARRIS, C. (forthcoming), *Food and Nutrition in Sri Lanka* (Oxford: Oxford University Press).

ASHTON, B., HILL, K., PIAZZA, A., and ZEITZ, R. (1984), 'Famine in China, 1958–61', *Population and Development Review*, 10.

BANISTER, J. (1987), *China's Changing Population* (Stanford, Calif.: Stanford University Press).

BARDHAN, P. K. (1974), 'On Life and Death Questions', *Economic and Political Weekly*, 9 (Special No.).

——(1984), *The Political Economy of Development in India* (Oxford: Basil Blackwell).

——(1987), 'On the Economic Geography of Sex Disparity in Child Survival in India: A Note', paper presented at the BAMANEH/American SSRC Workshop on Differential Female Mortality and Health Care in South Asia, Dhaka.

BHALLA, S. (1988), 'Is Sri Lanka an Exception? A Comparative Study of Living Standards', in Srinivasan, T. N., and Bardhan, P. K. (eds.), *Rural Poverty in South Asia*, vol. ii (New York: Columbia University Press).

——and GLEWWE, P. (1986), 'Growth and Equity in Developing Countries: A Reinterpretation of the Sri Lankan Experience', *World Bank Economic Review*, 1.

BOSERUP, E. (1970), *Women's Role in Economic Development* (London: Allen & Unwin).

CHEN, L. C., HUQ, E., and D'SOUZA, S. (1981), 'Sex-Bias in the Family Allocation of Food and Health Care in Rural Bangladesh', *Population and Development Review*, 7.

DAS GUPTA, M. (1987), 'Selective Discrimination Against Female Children in Rural Punjab', *Population and Development Review*, 13.

DASGUPTA, P., and RAY, D. (1986); 'Inequality as a Determinant of Malnutrition and Unemployment: Theory', *Economic Journal*, 96.

—— ——(1987), 'Inequality as a Determinant of Malnutrition and Unemployment: Policy', *Economic Journal*, 97.

DESAI, M. (1988), 'The Economics of Famine', in Harrison (1988).

DRÈZE, J. P. (1988), 'Social Insecurity in India', paper presented at a Workshop on Social Security in Developing Countries held at the London School of Economics, July.

——and SEN, A. K. (1989a), *Hunger and Public Action* (Oxford: Oxford University Press).

—— ——(1989b), 'Public Action for Social Security', Discussion Paper No. 20, Development Economics Research Programme, London School of Economics; to be published in Ahmad, S. E., Drèze, J. P., Hills, J., and Sen, A. K. (eds.) (1991), *Social Security in Developing Countries* (Oxford: Oxford University Press).

D'SOUZA, F. (1988), 'Famine: Social Security and an Analysis of Vulnerability', in Harrison (1988).

EICHER, C. (1988), 'Food Security Battles in Sub-Saharan Africa', paper presented at the VIIth World Congress for Rural Sociology, Bologna, 25 June–2 July.

HARRISON, G. A. (ed.) (1988), *Famines* (Oxford: Oxford University Press).

HARRISS, B., and WATSON, E. (1987), 'The Sex Ratio in South Asia', in Momsen, J. H., and Townsend, J. (eds.), *The Geography of Gender in the Third World* (London: Butler and Tanner).

ISENMAN, P. (1987), 'A Comment on "Growth and Equity in Developing Countries: A Reinterpretation of the Sri Lankan Experience" by Bhalla and Glewwe', *World Bank Economic Review*, 1.

JHA, P. S. (1980), *India: The Political Economy of Stagflation* (Bombay: Oxford University Press).

KANDIYOTI, D. (1988), 'Bargaining with Patriarchy', *Gender and Society*, 1.

KYNCH, J., and SEN, A. K. (1983), 'Indian Women: Well-Being and Survival', *Cambridge Journal of Economics*, 7.

LIPTON, M. (1987), 'Limits of Price Policy for Agriculture: Which Way for the World Bank?', *Development Policy Review*, 5.

MELLOR, J. W., DELGADO, C. L., and BLACKIE, C. L. (eds.) (1987), *Accelerating Food Production in Sub-Saharan Africa* (Baltimore, Md.: Johns Hopkins).

MILLER, B. (1981), *The Endangered Sex: Neglect of Female Children in Rural North India* (Ithaca, NY: Cornell University Press).

—— (1989), 'Changing Patterns of Juvenile Sex Ratios in Rural India, 1961 to 1971', *Economic and Political Weekly*, 24.

OSMANI, S. (1989), 'Food Deprivation and Undernutrition in Rural Bangladesh', paper presented at the 9th World Congress of the International Economic Association, Athens, Aug.

—— (ed.) (1993), *Nutrition and Poverty* (Oxford: Oxford University Press).

PARIKH, K., and RABAR, F. (eds.) (1981), *Food for All in a Sustainable World* (Laxenburg: IIASA).

PENG, X. (1987), 'Demographic Consequences of the Great Leap Forward in China's Provinces', *Population and Development Review*, 13.

PINSTRUP-ANDERSEN, P. (1989), 'Assuring a Household Food Security and Nutrition Bias in African Government Policies', paper presented at the 9th World Congress of the International Economic Association, Athens, Aug.

PYATT, G. (1987), 'A Comment on "Growth and Equity in Developing Countries: A Reinterpretation of the Sri Lankan Experience" by Bhalla and Glewwe', *World Bank Economic Review*, 1.

RAVALLION, M. (1987a), *Markets and Famines* (Oxford: Oxford University Press).

—— (1987b), 'Growth and Equity in Sri Lanka: A Comment', mimeo (Washington, DC: World Bank).

RAY, A. (1988), 'A Response to Lipton's (June 1987) Review of "World Development Report 1986"', *Development Policy Review*, 6.

RISKIN, C. (1987), *China's Political Economy: The Quest for Development since 1949* (Oxford: Oxford University Press).

SEN, A. K. (1977), 'Starvation and Exchange Entitlements: A General Approach and its Application to the Great Bengal Famine', *Cambridge Journal of Economics*, 1.

—— (1981), *Poverty and Famines* (Oxford: Oxford University Press).

—— (1983), 'Development: Which Way Now?', *Economic Journal*, 93.

—— (1984), *Resources, Values and Development* (Oxford: Basil Blackwell).

—— (1985), *Commodities and Capabilities* (Amsterdam: North-Holland).

—— (1988a), 'Africa and India: What Do We Have to Learn from Each Other?', in Arrow, K. J. (ed.), *The Balance between Industry and Agriculture in Economic Development*, i: *Basic Issues* (London: Macmillan).

——(1988*b*), 'Food and Freedom', Sir John Crawford Memorial Lecture, to be published in *World Development*.

——(1989*a*), 'Economic Methodology: Heterogeneity and Relevance', *Social Research*, 56.

——(1989*b*), 'Women's Survival as a Development Problem', talk given at the American Academy of Arts and Sciences, to be published in the *Bulletin* of the Academy.

STREETEN, P. (1987), *What Price Food?* (London: Macmillan).

SUKHATME, P. V. (1977), *Malnutrition and Poverty* (New Delhi: Indian Agricultural Research Institute).

——(ed.) (1982*a*), *Newer Concepts in Nutrition and Their Implications for Policy* (Pune: Maharashtra Association for the Cultivation of Science).

——(1982*b*), 'Measurement of Undernutrition', *Economic and Political Weekly*, 17.

WALDRON, I. (1983), 'The Role of Genetic and Biological Factors in Sex Differences in Mortality', in Lopez, A. D., and Ruzicka, L. T. (eds.), *Sex Differentials in Mortality: Trends, Determinants and Consequences* (Canberra: Australian National University).

World Bank (1986), *World Development Report 1986* (Washington, DC: World Bank).

LIST OF PAPERS

Volume 1: Entitlement and Well-Being

Volume 2: Famine Prevention

Introduction
Jean Drèze and Amartya Sen

Famine Prevention in India
Jean Drèze

Famine Prevention in Africa:
Some Experiences and Lessons
Jean Drèze

Ethiopian Famines 1973–1985:
A Case-Study
B. G. Kumar

Modelling an Early Warning System for Famines
Meghnad Desai

Market Responses to Anti-hunger Policies:
Effects on Wages, Prices and Employment
Martin Ravallion

The Food Crisis in Africa:
A Comparative Structural Analysis
Jean-Philippe Platteau

Volume 3: Endemic Hunger

Introduction
Jean Drèze and Amartya Sen

Feeding China:
The Experience since 1949
Carl Riskin

Public Policy and Basic Needs Provision:
Intervention and Achievement in Sri Lanka
Sudhir Anand and S. M. Ravi Kanbur

Growth and Poverty:
Some Lessons from Brazil
Ignacy Sachs

Malnutrition and Poverty in Latin America
S. M. Ravi Kanbur

Undernutrition in Sub-Saharan Africa:
A Critical Assessment of the Evidence

Peter Svedberg

Policy Options for African Agriculture

Francis Idachaba

Poverty and Food Deprivation in Kenya's Smallholder Agricultural Areas

Judith Heyer

The Contribution of Industry to Solving the Food Problem in Africa

Samuel Wangwe

The Food Problems of Bangladesh

S. R. Osmani

The Elimination of Endemic Poverty in South Asia:
Some Policy Options

Kaushik Basu

2

Food, Economics, and Entitlements

Amartya Sen

2.1. *Economics and the acquirement problem*

What may be called 'instant economics' has always appealed to the quick-witted layman impatient with the slow-moving economist. This is particularly so in the field of hunger and food policy. Of course, the need for speed is genuinely important in matters of food, and the impatience is, thus, easy to understand. But instant economics is also highly deceptive, and especially dangerous in this field. Millions of lives depend on the adequacy of the policy response to the terrible problems of hunger and starvation in the modern world. Past mistakes of policy have been responsible for the death of many millions of people and the suffering of hundreds of millions, and this is not a subject in which short cuts in economic reasoning can be taken to be fairly costless.

One common feature of a good deal of instant economics related to food and hunger is impatience with investigating the precise mechanisms for acquiring food that people have to use. People establish command over food in many different ways. For example, while a peasant owning his land and the product of his labour simply owns the food produced, a wage labourer paid in cash has to convert that wage into a bundle of goods, including food, through exchange. The peasant does, as it were, an exchange with 'nature', putting in labour, etc., and getting back the product, namely food. The wage labourer does repeated exchanges with others in the society—first, his labour power for a wage and then, the wage for a collection of commodities including food. We cannot begin to understand the precise influences that make it possible or not possible to acquire enough food, without examining the conditions of these exchanges and the forces that govern them. The same applies to other methods of acquiring food, e.g. through share-cropping and getting a part of the produce, through running a business and making a profit, through selling services and earning an income, and so on. I shall call the problem of establishing command over commodities, in this case food, the 'acquirement problem'. It is easy to

This is a shortened version of the fourth Elmhirst Lecture given at the triennial meeting of the International Association of Agricultural Economists, in Malaga (Spain), on 26 Aug. 1985. The paper was prepared at the World Institute of Development Economic Research in Helsinki. The author is grateful for discussions with Lal Jayawardena, Glenn Johnson, and Nanak Kakwani. An earlier version (the fourth Elmhirst Lecture) was published in the *Proceedings* of the conference (Maunder and Renborg 1986) and also in *Lloyds Bank Review*, 160 (Apr. 1986).

establish that the acquirement problem is really central to questions of hunger and starvation in the modern world.

The acquirement problem is often neglected not only by non-economists, but also by many economists, including some great ones. For example, Malthus in his famous *Essay on the Principle of Population as it Affects the Further Improvement of Society* (1798) leaves the acquirement problem largely unaddressed, though in his less-known pamphlet *An Investigation of the Cause of the Present High Price of Provisions* (1800), which deals with more short-run questions, Malthus is in fact deeply concerned precisely with the nitty-gritty of this problem.[1] The result of this neglect in the former work is not without practical consequence, since the popularity of the Malthusian approach to population and food, and of the particular metric of food output per head extensively used in the *Essay on Population*, has tended to give that metric undue prominence in policy discussions across the world.

Malthusian pessimism, based on the expectation of falling food output per head, has not been vindicated by history. Oddly enough, what can be called 'Malthusian optimism', i.e. *not* being worried about the food problem so long as food output grows as fast as—or faster than—population, has often contributed substantially to delaying policy response to growing hunger (against a background of stationary or rising food output per head). This is a serious enough problem in the case of intensification of regular but non-extreme hunger (without starvation deaths but causing greater proneness to morbidity and mortality), and it can be quite disastrous in the context of a famine that develops without a decline in food output per head, with the misguided focus leading to a hopelessly delayed response of public policy. While Malthus's own writings are by no means unique in focusing attention on the extremely misleading variable of food output per head, 'Malthusian optimism', in general, has been indirectly involved in millions of deaths which have resulted from inaction and misdirection of public policy.[2] While fully acknowledging the great contribution that Malthus has made in highlighting the importance of population policy, this negative feature of his work, related to his own bit of instant economics, must also be recognized.

The neglect of the acquirement issue has far-reaching consequences. For many years rational discussion of the food problems of the modern world was distracted by undue concentration on the comparative trends of population growth and the expansion of food output, with shrill warnings of danger coming from very respectable quarters.[3] The fear of population outrunning

[1] On the importance of the latter document, which has received much less attention than the former, see Sen (1981a).

[2] This issue is discussed in Sen (1982).

[3] The Club of Rome, despite its extremely distinguished leadership, had been responsible for some of the more lurid research reports of doom and decline. However, a later study sponsored by the Club, undertaken by H. Linnemann (1981), shows the picture to be both less gloomy and more easily influenced by policy. See also Parikh and Rabar (1981), especially on the role of policy.

food output on a global scale has certainly not been realized, and world food output per head has steadily risen.[4] This has, however, gone hand in hand with intensification of hunger in some parts of the world. In many—though not all—of the affected countries, food output per head has in fact fallen, and the anxiety about these countries has often been anchored to the statistics of food output per head, with Malthusian worries translated from the global to the regional or country level. But a causal analysis of the persistence and intensification of hunger and of the development of famines does, in fact, call for something more than attention being paid simply to the statistics of food output per head.

I shall have more to say on the policy questions presently, but before that I would like to discuss a bit further the nature and implications of the acquirement problem. I shall also discuss some arguments that relate to studying food and hunger in terms of what in my book, *Poverty and Famines*,[5] was called the 'entitlement approach'.[6] That approach has been extensively discussed, examined, criticized, applied, as well as extended, and I have learned a lot from these contributions.[7] But the approach has also been occasionally misinterpreted, and given the importance of the subject of food policy and hunger, I shall permit myself the self-indulgence of commenting—*inter alia*—on a few of the points that have been made in response to my earlier analysis.

2.2. *Famines and entitlements*

The entitlement approach provides a particular focus for the analysis of famines. It does not specify one particular causation of famine—only the general one that a famine reflects widespread failure of entitlements on the part of substantial sections of the population. Such failure can arise from many different causes.

The entitlement of a person stands for the set of different alternative commodity bundles that the person can acquire through the use of the various legal channels of acquirement open to someone in his position. In a private ownership market economy, the entitlement set of a person is determined by his original bundle of ownership (what is called his 'endowment') and the various alternative bundles he can acquire starting respectively from each initial endowment, through the use of trade and production (what is called his

---

[4] See e.g. FAO (1985).

[5] See Sen (1977, 1981a, 1981c); see also Ravallion (1987).

[6] Note that the use of the expression 'entitlement' here is descriptive rather than prescriptive. A person's entitlements as given by the legal system, personal circumstances, etc. need not command any moral endorsement. This applies both to the opulent entitlements of the rich and to the meagre entitlements of the poor.

[7] Particularly from Seaman and Holt (1980), Arrow (1982), Bliss (1982), Griffin (1981), Hayter (1981), Joshi (1981), Lipton (1981), Desai (1984), Solow (1984), Kahn (1985), Kumar (1985), Ravallion (1985, 1987), Snowdon (1985), among others.

'exchange entitlement mapping'). This is not the occasion to go into the formal characterizations of endowments, exchange entitlement mappings, entitlement sets, etc., which were discussed in *Poverty and Famines*.

A person has to starve if his entitlement set does not include any commodity bundle with enough food. A person is reduced to starvation if some change either in his endowment (e.g. alienation of land, or loss of labour power due to ill health), or in his exchange entitlement mapping (e.g. fall in wages, rise in food prices, loss of employment, drop in the price of the goods he produces and sells), makes it no longer possible for him to acquire any commodity bundle with enough food. I have argued that famines can be usefully analysed in terms of failures of entitlement relations.

The advantages of the entitlement approach over more traditional analysis in terms of food availability per head were illustrated with case-studies of a number of famines, e.g. the Bengal famine of 1943, the Ethiopian famines of 1973 and 1974, the Bangladesh famine of 1974, and the Sahel famines in the early seventies.[8] In some of these famines food availability per head had gone down (e.g. in the Sahel famines); in others there was no significant decline —even a little increase (e.g. in the Bengal famine of 1943, the Ethiopian famine of 1973, the Bangladesh famine of 1974). That famines can occur even without any decline in food output or availability per head makes that metric particularly deceptive. Since food availability is indeed the most commonly studied variable, this is a source of some policy confusion. It also makes 'Malthusian optimism' a serious route to disastrous inaction. But the point of entitlement analysis is not only to dispute the focus on food availability, but more positively also to provide a general approach for understanding and investigating famines through focusing on variations in endowments and exchange entitlement mappings.

Famine can be caused by various different types of influences, and the common predicament of mass starvation does not imply any one common fundamental cause. Droughts, floods, general inflationary pressure, sharp recessionary loss of employment, and so on can all in their own way deprive large sections of the population of entitlement to adequate food. A decline in food output or availability can, of course, be one of the major influences on the development of a famine, but even when that is the case (indeed even when food availability decline is the primary proximate antecedent), a serious study of the causal mechanism leading to the famine and the precise form it takes will require us to go into the behaviour of the determinants of the entitlements of the different sections of the population.

In *Poverty and Famines* two broad types of famines were distinguished from each other, namely boom famines and slump famines. A famine can, of course, occur in a situation of general decline in economic activity (as happened, for

[8] See Sen (1981*a*: chs. 6–10).

example, in the Wollo province of Ethiopia in 1973, due to a severe drought). But it can also occur in overall boom conditions (as happened, for example, in the Bengal famine of 1943, with a massive expansion of economic activity related to war efforts). If economic expansion is particularly favourable to a large section of the population (in the case of the Bengal famine, primarily the urban population including that of Calcutta), but does not draw into the process another large section (in the Bengal famine, much of the rural labouring classes), then that uneven expansion can actually make the latter group lose out in the battle for commanding food. In the food battle the devil takes the hindmost, and even a boom condition can lead to some groups losing their command over food because of the worsening of their relative position *vis-à-vis* the groups favoured by the boom.

2.3. *The entitlement approach and economic traditions*

It is important to emphasize that the entitlement approach is consistent with many different detailed theories of the actual causation of a famine. While the approach identifies certain crucial variables, different theories of the determination of the values of these variables may all be consistent with the general entitlement approach. For example, the entitlement approach does not specify any particular theory of price determination, but relative prices are quite crucial to the entitlements of various occupation groups. The entitlement approach by itself does not provide—nor is it intended to provide—a detailed explanation of any famine, and such an explanation would require supplementation by more specific theories of movements of prices, wages, employment, etc., causing particular shifts in the entitlements of different occupation groups.[9]

What the entitlement approach does is to take up the acquirement problem seriously. Rather than arbitrarily making some implicit assumption about distribution (such as equal division of the available food, or some fixed pattern of inequality in that division), it analyses acquirement in terms of entitlements, which in a private ownership economy is largely a matter of ownership and exchange (including of course production, i.e. exchange with nature). I would claim that this is not in any way a departure from the old traditions of economics. It is, rather, a reassertion of the continuing concern of economics with the mechanism of acquiring commodities. If I had the courage and confidence that Gary Becker shows in his distinguished work in calling his own approach '*the* economic approach',[10] I would have called the entitlement approach by the same bold name. While the price of timidity is to shy away from such assertive naming, I would nevertheless claim that economic tradi-

---

[9] See Sen (1981a: chs. 6–10). See also Svedberg (1984), Ravallion (1985), and Khan (1985).

[10] See Becker (1976, 1981).

tions stretching back centuries do, in fact, direct our attention to entitlements in analysing problems of wealth, poverty, deprivation, and hunger.

This is clear enough in Marx's case,[11] but the point is often made that Adam Smith was a great believer in the simple theory of food availability decline in explaining all famines, and that he would have thus had little patience for discussion of entitlements and their determinants. Indeed, it is true that in his often-quoted 'Digression Concerning the Corn Trade and Corn Laws' in Book IV of the *Wealth of Nations*, Adam Smith did remark that 'a dearth never has arisen from any combination among the inland dealers in corn, nor from any other cause but a real scarcity, occasioned sometimes, perhaps, and in some particular places, by the waste of war, but in by far the greatest number of cases, by the fault of the seasons'.[12] However, in understanding the point that Adam Smith is making here, it is important to recognize that he is primarily denying that traders could cause famine through collusion, and he is disputing the view that famines often follow from artificial shortages created by traders, and asserting the importance of what he calls 'a real scarcity'. I shall have the occasion to take up this aspect of Smith's observation presently when I discuss the issue of anti-famine policy.

We have to look elsewhere in the *Wealth of Nations* to see how acutely concerned Adam Smith was with the acquirement problem in analysing what he called 'want, famine, and mortality'. I quote Smith from the chapter called 'Of the Wages of Labour' from Book I of the *Wealth of Nations*:

But it would be otherwise in a country where the funds destined for the maintenance of labour were sensibly decaying. Every year the demand for servants and labourers would, in all the different classes of employments, be less than it had been the year before. Many who had been bred in the superior classes, not being able to find employment in their own business, would be glad to seek it in the lowest. The lowest class being not only overstocked with its own workmen, but with the over-flowings of all the other classes, the competition for employment would be so great in it, as to reduce the wages of labour to the most miserable and scanty subsistence of the labourer. Many would not be able to find employment even upon these hard terms, but would either starve, or be driven to seek a subsistence either by begging, or by the perpetration perhaps of the greatest enormities. Want, famine, and mortality would immediately prevail in that class, and from thence extend themselves to all the superior classes.[13]

Here Adam Smith is focusing on the market-based entitlement of labourers, and its dependence on employment and real wages, and explaining famine from that perspective. This should, of course, come as no surprise. In denying that artificial scarcity engineered by collusive traders can cause famine, Adam Smith was in no way closing the door to the economic analysis of various

---

[11] See e.g. the discussion on wages and capital in Marx (1887), Parts VI and VII.

[12] See Smith (1776).

[13] Smith (1776: Book I, ch. VIII, 26, pp. 90–1).

different real influences on the ability of different groups to command food in the market, in particular the values of wages and employment.

Perhaps it is useful to consider another argument presented by another great classical economist, namely David Ricardo, attacking the view that a famine cannot occur in a situation of what he calls 'superabundance'. This was in a speech that Ricardo wrote for delivery in Parliament in 1822, using the third person for himself as if the speech is reported in *Hansard*, though in the event Ricardo did not actually get to deliver the speech. The reference is to the famine conditions then prevailing in Ireland, and Ricardo examines the point made by another member of Parliament that this could not be the case since there was superabundance of food in Ireland at that time.

But says the honble. gentn. the people are dying for want of food in Ireland, and the farmers are said to be suffering from superabundance. In these two propositions the honble. gentn. thinks there is a manifest contradiction, but he Mr. R. could not agree with him in thinking so. Where was the contradiction in supposing that in a country where wages were regulated mainly by the price of potatoes the people should be suffering the greatest distress if the potato crop failed and their wages were inadequate to purchase the dearer commodity corn? From whence was the money to come to enable them to purchase the grain however abundant it might [be] if its price far exceeds that of potatoes. He Mr. Ricardo should not think it absurd or contradictory to maintain that in such a country as England where the food of the people was corn, there might be an abundance of that grain and such low prices as not to afford a renumeration to the grower, and yet that the people might be in distress and not able for want of employment to buy it, but in Ireland the case was much stronger and in that country there should be no doubt there might be a glut of corn, and a starving people.[14]

There is indeed nothing surprising in the fact that economists should be concerned with the acquirement problem, and dispute the instant economics that overlooks that aspect of the food problem based on confusing supply with command, as the 'honourable gentleman' quoted by David Ricardo clearly did. It is a confusion that has recurred again and again in actual discussions of the food problem, and the need to move away from instant economics to serious analysis of the acquirement problem and the entitlement to food is no less today than it was in Ricardo's time.[15]

It is not my purpose to assert that the entitlement approach is flawless as an economic approach to the problem of hunger and starvation. Several 'limitations' of the entitlement approach were, in fact, noted in *Poverty and Famines*, including ambiguities in the specification of entitlement, the neglect of non-legal transfers (e.g. looting) in the disposition of food, the importance of tastes and values in causing hunger despite adequate entitlement, and the relevance of disease and epidemic in famine mortality which extends far beyond the groups whose entitlement failures may have initiated the famine.

[14] See Ricardo's papers in Sraffa (1971: 234–5).
[15] See Taylor (1975) for an illuminating critique.

To this one should also add that in order to capture an important part of the acquirement problem, to wit, distribution of food within a family, the entitlement approach would have to be extended. In particular, notions of perceived 'legitimacy' of intrafamily distributional patterns have to be brought into the analysis, and its causal determinants analysed.[16]

Further, if the focus of attention is shifted from famines as such to less acute but possibly persistent hunger, then the role of choice from the entitlement set becomes particularly important, especially in determining future entitlement. For example, a peasant may choose to go somewhat hungry now to make a productive investment for the future, enhancing the entitlement of the following years and reducing the danger of starvation then. For entitlement analysis in a multi-period setting the initial formulation of the problem would require serious modification and extension.[17]

These changes and amendments can be systematically made without losing the basic rationale of introducing entitlement analysis to understand the problem of hunger and starvation in the modern world. The crucial motivation is to see the centrality of the acquirement problem and to resist the short cuts of instant economics, no matter how respectable its source.

2.4. Policy issues

(a) Famine anticipation and action

Focusing on entitlements and acquirement rather than simply on food output and availability has some rather far-reaching implications for food policy. I have tried to discuss some of these implications elsewhere, but I would like to pick a few issues here for brief comment. In particular, the problems of famine anticipation and relief are among the most serious ones facing the turbulent and traumatic world in which we live, and I shall comment on them briefly from the perspective that I have been outlining.

So far as famine anticipation is concerned, the metric of food output and availability is obviously defective as a basis, for reasons that follow from the preceding discussion. In fact, the anticipation of famines and their detection at an early stage have often in the past been hampered by undue concentration on this index, and specifically by what we have been calling 'Malthusian optimism'. Early warnings, as they are sometimes called, may not come at all from

---

[16] The consequences of particular perceptions of 'legitimacy' of intrafamily distributions do have something similar to those of legal relationships. Using that perspective, 'extended exchange entitlement' relations, covering both interfamily and intrafamily distributions, have been explored in an integrated structure in Sen (1985). The interrelations may be of real importance in understanding sex bias, e.g. the effect that outside earnings of women have on the divisions within the family. On this see also Boserup's (1970) pioneering study, and Sen (1984: essays 15, 16, 19, and 20).

[17] See Sen (1981a: n. 11). For some important and original ideas in this direction, see Svedberg (1986).

the output statistics, and it is necessary to monitor other variables as well, which also influence the entitlements of different vulnerable groups. Employment, wages, prices, etc. all have very direct bearing on the entitlements of various groups.

It is also important to recognize that famines can follow from many different types of causal processes. For example, while in a boom famine food prices will sharply rise, in a slump famine they may not. If the economic change that leads to mass starvation operates through depressing incomes and purchasing powers of large groups of people, food prices may stay low—or rise only relatively little, during the process of pauperization of these groups. Even when the slump famine is directly related to a crop failure due to, say, a drought, there may possibly be only a relatively modest rise in food prices, if the supply failure is matched by a corresponding decline in purchasing power due to the same drought. Indeed, it is easy to see that in a fully peasant economy in which food is eaten precisely by those who grow it, a crop failure will subtract from demand what it deducts from supply. The impoverished peasants would of course be later thrown into the rest of the economy —begging, looking for jobs, etc.—but they will arrive there without purchasing ability, and thus need not cause any rise in food prices even later. Actual economies are not, of course, that pure, but the impact on prices is very contingent on the relative weights of the different types of system and organization that make up the affected economy.[18]

Neither food output, nor prices, nor any other variable like that can be taken to be an invariable clue to famine anticipation, and once again there is no substitute for doing a serious economic analysis of the entitlements of all the vulnerable groups. All these variables have possible significance, and it is a question of seeing them as contingently important in terms of what they could do to the ability of different groups to acquire food. The search for some invariable indicator on the basis of which even the economically blind could see an oncoming famine sufficiently early is quite hopeless.

One of the major influences on the actual prevention of famine is the speed and force with which early hunger is reported and taken up in political debates. The nature and freedom of the news media, and the power and standing of opposition parties, are of considerable importance in effective prevention of famines.[19] But if the aim is to anticipate a famine even before early reports of hunger, that object cannot be satisfied by some mechanical formula on an 'early warning system'. The various information on prices, wages, outputs,

[18] In the Ethiopian famine in Wollo in 1973, food price rises seem to have been relatively moderate. Indeed, in Dessie, the capital of Wollo, the mid-famine food prices seem to have been comparable with prices outside the famine-affected province. There was more of a price rise in the rural areas, but again apparently not a catastrophic rise, and prices seemed to come down relatively quickly. On the importance of prices as a monitoring device for famine anticipation, see Seaman and Holt (1980) and Cutler (1984). See also Snowdon (1985).

[19] On this see Sen (1983).

the entitlements of the different occupation groups and of the rich variety of different ways in which the entitlements of one group or another can be undermined.

The different processes involved not only vary a good deal from each other, they may also be far from straightforward. For example, in various famines some occupation groups have been driven to the wall by a fall in the relative price of the food items they sell, e.g. meat sold by pastoral nomads in Harerghe in the Ethiopian famine of 1974, fish sold by fishermen in the Bengal famine of 1943. These groups may survive by selling these food items and buying cheaper calories through the purchase of grains and other less expensive food. A decline in the relative price of meat or fish will, of course, make it easier for the richer parts of the community to eat better, but it can spell disaster for the pastoralist and the fisherman. To make sense of them as signals of turmoil, the observed variables have to be examined in terms of their specific roles in the determination of entitlements of vulnerable groups.

(b)   Relief, food, and cash

Turning now from the anticipation to the relief of famines, the traditional form of relief has, of course, been that of providing free food in relief camps and distribution centres. There can be no doubt that relief in this form has saved lives in large scale in various famines around the world. But to understand precisely what free food distribution does, it may be useful to distinguish between two different aspects of the act of providing, which are both involved in the food relief operation. One is to give the destitute the ability to command food, and the other is to give him this ability in the actual form of food itself. Though they are integrated together in this form of relief, they need not in general be thus combined. For example, cash relief may provide the ability to command food without directly giving the food.

A person's ability to command food has two distinct elements, namely, his 'pull' and the supplier's 'response'. In the price mechanism the two elements are integrally related to each other. But in terms of the logistics of providing the person with food, the two elements may, in some contexts, be usefully distinguishable. If a person has to starve because he has lost his employment and has no means of buying food, then that is a failure originating on the 'pull' side. If, on the other hand, his ability to command food collapses because of absence of supply, or as a result of the cornering of the market by some manipulative traders, then this is a failure arising on the 'response' side.

One way of understanding what Adam Smith was really asserting (an issue that was briefly touched on earlier) is to see his primary claim as being one about the nature of 'response failure' in particular, saying nothing at all about 'pull failure'. His claim was that a response failure will only arise from what he called 'a real scarcity', most likely due to natural causes, and not from manipulative actions of traders. He may or may not have been right in this claim, but it is important to note that in this there is no denial of the possibility of 'pull failure'. Indeed, as is shown by his own analysis of 'want, famine, and mortality' arising from unemployment and falling wages (I quoted a passage from this earlier), Smith did also outline the possibility of famine originating on the 'pull' side. There is nothing particularly puzzling or internally inconsistent in Smith's various pronouncements on famine, if we distinguish between his treatment of pull and that of response. It is not the case, as is often asserted, that Adam Smith believed that hunger could not arise without a crop failure. Also he was not opposed to public support for the deprived, and in particular he was not opposed to providing relief through the Poor Laws (though he did criticize the harshness of some of the requirements that were imposed on the beneficiaries under these laws).

Smith's point that response failure would not arise from collusive action of traders has a direct bearing on the appropriate form of famine relief. If his point is correct, then relief could just as easily be provided by giving the deprived additional income and leaving it to the traders to respond to the new pull through moving food to the cash recipients. It is arguable that Smith did underestimate the extent to which traders can and do, in fact, manipulate markets, but at the same time the merits of cash relief do need serious examination in the context of assessing policy options.

Cash relief may not, of course, be quick enough in getting food to the starving in a situation of severe famine. Directly moving food to the starving may be the only immediate option in some situations of acute famine. There is also the merit of direct food distribution that it tends to have, it appears, a very immediate impact on nutrition, even in non-famine, normal situations, and it seems to do better in this respect than relief through income supplementation. These are points in favour of direct relief through food distribution. There is the further point that cash relief is arguably more prone to corruption, and that the visibility of direct food distribution does provide a better check. And the point about the possibility of manipulative actions of traders cannot, also, by any means be simply dismissed. These are serious points in favour of direct food distribution. But cash relief does have many merits as well.

First, the government's inefficiency in transporting food could be a considerable barrier to famine relief, as indeed some recent experiences have shown. In addition to problems of bureaucracy and red tape, there is the further problem that the transport resources (i.e. vehicles, etc.) in the possession of the private sector may sometimes be hard to mobilize, whereas they would be drawn into use if the actual trading and moving is left to the profit-seeking private sector itself. There is here a genuine pragmatic issue of the speed of response, and it cannot be brushed aside by a simple political judgement one way or the other.

Second, as was observed in the Wollo famine in 1973 and the Bangladesh famine of 1984, and most spectacularly in the Irish famines of the 1840s, food often does move *out of* the famine-stricken regions to elsewhere. This tends to happen especially in some cases of slump famine, in which the famine area is short of effective demand. Since such 'food countermovement' tends to reflect the balance of pulls of different regions, it may be preventable by distributing cash quickly enough in the famine-affected region.

Third, by providing demand for trade and transport, cash relief may help to regenerate the infrastructure of the famine-stricken economy. This has some merit in contrast with *ad hoc* use of transitory public intervention, which is not meant to continue, and the lasting benefits from expansion of normal trade and transport may be considerable for the local economy.

Fourth, it is arguable that cash relief is more usable for development investment needed for productive improvement, and this cannot be sensibly organized in relief centres. Even 'food for work' programmes, which can help in this direction, may sometimes be too unwieldy, given the need for flexibility for such investment activities.

Fifth, living in relief camps is deeply disruptive for normal family life as well as for pursuing normal economic activities. Providing cash relief precisely where the people involved normally reside and work, without having to move them to relief camps, may have very considerable economic and social advantages. Judging from the experience of an innovative 'cash for food' project sponsored by UNICEF in Ethiopia, these advantages are indeed quite real.[20]

This is not the occasion to try to form an overall judgement of the 'net' advantage of one scheme over another. Such judgements would have to be, in any case, extremely contingent on the exact circumstances of the case. But the general distinction between the 'pull' aspect and the 'response' aspect of entitlement failures is of immediate relevance to the question of the strategy of famine relief. Adam Smith's long shadow has fallen over many famines in the British Empire over the last two hundred years, with Smith being cited in favour of inaction and letting things be. If the analysis presented here is accepted, then inaction reflected quite the wrong reading of the implications of Smith's economic analysis. If his analysis is correct—and the honours here are probably rather divided—the real Smithian issue in a situation of famine is not 'intervention versus non-intervention', but 'cash relief versus direct food relief'. The force of the arguments on Smith's side cannot be readily dismissed, and the experience of mismanagement of famine relief in many countries has done nothing to reduce the aptness of his question.

(c) Food supply and food prices

In comparing the merits of cash relief with food distribution, it was not assumed that there would be more import of food with the latter than with the former. That question—of food imports from abroad—is a quite distinct one from the form that relief might take. It is, however, arguable that in a famine

---

[20] See Kumar (1985). See also Bjoerck (1984) and Padmini (1985).

situation direct food distribution is more thoroughly dependent on food import from abroad than a cash relief scheme need be. This is to some extent correct, though direct food distribution may also be based on domestically acquired food. But if we compare food distribution combined with food imports, on the one hand, and simple cash relief without such imports, on the other, then an arbitrary difference is brought into the contrast which does not belong there. In fact, the issue of food import is a separate one, which should be considered on its own.

This relates to an issue that has often been misunderstood in trying to work out the implications of the entitlement approach to hunger and famines, and in particular the implications of recognizing the possibility that famines can occur without any decline in food availability per head. It has sometimes been argued that if a famine is not caused by a decline in food availability, then there cannot be a case for food imports in dealing with the famine.[21] This is, of course, a *non sequitur*, and a particularly dangerous piece of nonsense. Consider a case in which some people have been reduced to starvation not because of a decline in total supply of food, but because they have fallen behind in the competitive demand for food in a boom famine (as happened, for example, to rural labourers in the Bengal famine of 1943). The fact is that the prices are too high for these victim groups to acquire enough food. Adding to the food supply will typically reduce prices and help these deprived groups to acquire food. The fact that the original rise in prices did not result from a fall in availability but from an increase in total demand does not make any difference to the argument.

Similarly, in a slump famine in which some group of people has suffered a decline in their incomes due to, say, unemployment, it may be possible to help that group by reducing the price of food through more imports. Furthermore, in each case import of food can be used to break a famine through public relief measures. This can be done either directly in the form of food distribution, or indirectly through giving cash relief to the famine victims combined with releasing more food in the market to balance the additional demand that would be created. There are, of course, other arguments to be considered in judging pros and cons of food imports, including the important problem of incentives for domestic food producers. But to try to reject the case for food imports in a famine situation on the simple ground that the famine has occurred without a decline in food availability (if that is the case) is to make a straightforward mistake in reasoning.

A more interesting question arises if in a famine situation we are, for some reason, simply not in a position to get more food from abroad. Would a system

---

[21] For a forceful presentation of this odd belief, see Bowbrick's paper (with a truly flattering title), 'How Professor Sen's Theory Can Cause Famines', presented at the Agricultural Economics Society Conference, 1985, at the Annual Conference of the Development Studies Association. (A revised version was later published in *Food Policy*; see Bowbrick (1986, 1987) and Sen (1986, 1987).)

of cash relief then be inflationary, and thus counter-productive? The answer is it would typically be inflationary, but not necessarily counter-productive. Giving the famine victims more purchasing power would add to the total demand for food. But if we want a more equal distribution of food, with some food moving from others to the famine victims, then the only way the market can achieve this (when the total supply is fixed and the money incomes of others cannot be cut) is through this inflationary process. The additional food to be consumed by the famine victims has to come from others, and this may require that prices should go up to induce others to consume less, so that the famine victims—with their new cash incomes—can buy more. Thus, while having a system of cash reliefs is not an argument against food imports in a famine situation, that system can have some desirable consequences *even when* food imports, are, for some reason, not possible. If our focus is on enhancing the entitlements of famine victims, the creation of some inflationary pressure —within limits—to redistribute food to the famine victims from the rest of the society may well be a sensible policy to pursue.

(d)   Entitlements and public distribution

So far in this essay my concentration on policy matters has been largely on what may be called short-run issues, including the anticipation and relief of famines. But it should be clear from the preceding analysis, with its focus on acquirement and entitlements, that long-run policies have to be geared to enhancing, securing, and guaranteeing entitlements, rather than to some simple formula like expanding food output.

I have discussed elsewhere the positive achievements of public food distribution policies in Sri Lanka and China, and also in Kerala in India, along with policies of public health and elementary education.[22]

The role of Sri Lanka's extensive 'social welfare programmes' in achieving high living standards has been the subject of some controversy recently. It is, of course, impossible to deny that judged in terms of such indicators of living standard as life expectancy, Sri Lanka's overall achievement is high (its life expectancy of 69 years is higher than that of any other developing country —even with many times the GNP per head of Sri Lanka). But by looking not at the *levels* of living but at their rate of *expansion* over a selected period, to wit 1960–78, it has been argued by Surjit Bhalla and others that Sri Lanka has performed only 'in an average manner'. Armed with these findings (based on international comparisons of expansion of longevity, etc. over 1960–78), the positive role of Sri Lanka's wide-based welfare programmes has been firmly disputed (asking, on the contrary, the general question: 'when does a commitment to equity become excessive?').[23]

The basis of this disputation, however, is extremely weak. 1960–78 is a

[22] See Sen (1981*b*, 1983).

[23] See Bhalla (1988).

period in which Sri Lanka's social welfare programmes themselves did not
grow much, and indeed the percentage of GNP expended on such programmes
came down sharply from 11.8 in 1960–1 to 8.7 by 1977.[24] If the expansion of
sowing is moderate, and so is the expansion of reaping, that can scarcely be
seen as a sign of the ineffectiveness of sowing!

The really fast expansion of Sri Lanka's social welfare programmes came
much earlier, going back at least to the forties. Food distribution policies (e.g.
free or subsidized rice for all, free school meals) were introduced in the early
1940s, and health intervention was also radically expanded (including taking
on the dreaded malaria). Correspondingly, the death rate fell from 21.6 per
thousand in 1945 to 12.6 in 1950, and to 8.6 by 1960 (all this happened *before*
the oddly chosen period 1960–78 used in Bhalla's much-publicized 'international comparisons' of expansions). There is nothing in the picture of
'expansion' that would contradict the fact of Sri Lanka's exceptional performance, if one does look at the right period, i.e. one in which its social welfare
programmes were, in fact, radically expanded, which happened well before
1960.[25]

The diverse policy instruments of public intervention used in Sri Lanka
relate closely to 'food policy' in the wider sense, affecting nutrition, longevity,
etc., going well beyond the production of food. Similar relations can be found
in the experience of effective public distribution programmes in other regions,
e.g. China and Kerala. It is right that the 'food problem' should be seen in these
wider terms, involving not only the production of food, but also the entitlements to food and to other nutrition-related variables such as health services.

(e)   Production and diversification

The problem of production composition is achieving economic expansion is
also, *inter alia*, an important one in long-run food policy. This complex
problem is often confounded with that of simply expanding food output as
such, treating it as largely a matter of increasing food supply. This is
particularly so in the discussions of the so-called African food problem. It is, of
course, true that food output per head in sub-Saharan Africa has been falling in
recent years, and this is certainly one of the major factors in the intensification
of hunger in Africa. But food production is not merely a source of food supply
in Africa, but also the main source of means of livelihood for large sections of
the African population. It is for this reason that food output decline tends to go
hand in hand with a collapse of entitlements of the masses in Africa.

The point can be easily seen by comparing and contrasting the experience of
sub-Saharan Africa in terms of food output per head with that of some

---

[24] These figures are given by Bhalla himself in a different context. He does not give the figure
for 1978, but in his table the percentage had further dropped to 7.7 by 1980. Other sources confirm
these overall declining trends during the 1960s and 1970s taken together.

[25] My reply to Bhalla's note (Sen 1988), spelling out the methodological issues as well as
empirical ones, is included in the same volume, with a further rejoinder by Bhalla.

countries elsewhere. Take Ethiopia and the Sahel countries, which have all suffered so much from famines. Between 1969–71 and 1980–2, food output per head fell by 5 per cent in Chad and Burkina Faso, 7 per cent in Senegal, 12 per cent in Niger, 17 per cent in Mali, 18 per cent in Ethiopia, and 27 per cent in Mauritania.[26] These are indeed substantial declines. But in the same period, and according to the same source of statistics, food output per head fell by 5 per cent in Venezuela, 15 per cent in Egypt, 24 per cent in Algeria, 27 per cent in Portugal, 29 per cent in Hong Kong, 30 per cent in Jordan, and 38 per cent in Trinidad and Tobago. The contrast between starvation in sub-Saharan Africa and nothing of the sort in these other countries is not, of course, in the least difficult to explain. Unlike the situation in these other countries, in sub-Saharan Africa a decline in food output is associated with a disastrous decline in entitlements, because the incomes of so many there come from growing food, because they are generally poor, and because the decline of food output there has not been outweighed or even balanced by increases in non-food (e.g. industrial) output. It is essential to distinguish between (1) food production as a source of income and entitlement, and (2) food production as a source of supply of the vital commodity food. If the expansion of food production should receive full priority in Africa, the case for it lies primarily in the role of food production in generating entitlements rather than only supply.

There are, of course, other reasons as well for giving priority to food production, in particular the greater security that the growers of food might then have since they would not be dependent on market exchange for acquiring food. This argument has been emphasized by many in recent years, and it is indeed an important consideration, the relevance of which is brought out by the role of market shifts in contributing to some of the famines that have been studied. But this type of uncertainty has to be balanced against uncertainties arising from other sources, in particular those related to climatic reasons. In the very long run the uncertainty of depending on unreliable weather conditions in parts of sub-Saharan Africa may well be eliminated by irrigation and afforestation. However, for many years to come this is a serious uncertainty, which must be taken into account along with other factors in the choice of investment policy in sub-Saharan Africa. An argument that is often encountered in public discussion in various forms can be crudely put like this: 'Food output in parts of sub-Saharan Africa has suffered a lot because the climate there is so unreliable for food production; therefore let's put all our resources into food production in these countries.' This is, of course, a caricature, but even in somewhat more sophisticated forms, this line of argument as a piece of economic reasoning is deeply defective. One does not put all one's eggs in the same highly unreliable basket. The need is surely for diversification of the production pattern in a situation of such uncertainty.

---

[26] *World Development Review 1984* (Oxford University Press, 1984), table 6.

2.5.   *Concluding remarks*

I have tried to comment on a number of difficult policy problems. The entitlement approach on its own does not resolve any of these issues. But by focusing on the acquirement problem, and on the major variables influencing acquirement, the entitlement approach provides a general perspective that can be fruitfully used to analyse the phenomenon of hunger as well as the requirements of food policy. I have tried to illustrate some of the uses of the entitlement approach, and have also discussed what policy insights follow or do not follow from it. The policy issues discussed have included problems of anticipation and relief of famines, forms of relief to be provided (including food distribution versus cash relief), the role of food supply and food prices in famine relief, and long-run strategies for eliminating vulnerability to famines and starvation (with particular reference to Africa).

I have also claimed that the entitlement approach is, with a few exceptions, in line with very old traditions in economics, which have been, in their own way, much preoccupied with the acquirement issue. The challenges of the terrible economic problems of the contemporary world relate closely to those traditional concerns, and call for sustained economic analysis of the determination and use of entitlements of diverse occupation groups.

References

ARROW, K. J. (1982), 'Why People Go Hungry', *New York Review of Books*, 29.

BECKER, G. S. (1976), *The Economic Approach to Human Behaviour* (Chicago, Ill.: Chicago University Press).

——(1981), *A Treatise on the Family* (Cambridge, Mass.: Harvard University Press).

BHALLA, S. (1988), 'Is Sri Lanka an Exception? A Comparative Study of Living Standards', in Srinivasan, T. N., and Bardhan, P. K. (eds.), *Rural Poverty in South Asia*, vol. ii (New York: Columbia University Press).

BJOERCK, W. A. (1984), 'An Overview of Local Purchase of Food Commodities (LPFC)' (UNICEF).

BLISS, C. (1982), 'The Facts about Famine', *South*, Mar.

BOSERUP, E. (1970), *Women's Role in Economic Development* (London: Allen & Unwin).

BOWBRICK, P. (1986), 'The Causes of Famine: A Refutation of Professor Sen's Theory', *Food Policy*, 11.

——(1987), 'Rejoinder: An Untenable Hypothesis on the Causes of Famine', *Food Policy*, 12.

CAMPBELL, R. H., and SKINNER, A. S. (eds.) (1976), *Adam Smith: An Enquiry into the Nature and Causes of the Wealth of Nations* (Oxford: Oxford University Press).

CUTLER, P. (1984), 'Famine Forecasting: Prices and Peasant Behaviour in Northern Ethiopia', *Disasters*, 8.

DESAI, M. (1984), 'A General Theory of Poverty', *Indian Economic Review*.

FAO (1985), *The State of Food and Agriculture 1984* (Rome: FAO).

GRIFFIN, K. (1981), 'Poverty Trap', *Guardian*, 7 Oct.

HAYTER, T. (1981), 'Famine For Free', *New Society*, 15 Oct.

JOSHI, V. (1981), 'Enough To Eat', *London Review of Books*, 19 Nov.

KHAN, Q. M. (1985), 'A Model of Endowment Constrained Demand for Food in an Agricultural Economy with Empirical Applications to Bangladesh', *World Development*, 13.

KUMAR, B. G. (1985), 'The Ethiopian Famine and Relief Measures: An Analysis and Evaluation', mimeo (UNICEF).

LINNEMANN, H. (1981), *MOIRA: A Model of International Relations in Agriculture* (Amsterdam: North-Holland).

LIPTON, M. (1981), 'The Analysis of Want', *The Times Literary Supplement*.

MARX, K. (1887), *Capital*, vol. i (London: Sonnenschein).

MAUNDER, A., and RENBORG, V. (eds.) (1986), *Agriculture in a Turbulent World*, proceedings of the 19th International Conference of Agricultural Economists, Malaga, Spain, 26 Aug.–4 Sept. 1985 (Aldershot: Gower).

MYINT, H. (1985), 'Growth Policies and Income Distribution', Discussion Paper, World Bank, Mar.

PADMINI, R. (1985), 'The Local Purchase of Food Commodities: "Cash for Food" Project', mimeo (Addis Ababa: UNICEF).

PARIKH, K., and RABAR, F. (eds.) (1981), *Food for All in a Sustainable World* (Laxenburg: IIASA).

RAVALLION, M. (1985), 'The Performance of Rice Markets in Bangladesh during the 1974 Famine', *Economic Journal*, 95.

SEAMAN, J. A., and HOLT, J. F. J. (1980), 'Markets and Famines in the Third World', *Disasters*, 4.

SEN, A. K. (1977), 'Starvation and Exchange Entitlements: A General Approach and its Application to the Great Bengal Famine', *Cambridge Journal of Economics*, 1.

——(1981a), *Poverty and Famines* (Oxford: Oxford University Press).

——(1981b), 'Public Action and the Quality of Life in Developing Countries', *Oxford Bulletin of Economics and Statistics*, 43.

——(1981c), 'Ingredients of Famine Analysis: Availability and Entitlements', *Quarterly Journal of Economics*, 95.

——(1982), 'The Food Problem: Theory and Policy', *Third World Quarterly*, 4.

——(1983), 'Development: Which Way Now?', *Economic Journal*, 93.

——(1984), *Resources, Values and Development* (Oxford: Basil Blackwell).

——(1985), 'Women, Technology and Sexual Divisions', *Trade and Development (UNCTAD)*, 6.

——(1986), 'The Causes of Famine: A Reply', *Food Policy*, 11.

——(1987), 'Reply: Famines and Mr. Bowbrick', *Food Policy*, 12.

——(1988), 'Sri Lanka's Achievements: How and When', in Srinivasan, T. N., and Bardhan, P. K. (eds.), *Rural Poverty in South Asia* (New York: Columbia University Press).

SMITH, A. (1776), *An Enquiry into the Nature and Causes of the Wealth of Nations*, repr. in Campbell and Skinner (1976).

SNOWDON, B. (1985), 'The Political Economy of the Ethiopian Famine', *National Westminster Bank Quarterly Review*, Nov.

SOLOW, R. M. (1984), 'Relative Deprivation?', *Partisan Review*, 51.

SRAFFA, P. (ed.) (1971), *The Works and Correspondence of David Ricardo*, vol. v (Cambridge: Cambridge University Press).

SVEDBERG, P. (1984), 'Food Insecurity in Developing Countries: Causes, Trends and Policy Options', mimeo (UNCTAD).

——(1986), 'The Economics of Food Insecurity in Developing Countries', mimeo (Stockholm: Institute for International Economic Studies).

TAYLOR, L. (1975), 'The Misconstrued Crisis: Lester Brown and World Food', *World Development*, 3.

3

Famine Prevention in India

Jean Drèze

3.1. *Introduction*

India's record of famine prevention in recent decades has often been presented as a highly impressive one, and several attempts have been made to draw out the possible lessons of this experience for other countries. This alleged success arguably needs to be put in proper perspective, and it has to be remembered that the various influences which combine to ensure the sustenance of the people in times of crisis do little more than keep them barely alive. As this chapter comes to completion, a frightening drought is hitting large parts of India, and while large-scale starvation will no doubt be averted once again, the hardships endured by the rural population offer a sobering picture.

Having said this, if India's recent 'success' in preventing famines is hardly a definitive achievement, it still remains a creditable one against the background of continuing failures elsewhere. While the 'lessons from India' are by no means easy to draw, the rich experience of this country with famine prevention strategies remains well worth scrutinizing.

How, then, has India avoided major famines since independence in 1947? It is tempting to attribute her relative success in this field to a steady improvement in food production. A close look at the facts, however, quickly reveals the

For many helpful comments and suggestions, I am extremely grateful to Harold Alderman, Arjun Appadurai, David Arnold, Kaushik Basu, A. N. Batabyal, Nikilesh Bhattacharya, Crispin Bates, Sulabha Brahme, Robert Chambers, V. K. Chetty, Stephen Coate, Lucia da Corta, Nigel Crook, Parviz Dabir-Alai, Angus Deaton, Guvant Desai, Meghnad Desai, V. D. Deshpande, Steve Devereux, Ajay Dua, Tim Dyson, Hugh Goyder, S. Guhan, Deborah Guz, Barbara Harriss, Judith Heyer, Simon Hunt, N. S. Iyengar, N. S. Jodha, Jane Knight, Arun Kumar, Gopalakrishna Kumar, Jocelyn Kynch, Peter Lanjouw, Michael Lipton, John Levi, Michelle McAlpin, John Mellor, B. S. Minhas, Shantanu Mitra, Mark Mullins, Vijay Nayak, Siddiq Osmani, Elizabeth Oughton, Kirit Parikh, Pravin Patkar, Jean-Philippe Platteau, Amrita Rangasami, N. P. Rao, J. G. Sastry, John Seaman, Kailash Sharma, P. V. Srinivasan, Elizabeth Stamp, Nicholas Stern, K. Subbarao, P. Subramaniam, V. Subramaniam, Peter Svedberg, Jeremy Swift, Martin Ravallion, David Taylor, Suresh Tendulkar, A. M. Vidwans, A. Vaidyanathan, Peter Walker, Tom Walker, Michael Windey, and Sheila Zubrigg. I owe even more to the many labourers, farmers, administrators, and activists who helped me during my field work in Bihar, Gujarat, and Maharashtra in 1986. Amartya Sen, who invited me to undertake this study, provided me with constant inspiration during several years of highly rewarding collaboration, and his own work on famine-related issues has greatly influenced the analysis presented in this paper. My greatest debt is to Bela Bhatia, not least for reminding me that India's relative success in averting large-scale famines in the recent past should not deflect our attention from the persistent and unnecessary sufferings of her people—the need for concern, pressure, and action remains as great as ever.

inadequacy of this explanation. Indeed, the half-century preceding independence witnessed steadily *declining* levels of food production per head, along with a reduction in the frequency of famines compared to the nineteenth-century experience. Since independence in 1947, total food output has admittedly grown at a healthy rate, but per capita food production levels have *not* dramatically increased; they appear, in any case, to remain lower than late nineteenth-century levels, and also lower than per capita food output levels in many countries affected by famines today. Moreover, the increase of production has resulted first and foremost in the reduction of imports and the accumulation of increasingly large stocks, so that the net consumption of food has stayed remarkably stagnant over the last forty years. Last but not least, almost every year large and heavily populated parts of India suffer from devastating droughts which, through the 'entitlement failures' they threaten to precipitate, remain quite capable of causing large-scale starvation.

It is more plausible to attribute the disappearance of large-scale famines in India during recent decades to the overall evolution of the economy. Sources of livelihood for the rural population are increasingly diversified, and in some areas at least the rapid advance of productivity in agriculture has substantially raised general living standards and further reduced the insecurity of rural life. The government's general food policy, though far from flawless, has largely succeeded in stabilizing food prices and in insulating consumption from fluctuations in production. In many States a wide array of more or less successful 'poverty alleviation programmes' provide a measure of protection against destitution to poor households, and by some accounts at least a discernible trend towards decreasing poverty has emerged since the mid-1960s. So goes the argument.

But even this optimistic interpretation of recent changes in economic opportunities and policies does not seem to be quite enough to account for the prevention of famines. In the semi-arid parts of India, the stagnation or near-stagnation of yields, population pressure, and the increasing frequency of droughts keep the rural population at the mercy of the monsoon. The vulnerability of impoverished classes (particularly agricultural labourers) remains extreme, and the need persists for a very extensive and effective *relief system*. When food crises have assumed unusual proportions (as in 1966–7, 1972–3, 1979–80, and 1985–7), this relief system has played an undeniably crucial role in averting large-scale starvation. This chapter examines the role played by famine relief policies in ensuring the prevention of famines in India in the last few decades.

This enquiry will inevitably involve a brief excursion into the historical origins of India's relief policies as they exist today. This is the theme of section 1.2, where attention is drawn particularly to the role and content of the Famine Codes introduced by the British administration towards the end of the nineteenth century.

Section 3.3 takes a closer look at the nature of entitlement crises in India since independence. On the basis of a tentative comparison between India and the Sahel, as well as of a reassessment of crisis management in the State of Bihar in 1966–7, India's continued exposure to famine threats is underlined.

The effectiveness of relief policies in dealing with these threats is illustrated in Section 3.4, which is devoted to a case-study of famine prevention in Maharashtra during the devastating drought of 1970–3. This example, it must be stressed at the outset, is not in any sense 'representative' of India's experience with famine prevention. Indeed, the scope and effectiveness of famine relief measures in India vary considerably between different regions and periods. Nevertheless, the drought of 1970–3 in Maharashtra is well worth studying, partly because it has the merit of bringing out the *potential* of India's relief system, and partly because it is extremely well documented and provides rich material for an empirical examination of many important problems connected with famine prevention in general. Close attention will be paid, *inter alia*, to the familiar issues of early warning, food availability, private trade, public distribution, cash relief, targeting mechanisms, employment programmes, cost-effectiveness, and political pressure. A summary of the findings, and some concluding remarks, are contained in the final section.

This chapter is based primarily on research carried out in 1985–6. Since little material was available at that time on droughts and famine prevention in the 1980s, this study essentially concentrates on the pre-1980 period. There is much to say on the developments that have taken place since then (including the alarming problem of ecological devastation), and in particular on famine prevention during the drought of 1985–7, but no attempt has been made here to cover these issues.[1] It would be surprising, however, if recent events called for a major reassessment of the analysis presented in this paper.

3.2. *The emergence of India's famine relief system*

The history of famine relief in India is a fascinating area of research, and deserves attention from everyone concerned with the problem of famines in the modern world—scholars and practitioners alike. It is beyond the scope of this paper to review this history in any depth, or to contribute fresh insights to it. The interested reader is referred to the large literature on the subject.[2] My wish here is only to provide a selective account of the emergence of a famine relief system in India, as a background for the study of famine prevention since independence. The following is a selective chronological sketch of the history

[1] For some relevant studies, see Pinstrup-Andersen and Jaramillo (1985), Caldwell *et al.* (1986), Bandyopadhyay (1987), Agarwal (1988), Bhatia (1988), Hubbard (1988), Kumar (1988), Rao *et al.* (1988), Reddy (1988), Chen (1989), Drèze (1989, 1990), the collection of papers in Centre for Social Studies (1988), Government of India (1989), and the further literature cited in Mac (1988).

[2] On the history of famines and famine prevention in India, see Dutt (1900, 1904), Loveday (1914), Ghosh (1944), Bhatia (1967), Srivastava (1968), Ambirajan (1978), Alamgir (1980), Jaiswal (1978), McAlpin (1983), Ghose (1982), Brennan (1984), Klein (1984), among others.

of famines and famine relief in India during the period on which this section will focus.

1770	Formidable famine in Bengal
1770–1858	Frequent and severe famines
1858	End of East India Company
1861	Report of Baird Smith on the 1860–1 famine
1861–80	Frequent and severe famines
1880	Famine Commission Report, followed by the introduction of Famine Codes
1880–96	Very few famines
1896–7	Large-scale famine affecting large parts of India
1898	Famine Commission Report on the 1896–7 famine
1899–1900	Large-scale famine
1901	Famine Commission Report on the 1899–1900 famine
1901–43	Very few famines
1943	Bengal Famine
1945	Famine Commission Report on the Bengal Famine
1947	Independence

(a) Famines in nineteenth-century India

Numerous famines occurred in India throughout the nineteenth century, and their victims were often counted in millions.[3] There is a fair amount of agreement among nineteenth-century analysts and later economic historians concerning the proximate causes underlying these catastrophes. In most (nearly all) cases, famine followed massive crop failures resulting from drought. The immediate effect of these crop failures was not only to reduce food availability in the affected region, but also, and more importantly, to *disrupt the rural economy*. In particular, landless agricultural labourers found little employment as field activity was brought to a standstill while general impoverishment simultaneously enlarged the supply of casual labour. Food prices increased as the less vulnerable groups strived to maintain reasonable food consumption levels (possibly by selling assets), while trade was often slow to move food to the affected area from other regions. Money wages lagged behind price increases, further aggravating the plight of agricultural labourers.[4] The operation of the so-called 'moral economy' did little to mitigate their sufferings, which all too often ended only in death. Thus severe famines

[3] For chronologies of Indian famines in the 19th century, and estimates of their impact on mortality, see Loveday (1914), Bhatia (1967), Dando (1980), Jaiswal and Kolte (1981), Greenough (1982), Visaria and Visaria (1982), and Government of India (1880).

[4] The reduction of real wages in rural India during periods of rapid price increases (including famines) has been observed by numerous authors—see e.g. the evidence, discussions, and further references provided in Breman (1974), Bhatia (1975), Bardhan (1977), Lal (forthcoming), Ravallion (ch. 5, vol. 2), and Government of India (1898).

frequently took place even when crop failures were only localized (as well as short-lived) and food was far from wanting in the country as a whole.

This recurring scenario was aptly summarized by Baird Smith's well-known statement to the effect that famines in India were 'rather famines of work than of food'.[5] The same verdict was arrived at later by successive Famine Enquiry Commissions, as well as by most independent analysts—though there has predictably been much more controversy about the underlying causes of mass poverty in the same period. The Famine Commission Report of 1880 (the first major report of its kind) is worth quoting here, not least as an early example of 'entitlement analysis':

The first effect of drought is to diminish greatly, and at last to stop, all field labour, and to throw out of employment the great mass of people who live on the wages of such labour.[6]

. . . distress is mainly among the agricultural portion of the population thrown out of work by the failure of their ordinary employment, and the few small trades and handicrafts which are chiefly dependent upon them for sale of their manufactures . . . among this class, distress arises, not so much from an actual want of food, as from a loss of wages—in other words, money to buy food . . . as a general rule, there is an abundance of food procurable, even in the worst districts at the worst time; but when men who, at the best, merely live from hand to mouth, are deprived of their means of earning wages, they starve, not from the impossibility of getting food, but for want of the necessary money to buy it.[7]

Two aspects of this description are particularly relevant to an appreciation of later relief policies. The first is the recognition of *agricultural labourers and rural artisans* as the main victims of traditional Indian famines. During very severe famines cultivators became vulnerable to starvation as well, in spite of the then widespread practice of storing large quantities of grain;[8] and when epidemics broke out they caused victims among large sections of the population. But these qualifications apart, the outstanding vulnerability of agricultural labourers and artisans has been widely noted.[9]

Another important aspect of the received analysis of nineteenth-century famines is the view that entitlement failures occurred amidst plenty rather than in the context of a fierce battle for scarce food. A rather striking degree of agreement on this question can be found in the official reports of the British administration at the time, as well as among commentators of very diverse

[5] Baird Smith (1861), quoted in Srivastava (1968: 53 n.).

[6] Government of India (1880: 35); this is the preamble of a fuller discussion of 'The Classes that suffer from famine'.

[7] Government of India (1880: Appendix I, p. 205).

[8] 'Everyone knows that all the well-to-do farmers have very large hoards of grain, which they keep in pits, especially in the dry districts, often for many years' (Government of India 1880: Appendix I, p. 204).

[9] See e.g. Bhatia (1967, 1975), Srivastava (1968), Ghose (1982), and the Famine Commission Reports (Government of India, various years).

persuasions (e.g. Baird Smith 1861, Naoroji 1900, Ray 1901, Ray 1909, Loveday 1914, Srivastava 1968, Ghose 1982, McAlpin 1983, and Guz 1987, among many others). The literature on nineteenth-century famines is replete with statements such as the following:

What does a drought mean? It is not a question of food; the scarcity of food in a district affected by drought is the least of the evils with which the Government of India have to deal. There is nearly always a sufficiency of food in India to feed all the people within its limits; and owing to the development of the railway, the British Government was able, no matter what part of the country may be affected, to pour in sufficient food to maintain the people of the district.[10]

The consensus on this question should, admittedly, be approached with caution. The view that aggregate food availability was never a serious problem during Indian famines was, after all, largely propagated by the official Famine Commission Reports.[11] These lean heavily on the initial calculations of the Famine Commission Report of 1880, which might have been misleading. The Famine Commission Report of 1898 formed its own view on the subject partly on the evidence of the non-exhaustion of stocks and continued food exports in famine years (see below). But this piece of evidence is not particularly convincing: it only proves that extra food was available *at the margin*—but not necessarily enough to feed the whole population. Finally, it may be argued that the dismissal of food shortage problems served the interests of the British authorities by obviating the need for intervention in grain trade, which—as we shall see—they were so obsessively anxious to avoid.

Detailed investigations would be required to ascertain whether or not the absence of a food availability problem during nineteenth-century famines in India was a myth propagated by the Famine Commissions. There is, however, little indication that the myth theory should be taken very seriously. The fabrication of a myth would have triggered dissent, of which there is very little trace. Indeed, it is rather striking that commentators of all persuasions, including many radical ones, concurred with the views of the Famine Commissions on the issue of food availability; the distinction of the radical writers was not to challenge the notion of sufficiency of food, but rather to trace the lack of purchasing power of the masses to colonial exploitation.[12] As far as quantitative evidence is concerned, several independent rounds of food availability calculations were carried out (in 1878, 1898, and 1902); they were based on

[10] Statement made by Lord George Hamilton (3 Feb. 1902), quoted in Ray (1909: 10).

[11] The idea, however, did not originate from the Famine Commission Reports. As we have seen, the very first report on an Indian famine under British rule (that of Baird Smith in 1861) already considered Indian famines as 'rather famines of work than of food; when work can be had and paid for, food is always forthcoming' (Smith 1861, quoted in Srivastava 1968: 53 n.).

[12] See e.g. Ray (1901) and Ray (1909). The former argued that 'Close students of Indian economical history know, and none have ever seriously questioned the fact, that India, on the whole, produces enough of crops every year, good or bad, to feed her aggregate population' (Ray 1901: 33).

food consumption allowances which were extremely generous by contemporary standards and yet they all arrived at the firm conclusion that a substantial surplus of food was available in India in normal years.[13] Since multi-year storage was a widespread practice in nineteenth-century India, and most famines were localized, the argument that most nineteenth-century famines had little to do with a problem of physical availability of food seems convincing enough.

An exception may, however, have to be made in this respect for the last two famines of the nineteenth century—those of 1896–7 and 1899–1900. In these two cases, famine occurred against an exceptional background of massive crop failures virtually throughout the country at times when stocks were already diminished, and much greater caution is required in assessing the aggregate food availability situation. I shall argue below that the case against the existence of a food availability problem is much less convincing in this context.[14]

(b) Early famine relief efforts

Famine relief has a very long history in India. One of the very first treatises on government, written more than 2,000 years ago and commonly attributed to Kautilya, pronounces that when famine threatens a good king should 'institute the building of forts or water-works with the grant of food, or share [his] provisions [with the people], or entrust the country [to another king]'.[15] According to Srivastava, 'the chief methods of famine relief adopted by Indian rulers included free distribution of raw grains, opening of free kitchens, opening of public grain stores to the people, remission of revenue, payment of advances, remission of other taxes, construction of public works, canals and embankments, sinking of wells, encouragement of migration, and increase in the pay of soldiers. Even sold children in the time of Shahjahan are reported to have been ransomed by the Government and restored to their parents.'[16] However, the evidence is inadequate to judge the real efficacy of relief efforts

[13] See e.g. Bhatia (1967: table 33), and Government of India (1898: para. 587).

[14] Bhatia (1967), for one, has challenged the idea of food sufficiency in 19th-century India, as a background to the thesis that the responsibility for 19th-century famines lay largely with the government's refusal to interfere with private trade. His counterargument, however, is not very persuasive. He criticizes the official food availability estimates of 1878, 1898, and 1902 for their lack of accuracy (pp. 225–8), but fails to show a systematic bias or to suggest more plausible magnitudes. The main piece of evidence he puts forward on the existence of food shortages is the substantial rise in prices *throughout India* during the late 19th-century famines. This observation, however, refers specifically to the famines of 1896–7 and 1899–1900 which, I have argued, should be regarded as exceptions in this regard. Indeed the Famine Commission of 1898 referred to 'the uniform level of prices all over the country' as 'one of the most remarkable features in the recent (1896–97) famine', underlying the novelty of the phenomenon (on this see also Loveday 1914). It is, in any case, argued below that the policy of complete non-interference with private trade in British India had little to do with any particular appraisal of the food availability situation.

[15] *Arthasastra*, quoted in Chetty and Ratha (1987: 3).

[16] Srivastava (1968: 28).

before the nineteenth century, and it is not implausible that they were often far from systematic and comprehensive.[17]

Under the rule of the East India Company, famines were frequent and severe—sometimes extremely severe, as with the calamitous famine of 1770 in Bengal. Relief efforts were, moreover, at best half-hearted, and in any case lacking in effectiveness. The laconic remarks of the Famine Commission of 1880 on this subject are revealing enough:

the earlier despatches of the Bengal Government, while breathing a tone of sincere compassion for the sufferings occasioned by famine, are busied rather with its fiscal results, as affecting the responsibility of the Company towards its shareholders, than with schemes, which would have seemed wholly visionary, for counteracting the inevitable loss of life.[18]

How did the 'breath of sincere compassion' gradually turn into a serious preoccupation with the prevention of famines after the British administration took over in 1858? In other words, why were the British rulers so concerned to avert famines in India? Oddly enough, the answers that have been proposed to this question have remained extremely fragmented and speculative.[19] The report of the Famine Commission of 1880 repeatedly invokes the 'duty of the State' in this context.[20] But what this rhetoric actually masked is rather hard to say. The desire to preserve political stability or the revenue base, a feeling of obligation to the people arising from the more obviously deleterious aspects of colonial expansion (such as the ruin of the weaving industry), the so-called 'weight of irresponsible public opinion in England',[21] concern with the administration's image in the eyes of the British public, and genuine humanitarian concern may all have played a more or less important role. It is unlikely that this issue could be satisfactorily resolved without also considering British policy in Ireland and even in Africa, where very similar situations and debates were encountered. This, however, would take us far beyond the scope of this chapter and can only be proposed here as a theme for further research.

[17] See Curley (1977) for an interesting account of traditional Mogul famine policy in 18th-century India.

[18] Government of India (1880: 31).

[19] For some useful discussions, see Bhatia (1967), Ambirajan (1976, 1978), and Brennan (1984).

[20] Under the heading 'Obligation of the State to give relief in time of famine', for instance, the Famine Commission Report of 1880 states that 'there can be no doubt that a calamity such as famine, exceptional in its nature and arising from causes wholly beyond human control, which deprives an entire population of its customary food supply, and arrests the ordinary employments of the wage-earning classes, is one which in a country such as India wholly transcends individual effort and power of resistance. It accordingly becomes a paramount *duty of the State* to give all practicable assistance to the people in time of famine, and to devote all its available resources to this end; and this duty is emphasized by the fact that the Government stands in the place of landlord to the agriculturists, who form the great mass of the population' (Government of India 1880: 31–2; my italics).

[21] Government of India (1880: Appendix I, p. 117).

Referring to caste prejudices against forbidden food, Sir Bartle Frere lamented, in an important prelude to the later Famine Codes, that 'no one whose experience is confined to the poor of other countries can imagine the difficulties of dealing with starving Hindoos, even when you have the most ample means at your disposal'.[22] However, the really important difficulties initially experienced by the British administration in organizing relief went much beyond the cultural idiosyncrasies of 'starving Hindoos'. In fact they were strikingly reminiscent of the familiar stumbling blocks of famine relief elsewhere even today: confused information, faulty forecasts, absence of contingency planning, weak motivation, delays, transport bottlenecks and other logistical nightmares, poor administration, inertia of private trade, etc. The Famine Commission Report of 1880 contains a vivid account of the nature of relief efforts before the Famine Codes:

What often happens now is that they wander from their village, crowd into towns, die about the roads, and otherwise attract the attention of the officials. Then a survey is made, a relief-work is started, and then follows all the train of difficulties attendant on the endeavour to get masses of wretched, demoralized, half-starved creatures to work and be paid after some sort of method. The work is generally started too late to save life; numbers, from one cause or another, do not get within its scope; every department is strained to supply supervision, and the supervision is generally quite inadequate for anything like real control; the wage is a hopeless dilemma; if you give a low rate, the people desert and die; if you give a high one, you drain the labour market and the thing gets beyond control.[23]

To be fair, the prevention of famines during the greater part of the nineteenth century was also handicapped by infrastructural deficiencies which were to diminish substantially in later decades. The Famine Commission Reports often laid great stress on the need to develop *irrigation* and, even more importantly, *communications* (mainly railways). For future reference, and given the considerable importance ascribed to public and private trade issues in discussions of famine relief, the role of communications is worth probing.

Before the large-scale development of the railways from the 1870s onwards, private trade in foodgrains within India notably lacked dynamism, and local scarcities precipitated very severe price hikes.[24] Often, the 'lack of satisfactory communications . . . severely restricted the movement of food grains so that while in one part of the country people died of lack of food, in another, only a few miles away, there was an abundance of cheap food'.[25] Entitlement failures were exacerbated by the sluggishness of trade and the large price disparities prevailing between adjacent regions:

[22] Frere (1874: 15).

[23] Government of India (1880: Appendix I, p. 113). For a more detailed account of mismanagement in famine relief before the Famine Codes, see e.g. Srivastava (1968: chs. 2–5) and Bhatia (1967: ch. 3).

[24] On this question see Bhatia (1967), Srivastava (1968), and particularly McAlpin (1983).

[25] Srivastava (1968: 7).

while in one bazar, famine prices of four rupees per maund might be ruling, in another, not thirty miles off, the price would be but about rupee one and a half for the same quantity, yet no flow from the full to the exhausted market could take place, because roads were not in existence and means of carriage unknown.[26]

In his famous *Report on the Past Famines in the Bombay Presidency*, Etheridge (1868) attributed the inertia of private trade in that period to the lack of 'animal spirits' among Indian merchants, who sometimes 'altogether failed . . . to take advantage of the high prices ruling'; 'the Hindoo merchant', said Etheridge, 'is slow of action even when [his] own interests are deeply concerned'.[27] But later experience belied this peculiar view of the Hindu merchant. Indeed, only a few years later the Famine Commission of 1880 described a completely different state of affairs:

The extension of railways, and the connection of trunk lines, has so increased the rapidity of communication that mercantile relations now subsist between the Native traders of all parts of India, and these traders keep themselves well posted up in the state of the most distant markets, being keenly alive to the advantage of the telegraphic communication . . . The combined effect of Railway and Telegraph extension throughout the length and breadth of India, has permitted Government to rely upon the activity of private trade for the supply of foods to all districts immediately served by railways . . . Moreover, the area from which food supplies can be drawn has been extended from the limit of 100 miles, which, with a cart-carriage, in a famine-striken country, destitute of fodder for cattle, or oxen with pack-bullocks or cooly labour, is a maximum to a range of over 2000 miles . . . as certainly as a strong demand arises for grain or other country produce, either for a famine district or for export, the railway stations of all districts from which export is possible, are crowded with stores of grain, while the railway officials are besieged by applicants for early despatch of their consignments.[28]

The sudden dynamism of private trade may have been somewhat exaggerated by the Famine Commission which, as we shall see, was very anxious to rationalize the policy of non-interference recommended—it thought—by what Etheridge called the 'supposed infallible laws of the great Masters of Economic Science'.[29] However, it was certainly not a myth, and as a matter of fact the 'remarkable tendency to a common level of prices throughout India' during the 1896–7 famine, and again during the 1899–1900 famine, has been reliably documented.[30] Nor can the key role played by the railways in this context be seriously questioned.

While the expansion of the railways was undoubtedly *effective* in promoting private trade, it is much less obvious how *beneficial* this development was to various sections of the Indian people. This question has, not surprisingly, been

---

[26] Baird Smith (1861), quoted in Srivastava (1968: 53).   [27] Etheridge (1868: 3, 11).

[28] Government of India (1880: Appendix I, pp. 198–9).   [29] Etheridge (1868: 3).

[30] See e.g. Holderness (1897), Loveday (1914), McAlpin (1983), and Government of India (1898). The expression quoted in the text is taken from the latter report, p. 359.

a matter of some debate.[31] In the Indian context as elsewhere, radical writers have often blamed the growth of commercialization for the impoverishment of the people, and even held 'capitalist penetration' responsible for the occurrence of famines. But it is arguable that the source of exploitation and persistent poverty should be sought in the domain of *ownership* much more than in the domain of exchange *per se*.[32] This is not the place to pursue this complex question, and our attention here will be confined to a somewhat narrower issue, namely the consequences of railway extension for food movements during famines.

The Famine Commissions regarded the greater 'market integration' permitted by the railways as an unambiguous, if not completely unmixed, blessing. They did feel uncomfortable about the occasional facilitation of *exports* from famine-stricken areas (see below). And they gave a rather muddled response to the criticism of growing disincentives against private storage.[33] But on the long-run advantages of the railways they had no doubt, and the Famine Commission of 1898 pronounced that 'one of the most remarkable features in the recent famine was the uniform level of prices all over the country which is attributable to the ever-extending system of railways and which, *if it increased the area, greatly diminished the intensity of distress*'.[34] Analysts such as Loveday emphatically concurred with this view, arguing that 'the desirability of a system by which the prosperous should help to bear the burden of the distressed is unquestionable'.[35] But there also existed another school of thought, which stressed the evils of the railway in general, and its possible role in facilitating exports from famine-striken areas in particular.

Economic analysis confirms the scope for ambiguity in the effects of railway extension on food entitlements. There can be little doubt that the expansion of the railways resulted in a greater tendency towards uniformity of

[31] For a useful introduction to the controversy, see Michelle McAlpin (1974, 1975, 1980, 1982, 1983). McAlpin herself has strongly argued, on the basis of detailed empirical work, that the expansion of the railways in India led to a considerable reduction in poverty and famine vulnerability, and in particular that 'probably by the end of the nineteenth century and certainly by the beginning of the twentieth century, the movement of grain into regions with harvest shortfalls was a routine process' (McAlpin 1983: 156). For rejoinders, see Appadurai (1984), Bates (1985), Rangasami (1985), and Guha (1986).

[32] As Marx emphasized, 'the relation of capitalist and wage labourer . . . has its foundation in the social character of production, not in the mode of exchange . . . It is, however, quite in keeping with the bourgeois horizon, everyone being engrossed in the transaction of shady business, not to see in the character of the mode of production the basis of the mode of exchange corresponding to it, but vice-versa' (Marx 1970: 120). On railways in India specifically, Marx predicted that 'the railways system will become, in India, truly the forerunner of modern industry' (cited in Bhatia 1967: 307).

[33] 'It is true that to a certain extent cultivators, who formerly stored grain, because it could neither be sold nor removed, have ceased to do so because they can see to advantage; and that, owing to their improvidence, the money slips through their fingers' (Government of India 1901: 74).

[34] Government of India (1898: 351) (italics added).

[35] Loveday (1914: 111).

prices.[36] One may also generally expect a reduction of price disparities to reflect greater food movements towards famine-affected areas, and to result in an improvement of the food entitlements of vulnerable sections of the population in these regions. However, it is easy to think of counterexamples, of which two are particularly important here.

First, in the absence of international trade regulation, the smoother flow of grain towards high price regions took place across, as well as within, national boundaries, and the large-scale export of grain abroad during famine periods was a frequent phenomenon in the nineteenth century.[37] It must be remembered in this context that while regional food price patterns within India could, by and large, be expected to reflect the severity of entitlement crises in different parts of the country, price differences between India and England could certainly not be given the same interpretation—if only because they were heavily influenced by the exchange rate, itself a reflection of numerous factors hardly related to food entitlements. The Famine Commission of 1880 recognized the problem with some embarrassment but viewed it as an 'inevitable' consequence of the broader and essential policy of non-interference with private trade:

Unluckily for the Indian consumer, there have been several bad harvests in England, and this and the exchange have stimulated a great export of grain for the last few years. This gain of the producing class and its adjunct, the bunyah [trader], has been so far the loss of the consuming class. This seems inevitable.[38]

Second, even within a country the reduction of disparities in prices need not always imply a reduction in the severity of famine. In fact, the greater spatial integration of markets can be expected to contribute to alleviating famine if, and only if, two conditions are satisfied:[39] (1) the moderation of price increases improves the entitlements of vulnerable groups, and (2) vulnerable areas are also, as a rule, those subject to strong upward pressures on food prices. The first assumption is safe enough, since few households benefit from higher food prices except those who have some food to *sell*. Regarding the second assumption, a broad correlation has indeed been observed during Indian famines between the level of food prices and the intensity of distress, and the Famine Commission of 1880 even boldly stated that 'it may be said approximately and

[36] See the references cited earlier on this point. It is noteworthy that McAlpin's critics have not seriously challenged the *evidence* she has presented on the progress of market integration towards the end of the 19th century.

[37] For evidence of this, and indeed of the very large *increase* in exports during the famines of the 1870s, see Bhatia (1967). For an interesting econometric study of international trade and food entitlements in British India, see Ravallion (1987*b*).

[38] Government of India (1880: Appendix I, p. 112).

[39] Strictly speaking, the *violation* of both these conditions would also do, but this possibility is little more than a theoretical curiosum. More importantly perhaps, note that when trade takes place *within* a famine-affected region, one also has to check whether the reduction of disparities in food entitlements within that region does result in lower aggregate mortality. For a detailed examination of this hypothesis, see Ravallion (1987*a*).

generally that, in time of very great scarcity, prices of food grain rise to three times their ordinary amount'.[40] This statement was admittedly followed by lengthy qualifications, and the use of prices as an indication of distress has met with some notable failures.[41] However, the general observation that famine-affected areas were also areas of high food prices was a robust one.

In sum, and with a major reservation applying to international trade, it is plausible that the improvement of communications towards the end of the nineteenth century did make a major contribution to the alleviation of distress during famines. However, it is also easy to see that this factor alone could hardly account for the very sharp reduction in the incidence of famines in the twentieth century. Indeed, the dynamism of private trade during famines has always been contingent on the existence of adequate *purchasing power* in affected areas. Even today, it is clear that the high level of market integration in India would be of little consolation for agricultural labourers if government intervention did not also protect their market command over food during lean years. The idea of preventing famines by generating purchasing power in affected areas and letting private trade supply the food was the basic inspiration behind the Famine Codes.

(c) The Famine Codes and their basic principles

The failure of famine prevention during the period 1858–80 (extending from the demise of the East India Company to the birth of the Famine Codes) was not a complete one. A measure of inverse correlation between the extensiveness of relief efforts and the intensity of distress was noticeable even at that time. In particular, during the 'Panic Famine' of 1873–4 in Behar massive relief efforts were quite effective in preventing the worst. However, the shortcomings of *ad hoc* responses were increasingly evident, and while the relative success of relief efforts in 1873–4 was recognized they were also regarded as excessively costly.[42]

[40] Government of India (1880: 27). On the relationship between food prices and famine mortality in 19th-century India, see Lardinois (1982, 1985).

[41] During the famine of 1860–1 in Moradabad, for instance, John Strachey had already observed that 'although the agricultural population has thus suffered comparatively little the prices of food have risen higher in Moradabad than in almost any district of these provinces' (Government of Bengal 1874: 363). The Famine Commission of 1880 itself concluded that 'much caution, however, is requisite in regarding prices as a sound standard by which to estimate the severity of famine or distress' (Government of India 1880: 27), and this point was made even more forcefully by later Famine Commissions.

[42] The Famine Commission of 1880, referring to the Behar famine of 1873–4, did not hesitate to deplore that 'life was preserved, but money was spent profusely' (Government of India 1880: para. 94). It is of some interest to note that the exceptionally large levels of expenditure incurred during this famine were to a great extent due to the costs of food transportation and distribution (both unusual measures), as well as to the poor 'targeting' inherent in a relief strategy largely based on the distribution or subsidization of food (see e.g. ibid. para. 57 and Appendix I, p. 109). For further elaboration of the many interesting issues pertaining to famine relief after 1858 but before the Famine Codes, see particularly the discussion of 'Principles of Famine Relief' in ibid. Appendix I, as well as Loveday (1914).

This period of 'trial and error' (as Srivastava puts it) came to an end after the Famine Commission of 1880, keenly aware of the vital importance of 'prompt and decided action' in matters of famine relief, recommended the promulgation of *Famine Codes* which would contain authoritative guidelines to the local administration for the anticipation, recognition, and relief of famines:

The duties involved in relief measures are complicated and multifarious; their successful performance necessitates the utilisation of large stores of accumulated experience and a carefully considered and prepared plan; they cannot be safely left to individual energy and resource, or be dealt with on a system improvised only when the emergency has arisen. Prompt and decided action in carrying out these measures is of primary importance, and by considering well beforehand the principles that should guide them, much of that hesitation and uncertainty of purpose, which have been found to be so detrimental in the past, will be avoided in the future. We recommend, therefore, that the Government of India should, as soon as possible, issue a set of rules embodying the main principles that should govern the administration of famine relief, and that these rules should be authoritative in all parts of British India.[43]

The introduction of the Famine Codes undoubtedly represented an essential (though not quite decisive) step towards the successful prevention of famines in India.[44] The provisions of these Codes are much too comprehensive to be discussed here in detail.[45] For future reference, however, it is of some interest to recall the basic strategy of famine prevention recommended by the Famine Codes, and its rationale.

The backbone of the famine relief strategy embodied in the Famine Codes was the organization of *massive public works*. More precisely, the first and foremost aim of this strategy was nothing less than to provide employment at subsistence wages and at a reasonable distance from their homes to *all* those who applied for it (wages were to be paid in cash, and public employment

---

[43] Government of India (1880: 37–8). For a detailed account of the historical events surrounding the birth of the Famine Codes, see Brennan (1984).

[44] The first 'Draft Famine Code' was submitted along with the Famine Commission Report of 1880. Each State was required to frame its own code by adapting the model contained in the Draft Code to its own circumstances. With the passage of time the State Famine Codes underwent occasional revisions, and in independent India they received the name of Scarcity Manuals. In some parts of the country the latter are no longer explicitly used today, but this is partly because the rules they embody have become a matter of routine response to the threat of famine.

[45] The chapter headings of the provincial Famine Codes are as follows: '(I) Duties of revenue and village officers in ordinary times; (II) When serious scarcity is imminent; (III) Duties of superior revenue and engineer officers (during famine); (IV) Circle organization and duties of circle officers; (V) Gratuitous relief; (VI) Famine relief works; (VII) Wages and rations; (VIII) Poor houses; (IX) Kitchens for children; (X) Other measures of relief; (XI) Measures for the protection of cattle; (XII) Utilization of forests; (XIII) Duties of police; (XIV) Duties of medical officers; (XV) Accounts' (Srivastava 1968: 175). These were the recommended chapter headings for the provincial Famine Codes, as per a resolution of the Government of India, 1893 (see Srivastava 1968). The present Bombay Scarcity Manual (Government of Maharashtra 1966) still follows a very similar pattern. For an introduction to the Famine Codes and their provisions, see Srivastava (1968: ch. 6). See also the discussions in Alamgir (1980), McAlpin (1983), Brennan (1984), and Government of India (1945).

was directed to the creation of public assets such as roads and canals). 'Gratuitous relief' for those unable to work, in the form of doles or kitchens, complemented public works to form the core of relief measures.

It is tempting to suspect that the motivation behind this predilection for public works lay with a puritanical prejudice against the provision of unconditional relief. This suspicion is all the more difficult to refute because the Famine Commission Report in fact explicitly referred on occasion to 'the demoralising influences of purely eleemosynary aid'.[46] It is, nevertheless, worth attempting to understand the arguments which the Famine Commissions put forward in defence of the strategy they advocated.

The problem of preventing famine was, naturally, seen by the British administration as one of protecting food entitlements in a situation where the physical availability of food was not itself problematic. One avenue of intervention could, of course, have been to aim primarily at preventing undue increases in food prices. But the success of such measures would have inevitably called for some form of 'interference' with the free market—either in the form of direct price *control*, or at least in the form of government *participation* in trade, storage, and distribution. And this was anathema to the British administration.

Why so? It is hard not to sympathize here with Ambirajan's view that 'when virtually every document relating to the formulation and execution of famine policy over a century refers to Adam Smith and/or John Stuart Mill, it becomes well nigh impossible to dismiss the role of Classical economic ideas in the formation of economic policy'.[47] Indeed these ideas were echoed with striking fidelity in the Famine Commission Reports themselves.[48]

Policies of direct price control had been emphatically criticized by classical economists. John Stuart Mill, for instance, pronounced:

In cases of actual scarcity Governments are often urged . . . to take measures of some sort for moderating the price of food. But the price of a thing cannot be raised by deficiency of supply beyond what is sufficient to make a corresponding reduction of the

[46] Government of India (1880: para. 111). Note, however, that what is referred to here is not so much the intrinsically 'immoral' character of gratuitous relief as the adverse effect of gratuitous relief on the 'moral economy': 'Even where the legal right does not exist, the moral obligation of mutual assistance is scarcely less distinctly recognized [in rural India] . . . Any form of relief calculated to bring these rights into obscurity or desuetude, or to break down these habits by showing them to be superfluous, would be an incalculable misfortune' (ibid. para. 108).

[47] Ambirajan (1978: 100); see also Stokes (1959) and Ambirajan (1971, 1976). Bhatia dissents on this point: 'It is difficult to explain this palpably mistaken policy [of free trade] simply in terms of the ideological attachment of the Government of those days to the teachings of Adam Smith and John Stuart Mill . . . It appears that behind the façade of the theoretical argument there was the fear that the Government would have to assume a gigantic financial responsibility in undertaking to feed a vast population during the period of a famine' (Bhatia 1967: 107). But it is hard to take seriously the suggestion that several decades of official writings were consistently manipulated to maintain this 'façade', and the single 'letter' which Bhatia refers to in support of his contention carries little weight in the face of the voluminous evidence gathered by Ambirajan.

[48] See e.g. the lengthy chapter on Food Supply in Government of India (1880).

consumption; and if a Government prevents the reduction from being brought about by a rise of price, there remains no mode of effecting it unless by taking possession of all the food and serving it out in rations as in a besieged town.[49]

This argument implicitly assumes competitive conditions, so that high prices reflect the 'actual scarcity' in the first place rather than collusive practices or speculative hoarding. But the disciples of classical economists did not think that assumption implausible for India, where 'a combination of large dealers with the object of keeping up prices is impossible'.[50]

It is more difficult to understand why the British administration viewed government participation in food trade with abhorrence. It can be argued that in many circumstances, and especially in the presence of important uncertainties and information costs, judicious government involvement in food trade can have many positive effects, including that of stabilizing food prices.[51] But the British administration was deeply sceptical of this view, and strongly feared that government participation in food trade would have harmful *disincentive effects* on private initiative. Here again the influence of classical economists is unmistakable:

Direct measures at the cost of the State, to procure food from a distance, are expedient when, from peculiar reasons, the thing is not likely to be done by private speculation. In any other case they are in great error. Private speculation will not, in such cases, venture to compete with the Government and though the Government can do more than any other merchant it cannot nearly do so much as all the merchants.[52]

It might even become necessary for Government to import grain for sale to the public in such an event as a combination of local dealers to refuse to sell, or only to sell at prices unduly raised above the rates of neighbouring markets . . . But much caution will be required in every case lest interference should aggravate the evil which it is designed to avert, and have the effect of preventing traders from entering the market while it is being operated upon by the Government.[53]

Whether the British administration's obstinate policy of complete non-intervention in the food trade was an effective route to the moderation of price increases in famine situations has been the subject of some controversy.[54] But in any case, the fundamental problem remained that the moderation of price increases could hardly suffice to restore the entitlements of the masses of labourers and artisans whose cash earnings virtually vanished for long periods during droughts. The need for a mechanism of income generation or transfer was therefore inescapable.

[49] J. S. Mill, quoted in Etheridge (1868: 7).

[50] Wallace (1900: 48).

[51] For further discussion, see Ravallion, ch. 5 vol. 2. See also Drèze and Sen (1989).

[52] Mill (1848), cited in Bhatia (1967: 107).

[53] Government of India (1880: para. 159).

[54] For different viewpoints, see e.g. Bhatia (1967), Srivastava (1968), Ambirajan (1978), Rashid (1980), McAlpin (1983), and Ravallion (1987b).

It remains to explain why public works (supplemented by 'gratuitous relief' for those unable to work) emerged as the preferred transfer mechanism. At this point it is important to recognize that the British administration, while anxious to prevent starvation deaths during droughts, was also deeply concerned with financial economy. It therefore felt a strong urge to concoct a system by which 'the proper recipients of public charity can be most effectively ascertained',[55] and to ensure that resources were concentrated exclusively on that category. Given the weakness of the administrative structure at the time, and the large numbers of people often affected by famine, it was also felt important that the selection mechanism should rely as far as possible on 'self-acting tests' rather than on discretionary procedures. The latter method, although found necessary for some forms of gratuitous relief (see below), was deemed impracticable as a general approach to the identification of the needy, and a few experiments in that direction were criticized by the Famine Commissions.[56]

Four varieties of 'self-acting tests' were seriously tried at various stages in the early days of famine relief under the colonial administration: (1) the *distance test*: relief is provided (in some form or other) in far-apart places, on the assumption that only those in greatest need will take the trouble of travelling long distances to avail themselves of it; (2) the *residence test*: beneficiaries are required to reside at the place of relief (e.g. a poor-house or worksite), and thereby forgo the presumed pleasure of ordinary social life; (3) the *test of cooked food*: relief is based on the distribution of cooked meals, a source of repulsion to many 'starving Hindoos' at that time (particularly when cooked by, or shared with, people belonging to other castes); and (4) the *labour test*: relief takes the form of subsistence wages in return for hard manual labour.

The distance test and the residence test, both of which required entire families of famine victims to leave their homes before obtaining relief, were quickly rejected because experience repeatedly showed them to be too dangerous. Famine victims were found to be strongly attached to their homes, and only abandoned them in search of food or relief when their physical condition was one of extreme weakness and great vulnerability to disease. The Famine Commission of 1880 had already discouraged recourse to self-acting tests of this kind; later experience repeatedly confirmed their danger, and the Famine Commissions of 1898 and 1901 categorically rejected them:

There is . . . a great accumulation of evidence to the effect that the feeling of people towards relief administered in this form is in most parts of India one of extreme repulsion; and that even in the North-Western Provinces in 1877–8 that repulsion was strong enough to cause many to lose their lives rather than to accept help on those terms;[57]

---

[55] Government of India (1880: para. 110).

[56] See e.g. Government of India (1880, 1898: 86, and 1901: 25).

[57] Government of India (1880: para. 140).

. . . we do not hold the view . . . that the fact that many will attend works when close to
their village, who will not follow them to a distance, necessarily proves that such
persons were not in need of relief;[58]

Labour should be the only test; neither a distance test, nor compulsory residence
should be imposed.[59]

The choice between the labour test and the test of cooked food was a more
subtle one. Three reasons (each prevailing with varying strength over time)
seem to have accounted for the precedence taken by the generation of
employment over the unconditional provision of cooked food in the Indian
system of famine relief. The first reason was the belief (discussed earlier) in the
'demoralizing' influence of gratuitous relief.[60] The second reason was the
impracticability of delivering relief on a large scale by means of cooked food:

Acceptance of cooked food is the truest and safest test of the need for gratuitous relief,
but the objection to relying exclusively on this form of relief is, that it would be difficult
to work on a large scale if there were widespread distress. When a large proportion of a
not very dense population has to be relieved, the organization of adequate distribution
of cooked food becomes almost impossible.[61]

The third reason appeared only with the Famine Commission of 1901. The
Famine Commission of 1898 had pronounced a rather favourable judgement
on relief kitchens (as a means of gratuitous relief specifically), and expressed a
general preference for kitchens over doles (of cash or grain) as a form of
gratuitous relief partly on the grounds that kitchens embodied a self-acting
test.[62] Indeed there was evidence from different parts of the country that 'the
people showed a very strong reluctance to accept relief in this form'.[63] But the
Famine Commission of 1901 radically reversed this judgement, altogether
dismissed the idea that kitchens embodied a self-acting test, and therefore
strongly favoured (grain) doles as the main vehicle of gratuitous relief:

gratuitous relief can properly be regulated by *personal selection* alone. Every
self-acting test that has been tried has broken down;[64]

Non-official opinion is almost unanimous, we gather, in favour of doles. It is now
generally admitted by the officers of the Central Provinces that *personal selection* is as
necessary for kitchens as it is for village relief. This conclusion deprives the kitchens of
the principal advantage expected from them, namely, the enforcement of an automatic
test of distress; while the disadvantages attaching to them remain.[65]

---

[58] Government of India (1898: 110).

[59] Government of India (1901: 18).

[60] See e.g. Government of India (1898: 233).

[61] Ibid. 18.   [62] See ibid. 286.

[63] Ibid. 23–4. See also pp. 18–26, 68–74, 80–1, 84–5, 88, 93, 178, 210, 286–7, and 322 of the
same report for discussions of the relative merits of kitchens and doles.

[64] Government of India (1901: 44) (my italics).

[65] Ibid. 47 (my italics). 'Village relief' refers to the distribution of doles.

In spite of their perceived superiority over the provision of cooked meals as far as *gratuitous* relief was concerned, doles in cash or grain could obviously not be adopted as a *general* form of relief. This followed from the assumed need for a test of distress, the impracticality of personal selection on a large scale, and the difficulties and confusion to which the granting of doles often led.[66]

The effectiveness of the 'labour test' as a self-acting test, on the other hand, was repeatedly confirmed by practical experience. Public works therefore emerged as the preferred vehicle of income transfers in the Famine Codes.

Having said this, it should be stressed that the provisions of the Famine Codes also included gratuitous relief (usually in the form of doles) for those to whom the labour test could not be applied. Although gratuitous relief has almost invariably assumed much less importance than public works in terms of numbers relieved and expenditure incurred, it has undoubtedly been an irreplaceable component of the 'safety-net' which the relief system sought to provide.[67]

At the risk of repetition, it is worth closing this discussion by quoting at some length the passage where the Famine Commission of 1880 succinctly summarizes the logic of the recommended approach:

we have to consider the manner in which the proper recipients of public charity can be most effectually ascertained. The problem to be solved is how to avoid the risk of indiscriminate and demoralising profusion on the one hand, and of insufficient and niggardly assistance on the other—how to relieve all who really need relief, and to waste as little public money as possible in the process . . . . Again where limited numbers have to be dealt with, and there is a numerous and efficient staff of officials, it may be possible to ascertain by personal inquiry the circumstances of every applicant for relief sufficiently for the purpose of admitting or rejecting his claim. But in an Indian famine the Government has to deal not with limited numbers, but with millions of people, and the official machinery at its command, however strengthened for the occasion, will inevitably be inadequate to the task of accurately testing the individual necessities of so great a multitude. Nor again is it possible to entrust the administration of public charity to a subordinate agency without providing sufficient checks against dishonesty and neglect on the part of its members. Some safeguards then are essential in the interests of the destitute people no less than of the public treasury, and they are best found in laying down certain broad self-acting tests by which necessity may be proved, and which may, irrespective of any other rule of selection, entitle to relief the person who submits to them . . . The chief of these tests, and the only one which in our opinion it is ordinarily desirable to enforce, is the demand of labour commensurate in each case with the labourer's powers, in return for a wage sufficient for the purposes of maintenance but not more. This system is applicable of course only to those from whom labour can reasonably be required . . . but for those who are able to work, we can feel no doubt that

---

[66] 'The drawbacks were that they [relief centres in the Central Provinces, where doles were distributed] tended to become centres of confusion and disorder, where relief was disbursed, without discrimination or enquiry into individual cases' (Goverment of India 1989: 72).

[67] There are, unfortunately, very few empirical studies of how this component of the relief system has worked in practice in different periods. For some recent evidence, see Drèze (1989).

it is the safest and most efficacious form of State help . . . The great bulk of applicants for relief being thus provided for, we believe that it will be possible for an efficient staff of officers to control with success the grant of relief, on the basis of personal inquiry and knowledge of the individual circumstances of each applicant, among the comparatively small numbers of destitute persons to whom the test of labour cannot be applied.[68]

The preceding discussion has attempted to identify the main ingredients of the Famine Codes. It would be naïve to regard the Famine Codes as embodying only enlightened pragmatism, and I have indeed pointed out the role of other influences such as the phobia of 'interference' with private trade and the distrust of gratuitous relief on sheer moral grounds. However, the strategy of open-ended employment for cash wages, supplemented by 'gratuitous relief' for the weak, undeniably had a sound rationale in terms of the objective of preventing all starvation deaths while achieving a measure of financial economy. Since this narrow objective remains, unfortunately, how famine prevention is often conceived, the Famine Codes and their basic principles have not lost their relevance.[69]

(d) Modern developments

It would not be easy to 'demonstrate' that the relief system which emerged and evolved from the Famine Codes had a dramatic effect on the incidence of famines before independence in 1947. Such questions are commonly investi-gated on the basis of famine chronologies,[70] but in the absence of reliable information on the actual excess mortality associated with different events the use of this piece of evidence is fraught with difficulties. In fact, crop failures resulting in a successfully averted threat of famine have sometimes been recorded in the annals of history as a 'famine', even though little or no evidence existed of substantial excess mortality.[71] Reliable data on crop failures and other possible sources of entitlement failures would also be needed in order to assess the severity of the *threats* confronted by the relief system in different periods.

Nevertheless, an examination of the incidence of famines in India before and after the Famine Codes strongly suggests a contrast between the earlier period

---

[68] Government of India (1880: paras. 110–11).

[69] Brennan (1984) has rightly emphasized the importance of 'personalities and politics' in the framing of the first Famine Code. He does not, however, imply that the actual content of that Code significantly reflected the uninformed prejudices or self-interested inclinations of the members of the Famine Commission of 1880. The remarkable continuity of the basic principles of famine relief in India to this day, in spite of substantial changes in 'personalities and politics', strongly discredits any implication of that sort.

[70] See n. 3 above for some references of famine chronologies for India.

[71] *Vide* the 'famine' of 1906–7 in Darbhanga, when 'the death rate was *unusually low* during the greater part of the famine period when relief measures were organised and in working order' (Government of India 1908: 30; italics added). The 'famine' of 1907–8 in the United Provinces is another example (see Bhatia 1967: 265–70). On the methodology of historical famine assessment, see Murton (1984).

of frequently recurring catastrophes, and the latter period when long stretches of relative tranquillity were disturbed by a few large-scale famines (see the 'chronological sketch' in Section 3.2). This pattern is unmistakable, for instance, in a comparison between the twenty years preceding and the twenty years following the Famine Commission Report of 1880. The period from 1860 to 1880 was a calamitous one. From 1880 to 1896, by contrast, great success was encountered in preventing local crop failures from developing into famines, allowing the Famine Commission of 1898 to assert that 'scarcities occurring over limited areas while the rest of the Indian continent is prosperous, can be successfully dealt with by a very moderate expenditure of money without disturbing the ordinary administration'.[72] Then, in 1896–7 and again in 1899–1900, disaster struck with renewed force. During the twentieth century, the incidence of famines was remarkably small even before independence; the main failure was of course the Bengal Famine of 1943.[73]

Why did the relief system experience these intermittent failures to prevent large-scale starvation?[74] Without attempting to assess their relative importance, I will suggest here four elements of answer to this question.

First, it is important to note that the existence of the Famine Codes does not automatically ensure their *application*, let alone their early and energetic application. The Famine Codes did include very specific (and 'authoritative') guidelines on how to recognize and 'declare' a famine, and it was not their least achievement to reduce the risk of deliberate ignorance or neglect of a crisis —an attitude which has been described as 'one of the most predictable responses by Government officials' in times of famine.[75] Nevertheless this 'early warning system' remained *within* the Famine Codes, and the problem of triggering remained an important one. During the Bengal Famine of 1943, for instance, the Famine Codes were deliberately ignored for political reasons —and this fault may well be responsible for a large part of the extraordinary excess mortality associated with that famine.[76]

Second, even for the narrow purpose of ensuring the mere survival of the population, famine relief under the British administration often had an

[72] Government of India (1989: 5). There are several interesting first-hand accounts of successful famine prevention in pre-independence India, e.g. Carlyle (1900).

[73] Considerable mortality also occurred in 1918–19, but this was mainly the result of a terrible influenza epidemic which affected many other parts of the world as well. On this see Mills (1986). On the prevention of famines during the first half of this century, see Christensen (1984), Kachhawaha (1985), and McAlpin (1985), among others.

[74] Note that even when famine did occur, the relief system may have succeeded in ensuring a considerable moderation of excess mortality. The Famine Commission of 1898, for instance, claimed that 'the success actually attained in the relief of distress was, if not complete, far greater than any that has been recorded in famines that are at all comparable with it in extent, severity, and duration' (Government of India 1898: 196). Demographic statistics also showed a clear inverse correlation between the extent of relief and that of excess mortality (Visaria and Visaria 1982: 130).

[75] Carlson (1982:9).

[76] On the Bengal Famine of 1943, and the question of non-declaration of famine in that event, see Sen (1981), Greenough (1982), Brennan (1988), and the literature cited in these studies.

excessively punitive character. In particular, the level of wages paid on relief works was extraordinarily low—the extreme of stinginess being reached with the so-called 'Temple ration' of 1lb of grain per day (this standard was fortunately abrogated without delay).[77] As a result, during the most severe crises the availability of work did not always prevent a considerable enfeeblement of affected people, and their enhanced vulnerability to epidemics. This factor seems to have played a particularly important role during the famines of 1896–7 and 1899–1900.[78]

Third, in the case of the latter two famines the policy of strict non-interference with private trade was particularly questionable because the existence of abundant food supplies in India as a whole could no longer be so safely assumed. The crop failures which triggered these famines had unique severity for the nineteenth century, and they also had the exceptional feature of affecting very large parts of the country. The collapse of production for the country as a whole was unprecedented, and prices rose throughout India. The fact of continued food exports during the 1896–7 famine, taken by the Famine Commission of 1898 as evidence of the persistence of a surplus, could obviously not be interpreted in that way. It is hard to deny that in this case the refusal to prohibit exports or arrange for imports may have had disastrous consequences.[79]

Finally, it must be recognized that while epidemics are often exacerbated or even triggered by food entitlement failures, they do have an influence of their own as well. This was most obvious in the case of the 1918 influenza epidemic, which affected large parts of the world. The Famine Commissions of 1898 and 1901 also stressed the independent role of cold weather, contaminated water, and epidemics during the famines of 1896–7 and 1899–1900. In his rejoinder to some of the conclusions of the Famine Commission Report of 1898, Holderness even argued that in some places excess mortality had altogether little to do with food deprivation.[80]

[77] The proper level of wages, keeping in view the objective of preventing starvation deaths while simultaneously ensuring the greatest possible measure of financial economy, was discussed at nauseating length in most Famine Commission Reports. The issue was all the more important because the supply of labour to public works was repeatedly observed to be extremely sensitive to the level of wages. For some examples of strong expansion or contraction of labour supply in response to small wage revisions, see e.g. Bhatia (1967: 85, 95, 249) and Government of India (1898: 25, 26, 34, 76, 77, 80, 83, 168, 177).

[78] See e.g. Bhatia (1967), Guz (1987), Hebert (1987), and particularly Klein (1984).

[79] This question is pursued at some length in Holderness (1897), with reference to the 1896–7 famine. Holderness argued that 'there is . . . a strong probability that the production of the year was much below the requirements of the population' (p. 11), estimated the decline in foodgrain production to represent as much as 18 or 19 million tons (p. 13), and cited a letter published in early 1897 in the *Gazette of India* invoking the usual reasons for not interfering with private trade in any way: 'The Governor-General in Council believes that the intervention of Government as a purchaser or importer would do infinitely more harm than good, as it would cripple and discourage the agency which is best able to gauge the need, which is impelled by self-interest to anticipate it, and which alone is best able to supply it effectively' (quoted on p. 33).

[80] See the Appendix of Government of India (1898).

While the control of epidemics obviously demands intervention measures beyond the mere restoration of food entitlements, the first three of the above factors point to defects of the entitlement protection system itself. As we shall see, these three defects were largely remedied after independence, an event which must count as marking the second turning-point in the history of famine relief in India over the last two centuries. The government of independent India rapidly did away with the policy of strict non-interference with private trade in food, and its price stabilization measures in particular have often played an important role in averting famine threats. The punitive and avaricious nature of relief provisions has not altogether disappeared (far from it), but the value attached to human life has nevertheless appreciated compared to the colonial days. Last but not least, commitment to respond to the threat of famine has increasingly assumed the character of a political compulsion.

3.3. *Food crises in India after independence*

This section consists of two fairly self-contained parts. The first is devoted to a general overview of food crises in India since independence. The second discusses famine relief in Bihar during the drought of 1966–7, with particular attention to its shortcomings. The intention of these explorations is essentially to strengthen the background against which relief operations in Maharashtra in 1972–3 (the subject of Section 3.4) will be evaluated. The reader familiar with the food situation in contemporary India and lacking interest in the Bihar crisis may wish to go straight to Section 3.4.

(a) *The reality and nature of recent food crises*

According to official statistics, per capita food production in India consistently declined in the first half of this century (see Table 3.1). In fact, official statistics unambiguously show consistently declining *total output* over this period.[81] Even if we take official statistics for the pre-independence period with a pinch of salt, it is clear that by the time of independence per capita foodgrain production levels in India were dangerously low, and they remained so until very recent years when a mild trend upward has slowly emerged. It is,

---

[81] This conclusion is extremely robust with respect to alternative manipulations of these statistics—for further discussion, see Blyn (1966), Mukerji (1965), Sen (1971), and Sivasubramoniam (1960, 1965). The fact that the Famine Commissions (in 1880, 1898, and 1901) asserted the existence of a surplus of foodgrains in India in normal years on the basis of consumption allowances which far exceeded contemporary standards provides further support for the thesis of declining per capita production levels in the first half of this century. In a widely discussed rejoinder, Alan Heston (1973, 1978, 1982) has expressed scepticism about the plausibility of output trends derived from official statistics because they imply (he argues) the doubtful finding of declining yields over the same period. Heston's own estimates of production trends, based on the assumption of stable yields, affect the force, but not the substance, of the argument presented in this section. Indeed, the growth of *acreage* of foodgrains lagged behind population growth during the first half of this century (see McAlpin 1985).

Table 3.1 Production and availability of foodgrains in India, 1893–1985

Period	Production per capita (1961 = 100)	Availability per capita (1961 = 100)
1893–4 to 1895–6	146	—
1896–7 to 1905–6	140	—
1906–7 to 1915–16	136	—
1916–17 to 1925–6	134	—
1926–7 to 1935–6	115	—
1936–7 to 1945–6	99	—
1956	94	92
1961	100	100
1962	98	99
1963	94	95
1964	92	96
1965	100	102
1966	79	87
1967	80	86
1968	99	98
1969	98	95
1970	100	97
1971	107	100
1972	101	99
1973	90	90
1974	96	96
1975	90	87
1976	106	91
1977	96	92
1978	107	100
1979	109	102
1980	89	88
1981	102	97
1982	103	97
1983	98	93
1984	113	102
1985	106	99

Notes: Availability is calculated (following the usual conventions in Indian food statistics) as net production + net imports − net additions to government stocks, where net production consists of production less 12.5% for 'feed, seed, and wastage'.

There are a number of other estimates of pre-independence trends in per capita food production (e.g. Blyn 1966, Mukerji 1965, Sen 1971, and Sivasubramoniam 1960, 1965); but all those based on official statistics lead to the same conclusion of a *declining* pre-independence trend (see text).

In the post-independence calculations based on the *Economic Survey*, 'foodgrains' is understood as the sum of 'cereals' and 'pulses' (following the usual practice in Indian statistics). For pulses, 'net availability' is taken to be synonymous with 'gross production'—the resulting bias in the estimates of foodgrain production is negligible.

Sources: pre-independence: calculated from Bhatia (1967: 315), itself summarizing the work of Daniel Thorner; post-independence: calculated from *Economic Survey 1985–86* (Government of India 1986: 120).

moreover, very striking that production gains after independence have resulted mainly in reduced imports as well as in the accumulation of large stocks, leaving net 'availability' remarkably stagnant (see Table 3.1, and also Fig. 3.2 below).[82] There are compelling reasons, therefore, to attribute India's success in preventing famines after independence to other factors than the improvement of food availability.

Another important point to note is that the growth of food and agricultural output since independence has been very uneven across different parts of India.[83] While in irrigated regions the so-called 'Green Revolution' has permitted impressive increases in yields and total output, large unirrigated tracts have (until very recently at least) experienced virtual stagnation against a background of rapidly growing population. Accordingly, there is little evidence of increasing rural incomes and employment in unirrigated areas, which still cover around two-thirds of the total cropped area. These regions have also experienced huge ecological problems (such as deforestation, soil erosion, and falling water tables), and in this respect it is far from clear that they have fared better than Sahelian countries. Last but not least, there have been droughts and crop failures almost every year in some part or other of the country since independence, and the 'entitlement failures' which threatened to ensue remained quite capable of causing massive starvation in the absence of a vigorous relief system. The case-studies of drought in the States of Bihar (1966–7) and Maharashtra (1970–3) analysed further in this chapter unambiguously confirm that the growth of food production alone would have fallen far short of ensuring the prevention of famines in India in the last few decades.

The latter point can also, to some extent, be appreciated from a comparison of the recent experiences of India and the Sahel in terms of vulnerability to famine. Needless to say, any comparison of this kind must remain highly tentative, considering the quality of the available data and the wide variations in country-specific circumstances; in fact it is attempted here only with the greatest reluctance. I have nevertheless assembled in Tables 3.2 and 3.3 some evidence on levels of production and 'availability' of cereals for India and the Sahel over the 1960–80 period (see also Figs. 3.1 and 3.2).[84] Here 'availability' simply refers to the sum of production (net of 12.5 per cent allowance for feed, seed, and wastage), net recorded imports, and, in the case of India, net depletion of government stocks. This definition, largely imposed by the nature of the available data, neglects unrecorded imports (e.g. all private imports in the case of Maharashtra and Bihar) and the depletion of private stocks; it will, therefore, usually overestimate the instability of consumption. The neglect of

---

[82] See Lipton (1984) for further discussion of this point.

[83] For a detailed analysis of District-wise output trends during the 1960s and early 1970s, see Bhalla and Alagh (1979).

[84] I follow the definition of 'Sahel' used in Sen (1981). The comparison with the Sahel is emphasized because for that region in recent decades food availability fluctuations have been particularly sharp and closely associated with famines.

Table 3.2 'Production' of cereals per capita, India and Sahel, 1961–1980 (½ kg/cap./day = 100)

Year	India	Sahel (A)	Sahel (B)	Maharashtra	Bihar	Palamau (A)	Palamau (B)	Chad	Mali	Mauritania	Niger	Burkina Faso	Senegal
1961	86	124	—	93	—	—	—	194	141	52	145	89	90
1962	86	130	—	75	—	—	—	172	156	52	150	108	90
1963	82	124	—	77	—	—	—	164	127	52	151	108	101
1964	82	127	—	74	70	—	—	146	115	51	144	140	110
1965	87	120	—	74	68	—	—	141	118	60	132	117	113
1966	**69**	113	—	49	**63**	—	—	124	116	49	130	117	91
1967	**72**	124	—	62	**35**	**12**	**20**	119	128	59	141	117	133
1968	88	126	—	68	75	—	—	120	110	27	133	115	79
1969	87	116	—	67	79	—	—	109	129	55	129	108	122
1970	90	98	—	63	—	—	—	101	89	41	135	105	75
1971	96	102	96	**51**	—	—	—	103	123	37	117	88	100
1972	92	75	**105[a]**	**46**	—	—	—	**59**	**89**	**25**	**97**	**85**	**51**
1973	83	78	**83**	**27**	—	—	—	**72**	**72**	**15**	**101**	**80**	**81**
1974	88	115	**76**	62	—	—	—	84	79	25	140	111	122
1975	82	95	**104[a]**	—	—	—	—	79	98	**15[b]**	104	124	87[b]
1976	96	104	**102[a]**	—	—	—	—	81	116	14	156	115	77
1977	87	93	—	—	—	—	—	81	96	11	171	91	54
1978	97	109	—	—	—	—	—	83	124	9	169	97	102
1979	99	99	—	—	—	—	—	82	101	15	173	99	66
1980	82	91	—	—	—	—	—	84	76	10	184	82	64

[a] Excluding Mauritania.

[b] Discrete jump in population estimates.

Note: Bold type indicates a year of famine or averted famine.

Sources: The estimates presented in the table were obtained as follows: India: calculated from the *Economic Survey 1985–86* (Government of India 1986: 120). Sahel: the estimates for individual Sahelian countries (Burkina Faso, Chad, Mali, Mauritania, Niger, and Senegal) have all been derived using the same formula, and the estimates for 'Sahel (A)' are calculated by aggregation over individual countries. Production as well as (mid-year) population estimates are taken from the *FAO Production Yearbooks* (the FAO population series, unlike those of the *United Nations Demographic Yearbook*, are adjusted to achieve consistency across years). Whenever different production (population) estimates for a given year appeared in different *FAO Production Yearbooks*, the figure mentioned in the *latest Yearbook* in which a production (population) estimate was available for that year has been used. The alternative estimates 'Sahel (B)' are calculated from Club du Sahel (1977) and the *United Nations Demographic Yearbook 1977*. They are not directly comparable to 'Sahel (A)' on a year-to-year basis because of differences in calendars. Maharashtra: production figures from the *Economic Review 1973–74* (Government of Maharashtra 1974) and the *Bulletin on Food Statistics*, 1975, 1976. Population estimates (mid-year) from the *Bulletin on Food Statistics*, 1975 and 1982–4. To obtain per capita production, population in calendar year *t* was combined with production in agricultural year $(t-1, t)$. Bihar: production figures from the *Bulletin on Food Statistics*, 1967, 1968, and 1971: table 4. Population figures from the *Bulletin on Food Statistics*, 1972. Palamau: See Table 3.7 below.

The *Economic Survey* production figures for India have been preferred to the FAO figures, because the latter include rice in the husk, which is about 50% heavier than husked rice (used in the *Economic Survey* figures); the latter is more directly comparable to other cereals (e.g. in terms of calorie content per kg) than rice in the husk. Apart from this discrepancy, however, the FAO figures are broadly comparable to the *Economic Survey* figures, and the latter are generally considered as fairly accurate. The FAO figures for the Sahel, on the other hand, can at best be regarded as rough estimates. I am grateful to the Statistics Division of FAO for helpful personal communications on these issues.

Table 3.3 'Net availability' of cereals per capita, India and Sahel, 1961–1980 (½ kg/cap./day = 100)

Year	India	Sahel (A)	Sahel (B)	Maharashtra	Bihar (A)	Bihar (B)	Palamau	Chad	Mali	Mauritania	Niger	Burkina Faso	Senegal
1961	80	115	—	—	—	—	—	170	123	66	121	79	109
1962	80	120	—	—	—	—	—	151	137	70	126	97	109
1963	77	114	—	—	—	—	—	145	112	63	125	96	120
1964	80	118	—	—	—	71	—	129	102	63	120	124	137
1965	84	113	—	—	65	68	—	124	106	74	110	104	139
1966	**72**	105	—	—	**62**	**63**	—	124	103	66	109	104	115
1967	**73**	115	—	—	**45**	**53**	≈55^b	106	113	67	118	106	150
1968	81	118	—	75	85	72	—	106	97	53	110	103	104
1969	80	111	—	74	75	74	—	97	117	73	107	97	151
1970	81	93	—	68	—	—	—	90	105	66	111	95	95
1971	84	101	95	**55**	—	—	—	91	114	67	96	95	136
1972	84	**76**	102^a	**57**	—	—	—	**53**	**85**	59	**80**	79	**83**
1973	76	**85**	90	**46**	—	—	—	**66**	**79**	**59**	**86**	**79**	**129**
1974	82	120	87	73	—	—	—	81	92	77	134	104	148
1975	73	92	98^a	—	—	—	—	70	97	51	90	110	99
1976	75	104	—	—	—	—	—	74	101	65	140	103	112
1977	77	94	—	—	—	—	—	74	84	64	152	84	91
1978	85	110	—	—	—	—	—	75	114	62	154	91	132
1979	87	101	—	—	—	—	—	74	91	43	153	93	108
1980	76	94	—	—	—	—	—	74	73	66	166	78	96

^{a} Excluding Mauritania.

^{b} This includes estimates of private imports.

Note: Bold type indicates a year of famine or averted famine.

Sources: As explained in the text, the definition of 'net availability' used here is the following: net availability = net production + recorded imports + recorded stock depletion, where net production is obtained by deducting 12.5% from gross production for 'feed, seed, and wastage'. The production and population estimates are the same as in Table 3.2 for every region. Other sources are as follows: India: all figures obtained from *Economic Survey 1985–86* (Government of India 1986: 120). Sahel: there are no recorded changes in stocks. Import and export estimates for each year were taken from the latest *FAO Trade Yearbook* for which figures for that year were available. Maharashtra: see Table 3.6 below. Bihar: see Table 3.18 below. Palamau: see Table 3.7 below.

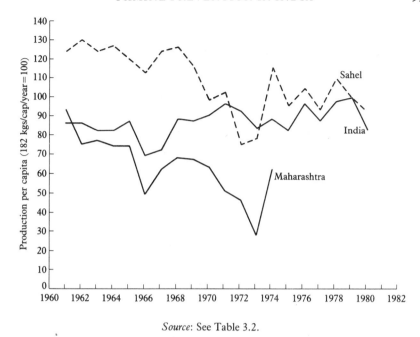

Fig. 3.1 Production of cereals per capita, 1961–1980

unrecorded trade is likely to be particularly serious in the case of individual States within India, and that of private stocks in the case of the Sahel. Note that much of the discussion in this section will concentrate on 'cereals' or 'food-grains' rather than 'calories'; however, a comparison between India and the Sahel based on available calorie data leads to broadly similar conclusions.[85]

Many complex issues are, of course, involved in deciding what these figures tell us about the potential severity of entitlement crises in different places at different times. It is arguable, for instance, whether the comparison made here should be primarily based on (1) *production* or *availability* figures; and (2) *levels* or *change*. Answers to these questions are highly contingent upon our view of how the food entitlement process works in a particular place. Regarding the first question, production and availability figures obviously give us different and complementary clues. While 'availability' sounds more closely related to consumption than production, it suffers particularly badly from being an aggregative measure. If entitlement failures are seen to arise mainly as a

---

[85] See also Sen (1986). For our purposes, foodgrains are probably not a bad proxy for calories in India, where they form an overwhelming proportion of total calories. Svedberg (1987) has argued that this approximation may not be too inaccurate for Sahelian countries either. Throughout this paper I shall use the usual convention in Indian statistics of defining 'foodgrains' as the sum of 'cereals' and 'pulses'. The share of pulses in total foodgrains in India was less than 10% in the early 1980s (Government of India 1986: 120).

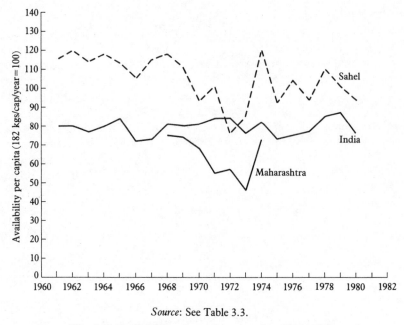

Source: See Table 3.3.

Fig. 3.2 Availability of cereals per capita, 1961–1980

consequence of the loss of employment or income associated with bad harvests, it is arguable that production is a more significant variable. In this case, however, it is total agricultural output rather than food output which is of interest. The recognition of this simple fact was indeed at the centre of the 'annewari' system of early warning in India, based on assessments of harvest quality.

The second question is also important, particularly in the case of availability figures. If food consumption responds little to income and price changes (except perhaps for pure 'income effects' at very low income levels), then even with a fairly high base consumption level small *declines* in net food availability are likely to have serious consequences, because the burden of adjustment will fall on the poorest. On the other hand, if food consumption is highly responsive to short-run price and income changes, then small changes in food availability around a high base level may be fairly unalarming, and the long-term level of food consumption may be the more important variable to focus on. The contrast is of some importance in this context, because the evolution of (aggregate) cereal production and consumption in India during the period 1960–80 seems to have been marked by much lower base levels but also smaller fluctuations than those experienced in the Sahel (see Figs. 3.1 and 3.2).

A further issue is that of appropriate standards for comparing availability levels. In principle, one should at least adjust for differences in calorie 'requirements' and in the importance of cereals in the diet. While the latter adjustment would not be likely to change the results, the basis of the former is a matter of fierce controversy (on this see Chapters 7 and 8 in the first volume of this book).

No attempt will be made here to take all these considerations explicitly into account. They are, to some extent, of secondary importance, in so far as our purpose is not primarily to compare actual or potential entitlement crises in India and the Sahel, but rather to show that the prevention of famines in contemporary India cannot be convincingly explained solely in terms of food production or availability. The data in Tables 3.2 and 3.3 allow us to compare both levels and change (for production as well as availability), and in the absence of fairly large differentials in consumption standards between India and the Sahel the following tentative observations would appear to be valid:

1. The interpretation of a comparison of food 'production' and 'availability' between *India as a whole* and *Sahel as a whole* over the 1960–80 period hinges greatly on whether one compares levels or change. India has not suffered from a declining trend in production over that period, but nevertheless production and availability levels have remained consistently lower in India than in the Sahel.

2. If one compares *Sahel countries* or groups of countries with *areas* of similar (or greater) population size in India, it always seems possible to find an area in India which has fared no better than the corresponding area in the Sahel (e.g. Maharashtra 1960–75 vs. Sahel 1960–75, or Bihar 1965–70 vs. Chad 1970–5). This holds in terms of both 'production' and 'availability'.

3. If we compare *India as a whole* with *individual Sahel countries*, some among the latter (e.g. Chad and Mauritania) have undoubtedly faced more severe food crises by any criterion.

Before moving on, it is worth reflecting for a moment on the issue of food security and national boundaries. The contrast between India and the Sahel suggests that food security tends to be enhanced by the integration of vulnerable areas within wider national boundaries. This observation is confirmed by an examination of State-wise cereal production and consumption data in India (Table 3.4). Not only do we find that consumption differences across States are much narrower than production differences, but consumption differentials themselves appear to be extraordinarily stable over time and therefore must have very little to do with production differentials as such. Thus, in contemporary India, consumption instability is very effectively insulated from production instability for individual States; though not perfectly, as the consumption 'dips' in Maharashtra (1972–3), Gujarat (1972–4), and West Bengal (1973–4)—all coinciding with local crop failures—illustrate.

The finding that a large country tends to achieve a greater level of food security, *ceteris paribus*, than a collection of small countries is hardly surprising. But the precise mechanism underlying this contrast deserves further

Table 3.4 Cereal production and consumption in India, State-wise (kg/cap./month)

State	Cereal consumption per capita				Cereal production per capita
	1970–1	1972–3	1973–4	1977–8	1977–8
Andhra Pradesh	16.05	15.25	15.80	15.85	14.30
Assam	15.70	14.81	15.33	14.38	11.18
Bihar	16.39	15.58	14.99	16.16	11.42
Gujarat	15.00	13.32	13.87	13.44	9.78
Haryana	18.13	17.57	16.56	15.22	30.16
Jammu and Kashmir	20.14	18.72	19.09	17.97	16.36
Kerala	(7.99)	(7.97)	(7.69)	(9.18)	4.44
Madhya Pradesh	16.51	17.28	17.12	16.08	17.51
Maharashtra	12.83	12.60	13.45	13.52	13.40
Karnataka	15.71	15.63	15.61	16.01	16.03
Orissa	16.12	15.22	15.80	15.97	16.27
Punjab	15.46	15.38	14.89	14.35	52.85
Rajasthan	17.91	18.17	18.76	18.18	13.56
Tamil Nadu	13.95	14.53	14.72	13.85	13.56
Uttar Pradesh	16.32	16.83	16.24	16.57	15.12
West Bengal	13.35	13.64	12.97	14.74	13.97
India	15.35	15.26	15.09	15.25	14.88

Note: Figures for Kerala are not strictly comparable with those for other States because of the great importance, in the former case, of food items classified as 'Cereal Substitutes' by the National Sample Survey.

Sources: Consumption figures for 1970–1, 1972–3, 1973–4 from National Sample Survey (25th, 27th, and 28th Rounds), as summarized in *Sarvekshana*, Jan. 1979. Consumption figures for 1977–8 from the Draft Report No. 311 of the National Sample Survey, relating to the 32nd Round. Production figures are calculated from the *Bulletin on Food Statistics*, 1980: 13–14, using population projections (for 1 Oct. 1977) from the *Bulletin on Food Statistics*, 1982–4: 8–9 (assuming a constant population growth rate during the 1971–81 decade, within each State).

investigation. Does a poor 'integration' of food markets across national boundaries obstruct some evening out of food surpluses and shortages? Does the restricted movement of factors impinge on the diversification of income sources and exacerbate the consequences of crop failures? Is there an un-utilized potential, within the Sahel for instance, for improving food security through co-operation or trade? All of these questions may well deserve prudently affirmative answers. But in the case of India it is also important to recognize a less frequently mentioned source of security, namely the possibility of implementing large *transfers* of resources towards vulnerable States during bad years. The financial resources allocated by the central government to drought-affected States have indeed reached impressive levels in recent years, and they certainly represent a very important factor of risk pooling at the national level.[86]

[86] These financial transfers have, in fact, become a bone of contention among economists and politicians. See Rangasami (1986) for a discussion of this and related problems.

This section will conclude with a brief overview of food crises in India since independence, as a background to the more detailed case-studies analysed in the remainder of the chapter. Over this period, localized crop failures (mainly due to drought) have occurred in different parts of the country almost every year.[87] In non-irrigated areas they recur at more or less frequent intervals. When crop failures are only local in character, food is usually forthcoming from neighbouring areas at reasonable prices, and hence the 'Famine Codes strategy' of generating purchasing power in the affected areas and stimulating private trade tends to work well. The actual determination with which relief has been provided has varied from State to State and from time to time, and some obvious failures have occurred (such as in Assam in 1974–5).[88] However, on the whole and by international standards the operation of the famine relief system in India in the context of local crises can undeniably be considered as impressive.

Besides dealing with these numerous local crises, India has had to cope with the threat of major disaster on three occasions since 1947: in 1966–7, 1972–3, and 1979–80.[89] The first of these crises occurred in the wake of a very rare instance of virtually country-wide crop failures for two consecutive years. In both 1965–6 and 1966–7, the all-India level of foodgrain production was nearly 20 per cent below the average for the previous five years (see Table 3.2 above). In terms of the magnitude and geographical coverage of crop failures, a disaster of this magnitude had not occurred since the catastrophic famine of 1899–1900. The situation was all the more precarious considering the very low base level of production, the large numbers of people affected, the sharp regional variations in distress, and the virtual disappearance of 'surplus areas'. In Bihar, a State then counting more than 50 million people (more than twice the combined population of all six Sahel countries at that time), foodgrain production in 1966–7 was only about 54 per cent of the average 1961–5 level.[90]

Disaster was narrowly avoided. Public food stocks being negligible at the time, massive imports were undertaken. But the net availability of food per capita remained dangerously low in several States (including Bihar), and a large-scale famine would undoubtedly have occurred in the absence of extensive measures of direct entitlement protection. These took the familiar form of a combination of employment generation and unconditional relief.

[87] It is worth remembering that when a 'localized' drought extends over, say, a single State, it still typically affects tens of millions of people! Note also that in the 19th century the vulnerability of agricultural labourers was so acute that localized crop failures occurring in a single year often caused famine—see e.g. Government of India (1880: paras. 76–7).

[88] See e.g. Prabhakar (1975) and Baishya (1975). It is noteworthy that this particular failure occurred in circumstances where the traditional 'early warning' system was likely to fail (because the famine was not, in this instance, caused by drought).

[89] The years 1985–7 were also a period of acute vulnerability. As stated in the introduction, however, this chapter focuses primarily on the pre-1980 period.

[90] Calculated from *Bulletin on Food Statistics*, various issues. See also Table 3.2 above, or Table 3.5 below.

Officially, no starvation deaths occurred. One is inclined to be suspicious of official figures in this respect when local authorities are accountable for starvation deaths, and indeed there were non-official allegations of starvation deaths. However, the numbers involved were undoubtedly very small. On the other hand, short of starvation deaths every possible kind of damage occurred to an alarming degree: hunger and severe nutritional deterioration, massive loss of livestock, depletion of assets, and possibly even substantial excess mortality. Eye-witness accounts of the situation evoke sadly familiar pictures of destitution and hunger.

In spite of this, the 1966–7 experience has been hailed as a grand 'success story' by many commentators.[91] Considering the gravity of the crisis this verdict may not be entirely exaggerated. I shall nevertheless express considerable reservations about it in the next section, where the 1966–7 crisis is further examined with special reference to Bihar.

India's great 'success story' of famine prevention is more justly dated in 1972–3, when another very severe drought hit large parts of the country. The worst affected State was that of Maharashtra (again, more than 50 million people at the time), which suffered the exceptional calamity of three successive drought years from 1970–1 to 1972–3. The cornerstone of relief operations consisted of open-ended public works of the cash-for-work type. At the peak of distress, as many as 5 million people attended the relief works in Maharashtra alone.

Inter-State private trade in foodgrains was prohibited, and the government undertook to fill the food deficit in affected States with food sales through the public distribution system. However, public food deliveries fell far short of needs, and crucial inter-State food movements also took the form of illegal private transactions. These were stimulated by large price differentials between States, and tolerated by pragmatic (or corrupt) government officials.

Even after allowing for these food movements, it appears that food consumption in Maharashtra during the drought was substantially lower than in normal years, but that famine was averted because the food deficit was rather well *distributed* among different socio-economic groups. There is also some evidence to the effect that nutritional damage during the Maharashtra crisis was not very great. Another important achievement of famine relief operations was to prevent a major and lasting disruption of the rural economy.

In many respects, therefore, famine relief in 1972–3 represented a great improvement over the 1966–7 experience. The former success was all the more impressive considering that it was achieved with little help from abroad, and with little resort to food imports. Section 3.4 is devoted to a case-study of the 1972–3 relief operations.

The drought of 1979–80 was short-lived, but its intensity and widespread geographical coverage were exceptional. Compared with the average of the

[91] See e.g. Nossiter (1967), Verghese (1967), Harvey (1969), Scarfe and Scarfe (1969), Berg (1972), Aykroyd (1974), and Singh (1975).

Source: Brass (1986).

Map 3.1 Bihar Districts, 1967

previous four years, foodgrain output fell by about 30 per cent in north India as a whole, and by much more in individual States. By then, however, India had accumulated large buffer stocks of foodgrains and these were used both to prevent excessive increases in food prices and to finance public works programmes. The crisis was anticipated with impressive foresight and a huge employment programme of the food-for-work type was undertaken. The country seems to have taken the drought in its stride with remarkable ease. This episode, however, will not receive further attention in this chapter.

(b)   Famine averted in 1966–1967: a reassessment

A proper 'case-study' of the 1966–7 drought is beyond the scope of the present enquiry. There is, nevertheless, some merit in attempting a brief re-examination of this important event, partly in order to question some of the interpretations it has lent itself to, and partly to bring out an instructive contrast with the Maharashtra drought of 1970–3 examined in section 1.4.[92]

Bihar is widely regarded as one of the most 'backward' regions of India. In the early 1980s this State had, among all the States of India, the lowest net domestic product per capita, the lowest proportion of non-agricultural employment to total employment, the second lowest literacy rate for both sexes, the third highest crude death rate, and the fourth highest incidence of rural poverty.[93] Bihar is also prone to droughts and floods, and in 1966 only a very small proportion of the cultivated area was irrigated. Yields were dangerously stagnating, and the State-level foodgrain deficit in an ordinary year around 1966 was officially estimated at 1.3 million tonnes.[94] By any account Bihar in the mid-1960s was a highly vulnerable spot.

In fact it can be said without exaggeration that India itself looked like a big 'vulnerable spot' at that time. In the early 1960s, output levels were pitifully low, yields were stagnating, the Green Revolution was hardly in sight, and output gains through expansion in cultivated areas were increasingly difficult

---

[92] An in-depth analysis of the 1966–7 drought would undoubtedly provide most valuable insights into many issues related to famine relief. Unfortunately, no comprehensive study of this event seems to be available. The most widely used source on the subject is Singh's (1975) very valuable book *The Indian Famine, 1967*. The author was District Collector in Palamau (one of the worst affected Districts) in 1967, and for this reason the book is well documented but not entirely detached; nor is it always a masterpiece of academic rigour. The Government of Bihar (1973) issued its own Report on the drought, and similar comments apply to this document. There exist a number of other interesting accounts and analyses of the 1966–7 events, including Indian Institute of Public Administration (1967), Sen (1967), Verghese (1967), Scarfe and Scarfe (1969), Swaminathan *et al.* (1969), Central Institute of Research and Training in Public Cooperation (1969), Ramlingaswami *et al.* (1971), Berg (1972, 1973), Gangrade and Dhadda (1973), and Brass (1986). None of them, however, provides a comprehensive and carefully documented analysis of the events. A further report by Professor Michael Windey, to whom a great deal of credit for orchestrating famine relief in Palamau should probably have gone, was handed to Indira Gandhi who later pronounced that it was 'too important to be disclosed' (Michael Windey, personal communication).

[93] These observations are based on Vaidyanathan (1987). All figures refer to 1982–3, except poverty incidence (1977–8) and crude death rate (average of 1979–81).

[94] Government of Bihar (1973: 75).

to achieve. India's future was not regarded with greater optimism in the early 1960s than Africa's future is today, and when widespread drought hit the country twice consecutively in 1965–6 and 1966–7, a terrible famine was widely predicted.

Massive imports were undertaken to augment available supplies of food. Most of the imported food consisted of food aid under the American PL-480 programme and there were, at times, complicated politics involved in securing the required supplies.[95] A policy of internal 'zoning' was in force, under which private trade in foodgrains across broad zones within the country was prohibited. The official purpose of this policy was to facilitate procurement from surplus zones—and presumably transfer this surplus to deficit zones.[96]

Complementary to these attempts at improving food supplies in deficit areas was the more traditional battery of relief measures, including relief works and unconditional relief. The efforts of the government were supplemented by those of voluntary agencies (local as well as international), which mainly organized free-feeding programmes.

The food situation in Bihar was very serious. Cereal production per capita was already on a dangerous downward trend, and collapsed dramatically in 1966–7 (see Tables 3.2, 3.3, and 3.5).[97] The final official estimates of cereal production in Bihar for the year 1966–7 (after a substantial *upward* revision of initial estimates) were put at 3.4 million tonnes.[98] If we use the average level of cereal consumption in Bihar over four rounds of the National Sample Survey in the 1970s as the 'normal consumption' standard, this represents barely *one-third* of cereal consumption requirements.

In order to arrive at an estimate of net availability of food in Bihar in 1966–7, the production figure needs to be adjusted in order to take into account (1) private stocks, (2) private trade, and (3) public distribution.[99]

No data exist, as far as I know, on private foodgrain stocks for that period; but there is every reason to believe that in this case the adjustment required to allow for private stocks would be minimal. As noted earlier, the practice of multi-year foodgrain storage by farmers was widespread in nineteenth-century India, but declined markedly towards the end of that century.[100] There are strong presumptions that nowadays the extent of on-farm storage across years

---

[95] On this see e.g. the contemporary issues of *Economic and Political Weekly*.

[96] See Bhagwati and Chakravaraty (1969), and Krishna and Chhibber (1983), for evaluations of zoning policies.

[97] In Bihar, the most damaging crop failure affected the *kharif* crop in the second part of 1966. The year 1966–7 covers both the 1966 *kharif* crop and the *rabi* crop (early 1967). Note that there is some discrepancy in India between the 'agricultural year' (July–June) and the 'financial year' (Apr.–Mar.).

[98] *Bulletin on Food Statistics*, 1968.

[99] Strictly speaking, one should also make an allowance for food aid not merged with central stocks, e.g. moved and distributed directly by international voluntary agencies such as CARE. But quantitatively this item was negligible (see Singh 1975: 201).

[100] See e.g. the discussions in Srivastava (1968: 331) and McAlpin (1974, 1983).

Table 3.5 'Outturn of crops' in Bihar, 1966–1967

District	'Outturn of crops' (in 000 tonnes)			1966–7 as % of 'normal'
	'Normal'	1965–6	1966–7	
Patna	540	542	119	22.0
Gaya	698	606	138	19.7
Shahabad	918	888	435	47.4
Saran	434	422	325	74.9
Champaran	437	488	280	64.1
Muzaffarpur	374	432	220	58.8
Darbhanga	515	473	246	47.8
Monghyr	484	487	283	58.5
Bhagalpur	251	291	129	51.4
Saharsa	178	161	122	68.5
Purnea	471	397	249	52.3
S. Pargana	523	522	323	61.8
Hazaribagh	297	252	79	26.6
Ranchi	362	335	179	49.4
Palamau	176	148	48	27.2
Dhanbad	85	85	21	24.2
Singhbum	383	280	156	40.7
STATE	7,403	7,122	3,564	48.1

Notes: It appears that 'outturn of crops' refers specifically to the output of *foodgrains*, and that 'normal outturn' is simply the outturn in 1963–4 (see Government of Bihar 1973: 87).

The District-wise figures do not precisely add up to the State figure because of the addition in the latter of 'Other crops for which district break-up not available'.

Source: Government of Bihar (1973: 108–9).

is extremely small, at least in north India.[101] Nor are the reasons for this difficult to understand. The confidence with which grain prices in India can be predicted to fall after a harvest is now so great (partly due to public storage and distribution policies) that storing grain across a major harvest is a very unattractive way of holding wealth, particularly with high interest rates. The same argument makes it unlikely that merchants store much grain across years. In any case, whatever the level of private storage might have been in Bihar in a normal year, foodgrain stocks in 1966–7 must have been particularly small since the preceding year itself was one of poor harvest. Singh (1975) confirms this hypothesis for Palamau District.[102]

[101] In the village of Palanpur (Uttar Pradesh), where I conducted intensive field work in 1983–4, the practice of grain storage across years (more precisely, storage across the main rabi harvest in Apr.–May) has virtually disappeared. Already in 1958, the reported total grain stocks held before the arrival of the rabi crop amounted to less than 5% of the current rabi harvest. During recent field work in other parts of north India as well as Maharashtra I have also been repeatedly told that only a small percentage of large farmers, at best, store across years.

[102] Singh (1975: 36, 227).

Private trade is also unrecorded, but again it is very likely that the adjustment required on this count would be minimal. Zonal restrictions of the 'single-State' type were in force at the time and they seem to have been effective.[103] Here again, a priori reasoning is directly confirmed for Palamau District.[104]

The report of the Government of Bihar (1973) on the drought (*Bihar Famine Report*) arrived at very similar conclusions on the importance of private stocks and unauthorized grain trade, and considered a margin of 10 per cent of food availability figures as a 'liberal allowance' on these counts.[105]

There remains the question of public distribution. The *Bulletin on Food Statistics* publishes State-wise annual series on 'Net Imports', 'Issues' (through the public distribution system), 'Procurement', and 'Closing Stocks' of cereals and foodgrains. 'Net Imports' refer to imports by 'Rail and River', which should closely coincide with total net imports on government account. When this is the case the identity

$$(\text{Net imports}) - (\text{Addition to stocks})$$
$$= \tag{3.1}$$
$$(\text{Issues}) - (\text{Procurement})$$

theoretically holds.[106] Unfortunately it is not possible to verify this identity on a year-to-year basis because net imports are reported for the 'financial year' (March to April), whereas other items refer to the 'calendar year' (January to December). However, this problem hardly arises if we attempt to verify the identity over a period of several years, and indeed over the period (say) 1964–5 to 1968–9 the figures tally well. Moreover, the *Bulletin on Food Statistics* figures are also consistent with the month-by-month figures on 'off-take' from the public distribution system appearing in Government of Bihar (1973: 162), and using these month-by-month figures we can check the above identity for the year 1966–7.[107] Again, the numbers tally fairly nicely. It seems, therefore,

---

[103] See e.g. ibid. 39, 98–9, 157, 227. On p. 156 of his book, Singh alludes casually to private trade 'not covered by zonal restrictions' of 1.3 million tonnes. But this is almost certainly a confusion with the same figure of 1.3 million tonnes for 'total net imports' mentioned in Government of Bihar (1973: 160). In fact, 1.3 million tonnes exceeds the likely magnitude of private trade even in a normal year (an idea of this can be obtained by comparing 'net availability' figures with 'consumption' figures from the National Sample Survey), and Singh himself emphasizes that private trade had slowed down considerably in 1966–7.

[104] See Singh (1975: 36, 46, 99).

[105] Government of Bihar (1973: 93–4).

[106] This is not strictly true because of minor details such as the fact that stocks are partly held by the central government and partly by the State government. But since stocks were anyway very small in this case we can safely ignore these qualifications.

[107] In doing this I have assumed that monthly issues over the period Apr.–Sept. 1966 (for which month-by-month data are not available in the Bihar Famine Report) were constant. This assumption is plausible and in any case rather unimportant. Monthly issues from July 1966 onwards for Palamau District are given in Singh (1975: 96), and they were fairly stagnant until Oct. 1966.

Table 3.6 Cereal availability in Bihar, 1966–1967

Year	Population[a] (000s)	Production[b]	Issues[c]	Procurement[c]	Closing stocks[c]	Net imports[d]	Net availability per capita (kg/year) (A)	(B)
1964 (1963–4)	49,580	6,282	765	—	74	—	—	129
1965 (1964–5)	50,552	6,293	758	36	214	436	118	120
1966 (1965–6)	51,537	5,902	806	67	169	662	113	115
1967 (1966–7)	52,532	3,377	2,092	10	195	1,288	81	95
1968 (1967–8)	53,536	7,343	658	44	186	1,891	155	132
1969 (1968–9)	54,547	7,864	485	76	184	532	134	134

[a] Mid-year estimates.
[b] Agricultural year (July–June).
[c] Calendar year.
[d] Financial year (Apr.–Mar.).

Note: Unless otherwise specified, all figures are in thousand tonnes.

Sources: All figures except 'net availability' are taken from the *Bulletin on Food Statistics*, 1967, 1968, 1971, and 1972, tables 1, 2, and 4. 'Net availability (A)' is calculated as 'net production' + 'net imports' + 'depletion of stocks'. 'Net availability (B)' is calculated as 'net production' + 'issues' − 'procurement'. 'Net production' is calculated by deducting 12.5% from 'production' for 'feed, seed, and wastage'. Series (A) and (B) are not quite comparable for a *single* year because they refer to different 12-month periods. But they should be compatible over a number of years. See text for details.

that one can alternatively use the 'Net Imports' figures or the 'Issues, Procurement and Closing Stocks' figures to arrive at net availability estimates. Table 3.6 presents two sets of estimates, based on these alternative series of figures. It is reassuring to note that these calculations are fairly consistent with those reported by Singh.[108]

The estimates of Table 3.6 ignore private trade and stocks altogether, but there is every reason to believe that both of these played a *greater* role in the years preceding 1966–7 than in 1966–7 itself: trade, because zonal restrictions were particularly stringent in 1966–7; and stocks, because in that year they must have been largely exhausted (see above). Thus, the figures in Table 3.6 probably *underestimate* the *change* in net availability in 1966–7 (as discussed earlier, they may also underestimate the *level* by up to 10 per cent).

Even then, an inescapable conclusion emerges: in spite of massive imports, a dramatic decline of net foodgrain availability accompanied the drought of 1966–7 in Bihar—a decline of the order of 30 per cent compared to ordinary levels.

There is, moreover, strong independent evidence of a sharp decline in aggregate consumption of foodgrains. By collating various bits and pieces of information contained in Singh (1975), we can perform similar calculations to the previous ones for Palamau District. This district, slightly more populated than Mauritania (1.19 million inhabitants according to the 1961 Census), was one of the worst-affected ones in 1966–7. But it was also one where relief measures were notoriously far-reaching,[109] and on balance there is no reason to believe that net food availability was better or worse in Palamau than elsewhere. Table 3.7 summarizes the possible calculations; the results for Palamau are quite similar to those for Bihar as a whole in the same year.

Further evidence can be gathered from direct consumption studies. In the 1960s the National Sample Survey was unfortunately not collecting data on quantities of foodgrains consumed, and inferring quantities from expenditure data is a hopeless exercise when prices change rapidly, as they did in 1966–7. However, three useful nutrition surveys were carried out during the drought by (1) the Public Health Institute, Patna (hereafter PHI); (2) the Nutrition Research Laboratories, Hyderabad (hereafter NRL); and (3) the All-India Institute of Medical Sciences, New Delhi (hereafter AIIMS). The quality of these surveys is difficult to ascertain, and the evidence they individually provide is very patchy; however, the tone of their common findings is clear enough.

Regarding the first of these surveys, Singh (1975) mentions that it found foodgrain intake to be 33 per cent lower in July–August 1966 compared to a similar baseline survey carried out in March 1964 (17.9 ounces per consumer

---

[108] Singh (1975: 146, 156).

[109] For instance, over the period Jan.–Sept. 1967, the 'daily number of persons receiving cooked food' in Palamau was about one-third of the total for the whole State—while its population was only around 2.5% of the State population (Government of Bihar 1973: 276–8).

Table 3.7 Net availability of foodgrains, Palamau District, 1966–1967

Period	Gross production (tonnes)		Public distribution (tonnes)	Private imports (tonnes)	Net availability (kgs/cap./year)	
	(A)	(B)			(A)	(B)
July 1966–Aug. 1967	29,400	48,000	73,972	26,390	97	107
Aug. 1966–Sept. 1967	29,400	48,000	80,665	26,126	101	112
Sept. 1966–Oct. 1967	29,400	48,000	85,812	22,235	102	113
Oct. 1966–Nov. 1967	29,400	48,000	87,836	17,976	101	111

Sources: For 'gross production (B)', see Table 3.5 above. All other figures except 'net availability' are calculated from Singh (1975: 8, 36, 96–9, 104) (the agricultural year 1966–7 being considered, following the usual practice, as the sum of *kharif* 1966 and *rabi* 1966–7). 'Net availability' is calculated as 'net production' + 'public distribution' + 'private imports', where 'net production' is obtained from 'gross production' by deducting 12.5% for 'feed, seed, and wastage'.

unit per day in 1966 as opposed to 26.6 ounces in 1964).[110] A resurvey in March 1967 found that foodgrain consumption had crashed to 8.1 ounces per consumer unit per day before rising again to 17 ounces per consumption unit per day as 'the nutrition and feeding programmes intensified and distribution of foodgrains extended'.[111]

The relevant results of the NRL survey conducted in May 1967 in four drought-affected districts are summarized in Tables 3.8–3.10. In this study, cereal intake in 'severely affected areas' was found to be 34 per cent below that in 'least affected areas' (44 per cent below for 'labourers' and 22 per cent below for 'cultivators'). Moreover, the NRL report states that 'there had been a substantial reduction in the dietary intake in the villages affected by drought, when compared to the diets of four selected districts surveyed prior to the onset of drought'.[112]

Both studies also reveal the sharp drop in *calorie* consumption which accompanied the drought (see Table 3.9, and Singh 1975: 241).

The third study, by the All-India Institute of Medical Sciences, presents no data on consumption but mentions that 'diet surveys conducted by the State Department of Nutrition at intervals of time in various parts of South Bihar between 1966 and 1967 showed that in several regions the calorie intake dropped from 2,200 per capita per day to nearly 1,200 calories'.[113]

Yet another confirmation of the large decline in food intake comes from socio-economic surveys. In a survey carried out by the Central Institute of Research and Training in Public Cooperation (hereafter CIRTPC) in the districts of Palamau and Gaya in 1967 and covering 555 households, 37 per cent of the respondent households reported 'missing meals' as a 'step to overcome their hardships'; and 95 per cent mentioned that food was one of the sources of 'hardship'.[114] A hint may also be taken from a report on a survey carried out in Dolchi (Uttar Pradesh, adjacent to Bihar and also severely affected by drought) in 1967, which states: 'During the preceding year 17 out of 24 households were taking three meals a day, 6 two meals a day and one household only one meal a day. But during 1966–67 the number of households taking 3 meals a day came down to 15 from 17 last year. On enquiry it was found that as many as 9 out of 24 households (37.5%) were either half-fed or on the brink of total starvation.'[115]

Finally, numerous eye-witness accounts of people eating wild leaves and roots, picking pieces of grain from the dust around railway sidings, undergoing appalling 'skeletonization', and even starving to death corroborate the finding of severe food deprivation.

[110] Singh (1975: 241). The area where the survey was conducted is not mentioned.

[111] Ibid. 246.   [112] Swaminathan *et al*. (1969: 214).

[113] Ramlingaswami *et al*. (1971: 95).   [114] CIRTPC (1969: 227, 231).

[115] Agricultural Economics Research Centre, Allahabad (1972: 18).

Table 3.8 Consumption of cereals and calories in drought-affected areas of Bihar, May 1967

	Cereal intake (gm/day)			Calorie intake (cal./day)			No. of households
	Cultivators	Labourers	All classes	Cultivators	Labourers	All classes	
SAFA	445	306	371	1,840	1,210	1,450	50
MAFA	453	312	388	1,740	1,280	1,510	42
LAFA	573	545	566	2,660	2,280	2,470	40

SAFA = 'Severely affected area'.
MAFA = 'Moderately affected area'.
LAFA = 'Least affected area'.

Notes: This table shows the results of a survey conducted by the Nutrition Research Laboratories (Indian Council of Medical Research, Hyderabad) in 7 villages of Gaya, Hazaribagh, Palamau, and Patna Districts in May 1967.

The data on cereal consumption do not take into account food intake in relief kitchens. But the authors describe the consumption at free kitchens as follows: 'It was observed that about 25–30% of the vulnerable segments of the population (preschool children, expectant and nursing mothers) surveyed, were deriving the benefits of the supplements provided through free kitchens functioning in the villages. This amounted to 300–500 calories per person per day.' Clearly, if calorie intake from relief kitchens was so low even among these narrowly defined 'vulnerable segments' of the population, the figures of average cereal intake in Table 3.8 can be taken as reasonably accurate.

Source: Swaminathan *et al.* (1969: tables III, IV, and V).

Table 3.9 Percentage distribution of calorie intake in
drought-affected areas of Bihar, May 1967

Level of per capita calorie intake per day	SAFA[a]	MAFA[a]	LAFA
<500	8.2	—	—
500–899	6.1	5.7	—
900–1,299	18.4	14.3	—
1,300–1,799	26.5	31.4	15.0
1,800–2,299	30.6	40.0	25.0
>2,300	10.2	8.6	60.0
TOTAL	100.0	100.0	100.0

[a] Including contribution of calories from feeding centres.

Note: See Notes and Source to Table 3.8.

Not surprisingly, food deprivation led to acute and widespread malnutrition. The findings of the NRL and AIIMS studies in this respect are reported in Swaminathan *et al.* (1969) and Ramlingaswami *et al.* (1971), respectively. The first study found a close relationship between malnutrition (assessed by anthropometric measures) and the severity of crop failures; a close positive relationship between nutritional status and the extent of relief measures; and a greater incidence of malnutrition among children than adults as well as among labourers than non-labourers.[116] The AIIMS study confirmed all these

Table 3.10 Income and assets in drought-affected areas of Bihar, 1967

Village	Per capita income (Rs./year)			% change in possession of livestock (1965–6 to 1966–7)	No. of households surveyed
	Agricultural sources	Other sources	Total		
SAFA					
Kundah	57	53	110	−49	21
Nawagarh	62	41	103	−36	22
Adarshagram	41	32	74	−38	7
MAFA					
Massaurah	35	77	112	−27	25
Tarwadi	56	46	101	−28	17
LAFA					
Ranipur	162	161	323	+33	17
Kothwan	177	180	357	+30	23

Note: See Notes and Source to Table 3.8.

[116] Swaminathan *et al.* (1969: 214–15).

findings; added 'the elderly' to the list of vulnerable groups; and noted the widespread prevalence of 'famine oedema'.[117] Significantly, out of 49 patients suffering from oedema and selected for intensive clinical study only four owned any land; five died in the hospital and the autopsies revealed that 'massive oedema was the characteristic feature and the body cavities were filled with fluid'.[118] The only consolation against this nutritional disaster was the absence of epidemics.

The occurrence of a sharp decline in food intake during the drought, accompanied by widespread nutritional damage, is thus clear enough. It is much more difficult to ascertain the consequences of deprivation in terms of excess mortality. The reasons are that (1) mortality estimates from various sources (such as the National Sample Survey, the ordinary system of Registration, and the new Sample Registration Scheme initiated in 1965) are not even remotely comparable, and (2) the use of a time-series for a given source is also fraught with difficulties, because the methods used to estimate vital statistics changed rapidly in the late 1960s. In principle, these problems could be circumvented by looking at month-wise data from a particular source over a short period covering the drought; but this method would itself have to deal with the sharp element of seasonality present in such statistics.

A rigorous analysis of the demographic impact of the drought is beyond the scope of this chapter. Some of the available evidence is summarized in Appendix 3.1, and with due reservations the following conclusions can tentatively be drawn:

1. the mortality figures reported in Singh (1975) for Bihar as a whole are internally inconsistent as well as in conflict with the published results from the Sample Registration Scheme, from which they are supposed to originate (Table 3.26);
2. the Sample Registration Scheme provides no evidence of a noticeable increase in mortality in Bihar as a whole during the crisis (Table 3.26);
3. National Sample Survey data suggest (quite implausibly) that while the death rate in Bihar was lower than in India as a whole during the years preceding the crisis, it was higher by about 20 per cent in the year 1966–7 (Table 3.27);
4. mortality estimates based on 'registered' deaths show a noticeable increase in Bihar as a whole during the crisis, the death rate being 34 per cent higher in 1967 than in 1968 (Table 3.28);
5. if the data reported in Singh (1975) for the severely affected Districts of Palamau, Hazaribagh, and Gaya are accepted (in spite of the discrepancies pertaining to Bihar as a whole), mortality appears to have shot up in these Districts during the crisis (Table 3.29); this is confirmed by published data on registered deaths, which show even larger increases in

---

[117] Ramlingaswami *et al.* (1971: 98–9).   [118] Ibid. 104.

mortality (of the order of 100 per cent for the infant mortality rate—see Table 3.28).

Of all these indications, those provided by published data on 'registered deaths' are probably the least unreliable. While registered deaths do not provide accurate estimates of *levels* of mortality, they are generally thought to be quite useful for the assessment of *change*. The fact that, according to this source, the death rate in Bihar in 1967 was 34 per cent above its 1968 value (with much higher increases for the more severely drought-affected Districts) is certainly alarming. Even if we reject these findings as based on unreliable data, one thing is clear: there is precious little evidence to support the self-congratulatory statements that have commonly been made about the Bihar famine, e.g. 'no exceptional mortality was recorded' or 'no one died of starvation'.[119]

While the severity of a famine is usefully measured by the extent of overall excess mortality, it may be worth commenting briefly on the question of 'starvation deaths' specifically. To the extent that the popular notion of 'starvation deaths' can be made precise, it seems to refer to deaths directly attributable to the inability to acquire any food, rather than to the indirect consequences of enfeeblement. The question of how many 'starvation deaths' occurred in 1966–7 was, as always, a highly sensitive one. Ever since the Famine Codes made it the clear duty of the authorities to protect the people against starvation, food crises have prompted public allegations of 'starvation deaths', and official refutations (or sometimes outright 'camouflage').[120] In fact, controversies around the existence and extent of starvation deaths have often provided a focus for public pressure, and played an important instrumental role in prompting the government to act. The 1966–7 drought was no exception.

Bihar alone accounted for almost half of the all-India total of 2,353 officially acknowledged 'alleged starvation deaths'.[121] At one point the government admitted 217 actual starvation deaths (all-India); but, as Singh puts it, 'later it was clarified that these were cases of suicide by "voluntary starvation" and had nothing to do with . . . the non-availability of food . . . the allegations about deaths from starvation were thus not substantiated'.[122] These statements need no comment, and eye-witness accounts leave no doubts as to the grim reality of numerous 'starvation deaths'.[123] I have already referred to the five patients

[119] Aykroyd (1974: 140). Authors such as Singh (1975) and Verghese (1967) went even further and asserted that health conditions *improved* during the crisis. What is, however, plausible is that mortality and morbidity did come down sharply after large-scale relief operations were undertaken. As we shall see, one of the main defects of remedial action in this event was its tardiness.

[120] The report of the Puri Famine Enquiry Committee of 1919, for instance, contains a convincing account of how starvation deaths were disguised by directly instructing the *chowkidars* —here village enumerators—to record starvation deaths as deaths due to sickness.

[121] Singh (1975: 182–3).   [122] Ibid. 182–3.

[123] Such accounts can be found, *inter alia*, in the journalistic literature on the drought of 1966–7 in Bihar.

who died from famine oedema while under clinical observation, and there is no reason to believe that they were isolated cases.

Let me conclude this overview of the effects of the Bihar drought by considering briefly the *distribution* of hardship. It may seem obvious that during a crisis of this magnitude the poor are the hardest hit. But the Maharashtra drought of 1970–3 will provide an interesting example of a remarkably egalitarian famine (or rather, 'non-famine'), and one may ask whether the Bihar crisis of 1966–7 was of the same type. Indeed it *has* been boldly asserted that the success of relief operations converted this potential tragedy into 'a bonus year . . . a year of great blessing' for the destitute masses.[124]

The evidence, however, strongly suggests a very different picture. First, we have already noted the high incidence of deprivation among landless labourers reported in the NRL and AIIMS studies (see also Tables 3.8–3.10). Informal accounts of the drought confirm this observation, which conforms to the traditional pattern of Indian famines (see Section 3.2). Second, there appears to have been a pronounced maldistribution of hardship across areas more or less severely affected by crop failures (see Tables 3.8–3.10, and also Appendix 3.1 on mortality estimates). Finally, informal reports strongly suggest that the peak of hardship occurred towards the end of 1966 (before the beginning of large-scale relief operations) and subsided considerably in the following months. This is plausible in itself considering the inverse correlation between relief and distress mentioned earlier. It is also confirmed by some interesting survey results reported by Singh (see Table 3.11). While the observation is a testimony to the effectiveness of relief operations, it also indicates the maldistribution of hardship across time caused by their notorious tardiness. Thus, the occupational, geographical, and temporal distribution of hardship during the drought of 1966–7 in Bihar appears to have been characterized by great unevenness.

A crucial question remains: were all these disastrous outcomes the inevitable consequence of an extremely precarious situation, or did they partly betray a failure of the relief system?

The received assessment, as was mentioned earlier, points in the former direction, and crisis management during the 1966–7 drought has indeed been hailed by many commentators as a grand success. However, there are good reasons to be suspicious of this received assessment, which has been based partly on the self-congratulatory writings of government administrators and partly on the writings of foreign observers who were inclined to contrast Bihar in 1967 with Bengal in 1943. The effectiveness of relief operations in 1966–7 needs to be re-examined.

A comprehensive reassessment will not be attempted here. I shall confine myself to pointing out three aspects of famine relief in 1966–7 which would

---

[124] Verghese (1967), quoted in Aykroyd (1974: 140).

Table 3.11 Subjective assessment of the severity
of hardship in different months, Bihar, 1966–1967

Months considered hard	Responses
June 1966	—
July 1966	3
August 1966	39
September 1966	171
October 1966	252
November 1966	361
December 1966	363
January 1967	368
February 1967	82
March 1967	14
April 1967	12
May 1967	90
June 1967	151
July 1967	166
Total response	2,072

Source: Singh (1975: 228).

call for serious scrutiny as part of the needed reassessment: the delayed 'declaration' of famine; the limited provision of employment; and the policy of zoning.

The Famine Commissions had all recognized the critical importance of diligence in starting relief operations. The Famine Commission of 1880 itself insisted that 'the great thing is to begin on time'.[125] Experience repeatedly showed that early relief measures promised a great economy of efforts and much better chances of success. This in fact was one of the very reasons for drawing up detailed contingency plans in the form of Famine Codes. The importance of a speedy response also explained the prominence given in the Famine Codes to an elaborate system of 'early warning', according to which the authorities had the obligation to 'declare' famine, and hence set in motion the provisions of the Famine Codes, once a number of well-defined signs of imminent distress manifested themselves (e.g. crop failures, rise in prices, unusual migration or sales of assets, etc.).

Famine was 'declared' in Bihar on 20 April 1967.[126] This was very late indeed. It is well known that once the monsoon breaks (normally in late June for Bihar), relief operations become extremely difficult to carry out, and declaring famine only two months ahead of the rains hardly seems worth the trouble. Relief operations did take place before the official declaration of

[125] Government of India (1880: Appendix I, pp. 119–20).
[126] Government of Bihar (1973: 77).

famine, but relief policy in that period was rather *ad hoc*, and in fact even later measures were explicitly confined to a mere 'intensification' of that policy.[127]

The reasons for delaying the declaration of famine were mainly of a political nature, and closely connected in particular with the general election of February 1967 as well as with centre–State intrigues. The reader is referred to Brass (1986) for further discussion of this issue.[128] The belated and politicized nature of relief efforts during the Bihar crisis in 1967 is undoubtedly an area of failure.

A second query, closely related to the first, concerns the failure to guarantee employment. According to the Bihar Famine Code, public works are supposed to form the backbone of relief operations, and moreover employment is to be provided through small-scale 'village works' near the homes of the affected people.[129] The actual pattern of relief operations in 1967 is summarized in Table 3.12. Clearly the contribution of public works to the overall relief strategy was rather small. The main plank of relief, in fact, was a huge free-feeding programme organized by CARE and UNICEF with the co-operation of the government. The beneficiaries of this scheme, mainly children and expectant or nursing mothers, received one meal a day at the local school. Also of great importance were free kitchens, organized mainly by the Bihar Relief Committee under the leadership of Jayaprakash Narayan. This pattern is quite interesting because it provides a rather impressive example of success-ful co-operation between government and voluntary agencies (both local and international). However, one suspects some abdication of responsibility on the part of the government.

In particular, it is very hard to believe that the 'employment guarantee' of the Famine Code was actually honoured, unless the free-feeding programmes induced a massive withdrawal of labour supply from public works.[130] Indeed, the figures of labour attendance on relief works are rather poor for a crisis of this intensity. Over the period January to June 1967 (the period of peak labour attendance), the average number of labourers employed on relief works was nearly 450,000 (Table 3.12). During the same months of 1973 in drought-affected Maharashtra, average attendance as a proportion of the population was nearly eight times as high! The difference may partly be due to the fact that the Maharashtra drought was a prolonged one, adding many farmers to the ranks of the drought victims along with agricultural labourers (see section 3.4). It is also hard to disprove the existence of a large 'withdrawal effect' due to free-feeding in the case of Bihar. However, *ex post* 'distress' in Bihar in 1967

---

[127] Singh (1975: 148); Government of Bihar (1973: 77).

[128] See also Singh (1975: 144–9), and CIRTPC (1969: 20).

[129] CIRTPC (1969: 42).

[130] There is some evidence that, to a certain extent at least, a withdrawal effect did operate. The CIRTPC study, for instance, noted that 'in many instances, it was true that people did not work on labour-schemes and hung around the free-kitchens' (CIRTPC 1969: 178).

Table 3.12 Relief operations in Bihar, 1967

Month	Average no. of people (000s) benefiting from				
	Cooked food	Mid-day meal (CARE/UNICEF) scheme	Red Cross scheme (free meals)	Relief works	'Red cards' (gratuitous relief)
	(A)	(B)	(C)	(D)	(E)
Jan. 1967	33	373	n/a	228	n/a
Feb. 1967	163	1,118	n/a	318	n/a
Mar. 1967	436	3,269	244	374	n/a
Apr. 1967	487	3,916	509	432	n/a
May 1967	636	4,282	500	607	n/a
June 1967	795	4,054	500	692	n/a
July 1967	700	4,549	n/a	324	783
Aug. 1967	537	4,767	n/a	68	n/a
Sept. 1967	527	4,553	n/a	22	n/a
Jan.–June average	425	2,835	n/a	442	n/a

Notes: In addition to relief works, 'plan schemes' employed 223,400 persons on average over the period Jan.–June 1967 (Government of Bihar 1973: 100).

Relief works started in Oct. 1966, and gratuitous relief started in Dec. 1966 (CIRTPC 1969).

Sources: (A) and (D) are from Government of Bihar (1973: Annexures 3.7 and 10.15). Other figures are from CIRTPC (1969).

was, as we shall see, much more severe by any criterion (food deprivation, nutritional damage, excess mortality, distress sales of assets, etc.) than in Maharashtra in 1973. Hence, unless Biharis have a much higher 'reservation wage' than Maharashtrians at a comparable level of income (an unlikely proposition), there must have been a large pool of unsatisfied labour supply in Bihar in 1967.[131] To take another point of comparison, peak labour attendance in Maharashtra in *1966* was itself of the order of 500,000, even though the drought affecting Maharashtra at that time was less severe, and the population less vulnerable, than was the case in Bihar in 1967.[132] The Bihar government appears not only to have delayed the application of the Famine Code, but also violated one of its most crucial provisions throughout the crisis.

Third, one may question how the national 'zoning' policy, prohibiting private trade in food across different States, affected food entitlements in different States of India. This is not the place to go into the controversy about

[131] Note that the observed contrast cannot be explained with reference to wage levels on public works: wage levels in Maharashtra in 1973 were extremely low (see Section 3.4), and they could hardly have been lower in Bihar in 1967.

[132] The figure is from Singh (1975: 177). Note that the total population of Maharashtra is *smaller* than that of Bihar.

the general merits or demerits of 'zoning' in India.[133] But a few remarks on the specific relationship between zoning and famine prevention are in order, if only because bureaucratic restrictions on private trade are often seen as essential in famine situations.

If private trade in grain is competitive, it is easy to show that a zoning system is essentially equivalent to a set of taxes on food movements.[134] As we have already seen in Section 3.2, a policy of this kind may well have some merit when vulnerable areas are *exporting* food; but this was definitely not the case in 1966–7 (see below). Otherwise, a case for zoning can still conceivably exist if the government desperately needs extra resources for financing relief measures and no socially preferable means exist of raising funds—but this is a rather remote possibility.

This argument, admittedly, runs in terms of a competitive food market. There is little evidence that food markets in India easily lend themselves to collusion and manipulation. But in any case, where collusive practices do exist it is rather hard to see how a policy of zoning helps to counter their deleterious effects. If anything, zoning is likely to facilitate such practices.

None of this implies, of course, that food trade, storage, and distribution offer no scope for a positive involvement of the government. On the contrary, public distribution schemes can definitely have a major impact on food entitlements, and the influence of public storage and food pricing policies on private expectations and hoarding decisions can be a decisive one in famine situations. But the point is that zoning does not, as a rule, strengthen the scope for this type of intervention.

To summarize, it is hard to see how a zoning policy could help to reduce the threat of famine under the conditions prevailing in India, and if anything one would expect its effects to operate in the opposite direction. Careful empirical studies strongly confirm that zoning policies, when in force, have considerably increased the dispersion of food prices across Indian States (and thus increased hardship for deficit households in deficit States). In fact, the dispersion of wheat prices reached an all-time high for the post-independence period precisely during the 1965–7 droughts.[135] In Bihar in 1967, the price of coarse rice (the staple cereal) increased by leaps and bounds and in August 1967 was more than four times as high as in Haryana (Table 3.13)! Price differentials of this magnitude between States are quite abnormal, and there undoubtedly existed a big untapped potential for advantageous food reallocation within the country in 1966–7. Without going as far as to claim that India could have taken

---

[133] For an introduction to the debate, see Bhagwati and Chakravarty (1969) and Krishna and Chhibber (1983).

[134] If procurement and/or public distribution take place at preferential prices rather than at open-market prices, the system will also involve the implicit lump-sum taxes and transfers associated with 'dual pricing' policies. These taxes and transfers may or may not be socially desirable, but in any case their operation is independent from that of zoning.

[135] See the work of Krishna and Chhibber (1983) on the effects of zoning in India.

Table 3.13 Cereal prices in North India, August 1967 (Rs/quintal)

	Bihar	Uttar Pradesh	Haryana	Punjab
Rice	288	150	63–7	83–9
Wheat	163	117–20	100–2	99–100
Maize	125	95–6	—	55–63

Source: Government of Bihar (1973: 98).

the drought in its stride in the absence of zoning, one does wonder how much this policy exacerbated the very problem it sought to relieve.

3.4. *A case-study: the Maharashtra drought of 1970–1973*

The drought of 1970–3 in Maharashtra offers ideal material for a case-study of successful famine relief operations: the crisis was of extreme severity, famine was uncontroversially averted, and the events are well documented. In this section we shall see how the sudden emergence of an alarming gap between food production and food requirements failed to develop into a famine. This gap was, in the first instance, considerably narrowed by the combined operation of the public distribution system and private trade movements—the latter stimulated by the generation of purchasing power in affected areas through public works programmes. Equally importantly, the remaining shortfall was very evenly shared between different socio-economic groups, as employment programmes protected the purchasing power of the more vulnerable groups. The role of markets, politics, public works, food distribution, informal security systems, and other contributing influences will be investigated.[136]

(a) *Background and impact of the drought*

In terms of several conventional indicators of 'development' (including literacy, urbanization, life expectancy, and average incomes), Maharashtra appears as one of the more 'developed' States of India. However, aggregate statistics hide enormous regional disparities, and this vast State strikes the

---

[136] The following case-study draws *inter alia* on the scattered but already voluminous literature (in English) on the Maharashtra drought. Important sources include Subramaniam (1975), who gives an extremely detailed and useful (though far from detached) account of the events from the point of view of a high-level government servant; Ladejinsky (1973), a vivid first-hand report; Oughton (1982), whose analysis, however, differs from mine in some important respects; the enquiry carried out by the Government of Maharashtra (1973b) itself; the studies of administrative, nutritional, and other specific issues in Jodha (1975), Krishnamachari *et al.* (1974), Mathur and Bhattacharya (1975), Mundle (1974a, 1974b), and Somwanski (1979); the detailed microstudies of Borkar and Nadkarni (1975), Brahme (1983), and particularly Kulkarni (1974); the field reports of voluntary agencies such as Oxfam (1972, 1973); various contributions to the *Economic and Political Weekly* from 1972 to 1974; and a large number of newspaper reports.

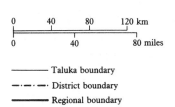

- ———— Taluka boundary
- —·—·—· District boundary
- ━━━ Regional boundary

Note: The area within the thick line indicates the 10 Districts most affected by drought in 1972–3 (see text).

Source: Brahme (1983).

Map 3.2 Political map of Maharashtra

traveller by its great diversity. The urban–rural contrast is particularly sharp, and the relative prosperity of the State as a whole hides a great deal of rural poverty. Thus, while Maharashtra had the third highest State Domestic Product per capita among all Indian States in 1977–8, it also had the third highest proportion of rural population below the poverty line, next only to Orissa and Madhya Pradesh.[137] Within the rural sector, there are enormous regional differences in productivity, particularly between the 'high' or 'assured' rainfall areas of coastal and eastern Maharashtra, and the semi-arid drought-prone areas of inland western Maharashtra.[138] Finally, even within fairly homogeneous rural regions, one cannot fail to be struck nowadays by the sharp contrast between irrigated and non-irrigated agriculture—not only in terms of yields but far more importantly in terms of incomes and employment. On the lush and busy patches of irrigated land (which constituted only 8.5 per cent of total gross cropped area in 1970–1),[139] 'progressive' farmers devote a large proportion of sown area to highly rewarding cash crops such as sugarcane, bananas, papayas, and even grapes, while in the non-irrigated expanses the meagre harvest of coarse grains remains a gamble on the monsoon and the land offers a spectacle of desolation and dust during the slack season.

At the time of the onset of the terrible drought of 1970–3, Maharashtra was facing problems of agricultural decline similar to those described earlier for Bihar: stagnant area under cultivation; stagnant yields; and rapidly increasing population pressure (Table 3.14). As a result, per capita food production was on a sustained downward trend.[140] This downward trend turned into a disastrous crash in the early 1970s, when the exceptional calamity of three successive drought years shattered the rural economy of Maharashtra. While the aggregate picture is bad enough, the District-wise figures of food production bring out even more clearly how in several Districts agricultural production and incomes, already so low to start with, were sharply depressed for several years (see Table 3.15). By any criterion, the severity of agricultural decline in Maharashtra before the early 1970s, and the extent of crop failures during the drought, dwarf the food crises which led to dramatic famines in the Sahel over the same period (see Tables 3.2–3.3 and Figs. 3.1 and 3.2 above). The sharply contrasting outcomes of these respective economic disasters in terms of human deprivation and mortality enhance the importance of understanding how famine was averted in the former case.

The sufferings occasioned by the Maharashtra drought were, indeed, very much smaller than one might have expected given the almost complete collapse

---

[137] Vaidyanathan (1987: table 1).

[138] The agroclimatology of Maharashtra, and its relation to drought and famine, is discussed in detail in Vincent (1981). See also Brahme (1983).

[139] Statistical Abstract of Maharashtra State for the year 1970–1, quoted in Brahme (1983: 14).

[140] In fact, this trend probably started several decades earlier—see the discussion of trends in food production in India during the first half of this century, in Section 3.3.

Table 3.14 Cultivated area, cereal yields, and cereal production in Maharashtra, 1956–1974

Year	Population (000)	Gross cropped area (000 ha)	Cereal yields (kg/ha)	Cereal production per capita kg/year	Three-year averages	
					Yields (kg/ha)	Production per capita (kg/year)
	(A)	(B)	(C)	(D)	(E)	(F)
1956–7	36,337	18,770	522	146		
1957–8	37,115	18,596	522	142	534	146
1958–9	37,909	18,764	559	151	530	143
1959–60	38,720	18,978	510	136	569	152
1960–1	39,880	18,823	637	169	560	147
1961–2	40,487	19,094	532	137	576	149
1962–3	41,806	18,963	560	141	547	138
1963–4	42,798	19,174	548	135	556	137
1964–5	43,825	19,216	559	134	497	120
1965–6	44,886	18,972	384	90	475	112
1966–7	45,982	19,191	482	113	471	109
1967–8	47,115	19,253	548	124	530	120
1968–9	48,284	19,367	561	122	553	120
1969–70	49,490	19,435	550	114	523	110
1970–1	50,709	19,398	458	93	478	97
1971–2	51,927	—	427	83	395	75
1972–3	53,159	—	301	49	—	82
1973–4	54,404	—	—	113	—	—

Sources: (A) *Bulletin on Food Statistics*, 1975 and 1982–4, for 1961 onwards (population figures correspond to the middle of the second of the two calendar years). Pre-1961 population figures were obtained by assuming a constant population growth rate (of 2.14%) between the 1951 and 1961 Censuses.

(B) Government of Maharashtra (1974: 72).

(C) Calculated from ibid. 72 and 74.

(D) See Table 3.2.

(E), (F) Calculated from (C) and (D). The three-year average for each year is calculated as an unweighted average for the preceding year, the current year, and the following year.

of agricultural incomes, employment, and wages in many areas for a prolonged period. Mortality rose only marginally, if at all, and disparities in mortality rates do not seem to have widened either between males and females or between infants and adults (Table 3.16).[141] There were no confirmed instances of 'starvation deaths'. Though no longitudinal studies of nutrition are available for that period, a survey conducted by the National Institute of Nutrition (Hyderabad) in February 1973 in the 'worst affected taluka' of each of four

[141] I am extremely grateful to Nigel Crook (SOAS) and Tim Dyson (LSE) for helping me to probe the evidence on this question. According to work in progress by Arup Maharatna (LSE), mortality during the last year of the drought *fell* in the most severely drought-affected Districts, and rose a little in the *other* Districts (where relief operations were less extensive).

Districts among the worst-affected observed that 'the incidence of the various deficiency signs is somewhat similar to that frequently seen among the poorest sections of rural population in many other parts of the country'.[142] Eye-witness accounts mention very little of the appalling emaciation that struck countless observers of the Bihar drought, and indeed a comparison of two nutrition

Table 3.15 District-wise cereal production in Maharashtra, 1969–1973

District	Index of cereal production (1967–8 = 100)				Cereal production per capita, 1972–3 (kg/year)
	1969–70	1970–1	1971–2	1972–3	
Ratnagiri	99	117	103	86	85
Yeotmal	131	65	104	85	86
Amravati	103	61	68	79	62
Chandrapur	129	109	105	71	118
Jalgaon	89	74	59	70	72
Wardha	97	59	73	68	80
Nagpur	96	71	76	67	49
Kolaba	78	101	81	67	131
Kolhapur	93	110	115	65	53
Buldhana	122	68	82	63	86
Akola	132	55	89	61	64
Bhandara	121	139	114	58	92
Dhulia	106	119	74	49	54
Osmanabad	108	54	58	45	61
Poona	90	70	73	43	38
Thana	88	110	97	42	46
Satara	98	103	91	41	45
Parbhani	76	54	42	41	66
Ahmednagar	109	80	59	33	47
Greater Bombay	77	81	54	31	n/a
Nanded	77	36	48	29	51
Nasik	81	107	55	26	32
Aurangabad	89	74	48	20	31
Sangli	90	86	90	18	20
Sholapur	92	51	63	18	27
Bhir	120	97	54	17	27
MAHARASHTRA	99	83	74	47	49

Source: Calculated from the Annual Season and Crop Reports (Government of Maharashtra) of the corresponding years. Per capita production figures for 1972–3 (last column) are based on District-wise population estimates (for 1973) obtained by assuming identical 1973–1971 population ratios for each District. District-wise population estimates for 1971 are from the Census (as given in Brahme 1983: 13–14).

[142] Krishnamachari et al. (1974: 22).

Table 3.16 Mortality in rural Maharashtra, 1968–1978

Year	Registered deaths		Sample Registration Scheme	
	Crude death rate	Infant death rate as ratio of crude death rate	Crude death rate	Male death rate as % of female
	(1)	(2)	(3)	(4)
1968	12.3	n/a	13.9	n/a
1969	12.9	n/a	15.5	n/a
1970	12.1	n/a	13.0	96
1971	11.3	6.19	13.5	96
1972	10.5	6.76	14.5 (13.2)[a]	95
1973	11.2	6.96	n/a (13.1)[a]	96
1974	9.1	6.59	12.6	95
1975	9.1	6.70	12.2	97
1976	8.6	6.28	12.5	94
1977	9.3	6.67	14.5	n/a
1978	7.3	6.44	11.3	n/a

[a] Figures in brackets relate to the first half of the calendar year.

Notes: The Sample Registration Scheme (SRS) in Maharashtra was disrupted during the second half of 1973. An explicitly 'unreliable' figure of 15.6 for the crude death rate in 1973 was later published by the *Sample Registration Bulletin* (July 1975 issue), apparently based on a rough extrapolation from 1970–2 figures.

While crude death rates based on 'registered deaths' are not very accurate estimates of mortality *levels*, they are generally thought to be useful for the assessment of *change*.

Sources: (1) *Vital Statistics of India*, various issues.

(2) Unpublished data kindly supplied by Nigel Crook (School of Oriental and African Studies, London).

(3) *Sample Registration Bulletin*, Apr. 1974 and June 1979.

(4) Unpublished data kindly supplied by Tim Dyson (London School of Economics).

surveys conducted respectively in Bihar (1967) and Maharashtra (1973) confirms the reality of the suggested contrast (Table 3.17). The loss of livestock was considerable, but the disposal of other assets was not large, and land sales (an indication of acute distress) were minute.[143] The extent of migration was also moderate (see below).

In contrast to Sahelian countries, of course, Maharashtra had the ability to draw fairly easily on the 'surplus' available in neighbouring areas. It also had the general advantage, discussed in the preceding section, of being integrated within a larger economic and political entity. I shall argue, however, that these factors fall far short of providing a satisfactory explanation for the successful

[143] Interesting observations on the disposal of assets and the loss of livestock during the Maharashtra drought can be found in a number of microstudies, including those reported in Kulkarni (1974), Borkar and Nadkarni (1975), Subramaniam (1975), and Jodha *et al.* (1977). Land sales are also discussed in Cain (1981), where a sharp contrast is drawn with the incidence of land sales during food crises in Bangladesh.

Table 3.17 Prevalence of nutritional deficiency signs among children (aged 0–5) in severely affected areas of Bihar (1967) and Maharashtra (1973)

Deficiency sign	Prevalence (%)	
	Bihar (1967)	Maharashtra (1973)
Without any clinical sign	37.9	69.1
Marasmus	16.1	2.4
Kwashiorkor	2.3	1.6
Number of cases observed	87	151

Sources: Swaminathan *et al*. (1969: table VI) and Krishnamachari *et al*. (1974: table III).

Notes: The Bihar survey was carried out in May 1967 among randomly selected households in areas classified by the State government as 'severely affected'. But the authors note that 'the pattern of malnutrition in the community could have been considerably influenced beneficially by the energetic ameliorative programmes which were already in operation' (Swaminathan *et al*. 1969: 215).

The Maharashtra survey was carried out in Feb. 1973 in 'the worst affected taluk of each of the Districts of Poona, Ahmednagar, Bihar and Aurangabad' (themselves among the very worst affected Districts—see text). The subjects were drawn from households of labourers (male and female) employed on relief works; but the authors argue that the people 'could be considered as representing the population of the surrounding drought stricken villages' (Krishnamachari *et al*. 1974: 20).

prevention of famine in Maharashtra—once again, the relief system played an essential role.

(b) *Production, availability and consumption*[144]

As in the discussion of nineteenth-century famines in Section 3.2, we have to consider here two closely related but nevertheless distinct effects of crop failures: the sharp reduction of food availability in affected areas, and the threat to food entitlements arising from the collapse of rural incomes. In the case of Maharashtra, it is quite clear that the improvement of food availability was an inescapable pre-condition to the protection of food entitlements. It is natural, therefore, to begin our investigation with a brief assessment of the food situation in Maharashtra in the year 1972–3, which marked the peak of the crisis.

Calculations of 'net availability' of foodgrains very similar to those performed in the previous section for Bihar can be carried out for Maharashtra using the same sources (mainly the *Bulletin on Food Statistics*). This has in fact already been done by Oughton (1982). Oughton takes the route of the left-hand side of equation (3.1) on p. 92 above, and I have attempted my own (rough) calculations via the right-hand side. Private stocks and private trade (the latter

---

[144] In arriving at the conclusions reached in this subsection, I have benefited from extensive discussions with several leading experts on Indian statistics, including N. Bhattacharya, B. S. Minhas, S. Tendulkar, A. Vaidyanathan, and A. M. Vidwans. I am also indebted to Michael Lipton for several useful suggestions.

again prohibited across States in 1972–3) are ignored throughout; I shall comment on this below. The results are summarized in Table 3.18.[145]

The two series of net availability estimates for foodgrains give a consistent picture of *change*, although in terms of *levels* my series appears to be somewhat lower than Oughton's. The discrepancy widens substantially in 1971 and 1972, and this may be due to the removal of zoning in 1970–1 and 1971–2 (if private trade takes place by rail or river, equation (3.1) ceases to hold). For the year we are concerned with, however, the discrepancy narrows down considerably. According to official statistics, then, net foodgrain availability per capita in Maharashtra for the year 1972–3 was somewhere between 90 and 100 kg, and roughly 60 per cent of the average 1968–70 level—a picture not very different from that obtained for Bihar in 1966–7.

This finding, however, is completely unbelievable. Field reports, nutrition surveys, socio-economic microstudies, and, finally, the National Sample Survey all converge to indicate that the decline in foodgrain *consumption* in 1972–3 must have been far smaller.

For the time being, let us neglect all other sources of evidence and only consider the most important one: the National Sample Survey (hereafter NSS). According to the 27th Round of the NSS (October 1972–August 1973), average monthly cereal consumption per person in Maharashtra in 1972–3

Table 3.18 Net availability of foodgrains in Maharashtra, 1968–1974

Year	Net production (000 tonnes)	Issues (000 tonnes)	Procurement (000 tonnes)	Net availability per capita (kg/year)		
				Oughton	Drèze	Drèze (cereals)
1968	5,972	1,942	567	167	156	137
1969	6,262	1,728	439	160	156	134
1970	6,050	1,609	400	167	147	124
1971	4,891	1,244	254	138	116	101
1972	4,334	1,677	122	132	113	103
1973	2,670	2,404	236	96	91	84
1974	6,230	1,979	231	157	147	133

Sources: Production, issues, and procurement are from the *Bulletin on Food Statistics*, 1971 to 1976. 'Net production' is obtained by deducting 12.5% from gross production for 'feed, seed, and wastage'. Production figures relate to the agricultural year (starting in July of the preceding calendar year). Issues and procurement figures relate to the financial year (Apr.–Mar.). Oughton's estimates of 'net availability' (see Oughton 1982: 180) are obtained as net production + net imports + net depletion of government stocks. My estimates are obtained as net production + issues − procurement (see text for details). Population estimates are as in Table 3.2.

[145] Brahme (1983: 79) presents similar calculations (for cereals), based on the various issues of *Maharashtra, An Economic Review* (1983). The broad picture is the same, though there are year-to-year discrepancies. Brahme, however, appears to have neglected changes in public stocks, and her results have, therefore, not been reported here.

Table 3.19 Cereal consumption in Maharashtra,
1972–1973

| | Cereal consumption per capita | | No. of households sampled |
	kg/month	kg/year	
Rural	12.60	153	5,249
Urban	8.95	109	6,181

Source: Sarvekshana, Jan. 1979: 133, reporting the results of the 27th Round of the National Sample Survey (Oct. 1972–Aug. 1973). The figures on yearly consumption are derived from those on monthly consumption, and are provided here to facilitate comparison with Table 3.18.

amounted to 12.6 kg in rural areas and 8.95 kg in urban areas (Table 3.19). With the rural–urban population proportions of the 1971 Census, this represents an average per capita consumption per year of 140 kg, and implies an embarrassing discrepancy of around 50 kg per head (a little more than 2.5 million tonnes) with our previous estimate.

Let us examine the possible sources of this discrepancy. First, could the NSS figures be wild overestimates? It is well known that NSS estimates of cereal consumption systematically exceed, at the all-India level, the 'net availability' estimates arrived at by the sort of method used in Table 1.18.[146] The reasons for this are an old and unsolved riddle in Indian statistics, and many experts believe that the NSS series are on the high side. However, even if we (unreasonably) put the whole blame for this chronic inaccuracy on the NSS series, we are only led to revise it downwards by about 15–16 per cent in the 1970–3 period and at most 20 per cent in 1972–3,[147] whereas our concern here is with an adjustment of about 35 per cent. We are still far off the mark.

Are there reasons why overestimation in the NSS figures should increase in a drought year? A complete answer to this question would lead us into the intricate (and rather boring) issue of the *source* of alleged overestimation in the NSS data, and only a few general conjectures can be made here. It is fairly well agreed that sampling errors in NSS data are small if one is concerned with aggregate magnitudes such as average cereal consumption. Among possible non-sampling errors leading to overestimation, the most frequently cited ones are the double counting or faulty recording of wages in kind, gifts (including meals at marriage feasts), animal feeding, and the like. But these sources of overestimation are not likely to increase in a drought year. A more relevant possibility is that respondents often report 'normal' or 'ideal' rather than

---

[146] For an excellent discussion of this problem, see Vaidyanathan (1986). On the quality of NSS data, see also Bhattacharya *et al.* (1985), Mukherjee (1986), Srinivasan and Bardhan (1974), and Suryanarayana and Iyengar (1986).

[147] See Vaidyanathan (1986: 133, table 3) and Bhattacharya *et al.* (1985: 275–83).

'actual' diets. Overestimation on this count *is* likely to increase in a drought year when people frequently miss meals but may fail to report the associated reduction in intake compared to usual levels. A similar conjecture is that NSS estimates partly reflect the perceptions of the investigator, and as a result underestimate change. Indeed Table 3.4 indicates astonishingly small year-to-year changes in cereal consumption, though this may also reflect robust consumption habits. What all this adds up to precisely is far from clear, but it hardly explains the gross discrepancy we are concerned with here.

Nor can migration solve the riddle. There is no trace of large-scale migration outside Maharashtra in the many first-hand accounts and newspaper reports on the drought. In his very careful survey of drought conditions in Sinnar taluka (Nasik District), Kulkarni (1974) found that a significant proportion of individuals and households had migrated in 1972–3, but 86 per cent of the migrating households had moved less than 50 miles away, and the author incidentally notes that 'most of the immigrants moved within taluka at the scarcity work centres'.[148] Subramaniam (1975) also forcefully denies the occurrence of large-scale population movements.[149]

What about the reliability of the 'net availability' calculations? Maharashtra is reputed to have one of the best statistical systems in India, and the transactions on government account (procurement, issues, changes in stocks, and imports) in all probability involve reasonable margins of error. Crop-cutting techniques are now well developed in India and production estimates are believed to be very accurate. It is sometimes suggested that individual States purposely and grossly 'falsify' production reports to the centre in order to achieve various political aims, but it is difficult to take these allegations very seriously. There remains the question of private stocks and trade. Private stocks can safely be ignored (for the same reasons as in the case of Bihar) since we are looking at the third successive drought year. We must, however, re-examine the issue of private trade.

During the year 1972–3, inter-State movements of foodgrains on private account were banned. The shortfall in food availability in Maharashtra was supposed to be met by the public distribution system. The Food Corporation of India organized the transport of foodgrains (mainly wheat) from other parts of the country, and their distribution at subsidized prices through a network of nearly 30,000 'Fair Price Shops' scattered all over the State. However, the achievements of the public distribution system fell far short of targets. Numerous formal and informal reports testify to the fact that all over Maharashtra the actual per capita allocation of grain in Fair Price Shops fell

---

[148] Kulkarni (1974: 207, and table 8.3). A 'taluka' is a small administrative unit within a District. One civil servant who had been Collector of one of the peripheral Districts at that time told me that large-scale employment programmes had attracted migrant labourers *into* Maharashtra during the drought.

[149] Subramaniam (1975: 463–5, 528–9).

pitifully short of the initial official allocation of 12 kg per month.[150] The quantum of actual allocations naturally varied from place to place, but the reported figures vary from 'hardly 2 kg per month' (Kulkarni 1974; Anon 1972b) and '5 to 10 per cent of needs'; (Patil 1973) to 4 kg per month (Brahme 1983). Subramaniam (1975), who is not inclined to admit government failures, concedes that 'the public distribution system was able to supply hardly 3 to 4 kg per month per adult'.[151] And indeed, according to official statistics themselves per capita issues of foodgrains through the public distribution system were only 2.7 kg per month in 1972 and 3.8 kg in 1973 (Table 3.18). By all accounts, public food distribution in 1972–3 represented only a very small proportion of consumption requirements.

Meanwhile, however, the purchasing power generated by huge public works programmes put an upward pressure on prices all over the State, and widening price differentials between Maharashtra and the neighbouring States promised huge profits to illegal private trade. Interestingly enough, private trade was also actively (though unofficially) encouraged by government authorities. During interviews with former District Collectors of the worst affected Districts, I have repeatedly heard the same story: 'smuggling' of grain across State borders was tacitly approved by government officials in Bombay, and openly promoted at the District level.[152] This policy was not just the result of common sense and concern for the people; in many cases its motivation arose directly from a strong anxiety about possible law and order problems ensuing from food shortages and price increases.[153] Illegal private trade was therefore brisk throughout the drought period in spite of the official ban. The microsurveys cited above all confirm that the bulk of food purchases drew on the 'open' (or black) market rather than on the public distribution system.

Attributing the whole of the discrepancy between the 'net availability' and the 'consumption' estimates to illegal private trade amounts to putting around 2.5 million tonnes of foodgrains on that account in 1972–3 (see above). This is a staggering figure: it exceeds the amount of foodgrains moved on government account over the same period, and suggests a picture of hundreds of trucks crossing the State borders every day 'illegally'. Thus while the most reasonable hypothesis seems to be to assign the bulk of the discrepancy to private trade, the other sources of inaccuracy discussed earlier may have played a significant role as well.

Let us now revert to the issue of the magnitude of food deprivation in

[150] See e.g. Kulkarni (1974: table 6.7), Borkar and Nadkarni (1975: 58), Brahme (1983: 69), Mody (1972: 2482), Oxfam (1972, 1973), Oughton (1982: 182), Patil (1973: 1617), Anon. (1972b), and Subramaniam (1975).   [151] Subramaniam (1975: 128).

[152] The State government also made representations to the central government in favour of the removal of 'zoning' (Subramaniam 1975: 254).

[153] One former District Collector even claimed that, fearing imminent food riots, he had literally 'hijacked' a large quantity of government-owned grain consigned by rail to Karnataka and emptied it in the nearest go-down! Law and order is one of the main responsibilities of the District Collector.

Table 3.20 Cereal consumption in rural India and Maharashtra, 1967–1978

Year	Cereal consumption (kg/cap./month)		
	India	Maharashtra	Maharashtra (10 drought-affected Districts)
1967–8	n/a	n/a	14.01
1970–1	15.35	12.83	n/a
1972–3	15.26	12.60	11.74
1973–4	15.09	13.45	13.90
1977–8	15.25	13.52	n/a

Sources: Figures for all-India and Maharashtra are from the Central Sample of the National Sample Survey, as reported in *Sarvekshana*, Jan. 1979: 133, and Bhattacharya *et al.* (1985). The 1967–8 and 1972–3 figures for the 10 worst-affected Districts are from Subramaniam (1975: 443), and are based on tabulations of the State Sample of the National Sample Survey. Figures for 1973–4 for these Districts have been calculated by Vijay Nayak and myself (using the Central Sample of the National Sample Survey, 28th Round) at the Development Economics Research Centre, University of Warwick, in Aug. 1986.

Maharashtra during the peak drought year. The figure of 12.6 kgs per capita per month for cereal consumption in rural Maharashtra in 1972–3 is the lowest ever for any State and for any round of the National Sample Survey for which such data are available (see Table 3.4).[154] It is also 17 per cent lower than the all-India figure for the same year; but this is not necessarily a good indication of the effect of the drought because, as was mentioned earlier, there seem to exist fairly substantial State-to-State variations in cereal intake which bear no obvious relation to price and income differentials and are more likely to be related (at least partly) to 'dietary habits'.

Table 3.20 presents cereal consumption figures for rural India and Maharashtra during the drought period as well as for the nearest years for which comparable data are available for the relevant regions. The table also shows similar figures for the ten Districts most affected by drought within Maharashtra, representing a combined population of more than 20 million in 1971 (nearly 80 per cent rural).[155] As before, it is worth noting the striking stability of cereal consumption estimates over time, and the fact that if

[154] This statement ignores Kerala, where there is a high propensity to consume food items classified in the National Sample Survey as 'cereal substitutes' (e.g. tapioca).

[155] Population figures are from Government of India (1979: 3–12). The definition of '10 worst-affected Districts' follows Subramaniam (1975) and includes Poona, Ahmednagar, Sholapur, Satara, Sangli, Aurangabad, Bhir, Osmanabad, Nasik, and Dhulia. Subramaniam does not motivate this definition explicitly, but implies that this was an official classification, and Table 3.15 above strongly suggests that the severity of drought was assessed on the basis of food or agricultural production estimates. An independent attempt at classification in Anon. (1972*b*) identifies the 8 worst-affected Districts, all of which belong to the above list.

Table 3.21 Cereal consumption and total consumer expenditure in the rural areas of 10 drought-affected Districts in Maharashtra

Household class	Monthly cereal consumption per capita (kg)	Per capita expenditure (nominal) (Rs/month)	Real per capita expenditure (1967–8 Rs/month)		No. of households
			(1)	(2)	
Large cultivators					
1967–8	15.55	33.50	33.50	33.50	147
1972–3	12.77	41.35	29.68	28.98	89
1973–4	15.26	57.71	38.07	37.67	130
Small cultivators					
1967–8	13.37	31.36	31.36	31.36	73
1972–3	11.08	33.87	24.31	23.74	50
1973–4	12.90	61.38	40.49	40.07	77
Farm labourers					
1967–8	14.47	24.01	24.01	24.01	111
1972–3	11.45	32.85	23.58	23.02	218
1973–4	13.68	44.69	29.48	29.17	166
Industrial workers					
1967–8	13.15	34.17	34.17	34.17	29
1972–3	12.02	37.23	26.72	26.09	28
1973–4	13.34	48.29	31.85	31.52	51
Others					
1967–8	12.38	33.14	33.14	33.14	40
1972–3	10.79	42.37	30.41	29.69	54
1973–4	12.07	79.83	52.66	52.11	59
All households					
1967–8	14.01	30.70	30.70	30.70	400
1972–3	11.74	36.34	26.08	25.47	439
1973–4	13.90	55.53	36.63	36.25	483

(1) = Calculated by using the Consumer Price Index (CPI) for Agricultural Labourers (General Index).

(2) = Calculated by using the Consumer Price Index (CPI) for Agricultural Labourers (Food Index).

Notes: The estimates of 'real' per capita expenditure are almost certainly overestimates, because the price indices used apply to Maharashtra as a whole, whereas the increase of prices (especially food prices) was more pronounced in the 10 worst-affected Districts. However, it is noteworthy that the difference in prices between these Districts and Maharashtra as a whole was in fact quite moderate (see text), so that the overestimation involved is not considerable.

'Small cultivators' are those with operational holdings of less than 7.5 acres.

Sources: Nominal consumption and expenditure for 1967–8 and 1972–3 are from Subramaniam (1975: 442–3, 435); they are based on the State Sample of the National Sample Survey (22nd and 27th Rounds). The corresponding figures for 1973–4 have been calculated by Vijay Nayak and myself, using the Central Sample of the 28th Round of the National Sample Survey at the Development Economics Research Centre (University of Warwick). Real expenditure figures are calculated by deflating the nominal expenditure figures. The deflator used to calculate real expenditure in 1972–3 is the ratio of the CPI for 1967–8 to the CPI for Oct. 1972–Sept. 1973 (unweighted average of monthly index), the period covered by the State Sample; and similarly for 1973–4 (using the sample period Oct. 1973–June 1974).

anything the NSS figures are likely to underestimate consumption fluctuations from year to year. In spite of this, a drop of 16 per cent in average cereal consumption is noticeable in 1972–3 for the 10 worst-affected Districts compared to either of the nearest two normal years for which comparable data are available. Given the possibility of a small underestimation of the consumption decline in the NSS figures, we can tentatively but reasonably conclude that average cereal consumption in rural areas of the 10 worst-affected Districts in 1972–3 was somewhere between 15 and 20 per cent below 'normal' levels.[156]

Consumption changes of this order of magnitude are nowhere as frightening as those which took place in Bihar in 1966–7. But when they affect such a large population they remain quite capable of entailing disastrous consequences. It is easy to see, for instance, that if the deficit had been concentrated on (say) the poorest 30 per cent of an already greatly impoverished population, the results in terms of excess mortality could have been catastrophic. This raises the question of the *distribution* of the food deficit, and brings us to a crucial aspect of the mechanism of famine prevention in Maharashtra.

Table 3.21 presents cereal consumption figures by socio-economic groups for the rural areas of the ten worst-affected Districts during the peak drought year (1972–3), as well as for the nearest two 'normal' years for which comparable data are available (see also Fig. 3.3). The emerging picture of consumption adjustments is interesting. Its most striking feature is the broad spread across socio-economic groups of the aggregate reduction in cereal intake, and the surprising *evenness* of the distribution of cereal intake in 1972–3. The consumption level of farm labourers in 1972–3, for instance, was very near the overall mean.

Taken on its own, this piece of evidence indicating a fairly 'egalitarian' reduction of food consumption during the Maharashtra drought is admittedly rather thin. However, further evidence from microstudies abundantly confirms the scope for relief measures to shift the burden of consumption adjustment away from the most deprived sections of the population. Indeed, reducing food intake (including cereal consumption) seems to be a common response to adverse changes in real income during droughts in rural India, not only on the part of landless labourers and poor artisans but also on the part of cultivators over a very wide range of landholding size groups. Some supporting evidence appears in Appendix 3.2, where I have assembled the results of several microstudies on food consumption during recent droughts in Maharashtra and other States.[157] The following findings are particularly noteworthy.

[156] More detailed and painstaking estimations, based on alternative inferences from NSS figures for all available years (Central Sample as well as State Sample), were carried out in an earlier draft of this paper (Drèze 1986). They led to very similar results.

[157] The findings reported in Appendix 3.2, and discussed here, are further supported by a recent study of drought in Gujarat in 1987 (see Chen 1989, especially table 39). In fact, there are many striking similarities between the episodes of drought and averted famine in Maharashtra in 1970–3 and in Gujarat in 1985–7 (see Drèze 1990).

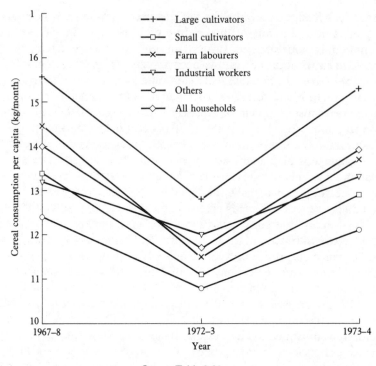

Source: Table 3.21.

Fig. 3.3 Cereal consumption decline in Maharashtra by household class, 1972–1973

A pioneering study of 144 'farming households' carried out by Jodha during the 1963–4 drought in Rajasthan (Table 3.30) clearly shows that (1) a very large proportion of households reduced their consumption of foodgrains during the drought, and (2) frugality in consumption set in largely before the process of asset depletion, mortgaging, and migration.

A study of 108 households during the drought of 1974–5 in Gujarat by Desai *et al.* (Table 3.31) arrived at strikingly similar results: the great majority of cultivators in all landholding size classes were found to reduce their cereal consumption, even though the depletion of assets only reached very moderate proportions.[158] Incidentally, much as in the case of Maharashtra in 1972–3 this study found that the proportion of households experiencing a reduction in cereal intake during the drought was significantly *lower* for labourers and artisans than for cultivators in any landholding size class (see Table 3.31). The authors themselves persuasively relate this phenomenon to the disproportion-ate involvement of labourers and artisans in relief works.

A somewhat similar, though less striking, pattern of cereal consumption

[158] The 'depletion' of assets in this case consisted mainly of livestock deaths (see Desai *et al.* 1979: 79–80).

changes is noted by Choudhary and Bapat during the 1969–70 droughts in Gujarat and Rajasthan (Table 3.32).

In a study of food consumption during drought and non-drought years in sample villages of Tamil Nadu, Pinstrup-Andersen and Jaramillo (1985) found, once again, that a large reduction of food intake was a feature of consumption patterns in drought years even for 'large farmers' (see Table 3.33). In this case, the relative deprivation of landless labourers in terms of food consumption during drought years remained important, possibly due to the apparent absence of extensive relief measures in these villages.

In their study of survival strategies during the 1983 drought in Karnataka, based on a survey of nearly 400 households, Caldwell *et al.* note: 'Eating less . . . was universal . . . The important point is that most families still regard their ability to weather droughts as being based on savage cutbacks in their living standards, dominated by reducing food to the minimum. The rich families moved from three to two meals a day, and many ordinary families from two to one.'[159] Once again, moreover, the protection of the productive base took precedence over the protection of consumption standards (see Table 3.34).

To the best of my knowledge, no comparable studies exist for Maharashtra in 1972–3. However, the survey of two villages in Aurangabad District by Borkar and Nadkarni in May–June 1973 contains some useful hints. This study does not cover cereal consumption as such, but presents data on purchases of cereals for different socio-economic groups (Table 3.35). No indication is given about the size of stocks, but these were most probably negligible by that time for most households. On the other hand the authors state that 'in May and June when they reported peak employment and earnings through scarcity works, the households purchased slightly in excess of their current requirements because of the expected rise in the prices of food articles and the decline in their incomes in the immediate future (due to discontinuance of scarcity relief works)'.[160] Thus purchases are not a very good approximation for consumption in this case. Nevertheless the rather egalitarian pattern of current purchases is itself revealing. The market command of agricultural labourers was, for instance, *greater* than average in both villages.

Two closely related objections can be raised against using these studies and surveys as evidence of 'equal sharing' of the food deficit during the Maharashtra drought. The first is that landholding size is not a good proxy for 'normal-year income', so that a fairly uniform pattern of food intake reduction across landholding size groups is quite compatible with a concentration of the burden of adjustment on the poor. The second objection is that, regardless of whether or not landholding size is a good proxy for average income, *within* each landholding class only the very poor may have suffered.

The first objection may seem surprising, but it has been seriously argued

---

[159] Caldwell *et al.* (1986: 687–8).   [160] Borkar and Nadkarni (1975: 58).

that, in the semi-arid areas of India, average 'normal-year' incomes do not increase with landholding size over a very wide range of landholding sizes at the lower end of the scale—there is a 'threshold effect'.[161] This is not the place to enter into a general assessment of this interesting theory—though it is worth noting in passing that the NSS data in Table 3.21 clearly show a large gap between the expenditure levels of farm labourers and 'small cultivators' in non-drought years. In Section 3.4c I shall comment on the available evidence on incomes and expenditure for Maharashtra around 1972–3, and suggest that if a 'threshold effect' existed at all in this context, it must have occurred at very low levels of landholding size. It would therefore be hard to invoke the threshold hypothesis to explain the observed adjustments in food consumption since, as Table 3.21 indicates, considerable reductions of food intake appear to have taken place even in the largest landholding size groups.

In any case, neither this first objection nor the second one square with further evidence on the pattern of reduction in food intake from the National Sample Survey. As Table 3.22 unambiguously shows, a significant proportion of the reduction in cereal intake in the ten worst-affected Districts took place among high-consumption groups: the percentage of all rural households consuming more than 15 kg of cereals per capita per month fell from 39.0 in 1967–8 to 15.9 in 1972–3, and rose again to 36.1 in 1973–4. Moreover, since 'cereals' invariably appear to have a positive and large expenditure elasticity in rural areas according to NSS data, high cereal consumption groups also correspond to high expenditure groups in this case.

A consistent and fairly solid picture emerges, then, indicating a significant reduction in aggregate cereal consumption during the peak drought year, spread rather evenly across different socio-economic groups—poor and less poor, landless and landed, blue-collar and white-collar and no-collar. If we trust consumer price indices, we may also conclude that every socio-economic group experienced a severe cut in 'real per capita expenditure' during the drought year, *except* farm labourers (see Table 3.21). The latter conclusion must be treated with some caution, especially because it is based on all-Maharashtra price indices whereas the increase of prices was somewhat more pronounced in the severely affected Districts than elsewhere.[162] Nevertheless, using a different price index would not invalidate the finding that the propertied classes suffered a much larger *percentage* reduction in real expenditure

[161] See Visaria (1978) and particularly Lipton (1985). It should be mentioned that the evidence presented by Visaria does not really provide much support for the 'threshold effect' hypothesis. Indeed, this evidence is precisely based on data relating to Maharashtra and Gujarat in 1972–3, when, as we shall see, the distribution of income and expenditure was very significantly less unequal than in normal years. In fact Visaria's evidence can be interpreted as *confirming* that, in normal years, per-capita income must be positively related to landholding size.

[162] On this, see e.g. the (fairly consistent) data on retail prices in Subramaniam (1975) and Brahme (1983). In June 1973, the price of cereals in 'Scarcity Areas' was higher than in 'Non-scarcity Areas; by a margin ranging from 6% for bajra to 34% for jowar (Brahme 1983: table 4.15).

Table 3.22 Percentage distribution of population by levels of per capita monthly cereal consumption in the rural areas of 10 drought-affected Districts in Maharashtra

Household class	Per capita intake of cereals (kg/month)			Total
	up to 12	12–15	15+	
Large cultivators				
1967–8	25.5	28.7	45.8	100.0
1972–3	44.7	30.0	25.3	100.0
Small cultivators				
1967–8	53.0	19.0	28.0	100.0
1972–3	61.2	25.2	13.6	100.0
Farm labourers				
1967–8	41.4	19.9	38.6	100.0
1972–3	60.9	25.3	13.8	100.0
Industrial workers				
1967–8	42.8	21.7	35.5	100.0
1972–3	65.3	27.1	7.6	100.0
All households				
1967–8	38.5	22.5	39.0	100.0
1972–3	58.9	25.2	15.9	100.0
1973–4	37.2	26.7	36.1	100.0

Note: For sample sizes and other details, see Table 3.21.

Source: All figures relating to the years 1967–8 and 1972–3 are from Subramaniam (1975: 446), and were derived from the State Sample of the National Sample Survey (22nd and 27th Rounds). The figures for 1973–4 were calculated as in Table 3.21.

than agricultural labourers. And this is itself quite striking, considering that famines are generally believed to exacerbate existing inequalities.[163]

The significance of these findings should not be exaggerated. Comparable percentage reductions of consumption at different income levels are not, of course, the same as comparable declines in well-being, and it is likely enough that the hardship endured by agricultural labourers remained much greater than the sufferings of the propertied classes. While many first-hand accounts of the Maharashtra drought go so far as to suggest that, thanks to bright employment prospects on relief works, agricultural labourers were actually *better-off* in the peak drought year than in normal years, there is little evidence supporting the view that agricultural labourers 'enjoyed the drought'.[164] The

[163] Even in the case of the Maharashtra drought, there remained some clear examples of widening inequalities. Oughton (1982), for instance, emphasizes the contrast between general impoverishment and the enrichment of large farmers growing cash crops on irrigated land.

[164] This view has been expressed in Anon. (1972b: 2480), Garcia (1981: 124), Subramaniam (1975: 491), Aykroyd (1974), and Oxfam (1972, 1973), among others. Liz Oughton, who conducted extensive field work in a village of Sangli District in 1982, met a poor labourer who told her that he 'liked droughts' because they improved his employment prospects (personal communication).

bulk of the evidence (reviewed in the next section) and of the better-informed first-hand accounts suggests a more plausible assessment closely agreeing with our previous observations: the plight of agricultural labourers during the drought varied from place to place and in some cases they may have found themselves better off than in ordinary years; as a rule, however, their real earnings declined.[165] The reason is simply that while labourers were getting more work than usual, and higher money incomes, their *real* wages were very meagre indeed.[166]

This said, the fact that the traditional victims of Indian famines not only remained safely protected from starvation but also experienced a surprisingly moderate deterioration in their living standards is remarkable enough. The precise mechanism underlying the observed 'redistribution of hardship' to-wards the more privileged classes is investigated in the next section.

(c) The entitlement process

Famines, it is now well understood, can and sometimes do occur without a substantial decline in aggregate food availability (Sen 1981). The symmetric question of whether, and to what extent, famines can be contained in spite of an irreducible decline in food availability has received comparatively little atten-tion. This question is of great importance for the design of famine relief policies, and in particular for the issue of whether the implementation of famine relief schemes in situations of food scarcity should be conditional upon the timely arrival of additional food supplies. The Maharashtra experience does seem to provide an example where famine was averted in spite of a partial failure of the food delivery system, mainly through *redistribution*. The factors which account for this success are worth exploring.

Why did cultivators in all landholding size classes reduce their food con-sumption during the Maharashtra drought? Why did people who owned many acres of land as well as other valuable assets such as animals and jewellery decide to go hungry rather than (or as well as) to deplete their wealth or to borrow? Before attempting to answer these questions, it is useful to take a closer look at the nature of income, expenditure, and price changes that accompany a drought of the kind that hit Maharashtra in 1970–3.

For this purpose, I have assembled in Appendix 3.3 such evidence as I could

---

[165] On this, see particularly the careful studies of Borkar and Nadkarni (1975), Kulkarni (1974), and Brahme (1983), as well as the National Sample Survey evidence presented above, and Ladejinsky (1973). On careful questioning (the distinction between money and real incomes always poses a problem), most of the eye-witnesses I interviewed myself concurred with the assessment proposed here. Labourers gave different answers in different places, according to the intensity of the drought and the effectiveness of relief measures in that area. In the worst affected places the events of 1972–3 often evoked very painful memories.

[166] Brahme estimated the average daily wage rate on relief works for Maharashtra as a whole at Rs. 1.90 for the period Apr.–July 1973 (Brahme 1983: 102). Using the figures which the same author presents on food prices in drought-affected areas in June 1973, this represented a little less than 1 kg of staple cereals!

gather from microstudies and household surveys on income and expenditure patterns in Maharashtra and adjacent States around 1972–3. Many of the studies reported there, it must be said, use rather rough survey methods— particularly when they attempt to estimate 'normal year income' retrospective- ly. Put together, however, they form a remarkably consistent picture, and their results can be summarized as follows. First, there is a clear correlation (in this region and for this period) between landholding size and 'normal year' per-capita income, at least across broad landholding size classes.[167] This correlation may or may not survive in a drought year, depending *inter alia* on the nature and effectiveness of relief measures. Second, during the Maharash- tra drought the distribution of *current incomes* was considerably more equal than in normal years. Third, a tendency towards much greater equality in *cur- rent expenditure* was also noticeable. Finally, greater equality was accompanied by a considerable reduction in *average* real incomes and expenditure; the latter resulted from the combination of a dramatic loss of output (pushing most households into the 'food deficit' category) and sharply rising prices.[168]

The observed changes in income patterns are not difficult to understand. In an ordinary year, large cultivators reap the profits of better endowments. In a drought year, however, cultivators may get only small returns on cultivation expenses, and 'net profits' per acre can drop to very low—possibly even negative—values. What happens to the distribution of income then depends largely on whether or not cultivators in different landholding size groups decide to join the relief works (when they exist). During an isolated drought following one or more 'good years', most cultivators commonly abstain from doing so, and this together with negative profits per acre accounts for the impressive 'reversal' of the ordinary income scale observed by Desai *et al.* (1979) during the 1974–5 drought in Gujarat (see Table 3.41). However, when droughts recur for several years in succession, cultivators gradually lose their resilience and start flocking to the relief works in increasing numbers. This is precisely what happened in Maharashtra in 1972–3 (see below), which ex- plains why in this event the distribution of current incomes, while far less unequal than in other years, retained the ordinary pattern.

It is, of course, not easy to predict how pronounced declines in current income for different socio-economic groups will affect their current expendi- tures. In principle, credit transactions and informal insurance arrangements (including patronage and reciprocity practices) could allow individual house- holds to protect their current expenditures from income fluctuations. To the

---

[167] The correlation does not always appear in small samples, partly because the variance of incomes is high. The relationship can also get blurred in places where small farms happen to have better access to irrigation facilities than large farms (presumably an exceptional situation).

[168] See Pandey and Upadhyay (1979) for similar results on the effects of the 1972–4 drought in Haryana. An important exception to the operation of equalizing forces must be made for the accentuation of inequality between irrigated and non-irrigated farming. See Brahme (1983) for a detailed discussion.

extent that the arrangements involved are imperfect and costly, a measure of correlation over time between income and expenditure would remain for individual households even if household incomes were largely uncorrelated and therefore potentially amenable to mutual insurance. In the event of a drought, however, we are concerned with income fluctuations which are not only large but also have a strongly collective nature. A reduction of living standards is especially inescapable in this context.[169]

There is plenty of evidence to support the validity of these speculations for rural India. Several careful empirical studies have indeed shown that informal insurance arrangements are active—though far from perfect—in rural India, and allow a substantial degree of insulation of expenditure levels from income fluctuations. During droughts, however, the effectiveness of insurance mechanisms is considerably eroded. In particular, the strategy of temporarily depleting assets to preserve ordinary consumption standards becomes extremely costly as widespread sales drive asset prices down. The insurance opportunities provided by alternative strategies such as borrowing, income transfers (including remittances), patronage, sharing, or storage are also severely limited in times of drought.[170]

Understandably enough, then, droughts in India do entail large cuts in household expenditures, not only for agricultural labourers but also for cultivators (large and small). Moreover, the available empirical evidence strongly suggests that the inclination of the propertied classes to protect their asset base during droughts by reducing consumption expenditure is much stronger than one might have thought (see the discussion in the preceding section, and the evidence presented in Table 3.21 and Appendices 3.2 and 3.3). This explains, *inter alia*, why household consumption expenditure during the peak year of the Maharashtra drought was found to be remarkably constant over a wide range of landholding sizes at the lower end of the scale (see particularly the NSS-based data in Table 3.40 of Appendix 3.3). As was discussed earlier, empirical studies also bring out clearly that reduction in consumption expenditure during droughts typically involves substantial reductions in food intake, even among the relatively privileged classes.

The widespread responsiveness of food consumption to sharp changes in real income has far-reaching implications for relief policies. Thus, even when some reduction of aggregate consumption appears inevitable, there is no reason why the burden of readjustment should necessarily fall on the most

[169] For further discussion of the theoretical issues involved, see Platteau (1988), Newbery (1989), and Martin Ravallion in ch. 5 vol. 2. The imperfection of insurance opportunities does not, of course, apply uniformly to all classes. The special disadvantages of agricultural labourers in this respect account for their traditional vulnerability to starvation, and the function of the relief system can be precisely seen as one of providing them with a form of insurance and shifting the burden of uncertainty towards the propertied classes.

[170] For reviews and discussions of the relevant empirical studies, see Torry (1986a), Agarwal (1988), Platteau (1988), Drèze and Sen (1989: ch. 5), and Martin Ravallion in ch. 5 vol. 2.

vulnerable groups. In principle, suitable income support measures (e.g. in the form of employment generation) can succeed in protecting their entitlements.

Before concluding this section, a word must be said about the role of prices in this scenario. At the risk of simplification, the changes in real incomes which took place in Maharashtra in 1972–3 can be seen as having resulted from the combination of three influences: (1) the loss of crops and agricultural employment; (2) direct income transfers through relief measures; and (3) the increase of prices (especially food prices).[171] The latter was due, in part, to the generation of purchasing power resulting from large-scale income support measures (mainly in the form of cash-for-work schemes). Exactly how much extra upward pressure relief measures were actually putting on food prices is, however, difficult to ascertain, and would have depended *inter alia* on the elasticity of supply. As was discussed earlier, the supply of food to Maharashtra in 1972–3 was far from completely inelastic, and it was not the least success of relief measures to attract large quantities of food from other parts of the country. Nevertheless, substantial increases in food prices did occur in Maharashtra in 1972–3.

If we ignore 'substitution effects', an increase in food prices operates very much like a lump-sum tax applying to all households *proportionately to their food purchases*.[172] The soundness of a relief strategy relying on an implicit tax of this kind to release the resources needed to support the entitlements of vulnerable groups depends largely on two conditions being satisfied. First, there must be a substantial pool of households whose food purchases are responsive to declines in real income but who are not immediately at risk. Second, the number of households who buy food but *are* at risk and have no access to the relief system must be small. In Maharashtra, the existence of many cultivators struggling to preserve their asset base in the face of massive crop losses ensured that the first condition was met. As we shall see, moreover, the policy of open-ended public works supplemented by unconditional relief for households without fit adult members ensured that the second condition was, by and large, also met. In these circumstances, it was hardly a mistake to provide massive cash relief to the poor without waiting for a definitive improvement in food availability.

If food consumption is also responsive to food price changes through substitution effects, the scope for using the incomes–prices mechanism to protect the entitlements of vulnerable groups can be expected to be correspondingly greater. Whether substitution effects are in fact important is hard to ascertain. Econometric studies would have us believe that the consumption of food (whether interpreted as 'total food', 'calories', or even

---

[171] For further details on incomes, wages, and prices in Maharashtra in 1972–3, see Oughton (1982). See also Appendix 3.3 below.

[172] This follows from the 'Slutsky equation'. A substitution effect is a change in consumption in response to a change in price occurring over and above the effect that one would expect merely on account of the induced change in real income (with unchanged relative prices).

Table 3.23 Per capita cereal
consumption in urban Maharashtra,
1970–1978

Year	Per capita cereal consumption (kg/month)
1970–1	9.75
1972–3	8.95
1973–4	9.24
1977–8	9.92

Source: National Sample Survey (25th, 27th, 28th, and 32nd Rounds), as reported in *Sarvekshana*, Jan. 1979: 133, and Draft Report No. 311 of the National Sample Survey.

'cereals') is subject to strong income *and* substitution effects at *all* income levels.[173] There are, however, good reasons to be cautious in interpreting these results,[174] and even if they are valid 'at the sample mean', they become quite suspect in the kind of price and income ranges relevant to a drought situation. This said, it is interesting to note that at least one clear case of a significant substitution effect can be detected for the Maharashtra drought: urban consumption of cereals fell in 1972–3 in response to sharp price increases, even though cereals appear to be an 'inferior' commodity group in urban Maharashtra (Table 3.23).[175]

One should not, of course, exaggerate the extent to which limited food supplies can be fairly 'shared' through the prices–incomes mechanism. In the event of a severe food shortage, the scope for redistribution will inevitably be limited. Further, it cannot be disputed that food entitlements are generally easier to protect the more comfortable the state of food supplies. Cash relief schemes should not (and need not) *substitute* for public involvement in food supply management.

The argument of this section can be summarized as follows. It is tempting to believe that, in a situation of severe food availability decline, the restraint of consumption will inevitably be concentrated on the poorest groups. Careful

[173] On this, see particularly the review of evidence in Alderman (1986).

[174] In the case of India, the need for caution arises particularly from (1) the virtually universal use of a single source of data (the National Sample Survey) in econometric studies of consumption; (2) the common practice of estimating functional forms (such as the Linear Expenditure System and its variants) which impose very strong a priori restrictions on substitution effects (or their relation to income effects); (3) the striking robustness, noted above, of cereal consumption for individual States in non-drought years.

[175] For evidence that cereals are an inferior commodity in urban Maharashtra, see e.g. the results of the 27th Round of the National Sample Survey reported in the Jan. 1979 issue of *Sarvekshana*.

reasoning as well as empirical evidence do not lend support to this presumption, at least for India. In the event of a severe crop failure, a broad section of the rural population experiences a dramatic decline in current income, to which food consumption appears to be responsive. In such a situation we can also expect food consumption to be widely responsive to price changes, if only through income effects. Hence, as long as the food deficit is not too large, income support policies for the most vulnerable groups should be successful (as they have been in Maharashtra) in spreading the burden of consumption reduction over a broad section of the population. This is not an argument for dealing with food shortages by engineering a redistribution of food from the poor to the poorest and neglecting the problem of food supply management. Rather, it is a plea to support the poorest by priority *irrespective* of the success achieved in improving food supplies. While this recommendation may sound trivial, it runs contrary to much current practice and thinking in famine relief.[176]

(d) Public works, public pressure and public distribution

By any criterion the drought of 1970–3 in Maharashtra must have marked an all-time record for the scale and reach of public works programmes in a famine relief operation. At the peak of employment in May 1973, nearly five million labourers attended relief works every day, and over the twelve-month period from August 1972 to July 1973 almost exactly one billion person-days of relief employment were provided. The average attendance in April–June 1973 exceeded 20 per cent of the total rural population in 7 out of 26 districts, and it was as high as 35 per cent in Bihar District.[177] Many informal as well as formal reports testify to the fact that in many villages, most of the labour force was employed on relief works. Even though real wages were very meagre, the contribution of relief works to total village income in 1972–3 was often enormous (see Table 3.24, and Table 3.36 in Appendix 3.3).

Wages were paid in cash. The idea was to enable labourers to purchase food themselves, mainly from 'Fair Price Shops' where grain rations of 12 kg per head per month were meant to be available. As was discussed earlier, the public distribution system actually met only a very small fraction of the population's food needs, and the bulk of purchases were made on the open market. The payment of cash wages ensured that delays and failures in public food delivery did not paralyse the provision of relief.

[176] It is noteworthy that even during the Maharashtra drought, when plenty of cheap food was available within India, the mode of intervention of international relief agencies still consisted mainly of importing wheat, biscuits, milk powder, and high-protein soya from countries as varied as Canada, Israel, and Australia, for direct feeding programmes.

[177] Figures calculated from Subramaniam (1975: table II.3). Strictly speaking, these figures are based on attendance on the last day of each month. One cannot rule out a margin of exaggeration in the official employment figures, and indeed there is some discrepancy between the employment and expenditure figures reported by Subramaniam (I am grateful to Siddiq Osmani for drawing my attention to this point).

Table 3.24 Earnings from relief works and total income in
70 drought-affected villages of Maharashtra, 1972–1973

Contribution of earnings on relief works to total income (%)	No. of villages
0.0–20.0	7
20.1–40.0	8
40.1–50.0	9
50.1–60.0	10
60.1–70.0	14
70.1–80.0	15
80.1–90.0	6
90.1–100.0	1
TOTAL	70

Source: Brahme (1983: 59). The villages were located in the Districts
of Poona, Ahmednagar, Sholapur, Aurangabad, Bhir, and Osmanabad (all severely drought affected).

The works undertaken had, initially at least, the intended 'productive'
nature (as with road building, soil conservation, and irrigation works). There
came a point, however, where the capacity to plan and implement productive
works on an increasingly large scale came under severe strain. Among the less
productive assets created under the relief programme was a mountain of nearly
30 million cubic metres of broken stones, which took years to utilize.[178] Some
authors have chosen to emphasize the productive value of relief works
(Ladejinsky 1973; Godbole 1973), others their wastefulness (Jaiswal and Kolte
1981; Morris 1975). There is little doubt that the total quantity of assets created
was impressive, but equally clearly the average productivity of labour must
have been extremely low. Serious cost–benefit studies of these questions are
not available, and would in any case face extremely complex methodological
problems.[179]

Productive achievements, however, are certainly not the most important
aspect of public works in the context of famine relief. While this is not the place
to go into a discussion of the general merits and shortcomings of employment
provision as a relief strategy, the Maharashtra experience does underline
particularly clearly a number of positive features of the approach. Special
mention should be made of the effectiveness of public works as a 'selection
mechanism'.

The importance of the 'selection problem' for famine prevention strategies

---

[178] Subramaniam (1975: 185). In some parts of Maharashtra the drought is remembered as 'the
drought of stone-breaking'.

[179] For a brave attempt at solving some of these problems, see Mundle (1974a, 1974b).

has been discussed elsewhere.[180] Any relief system must come to grips with the challenge of defining and reaching the population entitled to public support. In this context, a dilemma often arises between the 'security objective' and the 'targeting objective'. The security objective refers to the need to ensure that all those at risk of starvation are protected. The targeting objective is concerned with the possible importance of withdrawing public support from relatively privileged groups, in order to impart an adequately redistributive bias to the relief system.[181] The 'self-selection' feature of employment-based relief programmes is attractive from the point of view of both objectives. The experience of famine prevention in Maharashtra amply illustrates this point.

As far as the security objective is concerned, the open-ended provision of employment to all those who wished to join the relief works certainly went a very long way towards providing universal protection against starvation.[182] It may seem incredible that an actual guarantee of employment was successfully provided to a rural population of 35 million. Surely there were loopholes and people were deprived of work in many places? Because the question is so important, I have asked a large number of witnesses of the drought (in the administration, in voluntary agencies, in villages) whether they thought that the guarantee of employment had been effective in 1972–3. In the vast majority of cases the answer was basically in the affirmative, though occasional qualifications were expressed on account of short-run delays and bottlenecks.[183] And the employment figures, too, are eloquent enough.

Even more eloquent, to say the least, is Subramaniam's rather inflated but nevertheless revealing version of the story:

In every visit which was undertaken by the Chief Minister, he propounded a new slogan which in Marathi runs as 'maagel tyala kaam' or 'Work for all who want it'. The reverberations of this slogan from village to village, from worksite to worksite, coupled with the phenomenal industry displayed in the organisation of relief measures and the allotment of the necessary funds for implementing these measures, spread as it were a new gospel of faith and cheer and courage throughout the entire countryside, as a result

---

[180] See Drèze and Sen (1989), particularly ch. 7.

[181] The basic distinction between these two objectives is a familiar one in the income support literature, both for developed countries (see e.g. Atkinson 1987) as well as for developing ones (Cornia et al. 1987; Kumar and Stewart 1987).

[182] The guarantee of employment was supplemented with unconditional relief for those unable to work or to rely on able-bodied relatives. Unfortunately, the actual functioning of this component of the relief system has been little studied.

[183] An anonymous and impressionistic contribution to *Janata* in 1972 (Anon. 1972a), later quoted in Jaiswal and Kolte (1981: 19), themselves cited in Torry (1986a: 17), asserts that at one point in 1972 the amount of employment provided barely reached one-quarter of the amount demanded. Subramaniam himself admits that 'the number of works sanctioned in the initial stages fell far short of the number required to absorb the needy people' (Subramaniam 1975: 402), and Kulkarni also notes that 'in almost all the sample villages, scarcity works were available to the persons willing to work only since October 1972' (Kulkarni 1974: 169). There is clear evidence, however, that the lull of the first half of 1972 proved short-lived (see Fig. 3.5 below).

of which there was an electric charge in the rural atmosphere. The slogan of 'maagel tyala kaam' was not merely a myth; it was a reality.[184]

What accounted for this 'phenomenal industry' of the government machinery? Why did the Chief Minister suddenly prove so zealous and resourceful? One would like to think that humanitarian concern played a role, but other factors must obviously have been at work as well. Two different but highly complementary types of incentives can be identified here, arising respectively from the *meritocratic* nature of the Maharashtrian administration, and the *democratic* nature of Indian politics.

Meritocratic pressures were most evident in the behaviour of the District Collectors, who were often found to be incessantly working during the crisis. It must be remembered that District Collectors in India are very powerful, carefully trained, and often highly motivated individuals. In the event of a drought, they assume full responsibility for the management of relief operations typically covering several million people. This is a rare and often much awaited opportunity to achieve distinction, or, as one District Collector put it frankly, to 'boost one's ego'.[185]

Having said this, the reasons why the successful conduct of relief operations should be a cause for distinction in the first place cannot be understood without reference to the political influences and pressures which made the prevention of famine a chief preoccupation of the government. The role of opposition parties and the press in this context is obvious enough, if only from the 696 drought-related questions asked in the Maharashtra Legislative Assembly and Council in 1973 alone, as well as from the numerous journalistic reports which appeared in newspapers and periodicals such as *Economic and Political Weekly*, *Janata*, *Statesman*, *Times of India*, *Hindu*, and *Economic Times*, to mention only a few.[186] Popular demands for relief were also strongly backed by voluntary agencies (a very dynamic force in rural Maharashtra) and by local leaders (for whom the drought was an opportunity to build political capital).

Direct public pressure on the part of drought-affected populations also deserves emphatic mention. Employment for all was not only a clear instruction of the Bombay Scarcity Manual, it was also a *perceived right* which millions of poor men and (especially) women were determined to claim—if necessary

[184] Subramaniam (1975: 189–90). Many first-hand accounts of the public response to the drought provide a similar, if less flowery, picture of administrative dynamism.

[185] Personal communication from a former District Collector. It is hard to avoid a parallel with Mrs Thatcher's attitude during the Falklands Campaign: 'When you've spent half your political life with humdrum issues like the environment . . . it's exciting to have a real crisis on your hands' (quoted in *Pacifist*, 25/6, Nov. 1987, p. 16).

[186] A useful guide to many English-medium newspaper articles on the drought can be found in Luthra and Srinivas (1976). See also Subramaniam (1975: ch. IV.4), where many interesting details (including the figures cited above) can be found on the influence of newspapers and opposition parties during the drought. On the general role of adversarial journalism and politics in reducing the threat of famine in India, see Sen (1982), and ch. 4 of this volume.

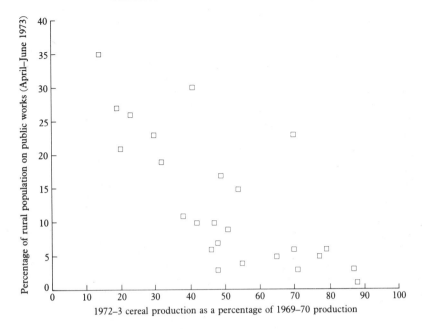

Source: Calculated from Subramaniam (1975: Appendix). Each point in the figure represents one District of Maharashtra.

Fig. 3.4 Drought intensity and public relief in rural Maharashtra by District, 1972–1973

by marching, picketing, and rioting. As one labourer aptly put it, 'they would let us die if they thought we would not make a noise about it'.[187]

It is, in fact, quite interesting that relief operations, particularly employment programmes, were the focus of a great deal of radical political activity, especially on the part of rural women.[188] This observation calls into serious question the common view that public works are merely short-term relief measures, which create 'dependency' and reduce the militancy of the masses.

[187] Cited in Mody (1972: 2483). Many vivid accounts of popular protest during the drought can be found in the columns of *Economic and Political Weekly* (see e.g. Mody 1972, Anon. 1973, and Patil, 1973). Women were commonly found to be 'more vociferous and articulate in voicing their needs and complaints than men' (Padgaonkar 1973). On this see also Bhatia (1986).

[188] On the long-term influence of drought-related political activity on the women's movement in Maharashtra, see Omvedt (1980). The success of a State-wide strike by relief labourers for higher wages in 1973 is another example. It could be argued, of course, that political activism had more to do with the impoverishment of the masses during the drought than with the relief operations. However, solidarity and organization are not typical features of famine situations, which lead more commonly to unorganized revolt and increasing individualism. See Kynch (1988), and Drèze and Sen (1989: chs. 4 and 5).

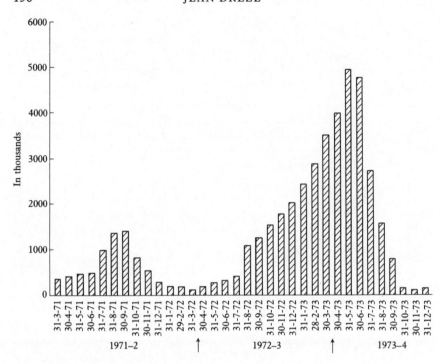

Source: Subramaniam (1975: Appendix).

Fig. 3.5 Month-by-month labour attendance on relief works in Maharashtra, 1971–1973

Turning to the 'targeting' objective, we can examine the redistributive effects of employment programmes along four distinct dimensions: (1) between areas more or less vulnerable to famine, (2) over time, (3) between different socio-economic groups at a given time and place, and (4) between different household members.

As far as the distribution of relief between different areas is concerned, Fig. 3.4 indicates a striking correlation, across Districts, between 'vulnerability' (as measured by the extent of crop failures) and 'relief' (as measured by the percentage of the rural population employed in relief works).

Regarding distribution over time, Fig. 3.5 suggests that relief operations in 1972–3 were highly concentrated on the period when the threat of famine was most serious: the summer months from April to June when, in the absence of relief, employment comes to a standstill and household resources run out. In both these respects (targeting over space and time), the Maharashtra experience sharply contrasts with the all too familiar nightmare of relief arriving at the wrong time and/or in the wrong place.

The distribution of relief between different socio-economic groups at a given time and place is less easy to assess. Usually the bulk of participation on public works schemes in India is accounted for by agricultural labourers, sometimes joined (particularly in non-irrigated areas) by marginal or small farmers. Income support through public works therefore typically assumes a strongly redistributive character.[189] During very severe droughts, however, the participation of cultivators is observed to increase sharply.[190] For this reason, the distribution of work in Maharashtra in 1972–3 was less progressive than usual if one takes landholding size as an indication of ordinary prosperity. In fact, the available evidence suggests that, during the peak months of the crisis and in the worst-affected districts, only a small measure of inverse correlation between household income from relief works and landholding size survived.[191]

However, a more sharply redistributive pattern would almost certainly emerge if one considered the entire drought period. Note also that the inverse correlation between relief employment and current (non-relief) *income* must have been much stronger than that between relief employment and landholding size. Indeed, large farmers were notoriously reluctant to join the crowd of lesser mortals on relief works, and those who eventually did so must have been driven by acute hardship.

Special mention should be made in this context of the employment of women on public works, because the redistributive effects of employment programmes arise partly from higher rates of female participation among the poorer groups. Maharashtra has a strong tradition of female wage labour, and women always form a very large proportion of the labour force on public works, often outnumbering men altogether. Relief works in 1972–3 were no exception to this rule.[192] Moreover, female wage labour tends to confer a low social status, and thus to be restricted to households of poor economic condition or (so-called) low caste. While in 1972–3 hardship was so widespread that no few stories of 'respectable' women joining the relief works could be heard, female participation must have remained significantly higher among

[189] This is evident, for instance, from the findings of Desai et al. (1979) for Gujarat in 1974–5, where participation on relief works was very strongly and inversely correlated with landholding size. Similarly, in her study of the Employment Guarantee Scheme of Maharashtra, Dandekar (1983) found that 90% of the labourers belonged to households owning less than 3 acres of land, almost always non-irrigated. See also Chen (1989: table 43) on participation in relief works during the 1987 drought in Gujarat.

[190] This phenomenon was already commonly observed during pre-independence famines (see Bhatia 1967), and was noticed by many observers of the Maharashtra drought including the authors of most of the microstudies cited earlier. For a more recent example, relating to the drought of 1985–7 in Gujarat, see Chen (1989).

[191] On this, see Borkar and Nadkarni (1975: table XI), Subramaniam (1975: table IV.3(iv)), Kulkarni (1974: table 7.21), and Brahme (1983: table 4.13).

[192] See Dandekar (1983) for an in-depth study of female employment on public works schemes in Maharashtra (her survey of 3,080 EGS workers in 1978–9 found females to outnumber males, though official statistics put the percentage of female labour to total EGS labour at about 40% only in 1979 and 1980). In his survey of Sinnar taluka (Maharashtra) during the 1972–3 drought, Kulkarni (1974) found female labourers to be almost as numerous as male labourers on relief works, even though women were heavily underrepresented in the total working population.

Table 3.25 Female participation in relief works, Maharashtra 1972–1973

Household class	% of female household members attending relief works	
	Ahmednagar District	Osmanabad District
Large cultivators	39.6	22.3
Small cultivators	47.8	38.8
Agricultural labourers	56.6	40.9
Village artisans	39.0	29.3

Source: Subramaniam (1975: table IV.3(iv)).

disadvantaged groups. The only piece of evidence I could find on this question is shown in Table 3.25, and confirms the hypothesis.[193]

The issue of female participation relates closely to that of intrafamily distribution—the fourth dimension of 'targeting' mentioned earlier. It may be argued that employment-based relief strategies fail to exert a positive influence on the distribution of resources (particularly food) within households. Indeed, the popularity of feeding programmes among relief agencies arises partly from the conviction that direct feeding can strongly tilt intrahousehold distribution towards more vulnerable individuals (e.g. women or children). It has been argued elsewhere that the benefits of individual targeting have often been exaggerated, partly because in practice it is extremely hard to exert a strong influence on intrafamily distribution, and partly because intrafamily inequalities typically supplement in a relatively minor way the debilitating forces operating in a famine situation.[194] Moreover, given the high involvement of women in public employment programmes in India, and the generally positive effects of this involvement on the position of women within the family, employment-based relief strategies can be seen as having some important advantages from the point of view of intrahousehold distribution. As was discussed earlier, mortality differentials between age and sex groups do not appear to have widened during the Maharashtra drought (see Table 3.16).

The performance of public works as a selection mechanism, in terms of both

[193] Hopefully there are better reasons for women outnumbering men on public works than that 'women themselves did not like their husbands to be employed as they are not in a mood to complete the given task and ultimately women have to assist in their work' (Lodha and Khunteta 1973). A distinct possibility is that the comparatively narrow wage differentials between men and women on public works make this employment opportunity relatively more attractive to women, who experience strong wage discrimination on the private labour market. Surveys carried out in Poona, Ahmednagar, and Osmanabad Districts of Maharashtra in 1972–3 indicate wage differentials of the order of 20% on relief works, arising mainly from the remuneration of men as 'diggers' and of women as 'carriers' (see Subramaniam 1975: 613, and Brahme 1983: 102–3).

[194] See Drèze and Sen (1989: chs. 4, 5, 7). On the general question of intrafamily distribution of food in India, see ch. 5 in this book. Gender issues in relation to Indian famines are examined in Kynch (1987) and Guz (1987).

the 'security' and 'targeting' objectives, contrasts especially favourably with that of the public distribution system. Clearly, if the resources which the Indian government was prepared to devote to famine relief in 1972–3 had been allocated through the indiscriminate (in fact, urban-biased) channel of the Fair Price Shops network, many of the impoverished labourers for whom relief was the main source of sustenance during the drought would have received too little support to survive. Once again, this is not to say that government intervention in foodgrain trade and distribution has no positive role to play. But the role of India's public distribution system needs to be put into proper perspective, because it is often given exaggerated credit for the elimination of famines in that country.[195]

The contrast between the strategy of relief works and the public distribution system also draws our attention to the merits of cash relief in this particular event. In spite of India's very considerable expertise with the logistics of food, the difficulties encountered in storing, transporting, and distributing large quantities of food made themselves very strongly felt.[196] It is quite plain that if the scale of relief had been limited by the capacity of the public distribution system to handle food, enormous hardship would have ensued. Under the cash-for-work strategy, however, the logistical resources of the public distribution system were effectively augmented by those of the private sector, and the relief system was largely protected from failures of public food delivery.

None of this, of course, amounts to a general and unqualified case in favour of the cash-for-work approach to famine relief. The choice of a relief strategy involves a broad range of issues, going well beyond the observations made in this section. Some of these issues are examined in other contributions to this book.[197]

3.5. *Summary and conclusions*

India's success in preventing droughts and other natural disasters from developing into large-scale famines since independence is not a spurious one. The entitlement system defined by the operation of the economy and the ordinary level of State provisioning leaves a large part of the population highly vulnerable to starvation in times of crisis. On several occasions, famine would undoubtedly have occurred in the absence of early and effective intervention to protect the entitlements of vulnerable groups. If the government of India can and should be criticized for having gone little further than espousing the earlier

---

[195] The public distribution system deserves credit for price stabilization, not direct income generation. The former goal depends on aggregate food supply management much more than on decentralized distribution through Fair Price Shops.

[196] See Subramaniam (1975: ch. 7) for further details.

[197] For a general discussion of alternative famine prevention strategies, see Drèze and Sen (1989).

colonial view that 'while the duty of the Government is to save life, it is not bound to maintain the labouring community at its normal level of comfort',[198] the measure of success it has achieved in the pursuit of this narrow objective is, by international standards, impressive.

At a general level, a reliable system of famine prevention can be seen to consist essentially of two distinct elements. The first is an intelligent and well-planned intervention procedure, based on a sound understanding of how the entitlements of vulnerable sections of the population may be threatened and can be protected. The second is a mechanism to ensure that an early decision to act is taken by the responsible authorities in the event of a crisis. This part of the system has, inevitably, an important political dimension. At the risk of some oversimplification, the emergence of these two components of India's famine prevention system can be traced to two historical milestones: the birth of the Famine Codes at the end of the nineteenth century, and the achievement of independence in 1947.

The Famine Commission of 1880 saw the loss of employment and wages for agricultural labourers and artisans during droughts as the primary cause of famines, while it pronounced that food was rarely in short supply for the country as a whole. Accordingly, the famine relief strategy embodied in the Famine Codes consisted of generating purchasing power in affected areas, and letting private trade ensure the physical supply of food. Moreover, the preferred income transfer mechanism consisted of open-ended public works supplemented by 'gratuitous relief' for the weak. The self-selection feature of relief works was relied upon to ensure financial economy while providing a universal guarantee against starvation. These principles remain at the core of the Scarcity Manuals of independent India.

It would be simplistic, however, to regard India's present relief system as a mere legacy of the British administration. In fact, important changes have occurred since independence. Some of these changes relate to the practicalities of a strategy of entitlement protection. In particular, the government of independent India has resolutely entered the previously sacrosanct domain of food supply management, and ensured a large measure of price stability through the public distribution system. However, the more fundamental changes have occurred in the political sphere, as the undependable commitment of the British administration to preventing starvation deaths evolved into a political compulsion to respond to famine threats.

A case-study of the drought of 1970–3 in Maharashtra, while admittedly concentrating on one of the most striking successes of public action for famine prevention in India, clearly underlines the high standards of effectiveness which the relief system is capable of achieving. Against the background of a dramatic and prolonged collapse of agricultural production and food availabil-

---

[198] Circular of the Government of India No. 44F, 9 June 1883, quoted in Government of India (1901: 35).

ity, massive programmes of income generation through public employment succeeded in attracting considerable amounts of food into Maharashtra, in a situation where the public distribution system had proved unequal to the task of filling the initial gap between availability and requirements. Large-scale provision of employment to the deprived sections of the population was also successful in ensuring that the remaining deficit was distributed with astonishing evenness between different socio-economic groups. The effectiveness of relief measures largely explains why this devastating drought caused relatively little damage in terms of excess mortality, nutritional stress, and asset depletion.

This case-study also highlighted the crucial role played (*inter alia*) by public pressure, cash relief, and public works in averting a tragedy. Public pressure from political parties, the media, voluntary agencies, and—last but not least—affected populations themselves galvanized the government into action at an early stage and kept it on its toes throughout the crisis. Cash relief enabled the logistical resources of the public sector to be supplemented with those of the private sector, and insulated income support strategies from food delivery failures. The reliance on public works as the main income transfer mechanism ensured both a sharp concentration of resources on the needy (the 'targeting objective') and, perhaps even more importantly, the provision of a nearly universal protection against starvation (the 'security objective').

It is fit to conclude this chapter by tempering its congratulatory tone. In fact, it can be argued that the diagnosis of success in crisis management is contingent upon the existence of acute and lasting famine vulnerability in the first place. The disappearance of large-scale famines in India has indeed coexisted with the resilient persistence of mass poverty and hunger. As with the prevention of famines, public action will be a crucial ingredient of success in confronting this colossal and inadmissible failure.

Appendix 3.1: Mortality in Bihar, 1966–1967

This Appendix presents some evidence on the impact of the food crisis of 1966–7 in Bihar on mortality rates. The findings are discussed in the text (Section 3.3b).

Table 3.26 Death rate in rural Bihar (Sample Registration Scheme)

Period	Source	
	Singh	Sample Registration Bulletin
July 1966–July 1967	16.8	
Aug. 1966–July 1967		15.4
July 1966–Dec. 1966	16.9	16.9
Jan. 1967–June 1967	14.2	
July 1966–June 1967		15.7
July 1967–June 1968	13.2	15.0
July 1967–Dec. 1967	10.3	
Nov. 1966–Oct. 1967		14.6
Jan. 1968–June 1968	11.6	11.8
1968		14.9
1970		14.5
1971		14.6
Jan.–June 1971		12.7
July–Dec. 1971		16.9
1972		19.0
Jan.–June 1972		15.1
July–Dec. 1972		22.6

Note: It can be seen that the figures reported by Singh are internally inconsistent (since 16.8 could hardly be an average of 16.9 and 14.2 with roughly equal weights), and also in conflict with the official figures of the *Sample Registration Bulletin*.

Source: Singh (1975: 243) and *Sample Registration Bulletin*, 1968, 1973, and 1974, various issues.

Table 3.27 Rural death rate in Bihar and India,
1963–1964 and 1966–1967 (National Sample Survey)

Period	Bihar	India
Feb. 1963–Jan. 1964	10.1	12.4
July 1966–June 1967	12.4	10.4

Notes: The individual observations consist of a death rate for
365 days before the date of interview. Hence, the reference
period '1963–4' (say) strictly speaking spans the period
Feb. 1962–Jan. 1964, but with a very small weight on the
beginning of the latter period.

Source: National Sample Survey, Report Nos. 175 (18th
Round) and 210 (21st Round).

Table 3.28 Registered deaths in Gaya, Palamau, and Hazaribagh Districts of Bihar
and in Bihar as a whole, 1966–1968

	Death rate (per 000)			Infant mortality rate (per 000 live births)		
	1966	1967	1968	1966	1967	1968
Gaya	14.7	24.6	8.1	107	132	63
Palamau	13.5	17.1	13.6	93	112	60
Hazaribagh	11.3	22.7	10.7	62	63	42
Bihar	11.4	13.9	10.4	74	72	51

Source: *Annual Report on Vital Statistics of Bihar, 1968* (Patna: Government of Bihar), and
Condensed Annual Vital Statistics Report for the Years 1966 and 1967 (Patna: Government of Bihar).

Table 3.29 Singh's mortality estimates for Gaya, Palamau, Hazaribagh, and Bihar,
1966–1967

Period	Death rate			
	Gaya	Palamau	Hazaribagh	Bihar
July 1966–Dec. 1966	17.2	19.2	19.8	16.9
July 1967–Dec. 1967	16.6	12.6	12.3	10.3

Source: Singh (1975: 243), who presents this as data collected by the Sample Registration Scheme
(but see Table 3.26 above).

Appendix 3.2: Food Consumption Adjustments during Drought Years in Rural India

This Appendix presents some evidence on food consumption adjustments by different socio-economic groups during drought years in Maharashtra, Gujarat, Karnataka, Rajasthan, and Tamil Nadu. It clearly emerges that even the relatively privileged classes often substantially reduce their food consumption in drought years, rather than maintaining ordinary food consumption levels by depleting their assets (see Section 3.4b for further discussion).

Table 3.30 Food consumption and asset depletion for a sample of 52 farming households from a village in Jodhpur District, Rajasthan, 1963–1964 (drought year)

(a)

Foodgrain consumption class (gm/day)	% of households in each consumption class						
	Oct. 1963	Nov. 1963	Dec. 1963	Jan. 1964	Feb. 1964	Mar. 1964	Apr. 1964
300–450	7.7	21.3	34.6	48.1	57.7	60.5	69.2
	(—)	(—)	(1.9)	(5.7)	(3.8)	(5.7)	(7.6)
451–600	21.2	25.0	38.5	34.6	35.5	32.7	25.0
	(67.3)	(73.0)	(69.2)	(74.9)	(76.8)	(78.7)	(78.7)
601–750	71.1	53.8	26.9	17.3	5.8	5.8	5.8
	(32.7)	(27.0)	(28.9)	(19.4)	(20.4)	(15.4)	(13.9)

(b)

Asset depletion step	% of households which took the indicated step						
	Oct. 1963	Nov. 1963	Dec. 1963	Jan. 1964	Feb. 1964	Mar. 1964	Apr. 1964
Sold inventories	22.9	40.9	55.0	50.1	52.2	35.3	36.7
Sold assets	—	1.4	—	—	2.1	0.7	4.2
Mortgaged assets	0.7	—	2.8	5.6	14.5	26.4	22.2

Notes: Figures in parentheses indicate the corresponding details for the year *following* the drought year.

'Inventories' here refer to items such as fuel wood, dung cakes, timbers, ropes and mats, spun wool, ghee, pickles, stocks of provisions, clothing, etc. (see Jodha 1975: 1620).

Source: Jodha (1975: 1613, 1615).

Table 3.31 Changes in cereal consumption for 108 households in Dandhuka taluka, Gujarat, 1974–1975

Household class and nature of change	All cereals	Wheat	Rice	Jowar	Bajra	No. of households
Large cultivators						24
Increased	—	5	—	22	14	
Decreased	75	22	59	5	7	
Stopped	—	—	23	—	36	
No change	25	73	18	73	43	
Medium cultivators						24
Increased	—	—	—	7	7	
Decreased	75	23	65	—	29	
Stopped	—	—	15	—	50	
No change	25	77	20	93	14	
Small cultivators						24
Increased	—	5	—	10	6	
Decreased	85	32	35	20	50	
Stopped	—	—	47	—	19	
No change	15	63	18	70	25	
Labourers						30
Increased	—	7	—	9	14	
Decreased	47	33	36	22	29	
Stopped	—	—	29	—	—	
No change	53	60	35	69	57	
Artisans						6
Increased	—	—	—	—	—	
Decreased	50	—	50	—	33	
Stopped	—	—	50	—	—	
No change	50	100	—	100	67	

Note: Each entry in the table indicates the percentage of households which were consuming the specified item in 1973–4 (a good year) and adopted the specified 'change' in 1974–5 (a severe drought year). Maize was not consumed by any household in 1973–4 and for this reason does not appear in the table.

Source: Desai *et al.* (1979: 4–5, 72).

Table 3.32 Consumption of foodgrains in Gujarat and Rajasthan villages, 1970–1971 (normal year) and 1969–1970 (drought year) (gm/adult unit/day)

Size of operational holding	Gujarat			Rajasthan		
	Normal year (1970–1)	Drought year (1969–70)	No. of households	Normal year (1970–1)	Drought year (1969–70)	No. of households
'Big'	956	895 (94%)	1	668	593 (89%)	7
'Large'	996	780 (78%)	10	715	605 (85%)	17
'Medium'	812	732 (90%)	29	595	507 (85%)	40
'Small'	648	577 (89%)	36	612	512 (84%)	31
Non-operators	557	523 (94%)	24	578	603 (104%)	5
All households	740	657 (89%)	100	626	535 (85%)	100

Notes: For Rajasthan, 'foodgrains' here includes foodgrain substitutes (*kair ki chhal, bhurat, chandalia*, etc.). During the drought year, the consumption of foodgrain substitutes virtually disappeared in each landholding size group, while that of foodgrains marginally increased. Numbers in brackets indicate 'drought year' consumption as a percentage of 'normal year' consumption.

Source: Choudhary and Bapat (1975: 394).

Table 3.33 Calorie and protein consumption in sample villages of Tamil Nadu during drought and non-drought years

	Calorie consumption per adult equivalent			Protein consumption (gm) per adult equivalent		
	Drought years		Non-drought year	Drought years		Non-drought year
	1973–4	1982–3	1983–4	1973–4	1982–3	1983–4
Large farmers	2,038	2,232	3,456	44	48	82
Small farmers	1,666	1,714	2,953	35	37	73
Landless labourers	1,662	1,783	2,572	33	40	67

Source: Pinstrup-Andersen and Jaramillo (1985: table 6.6).

Table 3.34 'Disaster-avoidance strategies' reported by 365 households during the 1983 drought in Karnataka

Type of strategy	Specific action	% of households concerned
Reducing consumption	Eating less food: all levels	'Nearly all'
	Eating less food: to point of hunger	35
	Changing type of food eaten	9
	Spending less on festivals	18
	Spending less on clothing	15
	Postponing marriages	7
	Spending less on entertaining and visiting	3
	Removing children from school	1
Selling possessions	Animals	6
	Valuables	2
	Land	1
Employment	Changing rural employment	3
	Changing to non-rural employment	3
	Working on natural resources	1
	Some family members migrating	2
Exchange transactions	Securing loans	13
	Food from members of their community	1

Note: This drought was far less severe than that of Maharashtra in 1970–3. On the other hand, relief operations were only undertaken on a modest scale (at least in the sample villages).

Source: Caldwell *et al.* (1986: table 1).

Table 3.35 Purchases of cereals in May–June 1973 in two villages of
Aurangabad District, Maharashtra

Household class	Quantity purchased (kg/head/month)		No. of households	
	Adul	Bhadji	Adul	Bhadji
Cultivating 50 acres and above	14.2 (25.0)	15.4 (25.0)	1	1
Cultivating 25–50 acres	14.8 (25.0)	12.6 (25.7)	3	5
Cultivating 15–25 acres	14.1 (25.0)	17.3 (26.6)	10	5
Cultivating 10–15 acres	14.9 (22.8)	14.5 (23.0)	5	6
Cultivating 5–10 acres	14.5 (24.3)	18.5 (31.2)	22	7
Cultivating less than 5 acres	14.7 (23.7)	18.7 (31.45)	17	4
Agricultural labour	14.7 (25.5)	16.4 (24.4)	17	4
Artisans	13.7 (26.6)	15.2 (29.6)	7	4
Others	13.3 (28.4)	—	10	0
All households	14.4 (24.9)	15.4 (26.9)	105	36

Notes: Figures in brackets indicate the percentage of purchases made at Fair Price Shops.

The authors note that 'in May and June, when they reported peak employment and earnings through scarcity works, the households purchased slightly in excess of their current requirements because of the expected rise in the prices of food articles and the decline in their incomes in the immediate future (due to discontinuance of scarcity relief works)' (Borkar and Nadkarni 1975: 58).

No indication is given about the size of initial stocks, but these were most probably negligible for most households.

Source: Calculated from Borkar and Nadkarni (1975: 14–15, 48–9).

Appendix 3.3: Income and Expenditure Patterns in Drought Years in Rural Western India

This Appendix presents some evidence on the relationship between landholding size and income or expenditure in drought and non-drought years for Maharashtra and nearby States around the time of the 1970–3 drought. The findings are discussed in the text (Section 3.4c).

Table 3.36 Incomes in two villages of Aurangabad District, Maharashtra, 1972–1973

Landholding size class (acres)	Village Adul					Village Bhadji				
	Household income per capita (Rs./year)				No. of households surveyed	Household income per capita (Rs./year)				No. of households surveyed
	Relief works	Farming	Other income	Total income		Relief works	Farming	Other income	Total income	
>50	91	—	—	91	1	188	61	1	250	1
25–50	165	−36	23	152	3	94	104	88	286	5
15–25	359	−22	25	362	10	167	−21	43	189	5
10–15	210	−7	21	224	5	138	−24	181	295	6
5–10	239	−22	7	224	22	193	−1	21	213	7
<5	240	−5	40	275	17	259	−11	1	249	4
Agricultural labour	287	16	30	333	17	193	13	168	374	4
Artisans	169	56	79	304	7	183	63	65	311	4
Others	83	−16	346	413	10					
All households	230	−6	59	283	92	153	28	76	257	36

Note: Adul was much more affected by the drought than Bhadji.

Source: Calculated from Borkar and Nadkarni (1975: tables I, II, and XI).

Table 3.37 Incomes in Nasik District, Maharashtra, 'normal year' and 1972–1973

Landholding size class (acres)	Household income per capita (Rs./year)		Population
	'Normal year'	1972–3	
>10	481	206	820
5–10	274	168	741
0.01–5	202	146	763
Landless agricultural labourers	138	152	288
Other landless	212	205	314
All households	293	175	2,926

Note: From the text in Kulkarni (1974), it seems that 'normal year' refers to 1971–2.
Source: Calculated from Kulkarni (1974: tables 7.21, 7.23).

Table 3.38 Incomes in six villages of Satara District, Maharashtra, 1972–1973

Landholding size class (ha)	Household income per capita (Rs./year)		No. of households surveyed
	'Normal year'	1972–3	
>4.0	446	283	139
2.1–4.0	251	218	204
0.1–2.0	260	213	526
Landless	215	208	121
All households	286	222	990

Note: A very similar pattern of income changes was observed in a village of Sholapur District (Brahme 1983: 73–5). In another sample of households in Poona District, incomes were found to be unrelated to landholding size both in the drought period and in the previous year, but (1) the sample was drawn exclusively from among relief workers, and (2) the author notes that large-scale relief works were in operation during both periods (Brahme 1983: 66–8).
Source: Brahme (1983: 76).

Table 3.39 Incomes in two Districts of Maharashtra, 1972–1973

Household class	Household income per capita (Rs./month)			
	Ahmednagar District		Osmanabad District	
	Latest normal year	1972–3	Latest normal year	1972–3
Large cultivators	36	24	32	23
Small cultivators	23	24	16	20
Agricultural labourers	21	24	16	22
Village artisans	18	17	28	24

Note: Small cultivators are those 'possessing' less than 7.5 standard acres of land.

Source: Subramaniam (1975: 436, 598). Based on a survey of 27 households for each household class in each District, carried out by the Directorate of Economics and Statistics, government of Maharashtra.

Table 3.40 Poverty and landholding size, Maharashtra and Gujarat, 1972–1973

Operational holding size	% of households below the 'poverty line'	
(acres)	Gujarat	Maharashtra
0	36.8	60.0
<1.0	44.0	63.6
1–2.5	39.8	66.6
2.5–5.0	41.2	59.4
5.0–7.5	37.3	58.8
7.5–10.0	29.9	57.5
10.0–20.0	24.4	47.7
>20	13.5	36.1
All households	34.7	57.3

Note: The 'poverty line' is defined here as an expenditure level of Rs. 15/month/capita at 1960–1 prices.

Source: Visaria (1978), itself based on a tabulation of the 27th Round of the National Sample Survey.

Table 3.41 Household incomes in Dandhuka taluka, Gujarat, 1972–1974

Household class	Income per household (Rs./year)				No. of households surveyed
	Relief works	Other wage income	Non-wage income	Total	
Large farms					
1973–4	0	33	4,213	4,246	24
1974–5	240	121	−764	−403	
Medium farms					
1973–4	0	65	3,326	3,391	24
1974–5	189	163	−763	−411	
Small farms					
1973–4	0	530	1,242	1,772	24
1974–5	254	2,260	−87	427	
Landless labourers					
1973–4	0	826	17	843	30
1974–5	447	413	7	867	
Landless artisans					
1973–4	0	1,533	0	1,533	6
1974–5	442	799	0	1,241	

Note: 1974–5 was a drought year in Gujarat, but *not* 1973–4.

Source: Desai *et al*. (1979: 4–5, 65).

Table 3.42 Household incomes in Panchmahal District, Gujarat, 1972–1973

Landholding size (ha)	Income per household (Rs./year)			No. of households surveyed
	Farm	Non-farm	Total	
Above 5.0	7,585	41	7,627	8
4.1–5.0	7,055	1,428	8,482	5
3.1–4.0	4,084	1,298	5,382	8
2.1–3.0	2,951	437	3,388	19
1.1–2.0	1,827	950	2,777	97
0.1–1.0	1,180	633	1,813	57
Landless	0	1,325	1,325	5
All classes	2,156	809	2,964	199

Source: Sambrani and Pichholiya (1975: 95–6).

Table 3.43 Household expenditure in rural Gujarat and Rajasthan,
1969–1970 and 1970–1971

Size of operational holding	Total household expenditure (Rs./year)			
	Gujarat		Rajasthan	
	Normal year (1970–1)	Drought year (1969–70)	Normal year (1970–1)	Drought year (1969–70)
Big	3,985	5,087	1,489	1,378
Large	3,693	3,812	1,950	1,743
Medium	2,124	1,595	1,766	1,581
Small	1,305	1,203	1,135	1,019
Non-operators	1,010	855	916	1,137
All households	1,737	1,532	1,540	1,398

Note: Data collected from two samples of 100 households each from villages of Gujarat and Rajasthan.

Source: Choudhary and Bapat (1975: table V.6).

Table 3.44 Incomes in 15 villages of drought-prone Districts of Andhra Pradesh,
Karnataka, and Tamil Nadu, 1978–1979

Household class	Total income per household (Rs./year)			
	Anantapur (Andhra Pradesh)	Bijapur (Karnataka)	Coimbatore (Tamil Nadu)	All villages
Large farmers (above 10 ha)	37,906	24,753	91,732	51,464
All cultivators	4,669	3,408	9,921	5,999
Marginal farmers (below 1 ha)	2,201	2,067	5,082	3,117
Agricultural labourers	1,942	1,812	2,954	2,236
Artisans	3,231	11,051	5,269	6,517
Others	4,442	3,137	8,609	5,396
All households	3,676	3,094	6,308	4,359

Source: Nadkarni (1985: table 9.1). The year 1978–9 was *not* a drought year.

References

AGARWAL, BINA (1988), 'Social Security and the Family: Coping with Seasonality and Calamity in Rural India', paper presented at a workshop on Social Security in Developing Countries held at the London School of Economics, July 1988; to be published in Ahmad, S. E., Drèze, J. P., Hills, J., and Sen, A. K. (eds.), *Social Security in Developing Countries* (Oxford: Oxford University Press).

Agricultural Economics Research Centre, Allahabad (1972), *Study of Drought Conditions in Dolchi*, Ad Hoc Study No. A.2(a) (Allahabad: AERC).

ALAMGIR, M. (1980), *Famine in South Asia* (Cambridge, Mass.: Oelgeschlager, Gunn & Hain).

ALDERMAN, HAROLD (1986), *The Effect of Food Price and Income Changes on the Acquisition of Food by Low-Income Households* (Washington, DC: IFPRI).

AMBIRAJAN, S. (1971), 'Political Economy and Indian Famines', *South Asia*, 1.

——(1976), 'Malthusian Population Theory and Indian Famine Policy in the Nineteenth Century', *Population Studies*, 30.

——(1978), *Classical Political Economy and British Policy in India* (Cambridge: Cambridge University Press).

Anon. (1972a), 'Scarcity: Government Accepts Reality but Fails to Do its Duty', *Janata*, 27/42–3.

Anon. (1972b), 'For Most, Metal-Breaking', *Economic and Political Weekly*, 7.

Anon. (1973), 'Food Riots: Hungry Stomachs Must Hunger On', *Economic and Political Weekly*, 28 Apr.

Anon. (1987), 'A Historical View of Famines and Famine Policy', mimeo (Ahmedabad: Centre for Social Knowledge and Action).

APPADURAI, A. (1984), 'How Moral is South Asia's Economy? A Review Article', *Journal of Asian Studies*, 43.

ATKINSON, A. B. (1987), 'Income Maintenance and Social Insurance: A Survey', in Auerbach, A., and Feldstein, M. S. (eds.), *Handbook of Public Economics* (Amsterdam and New York: North-Holland).

AYKROYD, W. R. (1974), *The Conquest of Famine* (London: Chatto & Windus).

BAISHYA, P. (1975), 'Man-Made Famine', *Economic and Political Weekly*, 10.

BANDYOPADHYAY, J. (1987), *Ecology of Drought and Water Scarcity* (Dehradun: Research Foundation for Science and Ecology).

BARDHAN, KALPANA (1977), 'Rural Employment, Wages and Labour Markets in India: A Survey of Research', *Economic and Political Weekly*, 12.

BATES, CRISPIN (1985), review of *Subject to Famine* (McAlpin 1983), *Modern Asian Studies*, 19/4.

BERG, ALAN (1972), 'Famine Contained: Notes and Lessons from the Bihar Experience', *Tropical Science*, 2; also in Blix *et al.* (1971).

——(1973), 'Nutrition in Disasters: A Case Study', Appendix A in Berg, A., *The Nutrition Factor* (Washington, DC: Brookings Institution).

BHAGWATI, J., and CHAKRAVARTY, S. (1969), 'Contributions to Indian Economic Analysis: A Survey', Supplement to *American Economic Review*, Sept.

BHALLA, G. S., and ALAGH, Y. K. (1979), *Performance of Indian Agriculture: A District-Wise Study* (New Delhi: Sterling Publishers).

BHATIA, BELA (1986), 'Drought Relief Work in North Sabarkantha: A Reality', mimeo (Ahmedabad: Centre for Social Knowledge and Action).

——(1988), 'Official Drought Relief Measures: A Case Study of Gujarat', *Social Action*, 38.

BHATIA, B. M. (1967), *Famines in India 1860–1965* (London: Asia Publishing House).

——(1975), 'Famine and Agricultural Labour in India: A Historical Perspective', *Indian Journal of Industrial Relations*, 10.

BHATTACHARYA, N., COONDOO, D., MAITI, P., and MUKHERJEE, R. (1985), *Relative Price of Food and the Rural Poor: The Case of India* (Calcutta: Indian Statistical Institute).

BLAIR, C. (1874), *Indian Famines: Their Historical, Financial and Other Aspects* (Edinburgh and London: W. Blackwood & Sons).

BLIX, G., HOFVANDER, Y., and VAHLQUIST, B. (eds.) (1971), *Famine: Nutrition and Relief Operations* (Uppsala: Swedish Nutrition Foundation).

BLYN, G. (1966), *Agricultural Trends in India, 1891–1947* (Philadelphia, Penn.: University of Pennsylvania Press).

BORKAR, V. V., and NADKARNI, M. V. (1975), *Impact of Drought on Rural Life* (Bombay: Popular Prakashan).

BRAHME, S. (1973), 'Drought in Maharashtra', *Social Scientist*, 12 July.

——(1983), *Drought in Maharashtra 1972*, Gokhale Institute Series No. 68 (Pune).

BRASS, PAUL (1986), 'Political Uses of Famine', *Journal of Asian Studies*, 45.

BREMAN, JAN (1974), *Patronage and Exploitation* (Oxford: Oxford University Press).

BRENNAN, LANCE (1984), 'The Development of the Indian Famine Codes: Personalities, Politics and Policies', in Currey and Hugo (1984).

——(1988), 'Government Famine Relief in Bengal, 1943', *Journal of Asian Studies*, 47.

CAHILL, KEVIN (ed.) (1982), *Famine* (New York: Orbis Books).

CAIN, M. (1981), 'Risk and Insurance: Perspectives on Fertility and Agrarian Change in India and Bangladesh', *Population and Development Review*, 7.

CALDWELL, J. C., REDDY, P. H., and CALDWELL, P. (1986), 'Periodic High Risk as a Cause of Fertility Decline in a Changing Rural Environment: Survival Strategies in the 1980–1983 South Indian Drought', *Economic Development and Cultural Change*, 34.

CARLSON, D. G. (1982), 'Famine in History: With a Comparison of Two Modern Ethiopian Disasters', in Cahill (1982).

CARLYLE, R. W. (1900), 'Famine in a Bengal District in 1896–1897', *Economic Journal*, 10.

Central Institute of Research and Training in Public Cooperation (1969), *Famine Relief in Bihar: A Study* (New Delhi: CIRTPC).

——(1970), *People can Avert Famine* (New Delhi: CIRTPC).

——(1971), *Famine Relief and Reconstruction (Report of a Workshop)* (New Delhi: CIRTPC).

Centre for Social Studies (1988), *Drought and Famine 1980s: Crises and Response* (Surat: Centre for Social Studies).

CHANDRA, N. K. (1982), 'Long-Term Stagnation in the Indian Economy, 1900–75', *Economic and Political Weekly*, 17.

CHARLESWORTH, N. (1982), *British Rule and the Indian Economy 1800–1914* (London: Macmillan).

CHATTERJEE, B. B., and SRIVASTAVA, H. P. (1968), *Challenge of Famine: A Study of the Working of Free Relief Kitchens in Naugarh, Varanasi* (Varanasi: Amitabh Prakashan).

CHEN, MARTHA (1989), 'A Gamble on the Monsoon: Coping with Seasonality and Drought in Western India', Ph.D. thesis, Harvard Institute for International Development; to be published as a monograph.

CHETTY, V. K., and RATHA, D. K. (1987), 'The Unprecedented Drought and Government Policies', mimeo (New Delhi: Indian Statistical Institute).

CHOUDHARY, K. M., and BAPAT, M. T. (1975), 'A Study of Impact of Famine and Relief Measures in Gujarat and Rajasthan', Research Study No. 44 (Ahmedabad: Agricultural Economics Research Centre, Sardar Patel University).

CHRISTENSEN, R. O. (1984), 'Famine and Agricultural Economy: A Case Study of Haryana during the British Period', *South Asian Studies*, 1.

Club du Sahel (1977), *Marketing, Price Policy and Storage of Food Grain in the Sahel: A Survey* (University of Michigan: Center for Research on Economic Development).

CORNIA, G., JOLLY, R., and STEWART, F. (1987), *Adjustment with a Human Face* (Oxford: Oxford University Press).

CURLEY, D. L. (1977), 'Fair Grain Markets and Mughal Famine Policy in Late Eighteenth-Century Bengal', *Calcutta Historical Journal*, 2.

CURREY, B., ALI, M., and KOHMAN, N. (1981), *Famine: A First Bibliography* (Washington, DC: Agency for International Development).

——and HUGO, G. (eds.) (1984), *Famine as a Geographical Phenomenon* (Dordrecht: Reidel).

DANDEKAR, KUMUDINI (1983), *Employment Guarantee Scheme: An Employment Opportunity for Women* (Pune: Orient Longman).

DANDEKAR, V. M., and PETHE, V. P. (1962), *A Survey of Famine Conditions in the Affected Regions of Maharashtra and Mysore (1952–53)* (Pune: Gokhale Institute of Politics and Economics).

DANDO, WILLIAM (1980), *The Geography of Famine* (New York: John Wiley).

DESAI, G. M., SINGH, G., and SAH, D. C. (1979), *Impact of Scarcity on Farm Economy and Significance of Relief Operations*, CMA Monograph No. 84 (Ahmedabad: Indian Institute of Management).

DIGBY, WILLIAM (1878), *Famine Campaign in Southern India*, 2 vols. (London: Longmans, Green & Co.).

DRÈZE, JEAN (1986), 'Famine Prevention in India', draft paper presented at a Conference on Food Strategies held at the World Institute for Development Economics Research, Helsinki, July 1986.

——(1989), 'Social Insecurity in India', mimeo (Development Economics Research Programme, London School of Economics).

——(1990), 'Famine Prevention', transcript of a presentation made at a conference on Hunger and Public Action held at WIDER (Helsinki), July 1990.

——and SEN, AMARTYA (1989), *Hunger and Public Action* (Oxford: Oxford University Press).

DUTT, R. C. (1900), *Open Letters to Lord Curzon on Famines and Land Assessment in India* (London: Kegan Paul, Trench Trubner & Co.).

——(1904), *The Economic History of India* (London: Kegan Paul, Trench Trubner; repr. 1969, New York: A. M. Kelley).

DYSON, TIM (1987), 'The Historical Demography of Berar, 1881–1980', mimeo (London School of Economics).

ETHERIDGE, A. T. (1868), *Report on the Past Famines in the Bombay Presidency* (Bombay: Education Society's Press).

FRERE, Sir BARTLE (1874), *The Bengal Famine: How it Will Be Met and How to Prevent Future Famines in India* (London: John Murray).

GANGRADE, K. D., and DHADDA, S. (1973), *Challenge and Response: A Study of Famines in India* (Delhi: Rachana Publications).

GARCIA, R. V. (1981), *Drought and Man: The 1972 Case History* (Oxford: Pergamon).

GHOSE, A. K. (1979), 'Short-Term Changes in Income Distribution in Poor Agrarian Economies: A Study of Famines with Reference to the Indian Sub-Continent', World Employment Programme Research Working Paper (Geneva: ILO).

——(1982), 'Food Supply and Starvation: A Study of Famines with Reference to the Indian Subcontinent', *Oxford Economic Papers*, 34.

GHOSH, K. C. (1944), *Famines in Bengal, 1770–1943* (Calcutta: Indian Associated Publishing Co.).

GODBOLE, A. (1973), 'Productive Works for the Rich', *Economic and Political Weekly*, 8.

GOPALAN, C. (1973), 'Nutrition Survey in Drought Areas of Maharashtra', *Hindu*, 21 Mar.

Government of Bengal (1874), *Administrative Experience Recorded in Former Famines* (Calcutta: Bengal Secretariat Press).

Government of Bihar (1957), *The Bihar Famine and Flood Relief Code* (Patna: Revenue Department).

——(1973), *Bihar Famine Report, 1966–67* (Patna: Secretariat Press).

——(undated), *Bihar Fights the Drought* (Patna: Secretariat Press).

Government of India (1880), *Report of the Indian Famine Commission 1880* (London: HMSO).

——(1898), *Report of the Indian Famine Commission 1898* (Simla: Government Central Printing Office).

——(1901), *Report of the Indian Famine Commission 1901* (Calcutta: Government Printing Office).

——(1908), *Final Report on the Famine Relief Operations in the District of Darbhanga during 1906–1907* (Calcutta: Bengal Secretariat Press).

——(1945), *Famine Inquiry Commission: Report on Bengal* (New Delhi: Manager of Publications).

——(1966), *Review of Scarcity Situation and Measures Taken to Meet It* (New Delhi: Ministry of Food, Agriculture, Community Development and Cooperation).

——(1967), 'Review of the Food and Scarcity Situation in India (January 1967, March 1967, July 1967, November 1967)' (New Delhi: Ministry of Food, Agriculture, Community Development and Cooperation).

——(1973): 'Review of Drought Situation in India', mimeo (New Delhi: Department of Food, Ministry of Agriculture).

——(1979), *Statistical Abstract, India 1978* (New Delhi: Central Statistical Organisation).

——(1986), *Economic Survey 1985–86* (New Delhi: Ministry of Finance).

Government of Maharashtra (1966), *The Bombay Scarcity Manual (draft)* (Bombay: Revenue Department).

——(1973a), *Scarcity: A Compendium of Government Orders*, 2 vols. (Bombay: Mantralaya).

——(1973*b*), *Report of the Fact Finding Committee for Survey of Scarcity Areas of Maharashtra State*, 2 vols. (Bombay: Mantralaya).

——(1974), *An Economic Review, 1973–74* (Bombay: Bureau of Economics and Statistics).

——(various years), *Maharashtra Season and Crop Report* (Bombay: Directorate of Agriculture).

GREENOUGH, PAUL (1982), *Prosperity and Misery in Modern Bengal: The Famine of 1943–1944* (Oxford: Oxford University Press).

GUHA, S. (1986), review of *Subject to Famine* (McAlpin 1983), in *Indian Economic and Social History Review*, 23.

GUZ, DEBORAH (1987), 'Population Dynamics of Famine in 19th Century Punjab, 1896–7 and 1899–1900', mimeo (London School of Economics).

HARRISS, BARBARA (1988), 'Limitations of the "Lessons from India"', in Curtis, D., Hubbard, M., and Shepherd, A. (eds.), *Preventing Famine* (London and New York: Routledge).

HARVEY, P. (1969), 'Development Potential in Famine Relief: The Bihar Model', *International Development Review*, Dec.

HEBERT, J. R. (1987), 'The Social Ecology of Famine in British India: Lessons for Africa in the 1980s?', *Ecology of Food and Nutrition*, 20.

HESTON, ALAN (1973), 'Official Yields Per Acre in India, 1886–1947: Some Questions of Interpretation', *Indian Economic and Social History Review*, 10.

——(1978), 'A Further Critique of Historical Yields Per Acre in India', *Indian Economic and Social History Review*, 15.

——(1982), 'National Income', in Kumar (1982).

HOLDERNESS, T. W. (1987), *Narrative of the Famine in India in 1896–97* (Simla: Government Central Printing Office).

HUBBARD, MICHAEL (1988), 'Drought Relief and Drought Proofing in the State of Gujarat, India', in Curtis, D., Hubbard, M., and Shepherd, A. (eds.), *Preventing Famine* (London and New York: Routledge).

Indian Institute of Public Administration (1967), *Administrative Survey of the Food and Relief Organisation of the Bihar Government* (New Delhi: IIPA).

——(n.d.), *Crisis Administration* (New Delhi: IIPA).

JAISWAL, N. K. (1978), *Droughts and Famines in India* (Hyderabad: National Institute of Rural Development).

——and KOLTE, N. V. (1981), *Development of Drought-Prone Areas* (Hyderabad: National Institute of Rural Development).

JODHA, N. S. (1975), 'Famine and Famine Policies: Some Empirical Evidence', *Economic and Political Weekly*, 10.

——(1978), 'Effectiveness of Farmers' Adjustment to Risk', *Economic and Political Weekly*, 13.

——(1980), 'The Process of Desertification and the Choice of Interventions', *Economic and Political Weekly*, 15.

——(1981), 'Role of Credit in Farmers' Adjustment against Risk in Arid and Semi-arid Tropical Areas of India', *Economic and Political Weekly*, 16.

——ASOKAN, M., and RYAN, J. G. (1977), 'Village Study Methodology and Resource Endowment of the Selected Villages', Economics Program Occasional Paper No. 16 (Hyderabad: ICRISAT).

——and MASCARENHAS, A. C. (1985), 'Adjustment in Self-Provisioning Societies', in

Kates, R. W., Ausubel, J. H., and Berberian, M. (eds.), *Climate Impact Assessment* (New York: John Wiley).

JODHA, N. S. and WALKER, T. (1986), 'How Small Farmers Adjust to Risk', in Hazell, P., *et al.* (eds.), *Crop Insurance for Agricultural Development* (Washington, DC: IFPRI).

KACHHAWAHA, O. P. (1985), *Famines in Rajasthan* (Delhi: Hindi Sahitya Mandir).

KLEIN, IRA (1973), 'Death in India, 1871–1921', *Journal of Asian Studies*, 32.

——(1984), 'When the Rains Failed: Famine, Relief and Mortality in British India', *Indian Economic and Social History Review*, 21.

KRISHNA, R., and CHHIBBER, A. (1983), 'Policy-Modelling in a Dual Grain Market', Research Report No. 38 (Washington, DC: IFPRI).

KRISHNAMACHARI, K. A. V., *et al.* (1974), 'Food and Nutritional Situation in the Drought-Affected Areas of Maharashtra: A Survey and Recommendations', *Indian Journal of Nutrition and Dietetics*, 11.

KULKARNI, S. N. (1974), *Survey of Famine Affected Sinnar Taluka* (Pune: Gokhale Institute of Politics and Economics).

KUMAR, B. G. (1988), 'Consumption Disparities, Food Surpluses and Effective Demand Failures: Reflections on the Macroeconomics of Drought Vulnerability', Working Paper No. 229 (Trivandrum: Centre for Development Studies).

——and STEWART, FRANCES (1987), 'Tackling Malnutrition: What Can Targeted Nutritional Intervention Achieve?', paper presented at a Conference on Poverty in India, Queen Elizabeth House, Oxford, Oct.

KUMAR, DHARMA (ed.) (1982), *The Cambridge Economic History of India*, vol. ii: (Cambridge: Cambridge University Press).

KYNCH, JOCELYN (1987), 'Some State Responses to Male and Female Need in British India', in Afshar, H. (ed.), *Women, State and Ideology: Studies from Africa and Asia* (London: Macmillan).

——(1988), 'Scarcities, Distress and Crime in British India', paper presented at the 7th World Congress of Rural Sociology, Bologna, July.

LADEJINSKY, W. (1973), 'Drought in Maharashtra: Not in a Hundred Years', *Economic and Political Weekly*, 8.

LAL, DEEPAK (1989), *The Hindu Equilibrium*, vol. ii: *Aspects of Indian Labour* (Oxford: Oxford University Press).

LARDINOIS, ROLAND (1982), 'Une conjoncture de crise démographique en Inde du Sud au XIXe siècle', *Population*, 37.

——(1985), 'Famine, Epidemics and Mortality in South India', *Economic and Political Weekly*, 20.

LIPTON, MICHAEL (1984), 'Conditions of Poverty Groups and Impact on Indian Economic Development and Cultural Change: The Role of Labour', *Development and Change*, 15.

——(1985), 'Land Assets and Rural Poverty', World Bank Staff Working Paper No. 744 (Washington, DC: World Bank).

LODHA, S. L., and KHUNTETA, B. K. (1973), *An Economic Survey of Famine in Beawar Sub-division* (Beawar: SD Government College).

LOVEDAY, A. (1914), *The History and Economics of Indian Famines* (London: A. G. Bell & Sons; repr. New Delhi: Usha Publications, 1985).

LUTHRA, S., and SRINIVAS, S. (1976), 'Famine in India: A Select Bibliography', mimeo (New Delhi: Social Science Documentation Centre).

MAC, M. R. (1988), *Drought, Famine and Water Management: A Select Bibliography* (Surat: Centre for Social Studies).

McALPIN, MICHELLE (1974), 'Railroads, Prices, and Peasant Rationality, India 1860–1900', *Journal of Economic History*, 34.

——(1975), 'Railroads, Cultivation Patterns, and Foodgrains Availability: India 1860–1900', *Indian Economic and Social History Review*, 12.

——(1980), 'Impact of Trade on Agricultural Development, Bombay Presidency', *Explorations in Economic History*, 17.

——(1982), 'Price Movements and Fluctuations in Economic Activity (1860–1947)', in Kumar (1982).

——(1983), *Subject to Famine: Food Crises and Economic Change in Western India, 1860–1920* (Princeton, NJ: Princeton University Press).

——(1985), 'Famines, Epidemics and Population Growth: The Case of India', in Rotberg, R. I., and Rabb, T. K. (eds.), *Hunger and History* (Cambridge: Cambridge University Press).

——(1987), 'Famine Relief Policy in India: Six Lessons for Africa', in Glantz, M. (ed.), *Drought and Hunger in Africa* (Cambridge: Cambridge University Press).

McMINN (1902), *Famine: Truth, Half-Truths, and Untruths* (Calcutta: Baptist Mission Press).

Maharashtra Economic Development Council (1974), *Droughts in Maharashtra* (Bombay: MEDC).

MARX, K. (1970), *Capital*, vol. ii (London: Lawrence & Wishart).

MATHUR, K., and BHATTACHARYA, M. (1975), *Administrative Response to Emergency: A Study of Scarcity Administration in Maharashtra* (New Delhi: Concept).

MAYER, JEAN (1975), 'Management of Famine Relief', in Abelson, P. H. (ed.) (1975), *Food: Politics, Economics, Nutrition and Research* (American Association for the Advancement of Science).

MENARIA, R. K. (1975), 'Famine Relief Operations in the Princely States during the British Period', *Economic Studies*, 15.

MEREWETHER, F. H. S. (1898), *A Tour Through the Famine Districts of India* (London: A. D. Innes & Co.).

MILL, J. S. (1848), *Principles of Political Economy*, ed. W. Ashley (New York: Reprints of Economic Classics, Augustus M. Kelley).

MILLS, I. D. (1986), 'The 1918–1919 Influenza Pandemic: The Indian Experience', *Indian Economic and Social History Review*, 23.

MODY, N. (1972), 'To Some, a God-Send', *Economic and Political Weekly*, 7.

MOOLEY, D. A., and PANT, G. B. (1981), 'Droughts in India over the Last 200 Years: Their Socio-economic Impact and Remedial Measures for them', in Wigley, T. M. L., Ingram, M. J., and Farmer, G. (eds.), *Climate and History* (Cambridge: Cambridge University Press).

MORRIS, M. D. (1974), 'What is a Famine?', *Economic and Political Weekly*, 9.

——(1975), 'Needed: A New Famine Policy', *Economic and Political Weekly*, 10.

MUKERJI, K. M. (1965), *Levels of Economic Activity and Public Expenditure in India: A Historical and Quantitative Study* (Bombay: Asia Publishing House).

MUKHERJEE, M. (1986), 'Statistical Information on Final Consumption in India and the National Sample Survey', *Economic and Political Weekly*, 21.

MUNDLE, S. (1974a), 'Relief Planning in Maharashtra', *Indian Journal of Public Administration*, 20.

MUNDLE, S. (1974b), 'Planning and Resource Deployment in Deought Relief Operations: A Study in Aurangabad District, Maharashtra, 1972–73', mimeo (New Delhi: Indian Institute of Public Administration).

MURTON, B. (1984), 'Spatial and Temporal Patterns of Famine in Southern India before the Famine Codes', in Currey and Hugo (1984).

NADKARNI, M. V. (1985), Socio-economic Conditions in Drought-Prone Areas (New Delhi: Concept).

NAOROJI, D. B. (1900), Poverty and Un-British Rule in India (London: Swan Sonnenschein & Co.).

NEWBERY, DAVID (1989), 'Agrarian Institutions for Insurance and Stabilization', in Bardhan, P. K. (ed.), The Theory of Agrarian Institutions (Oxford: Oxford University Press).

NOSSITER, B. D. (1967), 'Bihar's Famine Relief Viewed as a Model', Washington Post, 6 Nov.

OMVEDT, GAIL (1980), We Will Smash This Prison! Indian Women in Struggle (London: Zed).

OUGHTON, ELISABETH (1982), 'The Maharashtra Droughts of 1970–73: An Analysis of Scarcity', Oxford Bulletin of Economics and Statistics, 44.

OXFAM (1972, 1973), Unpublished field reports.

PADGAONKAR, D. (1973), 'Maharashtra after Rain', Times of India, 26–7 July.

PANDEY, S. M., and UPADHYAY, J. N. (1979), 'Effects of Drought on Rural Population: Findings of an Area Study', Indian Journal of Industrial Relations, 15.

PASSMORE, R. (1951), 'Famine in India: An Historical Survey', Lancet, 18 Aug.

PATIL, S. (1973), 'Famine Conditions in Maharashtra: A Survey of Sakri Taluka', Economic and Political Weekly, 8.

PINSTRUP-ANDERSEN, P., and JARAMILLO, M. (1985), 'The Impact of Technological Change in Rice Production on Food Consumption and Nutrition in North Arcot, India', mimeo (Washington, DC: IFPRI).

PLATTEAU, JEAN-PHILIPPE (1988), 'Traditional Systems of Social Security and Hunger Insurance: Past Achievements and Modern Challenges', paper presented at a Workshop on Social Security in Developing Countries held at the London School of Economics, July; to be published in Ahmad, S. E., Drèze, J. P., Hills, J., and Sen, A. K. (eds.), Social Security in Developing Countries (Oxford: Oxford University Press).

PRABHAKAR, M. S. (1975), 'Death in Barpeta', Economic and Political Weekly, 10.

RAMLINGASWAMI, V., DEO, M. G., GULERIA, J. S., MALHOTRA, K. K., SOOD, S. K., OM PRAKASH, and SINHA, R. V. N. (1971) 'Studies of the Bihar Famine of 1966–67', in Blix et al. (1971).

RANGASAMI, AMRITA (1978), 'A Study of Some Aspects of Famine-Affected Areas in India', unpublished Ph.D. thesis, University of Delhi.

——(1985), 'McAlpin's Capers', Economic and Political Weekly, 20.

——(1986), 'Mismanagement of Financing Drought Relief', paper presented at a Seminar on Control of Drought, Desertification and Famine, held at the India International Centre, New Delhi, May.

RAO, H. C. H. et al. (1988), Unstable Agriculture and Droughts (New Delhi: Vikas).

RAO, N. V. K. (1974), 'Impact of Drought on the Social System of a Telangana Village', Eastern Anthropologist, 27.

RASHID, S. (1980), 'The Policy of Laissez-faire during Scarcities', *Economic Journal*, 90.

RAVALLION, MARTIN (1987*a*), *Markets and Famines* (Oxford: Oxford University Press).

——(1987*b*), 'Trade and Stabilization: Another Look at British India's Controversial Foodgrain Exports', mimeo; forthcoming in *Explorations in Economic History*.

RAY, P. C. (1901), *Indian Famines: Their Causes and Remedies* (Calcutta: Cherry Press).

RAY, S. C. (1909), *Economic Causes of Famines in India* (Calcutta: Baptist Mission Press).

REDDY, G. P. (1988), 'Drought and Famine: The Story of a Village in a Semi-arid Region of Andhra Pradesh', mimeo.

RYAN, J. G., *et al.* (1984), 'The Determinants of Individual Diets and Nutritional Status in Six Villages of Southern India', Research Bulletin No. 7 (Hyderabad: ICRISAT).

SAMBRANI, S., and PICHHOLIYA, K. (1975), 'An Enquiry into Rural Poverty and Unemployment', mimeo (Ahmedabad: Indian Institute of Management).

SCARFE, W., and SCARFE, A. (1969), *Tiger On a Rein: Report on the Bihar Famine* (Melbourne: Geoffrey Chapman).

SEN, AMARTYA (1981), *Poverty and Famines* (Oxford: Oxford University Press).

——(1982), 'How is India Doing?', *New York Review of Books*, 29.

——(1986), 'India and Africa: What Do We Have to Learn from Each Other?', C. N. Vakil Memorial Lecture delivered at the Eighth World Congress of the International Economic Association, New Delhi, Dec.; pub. in Arrow, K. I. (ed.) (1988), *The Balance between Industry and Agriculture in Economic Development*, i: *Basic Issues* (London: Macmillan).

SEN, M. (1967), 'Famine in Purulia and Bankura', *Modern Review*, 121.

SEN, S. R. (1971), *Growth and Instability in Indian Agriculture* (Calcutta: Firma K. L. Mukhopadhyay).

SHUKLA, R. (1979), *Public Works during Drought and Famines and Its Lessons for an Employment Policy* (Ahmedabad: Sardar Patel Institute of Economic and Social Research).

——(1981), 'Employment Implications of Drought Situations: Issues and Experience', in *Employment, Poverty and Public Policy*, Monograph Series, No. 9 (Ahmedabad: Sardar Patel Institute of Economic and Social Research).

SINGH, S. K. (1975), *The Indian Famine, 1967* (New Delhi: People's Publishing House).

SIVASUBRAMONIAM, S. (1960), 'Estimates of Gross Value of Output of Agriculture for Undivided India, 1900–01 to 1946–47', in Rao, V. K. R. V., *et al.* (eds.), *Papers on National Income and Allied Topics*, vol. i (Bombay).

——(1965), 'National Income of India, 1900–01 to 1946–47', unpublished Ph.D. thesis, Delhi University.

SMITH, B. (1861), *Report on the North Western Provinces Famine of 1860–61* (London: HMSO).

SOMWANSKI, S. A. (1979), 'Impact of Drought on Cooperative Agricultural Credit in Aurangabad District', unpublished Ph.D. thesis, Marathwada University.

SPITZ, P. (1983), 'Food Systems and Society in India: A Draft Interim Report', mimeo (Geneva: UNRISD).

SRINIVASAN, T. N., and BARDHAN, P. K. (eds.) (1974), *Poverty and Income Distribution in India* (Calcutta: Statistical Publishing Society).

SRIVASTAVA, H. S. (1966), 'The Indian Famine 1876–79', *Journal of Indian History*, 44.
——(1968), *History of Indian Famines and Development of Famine Policy 1858–1918* (Agra: Sri Ram Mehra and Co.).
STOKES, E. (1959), *English Utilitarians and India* (Oxford: Oxford University Press).
SUBRAMANIAM, V. (1975), *Parched Earth: The Maharashtra Drought 1970–73* (Bombay: Orient Longman).
SURYANARAYANA, M. H., and IYENGAR, N. S. (1986), 'On the Reliability of NSS Data', *Economic and Political Weekly*, 21.
SVEDBERG, PETER (1987), 'Undernutrition in Sub-Saharan Africa', mimeo (Helsinki: WIDER).
SWAMINATHAN, M. C., *et al.* (1967), 'Food and Nutrition Situation in Drought-Affected Areas of Andhra Pradesh', *Indian Journal of Medical Research*, 55.
——*et al.* (1969), 'Food and Nutrition Situation in the Drought-Affected Areas of Bihar', *Journal of Nutrition and Dietetics*, 6.
TORRY, WILLIAM (1984), 'Social Science Research on Famine: A Critical Evaluation', *Human Ecology*, 12.
——(1986a), 'Drought and the Government–Village Emergency Food Distribution System in India', *Human Organization*, 45.
——(1986b), 'Morality and Harm: Hindu Peasant Adjustments to Famines', *Social Science Information*, 25.
VAIDYANATHAN, A. (1986), 'On the Validity of NSS Consumption Data', *Economic and Political Weekly*, 21.
——(1987), 'Poverty and Economy: The Regional Dimension', paper presented at a Workshop on Poverty in India held at Queen Elizabeth House, Oxford, Oct.
VERGHESE, G. (1967), *Beyond the Famine* (New Delhi: Bihar Relief Committee).
VINCENT, L. (1981), *Dry Spells, Drought Risk and Agricultural Production in Maharashtra State*, Monographs in Development Studies No. 9 (University of East Anglia).
VISARIA, L., and VISARIA, P. (1982), 'Population (1757–1947)', in Kumar (1982).
VISARIA, P. (1978), 'Size of Land Holding, Living Standards and Employment in Rural Western India, 1972–73', Working Paper No. 3 (Joint ESCAP-IBRD Project on the Evaluation of Asian Data on Income Distribution).
WALKER, T. S., SINGH, R. P., and ASOKAN, M. (1986), 'Risk Benefits, Crop Insurance, and Dryland Agriculture', *Economic and Political Weekly*, 21.
WALLACE, R. (1900), *Lecture on Famine in India* (Edinburgh: Oliver & Boyd).
World Bank (1984), 'Situation and Prospects of the Indian Economy: A Medium Term Perspective, vol. iii: Statistical Appendix', Report No. 4962-IN (India Division, World Bank).
——(1986), *Poverty and Hunger: Issues and Options For Food Security in Developing Countries* (Washington, DC: World Bank).
WRIGHT, A. (1968), 'Note on the Bihar Drought', *Journal of the Bombay Natural History Society*, 65.

4

An Independent Press and Anti-hunger Strategies: The Indian Experience

N. Ram

4.1. The problem from a media standpoint and some wider issues

The idea that information, and specifically the news media, can play a substantive and even a crucial role in shaping public policy for combating hunger is an appealing one in intellectual and socio-political terms. This discussion focuses on the role that a relatively independent press plays with respect to the phenomenon of hunger and distress resulting from a crisis (drought, other kinds of situations leading to 'food riots' or related mass-scale disturbances in society, and, where the situation is allowed to get out of hand, famine) and also regular, chronic hunger and subhuman poverty. In doing this, it calls attention to the need for a wider framework for the analysis of such media-related issues and suggests some reference points for such a framework.

The discovery that timely and relevant information on such vital matters makes a substantive difference to the way public opinion is shaped and official policy is made to respond is somewhat flattering to the self-image of professional journalism. In a sense, it begs a much larger question. It depends, obviously, on the kind of independent, or relatively independent, role that newspapers are allowed to play in society; and this in turn depends, equally obviously, on the political system and practice that prevail in the country in question.[1]

Journalism in the Third World—presumably the arena of mass hunger and

I am grateful to several people for contributing research assistance, notes, raw material, ideas, and encouragement for this essay: in particular, to Elizabeth Alexander, V. K. Ramachandran, and colleagues at the *Hindu* for either active research assistance or specific references; to the editorial departments of the *Statesman* and the *Times of India* for print-outs from old microfilms; to Lal Jayawardena for talking me into this venture; to Amartya Sen for providing ideas for the framework and for suggesting, 'have fun with it'; and to Steve Marglin for his critical evaluation as discussant when these ideas were presented in somewhat longer form at the WIDER conference on Food Strategies.

[1] Some media and communication specialists such as Hamelink (1983) have called attention to what they consider 'a constantly occurring distortion' in various discussions of the new world information order—the identification of information and mass media with news and press, the strong emphasis on the press, the news, and journalists 'as if they are the key actors in international communication'. In their view, this approach leaves the crucial questions concerning control over economic, technological, and marketing structures in international communication untouched. While legitimately attempting to correct the balance, such analyses probably undervalue the actual role independent newspapers and journalists play in a developing country, especially in the political arena. In any case, the role being analysed in this essay is not in the field of international communication; it is essentially in the arena of national politics and internal policy making.

battles over access to food that we are most concerned with—forms very much of a mixed bag. Third World journalism comes in such a pluralism of shapes and colours, historical experiences, socio-cultural, educational, infrastructural, and professional backgrounds as well as ideological and political persuasions that it becomes virtually impossible to distinguish its recent history, its practice, and its future as a meaningful category of experience in the manner this can be done for journalism as a professional field in America or Europe.[2]

At a rather obvious level, the character of the press, and therefore its role, bear the stamp of diverse, uneven environments. Third World journalists live as part of societies and cultures that, on the world map, present distinctive patterns. The histories they go back to, or take inspiration from, do not follow a uniform pattern, for among other things the civilizations they are part of extend from mankind's most ancient to the relatively recent, and their modern historical development involves significant divergences. They live in societies with quite different orders of per capita income, quality of life indices, human resource development, and institutional and infrastructural endowments. They live under systems which differ sharply in their basic structural features —in a handful of instances socialist, in the overwhelming majority of cases capitalist, in exceptional cases perhaps in some state of transition from one to the other, and only in a minority of situations (despite the encouraging progress registered recently in Latin America and also, to an extent, in Asia following the Philippine developments) providing their people with a measure of real democracy in the sense of a minimum 'bundle' of socio-economic, political, cultural, and intellectual rights being available to different sections of the people. Given these diversities, what can we say about the roles they play, and have played, in the past?

Generalizations can and must be attempted on the role of news media in overall developmental activity in the developing countries as a whole, necessarily in the context of the political, economic, and technological structures that increasingly shape this sensitive role in a situation of markedly unequal or unbalanced media resource development. But is is clear that such an exercise would need to wait for research on a wider and more systematic basis, if we are to go beyond impressions and, at best, tentative, fragmented analysis. In this essay, we advisedly restrict our discussion of the role of information and the press more or less to the Indian case. This experience seems to have both the breadth and depth of field to make possible a substantive consideration of the qualitative issues relating to anti-hunger strategies in a wider context. We begin with a brief reference to the contrasting experience of Africa where, in the main, the kind of role played by India's independent and pluralistic press in

---

[2] The experience of participating in the first media conference of the non-aligned (NAMEDIA) in the capacity of co-chairman of the conference's 'commission on imbalances—retrospect and prospect' brought this point about the extreme variability of Third World press situations home to this journalist.

relation to mass hunger and distress has seemed, if not absent, very weakly developed.

The case of the African famine, 1984–1985

The most important recent experience that provides a set of reference points for our broader discussion is that of the Ethiopian and African famine of 1984–5—specifically, the way it became an international media event and the results of that transformation. The effects of television coverage, in late-1984, of a full-blown crisis and what it actually meant for tens of thousands of Ethiopians are now fairly well known.

Activists of voluntary relief agencies, such as the Save the Children Fund and Oxfam, and a small number of sensitive reporters (and analysts of such organizations as the London-based Relief and Development Institute and, at a more substantive level, the World Bank group), were quite aware of the deepening of the crisis in Ethiopia and in the Sahel countries well before the African famine became the international media event of 1984–5. *South* magazine, based and published in London and run with an intelligently sustained sensitivity to Third World quality of life, development, and socio-political problems, had indeed featured on its cover 'Hunger: Who's to Blame?' (March 1984) and declared, in a factual analysis, Africa to be 'a continent at risk'. But since at this stage the impact of the specialist information network, and the media coverage, was not noticeable, such reporting, analyses, and warnings appear, upon media and scholarly resurrection today, marginal additions to what cynics might consider a we-told-you-so brand of development literature.

In his study of the challenge of hunger in Ethiopia, Hancock (1985), former East Africa correspondent of *The Economist*, sees the transmuting role of the October 1984 television coverage thus:

Reports of what was happening in Ethiopia made television news several times during the first nine months of 1984, but public reaction was small and editors gave the story little play. On 23 October, however, a seven-minute film by Visnews cameraman Mohamed Amin, with commentary by reporter Michael Buerk, was shown throughout the day on BBC news bulletins, and was subsequently picked up and networked around the world. This film, shot on location in the towns of Makalle and Korem in northern Ethiopia, portrayed a horrific human disaster on a scale that readily summoned up images of Hiroshima and Nagasaki, a disaster of hunger and suffering so great that it seemed to call into question the entire international system of aid, cooperation and control by which mankind governs its affairs in the late twentieth century . . . To this supplication . . . the international community has now responded by constructing a tremendous juggernaut of emergency aid and setting it rolling in the direction of Ethiopia.[3]

As Hancock relates it,[4] one of the harrowing elements of the prime time story told by the Amin visuals lay in the fact that at Makalle 150 starving people

[3] Hancock (1985: 7–8).   [4] Hancock (1985: 8–9).

were grouped 'for no special reason' in 'a patch of ground, like a sheep-pen, surrounded by a low stone wall about four feet high' while 'outside the wall there were about 10,000 other people, just as starved, just as near to death, who were not going to get fed that day, or the next day, or maybe were not going to get fed at all because there was almost no food in Makalle at that time'. Amin was particularly disturbed by the attitude of the people beyond the wall who 'just stood there and watched what was happening without any kind of greed and resentment. I think it was this calmness, this passivity, that got to me because I knew that if I had been in their position . . . I would have done anything, rioted, killed, to get the food I needed.' In Korem, the situation was a good deal worse:

about 60,000 starving people . . . camped in an open field outside the town. There was almost no food, and no real shelter, and the nights up there are cold, with temperatures falling to around zero . . . There was this tremendous mass of people, groaning and weeping, scattered across the ground in the dawn mist. I don't really know how to describe it but the thing that came to my mind at the time was that it was as if a hundred jumbo jets had crashed and spilled out the bodies of their passengers amongst the wreckage, the dead and the living mixed together as you couldn't tell one from the other. It still shatters me when I think back on what I saw. During the night, while I had slept, people had been slowly and steadily dying of exposure, and they were in this field—a mother cradling a dead child, a brother holding tight to the body of his dead sister, a husband and wife, dressed in rags, dead together on the ground. I went and filmed in the mortuary . . .

Such sensitive, professionally high-calibre reporting of the catastrophe in Ethiopia, and the feelings of solidarity brought into it, do help us to empathize with the powerful impact that hundreds of thousands of television viewers in Western countries felt when they watched the Amin and subsequent visuals or were exposed to more detailed press coverage. Information available from the BBC shows that the Buerk–Amin footage from northern Ethiopia was shown by 425 of the world's broadcasting organizations 'with a potential audience of 470 million people'.[5] We know that this television coverage made such a difference to public opinion in Western countries as to call for a very important official and voluntary life-saving response.

An important point to note is that journalism did not initiate either the insights or the campaign that brought about such positive results in terms of relief as well as understanding of the issues involved. In the words of Gill (1986), a participant journalist:

When Ethiopia's famine hit the headlines, it did so because of the relationship between private relief agencies and the television companies . . . In news coverage in October (1985) and beyond, the relief agencies provided most of the reference points—up-to-date information, places to visit, interviews in the field and at home, and a means of

---

[5] Gill (1986: 91).

response for concerned viewers. Our own *TV Eye* film 'Bitter Harvest' . . . had its origins in Oxfam's decision to purchase large quantities of grain for Ethiopia.[6]

The experience of organizing Live Aid, Sports Aid, and various other world-wide or nation-wide humanitarian projects, which have probably made a significant difference to the number of deaths in the African famine, is instructive; the whole experience provides valuable guidance for both analysis and practice.

In her often insightful essay on photography, Sontag (1978) takes on this question of impact and some determinant or shaping factors. For example: 'A photograph that brings news of some unsuspected zone of misery cannot make a dent in public opinion unless there is an appropriate context of feeling and attitude . . . Photographs cannot create a moral position, but they can reinforce one—and can help build a nascent one.'[7] She makes the point that there must be, ideologically speaking, 'space' for the impact to be made and also 'the existence of a relevant political consciousness' so that a moral impact is possible.[8]

An objection can be raised to Sontag's approach to the question of photographic or media impact, which appears to undervalue the initiative or trigger that the photo/media coverage can provide by way of influencing public opinion, or the public mood, in a particular direction. Nevertheless, the analysis helps us steer clear of exaggerated notions of the impact of media coverage, by itself, on the development of mass-scale phenomena or catastrophes such as famine or threatened famine. Alert, sensitive media coverage, if it is to be effective, must form part of an ideological and political context of attitude, feeling, and critical democratic values and practice. The role of the media within such a context in developing countries is clearly an under-researched area, certainly in the case of Africa. But we do know, from the empirical observation of those reasonably familiar with the situation in several African countries hit or threatened by famine, that neither the officially controlled mass media nor newspapers, which are usually controlled and manipulated by the state or otherwise severely restricted,[9] seem to perform the

---

[6] Gill (1986: 93).   [7] Sontag (1978: 17).   [8] Sontag (1979: 18–19).

[9] The case of Nigeria seemed to constitute a vigorous exception until the 1983 coup affected independent journalism. There are various sporadic discussions of the failure of the African press to perform a role considered vital to democratic practice. According to a report done for the Independent Commission on International Humanitarian Issues (1985), the Ethiopian government instituted in the wake of the 1972–4 famine 'the most complete early warning system of its kind in Africa', but its recurrent annual warnings lacked credibility with the aid donors. On the other hand: 'It is suggested that the reason there has not been a major famine in India since 1943 is not just because of the improved food production, but also because it has a free press functioning in a democratic framework. If an area within the country starts to slip towards crisis, victims can make their voice heard. Newspapers kick up a fuss, thus stirring the concern of the central authorities. Hence timely action. In Africa, regrettably, there is rarely the same link between countryside and urban politicians. In general, there is a lack of representative structures which allow rural voices to be heard. During the present famine, many of those in other continents who have seen starving people on television have been closer than many in Africa to what is happening'

role that the Indian press has played in relation to famine, drought, or other types of 'food crisis' over an extended historical period.

Towards analysis   The markedly dissimilar situations might be worth exploring more systematically. In some readings, the existence and flourishing of an independent, critical, watchdog press is usually regarded as a sensitive indicator of the level of civil society attained. Realization of this, in a context of being able to influence public policies in relation to issues such as mass hunger and poverty, gives the 'credible-informational' function a new, substantive content. Under certain circumstances, this makes for an 'adversarial', perhaps even a 'destabilizing',[10] role in the sense that the press tilts effectively against what begins, as a result of the communication impact or influence, to be popularly and politically perceived as unjust or otherwise unacceptable government policy. It is only in the latter sense that an independent press, by exposing facts on the ground relentlessly and by providing some kind of

---

(p. 43). As for the responsibility of the Ethiopian government, it 'had certainly been sounding the alarm internationally for over a year before a television team suddenly brought the crisis alive and galvanised international aid in October 1984. But the government had not come clean with its own people about the famine' (p. 43). In a commentary, 'Holding Back the Facts of Famine', *South* magazine (Dec. 1984) noted that while the government of Col. Mengistu Haile Mariam had 'not adopted a callous attitude to the famine', it had nevertheless 'up to a few months ago' been reluctant to 'reveal the true extent of the crisis'. For example, the head of state in a six-hour speech marking the tenth anniversary of the Ethiopian revolution in Sept. 1984 did not make a single reference to the catastrophe which was even then claiming the lives of tens of thousands of his people. Gill (1986), who is very critical of the attitude of Western governments towards the Ethiopian famine of 1984–5, refers to the phenomenon of official attention in mid-1984 being 'simply directed away from the likelihood of severe famine to the political priority in hand, the establishment of the new party and the anniversary celebrations' (p. 10). He refers to the fact that the government-run *Ethiopian Herald* did not focus on the famine raging in Ethiopia (pp. 4–15) and that while a new television transmitter costing some half a million pounds was opened in Makelle, the capital of Tigre (which along with Korem provided some of the most searing images of mass starvation on Western television screens in the autumn of 1984), the tasks on the political, economic, and social front designated officially for the expanded media 'did not include coverage of the famine' (p. 11).

[10] Some reservations have been expressed to this journalist about the use of the term 'destabilizing' in this context, and indeed Amartya Sen, in a written comment, suggested that 'the purpose of press activism may be to reform the government rather than to destabilise it even when it is acting in an "adversarial" role. In fact I like your term "adversarial" much better, as being less open to misinterpretation.' The point is persuasive; nevertheless, while characterizing the second function as 'adversarial' in the main, the question is kept open about the precise impact by the use of the term 'destabilizing' in a carefully qualified context. This usage carries none of the loaded, emotional connotations it has in the contemporary political vocabulary of, say, South Asia. Its essential content is not caught by the evocative phrase so familiar to the history of American journalism, 'muckraking'. But the term certainly covers the socio-political situation where what is legitimate and quite the professional-ethical thing to do for the press might naturally appear 'motivated destabilization' to an intolerant government. The accusation by the Rajiv Gandhi administration and the ruling Congress (I) party that the media disclosures relating to the Fairfax and defence deal controversies were part of a motivated plot to 'destabilize' the Indian government, the Indian Republic, and national security provide interesting confirmation of the typical tendencies of governments in trouble, or under pressure, to target the independent press. In Apr. 1987, when this note was written, it was a still developing story in India.

hunger-related discourse with policy implications, can prevent a government from pursuing disastrous policies and thus, in concert with other democratic institutions, can 'guarantee . . . the avoidance of acute starvation and famine'.[11] Thus in a deeper sense, the 'adversarial' or 'destabilizing' role makes for the relative stabilization of crisis-averting policies if the democratic rules of the game work reasonably. So far as a government is concerned, the second role might help to 'reform' its practice or, perhaps, to 'destabilize' it—this depends very much on the nature of the government, its attitude to democratic opposition and criticism, and the character of the policies it pursues.

In fact, it might be useful to make an analytical distinction between the 'credible-informational' and 'destabilizing' functions of an independent press in a developing country context, without attempting in any way to contrapose the functions. The first appears to be a prerequisite for the second; but without the latter, which on account of the content might imply some kind of 'adversarial' role in relation to government under typical circumstances, the former is not likely to thrive and develop, especially if it insists on living off historical memories, or on formalisms that might be sustained even in a substantively non-independent context for the press (as in Sri Lanka today). On the other hand, frequently heard complaints about the 'negative' role of the press from those in authority in countries such as India (where the system makes what must be recognized, by developing country standards, as an impressive allowance for an independent watchdog press) usually mean that the surface-level 'credible-informational' function and the more substantive 'adversarial' or 'destabilizing' political-developmental function in respect of unjust or wrong-headed or inadequate official policies relating to the vital affairs of society are being performed rather effectively.

Historically, of course, the 'credible-informational' function has something to do with a rule of law tradition which a particular colonialism, for all its barbarities and savage effects, was able to transplant to a particular country (in contrast to another colonialism in another country), but this function is also capable, it must be assumed, of being 'learned' or acquired consciously in a post-colonial context. Yet the more substantive and more progressive 'adversarial' role that a press may be able to play with respect to mass entitlements and their defence and expansion (and, at least at the conscious level, this might have nothing to do with the fight to overthrow one system and to replace it by another) needs much stronger nourishment in terms of ideological and political experience, context, institutions, and perceptions—such as those associated with a 'nationalist' or liberation movement, a struggle to consolidate and expand the content of independence, a major campaign for the people's socio-economic and political rights, a movement to overthrow authoritarianism in a post-colonial context, and so on. But lest this should sound too

---

[11] Sen (1985a: 77).

romantic a notion of journalism, we hasten to add that there appears to be a certain autonomy to the development of the profession in the sense of availability of indigenous media and intellectual resources, a stabilized practice with its own critical professional values and yardsticks, technological capabilities, advertising support to secure a measure of independence from the government, sophistication in production values, and so on. These might be present in one developing country and not in another, and this factor could make a vital difference to the role of the press.

The Indian press in relation to famine

At a conscious institutional and theoretical level, the idea that the independent press, and perhaps even professionally conscientious sections of the officially controlled electronic media, the journalism of 'sight and sound', can play a substantive role in anti-hunger strategies has come into its own in India only recently. There has been, of course, a kind of understanding of what this role means, and this is derived from long empirical experience. The Indian press—whose institutional memory goes back well over a century in the sense that major newspapers have files and archives going back to the 1860s and 1870s and also in the sense that there are to be encountered here and there inveterate long-term readers and newspaper veterans who can recall from their personal experience the way the press covered India's last famine, the Bengal famine of 1943—has a long-standing and fairly solid record in relation to situations where large-scale starvation and famine threatened. Over time, it has tended to bring out the facts in the field with elements of vivid descriptive and human interest detail; and to expose the failure of government authorities to recognize the problem, its causes and early symptoms, and to respond quickly and adequately in terms of crisis prevention, management, and relief.

By sensitizing and influencing public and political opinion in this way and also through editorial campaigns—especially in the strongholds of its influence or circulation, for example Calcutta and eastern India for the *Statesman*—the Indian press has tended to force public policy over time to face the challenge of crises which threaten to develop into famines. Developing in some sort of pre-historical or early form in the 1870s and gathering force and substance towards the end of the last century, this role became quite prominent during the first two decades of the twentieth century, as our case-study of the part played by an independent nationalist newspaper of record during the widespread 1918 'food riots' and related disturbances in the Madras Province makes clear.

But although the empirical practice and the institutional memory go back quite a long way, the substantive importance of the role played by newspapers in making it virtually impossible for governments and the political system to pursue obscurantist or otherwise damaging policies which might cause or usher in famine (or a mass-level food crisis) has hardly figured in media discussions in India.

It required the economist Amartya Sen to spotlight this role—so reassuring and so flattering to the self-image of Indian journalism—and even assign it central importance in an analysis of food crises and threatened famine. In his well-publicized 1982 Coromandel Lecture in New Delhi, Sen brought to national intellectual attention this somewhat surprising finding on the importance of the Indian press in the arena of mass access to food. At that time it might have appeared somewhat impressionistic, raised in a context of contrasting the situations of India and China, and substantiated chiefly in relation to the Bengal famine of 1943 and the role of the *Statesman*.[12] The strength of—as well as the apparent problem with—the formulation was that it seemed based on a clear-cut or unambiguous dichotomy between the Chinese and Indian situations, to which objection has indeed been raised. But the logic of the argument, and the fact that the Indian press found its way into a major economic theory of poverty and famine and into international discussions of it,[13] was persuasive.

The idea that independent newspapers in contrast to a controlled or manipulated press—along with genuine opposition parties—can, in a pluralistic political system, prevent a government from failing to intervene promptly in a crisis to avert famine is one that Indian journalists have warmed to, especially in a context where they have frequently heard homilies and lectures from those in authority to the effect that their practice was not 'positive', 'relevant', or 'development-orientated'.[14] The influence of the finding (and of a theoretical perspective which has influenced international policy thinking on access to food issues) on the self-awareness and practice of Indian journalism is difficult to measure, even as the impact made by the press on public opinion, official policy, and, in general, anti-hunger strategies is not at all easy to measure. But that the argument has had an influence on the profession and its internal perceptions and stances need not be doubted.

Indeed Sen's qualified tribute to the role of the Indian press seems to have struck such sympathetic or responsive chords in the better-informed sections of Indian journalism that there have been attempts to return the compliment in a rather obvious way. One is impressed by the variety and contexts of recent reports and articles (some by journalists, others by academics and pseudo-

---

[12] The contrast with China was presented in Sen (1982); and the observation on the positive role of the *Statesman* had appeared in Sen (1981: 195).

[13] See e.g. Independent Commission on International Humanitarian Issues (1985), esp. p. 43.

[14] This criticism was recorded on numerous occasions in the 1970s and 1980s by Prime Minister Indira Gandhi. After the highly damaging impact of Emergency policies on democratic institutions in India had become clear, and after the results of the very negative experience of censorship during 1975–6 which dissolved some 'liberal' illusions had been undone, the Indian press (in an institutional sense) increasingly saw the central government in an adversarial role, with Prime Minister Indira Gandhi consciously introducing strains and an element of stridency into press–government relations. With Prime Minister Rajiv Gandhi, the experience was mixed, although a tendency to blow hot and cold has been recorded (in press columns) in his case also.

academics) in Indian newspapers which make reference to, or imply, the idea of 'entitlements' or their collapse, sometimes in ways that would surprise the author. Popularization of an analytical and theoretical concept can be expected, after all, to proceed in this way—especially if we take into account the inherent tendencies of journalism which appears (from the analytical literature that derives from countries where it is practised seriously as a profession) as a state of incessant oscillation or interchange between the banal and the brilliant with some worthwhile attempts to find a middle ground.[15]

4.2. An Indian case-study

The Indian press is widely regarded as the most pluralistic, the least inhibited, and the most assertive or independent in all the Third World.[16] In terms of the number of newspapers published in a country, it ranks fourth in the world. The journalistic and production values of its most advanced contingents are rated among the better anywhere, even if the severe space constraint, reflecting major problems of government policy-dictated access to reasonably priced physical inputs—above all, newsprint—militates against editorial development and the comprehensiveness or relative completeness of coverage that might, otherwise, be possible. The fading out of the newspaper of record tradition in Indian journalism, and the increasingly visible incompleteness of news reporting and editorial featuring, are weaknesses that reflect the situation on the ground. One aspect of the pluralism is the considerable unevenness in professional and production quality among Indian newspapers and periodicals. And despite the relative sophistication and development of independent professional journalism and the substantial circulations and influence built up by major newspapers, including, more recently, several Indian language newspapers,[17] coverage of the population is not impressive even after making

[15] This is not meant to be as light-hearted a generalization as it might sound. Serious practitioners of journalism in various parts of the world recognize the problem in an intellectual sense and see several inherent weaknesses in the profession. Futile attempts in India and elsewhere to evolve or impose 'codes of conduct' on journalism reflect the dilemma. Given journalism's inherent tendency towards flashiness and making an impact, the pursuit of 'brilliance' cannot legitimately be blocked; the banal must, of course, be combated; but the 'middle ground' is probably the best bet for the profession in so far as it aspires to better intellectual (as distinct from entertainment world) standards.

[16] See e.g. the cover feature on 'The Indian Press' in the Far Eastern Economic Review, 18 July 1985. The review begins by noting: 'Among the world's largest and oldest, though not necessarily the best, the Indian press remains unmatched in the Third World . . . Indian publications are the most free of all their counterparts (in the developing world) . . .' This feature also takes note of the tensions between the press and government, various objective constraints such as 'the low diffusion rate in the rural areas', and the internal weaknesses of Indian journalism including, allegedly, 'the conformist ethos of the daily press'.

[17] Notable examples of rapid growth, over the last decade, of Indian language journalism would be two or three Malayalam daily newspapers, notably Malayala Manorama; some Bengali newspapers, notably Ananda Bazar Patrika; some Hindi newspapers; and perhaps most spectacularly Eenadu, a recently started Telugu newspaper.

allowance for the low literacy level. On the basis of officially collected circulation figures it has been estimated that the current dailies-to-people ratio in India is around 1:40, which compares unfavourably with the relevant statistics for a number of other developing countries, for example Malaysia and Sri Lanka. There are other constraints and handicaps, including the fact that remuneration and rewards in journalism—reflecting newspaper economics but also conservative management policies—are such that they do not make it easy for newspapers to compete for the best available educated or trained skills and talent, especially intellectual resources, in an increasingly diversified and sophisticated national recruitment pool.[18]

Overall, it appears that since the long-established tradition of free-wheeling pluralism and the independence of the Indian press which so impresses outsiders can be taken for granted (and this is in notable contrast to the regressive monotony and the narrowly construed propagandistic tone of state-owned and state-regimented television and radio, which are equally taken for granted) in the Indian democratic and political context, complaints against adversarial fiscal and import control policies of the government,[19] and self-criticism and implied criticism of others (usually competitors), seem to dominate the internal debate on the state of the Indian press.[20] Taken outside the very specific context in which the grievances and the self-criticism are expressed, the response would appear exaggerated, even misleading. In other words, the constraints, handicaps, and self-limiting factors (which can be attributed to slow-changing newspaper management as well as editorial development policies) should not make us lose sight of the fact that, in qualitative and historical terms, the practice of independent journalism in India is very nearly unique in the developing world.

[18] There is no systematic information available on recruitment policies and practices in newspapers relating either to journalists or to the non-journalistic workforce. A general editorial complaint pertains to the quality of the fresh input into journalism even if, in an objective evaluation, it might not be possible to substantiate a 'decline in standards' thesis. Many journalists would appear to be 'overqualified' in formal educational terms; and the induction of an increasing number of science and technology graduates into the profession points in a healthy direction in that it indicates an internal perception that journalism requires more rigorously trained skills (in the streaming out process in Indian higher education, students in science, technology, and professional fields are, as a group, rated higher than their counterparts in the 'arts', the humanities, and the social sciences). With respect to technical production departments such as photocomposition, offset printing, facsimile, and so on, the Indian newspaper industry has the advantage of being able to draw upon a fairly large pool of highly qualified skills, especially electronics engineers and technicians. However, the technological practices vary considerably even among the big newspapers and the overall situation with respect to the adoption of modern newspaper technology in India is extremely uneven.

[19] These are presented in numerous memoranda and representations by the Indian Newspaper Society (INS) to the central government over the past five years.

[20] At the media conference of the non-aligned (NAMEDIA) in 1983, several participants from outside South Asia appeared frequently taken by surprise by the sharp divergences in the views expressed by Indian participants on various media issues that came up in the discussions in the commissions into which the conference divided.

An attempt to evaluate and analyse the role of the independent Indian press in anti-hunger strategies must take into careful, balanced account the considerable historical and current strengths of this press, and also the constraints on its influence and 'powers', *vis-à-vis* public opinion and the making of official policy. But if, in balance, it is used analytically as a model against which to compare or evaluate other press traditions or experiences in the Third World, the role needs to be broken down in terms of the quality of response to essentially different types of situations of hunger on a mass scale.

One entry point into such an exercise would be offered by the kind of 'dichotomy' highlighted by the Sen (1982) analysis of the essential experiences of India and China. On the one hand,

India's record in eliminating endemic, non-acute hunger is quite bad and contrasts very unfavourably with the record of some other countries such as Sri Lanka and China . . . the astonishing tolerance of persistent hunger in India is greatly helped by our inclination to take a low-key approach to these deadly conflicts. It is indeed amazing that in a country with as much politicisation as India has, the subject of persistent hunger of a third of the rural population can be such a tame issue . . . non-acute, regular starvation . . . does not attract much attention in newspapers. These standard events in India seem to be not newsworthy . . .

On the other hand,

there is . . . one respect in which India has really turned a page on the food front. This refers not to the much publicised self-sufficiency of India in food, since the so-called self-sufficiency co-exists with—indeed survives on—keeping a large class of people in a position of having little entitlement to food in the market. The real achievement relates to the elimination of sudden large-scale starvation and famines. Given the . . . political system in India, including the ability of newspapers and opposition parties to pester the central and state governments, it is essential to avoid famines for any government keen on staying in power, and famines . . . are very easy to prevent if the government acts intelligently and in time.

India, the analysis goes on,

has not had a famine since independence, and given the nature of Indian politics and society, it is not likely that India can have a famine even in years of a great food problem . . . newspapers play an important part in this, in making the facts known and forcing the challenge to be faced. So does the pressure of opposition parties. In the absence of these pressures and free newspapers, famines can develop even in countries that normally perform much better than India.

Some elements in the analysis of the Chinese experience of 1959–61, and of the factors behind the development of the famine, have been questioned and indeed K. N. Raj has challenged the analysis on the ground that while 'I have no disagreement with Prof. Sen on the role that democratic institutions can play in checking tyranny and injustice in all forms . . . the precise relation of that set of issues to this specific question of political responsibility for the famine that took place in China is not so obvious as he seems to assume'.[21]

The academic controversy on this issue has been useful in that, among other things, it has posed rather sharply the problem of measuring the influence of the press and other democratic institutions on government policy and on the mass-scale socio-economic realities it is supposed to respond to. For the Indian press in a situation of weak coverage, historically and currently, of the population (as expressed by readership rates) but presumed strong influence on public policy, the problem of measurement of influence is particularly difficult. We shall not attempt to resolve this problem in terms of cause-and-effect relationships, but shall confine the present exercise to looking at the type of response and the quality of coverage by the independent press of issues relating to hunger, or problems of access to food, which affect very large numbers of people.

The historical experience: origins and continuities

The historical origins of an independent, critical, 'watchdog' role for the Indian press in relation to a sudden outbreak of hunger on a mass scale or to other kinds of 'food crisis' in society have not been precisely researched, even if the press has been tapped extensively in some fields of historical research as 'source'. Here the 'little traditions' in different parts of the country would be of obvious interest in so far as they might provide insights into a preparatory or 'pre-historical' phase. But in a generalized, institutional sense—involving in the main continuities, but also a few discontinuities—this role would appear to have taken shape in the late nineteenth century during a period of acceleration of the freedom movement in India.

While nascent nationalist newspapers saw themselves as performing this role consciously in relation to the rights and entitlements of the Indian people and in the face of what was perceived in the initial stages as benevolently inadequate, and increasingly as wrong-headed, callous, and unjust, official policies, it must not be assumed that the Anglo-Indian newspapers which generally aligned themselves with the Raj and its policies against the freedom struggle (and against the press associated with it) did not play such a role. Indeed for a later period, the way in which the *Statesman*, a British-owned newspaper, 'distinguished itself in its extensive reporting of the [1943 Bengal] famine and its crusading editorials'[22] throws light on a complex role for the Indian press with its 'credible-informational' and 'adversarial' or 'destabiliz-ing' traditions. The high quality, and authoritativeness,[23] of the role is

---

[21] K. N. Raj, letter to the editor, published in the *Hindu* of 7 Feb. 1983, under the heading 'China and Food Issues'.   [22] Sen (1981: Appendix D, p. 195).

[23] P. C. Mahalanobis, it is known, played a role in informing and influencing the line of the *Statesman* and in providing the newspaper with statistical information relating to famine deaths. This input from an academic who was engaged in empirical research on the famine doubtless provided authority and stature to the editorial assessment. I am grateful to a veteran in the profession, Nikhil Chakravartty, editor of *Mainstream*, for this information.

reflected in the editorials of 14 and 16 October 1943 titled 'Seen from a Distance' and 'The Death-Toll' respectively. It does suggest a certain auto-nomy for the role of journalism as a professional activity in the pre-independence period, which cannot simply be explained in terms of a political distinction between a nationalist press and a with-the-Raj or loyalist press. This factor is clearly a historical and institutional advantage for the development of independent Indian journalism.

There is a paucity of information on the precise role of newspapers in covering the terrible famines of the late nineteenth century and our sampling of the columns of *The Hindu* (founded in 1878) during the 1897–8 famine in different parts of the country, including the south, appears to suggest a formative, inchoate role for the independent press at this stage. Nevertheless, the spread and intensity of the 1897–8 famine—in which it reported that an estimated 150,000 people perished in the Central Provinces alone—was the topic of considerable editorial comment in the nationalist newspaper.

Reflecting the early stirrings of 'economic nationalism', some of the editor-ials relate the famine (in extremely general terms) to the wider consequences of British rule: '. . . but for the extreme costliness of British rule and the drain of millions of Indian money every year as the price of the good government that the country enjoys, India would be far more prosperous than she is, and there would be no such thing as famine' (*The Hindu*, 15 March 1897, 'Indian Famine and the British Exchequer'). Unlike famines which periodically occurred in the past, those of 'modern times'—which were spread over a wide area and affected millions of people—are attributed in large measure to the 'faults and errors of British rule'.

Within this broad framework, the editorials make a critical assessment of official attitudes, the 'niggardly outpourings' of British charity towards the Famine Fund, and the various difficulties relating to, and the tardy progress of, famine relief operations (points made in two editorials of 25 February and 1 March 1897, titled 'Governor and the Famine' and 'The Distribution of Famine Relief' respectively). The editorials express scepticism about the various Commissions appointed only in times of great distress:

When famine on a large scale is found to exist, the Government makes efforts to afford relief to suffering people, partly out of its own resources and partly by begging from other people. The moment the distress passes away the Government is quiet and happy again, and does not concern itself with the condition of the ryot until another similar calamity happens. Of course a Commission is now and then appointed; but the recommendations, so far as they interfere with the convenience of officials, are never carried out. ('The Starving Ryot', *The Hindu*, 24 March 1897)

Again to go by a limited sampling, the reporting is not vivid or detailed or sufficiently factual; the 'newspaper of record' function that was so strongly expressed by the same newspaper during another type of 'food crisis' a couple of decades later had not evolved during these famines. But the reports are indicative of a serious, factual approach to independent journalism. The reports in the nationalist newspaper on the 1897–8 famine refer to the proximate causes of the phenomenon, the slow pace of official response to the widespread distress, and various specific problems involved in famine relief works. Illustrative of this type of coverage is the report from South Arcot ('Notes from South Arcot') published in the newspaper on 15 July 1898:

The general outlook in the district is sufficiently gloomy, though the authorities are very slow and still unwilling to recognise the gravity of the situation and move betimes to the rescue of the suffering from the jaws of starvation and death. The price of rice, the simple article of food, has already risen to famine rates, when we see that five measures per rupee have succeeded in keeping many of those in the low strata of society beyond the reach of an adequate quantity of food-supply, nay in not a few instances of any food-supply at all. The supply of other foodgrains is not plentiful in the market. The famishing population is daily on the increase, and swarms of beggars have begun to infest our society.

This type of journalism has an old-fashioned ring to it, in relation to the confident, factually aggressive approach and style of 1918 dealt with subsequently, but it raises the relevant issues and points in a healthy direction. Research into newspaper coverage, in various parts of the country, of the famines of the late nineteenth century should throw more light on this point.

Responding to the 'food riots' and related disturbances in southern India, 1918: a new type of role

A new, far more substantive role is indicated for the independent nationalist press in response to another type of 'food crisis'—not famine or even threatened famine in this case, but the very extensive militant actions, protests, and 'disturbances' that broke out in Madras Province in 1918. The crisis, in fact, was expressed in the 'spate of looting and grain riots' which 'like the influenza, left hardly a town or district of the province untouched'.[24]

In his excellent little study of 'Looting, Grain Riots and Government Policy in South India 1918', Arnold (1979) brings out these features of the situation. The crisis, described as one of the two 'epidemics' of the time, surfaced in 1918 and its signs continued sporadically until the end of 1919. The bulk of the looting and related disturbances—numbering about 120 instances, in Arnold's count—occurred between the middle of May and the end of September 1918. The 'peak of unrest' was the first fortnight of September when 'serious looting [was] reported from fifteen of the twenty-five districts and three days of attacks on grain bazaars and warehouses in Madras city, the provincial capital'.

Arnold's analysis underlines the fact that although the partial failure in 1918 of the south-west monsoon was 'clearly of considerable economic and psycho-

---

[24] Arnold (1979: 111).

logical significance in the spreading of the looting epidemic', this factor does not adequately explain the origin and character of the crisis.

The failure of rains in this or any other part of India did not automatically provoke widespread rioting. The causes lay in a conjunction of factors, economic and social as well as climatic. Looting and rioting were expressions of the bewilderment, panic and anger felt by the poorer classes of the province when faced with abrupt price rises or the sudden disappearance of foodgrains from the bazaars while large quantities of grain were known to be stacked in warehouses or barges and in railway yards ready for export elsewhere . . . the poor of southern Indian reacted much as their counterparts in France, England and Scotland had done . . .

Arnold's study sheds light on the social composition of the looters and those involved in related disturbances, and this in turn provides insights into the basic features of the development of the crisis and also into the character of public policy and the role of an independent press in relation to the challenge. In sum, translating for the purpose of the argument into a conceptual framework that Arnold does not use, there was a widespread and alarming deterioration, if not collapse, of *entitlements* among various sections of the working people, calling for an emergency response from government and public policy. The role of the press in this situation—in making inputs into, although not perhaps shaping, colonial policy—was important. Factual reporting of the incidents of looting surfaced freely, especially in September 1918, in the columns of the nationalist press, notably *The Hindu, New India, Desabhaktan, Andhrapatrika, Swadesamitran,* and the *West Coast Spectator;* even the Anglo-Indian press, especially the *Madras Mail,* came up with accounts and, occasionally, criticism of the official handling of the crisis.

Before we come to our detailed study of the coverage of this crisis by *The Hindu,* let us make the general point that without such extensive reporting of the looting, the grain riots, and the related disturbances in far-flung parts of southern India, the influence of the event on public opinion and the element of pressure on official policy would have been significantly weaker. It is likely that the absence of a diverse and pluralist nationalist press, speaking in a range of narrative and critical editorial voices, would have tended to keep knowledge of the scope, the spread, the causes, and the gravity of the disturbances away from province-wide and nation-wide public awareness; officialdom, which was criticized by the press for attempting to underestimate or cover up the gravity of the situation and was itself engaged in an internal debate which is recorded in detail,[25] would have found it much easier to keep sensitive information on the

[25] This documentation is available in the Tamil Nadu Archives, Madras. For example, GO No. 593, dated 23 Sept. 1918, Miscellaneous Series, Revenue (Special), Confidential, includes correspondence from the Madras City Policy Commissioner's office to the Chief Secretary vacationing in Ooty, and also notes from the office of the Director of Civil Supplies, Madras, and other British bureaucrats. The documentation reveals a considerable variance in the approaches to this crisis.

crisis secret or fragmented in an attempt to manipulate public opinion and shape public policy in a direction which it deemed desirable.

This positive role of the press in relation to burning socio-economic issues in the Madras Province contrasts sharply with the role allowed to the nationalist newspapers around the same time by Sir Michael O'Dwyer in the Punjab. In an editorial published on 29 March 1920 titled 'The Agony of the Punjab', *The Hindu* raised this point bluntly on behalf of the nationalist press:

The 'Punjab manner' has become to the rest of India—bureaucratic India of course —an envious aspiration. If the people in their ignorance did not know what was good for them, heroic remedies must be adopted. The bane of their life is education . . . the kind of education which breeds what Kipling in his graphic way calls the 'beggar-taught' which teaches them ideas above their proper stations . . . when a man is bent on getting things done, getting them done quickly and getting them done regardless of consequences, it may easily be imagined how fierce must be his hatred of the formalities of procedure, how impatient he must be of criticism and how in the end he could have arrived at a hatred of what he must have considered hampering influences, amounting to a positive obsession. That, stripped of excessive verbiage, is his conception of the theory of Government . . . Sir Michael . . . interned hundreds of local men with little or no cause. He gagged the vernacular press, prevented the Nationalist papers edited outside the Punjab from circulating in the province, as for instance *New India*, the *Amrita Bazar Patrika*, the *Independent*; he prohibited the circulation of even pre-censored vernacular papers and brought a stage of things, whereby it became practically impossible for the people of the province to have free interchange of independent views, or a free ventilation of their grievances in the public press; and, having prevented free speech and free writing, he allowed himself to think, and gave outsiders to understand that the people of the Punjab were the happiest under his rule.

In contrast, in the Madras Province around this time, the nationalist newspapers, aside from publishing detailed factual reports of what happened at a particular place on a particular day, were able to sound warnings and draw lessons. For example, *New India* of 10 September 1918 noted in a dispatch (cited by Arnold):

Most of the poor obtain their supplies in the evening and have their only hot meal at night. The disturbances stopped all sales, and many families had to starve on Sunday night. Riots were therefore inevitable on Monday, if some plan were not arranged to supply the daily requirements.

At times, a note somewhat sympathetic to the looters was sounded. The *Madras Times* of 9 September 1918 noted, for example, on the Madras incidents (cited by Arnold):

One feature of the looting which deserves attention is that for the most part there was no attempt to steal goods from the shops looted. The looters seem to have contented themselves with destroying and spoiling goods, their motive presumably to cause loss to the shopkeepers, to deprive them . . . [of] the equivalent of what they regarded as their ill-gotten gains.

Using a number of methods to force the government to recognize, investigate, and do something about the crisis was not the only role the independent
press played during this period. Arnold (1979) detects a surprising tendency in
the press responses and relates this to the attitude of a section of district-level
officialdom. Before 'the climactic riots of September 1918' triggered government repression, many district officials showed 'an unmistakeable sympathy'
for popular complaints against traders' profiteering and, 'if they intervened at
all, it was invariably on the side of the public' to ask traders to sell at more
reasonable prices. Arnold observes that the newspapers, in their editorials,
dispatches from correspondents, and letters from readers, repeatedly came out
against high prices, artificial shortages, and gross profiteering; 'hardly a word
was to be heard or read in the merchants' defence', and until the September
'riots' made the salaried middle classes 'more wary', looting was held to be 'the
inevitable and not unreasonable response of the desperately poor'. Arnold's
unambiguous finding is that 'the press and officialdom helped to focus
discontent against the "avarice" and the "indecent profiteering" of the
merchants'.

The role played by an independent press under such circumstances, especially in a society with a very poor literacy rate, must not, of course, be
exaggerated to make out that this was a determining element.

Arnold's analysis appears to underestimate the influence of the nationalist or
freedom movement in providing a focus to the spontaneous grievances. Indeed
in Arnold's story of popular responses to the 1918 crisis, the ending is less than
inspiring. The government of Madras charged that 'nationalist agitation' had
contributed to the extent of the disturbances and the violent character of the
looting in its latest stages; cracked down in an increasingly repressive way on
the protesters; declined to admit the consequences of its own policies; ridi-
culed, and refused to adopt, 'heroic remedies', choosing instead the line of least
interference in the grain trade; and hardened its law and order posture.
Nevertheless, the role indicated for the press is a highly positive one. And this
includes the function of contributing to the 'destabilization' of the situation by
making a posture of official complacency or stupidity relatively difficult to
maintain—unless, of course, top officialdom adopted 'the Punjab manner' of
Sir Michael.

How precisely did the *The Hindu*, a nationalist newspaper which had taken
on the clear function of a newspaper of extensive record, cover the crisis and
the popular and official responses? Our detailed account is intended not just to
highlight the role of the independent press in a socio-economic crisis but also to
probe how a newspaper of record covers the events. The purpose is to provide
insights into the role and method of actively independent professional journalism which is given scope and which comes alive in response to extraordinary
circumstances.

This section is based on a reading of microfilms of issues of *The Hindu* from
3 September to 25 September 1918, the three-week period during which mass

action against a sudden rise in the prices of rice and other foodgrains, edible oil, chilli, tamarind, cloth, and other essential commodities—the 'food riots' of 1918—was at its peak. Information on the agitation and opinions on the events are available in daily reporting, in editorials, and in letters to the editor of the newspaper. Our account and assessment are based on material from the first two sources, reportage and editorials.

Reportage   By 1918, *The Hindu* was the region's pre-eminent newspaper and it served for the Madras province and the region as a newspaper of record. This role is brought out sharply in the content of the reports that appeared on the food agitation.

As high prices and unrest spread, reports on different aspects of the events—high prices, unrest, looting, attempted looting, looting averted, and measures to deal with the situation—came in from all parts of the region. An idea of the regional spread of reporting can be had from a summary listing of the places regarding which reports (of varying length, from a paragraph to two columns, and detail) were filed from 3 September to 25 September 1918: Madras; Chingleput, Conjeevaram, and Saidapet (Chingleput District); Arakkonam (North Arcot); Villupuram and Cuddalore (South Arcot); Salem; Coimbatore and Erode (Coimbatore District); Trichinopoly, Samayapuram, and Karur (Tiruchi District); Tanjore, Mayavaram, Kuttalam, Koranad, Shiyali, Negapatam, Mannargudi, Adirampatnam, and Kumbaconam (Thanjavur District); Madura; Kamuthi and Paramakudi (Ramnad District); Tinnevelly, Tuticorin, and Viranallur (Tirunelveli District); Ellore, Venkatagiri, Sullurpet, Nellore, Guntur, and Tirupati (all in the Telugu-speaking districts); as well as Coonoor, Bangalore, Mysore, Robertsonpet (the Kolar Gold Fields), Malabar District, and Cochin. Many of the reports included the names of surrounding villages from which agitators came to towns and weekly markets.

Considerable space was given—in what was then an eight-page newspaper —to these reports. Reports were regular and sequential, in that successive dispatches from a single centre attempted to follow up previous reports. Many of the reports are characterized by considerable detail: they state the scenes of action (the towns, quarters and streets of towns, the names of surrounding villages and hamlets), describe the sequences of events, often bringing the incidents alive through graphic reporting, and always explicitly state the (perceived) *cause* of looting—the sudden and calamitously steep rise in the prices of foodgrains and other necessaries of life. The reports bring out the fact that the price rise of the period was more than 'normal' inflation; prices rose sharply over the course of one, two, or a few days.

The targets of the looters were generally the shops and establishments of merchants, traders, and retailers and, in the districts, the weekly markets or shandies. (In Kamuthi, in Ramnad District, as *The Hindu*'s correspondent noted, the stress of the events of the market-place was compounded by the simmering conflict between the merchant-dominated Nadar community of the town and the Maravars of the surrounding villages, who on the day of looting shot dead two policemen and injured the rest, ransacked the market, and finally turned on residential buildings.) The reports also serve, incidentally, to underscore Arnold's (1979) point that the target of the agitators was not the government or government officials and we cite an example, from Madurai, further down, of the crowd turning to local officials for succour against those whom they had identified as profiteers.

These are some extracts from the body of reportage of our three-week reference period; they are meant to convey some of the vividness of 1918 food riot reporting by a nationalist newspaper of record.

(i) 'Attempted Looting in Madura' (FOOC)

Madura, September 3: Consequent on the heavy rise in the price of foodgrain and other commodities in the town, rumours had been widely circulated within the last two or three days, that looting of shops was under contemplation and was to be resorted to by the people. This had caused great panic and yesterday about 12 noon, the rumour had gathered considerable momentum. Looting was in the air and the shopkeepers one by one began to close their business . . . suddenly the news spread like wild fire that a paddy go-down in the Pattaraikara street had been looted; and people in town were running in groups to the place. I hastened to the scene and found a large concourse of people collected together in that broad street to a length of nearly two furlongs . . . Just about 1 o'clock some dozen persons, all robust and well built, went into a paddy go-down and enquired the price at which the paddy was sold. The answer came . . . that it sold at six measures a rupee. The previous day the rate was seven measures a rupee and the enquirers demanded the special reasons for inflating the prices so suddenly and at so short an interval. Hot words began to be exchanged between the sellers and purchasers; and the result was a huge commotion. A very large number of people had collected themselves in the *pettai* [locality] and these men were pushed outside and the gates were closed and locked against them. Great uproar was raised, the mob mad with fury then threw stones, big and small, on the gates and made an attempt to break into the go-down and commit looting inside . . . Mr. G. F. Paddison, I.C.S., the Collector . . . was driving in his motorcar from his residence . . . a number of people . . . laid themselves flat on the ground with a view to preventing the car from passing straightaway . . . The crowds . . . represented to him that the merchants in Madura were by a combination inflating the prices every day and it had now become impossible for the poor people to buy things and get on in life. Profiteering was going on to an enormous extent; and if something was not done to control the prices, they said, looting would become the order of the day. They prayed that the good and sympathetic Collector who recently intervened on behalf of the Mill strikers and gave redress to their grievances, might likewise alleviate their grievance by promulgating an order fixing the rate at which the merchants should sell to them cloths, foodstuffs and other necessaries of life.

(ii) *'Looting and Unrest at Madras: Madras under Military Guard'*

September 2, 1918: For the last four days loud complaints have been heard that prices of cloth, rice and chillies have risen very high and there was a persistent rumour that very soon the rice mandies in Wall Tax Road and the cloths bazaar in Devaraja Mudali Street would be looted. It would appear that even hand bills were circulated that such looting would occur. Vague rumours were also afloat that some of the mill hands in Choolai and some of the men to be sent to Basra would take part in the loot . . . rice and other [items] were thrown out into the street to be picked out by the mob . . . [at Pursewalkam] . . . another set of looters attacked the rice bazaar and cloth bazaar . . . but an alarm being raised a large crowd gathered and the Police also arrived on the spot . . . at Kotwal bazaar three shops selling rice, chillies, etc. were looted. Cocoanuts from a cocoanut shop were thrown in different directions and most of them destroyed. Vegetables, plantains, leaves etc. were trodden underfoot, shopkeepers were panic stricken and fled for their lives leaving the shops to their fate . . . the party that was driven back from the level crossing near the Salt Cotaurs rushed to Periamet along the Sydenham Road and arming themselves with bamboos kept on the road side in bundles for sale, attacked two or three marwari shops but no damage worth mentioning was done. Disappointed at this, they went into the Moore Market. The gates of the main building were closed. Birds were set free from their cages. A number of birds were killed and others were picked up by the mob. They then ran to the eastern building (Evening Bazaar) where several shopkeepers suffered heavy loss. Glasses, spectacles, toys, China wares, photos, etc. were destroyed. Shopkeepers in a body offered great resistance, and hand to hand fighting ensued. The police arrived on the spot and arrests were made.

(iii) *'At Tinnevelly'*

Tinnevelly, September 19—A Correspondent writes:

The infection of food riots has spread to Tinnevelly. At Viravanallur it is reported on Tuesday night a mob surrounded the bundles of paddy dealers who had just then purchased a stock and on their refusal to sell paddy, looted six bandy loads of paddy. The rioters were mostly peaceful and plodding Sowrashtra weavers who were reduced to the utmost destitution owing to high price of yarn and dyes . . . Some merchants of Tuticorin have received anonymous warnings to reduce their price lest they should share the fate of Madras profiteers. The police have conferred with the merchants and advised them against the danger of charging inflated prices.

Some of the reports attempted an occupational description of the people in the crowd. When they were from among the rural working people, they were often described in terms of caste: 'people belonging to the Mala and Madiga class' (report from Ellore, *The Hindu*, 4 September 1918); 'Pallars of the hamlets of Kannanur and Narsingamangalam' (report from Samayapuram, Tiruchi District, *The Hindu*, 9 September 1918); 'a mob of about 5000 people, mostly pariahs' (report from Shiyali, present-day Sirkazhi, *Hindu*, 20 September 1918). There were weavers, in Koranad (Thanjavur District) and Viravanallur (Tirunelveli District), and, in urban centres, industrial workers.

In Madras, textile workers were among the crowd; from Tanjore a report on the situation in Negapatam, described as a 'storm-centre of violent disturbances', warned that amongst the permanent population there are a considerable quantity of explosive material in the easily excitable and furiously ungovernable temperament of the workmen in the Railway shops and in the Harbour and business firms on the beach' (Report from Tanjore, *The Hindu*, 14 September 1918).

The opinion reflected in the reporting varied, of course, with the reporter. The 'mob' was a frequently used term for groups of agitators; and while the Madura correspondent could refer to the 'some dozen persons' at the paddy godown as 'robust and well-built' and a Madras correspondent described the crowd as 'on the whole a good-natured one', there were also reporters whose social predilections were explicit in their description of 'rowdies' or 'urchins'.

An important feature of our material is that as spontaneous protest spread to different regions, the response of the independent nationalist newspaper to the agitation *began to take on the character of a campaign*. This is most clearly reflected in editorial policy, but also shows itself in the way reportage was handled in the columns of the paper.

From 9 September, news of the agitation was published under a column titled 'Looting and Unrest'; on 17 September, the column title was quietly changed to 'High Prices and Unrest'. There is another interesting example of a neat intervention from the news desk: on 19 September, at the end of the 'High Prices and Unrest' column, after the reportage from the districts a small item was inserted, separated by a line but with no separate headline, of another food riot situation where the concerned Governor *had* intervened and the police played a somewhat non-traditional role: 'The rice riots in Japan are reported to have been noted for the presence of women among the mob in Kyoto. The Governor secured a supply of cheap foreign rice for sale and the police sympathise with the mob' (*The Hindu*, 19 September 1918). (This is followed by a report of places where 'disturbances and looting' took place.)

The editorials   There were five editorials, no less, on the subject of the food crisis and the people's agitation over the three-week period and they are characterized by an increasingly trenchant position *vis-à-vis* the government.

It is a characteristic of the editorials that they did not condemn the people's actions; the looting was seen as a response to the unbearable price situation:

The rise in prices of one article leads to a sympathetic rise in the rest. Chillies have gone up abnormally in prices. For what we paid 4 as. odd three months ago, today we are called upon to pay Rs. 1.10; black grams similarly has risen by about 50 percent, salt has gone up, we hear, by six annas a measure, a rise of 100 percent; rice also shows a marked tendency to rise; ghee and oils are characterised by the same feature . . . There is a belief which is, we think, justified in many cases, in many places in the mofussil especially, that profiteering remains unchecked on an immense scale. This, if it is a fact, must be put down with firmness; if it is not possible to do so by persuasion, compulsion must be unhesitatingly resorted to. The responsibility for eliminating profiteering and reducing the suffering of the people to a minimum rests on the Government . . . (editorial, 'The Food Problem', *The Hindu*, 5 September 1918)

Another editorial observed:

The Government have never had the high prices problem in hand. They are probably now considering the matter seriously. That prohibitive prices were prevailing Government have long been aware and only the other day a *communique* was issued on the sale of salt. But man does not live by salt alone, and we cannot conceive why Government have not dealt with the other necessaries of life in the same way. Their attentions have been directed to the matter over and over again, and these representations have resulted in a dissertation on the economic laws of supply and demand and a cut-and-dry programme for the publications of price lists through the cumbrous official machinery. Fine words butter no parsnips nor do statistical tables, which the proletariat never see nor care to see, stave off starvation, and the result is looting; not only in Madras but in other parts of the Presidency . . . (editorial, 'Looting in Madras', 10 September 1918)

Referring to the 'doings of a certain body in the City' charged with the supervision of mercantile activity:

Strange should be the constitution of the mind which, in spite of such unmistakeable signs of acute distress and depressing poverty, seeks to argue that no action is needed on the part of Government, that prices, though high, are not famine prices and that compulsory regulation of the trade in cloth and grain would alarm the merchants and create a panic. Such kind consideration for merchants may enable the merchants to clear huge profits part of which may be invested in war funds, but it is an altogether perverse and heartless view to take and speedy steps should be taken to see that the interests of the public do not suffer by such reactionary counsels being allowed to be made. (editorial, 'The Food Situation', 11 September 1918)

And another editorial pointed out:

Whatever may be the defects of Lord Pentland's Government, the charges at least cannot be laid at its doors that it ever acts with undue precipitation . . . The *Laissez faire* theory is so comfortable a one to hold that we need not be surprised at the assiduity with which our local Government pursues the great act of doing nothing. An endless supply of red tape, however, offers but indigestible fare for a population on the verge of starvation . . . (editorial, 'The Food Crisis', 19 September 1918)

The government was continuously faulted in the editorials and, as the campaign built up, in progressively stronger terms for mishandling the situation. It was faulted for not keeping prices in check and effectively controlling the market; for not ensuring supplies and clearing the bottlenecks in transportation; for not keeping the public informed about the measures it was taking to deal with the situation; and for a certain Olympian indifference, vividly captured by the fact that its major representatives continued their Hot Weather sojourn at the summer capital of Ootacamund while the crisis was at its peak. The editorial of 10 September 1918 stated clearly that the answer to the situation was to solve the food crisis, not to turn the police and army on the people. The editorials also stressed that the agitation sprang spontaneously from crisis conditions, and was not organized by the Home Rulers.

The other policy recommendations by the newspaper are worth noting. The first appeared in the editorial of 3 September, when the paper called for *state control* of the market in essential commodities during a period when a 'legitimate level' of prices was 'exceeded abnormally'. The second was a suggestion that a system of *food zoning* be introduced during a period of crisis. While acknowledging that this was a suggestion that the Madras government had made earlier, the *The Hindu* picked up a statement by the Collector of Guntur during this period to call attention to the point:

Mr. Davies pointed out virtually that Guntur had to starve in the midst of plenty, because the Director of Civil Supplies would not allow him to restrict exports . . . The curious thing . . . is that though the Director refused to restrict exports, he consented to allow imports from the north. In fairness to the Madras Government, they appear to have recommended the prohibition of export of products whenever it was deemed that the exporting area would thereby suffer acute distress. The Government of India . . . overruled the Local Government's decision to prohibit exports, on the extraordinary ground that the whole of India constituted a single economic unit! (editorial, 'The Government and Prices', 12 September 1918)

This was also the period when a major preoccupation of the government was the war effort, and its representatives were busy raising the Second War Loan which was advertised on the newspaper's front page every day of our three-week period. The editorials intertwined references to war with discussions of the crisis in the Presidency. The editorial of 10 September mentions the war effort only to observe that the activity of raising the War Loan was matched by inactivity on the food front, putting the observation down to what 'the people say':

Meanwhile the people say that when the Government want money for the war loan or soldiers for the King, the Governor finds it convenient to tour to Calicut and to preside at meetings at which the wealthy subscribe liberally, while, when the poor are suffering and unable to make two ends meet, the Governor and his Councillors are enjoying the climate of Ootacamund and are oblivious to their suffering. (editorial, 'Looting in Madras', 10 September 1918)

The last Indian famine: Bengal, 1943, and the role of the press   India's last famine was the Great Bengal Famine of 1943 in which an estimated three million people died, with a particularly heavy toll among agricultural labourers, fishermen, transport workers, and non-agricultural labourers in rural areas. Sen (1981) finds the role of the *Statesman* very significant. It highlighted 'the conspicuous failure of the Government to anticipate the famine and to recognise its emergence' and its 'powerful campaign with news reports, photographs and editorial comments on the calamity' won praise later from the

Famine Inquiry Commission and also contributed an important insight into the role of an independent professional press in relation to famine and poverty.[26]

The two editorials from the *Statesman* (of 14 and 16 October 1943) referred to by Sen (1981) demonstrate the high competence, the critical initiative, and the active nature of the role. The colonial authorities were virtually indicted by this British-owned newspaper (edited by Ian Stevens) for grave misjudgement of the crisis and for covering up the facts. In the editorial of 14 October, titled 'Seen from a Distance', the Secretary of State for India was pulled up thus:

Mr. Amery's speeches would be more acceptable in this country were they less habitually smug. His Parliamentary utterance last Tuesday on what he euphemistically called the Indian food 'situation' seems, from the long cabled text, intended to suggest to the British public that, so far as the Government of India and the India Office were concerned, all that could have been done was . . . Nasty words such as famine, starvation, corpse or cholera were carefully avoided. The Central Government's unexplained and amazing omission to establish a Food Department for a full year after Japan's declaration of war gained no mention.

As for citizens' feelings, they had been roused by the remarkably insensitive content and tone of Amery's speech and mounting evidence of a much higher famine toll than the authorities had accepted earlier. Referring to Amery's boast that it was largely due to the central government's exertions that 'a situation of widespread distress' has been confined to Bengal, Cochin, Travancore, and parts of the Deccan, the *Statesman* commented: 'As an example of the politician's art of smoothly evasive meiosis this takes memorably high place. Bengal alone contains a population larger than Britain's . . . Yet the distant Mr. Amery can imply that her distress does not by itself justify such adjectives as serious or widespread.'

The second editorial, 'The Death-Roll' (16 October 1943), is an outstanding example of informed, precise journalism. It looks closely at the government's figures on the weekly death-roll in the light of different aspects of the evidence. The newspaper deplored 'the continuous appearance of effort on the part of persons somewhere within India's Governmental machine, perhaps out here, perhaps in Whitehall, to play down, suppress, distort, or muffle the truth about Bengal' (even if a somewhat loyalist note was sounded through the remark that such an attitude was 'dragging the fair name of the British Raj needlessly low' and a somewhat sweeping assertion was recorded to the effect that during the famines near the end of the nineteenth century, 'the heyday of British imperial responsibility', no effort was spared 'to probe and proclaim the truth about any maladministration, so that it might be promptly dealt with and the blot on the honour of the Indian Empire removed').

The *Statesman*'s factual reporting, exposés, and editorial campaign had much value in the situation; they reflected both the active function of

[26] See Sen (1981: 52–85 and also 195–216).

independent journalism and the professional credibility and influence of a serious newspaper. But what can we say about the role of nationalist publications during this period? To call attention to another approach and perspective, we cite an editorial from the Birla-owned *Eastern Economist* belonging to the *Hindustan Times* group (the editorial, titled 'The Bengal Famine: India and Her People on Trial', was published in the issue of 5 November 1943). The perspective adopted in this editorial is not loyalist in any way; it is the perspective of contraposing the inherent tendencies and the interests of British colonial rule to the interests of the Indian nation. Apart from indicting the British government for 'such a woeful lack of imagination and efficiency that they have allowed a situation to develop which has gone out of control', it asserted that it was 'not the scarcity of food during the last few months alone' that had brought about the tragedy. The causes were clearly 'more deep-seated'.

The editorial analysis moved without inhibition into the field of economics: today it reads like a somewhat old-fashioned admixture of instant economics and perceptive political economy-orientated concerns. There is an element of exaggeration or overblown rhetoric and a lack of precision and nuance which were later to become one of the inherent features of Indian journalism in covering droughts and other types of 'food crisis'. 'Bengal's famine', the editorial assertion ran, 'is only a portent. Famine stalks all through the land and is not confined to Bengal, though it is seen at its worst in that province. In Travancore, Cochin and Malabar the situation is, if anything, worse than in Bengal, as the Dewan of Travancore has pointed out. In the Ceded Districts in Madras, in Orissa and in parts of Bombay conditions are as near famine as one can think of.'

Aside from the burden of contributing financially to the war, policy-related weaknesses in handling India as one integrated economic unit, transport bottlenecks, and the poor distribution system were blamed as factors that had contributed to the terrible crisis. The prescription concentrated on the short-term and long-term responsibility of the state in controlling famine and preventing its appearance in the same region or in other areas. 'Preventing the recurrence of famine', noted the editorial in the *Eastern Economist*, 'requires a complete reversal of our financial and economic policies. The country should not be asked to undertake any further responsibility for feeding the armed forces quartered in India. A big production drive should be organised . . . India should be administered as one economic unit, and no amount of provincial autonomy should be allowed to make inroads into the economic integrity of India.'

The editorial emphasized that while there was an imperative for emergency famine relief and famine combat measures, 'the after-famine problem is even more important'. It called for basic measures to tackle such massive problems as 'the pauperisation of millions of people', for a determination to go beyond the miserable inadequacy of the 'gruel kitchen' approach, for plans to make the economy more productive in both agriculture and industry and provide for the 're-employment of all labour that is seeking employment'.

The role of the nationalist press, and of conscientious independent investigation, in relation to the great crisis of 1943 is brought out vividly in a collection compiled by Santhanam (1943). It includes cartoons by Shankar and a moving collection of photographs assembled with the co-operation of the publications *People's War*, Bombay, the *Amrita Bazar Patrika*, and the *Hindustan Standard*, and organizations such as the Cyclone Relief Committee, Contai, the All-India Women's Association, Calcutta, and the Friends' Ambulance Unit, Calcutta. (Some of these searing images of human suffering and desperation have resurfaced in the attempts by Satyajit Ray and also Mrinal Sen to recreate through the cinematic medium the experience and essence of the Great Bengal Famine of 1943.)

Necessarily characterized by unevenness, elements of propaganda in defence of people's rights against the policies of the Raj, and an inclination towards instant economics, the Santhanam collection offers valuable documentary insight into the strong and aggressive role various sections of the independent press played during India's last real famine.

Current role and tendencies: vis-à-vis *two kinds of hunger*   The phenomenon of hunger and poverty on a mass scale and in specific places finds a great deal of coverage in Indian newspapers and magazines today. Reports, semi-investigative feature articles, occasional interventions by economists and other specialists, editorial observations, and letters from readers dealing with the subject in one form or another would, for the Indian press as a whole, run into tens of columns per day. This coverage, as is to be expected, gets significantly expanded during a period of widespread drought covering several states and affecting millions of people and their basic conditions of life and work. It goes without saying that given the pluralism of the press on the one hand and of society and politics on the other in a country as vast as India, coverage of the phenomenon of hunger and poverty is quite uneven. For the sake of manageable analysis, it may be assumed that about twenty influential newspapers and magazines—among daily newspapers, say the *Indian Express*, the *Times of India*, *The Hindu*, the *Statesman*, the *Telegraph*, plus several Indian language newspapers such as *Malayala Manorama* and *Mathrubhumi* of Kerala, *Eenadu of Andhra Pradesh*, *Ananda Bazar Patrika* of West Bengal, *Gujarat Samachar* of Gujarat, and a couple of newspapers active in the Hindi-speaking belt, and among the magazines *India Today*, *Frontline*, *Sunday*, *Illustrated Weekly*, plus a couple of mass-circulated periodicals published in Indian languages—would constitute a useful sample of current coverage of hunger and poverty. Such a sample is likely to miss out much in the experience of Indian journalism, which is characterized by a tremendous diversity in standards and resources available to publications, but since the sample would be very influential in terms of circulation and the impact on the decision-making process it would be strong in serving our purpose. We do not attempt a systematic content analysis, but offer instead a preliminary description and a somewhat impressionistic assessment of the current role and tendencies of the independent Indian press in relation to the phenomenon of hunger and poverty.

How valid is the 'dichotomy' in the role observed by Amartya Sen in his analysis of famine and poverty and brought to the fore in his 1982 Coromandel Lecture in New Delhi? The current contribution made by the press in reporting extensively on the drought is in line with the historically well-observed role and the important place it is given in Sen's analysis. On the other hand, the criticism that Indian newspapers have not been sensitive or responsive to 'regular', chronic hunger and subhuman poverty has been heard frequently from inside the journalistic profession. At one level, the criticism is obviously valid, although—for what it is worth—the Indian press is inclined increasingly to wrestle with the enormous challenge of discovering and doing something about the phenomenon of poverty and hunger in a country that has, for all its advantages, a greater mass of it than probably any other. From a sensitive or progressive social science standpoint, however, this coverage does appear 'low-key' or 'tame', aside from proving frequently incompetent.

The reasons for this would need to be looked for at several levels of the newspaper field: policy orientation and bias, entrenched professional routine and habits, the ideological and political predilections of journalists and the influential and trendy currents of the national and international literature they are exposed to, a variety of mundane practical constraints, the quality of resources available to the press, and so on. But as a generalization applicable to most of the field, it would be probably accurate to say that the basic problem is not that the rules of the game tie the press's hands in some unwritten way in relation to this sensitive subject. It is that the intellectual and methodological resources and competence required to investigate the complex, mixed-up socio-economic realities of India in anything other than superficial terms, to handle data and sources meticulously and critically, to make sense in a popular medium of a body of sophisticated but sharply varying analyses, findings, and prescriptions available to it, in principle, from the academic field, and to do all this interestingly, would demonstrably be beyond the press's current level of capability or competence. In the concluding section of this essay, we propose a line of achievable advance based on the strengths and capabilities available to the Indian press from the quite developed resource pool of certain branches of Indian social science—notably economics which has paid much empirical, and a certain amount of theoretical, attention to hunger and poverty across the land. In relation to the wealth of poverty studies in India, the coverage in what is supposed to be an increasingly sophisticated medium is underdeveloped.

Coverage of drought, 'food crisis' and anticipated famine   There is no doubt that the phenomenon of hunger and distress resulting from the recent spells of drought affecting several states and millions of people, especially agricultural labourers and other sections of the rural poor, has been given major attention in both the national and local press in various parts of the country. Reporters have turned up a considerable amount of descriptive detail from the field, sympathetic accounts of rural distress and even desperation reflected in the migration of thousands of families and in distress cattle sales, human interest stories focusing on individuals, and exposés of official incompetence, insensitivity, and cover-up tendencies. The itinerary of Prime Minister Rajiv Gandhi's visit in 1985–6 to areas of extreme poverty, hunger, and distress was as often as not influenced by press coverage which could at times be 'hyped-up journalism'. But the field reports have generally been valuable: they have tended, in state after state, to challenge official claims relating to drought relief efforts, the efficacy and destination of funds spent on creating employment and elementary purchasing power in a situation of near-collapse of the economy of the afflicted households, and in general the drought policies of the state and centre. So much so that a general political theme encountered in the campaign conducted by opposition parties and independent critics in various states against official drought management policies was that newspapers showed up the realities on the ground in the face of official untruths and suppression of facts. This applied to the situation in Congress (I)-ruled states such as Maharashtra, Gujarat, Rajasthan, and Orissa as much as it did to the exceptionally severe and recurrent drought in Janata-ruled Karnataka, and the situations in Telugu Desam-ruled Andhra Pradesh and AIADMK-ruled Tamil Nadu.

A cover story in the Sunday magazine section of the national daily the *Indian Express* (of 1 June 1986), reviewing the situation of the 1985–6 drought in four states—Maharashtra, Gujarat, Rajasthan, and Karnataka—and official responses to the crisis, noted that Karnataka witnessed 'the distress sale of tens of thousands of cattle last winter. The cattle population affected by the drought has been estimated as 107.39 lakhs while the human population exposed to it has been about 210.32 lakhs . . . the State's economy is in a shambles.' The article noted, in this connection, that 'it was only in the last two months of 1985 that the State Government took note of the serious shortage of fodder, and *that too after* newspapers carried detailed reports on cattle sales' (emphasis added). The newspapers referred to were local Kannada newspapers, such as *Samyuktha Karnataka*, and national dailies like *The Hindu* and the *Indian Express*.[27]

What is the kind of socio-economic and human interest detail that Indian newspapers bring to the attention of their readers in such circumstances? A sampling of reports from national dailies and magazines published in English is revealing:

---

[27] Some of the coverage, especially in the Kannada newspaper *Samyuktha Karnataka*, which is associated with the Congress (I) party, reflected oppositional politics. This bears out Sen's (1982) impression that the pressure from the independent press combined with campaigns by opposition parties would make it virtually impossible for any government keen on staying in power to shut its eye to a major crisis and to avoid pursuing famine-averting policies.

The story is the same every year—only the dates and the statistics are different. The vocabulary, too, remains unchanged . . . the same tired phrases are conjured up year after year to describe a countryside 'reeling under', 'in the grip of' or 'afflicted by' drought. The suffering, real and intense, comes through in a few revealing images —people elbowing each other out of the way in the frenzied race towards the water tanker; the worn and dehydrated faces of labourers toiling mechanically at 'drought relief works' while their babies crawl around in the heat and the dust, sad-eyed, fodder-starved cattle lined up for the short journey to the slaughterhouse . . .

The people of Rajkot and Jamnagar are facing the worst drinking water scarcity in living memory. Broken pipelines and ditches in the middle of the road are a common sight in Rajkot. People run after water tankers, like crazy animals, while some racketeers mint money by selling water pilfered from the pipeline right under the nose of the government. Private operators provide as much as two lakh gallons of water to the needy in Rajkot at about Rs. 150 per 10,000 gallons . . .

[In Karnataka] on account of both the kharif and rabi crops failing this year, about 30 per cent of the targeted food production has been lost and most farm labourers, along with a large number of small and marginal farmers, have lost their means of livelihood. In over 12,000 villages in 110 talukas spread over 17 districts, the average crop yield per acre has been less than 25 per cent. The State has witnessed the distress sale of tens of thousands of cattle last winter . . . the State's economy is in a shambles and resource mobilisation has been severely hit . . . One area in which the government has scored heavily is the provision of drinking water, as a result of a massive operation, which included sinking borewells, implementing mini-water supply and piped water supply schemes . . . [But] it appears that the government has not been able to go beyond the conventional concept that relief works mean mainly the building and repair of roads . . . One consolation is that as many as 32,213 hectares have been covered under afforestation schemes. But this is too small an area compared to the vast 'treeless' areas of the northern districts. (*Indian Express*, Sunday magazine section, 1 June 1986)

A 1600 km drive through some of the badly hit districts brought this reporter face to face with that agonising reality. Of the State's 175 taluks, 154 are reeling under the drought. Nearly 1.59 crore [15.9 million] people and 90 lakh [9 million] head of cattle are affected. Both kharif and rabi output has been hit and the shortfall in the targeted production of 85 lakh tonnes is expected to be a staggering 45 lakh tonnes. An estimated 15 lakh people need to be sustained daily on relief employment until the South-West monsoon in June. As much as Rs. 160 crores has already been funnelled from Government coffers into relief measures.

All one hears from the demoralised peasants is an endless narration of misery . . . It is being described as the worst drought of the century, though few have called it a 'famine' mainly because people, though not cattle, have so far escaped starvation . . .

Gaollara Kyathanna of Dodderi village in the almost barren Chellekere taluk of Chitradurga district is an illiterate marginal farmer who does not even know his age. He looks past 70. The three bagas of sajje, a coarse grain his sons had grown last year on their dry land, were not sufficient to feed the family of six. Now the family lives on the Rs. 7.80 a day one of the sons and his wife each earns on a Government relief work. Village-level officials have not issued the family the most sought-after 'green card' which ensures a ration of about 10 kg of grain a month besides clothes . . . The distress, coupled with the abolition of the . . . mid-day meal schemes, has affected school attendance. When those who have studied up to the SSLC are jobless and are tending goats, why should we send our children to school, ask the Harijans of Purlihalli in Chellakere taluk. Inducements like free education, text-books and uniforms work only during 'fair weather'.

All over northern Karnataka people complained of a sharp spurt in the prices of foodgrains. The revenue authorities maintain that the situation is not so grave as to warrant the opening of gruel centres . . . Some women scratching the scorched land were seen near Madhugiri town in Tumkur district. They were looking for groundnuts in the roots of plants harvested last season. One of them, Gowramma, had got four nuts after the morning-to-noon drudgery. Peanuts? But that is how the poor literally eke out a living. . . .

Karnataka, which has received migrants from the dry tracts of tamil Nadu and Andhra Pradesh for ages, is sending out its people this year to other States . . . Aggravating the problem in Kolar and Tumkur districts is the inflow of people from the Rayalaseema region of Andhra Pradesh which is also facing drought . . . Karnataka has wet patches and dry expanses . . . The crucial period is March to June. For the present, the rural and urban folk scan the spotless blue skies for that speck of cloud that might bring some succour. (A. Jayaram, 'On a Tour of Drought-Hit Areas', in *Frontline*, 22 February–17 March 1986)

In the state of Andhra Pradesh the 1985–6 drought was very widespread, with 250 taluks out of 330 declared drought affected. Telugu newspapers such as *Andhra Bhoomi*, *Andhra Prabha*, and *Eenadu* provided detailed and lively coverage of the impact on crops, cattle, and the conditions of the most vulnerable sections of the rural poor. So did the English language newspapers.

Detailed and sensitive coverage of a drought, its early signals, its effects in terms of the conditions of life and work of the people affected, and governmental performance in this crisis has for long been a strength of the independent Indian press, its local as well as national, its small as well as medium-sized and big components.

In his study of the political responses to the Bihar 'famine' of 1966–7, the political scientist Brass (1986) found that both 'the press reports about the developing crisis situation and the responses of the politicians and authorities to the situation turned the Bihar Famine of 1966–67 into a political drama in which many of the principals self-consciously played their roles on the public stage'. And more specifically:

framing the whole drama—commenting on it, in fact, virtually creating it—were the local and national press. The Bihar press, particularly two Patna English-language dailies, *Searchlight* and the *Indian Nation*, adopted vigorously critical positions towards the Congress Government and the administration of the State. Their correspondents toured the countryside during the drought and wrote numerous reports of famine conditions and starvation deaths that contradicted the statements of the Government and the administration, which said that the situation was under control.

Brass discovered that the reporters who accompanied Ministers and political bigwigs on their tour of the crisis-affected areas set the tone for the strong descriptions and characterizations of the overall situation and, in fact, created or evoked the language of 'unprecedented' crisis. For example, in one sample scrutinized by Brass, the reporter was moved to describe 'the rice-belt of Bihar' near Patna as looking 'like the desolate wastes of the Rann of Kutch in mid-summer'.

In this particular case, there were several weaknesses in the press coverage of the 'famine': Brass's study showed 'no systematic reports . . . at this time [October 1966] of various other signs and symptoms of famine, such as wandering, migration, increases in criminal activity, and the like. At this stage, much of the expressed concern was premonitory rather than immediate.'

More serious was the fact that the Bihar newspapers did not or could not see through official attempts to explain the major crisis in terms of 'drought-induced crop failure that led to a further food availability decline [FAD] in an already food-deficit State' whereas the evidence, including official statistics, clearly argued otherwise. Brass's analysis suggests that in such cases, the retention of the FAD theory as an explanation of 'famine' and scarcity

serves three important functions for the authorities . . . first, it equalises need within the area defined as famine-stricken or suffering from scarcity. All regions and all classes are said to suffer equally, if in different ways. . . . Second, the theory serves to minimise the ability of the authorities and people to help themselves, thereby justifying external assistance. Third, the theory diverts attention from inequalities and suffering that exist in normal times in particular regions and among disadvantaged social groups.

Nevertheless, for all the weaknesses and distortions in the response to the crisis that it allowed itself to reflect, the Bihar press in 1966–7 played a significant democratic role. Brass's study poses for us sharply the issue of the relationship between the severity of the 'famine'/drought/scarcity situation and its 'informatization' (a clumsy, but unavoidable, word in this context) and politicization; it highlights the world of difference which relatively independent information and news media can make to the consequences and impact of a crisis. One of Brass's conclusions relates to the 'high degree of politicisation' of the Bihar crisis of 1966–7. This point is vital to our analysis: 'Famine and scarcity have occurred before and since the Bihar Famine, and both have occurred with a lesser degree of politicisation or have been ignored by politicians and the press . . . In a democratised crisis, the crisis for the people becomes a crisis for the politicians as well.'

Several local and national newspapers covered actively, and generally with a greater sense of sophistication and nuance than in the Bihar case, the Maharashtra droughts of 1970–3. In particular, the *Times of India* distinguished itself in this coverage. There were numerous reports, editorial page assessments, and leaders over this period. In the 1980s, food crises which have developed or threatened to develop elsewhere, in other states and localities, have tended to get covered in increasing detail by various sections of the press which have provided growing evidence of being aware or conscious, in a professional or institutional sense, of the adversarial role performed. The contemporary coverage of the extensive situation of drought (in the summer of 1987) by various newspapers round the country appears to be a data-rich field that can be examined systematically by scholars interested in this role.

Tendencies of overstatement and sensationalism

There is increasingly, in sections of the Indian press, a tendency to dramatize and sensationalize the coverage of poverty and hunger on a mass scale, usually when a crisis threatens, but also in the 'regular', persistent form. While the approach might seem to serve a positive function in that it highlights the problem and brings it to the fore, the quality of the treatment, the obscuring of contours and certainly nuances, the blurring of definitions and specifics, and the dramatizing of poverty and hunger lowers credibility among serious readers and, from the standpoint of serious analysis, proves counter-productive. Unfortunately, international experience demonstrates that tendentious or 'populist' journalism and also propaganda tones can make a mark and set the pace and some of the trends in a quite competitive field.[28]

A widely read example in mainstream Indian journalism of sensationalizing a crisis and, in fact, transforming through journalistic overstatement (with propaganda tones) a widespread drought into an unprecedented 'famine' is the cover story in the *Illustrated Weekly* of 16 January–1 February 1986 by Nikhil Lakshman. The feature titled 'Hunger' carries the cover page announcement: 'As the Republic Celebrates Its 36th Anniversary, 100 Million Indians are Threatened by Famine.' The ten-page article treats as quite 'academic' any boundary line between *drought* and *famine*, predicts the direst consequences for India—including 'ecological disaster'—and indicts the government for remaining 'cool to the famine' (up to the time of writing of the article) and for playing 'semantic games'.

---

[28] The most detailed and trenchant criticism of the interrelationship between the structure, content, and tendencies of the American media come from an insider, Bagdikian (1983), who argues that the monopoly structure and control of the media have produced 'social and political sterility' in the reporting of events and 'silence on fundamental forces behind major news events'. Unfortunately, the media monopoly fosters viability and great commercial success in the market. Bagdikian (1983) concludes that 'the news media—diluted of real meaning by apolitical and sterile context, homogenised with the growth of monopoly, overwhelmingly more of service to merchants than to the audience, and filled with frivolous material—are a threat to their own future but also to the body politic . . . When the news is designed to exclude a third or a half of the population, it has sacrificed much of its standing as a democratic mechanism' (pp. 206–9). Again, Bagdikian (1985) observes, 'Gross propagandising, it is true, can reduce profits. But where monopoly reigns, as in 98 per cent of the cities with local papers, consumers have no alternative and owners have great latitude . . . The major media have enormous political and social influence. Those who control the media can make the most empty-headed political hack sound like a Founding Father and the most self-serving piece of legislation resemble the Golden Rule' (pp. 16–17). And so on. Some of these assessments might sound like overstatements, but there is little question among the serious Western media critics that bad journalism sells and, under certain circumstances, is quite capable of edging the better product out of the market. In India itself the *Hindustan Times*, which is generally recognized by professionals as having the weakest content among the major English language national dailies, is an established commercial success, especially in the national capital where it reigns as the top-circulated newspaper.

The feature claims to be based on an 'investigation' by one journalist into the phenomenon of unprecedented mass hunger in 1985–6—'now it's famine. Spreading its tentacles across nine States; affecting the lives of millions of men, women and children.' The article is right through a mixture of some well-observed verities and obvious exaggeration, with a turn of phrase, a quote, a verbal sweep, a stroke of journalistic breathlessness heightening the effect. The contrast between 'a nation which is held up as an example of agricultural glory in the Third World', a nation of 'foodgrain surpluses' on the one hand and a nation in which mass hunger is 'an unpleasant but integral part of our lives', is drawn legitimately enough. But the assertion that famine threatens 100 million people in nine states goes along with the rather tame statement that 'accurate information is unavailable' on starvation deaths—which are guessed to be over 500 in Orissa, 'victims of the epidemics that inevitably accompany the pestilence'.

The cover feature in the *Illustrated Weekly* charges that 'so far, the [Rajiv] Gandhi Government has remained cool to the famine and not taken any steps to channelise some of the excess stock toward scarcity-hit areas. It has been hostile to the States' urgent appeals for aid as well . . . three years into a crisis on a war footing, the government has chosen to play semantic games. This is a dangerous trend.' Aside from the centre, state government after state government is indicted for doing too little, too late. And such breathless assertions back up the argument:

Rajasthan, according to Chief Minister Harideo Joshi, is in the vice-grip of the worst famine in living memory . . . the overall situation in Maharashtra continues to be grim . . . In Orissa . . . large areas continue to be battered by famine with the result that cultivators have lost their zest for agriculture . . . For Karnataka, it is the worse famine this century . . . 27 out of the 45 districts in Madhra Pradesh are presently victims of famine . . . Gujarat was in trouble . . . [with] famine conditions existing in . . . 17 districts.

Only in the case of Andhra Pradesh does the writer settle for the lesser term, *drought*, and there too it is asserted for Rayalaseema that 'the current famine is the 20th in the last 28 years'.

There is in the article no careful examination of the specifics of mass hunger and distress, no attempt to identify possible factors that might have brought about the collapse of employment, purchasing power, and the economy of these people. The criticism of the central and state governments fails to be specific and becomes a stance of alleging that they were slow to recognize the symptoms of the phenomenon of 'famine' or tried to cover them up, moved far too slowly into miserably inadequate action, did not take efficient measures (in most cases) to implement the relief schemes, and did not, at any rate, have any worthwhile long-term or 'permanent' policy to combat the phenomenon.

Has not more land been brought under the plough and under irrigation over the past three decades? Have not cropping patterns diversified and foodgrain production *in toto* been raised rather impressively? Has not agricultural technology been transformed in important parts of India, making self-sufficiency in food a going proposition? And is there not evidence of some kind of impact of all this on rural poverty and hunger? Does not this objective side of the picture have to be taken into account while evaluating the poor record of the government in relation to the challenge of doing away with crisis hunger 'permanently'? Our journalist will have none of this. Nor does he look seriously at the other side of the picture and raise questions and issues that Indian economists have been discussing for long relating to a bleak development record in combating endemic 'regular' hunger.

The *Illustrated Weekly* article on the Great Indian 'Famine' of 1985–6 highlights another tendency in current Indian journalism: the meshing of *instant economics*[29] with *instant ecology*,[30] with the latter increasingly emphasized. The basic explanation advanced for the crisis, aside from government inaction and stupidity, is *ecological*. The 'ecological crisis', it is asserted, will intensify with man-induced 'gradual desertification of the terrain' which is generally regarded as the function of the current agricultural strategy. 'Authorities' and 'experts' are selectively cited to allege 'destruction of water resources' (by 'land mismanagement' and various other blunders), a wholesale neglect of the vital importance of afforestation, dangerously ill-conceived irrigation schemes, totally misplanned cropping patterns, and 'a steady erosion in our national resources'. Anil Agarwal, a writer who has made some sort of input into ecological journalism in India and is treated as a kind of cult figure by

---

[29] For an excellent discussion of what *instant economics* could mean to public policy in the field of food economics and hunger, see Sen (1985b): '"Practical" people are easily convinced that they know precisely what the problem is, and even though what they "know" with such certainty varies from person to person, they are impatient with the economists' tendency to use complicated ideas to tackle apparently simple problems. What may be called "instant economics" has always appealed to the quick-witted layman impatient with the slow-moving economist. In the field of hunger and food policy, the need for speed is of course genuinely important, and this impatience does have considerable sense. But instant economics is also dangerously deceptive, particularly in this field. Millions of lives depend on the adequacy of the policy response . . . Past mistakes of policy have been responsible for the death of many millions of people and the suffering of hundreds of millions, and this is not a subject in which short-cuts in economic reasoning can be taken to be fairly costless.'

[30] *Instant ecology* is a tendency that has surfaced in the Indian press over the past decade, although there is little doubt that there are parallel developments in other parts of the world. Some of the concerns might be progressive or legitimate, and in this sense some of the press coverage, particularly on ecological and political controversies such as the *Silent Valley* episode, has performed a worthwhile public service. Typically, however, the ecologically orientated journalist in India, recognizing a 'soft' and permissive field (in contrast to development economics), makes the most sweeping and extravagant claims about what he or she knows will be the ecological impact of, say, the new technology in agriculture, the effects and linkages with other problems, and plays the role of a pundit. Ecological overstatements, and assertions about desertification, the impact on rainfall trends, and so on that the journalist need not even bother to attempt to substantiate (beyond quoting some 'specialist' in a field where specialists might differ considerably), abound in certain sections of the Indian press. Such trends have obviously been influenced by international currents of instant ecology which Indian journalists and intellectuals are exposed to.

several of his followers, is quoted as saying: 'India is on the road to ecological, economic and social disaster.'

Articles of this kind, and the sensational manner of featuring them, lower the credibility of Indian magazine journalism with respect to socio-economic problems and issues and appear to be misconceived and misdirected responses to the need to provide support to anti-hunger strategies.

Coverage of endemic, 'regular' hunger

We shall begin this section by citing the opinions of some professionals on the role the Indian press plays in highlighting (or not highlighting) the problem of persistent 'regular' hunger and in motivating (or not motivating) public opinion to push for sustained and intelligently targeted anti-hunger policies.

[On] the point whether newspapers are sensitive to the problems connected with poverty or . . . other problems facing the majority of the people in this country . . . my own impression is that the English language newspapers do more in this respect than the regional language newspapers . . . the distance from the area of conflict or the type of readership which a particular paper might be catering for plays a part. (Nikhil Chakravartty, editor, *Mainstream*, and Chairman of the first NAMEDIA conference, 1983, in an interview 'Is the Indian Press Free and Fair' published in *Communicator*, 15/2, April 1980)

In an article titled 'News Coverage and Values in Official Media' published in *Mainstream*, 24/29, 22 March 1986, M. V. Desai, a veteran in the media field, noted that Indian newspapers reported much 'official' news, even if they were often critical of government action. They provided little news from mofussil towns and villages. As for news about hunger as in the recently highlighted case of the people of Kalahandi in Orissa, it was not broken until after the visit of a VIP (Prime Minister Rajiv Gandhi who visited the area in July 1985).

Drought, food, sales and starvation deaths in Kalahandi did seem to scandalise mediamen throughout the country. Almost every national English daily wrote editorials condemning the situation—State government officials, local politicians and journalists however are not surprised at the situation and ask why the nation's press has suddenly taken up cudgels on behalf of the starving people of Kalahandi who have been suffering from two decades of chronic drought. (Saibal Dasgupta, 'Orissa: In the Shadow of Neglect', *Indian Express* magazine, 25 August 1985)

We shall take up the somewhat rhetorical question posed at the end of this last evaluation by the journalist. In the main, Indian newspapers probably take a less 'low-key' approach to persistent hunger—and to the 'deadly conflicts' over capturing enough food to eat and survive—than they did a decade ago. However, the problem of persistent hunger and conflicts over access to food remaining, in effect, a 'tame issue' to Indian newspapers continues. The journalistic rationalization of this might run as follows. Since poverty and hunger have been around for a long time and since they exist on a forbiddingly vast scale in this society, newspaper coverage of them has to carry some element of novelty, some unusual facet, some waking-up quality in order to qualify as more than a 'tame' or 'soft' item. In newspaper parlance, you need some kind of news or topical peg to hang your hunger and poverty story on—if you are to convince your news editor or editor. Slowly and sporadically, this conception of journalism has begun to change, but the old approach is bolstered by news/editorial values and the impression that the space constraint and presumed reader interest do not make anything other than the present approach realistic.

Another occupational problem which is widely recognized by the critics is the 'essential dilettantism' of journalism. Now it is true that changes in the nature and scope of news coverage, the emphasized interest in science and technology, the importance of finance, economic journalism, and so on have pushed reporters into more specialization as *journalists* than used to be the case. At least in the more serious news organizations in India, the search is on for increasingly sophisticated science reporters, economic reporters, legal and industrial relations correspondents, energy, defence, and national security affairs writers, and so on. Even so, some familiarity with the content of the economic/financial/business newspapers in India suggests that there is no persuasive evidence that this supposedly specialized branch of Indian journalism does any deep-going, sustained investigation into the situation of persistent hunger and extreme deprivation in the land.

There is another basic problem inherent in the practice of journalism whether it is in a developing society such as India or a highly developed society such as the United States. For all its advantages and clout, journalism as a profession deservedly carries a reputation for *superficiality*, so much so that in English language usage, to be 'journalistic' is to merit a certain kind of condescending or otherwise unflattering response from serious intellectuals, scholars, and so forth. The insider critics point to the press's preoccupation with action, sensation, measurable developments, organized movements, personalities, surprises, and novelties as limiting its quality, role, and impact. Journalists might, to themselves and to superficial external observers of the profession, seem constantly to be participating in the making of history, but they clearly lack—as a professional group—the sensitivities, the nuances, and the rooted opportunities of the participant observers. The caricature of the successful journalist would be that of a fleet-footed participant observer who comes, sees, scribbles notes, conquers news space—and then moves on to something else.

This general observation can be related to an interesting small-scale phenomenon that has surfaced in Indian journalism during the last decade and a half: the journalist who turns researcher and undertakes to offer deeper insight, a better class of analysis, and more meaningful prescriptions on socio-economic subjects than garden variety colleagues. To the extent that this move by a small section of journalists who have made some kind of mark in their professional field is triggered by a restlessness with the superficialities and staleness of routine journalism it would seem to hold some promise. But the specific results of this move 'beyond journalism', to the extent they can be sampled in the columns of readily available publications, are not inspiring thus far.

Finally, we shall cite this influential example of socially sensitive journalism making a difference.

The *Indian Express* has, on several occasions, brought to the fore cases of bonded labour, the cruelty and indignity imposed on indigent women in specific rural contexts, starvation deaths in parts of the country, and so on. In 1985 it took the lead among national newspapers in covering starvation deaths amidst appalling socio-economic circumstances in Kalahandi district in Orissa. Kalahandi is one of the seventy-four vulnerable areas identified and covered by the Drought Prone Areas Programme. The first revelation of the long persistent hunger and of starvation deaths here appeared in the national media around the time of Prime Minister Rajiv Gandhi's visit to the area in July 1985. On 26 July 1985, the *Indian Express* (Madras edition) brought out a front page news item titled 'Starvation Deaths in Kalahandi District' with a Komna (Orissa) dateline. It reported the death on account of starvation of at least six persons in the preceding fortnight and the struggle for life of many more in the Komna block of Kalahandi district. Details of the dead were provided. It was noted that hungry people in Komna and surrounding villages had been eating leaves and roots for want of foodgrains after the crops failed three months earlier in the locality.

The failure of government to bring such a grave situation to light was noted. The Chief Minister of Orissa, it was reported, got first-hand knowledge of four deaths on 20 July 1985 but kept it to himself. The tribal people complained to the newspaper's correspondent that they were not provided with work or relief despite the Chief Minister's visit. All they got was a little foodstuff for babies under the drought feeding programme, but 'that is inadequate', they pleaded. On 28 July 1985, reports appeared in various newspapers round the country on the Prime Minister's visit to Phulbani district, and his fifteen-minute conversation with Parasi Punji, the woman who had sold her sister-in-law on account of an inability to support her, made the national media headlines. The tribal people were also reported to have told Rajiv Gandhi about the roots and wild leaves they were eating and to have complained that no official had ever visited their villages. 'Emaciated' Adivasi men and women were quoted as pleading with the Prime Minister's wife: 'Ma, give us food and work.'

The *Indian Express* continued its survey work in the area. In its issue of 7 August 1985 appeared a story by Saibal Dasgupta headlined 'Orissa Tribes live on Seeds and Leaves'. It described the 'traditional famine food' of tribal people in Koraput and Kalahandi districts—cakes made of powdered tamarind seeds, dried kernel or mango, mushrooms, wild leaves, mahua flowers, bamboo shoots, and tuberous roots—but noted that even when there was no drought, large sections of the people sustained themselves on a miserable diet. Once again, criticism was recorded of the official attitude and performance. There was an independent follow-up by the newspaper, and on 23 August 1985 fourteen more starvation deaths in just one Kalahandi village were reported. Feature articles in the newspaper's magazine section, other reports, and responses from readers demonstrated that a serious, independent, and sustained journalistic effort in such matters did make a difference to public opinion and did put pressure on impervious official hides.[31]

The fairly detailed coverage in the press of the issues concerning the midday meal (free school lunch) scheme which was introduced in 1982 in the southern state of Tamil Nadu and expanded to cover some nine million preschool and school children between the ages of 2 to 15 and which cost the state exchequer approximately Rs. 2,000 million annually represents another example of relevant journalism focusing on nutrition and hunger, even if the evaluations are somewhat divided. The motivations, implementation, financing, and impact have made it a target for political and media controversy, but there is a clear and persistent strand of support within an influential section of the press for such policy interventions in the vast arena of malnutrition and hunger.

Another example is the active interest taken by various newspapers and magazines in 1986 in exposing the story of injustice meted out to hundreds of bonded labourers, living under conditions of semi-starvation and social isolation, in the Kodaikanal area in Tamil Nadu. In this case, the press acted in association with official and unofficial allies in the democratic system to make a difference to a specific case of gross inequity and hunger. The Supreme Court's intervention in favour of the bonded labourers—clearly recognizing their entitlements, interpreted in a minimum sense, as justiciable rights—is likely to encourage the practice of such socially sensitive journalism.

In the most recent period, there has been a new interest shown by national newspapers in the content and methodology of the Left Front government's land reform and rural relief programme in West Bengal. With the interest heightened in the wake of the Left Front's decisive electoral victory in the state in March 1987 (for the third successive time) the experiment is widely recognized as a more imaginative and serious response to the challenge of chronic hunger and inequity in the countryside than the responses seen in other states. Studying the results of such broad-based socio-economic and political experiments in a relatively objective way, without ideological obfuscation or the mediation of crude prejudices, will undoubtedly represent an advance for Indian journalism.

Such cases provide insights into the strengths, but also the inadequacies, of Indian journalism in relation to endemic, regular hunger. Press coverage

---

[31] The situation in Kalahandi continued to figure on magazine covers a couple of years after the problem was highlighted by a daily newspaper. See for example, 'The Sorrow of Kalahandi' by S. N. M. Abdi in the *Illustrated Weekly* of 26 April–2 May 1987.

makes an observable difference, but almost invariably the press comes in only after another source of investigation has set in motion the events or triggered the controversy. A perceptive essay on the Indian judicial system by an American scholar, Galanter (1986), makes the point that the practice of law in India, for all the courtroom skills and sophistication it exhibits, suffers from serious inadequacies: for example, there is no tradition of independent investigation developed for situations outside the courtroom, technical specialization, and so on.[32] Such a criticism would apply even more to Indian journalism in relation to socio-economic fields where its independent or internal resources are clearly inadequate. With respect to exploring hunger and poverty across the land and yielding popular support to anti-hunger strategies, a major line of advance for the independent press would be directed towards bringing about a purposeful, critical, precisely targeted interaction between intelligent journalism and the relevant specialized disciplines in the social sciences or in other fields. This could help provide some focus, nuance, and sophistication in description, analysis, and prescription to journalistic coverage of complex socio-economic realities. Journalists must, making a decisive break with the tendencies we have remarked on in this paper, demonstrate a willingness to seek the aid of specialists in a much bigger way in the knowledge that *self-reliance* in this profession is guaranteed to push journalism further in the direction of superficiality, misleading analysis, and habitually missing the mark. On the other side, economists, historians, sociologists, anthropologists, political scientists, those involved in the study of science and technology and various other disciplines relevant to the concerns of wide-ranging journalism must show a willingness to utilize and develop the channels available in the relatively independent press (and perhaps even in the non-independent electronic media) to popularize the knowledge and insights they have gained from serious research. This they must do especially if they are concerned with influencing public policy in directions they deem desirable.

To an extent, the *Economic and Political Weekly* (*EPW*), a unique publication in the developing world, has promoted such an interaction over the years. Taking some kind of vantage position between journalism and the scholarly world, it has drawn from both and, perhaps, to that extent influenced sections

[32] Galanter (1986) offers an excellent review of the strengths and weaknesses of the Indian judicial system. He observes: 'The Indian lawyer is primarily a courtroom advocate, rather than advisor, negotiator, planner, or investigator . . . Lawyering revolves around courtroom manœuvre and argument with hardly a trace of the investigative, fact-development side of law practice. Lawyers do not employ specialist investigators or para-legals trained to conduct factual inquiries. Experts in scientific and technical fields with the exception of medicine are seldom utilised. Factual investigation is generally considered the responsibility of clients rather than of their lawyers. The low priority to fact-gathering and research is reflected in lawyers' fee arrangements: Lawyers typically charge their clients by the court "appearance" . . . India's lawyers are far from unenterprising. But it is an inventiveness within the severe limits imposed by the present format of law practice.' This criticism is of obvious relevance to the 'fact-development' side of journalistic practice in India.

of Indian journalism and also introduced the academic researcher to some of the requirements and strengths of serious journalism. Especially in the field of hunger, food economics, and poverty, the *EPW*—which, one must assume, has an influence beyond its limited circulation and is taken seriously by policy makers—has distinguished itself over the years in both its academic and journalistic sections. If there has been one major theme running through its issues it is the structural inadequacy of anti-hunger strategies pursued in India; its criticism of official policies has been detailed, sensitive, and credible. (However, in the recent period, the *EPW* has also tended to reflect trends in *instant economics* and *instant ecology*.) Provided the standards are not consciously lowered in an attempt to gain circulation and provided the temptation to compete with non-comparable publications on purely journalistic terms is resisted, there is clearly a future for this type of informed, research-orientated journalism. *South* magazine is another example of this intellectually serious approach to journalism, with some differences from the *EPW* in terms of focus, length of articles, and presentation and also international reach. (A deficiency in comparison with the *EPW* seems to be a less clearly focused critical editorial standpoint.)

If the capabilities and role of the independent press *vis-à-vis* hunger and poverty are to be strengthened, practical attention must be bestowed on the task of systematic interaction between journalism and specialized disciplines. If scholars who want to go public, or reach a wider audience, have something to learn from journalism, the press has a great deal to learn from academic disciplines on questions of sources, substantiation, precision, making a distinction between narration, description, descriptive richness, and analysis, and focusing on issues.

For too long has India's independent press got by on the strength of empiricism (if so eclectic an activity can be given that description), an inchoate realization of its own history, accumulated strengths, and unrealized potential, and a methodology that is *ad hoc* and, on most issues, hit-or-miss. What it needs to acquire in order to develop further is an active consciousness, a coherent theory of its own role in relation to society, a better informed socio-political and ethical[33] side to its practice, a break with the illusion of professional self-sufficiency, a systematic critical monitoring of its own performance, an internal accountability to higher intellectual standards, a more precise and less breathless style, and an active public advocacy of its own role as an indispensable part of the striving for a democratic, just system. Our study of the role of India's independent press in relation to hunger and poverty and the direction of public policy points strongly to these conclusions.

---

[33] Two recent studies of the ethical side of journalism, as it is practised in America, are Goldstein (1985) and Lambeth (1986); the findings would be, in some cases, of recognizable relevance to the practice of the Indian press. The first is a revealing critique and exposé of 'how journalists compromise their ethics to shape the news', and the second is a more formal academic treatment on 'enduring principles' and 'an ethic for the profession'.

4.3. *Conclusions*

1. It is an attractive intellectual proposition that information, and especially the news media, can play a substantive and progressive role in shaping public policy combating hunger. Our study, which is confined to the role of an independent press in relation to two kinds of hunger—a 'crisis' such as drought or famine on the one hand, and 'regular', endemic hunger and subhuman poverty on the other—substantiates this impression. It demonstrates that where the political system and practice allow it, timely and relevant journalism does make a real difference. Further research is required to explore why this role is so unevenly developed in the Third World. This case-study of the Indian experience yields a highly positive conclusion on the role of an independent press, but cautions against overestimating this role, especially as measurement of influence is virtually impossible. The contrast with the contemporary experience of much of Africa suggests a framework in which the 'power' of a relatively independent press—with a long-established tradition of playing a credible-informational and also a critical-adversarial role in relation to official authority—can be contrasted usefully with the absence of any such tradition and current role.

2. The role of an independent press such as India's must be viewed and analysed as part of a wider institutional value and ideological-political context. Alert, informative media coverage, if it is to be effective, must form part of an ideological and political context of attitude, feeling, and critical democratic values and practice; but merely to emphasize this would appear to undervalue the initiative or trigger that media coverage can provide to influencing the public mood or public opinion in a particular direction. Where the system allows no role for an independent press, policies could take a damaging course—at least in part on account of this absence.

3. The Indian press experience set in a broader framework suggests an analytical distinction between the 'credible-informational' and 'adversarial' or 'destabilizing' roles of an independent press in a developing country context. The first function has usually to do with a rule of law tradition, but it must be assumed that it can also be 'learned'; the more progressive 'adversarial' role that a press may be able to play with respect to public policy and in defence of mass entitlements and their expansion needs much stronger ideological and political nourishment. The first role appears to be a prerequisite for the second; but without the latter, which might imply some kind of 'adversarial' function in relation to government under typical circumstances, the former role might fade away through sheer disuse. Discussion of the independent strengths of a press in terms of these two roles does not imply ruling out a certain autonomy for the development of professional journalism. At its best, an independent press combines the two roles with professional competence and sophistication and works in favour of the stabilization of crisis-averting policies. But even under the best conditions, performance of the roles with professional serious-

ness might involve tensions and strains in the relationship with the government and in the arena of public policy making. Possibly the most important application of our positive finding is in the field of anti-hunger strategies.

4. A study of the historical and current performance of the independent Indian press in relation to hunger and poverty does seem to validate the 'dichotomy' suggested by Amartya Sen in his analysis of the essential experiences of India and China. The analysis suggests that while India's record in eliminating endemic, non-acute hunger contrasts unfavourably with the record of some other countries, such as China and Sri Lanka, independent newspapers along with opposition parties play a valuable role in making governments in India face realities and take steps in time to prevent famine. On the other hand, the disastrous Chinese experience of 1959–62 suggests that the absence of effective opposition parties and independent newspapers could, under certain circumstances, leave a government free to pursue disastrous policies even if they cause, or are unable to avert, a famine. The historical record of the Indian press with respect to a sudden outbreak of hunger on a mass scale—with famine as the worst case possibility—is a solid and valuable one. Recent and current coverage of crises such as droughts has been a strong point in the performance. On the other hand, the criticism that 'regular', chronic hunger and subhuman poverty are 'tame' issues to the Indian press is legitimate, even if recent coverage does suggest some improvement. The reasons for the 'low-key' treatment of endemic hunger and poverty must be explored in terms of policy orientation and bias, professional routine, the ideological and political predilections of journalists, influential or trendy currents in the literature journalists are exposed to, and a variety of practical constraints. But the basic problem seems related to inadequate intellectual and methodological resources and competence to investigate complex, mixed-up socio-economic realities in a non-superficial way. If this problem is addressed, the qualitative performance and impact could be improved significantly even within the context of the other limitations and constraints.

5. The Indian experience suggests that while the overall role and concerns are valuable, habits of imprecision, exaggeration, and oversimplification might detract from this role. There is a tendency to dramatize and sensationalize the coverage of poverty and hunger on a mass scale while missing out deeper structural features and processes. This tends to lower credibility among serious readers and, from the standpoint of serious analysis, proves counter-productive. The inherent problems of journalism—the constant search for a 'wake-up' quality for the less serious reader, dilettantism, and built-in tendencies of superficiality—make sensitive and sustained coverage of complex socio-economic realities difficult.

6. Aside from working towards a better material basis on which to develop, the independent press in India needs to go beyond the informational and methodological capabilities it has acquired professionally. A major line of advance would be stronger and more systematic interaction between serious

journalism and specialized disciplines, especially the social sciences; the pursuit of self-reliance in journalism would clearly be retrograde. The press also needs an internal accountability to higher intellectual standards, a more precise and less breathless style of work, and public advocacy of its role as a vital part of the striving for a democratic, just society. Provided these tasks can be undertaken seriously, it has a real future—even if majority practice in the Third World suggests that the Indian experience will be very hard to extend or replicate.

References

ARNOLD, D. (1979), 'Looting, Grain Riots and Government Policy in South India 1918', *Past and Present*, 84.

BAGDIKIAN, B. H. (1983), *The Media Monopoly* (Boston: Beacon Press).

——(1985), 'The Media Grab', *Channels*.

BRASS, P. R. (1986), 'The Political Uses of Crisis: The Bihar Famine of 1966–1967', *Journal of Asian Studies*, 45.

GALANTER, M. S. (1986), 'Affidavit in the United States District Court, Southern District of New York in Union Carbide Corporation Gas Leak Disaster at Bhopal, India', in *Mass Disasters and Multinational Liability: The Bhopal Case* (Bombay: Indian Law Institute).

GILL, P. (1986), *A Year in the Death of Africa: Politics, Bureaucracy and the Famine* (London: Paladin Grafton Books).

GOLDSTEIN, T. (1985), *The News at Any Cost: How Journalists Compromise Their Ethics to Shape the News* (New York: Simon & Schuster).

HAMELINK, C. J. (1983), *Cultural Autonomy in Global Communications* (London: Gollancz).

HANCOCK, G. (1985), *Ethiopia: The Challenge of Hunger* (London: Gollancz).

Independent Commission on International Humanitarian Issues (1985), *Famine: A Man-Made Disaster?* (London: Pan Books).

LAMBETH, E. B. (1986), *Committed Journalism: An Ethic for the Profession* (Bloomington, Ind.: Indiana University Press).

SANTHANAM, K. (1943), *The Cry of Distress: A First-Hand Description and an Objective Study of the Indian Famine of 1943* (New Delhi: The Hindustan Times).

SEN, A. K. (1981), *Poverty and Famines: An Essay on Entitlement and Deprivation* (Oxford: Oxford University Press).

——(1982), 'Coromandel Lecture' (New Delhi: as published in the *Hindu*).

——(1985a), 'Some International Comparisons', in *Commodities and Capabilities* (Amsterdam: North-Holland).

——(1985b), 'Food, Economics and Entitlements', mimeo (WIDER); reproduced as ch. 2 above.

SONTAG, S. (1978), *On Photography* (Harmondsworth: Penguin).

5

The Intrafamily Distribution of Hunger in South Asia

Barbara Harriss

5.1. *A narrative string of quotations*

All actions stem from food . . . Food depends on food. (Rig-Veda; Taittiriya Upanishad, III.ix.1)

Food is a language of power. (Macdonald 1955)

The logic of the hearth is the logic of the Hindu cosmos in miniature. (Appadurai 1985)

The concept of 'the Indian family' has no analytical value. (Mies 1980: 73)

The son is oneself, the wife is one's friend but the daughter is indeed a humiliation. (Mahabharata Adi, 159.11)

Men owe their birth to women; O ungrateful wretches! How can happiness be your lot when you condemn them? (Bratsamhita (74) of Varahamira)

In India and Bangladesh . . . a pattern of sex bias—against women—in the distribution of food . . . has come through strikingly. (Sen 1985*a*: 15)

The data clearly demonstrate the non existence of sex discrimination in the intrahousehold allocation of food to women beyond what can be accounted for by body size, activity and physiological differentials. (Abdullah 1983: 143)

The primary target group . . . of relatively deprived individuals . . . has been identified beyond doubt as the child of either sex in the age group from 7 to 18 months. (Cantor *et al.* 1973: i.92)

Food is an emotional and moral meta-language . . . To miss the abstract notion of food is to see the place of practice very differently. (Khare 1976*a*: 5, 267)

These quotations commend themselves because they show the extent to which this essay will thread its way through a maze of both subtle ambivalences and gross contradictions with respect to a number of social issues which bear upon any discussion of food distribution within the South Asian household. These are the *modus operandi* of patriarchy, the measurement and interpretation of hunger, the cultural meanings of material phenomena, and the conception of the policy process. We shall consider these issues, in the course of this essay.

I am very grateful to Erica Wheeler, Simon Strickland, Philip Payne, and Mary Griffiths of the Department of Human Nutrition, London School of Hygiene and Tropical Medicine, for their helpful responses to earlier versions; to Amartya Sen, Qaiser Khan, Judith Heyer, and especially Jean Drèze for comments at and after the WIDER Conference in Helsinki (1986); to Terry Byres, Chris Langford, and Maureen Mackintosh who reacted to it elsewhere; to ICRISAT, especially Tom Walker, for permitting access to their food intake data; and to Nicola Dunn of the London School of Hygiene and Tropical Medicine who reworked some of the ICRISAT data for WIDER, though I alone am responsible for this revision.

5.2. *The context*

Malnutrition has been related to low household income and to inadequate entitlement to food at the level of the household.[1] But some members of households with inadequate aggregate food intake may not be malnourished,[2] and not all malnourished individuals come from households with inadequate aggregate food intake.[3] Shares within the household are unequal throughout the entire world including Western referents. Although it is necessary to explain the aetiology of malnutrition in terms of factors operating on the household, malnutrition does not often affect every household member equally at any given time.[4]

If malnutrition is difficult to define (a social construct as much as a biological state or process, an economic input as well as an outcome), it is even more the case with the idea of hunger. As Payne has observed, 'hunger is a euphemism for want and deprivation, an expression of appetite, a manifestation of the biological regulation of energy balance'.[5] Lipton has identified hunger as a probabilistic state of energy deprivation not intense enough to cause physiological damage through severe undernutrition, which is a state he associates with ultrapoverty.[6] We shall define 'hunger' carefully, restrictively (and with reference to its opposite), when we come to its measurement (Section 5.3).

There is a widely held set of views about the allocation of food and nutrients within the South Asian household, summarized recently by Wheeler.[7] This is:

- that men take a disproportionate share of household food resources at the expense of other members and that women and children get less both than adult men and than what they need physiologically;
- that the consequences of getting less are more serious in households with insufficient food entitlements;
- that women permit this distribution and therefore acquiesce to the reproduction of malnutrition.

The reasons for this are thought to be not only material but also related to Hindu cultural principles.[8] So we begin by examining the culture of food in South Asia, after which we turn to the material relations of provisioning. Great interpretative caution is needed. While fine ethnographic accounts have been

---

[1] Respectively Lipton (1983); Sen (1981); Khan (1984).

[2] Mathews (1979: 100–3).

[3] Munoz de Chavez *et al.* (1974); Ryan *et al.* (1984: 30, 39).   [4] Sen (1985*a*, 1985*b*).

[5] Payne (1985*a*).   [6] Lipton (1983: 23).   [7] Wheeler (1984).

[8] 'Hindu' refers here to what Khare has called 'para-ideology': although Hindu does not mean Indian 'it is wrong to assume that there are as many types of cultural genesis of food problems as regional, religious or cultural communities'. For long, there has been exchange of information and technique such that people of all regions and religions are bound by interconnected effects with respect to the production and distribution of food (Khare 1976*b*: 173).

provided by Khare and by Appadurai,[9] it would seem that quantitative and gender aspects of allocation are so underresearched by anthropologists, and the small body of nutritional evidence is presented in such a timeless and classless way by nutritionists, that statements of general principle are made at one's peril. Caution is also needed over the discrepancies between what people say and believe, what they actually do, and what they think about these discrepancies.[10]

(a) The control of food

It is often assumed that men make decisions about food production while women control household food budgets and food distribution.[11] Whitehead, however, has shown the household to be an arena of unequal material exchanges. These exchanges, and the control they involve, work to male advantage in both peasant society in Ghana and working-class households in the English Midlands.[12] That there are no equivalent studies in South Asia does not mean that her observation would not hold. Certainly both ancient customary law and modern practice show that the provision of a shared source of food appropriate to each member's needs is one of the obligations of the male householder. In practice, this distributive obligation involves the unequal work of almost all household members in rural society the needs of whom are culturally defined.[13] Control can be exercised over material stocks, over decisions about their use, and over their preparation within the household from the state of raw material to that of product, ready for consumption.

Attempts have been made recently to relate *female* control over food decisions to the class position of their households and their individual economic status as wage workers. Evidence exists from Maharashtra that the nutritional status of children is better if women rather than men directly control grain and/or cash with which to purchase grain.[14] The question at issue is whether cash or kind contributions by wage-working women to the household budget are translated into greater control over the use of that cash in subsistence decisions. Existing evidence suggests the answer is no. In three contrasted villages in North Arcot District of Tamil Nadu, although patterns of control were surprisingly diverse, the male household head enjoyed sole control of market decisions relating to domestic food in nearly 60 per cent of cases, and jointly with his wife in another 15 per cent. Women were responsible in a slight majority of households for the choice of ingredients, but with respect

---

[9] Khare (1976a, 1976b); Appadurai (1981, 1985).

[10] Khare (1976b); Dube (1983: 228).   [11] White (1984: 24).

[12] Whitehead (1981).   [13] Kane (1941: ch. 9, esp. p. 428); Greenough (1982: 215).

[14] ILO (1979). It is possible that factors other than female control (such as income) are involved in this relationship. There is evidence that nutritional status does not improve in female-headed households where female control is not a cultural artefact but a necessity in a slum in urban Bangladesh (Pryer 1987).

to quantities of food prepared there is no discernible pattern of control. Certainly women do not dominate quantitative decisions. There were no significant associations between female wage-work participation and their control over food expenditure and purchase decisions. Nor was there any consistent association between the gender of food controllers and their social class. In two villages women were more important controllers of food in the propertied classes while men dominated in assetless, labouring families.[15] This was not true for a third where male control was more frequent than joint or female control throughout the social spectrum.[16] This lends qualified support to a general conclusion made by Jain that 'income does not guarantee improved female status within household or society' if we understand 'status' to be defined at least in part by control over the most important expenditure head.[17]

(b)   The food cycle

The domestic preparation of food has developed elaborate structures based on principles of rank and hierarchy according to purity, social and ritual debt over the last two thousand years.[18] These structures testify to individual material rights and obligations which are not symmetrical, but which are not always easily reducible to female inferiority. Khare has described the preparation of a meal as a 'food cycle', and identified its elements and its social and cultural scope. Its rules, as derived from ethnographic material for Lucknow Brahmins, are recognized as 'remarkably similar' for Tamil Brahmins by Appadurai,[19] and so they may have wide geographical relevance. Khare's treatment of food cycles in poverty-stricken and/or low-caste households is to itemize and analyse the respects in which they deviate from Brahminical orthodoxy, an approach latent in Appadurai's most recent work on food cycles in poor agricultural households in Maharashtra.[20]

The elements of a food cycle consist of the food area, cook, utensils, technique, ingredients, feeding, and the reinstatement of purity by cleaning. To summarize: the cleaning of the food area is a female act; the food area may be subdivided into cooking, storing, and eating areas, the former generally female and the latter male. The cooking crews for the most exclusive food and in the most exclusive food area tend to be female.[21] Cooking utensils are

---

[15] Harriss (1986: 79–81).   [16] Gibbs (1986).   [17] Jain (1980: 4).

[18] On its history, see Chakravarty (1972: 33–7). Note that 'cooking' means an act of preparation not necessarily involving the application of heat, but almost invariably involving progressive social restrictions on consumption according to mode of preparation. Preparation without fire is more inclusive than with fire, and frying is more inclusive than boiling. Culinary expertise is derived from knowledge of the ritual rules of handling food rather than from any accomplishment in culinary aesthetics. Culinary orthodoxy rests with the individual not with the household (Khare 1976a, 1976b: 36; Appadurai 1985). The principles of orthodoxy, of purity, and of service are part and parcel of all other aspects of household behaviour (Dube 1983: 229–31).

[19] Appadurai (1981: 497).   [20] Appadurai (1985).

[21] Even in urban scavenging households it is women who 'cook' i.e. in this case who collect the food from their 'client' households (Trivedi 1976: 43).

classified in terms of material and context into a hierarchy of auspiciousness
and gender. Cooking technique is not sophisticated, in contradistinction to its
'ontological mode' which is sophisticated and is not yielding to technological
change.[22] 'To perfect the pampering of the body is to have labour lost for a
decidedly trifling cause.'[23] Ingredients are subject to a large number of
simultaneous and interacting classification systems, which we need to discuss
later. But as Appadurai observes for the village of Vadi in Maharashtra, the
provision of ingredients is not a task framed by rigid conceptions or measures
of need or requirements but rather by seasonality of crops in relation to
the cycle of village rituals and festivals, and to idiosyncratic household
celebrations of the life-cycle rituals.[24]

'A meal' is consumed by different household members in different places at
different times and with specific types of company. Eating is a ritually lowering
act for the (male) eater and tends to be carried out after cleansing rather quickly
and in silence.[25] For men to eat in the company of women has been considered
improper since the first century AD.[26] In general, eating order obeys certain
principles, with age and male sex taking precedence, and with husbands'
relatives and patrikin taking precedence over wives' relatives and matrikin.[27]
Women (not necessarily those who cook) serve using the right (male/pure)
hand only, and they assign quantities despite male silence or refusal.[28]
Whereas women eat last, the position of children is not so determined. They
have been reported to eat in any order: before other household members (so
that the wife serves her husband with undivided attention);[29] after men but
before women (fed by other brothers and sisters; not subject to special favours
from the server); and/or with the women.[30] In the latter circumstances, men

[22] Khare (1976a: 35–6, 70).

[23] Ibid. 63.

[24] Appadurai (1985). The classification of foods is often referred to derogatively by nutritionists
as 'food fads' or 'taboos'. Judgements of these systems as 'pernicious', 'detrimental to good
nutrition', 'deplorable' (e.g. Cantor et al. 1973: i. 116, 120) may have been informed by the
concept of the balanced diet which has come under criticism for its tendency to equate food types
with types of nutrient.

[25] Khare (1976a: 8).

[26] Chakravarty (1972: 37).

[27] Khare (1976a: 76). Ambiguities of rank in large joint families with systems of cross-cousin
marriage, resolved by statements with portions and ingredients, are the subject of Appadurai's
'Gastropolitics' (1981). See also Sharma (1983) for Rajasthan; Abdullah (1983) for Bangladesh.

[28] The left hand is reserved for dealing with the impure opposite of food: faeces. Women are
proscribed from either cooking or serving while menstruating (when the woman is most removed
from the role of genetrix) at which point, in houses where there is no alternative, roles are reversed
and the male cooks and serves. This reversal is observed by the cremator who is cook at death
rituals (Khare 1976a, 1976b).

[29] A case-study for Bengal is by Chakravarty (1972: 100–2).

[30] Khare (1976a) for north India, Appadurai (1981: 498); McNeill (1986: ch. 3.1); Thiagarajan
(1973: 80) for south India.

will not know the quantities of food consumed by their women and children. Age and sex play a role in the degree of indulgence displayed over infantile transgressions of food rules. Women may in turn themselves obey an eating (and serving) order based on age and husband's rank within the household, or may eat communally at their convenience with 'prolonged gossiping'.[31]

Special food for women is often called 'leftovers'. Husband's leftovers are appropriate for the wife alone, otherwise polluted. But it is worth understanding that there are at least three types of leftover, only one of which has the wife eating the scraps on her husband's leaf or plate. The others are unserved residues: uneaten food in the serving pots and unserved reserves in the kitchen.[32]

There is a category of food recognized throughout South Asia as signifying status or prestige. Although the precise items vary, we tend to be referring with this concept to meat, fish, and sometimes milk products, fruit, and 'English' (temperate) vegetables. North Indian evidence suggests that this food is either never eaten by women, or reserved for men if supplies of it are scarce.[33] In Sharma's poor households in Rajasthan even vegetables were eaten mainly by men, and pulses were not given to young children.[34] However Khare cautions that meat, milk, and status vegetables are 'seldom encountered delicacies', not of great quantitative importance in the daily diet. Moreover, dietary variety does not by itself indicate variety or appropriateness of nutrients. A further caution comes from evidence from the south of an absence of gender difference in food variety in agricultural castes in Tamil Nadu, among scheduled castes in Kerala, and tribals in Andhra Pradesh. Finally, items taboo to women may also include narcotics and other appetite suppressants.[35] Given such variations and given trade-offs and substitutions between quantities and prices of food items in male and female diets it is not possible to make assumptions or generalizations about gender differences in the costs of nutrients in South Asia.

Three major sources of change in this model of daily food behaviour have been noted by ethnographers. One, poverty, appears to lead to a relaxation of rules with respect to every element. However, the orthodox rules are observed in ceremonial feasting by the poor, which is taken to signify their importance as reference points.[36] The second source of change is commensal derestriction. This has been described as practised by men, opposed by women, and understood not as a change in the rules but as a flouting of them.[37] The third is the education of women which may lead to a change in the rules surrounding

[31] Chakravarty (1972: 100–1); Khare (1976a: 76); Caldwell et al. (1983).

[32] Chakravarty (1972: 33); Khare (1976a: 76); Appadurai (1981: 498).

[33] Thiagarajan (1973); Abdullah (1983); Gulati (1978); Appadurai (1985).

[34] Sharma (1983).

[35] Khare (1986: 95); McNeill (1986: ch. 3); Trivedi (1976: 41); Gillespie (1986; personal communication).

[36] Khare (1976a: 65–99).   [37] Ibid. 245–54.

food as in those surrounding other aspects of domestic life.[38] We shall return to discuss certain policy implications of these changes later.

(c) Gender, food cycles, and life cycles

The food cycle is further shaped by culturally defined needs associated with equally culturally defined stages of life.[39] From birth, the gender of an infant testifies to its cultural needs. While a child is breast-fed he or she gets a nutritionally balanced diet with anti-infective properties. No evidence yet exists that gender affects the number or duration of feeds while a suckling is breast-fed. But evidence from villages as dispersed as Morinda in Punjab, Matlab thana in Bangladesh, Karnataka and DR Kuppam in Tamil Nadu suggests that male babies are breast-fed for longer than females. In the southern case the difference was five months. The difference between the most propertied and the assetless classes was a further five months so that a male child in a landed household would be likely to be breast-fed for ten months longer than a female child in an agricultural labouring household.[40] The decisions to wean and to cease breast-feeding, as Caldwell et al. also report with respect to the decision to end post-natal sexual abstinence, have until recently been a matter for female elders rather than for the mother herself and may be being taken over in some areas by husband or by husband and wife together.[41] Despite the listing of special diets for weaning in ancient texts, it is rare to find their use now and it is apparently usual to find children weaned on to a bland version of 'household food' (if this term can now be used). The relatively low energy density of such food is thought to result in frequent, time-consuming feeding of the weanling. Das Gupta, in her surveys of Ludhiana villages in Punjab, notes a tendency towards daughters being weaned on to a vegetarian diet and sons on to a non-vegetarian one.[42] Levinson, however, reminds us that gender differences in weaning do not necessarily signify nutritional differences. In the richer Jat households in Morinda the weaned girl was on a par with the semi-weaned boy in terms of total nutrients. This was not true of the poorer Ramdasia caste, where girls were at a disadvantage from an early age.[43]

[38] Dube (1983: 230–6) attributes this to the anomic nature of institutions of education and to the dissolving effect on domestic life of the intrusion of various forms of secular state institutions into it.

[39] Greenough (1982). Even at birth a distinction is made. The dhai in Kodiur village in Tamil Nadu is paid twice as much for a boy as for a girl (Mathews 1979: 150). Useful accounts of food and the life cycle are given for two villages in Tamil Nadu by Krishnamurthy (1973) and Thiagarajan (1973). Comparisons of different regions are made by Apte (1973).

[40] Levinson (1972); McNeill (1984); Caldwell et al. (1983); Koenig and d'Souza (1986); Visaria (1987).   [41] Caldwell et al. (1982).   [42] Das Gupta (1987).

[43] Levinson (1972). See also Chakravarty (1972) and Mathews (1979: 103–7). The Tamil Nadu Nutrition Study reports no gender discrimination in food behaviour, notes a large number of foods as being recognized as good for the weanling and concludes that cultural practices limit quantity rather than variety (Cantor et al. 1973: i. 123).

Appadurai reports that the gastropolitical socialization of children into roles of demand, aggression, and authority (boys) and deference, meekness, stoicism, and self-preservation (girls) proceeds from the age of about 5.[44] The Caldwells additionally observe gender differences in foraging for food and in snacking (both done more by boys). Children in their Karnataka studies were reported to eat together (in such a way as to make gender differences in the socialization of eating difficult to administer) until the age of 6 among the rich but until adolescence among the poor.[45]

Unless unusually poor nutritional status throughout childhood delays menarche, the girl reaches the stage of adulthood at puberty and several years before the boy.[46] If married prior to puberty she now migrates (if not, she is married) and starts to climb from the bottom the rungs of rank in her husband's household. This climb depends on the outcomes of her pregnancies. Food restrictions, commonly imposed in pregnancy and lactation,[47] actually leave a wide range of food available for women made to observe these rules. Evidence from a North Arcot village shows increases in food variety for pregnant and lactating women, together with slight increases in energy intake and marked compensating reductions in activities involving high energy expenditure in the third trimester.[48] According to Khare, the mother of a girl is freed from post-natal dietary restrictions earlier than is that of a boy because at birth the girl is less polluting. During lactation however the mother of a boy is allowed greater dietary variety than that of a girl[49] (though recall that dietary variety *per se* indicates nothing necessarily about nutrition). Other aspects of food behaviour for adults in the sexually active, working, householder stage of life have been described earlier.

The elderly are defined demographically as over 44 and supposedly post-menopause ('dried-out' is a common description in Indian languages). Calorie needs are thought to begin declining after the age of 55. About the diet of the elderly (who have been found recently to have major and time-consuming roles in child care[50]) little is known. In Kodiur, a village also in North Arcot, an orthodox widow in an agricultural caste would eat but one meal a day composed of a highly restricted range of foods.[51]

[44] Appadurai (1981: 498).

[45] Caldwell and Caldwell (1987).

[46] Evelath (1985); Greenough (1982: 247).

[47] Mathews (1979); Krishnamurthy (1973); Thiagarajan (1973).

[48] Sundaraj and Pereira (1973, 1975); McNeill (1986); see also Roberts *et al.* (1982) for activity reductions during pregnancy in Gambia.

[49] Khare (1976a: 162).

[50] McNeill (1984). In India as a whole, however, 65% of male children are cared for by their mothers in contrast to 55% of female children (Nagaraj 1986: 65–6).

[51] Mathews (1979: 226–31); see also proscriptions on meat, fish, and alcohol in old age, in Chakravarty (1972: 36).

The food cycle is embellished not simply by life cycles but also by responses to illness. Errors in the food cycle *inter alia* are also widely understood to cause illness. 'The local medical system' (though there are at least three non-allopathic systems) 'encourages a view of a good diet which centres on food type rather than food quantity.'[52] This is because health is understood as a balance between three elements composing the material and spiritual body and corresponding broadly with three types of food.[53] Most major diseases recognized by allopathic medicine including those of malnutrition therefore have a dietary explanation vested in type of food rather than quantity.[54] Treatment accordingly is not conceived in terms of quantity but instead in terms of food items with qualities opposite to those manifested by the illness. For instance, the practice in DR Kuppam village of feeding millet rather than rice to workers engaged in heavy agricultural labour and vulnerable to malnutrition is understood in terms of millet's quality of 'coolness' which makes it appropriate for work in hot weather.[55]

While nutritionists have strained to study the quotidian food cycle, anthropologists have devoted attention to ceremonies. For our purposes a few points suffice. First festivals, whether to do with the calendar, or with national, village level, or household religious occasions, or with life-cycle rituals, are numerous and involve increased consumption of food, 'perpetuating the myth of abundance and dissipating collective scarcity', as Khare puts it. Secondly they involve a social expansion of every aspect of the food cycle extending in the case of marriages to public meals. And they are not captured, indeed they are studiously avoided, in dietary surveys by nutritionists, so their positive quantitative effects are unknown.[56]

The converse is also true. Nutritionists have also avoided fasting subjects when studying the diets of so called 'free living' people. A fast, like a leftover, needs defining. Fasting means the abstinence from 'exciting' food (spices, fried and/or salty food) or from food raised through ploughing for half or a whole day. Boiled potatoes, tapioca, milk and its products, including sweets and fruit, are all fasting foods. So fasting involves changing the source of energy intake but not always reducing it. There are strong gender differences in fasting, male fasts being for individual spiritual purpose and female fasts being for the auspiciousness of the household collective (i.e. for husband, son,

[52] McNeill (1986: ch. 3.2); Mathews (1979: 96–141) according to whom other causes of illness are supernatural; injury, accident, and stress; dirt and pollution; and cultural errors in the practice of sexual intercourse.

[53] Marriott (1978); Kakar (1982: 219–51); Caldwell *et al.* (1982); Thiagarajan (1973: 84–6).

[54] Mathews (1979: 141); Krishnamurthy (1973: 60–4); see also Kynch and Maguire (1986) for evidence of reluctance to attribute disease to lack of food in Palanpur, UP.

[55] McNeill (1986: ch. 3.1); Krishnamurthy (1973).

[56] Excellent sources on food and feeding ritual in ceremonies can be found in Khare (1976a: 162–228); Appadurai (1981: 502–5; 1985); and Mathews (1979: 211–63).

brother).[57] In Vadi in Maharashtra 'most households have at least one member who fasts on at least one day a week and if it is just one person who fasts it is likely to be the senior female'.[58] Female fasts according to Khare are more varied, numerous, and austere than those of men. In Lucknow in the north, out of a total of 105 possible fasting days in the year, orthodox Brahmin women observed fasts on average on 55 days, while poor urban women observed from 5 to 15. Yet in DR Kuppam in the south, McNeill found no gender difference in those having fewer than three meals a day (whether voluntary or involuntary).[59] Both Khare and Appadurai remark that fasting among the poor may be an occasion for sociability and supportive exchange by the women of the immediate neighbourhood.[60] Again the quantitative negative effects of fasting on adult men and women are unknown.

This review of Hindu food behaviour lends very qualified support to the generalizations marshalled by Wheeler to the effect that women are residual claimants and that their lack of eligibility to certain types of food leads to malnutrition. Women and girls tend to act domestically according to a paradigm of service (both sexual and culinary). But just as there is great variety in types of household and types of food cycle so there is great variety in structural types of woman. Our model of subordination in food allocation is the bride. The new bride and apprentice cook in an orthodox house may well eat last and alone (less likely in tribal and/or Dravidian society and among the very poor). As the mother of a son she may eat well and in the company of her mother-in-law.[61] As a widow she may eat, taking precedence but separately, close to the biological minimum for survival. The separate interactional worlds of women both dictate gender differences in eating patterns and permit nutritional subterfuge. Small children appear to be a collective responsibility in a joint family, with elderly male and female relatives and/or older children, aunts, and servants figuring as importantly in their general care and their feeding as the mother, so often assumed to be the sole feeder. Notions of female rank and deconstructions of female gender have not by and large informed nutritionists' classifications of adult women and seem to be outside the range of their policy prescriptions.[62] Perhaps this is because rank and gender are modified by region, poverty, and caste or tribal group, in complex ways not easily accommodated by the policy process.

(d)   Material aspects of patriarchy

Food behaviour and culture have been interpreted as manifestations of patriarchy[63] and, consistent with other indicators, as manifestations of rela-

---

[57] Macdonald (1955); Khare (1976a: 130–3); Dube (1983: 229).

[58] Appadurai (1985).   [59] McNeill (1986: ch. 3).

[60] Khare (1976a: 144–9); Appadurai (1985).   [61] Appadurai (1981: 500).   [62] ICSSR (1977).

[63] For example Mies (1980); Bardhan (1985). On the general phenomenon of patriarchy, see Mackintosh (1981).

tions and states of 'discrimination' and female subordination.[64] Pursuit of evidence of these states and indicators contextualizes food behaviour with other aspects of life inside and outside the household. With apologies to authors and readers of a large literature, we have to be brief. The oft-quoted law of Manu belies a profound ambivalence towards women in the minds of the male makers of and commentators on customary law, an ambivalence also attested by contemporary psychologists.[65] (The customary rights of the male householder over children of either sex, we also ought to note, are said to have been as absolute as those over women until earlier this century.)[66] The material subordination of women and children has operated through male control over land, property, labour and the expression of sexuality. It has had historically specific outcomes in welfare as measured by health and nutritional status, by mortality, in particular by the age distribution of excess female or male mortality rates.

Despite the enactment of legislation after Independence in India and Bangladesh to guarantee equal inheritance rights to men and women, the control of women over property is thought to have diminished throughout the subcontinent over the past fifty years, although there remain notable differences between 'the south' and 'the north', with southern (and possibly tribal) women having greater access to property than northern women.[67] Similarly despite the Dowry Prohibition Act of 1961, the practice of transferring resources on marriage as dowry is said to be increasing in both prevalence and size and colonizing the south of the subcontinent, where previously bride price was more common.[68] Controversial issues include the economic significance of the dowry,[69] the nature of the north–south difference in marriage transfers, whether or not dowry is diffusing south,[70] and whether its diffusion is related to a decline in female participation in the wage labour force.[71] But there is

---

[64] The dictionary definition of discrimination is the 'observation of distinct differences'. Sen does not distinguish between states and indicators of discrimination in his concept of (measurable) 'functionings' (Sen 1985*b*).

[65] Manu (v. 146–8): 'In childhood a female must be subject to her father, in youth to her husband, when her lord is dead to her sons. A woman must never be independent.' The ambivalence between scorn (of her pettiness), fear (of her sexuality), and veneration (of her as a mother of sons) is magnificently discussed in relation to customary law in Kane (1941: vol. ii, part 2, chs. 9–11) and see also Sharma (1980) for contemporary evidence for northern India. (Male) ambivalence towards the nurturing, protective, and destructive role of the mother is equally well described in Kakar (1981: 53–112).

[66] Kane (1941: 507). [67] Omvedt (1978); Cain (1977); Miller (1981).

[68] Rajaraman (1983).

[69] Dowry can be interpreted economically as a rotating capital fund; as a compensation for an economically unproductive member; as a symbolic selling; as a response to a shortage of marriageable men; and as a premortum inheritance for the bride (Woodley 1986).

[70] Dyson and Moore (1983); compare Sharma (1980) for the north with Gough (1981) for the south.

[71] Compare Rajaraman (1983) with Randeria and Visaria (1984).

agreement that the commercialization of females via resource transfers at marriage is punitive for households with a preponderance of daughters.

Also material and real for those women to whom it pertains is the practice of seclusion. This may restrict the secluded woman to the interior of the home. It may prohibit interaction of any sort between a young woman and senior men. It may restrict public movement, participation in the labour force, and the making of cash transactions.[72] A sociological verdict on its operation in a Hindu village in central India is that it creates a smaller yet much more intricate interactional world than that of men.[73] Other ways by which female behaviour may be controlled in exogamous patrilineages include age differences between spouses, distance from the natal home, and frequency of natal visits (the latter regarded by demographic anthropologists of South Asia as having crucial bearing upon female welfare).[74]

Female disadvantage is expressed in wage work. In many parts of central and south India, for instance, men and women play a roughly equal role in the labour inputs to agricultural production, yet women are remunerated less for it both because more of their productive agricultural work is unwaged, and because daily wage rates are lower, in the region of 50–70 per cent of those of men.[75] Male control over the labour process is argued to render acceptable both the exclusion of women from secure work and a greater probability of involuntary unemployment. Other restricted sectors of female activity such as petty production and trade are dependent on male sanction for physical premises, credit, and prices.[76] This male control has implications for female welfare.

Girls' survival chances have been related to their anticipated earnings as adults and to the size of the gender gap in daily earnings.[77] Yet legislation in certain states expresses acceptance of this gender difference.[78] These differences cannot be explained by productivity. For a start, it is impossible to

[72] Respectively Sharma (1978, 1980) for north India; Gough (1981: 383–5) for the south; Cain *et al.* (1979) for Bangladesh.

[73] Appadurai (1985).

[74] Das Gupta (1987); Jeffery *et al.* (1987); and Visaria (1987) who records that in Kachch District of Gujarat a shroud is commonly given with a dowry, symbolic of the complete lack of future contact on the part of the bride with her natal home.

[75] See Parthasarathy and Rama Rao (1973); Ryan and Ghodake (1984), Behrman and Deolalikar (1986a) for evidence in agriculture, and Harriss (1981) for evidence in trade and agroprocessing.

[76] Harriss (1976a).

[77] Rosenzweig and Schultz (1980). See also Bardhan (1987) and Bardhan (1985). On gender differences adverse to women in rural trade see Harriss (1976a); on greater insecurity and on the lack of relation between participation rates and the probability of employment for women in contradistinction to men, see Ryan and Ghodake (1980); on a general statement about women's subsidy to capitalist exploitation, see Deere (1979).

[78] Bardhan (1982).

measure gender productivity when, as in agricultural production, the gender division of labour requires men and women to perform non-comparable tasks; and where jobs are comparable, productivity differences have been found not to determine wage rate differentials.[79] Whether wage rates are determined by supply and demand is still unresolved despite a substantial econometric input,[80] and the gender division of labour, within which supply and demand operates, is taken as given in this work.

Striking regional variations in the extent, forms, and conditions of female participation have been mapped, and attempts have been made to explain them materially. Although higher rates of female participation in wage work are observed in the south and east than in the north and north-west, explanations based on regional variations in agricultural ecology and on the labour needs of agriculture have not stood the test of empirical scrutiny.[81] This failure has strengthened the hand of those invoking the power of the varied manifestations of patriarchy.

Trends toward declining female participation have been observed from as far back as the 1911 census. This trend has been carefully reinterpreted as not being an artefact of the several census redefinitions of work.[82] Attempts have been made to relate the male control of new production technology in agriculture to the recent displacement of female labour and the intensification of capitalist production relations.[83] It is likely, however, that several contradictory processes are involved: changes in the gender division of labour; changes in the crop composition of certain farming systems with implications for the gender division of labour; 'voluntary withdrawal' of upper-class rural women; and forced displacement of women from assetless households.[84] There is incontrovertible evidence of massive masculinization and net labour displacement due to technological change in post-harvest processing.[85]

Women combine waged and unwaged productive work with unwaged reproductive work for much of their lives. While biological production and field work may be the preserve of adult women, social reproduction and household production is carried out by girls, adult women, and the elderly.

---

[79] Rosenzweig (1984).

[80] Ibid.; Binswanger and Rosenzweig (1984).

[81] Miller (1981); and see literature which qualifies her 'agrarian determinist' explanation of female participation: Mencher and Saradamoni (1982); Gulati (1975a, 1975b) in Kerala; Harriss et al. (1984); Ryan and Ghodake (1980) for central and southern dryland agricultural villages. For complicating and contradictory effects of poverty see Sen (1982); of caste see Gulati (1978); of dependency see Cain et al. (1979); of urban and rural location see Kynch and Sen (1983).

[82] ICSSR (1977: 5–6); Omvedt (1978).

[83] Mies (1980); Mencher (1980); Agarwal (1984).

[84] Agarwal (1984); Sharma (1980); Maclachlan (1983).

[85] See Sharma (1980) for Punjab and Himachal Pradesh; Harriss (1976b) for Tamil Nadu; Harriss (1982) and Mukherjee (1983) for West Bengal; Harriss (1979) and Greeley (1986) for Bangladesh.

This unremunerated work has been argued to subsidize wages paid to both male and female labour. Recent trends towards the nuclearization of the household in rural north India have been shown to have contradictory effects upon female autonomy. While on the one hand the relative power of the adult woman *vis à vis* the adult relatives in her household over decisions pertaining to provisioning, birth spacing, and child care may be increased, on the other hand so also are her burden of work and her energy needs, particularly about the time of childbirth. It is possible to generalize neither about trends in household composition and type nor about their implications for female autonomy.[86]

Given that female education may be a major source of change in domestic productive and reproductive behaviour (especially fertility decisions) advantageous to the welfare of women, the rise in their literacy rates and the increasing confinement of illiteracy to those over the age of 25 indicates the possibility of a rise in female status over the next two decades. Yet female literacy lags behind that of males, especially in the north and centre of India in areas with a high concentration of scheduled castes and tribes. In the latter case, there are high adult female participation rates in wage work to which low education may be expected to act as a countervailing force.[87] The relationship between education and demographic indicators of welfare is not clear cut. The Caldwells show for Karnataka that rising female educational status is associated with a reduction in child mortality rates but with no reduction in male–female differentials. Das Gupta presents evidence from Ludhiana region where there is a relatively high rate of female literacy that education has no impact upon either child mortality rates or gender differentials. Behrman finds that the ICRISAT data for villages in central and southern India reveals the educational status of the male household head as being positively associated with pro-male bias in the food allocation and intake of children under 13, an activity actually undertaken by women.[88]

Well-being, measured most directly by mortality, is the outcome not only of work burdens and status, and of education, but also crucially of the interaction between nutrition, physiological state, and disease. While female mortality rates in excess of male rates in the reproductive years are likely to reflect the hazards of childbirth,[89] and while high levels of parity and reproductive wastage are well-acknowledged health risks, the evidence for differential morbidity which is not directly or indirectly related to reproduction is not clear. On the one hand there is historical data to show greater female mortality

---

[86] Jeffery *et al.* (1987); Wadley and Derr (1987).

[87] Dube (1983); Caldwell *et al.* (1982); ICSSR (1977); Khan (1985); Jain and Nag (1986).

[88] Caldwell *et al.* (1983); Das Gupta (1987); Behrman (1986). An indication of the importance of countervailing factors to that of education is found in Sri Lanka where the far less well-educated Tamil women have lower fertility than more highly educated Sinhalese women (Langford 1982).

[89] ICSSR (1977: 4–7); Karkal (1987).

from epidemics of plague and influenza.[90] Closer to the present time, evidence on morbidity from the Calcutta Metropolitan Development Area shows that while 1.9 per cent of men were 'clinically ill', 2.2 per cent of women were 'clinically ill'.[91] On the other hand, Chen et al. and Koenig and d'Souza in Bangladesh, and McNeill in Tamil Nadu, all conclude that while there is no gender difference in the incidence of disease, there may be gender differences in the duration and intensity of illness.[92] Gender differences in sanitation have also been hypothesized as having an impact on morbidity in rural (north) India where the quantity, source, and degree of (faecal) contamination of bathing and clothes-washing water may be gender specific. Gender differences in quality of and expenditure upon clothing may also influence health status.[93]

Perceptions of health are another matter. Sen reports Bengali women as much more unwilling to declare indifferent or ill health than men. Gillespie shows that health is perceived by men of the Koya and Lambardi tribes in Andhra Pradesh as an individual state related to occupation and task. By contrast, tribal women see health as a collective household state related to household environment.[94]

Less ambiguity surrounds female disadvantage in the treatment of disease. We want to emphasize six aspects of this type of female disadvantage because of their implications for nutrition. First, lack of establishment of and/or access to maternity facilities represents a significant female disadvantage.[95] Second, if gynaecological and obstetric disorders are removed from data sets, it would seem that, while the gap between female and male treatment per death is narrowing, the gender gap in treatment of disease remains. But the evidence is not all one-way. In cases from north India and Bangladesh, a marked gender imbalance in health expenditure on children has been recorded (Das Gupta noting a factor of two for infants under 12 months). Females also appear to be less often referred for allopathic treatment than are males. Females are more often treated using the three other indigenous health systems (though we have to note criticisms about the iatrogenic character of rural primary health care interventions of whatever system of medicine). By contrast, in Karnatakan

---

[90] Kynch (1985a). These excess deaths may have been modified by relative lack of treatment, while the reasons for excessive female mortality from plague were ascribed by the British authorities not to poorer nutrition but to female service roles which brought them into contact with soiled clothes, infested grain, and which had them living in poorly ventilated rooms (ibid. 25).

[91] See Sen (1985b: 101–4). Here the relative excess of women suffering a combination of indifferent and ill health was only very slightly greater than the gender ratio for ill health by itself. Interestingly, the gender ratio for ill health was more adverse to women in improved slums than it was in unimproved slums and it was adverse to men in the town and villages surrounding Calcutta.

[92] Chen et al. (1981); McNeill (1986); Koenig and d'Souza (1986).

[93] Das Gupta (1987); Pettigrew (1987).

[94] Gillespie (1986).

[95] ICSSR (1977).

villages the Caldwells note no gender differences in treatment; and much more controversially neither does Visaria for infants and children in Gujarat.[96] Third, the (northern) gender gap seems to be greater for children than for adults.[97] Fourth, Mitra found that gender differences in child mortality rates from respiratory, gastrointestinal, and vitamin deficiency diseases arise not from gender differences in morbidity or differences in treatment but from the relatively later stage in illness at which girls were brought for treatment.[98] Fifth, mortality rates are highest in regions where the provision of health facilities and public expenditure on health per capita are lowest.[99] Gender differences in mortality rates have been shown to vary positively with distance of home from centre of treatment.[100] Lastly, it has been found in Bangladesh (and remains a hypothesis for testing elsewhere) that mothers of sons are less morbid than mothers of only daughters.[101]

Disadvantage in female access to treatment, especially at a young age, may be the most important influence on female health, a matter to which we need to return later. But as a corollary here we should note that these gender differentials in access to state medical facilities may be extended into other types of access to the state and into political life at village level and beyond.[102]

It comes as no surprise then that there is gender bias in basic demographic indicators (such as life expectancy, mortality, and the sex ratio) in South Asia. Although life expectancy has increased from the 1930s, when it was very low (mid-twenties) and had no marked gender bias, up to the present (when it is in the early fifties), improvement for women historically has lagged behind that for men. Aggregate female life expectancy, however, has been on a convergence course with that of men since the 1970s and is estimated actually to have converged in 1987.[103] Regional and social differences in this trend require research.

Similar general trends and relations are observed in mortality rates. The sex ratio is unusually masculine in South Asia and has become more masculine during this century.[104] Dyson concludes from a careful scrutiny of the Indian

[96] Singh et al. (1962); ICSSR (1977: 29); Aziz (1977); Aziz and Rassaque (1987); Caldwell et al. (1983); Kynch and Sen (1983); Kynch (1985a); Das Gupta (1987); Visaria (1987).

[97] Wyon and Gordon (1971); Chen et al. (1981); Chen (1982); Kielmann et al. (1983); Das Gupta (1987).

[98] Mitra (1978).

[99] Bardhan (1974).

[100] Rahaman (1982).

[101] Koenig and Wojtnyiak (1987). Whether this relation stems from the intrinsically more auspicious state of the mother of sons, or whether it is her sons who pay for her treatment, is a matter of conjecture.

[102] ICSSR (1977); Sharma (1978, 1980); Gough (1981).

[103] ICSSR (1977: 3, 19). Women's survival may have been affected by the gender of their children. The sex ratio is more masculine the greater the age of the respondent (Dyson 1987).

[104] Bardhan (1974); Padmanabha (1982); Sen (1985b: 85–6); Sen (1986); Nagaraj (1986).

data that the increasing masculinization of the sex ratio in successive censuses since 1921 is associated with the trend of decline in the general mortality rate *per se* 'independent of any change in the relative life chances between the sexes'.[105] Mortality is related to fertility and this too is declining. As a rule of thumb for South Asia, male neonatal mortality rates exceed those of females but are about-turned at one month of age. Excess female mortality persists through most of childhood and throughout the reproductive, householder stage of life. Roughly one-third of excess female mortality occurs during the first twelve months of life, another third occurs in the years 1–4, and the remaining third is spread throughout reproductive adulthood.[106] Recently, the life chances of females above the age of 5 have increased as have those of women at ages beyond the prime reproductive years. By contrast, excess male mortality in the age group above 35 has been rising rapidly, reasons for which are underresearched.[107] The sex differential, however, is never the most important component of mortality. Regional location is.

States with highest general mortality rates have the highest excess female mortality rates: Punjab, Haryana, and Uttar Pradesh. But, as Dyson and Das Gupta have each concluded, despite these very important redoubts, excess female mortality is declining and being gradually reduced to certain age groups, certain regions, and within them certain types of vulnerable female, notably the second and third daughters.[108] Historical case-studies in north-western India emphasize the role of female infanticide in the acquisition and retention of social and economic power and hint that despite legislation prohibiting this practice, it may still occur occasionally.[109] In the south, by contrast, gender differences in aggregate and infant mortality approach parity and even favour females in a number of districts in Tamil Nadu and in Kerala.[110] A spatial trend from parity in the sex ratio in the south-western extremity towards high masculinity in the north has been well described.[111] But the trend is less visible when data are disaggregated by caste or income

---

[105] *Pace* ICSSR (1977: 21). In Utopian agricultural conditions, if all mortality were slowly banished, a population sex ratio would increase to approach that at birth (approximately 105) (Dyson 1987).

[106] See Sathar (1985) for Pakistan; Koenig and d'Souza (1986) and Koenig and Wojtyniak (1987) for Bangladesh; Dyson (1987) for India; and Langford (1984) for Sri Lanka. Even in Sri Lanka, where the male mortality rate has exceeded that of the female since 1971, there is still excess female mortality among the under-5s (Langford 1984).

[107] Sen (1985b: 94–5); Padmanabha (1981, 1982); Chen *et al.* (1981); Dyson (1987).

[108] Bardhan (1974, 1987); Visaria and Visaria (1973) show that complications to this surface trend arise if the data are disaggregated according to social class.

[109] Clark (1983); Parry (1979): 'Mians do not feel it necessary to repudiate their past conduct and even view the allegation that the practice is not altogether extinct with a certain amount of complacency' (ibid. 215).

[110] Caldwell and Caldwell (1987); Das Gupta (1987).

[111] Miller (1981); Sopher (1980).

group. Regional variations in factors such as the age of marriage, the under-enumeration of women in censuses, the distance and frequency of visits to natal home, patterns of fertility and morbidity, gender and social differentials in the extent of assetlessness and poverty, property rights, the age and gender division of work and work burdens, have been invoked to explain regional variations in the sex ratio, and muddy the simple picture.[112]

So what? Far from being a digression, this summary of the *modus operandi* of patriarchy in South Asia shows that there is a material base to religiously justified son preference. Food behaviour cannot usefully be abstracted (either for analytical or for 'policy' purposes) from the social relations of patriarchy. The discriminatory practices of patriarchy may be unrelated to the wealth and economic status of households.

Female disadvantage which was most strikingly manifested in the sex ratio is not the necessary and inevitable result of underfeeding alone. A bundle of reciprocally causing variables, in particular reproductive burdens, work burdens, sanitation, and the treatment of disease, interact with the need for food to affect mortality. Lastly gender-based categories cannot be universalized even under the South Asian brands of patriarchy. There would appear to be sufficient contrariness in the relationships between the culture of food and the material subordination of women to justify a re-examination of nutritional evidence of intrahousehold food allocation. This forms the burden of the next section.

5.3.   *The measurement of hunger within the household*

'Hunger' or food-related deprivation in populations is measured by nutrient intakes, heights, weights, and ages, interpreted against yardsticks representing norms or averages.[113] Although we shall examine the intake of micronutrients, we focus on energy. The reasons for this are (1) that almost all components of the diet (including protein) are broken down to energy in the normal course of events, (2) that there are few deficiency diseases of which low energy intake is not a correlate, and (3) that appetite is probably most closely related to energy sufficiency.[114]

Hunger within the family is exceptionally difficult to research. Much

---

[112] ICSSR (1977: 4–5); Dyson and Moore (1983); Harriss and Watson (1987). It has been recently suggested by the Caldwells that 'north' and 'south' are misleading regionalizations, and that the more influential contrasts are between, on the one hand, regions of long-settled peasant agriculture with strongly differentiated age and sex roles, high fertility, and lower rates of fertility decline and, on the other, southern frontier agriculture with less-differentiated sex roles and lower fertility (Caldwell and Caldwell 1987).

[113] Clinical signs and symptoms conventionally indicate micronutrient deficiency rather than hunger.

[114] Payne (1985a); LSHTM (1985: 7, 24). This also means that most nutrient deficiencies can be rectified straightforwardly with an increase in the usual diet.

research (and also much policy advocacy) assumes the identity of the malnourished and sets out to verify the prevalence and intensity of
malnutrition.[115] Hence there is a disproportionate number of studies on
samples of pregnant and lactating women and on infants and preschool
children (the latter often undifferentiated by sex)[116] and correspondingly a
dearth of measurements on adult men, older children and adolescents, and the
elderly, let alone whole households.[117] This situation limits the inferences that
can be made about gender differences for they cannot be sustained by evidence
from children alone.[118] It also qualifies inferences about gender differences
according to stages of life, whether physiologically or culturally defined.

That said, two types of measurements may be made on individuals within a
household: (1) their food intake, subsequently converted to nutrients, and (2)
their heights and weights (and ages), subsequently converted into anthropometric indices. Sen, concerned to evaluate ways of measuring function and
capability, has put the case against food intake and for anthropometry for the
measurement of well-being. In essence this case rests on measurement precision, the intervention of other, possibly confounding (physiological), factors
preventing a direct stimulus–response relationship between food intake and
well-being, and the interpretation of measurements given the ragged state of
standards for evaluation.[119]

Yet exactly the same comments may be levelled at anthropometry.[120] First,
measurements of heights, weights, and especially ages in children are as
practically difficult and subject to as many sources of error as are those of food
intake.[121]

Second, diagnosis based on anthropometric status does not reflect aetiology.
Malnutrition is a combination of inadequate food intake and infections.[122]
Feedback relations operate through increased needs for energy in fever and

---

[115] Gopalan (1985).

[116] Waterlow (1972, 1973). Two recent examples from north-east India where disaggregation
by gender would have been very helpful are Khan (1980) and Chattopadhyay (1985).

[117] See Satyanarayana et al. (1979, 1980) for adolescents; McNeill (1986) and references therein
for adults and the elderly; and Dugdale (1985) for household measurements.

[118] Birth weight is influenced by maternal nutritional status (Prema 1978; Sibert et al. 1978).
Interestingly, Tanner et al. (1970) show that there are even different degrees of gender difference
in birth weight according to maternal body weight. The influence of the environment comes into
play from early in infancy.

[119] Sen (1985b: 83). Sen also discusses other welfare indicators including mortality, morbidity,
and clinical signs and symptoms.

[120] To call the result of anthropometry 'nutritional status' is as misleading as to call it 'health
status' (Deolalikar 1984), and to use the anthropometric status of children as the basis of inferences
about the 'nutritional status' of whole populations is an act of perhaps misleading heroism because
of health events specific to childhood (Payne 1985a).

[121] Abdullah (1983) and McNeill (1986) have carried out both methods of assessment and
discussed them critically.

[122] Pacey and Payne (1985: ch. 5).

tissue repair, reduced absorption of (up to 9 per cent of) nutrients because of intestinal dysfunctions, and reduced food intake because of mouth lesions, anorexia, and the withholding of food from the sick. All these mechanisms may serve to reduce the capacity to cope with infection.[123] The nutritional outcome of these feedback relations upon need and upon appetite for food cannot be generalized. Feedback relations are of course the basis of non-allopathic theories of illness. The complexity of environmental influences on both food supply and infection is traced in Fig. 5.1. Apropos of which, we have already seen how morbidity may be modified by gender differences in health care. It may be affected further by the quality of childcare.[124]

Third, the interpretation of anthropometric indices is problematic. Conventional arbitrary cut-offs for different grades of malnutrition (other than severe) are not helpful for assessing individuals because of interindividual variation in genetic potential. Local standards derived from populations affected by sex bias would lead to evaluations which are underestimates of discrimination. The meaning of mild to moderate malnutrition both for risk of current clinical conditions and for the probability of adverse current, seasonal, or long-term future effects on earnings, physical productivity, physiological and mental function is not clear.[125] Nor is the significance for adult functioning of the duration and incidence of the severe category of malnutrition during the period of growth.

Anthropometry cannot tell us whether there is 'failure in the equity of intrahousehold food distribution' but it can tell us about growth differences in children. We will not throw this particular baby out with the methodological bath water, so let us turn to what the South Asian data show (Map 5.1).

(a) The anthropometric evidence

Some of this evidence is not socio-economically disaggregated but indicates gross regional variations. At the extremities of the subcontinent, in the Nepalese Terai and in Sri Lanka, there are no gender differences in the growth

[123] LSHTM (1985: 63). According to Sukhatme, in a given population, barely half the variance in anthropometric status is linked to nutritional history, the rest is because of illness or it is genetic (1981: 6). Martorell, reviewing the literature on anthropometric status and risk of infection, also finds that anthropometric status affects the intensity of illness but not the risk (1985: 22).

[124] Nagaraj (1986); Visaria (1987).

[125] For the interpretation of grades see Gworinath Sastri and Vijayaraghavanlk (1973). For difficulties in matching anthropometric grades with clinical signs and symptoms, see Pacey and Payne (1985: 84–94) and Montgomery (1977). For problems with the concept of genetic potential see Payne and Cutler (1984). For controversy over the possible relationships between childhood malnutrition and adult productivity see Immink *et al.* (1984); Gwatkin (1983); Viteri (1971); Satyanarayana *et al.* (1979, 1980); Lipton (1983). On controversies over the relationships between childhood anthropometric status and physiological function see Pereira *et al.* (1979); Madhavan (1965); Rajalakshmi (1981); Klein (1981); Freeman *et al.* (1980); Evelath (1985); McNeill (1986). On anthropometric status and mental performance see Madhavan (1965); Rajalakshmi (1981). On seasonal changes in anthropometric status being socio-biological adaptation to the duration and periodicity of physical work, see Dugdale and Payne (1986).

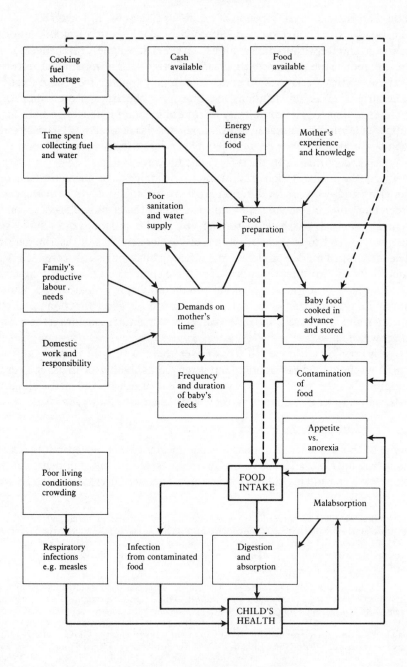

Source: Payne and Pacey (1985: 103).
Fig. 5.1. Factors operating at the household level which affect the state of nutrition of children

retardation of children.[126] There is a conflict in the results from Bangladesh. On the one hand Chen et al. find that whereas 14.4 per cent of girls under 5 years old were 'severely malnourished' in terms of weight for age, only 5.1 per cent of boys were.[127] Abdullah, however, found no gender distinctions in anthropometric status for children of any age. Male children under 5 (and male adults) in labouring households were more likely than their female counterparts to lose weight in the scarce seasons.[128] Sen, discussing the impact of the 1978 floods in West Bengal, shows that girls bore the brunt of the growth retardation in children under 6 years.[129] Kynch and Maguire in Palanpur village of Uttar Pradesh also found that young girls had a lower frequency distribution of anthropometric status than young boys and more frequent seasonal weight losses for girls against boys; but they noted a progressive decline in the status of boys with increasing age such that adult men were of as much concern as young girls.[130] In the north-west, in Kuchch District of Gujarat, no significant gender differences in anthropometric status have been found among preschool children.[131] Pushpamma and colleagues, investigating differences among adolescents in the three cultural and ecological regions of Andhra Pradesh, also found no gender differences.[132] In Tamil Nadu Pereira noted that girls' weights were closer to standards than boys',[133] and McNeill found the same relationships with respect to adult body mass indices, and found insignificant seasonal changes and no seasonal differences between the sexes.[134]

These findings are commonly presented in a historically decontextualized manner. They show regional variations but they are curiously classless. Gender differentiation in growth retardation among children appears to be a phenomenon confined to the north of the subcontinent and not always evident there.

Less field work is concerned with the social profile of anthropometric status. A general hypothesis about female economic status has been borrowed for testing from the mortality literature: excess female mortality (and hence anthropometrically measured female neglect) is greatest not among the poor but among the asseted where women are banned from participation in productive agricultural work.[135] This tends to be refuted in the 'north'.

---

[126] Martorell et al. (1984) for Nepal; Perera (1983) for Sri Lanka.

[127] Chen et al. (1981).   [128] Abdullah (1983).   [129] Sen (1981).

[130] Kynch and Maguire (1986).   [131] Visaria (1987).

[132] Pushpamma, Geervani, and Lakshmi Devi (1982).   [133] Pereira et al. (1979).

[134] McNeill (1986), thereby casting doubt on Chambers et al.'s model of the effects of seasonality of energy expenditure, input food stocks, and disease on nutritional status (Chambers et al. 1981). See also Behrman and Deolalikar (1986b) for similar results using the ICRISAT data for rural households in central and south India.

[135] Miller (1981). Bardhan (1987) finds a correlation coefficient of -0.82 between Bhatia's index of son preference and the statewise proportion of households possessing assets of less than Rs 1,000.

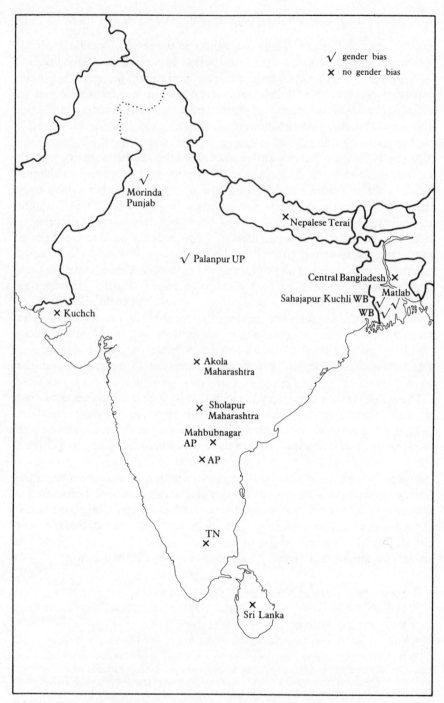

√ gender bias
✗ no gender bias

Morinda
Punjab √

✗ Nepalese Terai

√ Palanpur UP

Central Bangladesh ✗

Sahajapur Kuchli WB √ √ Matlab
WB

✗ Kuchch

✗ Akola
Maharashtra

✗ Sholapur
Maharashtra

Mahbubnagar
AP ✗

✗ AP

TN
✗

✗
Sri Lanka

Sources: Abdullah (1983); Chen *et al.* (1981); Kynch and MaGuire (1986); Levinson
(1972); Martorell *et al.* (1984); Perera (1983); Pushpamma *et al.* (1982); Ryan *et al.*
(1984); Sen (1981); Sen and Sengupta (1983).

Map 5.1. Gender bias in anthropometric status in S. Asia

Sen and Sengupta's study in two contrasting villages of West Bengal reveals gender differences in growth status which were greatest in landless labouring households.[136] Khan shows that whereas the heights and health status of Bangladeshi males aged 5 to 19 were not affected by household energy supplies, those of females were.[137] In Punjab, Levinson found anthropometric gender differences to be pronounced only among the poor Ramdasia caste.[138]

In central and southern India there is evidence of gender bias, but not in the expected direction. Ryan *et al.*'s anthropometric research in six villages selected as representative of agrarian conditions in the semi-arid tropics shows gender differences confined to the children of landless and small farmer households where it was boys who were at a disadvantage.[139] Such results reinforce the view of some demographic anthropologists that it is not economic hardship or aggregate energy availability *per se* which cause discrimination against the female sex. Rather, where it happens, it is to be considered the outcome of kinship and culture.[140]

(b) Indicators of intake

But our subject is hunger. Hunger is a direct appetite for an input, hence the appropriate measure is nutrient intake. As is the case with basic micro-economic data (income, employment, time allocation, costs of production, etc.), this is easier said than done. Data for individuals comprising households sampled throughout a local society are needed because it cannot be assumed that hunger is not felt within families identified in terms of their aggregate energy supply as being adequately supplied with food. Seasonal data are needed because intake, work loads and activity levels, and maintenance requirements are known to vary seasonally. It is not to be supposed that food allocations will be constant over the labouring year. Female interviewers are appropriate for female respondents and are more likely to gain access to the individual portions, necessary for weighing and for subsequent biochemical analysis. Continuous on-site observation captures subsidiary feeding and gender specific supplements to main meals. Exceptional events bias 24-hour

---

[136] Sen and Sengupta (1983).

[137] Khan (1984).

[138] Levinson (1972). Village-level data on excess female mortality are consistent with the north Indian anthropometric results for cases in UP (Jeffery *et al.* 1987; Wadley and Derr 1987); and Pakistan (Sathar 1985). But in Punjab, Das Gupta (1987) finds that although the landless are not distinguished by greatest total excess female mortality, the mortality rates for the second daughter are highest in this group. By contrast Houska finds no gender bias in mortality among sweepers in Allahabad (1981).

[139] Ryan *et al.* (1984); confirmed by Behrman (1986). With respect to mortality, the Caldwells found less gender bias among the landless in Karnatakan cases than among the landed (1987).

[140] Das Gupta (1987).

observations unless supplemented with food frequency information based on recall. Periods of measurement of between three and seven days are therefore necessary. The subject cannot be investigated, as nutritionists are wont to do, by taking random samples of men, women, and children, measuring their portions separately in different households, aggregating and contrasting the results, and leaving the readers free to recreate model households under their own assumptions about composition. Ideally each household member's food must be compared with others in the same household. This is rarely done.

As with anthropometry, there are many ways in which measurement errors may creep in. The methods by which intake is measured are said to suffer from trade-offs between precision and cost and invasiveness.[141] Errors of omission include 'snacking' (which may be the normal way of feeding little children), the measurement of consumption of breast milk, condiments, and spices, eating outside the household, and the exclusion of extraordinary food cycles.[142] Errors of commission may arise from the standardization of volumetric measurements, and from variations in the nutrient content of foods (especially consequent to cooking with heat), in its digestibility, in the accuracy of food composition tables, in dietary duplication for chemical analysis, and in behavioural modifications in 'subjects' due to their being observed.[143] Comparisons of recall with weighing have produced estimates of error of 10 to 40 per cent, though recent comparative studies tell of low levels of error.[144] To acknowledge the possibility of errors does not mean however that we can wish away the results of careful research.

A fair distribution of food among members of a household is not an equal one. Intakes attain significance (and 'nutritional justice' is achieved) in relation to need. Analysis of interindividual adequacy requires information about individual need. Need is arguably the most controversial concept in human nutrition. Need is thought to consist of three components: growth, activity, and maintenance. Body maintenance is by far the largest and most constant

---

[141] The methods are recall over 24 hours, record keeping, food frequency listing, with or without the testing of local household volumetric measures, the weighing of stated inventories for individuals, the weighing of cooked portions, and chemical analysis. Combinations of these methods are frequently used (Ferro-Luzzi 1982). 'There is no perfect method' (Pekkarinen 1970).

[142] Khare (1976a) describes the more or less numerous and casual meals fed to under-4s in his Lucknow households. See also Sundaraj and Pereira (1973, 1975). In studies on the allocation of food, breast milk is not conventionally measured and sometimes children under 2 are omitted from the analysis. However, for children above the age of 2, the energy from breast milk is not thought to introduce 'normally' a major error. (But for evidence to the contrary, see Ryan et al. 1984.)

[143] Ferro-Luzzi (1982); Pushpamma, Geervani, and Usha Rani (1982); Chacko et al. (1984). Note that in economic research the conversion of expenditure data into quantities introduces errors due to assumptions made about prices.

[144] See McNeill (1986) for a review of research. Her own work suggested that weighing methods lead to the omission (if at all) of drinks, pickles and chutneys, and (fried) snacks which are of significant importance to energy intake. Recall leads to the omission (if at all) of meal accompaniments (rasam and side dishes) which are not of importance to energy estimates.

component of need.[145] Women are known to be physiologically more efficient than men (even girls under 5 seem to be more efficient than boys under 5) and therefore to need less, and an 'average' Western man expends and needs to eat about 36 per cent more energy each day than his female counterpart.[146] Growth is a very small component of need even in children.[147] Evidence of the energy costs of pregnancy shows considerable variation.[148] It is the energy cost of activity which displays greatest interindividual variation.[149] Here there are many traps for unwary makers of assumptions. Time allocation studies may show that adult women have both much longer working days and less seasonal variation than can be accounted for by either wage work or farm work because of their widespread responsibility for the reproduction of the household.[150] But this may be set against physiological evidence that the energy costs of women's common daily activities (which subjectively seem quite demanding) are low.[151]

In the orthodox model of human nutrition, needs are converted into requirements[152] as a yardstick by means of which the adequacy of intakes may be evaluated. Requirements are defined as an estimated average value of a given nutrient intake and refined, according to further estimates, in relation to body weight, sex, activity, growth, and physiological state. From this account it will be evident that these estimates are subject to different margins of

[145] These are at present assumed not to interact or to vary with the composition of the diet (Rivers and Payne 1982). Activity accounts for only about 13% of energy need in a moderately active adult; growth accounts for only 4% of the intake of an average 1-year-old, only 2% after infancy. Growth accounts for only 18% during recovery from severe malnutrition in infancy (LSHTM 1985: 15).

[146] The female is physiologically more efficient because she is genetically smaller, has a lower proportion of metabolically active lean tissue and therefore, cet. par., lower protein and energy requirements. For reasons as yet unknown, her energy costs for activity are also lower, even per unit of lean body mass (Rivers 1982; LSHTM 1985: 18; Nelson 1986).

[147] On growth, see the Gambian studies of Flores et al. (1984); Gorsky and Calloway (1983). Ferro-Luzzi (1982) queries conventional deductions in energy requirements for ageing. Empirical evidence shows no reduction in energy intakes and wide variation in intakes with increasing age.

[148] Estimates of the energy needs of pregnancy vary from 27,550 calories (Ebrahim 1979) through the official 61,600 calories (UK, Colombia, and Guatemala) to 141,120 (Canada); see Lipton (1983). Both Lipton and McNeill conclude that there is no need for a special energy allowance for pregnancy, the calorie needs of the third trimester being straightforwardly compensated for by reductions in activity.

[149] Ferro-Luzzi (1982); Lawrence et al. (1985).

[150] McGuire (1979); Immink et al. (1984); Batliwala (1982, 1985); Ryan et al. (1984); McNeill (1986: ch. 4).

[151] Lawrence et al. (1985).

[152] Requirement (estimated average) must be distinguished from recommendation (set at above average to cater for people whose requirement is greater than average). Intake (what is eaten) must also be distinguished from allowance (what should be provided) (Waterlow 1979). In practice there is much confusion over the use and meaning of these terms.

error[153] not to mention variability,[154] sheer ignorance,[155] and political manipulation.[156] Furthermore, individual need (supposing it is normally distributed) will be below estimated requirements quite legitimately in half the cases. So requirements are abused if applied to individuals.

The revolutionary concept of adaptation has set the cat among these pigeons. 'Adaptation' arose from attempts to explain observations of habitual low and variable energy intake, capacity to adjust to which has been thought to be 'a form of fitness'.[157] Adaptation means many things. It can be behavioural, as when intake does not change during the third trimester of pregnancy but activity is much reduced.[158] It may be physiological: changes in body composition accompanying changes in intake.[159] But it may also involve the human body's adjusting the efficiency with which it metabolizes energy in a benign autoregulatory manner over a range of levels of supply, which puts paid to the concept of a fixed efficiency machine, a fixed requirement, and a determinate entitlement.[160] Adaptation could involve a combination of these factors. Beaton[161] notes a 'general failure to demonstrate metabolic adaptation' and Lipton, while acknowledging its conceptual importance, reckons that its quantitative impact may be small.[162]

In relation to intrahousehold food allocation, an adaptationist interpretation of low individual shares would be a counsel of caution against concluding that they are the result of 'discrimination'. In this study, since the range of intakes comprising thresholds for adaptation has not been specified, we do not have any option but to proceed to evaluate the sharing of food against requirements.

---

[153] Requirements of vitamins and minerals are set by evidence on intakes and deficiency diseases; the minima associated with disappearance of deficiency diseases (Anon. 1976).

[154] Recommended daily allowances for 41 countries show massive variations (as much as the variations in RDAs in the 19th century (Rivers and Payne 1982; Anon. 1976)) because of different assessments of the needs of age, sex, physiological status, different concepts of RDA, different criteria of adequacy, and different foods.

[155] Ignorance is deepest for aminoacids, trace elements, and minor vitamins; and for nutrients for the child from 6 months to 5 years, for adolescents, and for adults. Knowledge is most advanced with respect to energy, protein, calcium, iron, and vitamins A, B, and D and for young adults and the infant from birth to 6 months (Anon. 1976). See Lipton (1983) for a convincing argument that Western requirements are set too high and that modifications for body weight, activity, pregnancy, and climate are also exaggerations (pp. 13–29).

[156] Rivers and Payne (1982).   [157] Payne (1985a); Payne and Cutler (1984).

[158] Gorsky and Calloway (1983); Waterlow (1985).   [159] McNeill (1986).

[160] Sukhatme (1981, 1982); Seckler (1982); Payne (1985a, 1985b).

[161] Beaton (1985: 225); see also McNeill (1986).

[162] The idea has also been criticized as a tautology ('So long as you are not dead you are adapted' (Waterlow 1985)), and for its policy implications ('adaptation generates the impression among policy makers that undernutrition is not a serious problem in the country any more' (Gopalan 1983)). But the counter-arguments to these are that it is serious undernutrition that is 'the problem' and that it is neither accurate nor responsible to describe what is actually a process, as being a pathological state, by implication amenable to rectification (Rivers and Payne 1982; Payne 1985a, 1985b).

We derive a certain consolation from the fact that the Indian requirements estimates are among the most carefully determined and most regularly revised. They indicate that the female adult needs 85 per cent of the male's energy intake. Comparison with Western norms and recent empirical research (which suggest, respectively, that adult females need 27 and 32 per cent less than men[163]) open up the possibility that the Indian norms err on the side of generosity to women. In which case using them as a standard will tend to lead to overestimation of anti-female discrimination.

5.4. *Results*

Our search, which does not pretend to be exhaustive and extends to 1986, unearthed 24 cases of household surveys in India and Bangladesh relevant to the subject of food allocation (Table 5.1). They may be considered representative in regional terms, but they proved impossible to standardize. Sample sizes vary from 50 to 2,800 households. Sample selection varies from taking a population (Abdullah in Bangladesh), through random sampling of a preidentified stratum of the poor (Sharma in Rajasthan; Gopaldas in Gujarat; Pushpamma in Andhra Pradesh); spatially stratified random sampling (Tamil Nadu Nutrition Study); a combination of representative, purposive sampling for the landed and random sampling for the landless (ICRISAT in Madhya Pradesh, Maharashtra, and Andhra Pradesh) to purposive selection for accessibility (Chen in Bangladesh). With the exception of the Tamil Nadu study (estimated to be carried out in 1971–2) they date from the late 1970s and early 1980s. Only in Abdullah's and ICRISAT's 6 village cases is there any socio-economic disaggregation.[164] The length of observation varies; 3 sets (done by nutritionists Abdullah in Bangladesh, Pushpamma in AP, and Sharma in Rajasthan) consist of 72-hour continuous observation, the rest of 24 hours. Only 3 cases (the two Bangladesh studies and ICRISAT's 6-village one) comprise seasonally repeated observations. All aim for precision by weighing and/or volumetric estimation supplemented by recall, except for the Tamil Nadu Nutrition Study which relies only upon recall.[165] Coverage of micronutrients, classification by age, and disaggregation by sex are all unstandardized. Frustratingly few studies present disaggregates by sex for children under 13 and even fewer give data separately for the elderly. The routine inclusion of elderly men who

---

[163] LSHTM (1985); Nelson (1986).

[164] It should be pointed out that the Rajasthan, Gujarat, and AP case-studies are confined to the poor and permit little further disaggregation.

[165] The Tamil Nadu Nutrition Survey (Cantor *et al.* 1973, while being a model for detailed presentation, is the result of the least accurate method of measurement and contains what one suspects are at least a few spuriously precise and arbitrary results. Note an idiosyncrasy characteristic of the entire data set: that the results which deviate most from expectations (especially in relation to micronutrients) are for the smallest cell sizes in their samples.

Table 5.1 Household surveys on food allocation in India and Bangladesh

Source	Location	Sample	Method	Problems
Abdullah (1983); Abdullah and Wheeler (1985)	Bangladesh: an unnamed village 85 kms from Dhaka selected for isolation and unmodernized agriculture	53 households, being the population of households with one or more children under 5, surveyed four times (seasonally) in 1983	3 consecutive days of 24-hour weighing of total raw and cooked food and of individual portions of cooked food plus recall of snacks	Micronutrients omitted except retinol/carotene
Chen et al. (1981)	Bangladesh: 4 villages of Matlab thana	130 households purposively selected to be accessible and with one or more children under age 5, surveyed 1978–9.	Bimonthly 24-hour measurement of household food supplies prior to intake and individual food intake via volumes of cooked food in vessels before and after each serving	No measurement for calcium, iron, carotene, thiamine, riboflavin, and ascorbic acid
Sharma (1983)	Rajasthan: a drought-affected village in Jodhpur	100 households randomly selected from among small and marginal farmers, share-croppers, and landless agricultural labour households	66% of households subject to weighment of raw and cooked portions over 3 days. 33% of households subject to 24-hour recall (no significant difference between the 2 methods)	

Source	Sample	Method	Comments
Gopaldas *et al.* (1983)	Gujarat: 5 hamlets purposively selected for socio-economic representativity among Rathwakoli tribals	78 households, means of sampling not stated, surveyed in October 1980.	25-hour recall plus one day's weighment of raw food	No gender difference in data presentation prior to adulthood, no adult non-pregnant non-lactating women. Vitamin A presented as retinol equivalents and not as carotene.
Sadasivam *et al.* (1980)	Tamil Nadu: village 20 kms from Coimbatore	50 households randomly sampled (36% of which were agricultural labour, 38% industrial labour)	3-day measurement of cooked individual portions, subjected to biochemical analyses	Gender not distinguished prior to age 13
Pushpamma, Geervani, and Lakshmi Devi (1982); Pushpamma, Geervani, and Usha Rani (1982)	Andhra Pradesh: 18 semi-arid villages	280 households: 3% of small and marginal farms	3-day consecutive weighings of individual portions	
Cantor *et al.* (1973)	360 villages and 240 urban blocks selected randomly subject to a minimum of 16 villages per district in rural cases	12,953 individuals from 2,800 households with pregnant and/or lactating women and/or with children under 13, surveyed in 1971–2	One 24-hour recall of individual quantities of ingredients	Least accurate method together with a certain arbitrariness in the numbers

Table 5.1 cont.

Ryan et al. (1984)	Madhya Pradesh, Maharashtra, Andhra Pradesh: 6 villages purposively selected so as to represent typical conditions of 3 agro-ecological zones of the semi-arid tropics	240 households selected as follows: in each village 30 cultivator households representative of all size categories of farm plus 10 randomly selected landless households, surveyed from Sept. 1976 to Jan. 1978.	24-hour recall at 3–4-month intervals supplemented by volumetric estimations by respondents using 13 local size/volumetric vessels	Aggregation of different, village-specific size categories for types of cultivator; aggregation of random and representative samples with different sampling fractions; no gender classification prior to age 13; inclusion of breast-fed children but not of nutritional composition of breast-milk intakes in group 1–3; results are of 4×1 day's recall rather than of measurement or recall over longer periods though fasting and feasting were ignored in the surveys; no data for iron or calcium

may both need and eat less energy than younger adults leads to underestimations of the shares of male household heads in their reproductive years. A lamentable state of methodological disarray, but no worse than that of most areas of microeconomic rural research in South Asia and elsewhere.

All analysis of such data suffers bias. We have adopted the following method to pick our way through this minefield and construct an index of the intrafamily distribution of hunger.

Average (actual) nutrient intakes for individuals in specific age and sex groups have been expressed as a proportion of the average (actual) nutrient intake of the adult male group, yielding ratios of *relative intake* (RI). Sources of bias here are, first, the mean and extent of variation of the adult male intake unstandardized for occupation, income, age, and activity, and second, as we have observed, the accuracy of measurement. To facilitate a comparative evaluation, each RI is then expressed as a proportion of the corresponding *recommended relative intake* (RRI), where the latter is defined as the proportion of the recommended intake for the group under consideration to the recommended intake for adult males. Recommended relative intakes are derived from the latest (1981) recommendations for moderate activity levels of the Indian Council of Medical Research. The *index of relative intake* (IRI) is the ratio of actual relative intake (RI) to recommended relative intake (RRI).

The index of relative intake so constructed indicates the relative deprivation of specific groups compared to adult males, where deprivation is seen in terms of the deficit of intake in relation to need. Thus, an IRI of 1.0 indicates that the relevant group has the same share as that recommended by the ICMR. An IRI greater than unity indicates a favourable share of food, and conversely for an IRI lower than unity.

Extreme deviations of IRI from unity, ranging from 0.1 to 2.44, are observed for carotene (Map 5.7) and are characteristic of vitamin consumption. The ICMR index of RRI must be acknowledged as merely a probabilistic criterion of evaluation, and is biased by the degree of accuracy of recommendations.[166] Cells with the largest number of observations have been mapped (Maps 5.2 to 5.7). We shall compare our interpretation with those of the authors concerned. We then proceed to a reworking at the household level of some of ICRISAT's data. This exposes further methodological problems, and untoward results.

(a)   The regional geography of intrafamily energy and protein allocation

No group of adult women consumed absolutely more energy or protein than adult men, but our concern is with distribution rather than with absolute intake. Two pieces of research from Bangladesh provide the strongest evidence of low IRIs for young children (especially for girls under 4 years who are

---

[166] Nelson (1986) gives a full treatment of such analytical problems in relation to a UK case-study.

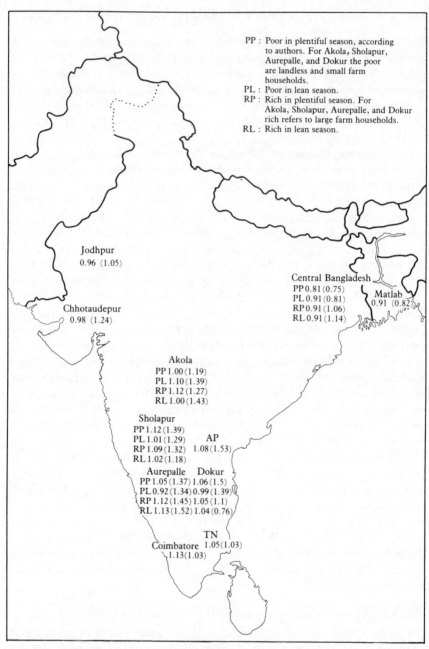

PP : Poor in plentiful season, according to authors. For Akola, Sholapur, Aurepalle, and Dokur the poor are landless and small farm households.
PL : Poor in lean season.
RP : Rich in plentiful season. For Akola, Sholapur, Aurepalle, and Dokur rich refers to large farm households.
RL : Rich in lean season.

Jodhpur
0.96 (1.05)

Central Bangladesh
PP 0.81 (0.75)
PL 0.91 (0.81)   Matlab
RP 0.91 (1.06)   0.91 (0.82)
RL 0.91 (1.14)

Chhotaudepur
0.98 (1.24)

Akola
PP 1.00 (1.19)
PL 1.10 (1.39)
RP 1.12 (1.27)
RL 1.00 (1.43)

Sholapur
PP 1.12 (1.39)
PL 1.01 (1.29)   AP
RP 1.09 (1.32)   1.08 (1.53)
RL 1.02 (1.18)
Aurepalle   Dokur
PP 1.05 (1.37) 1.06 (1.5)
PL 0.92 (1.34) 0.99 (1.39)
RP 1.12 (1.45) 1.05 (1.1)
RL 1.13 (1.52) 1.04 (0.76)

TN
Coimbatore   1.05 (1.03)
1.13 (1.03)

Sources: Central Bangladesh: Abdullah (1983); Matlab: Chen *et al.* (1981); Jodhpur: Sharma (1983); Chhotaudepur: Gopaldas *et al.* (1983); Akola, Sholapur, Aurepalle, and Dokur: Ryan *et al.* (1984); AP: Pushpamma, Geervani, and Usha Rani (1982); Pushpamma, Geervani, and Lakshmi Devi (1982); Coimbatore; Sadasivan (1980); TN: Cantor *et al.* (1973). On the construction of the indices, see text.

Map 5.2. Indices of relative intake of calories: adult women and (in brackets) adolescent girls (aged 13–18)

obtaining 16 per cent less energy than boys on the average) and for elderly women. These relations seem most accentuated amongst the poor under conditions of scarce food availability (Maps 5.2–5.4). Similar trends are found for protein as well (Maps 5.5 and 5.6). Those responsible for this work have been cautious in their interpretations. Abdullah, while acknowledging the statistically significant gender difference in energy intake among preschool children, states with respect to other age groups: 'The data clearly demonstrate the non existence of sex discrimination in the intrahousehold allocation of food to women beyond what can be accounted for by body size, activity and physiological differentials'.[167] Chen and colleagues also compare their intake data with those for requirements, adjusted in a necessarily arbitrary way but according to the best state of knowledge, for body size, pregnancy, and lactation in women and for calorie increments necessary for labour in adult men. They also conclude: 'For all age groups male to female intake/requirement ratios are near parity although marked male predomination persists among young children'.[168]

The average level of energy intake of adult males in the data set for the north-east is identical to that in the north-west of the subcontinent but the pattern of sharing differs (Maps 5.2–5.6). The data show high IRIs of both calories and protein for adolescent girls, rough parity of IRIs for adult women in Rajasthan, and low IRIs for elderly women in a tribal population in Gujarat where male and female children were already known to be treated, in food as in other aspects of life, with equality. Intakes of all measured nutrients were significantly different from those of the adult head with the exception of those of adolescent males in Rajasthan and that of calcium in Gujarat. Their authors have concluded respectively: 'The major portion of the diet was received by the adult male';[169] 'The head of the family did receive the lion's share of the family diet'.[170]

Adult male energy intakes average about the same amount in central India, where the research carried out under the auspices of ICRISAT's village studies programme reveals a different pattern. In the entire set of cases from ICRISAT the age group under 5 appear to have low IRIs for energy. Children who are being partially breast-fed have been included in this group but when notional allowances are made for the energy content of breast milk, their nutritional deficits are said to be greatly reduced.[171] In these four villages it is adult males who appear to have low IRIs compared with adult women and adolescent girls, while protein RIs are close to RRIs throughout the age and sex distribution. Regression analysis and t-testing for 10 nutrients for 938 children has provided a statistical basis for ICRISAT's own conclusion that 'There is no significant difference between boys and girls in the intake of the 10 nutrients'.[172]

[167] Abdullah (1983: 134).   [168] Chen et al. (1981: 63).
[169] Sharma (1983: 5).   [170] Gopaldas et al. (1983: 73).   [171] Ryan et al. (1984: 25).
[172] Ibid. 38.

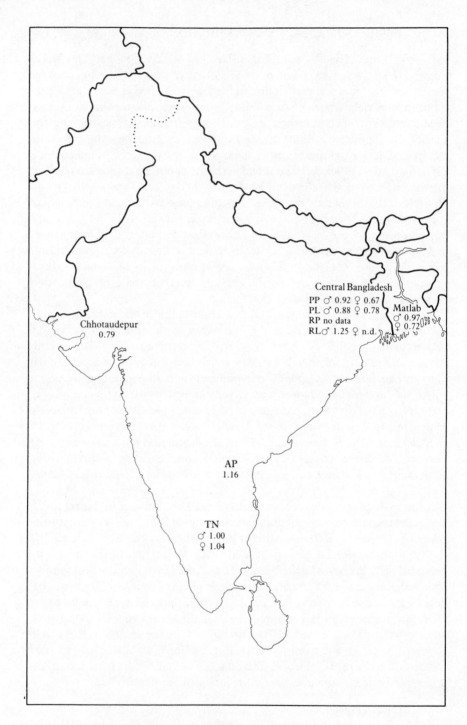

Central Bangladesh
PP ♂ 0.92 ♀ 0.67
PL ♂ 0.88 ♀ 0.78
RP no data
RL♂ 1.25 ♀ n.d.

Matlab
♂ 0.97
♀ 0.72

Chhotaudepur
0.79

AP
1.16

TN
♂ 1.00
♀ 1.04

Sources: As for Map 5.2

Map 5.3 Indices of relative intake of calories: the elderly

Somewhat the same pattern is revealed from two of ICRISAT's villages in south India together with two other studies. Here, the average energy consumption of the adult male is at least 300 calories less per day than elsewhere in the subcontinent. A given RI thus refers to absolutely less. Adult men seem to have relatively low intakes judged by the IRIs of all other age–sex groups. In Pushpamma et al.'s survey of 18 villages in Andhra Pradesh adult men receive 40 calories per kg of body weight contrasted with adult women who eat 44 calories per kg.[173] Exceptions to this trend occur among the poorest of ICRISAT's sample in the lean season where adult women (though not adolescent girls) are slightly disfavoured. In the southernmost villages again it is children of both sexes under 13 who have low IRIs. By contrast protein RIs are close to RRIs, except for poor preschool children in Aurepalle village.

While ICRISAT's conclusions have already been set out, and while Pushpamma et al. find adolescents of both sexes to be consuming absolutely more than male adults, Sadasivam and colleagues note the reverse. Adolescent girls and adult women are found to consume lower absolute levels than adolescent boys and adult men. They do not pursue this aspect of their interpretation further.[174] The authors of the Tamil Nadu Nutrition Study evaluated consumption by comparing absolute intakes with FAO references and concluded that weanlings of both sexes were subject to greatest deprivation while children under 4, adolescents, and young adults of both sexes but especially pregnant women were disadvantaged. Intake–requirement ratios rose with age: a system of gerontocratic favouring.[175]

(b) Seasonal and social aspects of energy and protein allocation

It is difficult to disentangle seasonal effects from those of socio-economic status because most of the data sets which disaggregate for the one disaggregate for the other. Hence both will be considered here, greatly facilitated by evidence that income or seasonal trends in shares are usually consistent throughout the age ranges.

Testing the hypothesis that if food is given preferentially to active participants in the wage labour market, then unproductive people (women and children in Bangladesh) will receive lower shares when overall food supply to the household is scarce than they do at times of plenty, Abdullah and Wheeler found cause to reject it.[176] A seasonal analysis of RIs of household energy in a village in central Bangladesh showed that the intake of women varied as a constant percentage of that of men at all seasons. Furthermore whereas the

---

[173] Pushpamma, Geervani, and Usha Rani (1982).

[174] Sadasivam et al. (1980: 250).

[175] Cantor et al. (1973: i. 79–86); also Pushpamma et al. (1981). But note that McNeill, studying adults but not children, found the reverse (1986: ch. 7).

[176] Abdullah and Wheeler (1985).

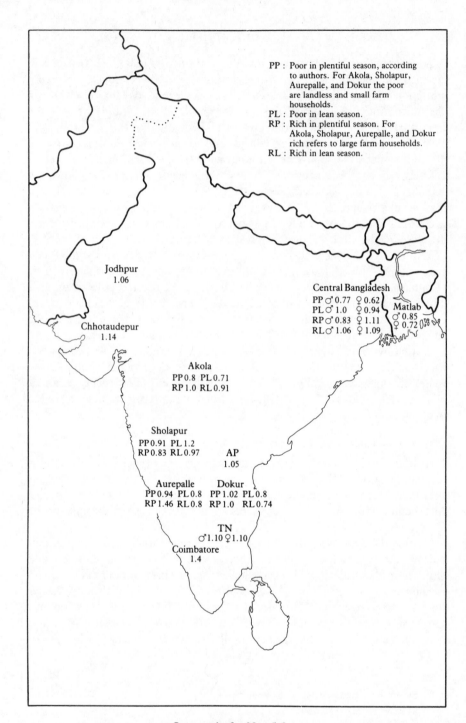

PP : Poor in plentiful season, according
to authors. For Akola, Sholapur,
Aurepalle, and Dokur the poor
are landless and small farm
households.
PL : Poor in lean season.
RP : Rich in plentiful season. For
Akola, Sholapur, Aurepalle, and Dokur
rich refers to large farm households.
RL : Rich in lean season.

Jodhpur
1.06

Central Bangladesh
PP ♂0.77 ♀0.62
PL ♂1.0   ♀0.94
RP ♂0.83 ♀1.11
RL ♂1.06 ♀1.09

Matlab
♂ 0.85
♀ 0.72

Chhotaudepur
1.14

Akola
PP 0.8 PL 0.71
RP 1.0 RL 0.91

Sholapur
PP 0.91 PL 1.2
RP 0.83 RL 0.97

AP
1.05

Aurepalle
PP 0.94 PL 0.8
RP 1.46 RL 0.8

Dokur
PP 1.02 PL 0.8
RP 1.0   RL 0.74

TN
♂1.10 ♀1.10

Coimbatore
1.4

Sources: As for Map 5.2

Map 5.4 Indices of relative intake of calories: children under 5

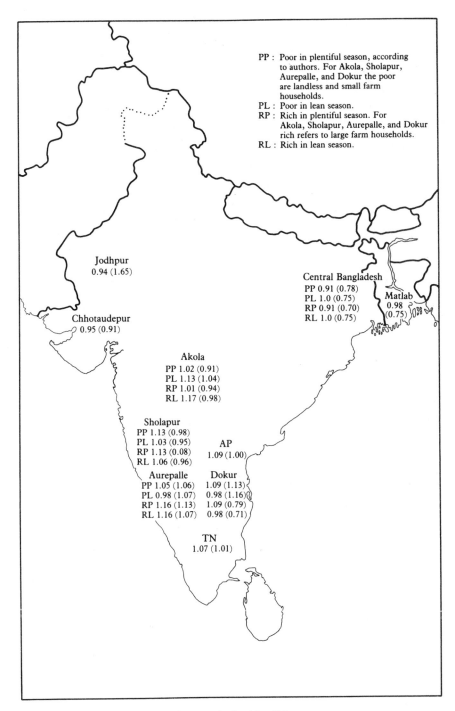

PP : Poor in plentiful season, according to authors. For Akola, Sholapur, Aurepalle, and Dokur the poor are landless and small farm households.
PL : Poor in lean season.
RP : Rich in plentiful season. For Akola, Sholapur, Aurepalle, and Dokur rich refers to large farm households.
RL : Rich in lean season.

Jodhpur
0.94 (1.65)

Central Bangladesh
PP 0.91 (0.78)
PL 1.0 (0.75)
RP 0.91 (0.70)
RL 1.0 (0.75)

Matlab
0.98
(0.75)

Chhotaudepur
0.95 (0.91)

Akola
PP 1.02 (0.91)
PL 1.13 (1.04)
RP 1.01 (0.94)
RL 1.17 (0.98)

Sholapur
PP 1.13 (0.98)
PL 1.03 (0.95)
RP 1.13 (0.08)
RL 1.06 (0.96)

AP
1.09 (1.00)

Aurepalle   Dokur
PP 1.05 (1.06)   1.09 (1.13)
PL 0.98 (1.07)   0.98 (1.16)
RP 1.16 (1.13)   1.09 (0.79)
RL 1.16 (1.07)   0.98 (0.71)

TN
1.07 (1.01)

Sources: As for Map 5.2

Map 5.5 Indices of relative intake of proteins: adult women and (in brackets) adolescent girls (aged 13–18)

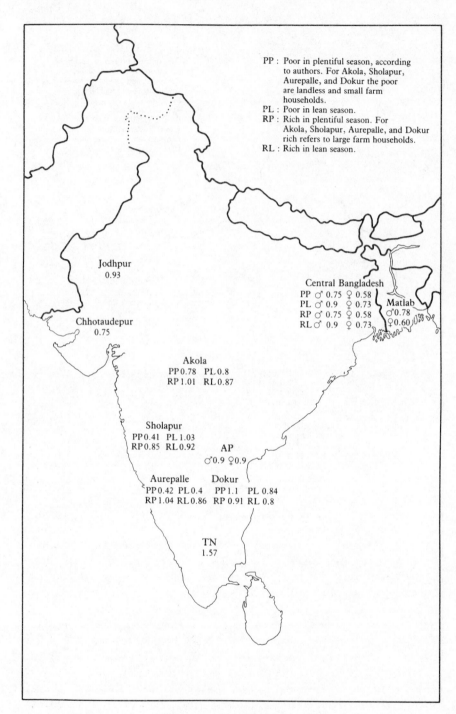

PP : Poor in plentiful season, according
to authors. For Akola, Sholapur,
Aurepalle, and Dokur the poor
are landless and small farm
households.
PL : Poor in lean season.
RP : Rich in plentiful season. For
Akola, Sholapur, Aurepalle, and Dokur
rich refers to large farm households.
RL : Rich in lean season.

Jodhpur
0.93

Chhotaudepur
0.75

Central Bangladesh
PP ♂ 0.75 ♀ 0.58
PL ♂ 0.9 ♀ 0.73   Matlab
RP ♂ 0.75 ♀ 0.58   ♂0.78
RL ♂ 0.9 ♀ 0.73   ♀0.60

Akola
PP 0.78 PL 0.8
RP 1.01 RL 0.87

Sholapur
PP 0.41 PL 1.03
RP 0.85 RL 0.92   AP
                    ♂0.9 ♀0.9

Aurepalle   Dokur
PP 0.42 PL 0.4   PP 1.1 PL 0.84
RP 1.04 RL 0.86 RP 0.91 RL 0.8

TN
1.57

Sources: As for Map 5.2

Map 5.6 Indices of relative intake of proteins: children under 5

Table 5.2 Seasonal and socio-economic relationships in energy intake, India

Region	Season	
	Lean	Plentiful
North		
A	p < r	p ≤ r
B	p ≤ r	p < r
Central		
A	p = r	p ≥ r
B	p > r	p > r
A	p < r	p = r
B	p = r	p = r
South		
A	p > r	p < r
B	p < r	p < r
A	p = r	p < r
B	p = r	p > r

Notes: A: absolute level of energy intake by male adult.
   B: relative intakes of other age/sex categories.
   p: poorest (landless).
   r: richest (landed).
   For 'Central' and 'South', data are given for two locations within the region.

absolute intakes of young children remained well below recommended levels, the RIs of the most disadvantaged (girls under 4 years) actually rose at times of scarcity in such a way as to suggest that the seasonal shortages were absorbed by men rather than by women. Whereas the poor increased their consumption in times of plenty, it seemed that the richer households reduced their consumption of energy, possibly commensurate with reduced activity levels after harvest.[177]

Aggregate data for six villages in central and southern India reveals no easily interpretable seasonal relationships (Table 5.2). In the four central Indian villages discrepancies in consumption between rich and poor individuals during the lean season are reduced during seasons of plenty, because of a drop in the consumption of the rich. By contrast, in the south the rich consume absolutely more in times of plenty. There is, however, no consistent trend in the RIs of other household members. Testing Chambers's hypothesis that there are marked seasonal variations in nutrient intake (calorie lows coinciding dysfunctionally with high work burdens, high levels of morbidity, and the peaking of energy costs of pregnancy and lactation), Ryan *et al.* partially reject it.[178] Their regression analysis, confined to the intakes of children, shows no significant seasonal effect on nutrient intake despite the highly seasonal agricultural ecology of the semi-arid tropics. Two comments are in order: first

[177] Abdullah (1983); Abdullah and Wheeler (1985: 1312).

[178] Ryan *et al.* (1984: 39).

their analysis excluded the intakes of adults.[179] Second, their aggregated regression analysis may mask (possibly contradictory) seasonal relationships specific to individual villages. With respect to income, their finding of an absence of any income effect on the consumption of energy or protein is hard to square with an absence of change in RIs attributable to increasing income.[180] Constant RIs should mean rising absolute consumption (if income relates positively to holding size) when holding size is positively associated with nutrient consumption, as is found. It is possible that the range of agricultural income is low in these villages. If so, this would indicate the important nutritional role of off-farm income. Behrman's reworking of ICRISAT's seasonal data on food intake, anthropometric status, and expenditure shows a 5 per cent pro-male bias in nutrient allocation in the lean season, a bias more marked in low-caste (low-income) groups. To put this in its context, it is a gender bias in allocation less than that found in the USA.[181] The Tamil Nadu Nutrition Study, which did not investigate seasonal effects, shows incontrovertibly that the pattern of RIs in this southern state does not vary with aggregate household intake or with differences in household income.[182]

An important socio-economic variable in the ICRISAT data set (with effects upon consumption that overrode those of other variables) is household size. As household size increases so the individual consumption of energy and protein (as well as certain micronutrients) decreases. This is a marked general effect while the specifics of birth order have no explanatory mileage for this set of 938 children.[183]

(c)   Class and allocative behaviour in scarcity: a village-level case in central India

The issue of social differences in the intrafamily distribution of energy under seasonally varying conditions of household energy availability demands further attention. ICRISAT's data on energy intake can be reworked at the level of individual households to compute RIs and IRIs. These can be examined under extreme conditions of energy supply to households to investigate three aspects of this subject:

1. whether allocative practice changes in scarcity;
2. whether allocative reactions take different forms according to agrarian class position;

---

[179] Note that McNeill in her semi-arid village found no socio-economic difference in the share except for greater variability in the female share among the landless and marginal peasantry than in other classes (1986).

[180] Ryan *et al.* (1984: 35).

[181] Behrman (1986).

[182] Cantor *et al.* (1973: i. 100). But note that levels of intake were associated inversely with ritual status 'regardless of economic position' (ibid. 94).

[183] Ryan *et al.* (1984: 35).

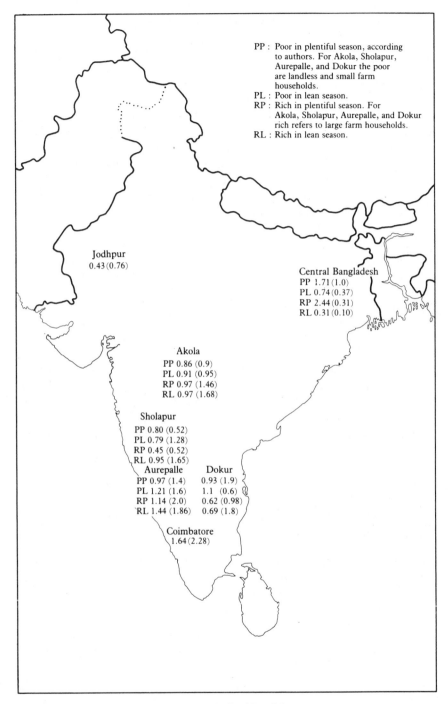

PP : Poor in plentiful season, according
　　to authors. For Akola, Sholapur,
　　Aurepalle, and Dokur the poor
　　are landless and small farm
　　households.
PL : Poor in lean season.
RP : Rich in plentiful season. For
　　Akola, Sholapur, Aurepalle, and Dokur
　　rich refers to large farm households.
RL : Rich in lean season.

Jodhpur
0.43 (0.76)

Central Bangladesh
PP 1.71 (1.0)
PL 0.74 (0.37)
RP 2.44 (0.31)
RL 0.31 (0.10)

Akola
PP 0.86 (0.9)
PL 0.91 (0.95)
RP 0.97 (1.46)
RL 0.97 (1.68)

Sholapur
PP 0.80 (0.52)
PL 0.79 (1.28)
RP 0.45 (0.52)
RL 0.95 (1.65)

Aurepalle　　Dokur
PP 0.97 (1.4)　0.93 (1.9)
PL 1.21 (1.6)　1.1 (0.6)
RP 1.14 (2.0)　0.62 (0.98)
RL 1.44 (1.86)　0.69 (1.8)

Coimbatore
1.64 (2.28)

Sources: As for Map 5.2

Map 5.7 Indices of relative intake of B carotene: adult women and (in brackets)
children under 5

3. whether such forms are generalized across different local agrarian ecologies.

The data set has already been introduced and discussed, both in the text and in Table 5.1, but further familiarity is advisable.

It has had to be assumed that ICRISAT's village-specific, different land-holding classes for categories of small, medium, and large farmers generate comparable economic groups and we worked with these categories (plus that of landless labour—four classes in all). It is also assumed that energy expenditure is more or less constant and moderate in all seasons. The type and size of samples make it clear that the possibility of non-trivial intervillage variation in nutrition was discounted when the field surveys began. This also has to be accepted. Disaggregated analysis by agrarian class in a given village shows that it is not possible to know whether some statistically insignificant results are 'real' or result from small cell sizes. This problem of cell size (along with a trial and error process of experimental aggregation) also informed our three age groupings (Table 5.3).

The first rock hit concerns the identity of the 'adult male' forming the referent for the construction of RIs and IRIs for all other household members. Social and economic power and decision-making responsibility do not require energy and may not be a characteristic of the male with the largest energy intake who is typically in his teens (as he is in the UK[184]). It is also possible for adolescent males to have an IRI exceeding 1.0.[185] In complex households, our household head is therefore the male between the age of 20 and 55 who consumes most energy. In the absence of such a male, it is a male over the age of 55. It is always possible that this nutritional household head is not the political head.

Another rock hit concerns seasons. ICRISAT classifies its four rounds of data as 'surplus' or 'lean' in season. T-tests, performed on the relative intakes for males and females under 3 and over 18, in order to examine whether interseasonal variation exceeded intraseasonal variation, demonstrated conclusively that ICRISAT's categories of 'surplus' and 'lean' are not meaningful indicators of household energy supplies in any social group. The variation in household energy supply between the two surplus seasons was more significant than any other seasonal difference. Thus it would seem that agricultural

---

[184] Nelson (1986).

[185] Seasonally female-headed households due to male migration are another problem, although in this case a quantitatively small one. In 2% of cases the RI ratio is constructed on the adult female. Another frustration, given our advocacy of the deconstruction of terms such as 'female', is our inability to do just that. We cannot distinguish between bride and daughter, between married elderly mother of sons and widow of daughters. Many big households in this data set include servants, kin, and guests. We have ignored their consumption in this exercise, though this is potentially researchable with ICRISAT's data set; as is the issue of deliberate discrimination against the second or third daughter (or son) in the subset of households simple enough to clarify this kinship relation.

production seasons cannot be assumed to be nutritional seasons in the diverse rural economy of the semi-arid tropics of South Asia. Nor will agricultural seasons in widely scattered villages be conterminous. Household energy entitlement will result from farm and non-farm assets, employment, other forms of exchange, and energy stocks stored. Disregarding ICRISAT's classification, the four sets of seasonal data for each household were therefore ranked according to aggregate household energy availability per consumption unit. Each household member's IRI in the period of maximum and minimum energy supply to the household was computed. Households were then grouped into agrarian classes, following ICRISAT's categories, and individuals within the households of given agrarian classes were grouped according to age and sex.

Four villages are studied separately here because of intervillage variation in their agricultural economies. Two, Aurepalle and Dokur, are on alfisols in a low rainfall region of Andhra Pradesh (Mahbubnagar District). Both have agricultural economies characterized by complexity and diversity in cropping patterns, which include monocropped paddy and monocropped and inter-cropped groundnut, sorghum, pearl millet, and pigeon pea.[186] Aurepalle has about a quarter of its cropped area irrigated by tank. By contrast Dokur has 60 per cent of its gross cultivated area irrigated by tank and well. Production resources tend to be concentrated upon irrigated land in Dokur where the specialized commercialization of monocropped agroindustrial crops such as sugarcane and cotton is on the increase. Large farms are those exceeding 5.25 ha in Aurepalle and 3 ha in Dokur (where average holding size is 2.6 ha). Both villages rely substantially upon female labour in production, Dokur, where labour inputs are twice as intense, more than Aurepalle. From 63 to 88 per cent of all hired labour is female and participation rates are (relative to other villages in the semi-arid tropics) high and stable. Female wages are, however, about 56 per cent of male wages.

Kalman village in Sholapur District of Maharashtra lies on deep vertisols, which, together with the bimodal pattern of the monsoons, means that land is fallowed during the rains. Only a tenth of the land is irrigated, upon which sugarcane, vegetables, and wheat are grown. The rest of the dryland is put to sorghum-led, complex intercropping. Large farms are those in excess of 10.75 ha. The intensity of labour use in Kalman is only one-fifth that of Dokur and a slight majority of the labour force is male. Female participation rates are lowest here, while the seasonal variability of both male and female employment is highest. Kanzara village in Akola District of Maharashtra has shallow soils and least irrigation (5 per cent of cropped land upon which cotton tends to be grown) but, like Dokur, it has a relatively assured moisture regime based in this case upon a dependable pattern of rainfall. The rainfed land, like that of

---

[186] Jodha (1980). Intercropping increases gross returns on rainfed land, evens out demand for labour, phases harvests with crops of different maturation (and thus phases actual or implicit income streams), and minimizes risk. It is particularly practised by small farmers.

Table 5.3 Statistically significant changes in indices of relative intake for calories in times of relative scarcity by agrarian class and sex, central Indian villages

Landholding class	Females		Males		% mean deviation of RI from RRI in period of:						Age-sex group compensating for change observed
	Age group	P value	Age group	P value	max. supply			min. supply			
					%	SE	n	%	SE	n	
Aurepalle, Mahbubnagar Dt., AP											
III	≥ 20	0.008			+8	6.6	9	−18	5.3	8	M + F, 1–10; M ≥ 20
III + sf			1–10	0.03	−1	4.7	22	+19	8.0	16	F ≥ 20
mf			1–10	0.03	−2	3.1	8	+27	12.4	7	M HHH
lf	1–10	0.040			+2	4.8	5	+67	28.5	4	M HHH
lf	11–19	0.020			−9	2.4	8	+6	5.6	7	M HHH
mf + lf	11–19	0.050			−8	2.5	9	+34	1.8	10	M HHH
mf + lf			1–10	0.02	0	2.9	10	+25	8.8	11	M HHH
Dokur, Mahbubnagar Dt., AP											
III sf	11–19	0.030			−12	6.9	8	+10	6.0	8	F, 1–10
mf lf	1–19	0.060			−4	2.7	14	−17	23.6	13	M ≥ 20 + HHH
Kalman, Sholapur Dt., Maharashtra[a]											

Kanzara, Akola Dt., Maharashtra

III	1–19	0.020			+2	2.6	11		−11	4.3	9	M HHH
sf			1–10	0.05	+8	8.8	9		−12	4.1	10	F, 11–19
III + sf	1–10	0.020			−1	2.7	11		−14	3.1	12	F, 11–19
III + sf			1–10	0.02	+5	7.5	11		−15	3.9	13	F, 11–19
mf	all	0.050			+5	3.4	22		−5	3.7	18	M HHH

Notes: III: landless
sf: small farm households (Aurepalle 0.21–2.5 ha; Dokur 0.21–1.0; Kalman 0.21–6.0; Kanzara 0.21–2.25).
mf: middle farm households (Aurepalle 2.51–5.25 ha; Dokur 1.01–3.0; Kalman 6.01–10.75; Kanzara 2.26–5.6).
lf: large farm households (Aurepalle >5.25 ha; Dokur 3.0; Kalman >10.75; Kanzara >5.6) (Jodha 1980).
HHH: household head.
M: male.
F: female.
SE: standard error.
n: cell size.
Age groups are as follows: 1–10; 11–19.
[a] No significant changes.

Source: ICRISAT raw data.

Kalman, has sorghum- and chickpea-based intercropping. By contrast, the labour markets resemble those of the Mahbubnagar villages. The labour intensity, despite the domination of dry agriculture, resembles that of Aurepalle. Large farms exceed 5.6 ha.[187] Landless labourers account for 32 per cent of households.

We tested statistically the hypothesis that IRIs differ significantly in times of relative abundance and scarcity (as defined earlier). Separate tests were carried out for different cells disaggregated by sex, 3 age groups, 4 agrarian classes for each of four villages (96 tests), and also for experimental aggregations of classes and age groups to increase cell sizes. Of the 192 t-tests performed in all, only 14 were significant at the 5 per cent level and only 2 at 1 per cent. No significant changes in IRIs were recorded for Kalman village, one of the least irrigated and most uninnovative dryland villages, and that with the highest proportion of landless labour, the lowest female participation rate, and the greatest class variability in female employment. It was precisely in this type of village that we expected to find evidence of class-specific seasonal modifications to allocative practice. But such behaviour could not be detected. At the very least this calls

Table 5.4 Statistically significant changes in IRIs for calories by age group, central Indian villages

Landholding class	Sex	Age group			
		1–10	11–19	1–19	≥20
Aurepalle					
III	F				D
III + sf	M	I			
mf	M	I			
lf	F	I	I		
mf + lf	F		I		
Dokur					
III + sf	F		I		
III + sf	F	D			
Kanzara					
III	F			D	
sf	F	D			
III + sf	F	D			
	M	D			

Notes: I: increase in RI.
  D: decrease in RI.
  RI: relative intake; for definition, see text.
  For other abbreviations see notes to Table 5.3.
Source: ICRISAT raw data.

<hr/>

[187] Jodha (1980); Ryan *et al.* (1980).

into question the value of female participation as a sensitive indicator of female advantage.

Age and gender groupings which showed statistically significant changes are recorded in Table 5.3 by sex and Table 5.4 by age. Table 5.3 also presents the deviation of RI from RRI for the class, both in times of abundance and in times of scarcity. On the right, the movements (rarely ones of statistical significance) in other gender and age groups' IRIs have been analysed to show the beneficiaries of, or the casualties from, the significant changes.

In the two Mahbubnagar villages significant changes in IRIs occurred among both sexes. In Aurepalle this change is complex. In the landless class, the RI of adult women was 8 per cent more than their RRI in the maximum time of plenty to each household, but dropped very significantly to 18 per cent less than RRI at the time of scarcity. Those to gain in times of scarcity were young children of both sexes (but especially boys) and adult men. In the asseted classes, the IRIs of young and adolescent girls increased in times of scarcity, as did those of young boys, at the expense of the male household head.

In Dokur, significant change was confined to girls and adolescent females and socially contradictory trends emerged. Among the labouring peasantry, adolescent girls increased their RIs from 12 per cent below the RRI in times of plenty to 10 per cent more than the RRI in times of scarcity. The casualties of this increase were girls under 10. Among the asseted, the share of young and adolescent girls decreased in scarcity. Adult men gained most from this.

In Kanzara, among labouring households young girls and boys under the age of 10 who had fair (girls) or 8 per cent more than fair (boys) shares in plenty saw their RIs reduced in scarcity by 13 per cent (girls) and 20 per cent (boys). The beneficiaries were girls aged 11 to 19. In the richer classes, there was a clear gender bias throughout all age groups. All female IRIs tended to fall in times of scarcity to the benefit of adult men, especially the male household head.

Analysis of variance tests (conducted on IRIs according to agrarian class, sex, and periods of maximum and minimum scarcity) showed that in the three latter villages agrarian class was the only significant variable affecting the IRIs. Gender and aggregate energy supplies to households (which must be affected by entitlements other than land) do not appear to be significant determinants of the pattern of intrahousehold shares.

It has been hypothesized from Bangladesh that, in times of scarcity, relative intakes will be chosen to relative needs, i.e. IRIs will be closer to unity (Abdullah 1983). The data examined here do not demonstrate any systematic relation of this sort, either according to age or gender, or between two villages in the same district, or within a social class. With the eye of faith we can discern two patterns. The changes in Dokur and Kanzara are somewhat similar. But Aurepalle is different. Separate trends are distinguishable for the asseted medium and large farm households on the one hand and the labouring peasantry (the small farm households and the landless labouring class) on the other. Among the labouring peasantry in Dokur and Kanzara, scarce food enables adolescent girls to increase their shares but young boys and girls to reduce theirs. Among the labouring people of Aurepalle, scarce food makes adult women reduce their share to the benefit of young children of both sexes and adult men. Among the richer households in Dokur, relative scarcity forces young and adolescent girls to reduce their shares in favour of the male household head. In Kanzara, it is all women who reduce their shares for the sake of the household head. By contrast in Aurepalle when food is relatively scarce, the male household head drops his share in favour of young children of both sexes.

It has also been hypothesized that unproductive people have lower relative intake in scarcity (Abdullah and Wheeler 1985). In the absence of information on economic participation, all we can report is that there is no social trend common to all four villages. While female chidren lose out in scarcity in all classes in Dokur and Kanzara, there is no change in Kalman. In Aurepalle, children of both sexes seem to be protected in scarcity (by mothers in poor families; and by fathers in those of the more propertied). Unfortunately there is no way of pursuing explanations for village- and class-specific behaviour, given the confines of the database.

We can now return to the three questions posed at the beginning of this section. With respect to the question whether allocative practice changes significantly with scarcity, we may conclude from the preponderance of insignificant results of t-tests that much allocative behaviour in these villages appears rather insensitive to conditions of aggregate household food availability. We are aware however that this conclusion, though based on a comparatively large sample, results from a disaggregation which has yielded many small cells. Yet by examining IRIs according to agrarian class and taking each village in turn, we do see certain significant changes in intrahousehold energy distribution. Certain classes in certain villages show age–sex responses in the allocation of energy which are most unlikely to be caused by chance. These allocative responses are to scarcity irrespective of the calendrical season of its occurrence. They are not responses to 'seasonality' per se.

So the answer to the second question (concerning the class specificity of allocative adjustments) is that some class-specific patterns have been distinguished in age–sex groups where allocative adjustments are significant. The answer to the third question (as to the similarity of class-specific behaviour across villages) is that this behaviour is so idiosyncratic as to defy generalization.

Such allocative patterns have not been revealed in previous analyses of the same data (Ryan et al. 1984; Behrman 1986). Other studies have focused upon absolute child intakes rather than the shares of each household member, and on the aggregate data set, which clearly masks varied and countervailing village- and class-specific trends. Other studies have assumed that agricultural seasons are congruent with nutritional seasons and that households do not have countervailing nutritional experiences during series of seasons defined as 'lean' and of 'plenty'. This case-study has exposed the limitations of such foci and assumptions. It has also exposed complex allocative behaviour explicable only by further field research. The specificities of the village economy, especially its class configurations, seem to be more powerful influences on changes in intrahousehold energy allocation than do levels of household energy intakes, agricultural seasons, or even gender *per se*. There is no quick fix for policy.

(d) The allocation of micronutrients

Imbalances in the shares of micronutrients in relation to estimates of need are far more marked and varied than those of energy and protein. They are also harder to interpret. The role of many vitamins is imperfectly understood. The absorption of certain minerals by the gut varies and is far from complete. It seems to depend as much on the presence or absence of other factors as on the mineral content of the diet. So the scientific basis for the RRIs is more uncertain than those for energy and protein. We present data for two minerals (iron and calcium (Table 5.5)) and for B carotene for vitamin A (Map 5.7).

Deficiencies in iron and in vitamin A are thought to be more significant for health than those of other vitamins and minerals.

Age/sex patterns in the allocation of iron and calcium are similar for the three cases for which we have evidence. Children under 5 have low IRIs (with relative intake about or under half the recommended norm). In disaggregated cases, girls and female adolescents get less than boys. Adult women have very low IRIs (with one exception for calcium).

Those familiar with policy-orientated debates over energy undernutrition may be interested in the conclusion of Ryan *et al.*:[188] 'The deficiency of vitamin A is probably the most serious nutrient deficiency in India.' Our data (22 cases, Map 5.7) show that, in the north, the aetiology of this deficiency is likely to be due to the way carotene is shared within the household, while in the south, it is likely to be due to very low absolute levels of household supply which are allocated relatively more equitably. Allocations lead to low IRIs for children of both sexes and for adult women in the north; and to low IRIs for adolescents and adult women in the central region. In 16 of the 22 cases, the IRI of adult women is more severely in deficit than that of children.

Data not presented here show that IRIs of thiamine (vitamin B1) follow a similar type of pattern with respect to age, gender, and the tendency for relative intakes to be more proportional to apparent need in the south, even though absolute levels may be low. The consumption of ascorbic acid (vitamin C) leads in the majority of cases to very low shares for children and to a lesser extent for adolescent and adult women. By contrast the sharing of riboflavin (vitamin B2) appears to discriminate in almost every case against adult men or is 'fair'.

An attempt to explain the absolute consumption levels of children (though not the intrahousehold shares) was made by Ryan *et al.*[189] It produced cases of

[188] Ryan *et al.* (1984).   [189] Ibid.

Table 5.5 Indices of relative intake for minerals

	Iron (μg)						Calcium (mg)					
	<5	10–12		13–18		≥18	<5	10–12		13–18		≥18
		m.	f.	m.	f.	(f.)		m.	f.	m.	f.	(f.)
Rajasthan	0.50	0.93	0.72	0.85	0.43	0.62	0.44	0.56	0.50	0.70	0.39	0.59
Gujarat	0.49	0.65		0.89		0.80	0.44	0.82		0.86		1.11
Tamil Nadu	0.56	0.91		0.98		0.54	0.36	0.64		0.62		0.80

Sources: Rajasthan: Sharma (1983); Gujarat: Gopaldas *et al.* (1983); Tamil Nadu: Sadasivam *et al.* (1980).

swings and roundabouts. On the one hand, it appears that the level of education of the mother accounts significantly and positively for the consumption of calcium and carotene by her children, by means, it is suggested, of her knowledge of the benefits to be gained from the consumption of milk (though there is an income as well as an education effect here). And the children of houses with larger agricultural holdings had larger absolute levels of consumption of calcium and all the measured vitamins; perhaps because land and labour could be spared for the vegetable garden. On the other hand, female participation in the agricultural wage labour force is associated positively with consumption of ascorbic acid. It is speculated that children who travel to the fields with their (uneducated and landless) mothers have ready access during the day to greens, chillies, tamarind, all rich in vitamin C. Furthermore, to the extent that they consume millet rather than milled rice their diets will probably be richer in iron and vitamin B1.

There are two further aspects to intrahousehold food distribution, for which we have to refer to information additional to that presented here. The first subject is alcohol. The second is food behaviour in times of crisis and famine.

(e) Alcohol

The consumption of alcohol in non-tribal and, for different reasons, non-Muslim areas of South Asia is almost exclusively the preserve of males from their mid-teens to their late thirties.[190] It represents a private appropriation of costly calories (though it also dampens appetite and may lead to a reduction in food consumption).[191] About a third of male adults are estimated to drink.[192] The habit is not the preserve of harijans and is found throughout the social spectrum.[193] About half South Asia's drinkers drink heavily. Heavy or excessive drinkers tend to come from the social extremes in rural society.[194]

Drinking affects the household economy. Research from Punjab shows that the 'average' household with a heavy drinker spends 40 per cent less on food per capita than the average non-drinking household.[195] In two villages in

---

[190] Deb (1977: 1–9); Mohan et al. (1980); Mitchell (1984).

[191] Van Estenk and Greer (1985); Priyardarsiri and Hartjen (1982). Note that alcoholic drinks often contain sugar and small quantities of vitamins and minerals as well as alcohol (LSHTM 1985: 30).

[192] Thimmaiah (1979). Prevalence is higher in Sikh and Christian areas. Note that policy on alcohol consumption is a dilemma for the secular state, being a very important source of revenue (Mamoria 1980; Priyardarsiri and Hartjen 1982).

[193] Deb (1977); Harriss (1989). This is consistent with an account of a village in nearby Chinglepet (Djurfeldt and Lindberg 1975).   [194] Deb (1977); Harriss (1989).

[195] Deb (1977: 53). Deb also provides evidence that 'drinking households' spend less than non-drinking households on cash inputs to agricultural production, and on non-food consumption items (clothing, education, and medicine). Drinking is associated with lower gross income per acre from cultivation and with lower net income per capita. It is associated with higher expenditure on litigation (ibid. 41–53)!

North Arcot District, 10 per cent of households had both very low aggregate energy intakes and one or more drinkers. In these households there was a statistically significant negative relationship between expenditure on alcohol and expenditure per capita on food. A simulation of the diversion of alcohol expenditure to millet for the entire subsample of such households showed this would rectify household level energy deficits in every case.[196] Alcohol is usually excluded from dietary surveys, but it seems to lead to a reduction in food intakes for the household.

(f) Famine

Extreme events have been interpreted by some as an accentuation of the 'normal order' and by others as a reversal of it.[197] By criteria of absolute mortality rates, the most vulnerable individuals during the 1878 famine in southern India were infants under 1, and people over 50. The least vulnerable were those aged between 12 and 50. In relief camps male mortality exceeded female mortality, and the population as a whole apparently became more feminine after the event. McAlpin has concluded from this that females have a survival capacity not affected by social factors.[198] The most vulnerable individuals during the 1943 Bengal famine appear to have been people over 50 and children aged 5 to 10. The least vulnerable were adults aged 20–40, men less than women.[199] Sen found greatest vulnerability among women of all age groups up to 61 in the wake of the West Bengal food emergency of 1978, and Bairagi found girls to be of lower nutritional status than boys after the food crisis in Bangladesh in the early 1980s.[200] Greenough explains that 'behind the cultural ideal of a co-resident sharing family' (an ideal which may not be practically manifest even in normal times) 'is a more powerful idea of family continuity held to depend on the adult male'.[201] Greenough argues that under conditions of acute scarcity the household is centralized into one agent, the householder, and other instruments are shed. Appadurai offers an alternative hypothesis that the destruction of the family during famine, including the abandonment of women and children by men, actually serves to maximize the life chances of individuals.[202] The evidence on the effects on food allocation

[196] Mitchell (1984: appendices 12–15).

[197] Sen (1985a: 16–17 nn.); Appadurai (1985).

[198] McAlpin (1983: 56–63). See also Kynch (1985a) on the gender impact of colonial policy on famine relief which became more biased against women as time went on. And contrast with Caldwell et al. (1982) for contemporary Karnataka where the increasing cost of raising children is suggested as the reason for improved allocation to 'the weak' during crisis nowadays.

[199] Greenough (1982: 217–50).

[200] Sen (1984: 352–4); Bairagi (1986). Pryer (1987) also shows that even female-headed households in acute (personal) food crisis do not alter the bias in food allocation against girls in Khulna slums in Bangladesh.

[201] Greenough (1982: 224).

[202] Appadurai (1984: 484–5).

within the household of extreme food scarcity defies generalization about gender for South Asia. If one looks at absolute mortality rates by age and sex during famines, the very young and the elderly of both sexes seem most expendable. It is also possible to study age and sex patterns of increase in mortality during famines and to compare them with ordinary times. This approach can lead to quite different conclusions, in many cases children being protected. On this, see Drèze and Sen (1989).

(g)   Conclusions

If the average actual relative intake ratios (RIs) of each of the 24 different sets of derived data on the allocation of calories according to age group and sex are plotted (Fig. 5.2), four tentative conclusions can be drawn which might best be regarded as hypotheses for further testing:

1. While the ratio of the adult woman's average energy intake to the adult male's is 0.85, the corresponding ratio for the '4 to 6 year old' (unfortunately the only non-adult category where the classification of age and sex groups gives us a useful number of variates (19)) is 0.47. These aggregate average ratios are commensurate with the RRI ratios obtained from ICMR recommendations.

2. However, whereas the variability of adult male and female absolute energy intake in these 22 regional cases appears similar (coefficient of variation: 15 per cent) that for 4- to 6-years-olds is over twice as great (37 per cent). This greater variability might be explained either by differences in the age distribution of children within this age group or by greater variability of energy

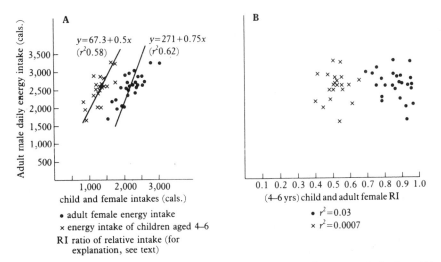

Fig. 5.2 Relationship between absolute adult male intakes of energy and absolute (A) and relative (B) intakes of adult females and children aged 4–6 years in South Asia

intakes, holding age constant (likely because of the feeding habits of this group), or by a combination of both.

3. About two-thirds of the absolute energy intakes of adult women and of children aged 4 to 6 appears to be explained statistically by the absolute level of intake of the adult male; so that one-third is to be explained by other factors, among which will feature intrahousehold allocation.

4. The absolute energy intake of adult men does not appear to explain the relative intake (the RI) of either adult women or children aged 4 to 6. Analysis of this data set (hedged crudely with *cet. par.* assumptions) does not support the hypothesis that in times of aggregate scarcity to a household there is a general trend towards intakes more proportional to need, despite the fact that individual cases such as Abdullah's (1983) show this behaviour pattern.

Other similarly tentative conclusions are:

5. Discrimination in energy and protein intakes through the allocation of food within the household seems to be greater in the north than in the south.

6. In the north it is least 'fair' for very young and very old females, and probably for adult women with special needs associated with pregnancy and lactation.

7. In the centre and south, where absolute intake is lower, shares are relatively low for weanlings, for young children of both sexes in the poorest households, and possibly, though controversially, for adult men.

8. Fifteen of the 31 observations of intakes of preschool children show relatively low shares, even among the comparatively rich and even among boys. This behaviour is concentrated in (though not exclusive to) the northeast and centre of the subcontinent. As with the mortality data, the greatest vulnerability is found in the 0–5 age group.

9. In the centre and south, socio-economic class rather than gender or aggregate household entitlement appears to be the most important influence upon distributional patterns within the family, though this does not necessarily mean that class position is the strongest influence upon anti-female discrimination.

10. Micronutrients are not distributed according to contemporary understanding of need. Children of both sexes and adolescent and adult (menstruating, pregnant, or lactating) women receive low shares, while adult men may be eating not only relatively large shares but also more than they are estimated to need, a factor especially important with respect to iron and vitamin A. There is more agreement about this aspect of food behaviour, although it is less strongly evident in central and southern India.

11. The consumption of alcohol, *ceteris paribus*, certainly reduces household food intake but its actual effects on the sharing of energy have not been measured.

5.5. *The chronicle of explanations*

In view of the contradictory nature of the evidence on intrafamily food allocation for South Asia as a whole, our approach here is to list the types of explanations (material then cultural) which have been put forward for low individual shares. Interestingly, little attention has been paid to the economics of the relative underfeeding of the elderly, who may perform important reproductive roles within the household, and may liberate adult women for wage work.

Earlier, in Section 5.2(*d*) on patriarchy, we examined discrimination against the female sex as a whole, summarized by the sex ratio. Material explanations for its history and geography have involved notions of economic status and utility derived from female participation in wage work, or notions of autonomy derived from property rights and transfers. But existing ethnographic evidence shows the inadequacy of both types of explanation for regional variations in the masculinity of the sex ratio and tends to emphasize what the entire South Asian region has in common materially and culturally.

(*a*) Discrimination against women and children

Economic explanations turn around discrimination's being an efficient survival strategy (and presuppose scarcity of household food supplies, and a given gender division of labour). For south India, positive relationships between male anthropometric status and daily earnings from wage work, productivity on the household farm, or earnings from fish catches have been established.[203] The relative overfeeding of adult men has then been explained as necessary for the major income earner to secure work in uncertain and risky labour markets.[204] A disproportionate allocation to men is thus not a cause of (female) child undernutrition. Rather it is to be seen as a response to labour markets structured in favour of males and boys (and perhaps a means of contributing towards maintenance of women and children).

(*b*) Discrimination against the female child

Economic explanations focus on differentials in income or earnings and expenditure. State-level data show a significant relationship between low adult female earnings relative to those of adult men and the low survival chances of

---

[203] Ryan (1982); Deolalikar (1984); Abraham (n.d.); Ramprasad (1985).

[204] Lipton (1983: 54), though the introduction of uncertainty into the economic argument has to be squared with the facts—at least for the semi-arid tropics of India—that female hired labour is more important in production than is male hired labour, and that female labour markets are characterized by greater uncertainty than those for males (Ryan and Ghodake 1984; Harriss *et al.* 1984).

female children under 5.[205] Furthermore if the recurrent cost of raising boys is higher than that of girls, then girls, being cheaper to replace, may be more expendable.[206] The same may follow if boys have a greater earning power than girls prior to adulthood.[207] Calculations of future costs and returns may determine the reproductive strategy of a household. Girls may be disfavoured because their income earning capacity (in those regions where they participate in wage work) is removed from a household when they migrate at marriage. Conversely boys may be allocated preferential resources in order to attract brides.[208] The cultural corollary is that relative deprivation in food is part of the socialization of girls into the roles of deference and service that they will play as future daughters-in-law. In turn this involves authority and complicity on the part of the mother herself.[209] The religious role of the son upon the death of his parents is another crucially important cultural factor said to predispose households with children of both sexes to neglect the girl child in favour of the boy in times of scarcity.

(c)   Discrimination against small children of both sexes

Discrimination against the male child when it occurs is the more extraordinary given the emotional and ritual centrality of the mother–son relationship in South Asia. A material explanation for discrimination against small children, whether male or female, is that feeding is part of a punitive conditioning appropriate to conditions of scarcity in adulthood.[210] There are also biological explanations, one termed the 'silhouette hypothesis': food is allocated according to the two-dimensional size of individuals, ignoring the higher rate of energy expenditure per unit of body weight in the young child, also ignoring

[205] Parthasarathy and Rama Rao (1973); Cain (1977); Miller (1981). It seems simplistic to confine measurements of costs and benefits to wage work. In rich households the male child may serve an unwaged apprenticeship in productive agriculture while female children in all conditions of household serve an unwaged apprenticeship which is both productive and reproductive. Caldwell et al. (1982) have used this type of reasoning to explain a relative shift in power and resources within households in Karnataka towards children and females. Children being more costly to raise (girls are increasingly being educated), they are not dispensed with as easily as before.

[206] Sen and Sengupta (1983).   [207] Kynch (1985b).

[208] Mies (1980: 93–100). Kane (1941: 510) quotes Bana the poet expressing parental caution over 'one whom one would never forsake, taken away all of a sudden by persons [husbands] who were till then quite unfamiliar'. But Abdullah uses this argument to explain the relative pampering of the prepubescent girl in Bangladesh (1983)!

[209] Lannoy (1971: 91–3). Feeding may be a similar sort of punitive experience as are bathing and disease, and, when combined with maternal indulgence, strengthens the child's ambivalence towards his/her mother.

[210] Cantor et al. (1973: i. 105–15). The silhouette hypothesis is used to explain their observation of the relative overfeeding of the ('inactive') elderly; though it must be said that their reference of need for the elderly may be underestimated; and that neither overfeeding nor the relative inactivity of the elderly has been confirmed more recently (McNeill 1986. See also LSHTM 1985: 18).

adult needs of activity, physiological state, etc.[211] A sociological explanation for the underfeeding of small children, when it occurs in joint households, is that it is not the mother but less well-motivated older siblings who help the young child to eat.

This array of explanations suggests that they are best considered as specific rather than as general, which is consistent with the variation found in our evidence.

But, as Sen says, 'in dealing with within-family distribution, the perception of reality—including illusions about it—must be seen to be an important part of reality'.[212] Subjective and objective criteria of taste, sufficiency, satisfaction, and survival interact in nutrition. A meal can be nutritious but dissatisfying, satisfying but insufficient, or malnourishing as well as insufficient and dissatisfying.[213] It is thus necessary to consider the cultural explanation of scarcity, the meaning of deprivation to those who experience it.

(d) Cultural explanations of deprivation

'A cultural explanation, even if not yielding uniquely profound truth may allow us to see how and why a culture may have failed in responding to forces of reality.'[214] It is significant, then, that types of individual have not so far figured in existing cultural explanations of deprivation and scarcity. The notion of exclusion from items of food is a corollary of systems of classification of food which simultaneously emphasize rank, periodicity, auspiciousness, and medicinal properties in an effort to achieve a state of satisfaction signifying personal health.[215] As part of this effort, to have certain types of food forbidden temporarily or permanently for purposeful, ritual reasons is the common experience of life. Exclusion per se should not concern us so much as should the deprivation associated with mass poverty. Khare, in seeking to explain why chronic deprivation does not provoke a massive action for its removal in India, has advanced the idea that it is because of the Hindu conception of food that South Asian society tolerates extreme scarcity.

The first element in this cultural conception of food is that of the jati and varna orders within which the food available to one depends on one's past karma. These concepts offer stubborn resistance to forces of technological and social change.[216] The second element is that of the Hindu myth of abundance. 'To eat and to feed are matters of inalienable moral responsibility.' Scarcity therefore conveys a moral message. Even when food is scarce and nutritional

---

[211] Wheeler (1984).   [212] Sen (1985b: 83).   [213] Khare (1976b).

[214] Khare (1976b: 72).

[215] Ibid. 123. Food is 'an item of great semiotic virtuosity' (Appadurai 1981: 494). It may be classified simultaneously in the following terms: purity and pollution; right- and left-handedness; exclusiveness; organoleptic qualities; medicinal properties (heat, coolness, and windiness; digestibility; weakness and strength); and auspiciousness over time (Kakar 1982: 219–68; Chakravarty 1972: 41–53; Khare 1976a, 1976b).

[216] Khare (1976b: 168–70).

well-being is materialized only for few, abundance is thought by Khare to continue to be approximated both ceremonially and as an image of the future.[217] Hunger as a state of helpless deprivation does not receive any support in Indian cultural norms. The third element is the cultural 'taking for granted' of production. Cultural emphasis lies not in the material aspects of the production of food, but instead in invisible divine and moral aspects of the distribution of food within society to individuals whose nutritional needs are culturally prioritized according to the duties of the life stages.[218]

The nub of Khare's argument is this. Food produced by the farmer does not reach the eater without the observance of the moral order governing distribution. When this is weakened (as happens under conditions of material scarcity) there is no equally viable, universal, alternative regulation of distribution. 'Though we find profuse culturally backed incentives for distributing foods and feeding different types of members of society . . . we do not obtain any substantive or well focused idea that the cultural system had been geared to retaining sufficiency in foods.'[219] Moderation is thus simultaneously a value of luxury and a condition of necessity of the poor. Khare concludes that such cultural conceptions may reinforce the material neglect of production, may obscure the assessment of food shortage, and may contribute to apathy in the implementation of policy directed from the top down to remedying the problems of scarcity which appear.[220] Intrahousehold discrimination is thus culturally problematic only under deviant conditions of persistent scarcity when the provisioning responsibility of the male householder breaks down. Generalized subsistence for survival as substantiated for South Asia by food economists is for the cultural anthropologist an abnormality.

5.6. *Issues for policy*

Feeding is fundamental to biological, cultural, and political processes. Feeding is the expression of reproductive strategy. This can be expected to vary according not only to culture but also to class position. It is hardly surprising, therefore, that the literature cannot be construed as saying that there is a pan-Indian gender problem in the allocation of food. Evidence of discrimination in feeding practices and nutrient allocation within the family in South Asia certainly exists. It is rarely of a dramatic nature. Young children and the elderly are the groups most generally discriminated against. The absolute entitlement of the male household head, affected by the class position of the household, is probably the most important influence upon hunger within the family. Nutrient allocation is certainly problematic under conditions of

[217] Khare (1976b: 169).

[218] Chapman (1983) provides a similar example of the interaction between different systems of knowledge about agricultural production in Bihar.

[219] Khare (1976b: 161–4).   [220] Ibid. 164–9.

scarcity, but no consistent allocative pattern emerges, even within the large class of the poor in times of scarcity. Instead, the age and gender impact of discrimination, its social and seasonal incidence and severity all vary regionally through the subcontinent. The scale of such geographical variation is below that at which the policy processes of agenda formation, authorization, and resource mobilization and allocation normally operate.[221] It is most unlikely that this conclusion would be changed by further research. As Gwatkin concluded after an exhaustive review of nutrition–productivity relations: 'The more thorough the study the lower the likelihood of an unambiguously positive result'.[222] What will be improved by future research on material strategies of reproduction is our understanding of the reasons for the apparent great diversity of allocative practice.

It can be objected that in the context of the reciprocally causing relations of patriarchy, it is counter-intuitive that there be no general sex bias in food intake. This chapter has shown, however, that discrimination in feeding does not automatically imply discrimination in nutrition, and that discrimination in nutrition does not automatically imply disadvantage in welfare. Females need absolutely less of most nutrients than do males. It is also clear that there are class, caste, and regional differences in the operation of patriarchy. Further- more, discrimination may exist and yet not be picked up even in welfare indicators. That average life expectancy for example has probably reached gender parity in India says little about sex bias under patriarchy. Mortality and morbidity differentials can be explained by gender differences in access or entitlement to health care as well as by access or entitlement to nutrients. Then gender is not just a biological characteristic. It is also a social relationship affected by a material career, the content of both of which is undergoing change. Women are assumed to justify and condone 'inequitable distribu- tions'. If, in a changing society, they actually do not condone allocative practice, they may be supposed to resist the system of ordering of power and subjugation at points where they may exercise certain control. Feeding is one such point.

We cannot assume therefore that the household is a castellated fortress defending patriarchy against the state. In fact, despite or because of the reciprocally causing relations of patriarchy, the household has long been sectoralized, split up, and relabelled for policy purposes, a process often undeterred by lack of information. In the case of intrafamily hunger: the nutritional vulnerability of children and the role of feeding practice in creating vulnerability were a basis for policy long before nutritional discoveries about vulnerability had been made. And, conversely, existing research is translated into clarion calls to planning in such a way as to make the policy analyst suspect that data often have a symbolic value rather than an informational role in the

---

[221] Schaffer (1984).   [222] Gwatkin (1983: 56).

process of policy. 'We need gender specific plans to improve the chances of survival of the girl child', concludes the *Indian Express*,[223] exemplifying the sort of faith in the ability of planning to deliver, in the ability of delivery systems to target, and in the ability of 'us' to benefit, that has been interpreted by Schaffer as institutional irresponsibility.[224] In fact there is no shortage of advocacy for more or less highly targeted therapeutic interventions to remedy nutritional discrimination. In this concluding section we shall describe the form it takes.

First, food behaviour is thought to be amenable to change by ideas and knowledge, hence nutrition education aimed at mothers is advocated. The paternalistic assumptions of maternal ignorance embodied in conventional nutrition education and the irrelevant and sometimes humiliating experience it can be for the target group have been exposed by Wheeler.[225] One could as well conclude from the evidence marshalled in this paper that men should be the target for education, especially about the allocation of micronutrients. More importantly there is no evidence that nutritional knowledge by itself can change the meaning of the food share, embedded in its culture. Others have argued further along these lines that women's education may change house-hold culture. There is evidence that this is true among the rich but judgement must be reserved for the poor. 'The fact is clearer than the mechanics.' If women's education leads to an increase in their age at marriage and a reduction in the gap in age and experience between bride and groom, it may be more likely to change culture.[226]

A second strand of advocacy favours the extraction of the mother and child or the child alone from the household for the administration of gender-neutral or positively discriminating nutritional therapy, as in on-site or take-home supplementary feeding schemes and mother and child health schemes. Free, decentralized, and locationally dispersed health care appears to reduce gender inequities in medical treatment. If nutritional therapy is successful, both absolute intake and relative shares within the household can be supplemented from outside. However, if the nutritional therapy is shared with untargeted household members or if it acts as a substitute rather than as a complement, changes in individual intakes and shares may not come about. Interestingly supplementary feeding has been most successful at reaching poor children, especially girls, in the south of the subcontinent where its need is arguably not the greatest, and amongst age groups which are not identified as most vulnerable, by schemes such as Tamil Nadu's Noon Meals Scheme which is minimally targeted, not beamed preferentially at girls, extremely costly, and which flouts many principles of good planning.[227] Alternatives to sup-plementary feeding have included feeding schemes for adult men, where the

---

[223] *Indian Express*, 17 Oct. 1985.   [224] Schaffer (1984).   [225] Wheeler (1985).
[226] Caldwell *et al.* (1982); Woodley (1986).   [227] Harriss (1986).

supplement is known to have 'leaked';[228] and schemes abstracting the child and offering an 'integrated' therapy not confined to food alone.

A third type of policy aims to increase the economic status of women via subsidized support: special credit, nurseries for working women, vocational training,[229] even reform of the gender division of labour and of gender differentials in wage rates[230] extending to the organization of women into trade unions and co-operatives[231] to claim *inter alia* land and property rights. But there is little evidence yet that improved economic status becomes translated into increased food shares, or that increased control by women over household resources changes their food behaviour. And with respect to the organization of women there is no evidence to date for this as a means of obtaining improved rights within the household.[232] As Sharma says: 'Women tend to see their position as problematic only when the machinery breaks down'. At this point they have little power and their customary forms of small-scale and individualized resistance are inadequate, against men within families and against the state in circumstances when it appears to be the castellated fortress defending patriarchy.[233]

A fourth tack is for the state to administer a general income supplement and an increase in aggregate household food supply through the public distribution system such that maldistributivist practices, if they exist, have less nefarious consequences. The public distribution system has no inevitable effect upon age or sex bias in food allocation. One example from Karnataka shows that a well-administered PDS may lead to a reorientation of the food-allocative priorities of households in time of scarcity.[234] But as PDS administered according to a perverse logic (supplies withdrawn in scarcity and increased at times of abundance, as has occurred elsewhere) could equally well have an opposite, retrenching effect.[235] Sex or age bias will not disappear with increases in income or household entitlement even if the visible, measurable welfare consequences of such biases do. An alternative but variable income supplement for about a third of rural households would be the prohibition of alcohol consumption.

Lastly, perusal of environmental linkages suggests a number of other policy options: measures to reduce female activity levels via a reduction in the energy costs of the acquisition of fuel and water, improving the efficiency of cooking stoves,[236] and reducing the 'secret sharers of food' by eliminating intestinal parasites.[237]

A few comments are in order. First, existing nutrition policy comprises interventions in the realms of incomes and prices (of changes to exchange

[228] Ryan (1982).   [229] ICSSR (1977); Nagaraj (1986).   [230] Lipton (1983: 54).

[231] Bardhan (1985).   [232] Ibid.   [233] Sharma (1980).

[234] Caldwell *et al*. (1982; 1987).   [234] Harriss (1985).   [236] Batliwala (1982).

[237] Lipton (1983).

entitlements) and not reforms of asset distributions (of changes to ownership entitlements). Second, it is still difficult to evaluate which options are available. There is no database for implemented policy such as to enable a technical choice between these options or permutations and combinations of them.

Third, the state has long addressed itself to the rectification of inequalities in rights, without demonstrating a corresponding capacity to discharge its legal obligations to other than a small proportion of the population.[238] All the states of South Asia are signatories of the Universal Declaration of Human Rights which includes a right to food, and to the International Covenant on Economic, Social and Cultural Rights guaranteeing the right to be free from hunger.[239] But the policy options which we have listed here have never been legal, mandatory obligations, and the international right appears tantamount to impossible to operationalize.[240] None the less, 'hunger within the family' can be reduced by supporting pressures on the state to make it more accountable to the organized claims of the hungry for those food-related resources that the state has professed itself obliged to provide. This requires an understanding of how state policy affects the organization and claims of different classes and types of women. It also entails understanding the interests of a given state in unequal allocations within different classes of households: a conceptual linking of reproductive strategy at the level of the family and at the level of the state.

[238] ICSSR (1977).   [239] Alston (1984).   [240] Zalaquette (1984).

References

ABDULLAH, M. (1983), 'Dimensions of Intra-household Food and Nutrient Allocation: A Study of a Bangladeshi Village' (Ph.D. thesis, Faculty of Medicine, London University).

——and WHEELER, E. F. (1985), 'Seasonal Variations and the Intra-household Distribution of Food in a Bangladeshi Village', *American Journal of Clinical Nutrition*, 41.

ABRAHAM, A. (n.d.), 'A Socio-economic Analysis of Food and Nutrition among Traditional Fishing Households (Kerala): Intra-family Food Allocation' (Brussels).

AGARWAL, B. (1984), 'Rural Women and High Yielding Variety Rice Technology', *Economic and Political Weekly*, Review of Agriculture, 19.

ALSTON, P. (1984), 'International Law and the Right to Food', in Eide *et al.* (1984).

Anon. (1976), 'Recommended Dietary Intakes and Allowances Around the World: An Introduction', *Food and Nutrition Bulletin*, 4.

APPADURAI, A. (1981), 'Gastropolitics in Hindu South Asia', *American Ethnologist*, 8.

——(1984), 'How Moral is South Asia's Economy? A Review Article', *Journal of Asian Studies*, 43.

——(1985), 'Dietary Improvisation in an Agricultural Economy' in Sharman *et al.* (1985).

APTE, J. (1973), 'Food Behaviour in Two Districts', in Cantor *et al.* (1973).

AZIZ, K. M. A. (1977), 'Present Trends in Medical Consultation Prior to Death in Rural Bangladesh', *Bangladesh Medical Journal*, 6.

——and RASSAQUE, A. (1987), 'Sex Differential in Mortality and Medical Consultation during 1975–1984: A Study in Matlab Upaz of Bangladesh', mimeo, paper presented at BAMANEH/American SSRC Workshop on Differential Female Mortality and Health Care in South Asia, Dhaka.

BAIRAGI, R. (1986), 'Food Crisis, Nutritional Status and Female Children in Bangladesh', *Population and Development Review*, 12.

BARDHAN, K. (1985), 'Women's Work, Welfare and Status', *Economic and Political Weekly*, 20.

BARDHAN, P. (1974), 'On Life and Death Questions', *Economic and Political Weekly*, 9.

——(1982), 'Little Girls and Death in India', *Economic and Political Weekly*, 17.

——(1984), *Land, Labor and Rural Poverty* (New Delhi: Oxford University Press).

——(1987), 'On the Economic Geography of Sex Disparity in Child Survival in India: A Note', mimeo, paper presented at BAMANEH/American SSRC Workshop on Differential Female Mortality and Health Care in South Asia, Dhaka.

BATLIWALA, S. (1982), 'Rural Energy Scarcity and Nutrition', *Economic and Political Weekly*, 17.

——(1985), 'The Energy, Health and Nutrition Syndrome', in Jain and Banerjee (1985).

BEATON, G. H. (1985), 'The Significance of Adaptation in the Definition of Nutrient Requirements and for Nutrition Policy', in Blaxter and Waterlow (1985).

BEHRMAN, J. R. (1986), 'Intra Household Allocation of Nutrients in Rural India: Are Boys Favoured? Do Parents Exhibit Inequality Aversion?', mimeo (Population Studies Center, University of Pennsylvania).

BEHRMAN, J. R., and DEOLALIKAR, A. B. (1986a), 'Agricultural Wages in India: The Role of Health, Nutrition and Seasonality', mimeo, IFPRI/FAO/USAID Conference on Seasonal Causes of Household Food Insecurity, Annapolis, USA.

——————(1986b), 'Seasonal Demands for Nutrient Intakes and Health Status in Rural South India', mimeo, IFPRI/FAO/USAID Conference on Seasonal Causes of Household Food Insecurity, Annapolis, USA.

BENERIA, L. (ed.) (1982), Women and Development: The Sexual Division of Labour in Rural Societies (Geneva: ILO).

BHATIA, J. C. (1978), 'Ideal Number and Sex Preference of Children in India', Journal of Family and Welfare, June.

BINSWANGER, H. P., and ROSENZWEIG, M. R. (eds.) (1984), Contractual Arrangements, Employment and Wages in Rural Labour Markets in Asia (New Haven, Conn.: Yale University Press).

BLAXTER, K., and WATERLOW, J. C. (eds.) (1985), Nutritional Adaptation in Man (London: John Libbey).

CAIN, M. T. (1977), 'The Activities of Children in a Village in Bangladesh', Population and Development Review, 3.

—— SYED, S. K., and NAHAR, S. (1979), 'Class, Patriarchy and Women's Work in Bangladesh', Population and Development Review, 5.

CALDWELL, J. C., REDDY, P. H., and CALDWELL, P. (1982), 'The Determinants of Fertility Decline in India', Population and Development Review, 8.

——————(1983), 'The Social Component of Mortality Decline', Population Studies, 37.

CALDWELL, P., and CALDWELL, J. (1987), 'Where There is a Narrower Gap between Female and Male Situations: Lessons from South India and Sri Lanka', mimeo, paper presented at BAMANEH/American SSRC Workshop on Differential Female Mortality and Health Care in South Asia, Dhaka.

CANTOR, S. M., et al. (1973), Tamil Nadu Nutrition Study (6 vols.) (Haverford, Penn.: Cantor Associates).

CHACKO, A., BEGUM, A., and MATHAN, V. I. (1984), 'Absorption of Nutrient Energy in Southern Indian Control Subjects and Patients with Tropical Sprue', American Journal of Clinical Nutrition, 40.

CHAKRAVARTY, I. (1972), Saga of Indian Food (New Delhi: Sterline).

CHAMBERS, R., LONGHURST, R., and PACEY, A. (eds.) (1981), Seasonal Dimensions of Rural Poverty (London: Frances Pinter).

CHAPMAN, G. P. (1983), 'The Folklore of Perceived Environment in Bihar', Environment and Planning A, 15.

CHATTOPADHYAY, B. (1985), 'Per Capita Per Diem Intake of Calorie Protein and Fat and Estimate of Clinical Undernutrition in Children for the Rural Paper in Selected Village Clusters of Districts in West Bengal', mimeo (Calcutta: Cressida).

CHEN, L. C. (1982), 'Where Have All the Women Gone?', Economic and Political Weekly, 17.

—— HUQ, E., and D'SOUZA, S. (1981), 'Sex-Bias in the Family Allocation of Food and Health Care in Rural Bangladesh', Population and Development Review, 7.

CLARK, A. (1983), 'Limitations on Female Life Chances in Rural Central Gujarat', Indian Economic and Social History Review, 20.

CLAY, E. J., and SCHAFFER, B. B. (1984), Room for Manœuvre: An Exploration of Public Policy in Agriculture and Rural Development (London: Heinemann).

COHEN, R., GUTKIND, P. C. W., and BRAZIER, P. (eds.) (1979), *Peasants and Proletarians: The Struggle of Third World Workers* (London: Hutchinson).

COREA, G., *et al.* (eds.) (1985), *Man-Made Women* (London: Hutchinson).

DAS GUPTA, M. (1987), 'The Second Daughter: Sex Differentials in Child Mortality, Nutrition and Health Care in Punjab, India', mimeo, paper presented at BAMANEH/American SSRC Workshop on Differential Female Mortality and Health Care in South Asia, Dhaka.

DEB, P. C. (1977), *Liquor in a Green Revolution Setting* (Delhi: Research Company Publishers).

DEERE, C. D. (1979), 'Rural Women's Subsistence Production in the Capitalist Periphery', in Cohen *et al.* (1979).

DEOLALIKAR, A. B. (1984), 'Are There Pecuniary Returns to Health in Agricultural Work?', Progress Report No. 66, Economics Programme (Hyderabad: ICRISAT).

DJURFELDT, G., and LINDBERG, S. (1975), *Pills Against Poverty*, Scandinavian Institute of Asian Studies, Monograph Series No. 23 (London: Curzon Press).

DRÈZE, J., and SEN, A. K. (1989), *Hunger and Public Action* (Oxford: Oxford University Press).

DUBE, S. C. (1983), 'Changing Norms in the Hindu Joint Family', in O'Flaherty and Devett (1983).

DUGDALE, A. E. (1985), 'Family Anthropometry: A New Strategy for Determining Community Nutrition', *Lancet*, 21 Sept.

——and PAYNE, P. R. (1986), 'A Model of Seasonal Changes in Energy Balance', mimeo (London: London School of Hygiene and Tropical Medicine).

DYSON, T. (1987), 'Excess Female Mortality in India: Uncertain Evidence on a Narrowing Differential', mimeo, paper presented at BAMANEH/American SSRC Workshop on Differential Female Mortality and Health Care in South Asia, Dhaka.

——and MOORE, M. P. (1983), 'Kinship Structure, Female Autonomy and Demographic Behaviour: Regional Contrasts within India', *Population and Development Review*, 9.

EBRAHIM, G. (1979), 'The Problems of Undernutrition', in Jarrett (1979).

EIDE, A., EIDE, W. B., GOONATILEKE, S., GUSSOW, J., and OMAWALE (eds.) (1984), *Food as a Human Right* (Tokyo: UNU).

EVELATH, P. B. (1985), 'Nutritional Implications of Differences in Adolescent Growth and Maturation and in Adult Body Size', in Blaxter and Waterlow (1985).

FERRO-LUZZI, A. (1982), 'Meaning and Constraints of Energy Intake Studies in Free Living Populations', in Harrison (1982).

FLORES, R., *et al.* (1984), 'Functional Consequences of Marginal Malnutrition among Agricultural Workers in Guatemala 1984', *Food and Nutrition Bulletin*, 6.

FREEMAN, H., *et al.* (1980), 'Nutrition and Cognitive Development among Rural Guatemalan Children', *American Journal of Public Health*, 70.

GIBBS, C. (1986), 'Characteristics of Household Expenditure in a Tamil Village, South India' (BA dissertation, Newnham College, Cambridge).

GILLESPIE, S. (1986), 'Perceptions of Health and Seasonality in Two South Indian Tribal Groups', mimeo (London: London School of Hygiene and Tropical Medicine).

GOPALAN, C. (1983), 'Measurement of Undernutrition: Biological Considerations', *Economic and Political Weekly*, 18.

——(1985), 'The Mother and Child in India', *Economic and Political Weekly*, 20.

GOPALAN, C., and NADAMUNI, N. A. (1972), 'Nutrition and Fertility', *Lancet*, 18 Nov.

GOPALDAS, T., SAXENA, K., and GUPTA, A. (1983), 'Intrafamilial Distribution of Nutrients in a Deep Forest Dwelling Tribe of Gujarat, India', *Ecology of Food and Nutrition*, 13.

GORMSEN, E. (ed.) (1976), *Market Distribution Systems*, Mainzer Geografische Studien, No. 10.

GORSKY, R. D., and CALLOWAY, D. H. (1983), 'Activity Pattern Changes with Decreases in Food Energy Intake', *Human Biology*, 55.

GOUGH, K. (1981), *Rural Society in Southeast India* (London: Cambridge University Press).

Government of Sri Lanka (1983), *Nutritional Status: Its Determinants and Intervention Programmes* (Colombo: Colombo Food and Nutrition Policy and Planning Division, Ministry of Plan Implementation).

GOWRINATH SASTRY, J., and VIJAYARAGHAVANLK (1973), 'Use of Anthropometry in Grading Malnutrition in Children', *Indian Journal of Medical Research*, 61.

GREELEY, M. (1986), 'Rice in Bangladesh: Post Harvest Losses, Technology and Employment' (Ph.D. thesis, University of Sussex, Brighton).

GREENE, L. S. (ed.) (1977), *Malnutrition, Behaviour and Social Organization* (New York: Academic Press).

GREENOUGH, P. R. (1982), *Prosperity and Misery in Modern Bengal: The Famine of 1943–1944* (New York: Oxford University Press).

GULATI, L. (1975a), 'Female Work Participation: A Study of Interstate Differences', *Economic and Political Weekly*, 10.

—— (1975b), 'Occupational Distribution of Working Women: An Interstate Comparison', *Economic and Political Weekly*, 10.

—— (1978), 'Profile of a Female Agricultural Labourer', *Economic and Political Weekly*, 13.

GUPTA, S. C. (1986), 'Sex Preference and Protein Calorie Malnutrition', *Journal of Family Welfare*, 32.

GWATKIN, D. (1983), 'Does Better Health Produce Greater Wealth? A Review of the Available Evidence Concerning Health Nutrition and Output', mimeo, Report to USAID, Overseas Development Council (Washington, DC).

HARRISON, G. A. (ed.) (1982), *Energy and Effort*, Symposia of the Society for the Study of Human Biology (London: Taylor and Francis).

HARRISS, B. (1976a), 'Social Specificity in Rural Weekly Markets', in Gormsen (1976).

—— (1976b), 'Paddy Processing in India and Sri Lanka: A Review of the Case for Technical Innovation', *Tropical Science*, 18.

—— (1979), 'Post Harvest Rice Processing Systems in Rural Bangladesh: Technology, Economies and Employment', *Bangladesh Journal of Agricultural Economics*, 2.

—— (1981), *Transitional Trade and Rural Development* (New Delhi: Vikas).

—— (1982), *Transitional Trade and Rural Development* (New Delhi: Vikas).

—— (1983), 'Food Systems and Society: The System of Circulation of Rice in West Bengal', *Cressida Transactions*, 2.

—— (1986), 'Meals and Noon Meals in South India: Food and Nutrition Policy in the Rural Food Economy of Tamil Nadu State', Development Studies Occasional Paper No. 31 (Norwich: School of Development Studies, University of East Anglia); published as *Child Nutrition and Poverty in S. India* (New Delhi: Concept Pub. Co., 1990).

——(1989, *Child Nutrition and Poverty in South India* (New Delhi: Concept).

——with CHAPMAN, G. P., McLEAN, W., SHEARS, E., and WATSON, E. (1984), *Exchange Relations and Poverty in Dryland Agriculture* (New Delhi: Concept).

——and WATSON, E. (1987), 'The Sex Ratio in South Asia', in Momsen and Townsend (1987).

HOUSKA, W. (1981), 'The Characteristics of Son Preference in an Urban Scheduled Caste Community', *Eastern Anthropologist*, 34.

Indian Council of Social Science Research (1977), *Critical Issues on the Status of Women* (New Delhi: ICSSR).

ILO (1979), *The Impact of Women Workers of the Maharashtra Employment Guarantee Scheme* (New Delhi: ILO).

IMMINK, M. D. C., VITERI, F. E., FLORES, R., and TORUN, B. (1984), 'Microeconomic Consequences of Energy Deficiency in Rural Populations in Developing Countries', in *Energy Intake and Activity* (New York: Alan Liss Inc.).

JAIN, A. K., and NAG, M. (1986), 'Importance of Female Primary Education for Fertility Reduction in India', *Economic and Political Weekly*, 21.

JAIN, D. (1980), *Women's Quest for Power* (New Delhi: Vikas).

——and BANERJEE, N. (eds.) (1985), *Tyranny of the Household: Investigative Essays on Women's Work* (New Delhi: Shakti).

JARRETT, R. J. (ed.) (1979), *Nutrition and Disease* (London: Croom Helm).

JEFFERY, P., JEFFERY, R., and LYON, A. (1987), 'Domestic Politics and Sex Differences in Mortality: A View from Rural Bijnor District, Uttar Pradesh', paper presented at BAMANEH/American SSRC Workshop on Differential Female Mortality and Health Care in South Asia, Dhaka.

JODHA, N. S. (1980), 'Some Dimensions of Traditional Farming Systems in Semi Arid Tropical India', in *Socio-economic Constraints to the Development of Semi Arid Tropical Agriculture* (Hyderabad: ICRISAT).

KAKAR, S. (1981), *The Inner World: A Psychoanalytic Study of Childhood and Society in India* (New Delhi: Oxford University Press).

——(1982), *Shamans, Mystics and Doctors: A Psychological Enquiry into India and Its Healing Traditions* (New Delhi: Oxford University Press).

KANE, P. V. (1941), *History of Dharmasastra*, vol. ii (Pune: Poona Bhandarkar Oriental Research Institute).

KARKAL, M. (1987), 'Differentials in Mortality by Sex', paper presented at the BAMANEH/American SSRC Workshop on Differential Female Mortality and Health Care in South Asia, Dhaka.

KHAN, M. (1980), 'Infant Feeding Practices in Rural Meheran, Comilla, Bangladesh', *American Journal of Clinical Nutrition*, 33.

KHAN, Q. (1984), 'Impact of Household Endowment Constraints on Nutrition and Health', *Journal of Development Economics*, 15.

——(1985), 'Household Wealth, Mother's Education and Female Child Mortality in South Asia: An Empirical Test of Intrahousehold Resource Allocation', Discussion Paper Centre for Analysis of Developing Economies, University of Pennsylvania).

KHARE, R. S. (1976a), *The Hindu Hearth and Home* (New Delhi: Vikas).

——(1976b), *Culture and Reality: Essays on the Hindu System of Managing Foods* (Simla: Indian Institute of Advanced Study).

——(1986), *The Indian Meal: Aspects of Cultural Economy and Food Use*, in Khare and Rao (1986).

KHARE, R. S., and RAO, M. S. A. (eds.), *Food, Society and Culture: Aspects of South Asian Food Systems* (Durham, NC: Academic Press).

KIELMANN, A. A., *et al.* (1983), *Child and Maternal Health Services in Rural India: The Naragwal Experiment*, vols. i and ii (Baltimore: Johns Hopkins).

KISHWAR, M. (1985), 'The Continuing Deficit of Women in India and the Impact of Amniocentesis', in Corea *et al.* (1985).

KLEIN, R. (1981), 'Relationship of Pre-school Nutritional Status, of Family Socioeconomic Status and Preschool Ability to School Performance and School Age Intellectual Ability', mimeo (INCAP).

KOENIG, M. A., and D'SOUZA, S. (1986), 'Sex Differences in Childhood Mortality in Rural Bangladesh', *Social Science and Medicine*, 22.

——and WOJTYNIAK, B. (1987), 'Excess Female Mortality during infancy and Early Childhood: Evidence from Rural Bangladesh', mimeo, paper presented at BAMANEH/American SSRC Workshop on Differential Female Mortality and Health Care in South Asia, Dhaka.

KRISHNAMURTHY, L. (1973), 'A Life Cycle: Tiruvanmiyur Village, Chinglepet District', in Cantor *et al.* (1973).

KYNCH, J. (1985a), 'Some State Responses to Male and Female Need in British India', mimeo (Oxford: Institute of Economics and Statistics).

——(1985b), 'How Many Women are Enough? Sex Ratios and the Right to Life', *Third World Affairs*, 156–71.

——and MAGUIRE, M. (1986), 'Report on the Nutritional Status of Families in Palanpur, Utar Pradesh, India', mimeo (Oxford: Institute of Economics and Statistics).

——and SEN, A. K. (1983), 'Indian Women: Well-Being and Survival', *Cambridge Journal of Economics*, 7.

LANGFORD, C. M. (1982), 'The Fertility of Tamil Estate Workers in Sri Lanka', International Statistical Institute, Scientific Report (Voorburg: World Fertility Survey).

——(1984), 'Sex Differentials in Mortality in Sri Lanka: Changes since the 1920s', *Journal of Biosocial Science*, 16.

LANNOY, R. (1971), *The Speaking Tree* (London: Oxford University Press).

LAWRENCE, M. L., SINGH, L., LAWRENCE, F., and WHITEHEAD, R. G. (1985), 'The Energy Cost of Common Daily Activities in African Women: Increased Expenditure in Pregnancy?', *American Journal of Clinical Nutrition*, 42.

LEVINSON, F. J. (1972), *Morinda: An Economic Analysis of Malnutrition among Young Children in Rural India* (Ithaca, NY: Cornell University Press and MIT).

LIPTON, M. (1983), 'Poverty, Undernutrition and Hunger', World Bank Staff Working Paper No. 597 (Washington, DC: World Bank).

London School of Hygiene and Tropical Medicine (1985), 'Basic Nutrition and Malnutrition', *Nutrition in Practice*, 1 (London: Department of Human Nutrition, London School of Hygiene and Tropical Medicine).

McALPIN, M. B. (1983), *Subject to Famine: Food Crises and Economic Change in West India, 1860–1920* (Princeton, NJ: Princeton University Press).

MACDONALD, A. W. (1955), 'Le Concept de Sambhogakaya', *Journal asiatique*.

McGUIRE, J. S. (1979), 'Seasonal Changes in Energy Expenditure and Work Patterns of Rural Guatemalan Women' (Ph.D. thesis, MIT, Cambridge, Mass.).

MACKINTOSH, M. (1981), 'Gender and Economics: The Sexual Division of Labour and the Subordination of Women', in Young et al. (1981).

MACLACHLAN, M. D. (1983), 'Why They Did Not Starve: Biocultural Adaptations in a South Indian Village' (Philadelphia: Institute for Study of Human Issues).

McNEILL, G. (1984), 'Energy Undernutrition in Adults in Rural South India', Progress Report, mimeo (London: London School of Hygiene and Tropical Medicine).

——(1986), 'Energy Nutrition in Adults in Rural South India', Final Report to Ford Foundation, UNICEF, and ODA (London: London School of Hygiene and Tropical Medicine).

MADHAVAN, S. (1965), 'Age of Menarche of S. Indian Girls Belonging to the States of Madras and Kerala', Indian Journal of Medical Research, 53.

MAMORIA, C. B. (1980), Social Problems and Social Disorganisation in India (Allahabad: Kitabimahal).

MARRIOTT, M. (1978), 'Intimacy and Rank', mimeo, New Delhi Tenth Internal Conference of Anthropological and Ethnological Sciences.

MARTORELL, R. (1985), 'Child Growth Retardation: A Discussion of Its Causes and Its Relationship to Health', in Blaxter and Waterlow (1985).

——LESLIE, J., and MOOCK, P. R. (1984), 'Characteristics and Determinants of Child Nutrition Status in Nepal', American Journal of Clinical Nutrition, 39.

MATHEWS, C. M. E. (1979), Health and Culture in a South Indian Village (New Delhi: Sterling Publications Pvt. Ltd.).

MENCHER, J. (1980), 'The Lessons and Non-lessons of Kerala; Agricultural Labour and Poverty', Economic and Political Weekly, 15.

——and SARADAMONI, K. (1982), 'Muddy Feet, Dirty Hands: Rice Production and Female Agricultural Labour', Economic and Political Weekly, Review of Agriculture, 17.

MIES, M. (1980), Indian Women and Patriarchy (New Delhi: Concept).

MILLER, B. (1981), The Endangered Sex: Neglect of Female Children in Rural North India (Ithaca, NY: Cornell University Press).

MITCHELL, J. (1984), 'Patterns and Prevalence of Alcohol Consumption in Two Tamil Nadu Villages' (M.Sc. thesis, London School of Hygiene and Tropical Medicine).

MITRA, A. (1978), India's Population: Aspects of Quality and Control (New Delhi: Abhinar Publications).

MOHAN, D., SHARMA, H. K., SUNDARAM, K. R., and NEKI, J. S. (1980), 'Patterns of Alcohol Consumption in Rural Punjab', Indian Journal of Medical Research, 72.

MOMSEN, J. and TOWNSEND, J., (eds.) (1987), The Geography of Gender in the Third World (London: Butler & Tanner).

MONTGOMERY, E. (1972), 'Stratification and Nutrition in a Population in Southern India' (Ph.D. thesis, Colombia University, Colombia).

——(1977), 'Social Structuring of Nutrition in a South Indian Village', in Greene (1977).

MUKHERJEE, M. (1983), 'Impact of Modernisation on Women's Occupations: A Case Study of the Rice Husking Industry of Bengal', Indian Economic and Social History Review, 20.

MUNOZ DE CHAVEZ, M., et al. (1974), 'The Epidemiology of Good Nutrition in a Population with a High Prevalence of Malnutrition', Ecology of Human Nutrition, 3.

NAGARAJ, K. (1986), 'Infant Mortality in Nadu', Bulletin, Madras Development Seminar Series, 16.

NELSON, M. (1986), 'The Distribution of Nutrient Intake within Families', *British Journal of Nutrition*, 55.

O'FLAHERTY, W., and DEVETT, J. D. M. (eds.) (1983), *The Concept of Duty in Southern Asia* (New Delhi: Vikas).

OMVEDT, G. (1978), 'Women and Rural Revolution in India', *Journal of Peasant Studies*, 5.

PACEY, A., and PAYNE, P. R. (1985), *Agricultural Development and Nutrition* (London: Hutchinson).

PADMANABHA, P. (1981), 'Survey on Infant and Child Mortality (1979)', quoted in Kynch and Maguire (1986).

——(1982), 'Mortality in India: A Note on Trends and Implications', *Economic and Political Weekly*, 17.

PARRY, J. P. (1979), *Caste and Kinship in Kangra* (London: Routledge).

PARTHASARATHY, G., and RAMA RAO, G. D. (1973), 'Employment and Unemployment among Rural Labour Households: A Study of West Godavari', *Economic and Political Weekly*, 8.

PAYNE, P. R. (1985a), 'Public Health and Functional Consequences of Seasonal Hunger and Malnutrition', paper for Workshop on Seasonal Causes of Household Food Insecurity: Policy Implications and Research Needs, Washington, IFPRI.

——(1985b), 'Nutritional Adaptation in Man: Social Adjustments and Their Nutritional Implications', in Blaxter and Waterlow (1985).

—— and CUTLER, P. C. (1984), 'Measuring Malnutrition: Technical Problems and Ideological Perspectives', *Economic and Political Weekly*, 19.

PEKKARINEN, M. (1970), 'Methodology in the Collection of Food Consumption Data', *World Reviews, Nutrition and Dietetics*, 12.

PEREIRA, S. M., SUNDARAJ, R., and BEGUM, A. (1979), 'Physical Growth and Neuro Integrative Performance of Survivors of Protein Energy Malnutrition', *British Journal of Nutrition*, 42.

PERERA, W. D. A. (1983), 'The Nutritional Status Surveys of Preschool Children in Sri Lanka', in Government of Sri Lanka (1983).

PETTIGREW, J. (1987), 'The Household and Community Context of Diarrhoeal Illness among the under Twos in the Rural Punjab', mimeo, paper presented at BAMANEH/American SSRC Workshop on Differential Female Mortality and Health Care in South Asia, Dhaka.

PREMA, K. (1978), 'Pregnancy and Lactation: Some Nutritional Aspects', *Indian Journal of Medical Research*, 68.

PRIYARDARSIRI, S., and HARTJEN, C. A. (1982), 'Legal Control and Alcohol in the United States and India', *International Journal of the Addictions*, 17.

PRYER, J. (1987), 'The Production and Reproduction of Malnutrition in a Bangladesh Slum', in Momsen and Townsend (1987).

PUSHPAMMA, P., GEERVANI, P., and KRISHNA KUMARI, K. (1981), 'Anthropometric and Dietary Pattern of Adults and Elderly Population of Andhra Pradesh', *Nutrition Reports International*, 23.

—— ——and LAKSHMI DEVI, N. (1982), 'Food Intake, Nutrient Adequacy and Anthropology of Adolescents in Andhra Pradesh', *Indian Journal of Medical Research*, 75.

—— ——and USHA RANI, M. (1982), 'Food Intake and Nutritional Adequacy of the

Rural Population of Andhra Pradesh, India', *Human Nutrition: Applied Nutrition*, 36A.

RAHAMAN, M. (1982), 'A Diarrhoea Clinic in Rural Bangladesh: Influence of Distance, Age and Sex on Attendance and Diarrhoeal Mortality', *American Journal of Public Health*, 72.

RAJALAKSHMI, R. (1981), 'Behavioural Development of Underprivileged and Malnourished Children', *Baroda Journal of Nutrition*, 8.

RAJARAMAN, I. (1983), 'Economics of Bride Price and Dowry', *Economic and Political Weekly*, 18.

RAMPRASAD, V. (1985), 'Food and Nutrition Assessment of Fishing Communities in Tamil Nadu', Bay of Bengal Fisheries Project Consultancy Report (Madras: FAO).

RANDERIA, S., and VISARIA, L. (1984), 'Sociology of Bride Price and Dowry', *Economic and Political Weekly*, 19.

RIVERS, J. P. W. (1982), 'Women and Children Last: An Essay on Sex Discrimination in Disasters', *Disasters*, 6.

—— and PAYNE, P. R. (1982), 'The Comparison of Energy Supply and Energy Need: A Critique of Energy Requirements', in Harrison (1982).

ROBERTS, S. B., PAUL, A. A., COLE, T. J., and WHITEHEAD, R. G. (1982), 'Seasonal Changes in Activity, Birth Weight and Lactational Performance in Rural Gambian Women', *Transactions of the Royal Society of Tropical Medicine and Hygiene*, 76.

ROSENZWEIG, M. R. (1984), 'Determinants of Wage Rates and Labour Supply Behaviour in the Rural Sector of a Developing Country', in Binswanger and Rosenzweig (1984).

—— and SCHULTZ, T. P. (1980), 'Market Opportunities, Genetic Endowments and the Inframily Distribution of Resources: Child Survival in Rural India', *American Economic Review*, 63.

RYAN, J. G. (1982), 'Wage Functions for Daily Labor Market Participants in Rural South India', Progress Report No. 38, Economics Programme (Hyderabad: ICRISAT).

—— BIDINGER, P. D., PRAHLAD RAO, N., and PUSHPAMMA, P. (1984), 'The Determinants of Individual Diets and Nutritional Status in Six Villages of Southern India', *Research Bulletin*, 7 (Hyderabad: ICRISAT).

—— and GHODAKE, R. D. (1980), 'Labor Market Behavior in Rural Villages of South India: Effects of Season, Sex and Socioeconomic Status', Progress Report No. 15, Economics Programme (Hyderabad: ICRISAT).

—— —— (1984), 'Labor Market Behavior in Rural Villages in South India: Effects of Season, Sex and Socioeconomic Status', in Binswanger and Rosenzweig (1984).

—— —— and SARIN, R. (1980), 'Labor Use and Labor Markets in Semi Arid Tropical Rural Villages of Peninsular India', in *Socio-economic Constraints to the Development of Semi Arid Tropical Agriculture* (Hyderabad: ICRISAT).

SADASIVAM, S., KASTHURI, R., and SUBRAMANIAM, S. (1980), 'Nutritional Survey in a Village of Tamil Nadu', *Industrial Journal of Nutrition Dietetics*, 17.

SATHAR, S. (1985), 'Infant and Child Mortality in Pakistan: Some Trends and Differentials', *Journal of Biosocial Sciences*, 17.

SATYANARAYANA, K., NADAMUNI NAIDU, A., and NARASINGA RAO, B. S. (1979), 'Effect of Early Childhood Undernutrition and Child Labour on Growth and Adult Nutritional Status of Rural Indian Boys around Hyderabad', *American Journal of Clinical Nutrition*, 32.

SATYANARAYANA, K., NADAMUNI NAIDU, A., and NARASINGA RAO, B. S. (1980), 'Agricultural Employment, Wage Earnings and Nutritional Status of Teenage Rural Hyderabad Boys', *Industrial Journal of Nutrition and Dietetics*, 17.

SCHAFFER, B. (1984), 'Towards Responsibility: Public Policy in Concept and Practice', in Clay and Schaffer (1984).

SCRIMSHAW, N. S., and ALTSCHUL, A. M. (eds.) (1971), *Amino Acid Fortification of Protein Foods* (Cambridge, Mass.: MIT Press).

SECKLER, D. (1982), 'Small but Healthy: A Basic Hypothesis in the Theory, Measurement and Policy of Malnutrition', in Sukhatme (1982).

SEN, A. K. (1981), *Poverty and Famines: An Essay on Entitlement and Deprivation* (Oxford: Oxford University Press).

——(1984), 'Family and Food: Sex Bias in Poverty', in *Resources, Values and Development* (Oxford: Basil Blackwell).

——(1985a), 'Women, Technology and Sexual Divisions', *Trade and Development (UNCTAD)*, 6.

——(1985b), *Commodities and Capabilities* (Amsterdam: North-Holland).

——and SENGUPTA, S. (1983), 'Malnutrition of Rural Indian Children and the Sex Bias', *Economic and Political Weekly*, 18.

SEN, G. (1982), 'Women Workers and the Green Revolution', in Beneria (1982).

SEN, I. (1986), 'Geography of Secular Change in Sex Ratio in 1981', *Economic and Political Weekly*, 21.

SHARMA, S. (1983), 'Food Distribution Pattern in Drought Affected Farm Families of Rajasthan', M.Sc. thesis, University of Udaipur.

SHARMA, U. (1978), 'Women and Their Affines: The Veil as a Symbol of Separation', *Man*, June.

——(1980), *Women, Work and Property in North-West India* (London: Tavistock Publications).

SHARMAN, A., THEOPANO, J., CURTIS, K., and MERCER, E. (eds.) (1985), *Diet and Domestic Life in Society*.

SIBERT, J. R., YADHAV, M., and INBARAJ, S. G. (1978), 'Maternal and Foetal Nutrition in Southern India', *British Medical Journal*, 1.

SINGH, S., GORDON, J. E., and WYON, J. B. (1962), 'Medical Care in Fatal Illness of a Rural Punjab Population: Some Social, Biological and Cultural Factors and Their Ecological implications', *Indian Journal of Medical Research*, 50.

SOPHER, D. E. (ed.) (1980), *An Exploration of India* (London: Longman).

SUKHATME, P. V. (1981), 'Relationship between Malnutrition and Poverty' (New Delhi: Indian Association of Social Science Institutions).

——(ed.) (1982), *Newer Concepts in Nutrition and Their Implications for Policy* (Pune: Maharashtra Association for the Cultivation of Science).

SUNDARAJ, R., and PEREIRA, S. M. (1973), 'Diets of Pregnant Women in a South Indian Community', *Tropical Medicine*, 25.

—— ——(1975), 'Dietary Intakes and Food Taboos of Lactating Women in a South Indian Community', *Tropical Medicine*, 27.

TANNER, *et al.* (1970), 'Standards for Birth Weights at Gestational Periods from 32 to 42 weeks Allowing for Maternal Height and Weight', *Archives of Diseases of Children*, 45.

THIAGARAJAN, D. (1973), 'A Life Cycle: Olappalayam Village, Coimbatore Dt.', in Cantor *et al.* (1973).

THIMMAIAH, V. (1979), *Socio Economic Impact of Drinking, State Lottery and Horse Racing in Karnataka* (New Delhi: Sterling Pub. Co.).

TRIVEDI, H. R. (1976), *The Scheduled Caste Woman: Studies in Exploitation* (New Delhi: Concept).

VAN ESTENK, P., and GREER, J. (1985), 'Beer Consumption and Third World Nutrition', *Food Policy*, 10.

VISARIA, L. (1987), 'Sex Differentials in Nutritional Status in a Rural Area of Gujarat States, India', mimeo, paper presented at BAMANEH/American SSRC Workshop on Differential Female Mortality and Health Case in South Asia, Dhaka.

VISARIA, P., and VISARIA, L. (1973), 'Employment Planning for the Weaker Sections in Rural India', *Economic and Political Weekly*, 8.

VITERI, F. E. (1971), 'Considerations on the Effect of Nutrition as the Body Composition and Physical Working Capacity of Young Guatemalan Adults', in Scrimshaw and Altschul (1971).

WADLEY, S., and DERR, B. (1987), 'Child Survival and Economic Status in a North Indian Village', mimeo, paper presented at BAMANEH/American SSRC Workshop on Differential Female Mortality and Health Care in South Asia, Dhaka.

WATERLOW, J. C. (1972), 'Classification and Definition of Protein-Calorie Malnutrition', *British Medical Journal*, 3.

——(1973), 'Note on the Assessment and Classification of Protein-Energy Malnutrition in Children', *Lancet*, 14 July.

—— (1979), 'Uses of Recommended Intakes: The Purpose of Dietary Recommendations', *Food Policy*, 4.

——(1985), 'What Do We Mean by Adaptation?' in Blaxter and Waterlow (1985).

WHEELER, E. F. (1984), 'Intra Household Food Allocation: A Review of Evidence', Bad Homborg, mimeo, paper presented at meeting on 'The Sharing of Food', London School of Hygiene and Tropical Medicine, London.

—— (1985), 'To Feed or to Educate: Labelling in Targetting Nutrition Interventions', in Wood (1985).

WHITE, B. (1984), 'Measuring Time-Allocation, Decision Making and Agrarian Changes Affecting Rural Women: Examples from Recent Resources in Indonesia', *IDS Bulletin*, 15.

WHITEHEAD, A. (1981), ' "I'm Hungry Mum": The Politics of Domestic Budgeting', in Young *et al.* (1981).

WOOD, G. (ed.) (1985), *Labelling in Development Policy* (London: Sage).

WOODLEY, R. (1986), 'Women's Marriage and Migration in Rural South India' (BA dissertation, Downing College, Cambridge).

WYON, J. B., and GORDON, J. E. (1971), *The Khanna Study: Population Problems in the Rural Punjab* (Cambridge, Mass.: Harvard University Press).

YOUNG, K., WOLKOWITZ, C., and McCULLOGH, R. (1981), *Of Marriage and the Market: Women's Subordination in International Perspective* (London: CSE Books).

ZALAQUETTE, J. (1984), 'The Relationship between Development and Human Rights', in Eide *et al.* (1984).

6

Public Policy and Basic Needs Provision: Intervention and Achievement in Sri Lanka*

Sudhir Anand and S. M. Ravi Kanbur

6.1. *Introduction*

In academic and policy discussions of development strategy, Sri Lanka has become a test case. It is well known that the country has exceptionally high achievements in the areas of health and education. The life expectancy at birth of a Sri Lankan is almost 70 years, which is a figure approaching that found in industrial market economies, and much higher than that typical of developing countries at similar or even considerably higher levels of per capita income. Infant mortality rates in Sri Lanka are below 40 per 1,000 live births, which compares with figures in excess of 100 for most countries at similar levels of per capita income. Literacy rates are 80 per cent or more, compared with the developing countries' average of around 50 per cent.

Assuming that one of the major objectives of development is to enhance the quality of life along the dimensions of health, education, and other basic needs, Sri Lanka appears to have been remarkably successful. Yet the growth of its per capita income has been modest in comparison with other developing countries, and it remains part of the 'low-income' group of developing countries. The remarkable record in achievement is attributed by some to a systematic and sustained policy of government intervention in the areas of health, education, and food over a long period. The counter to this position comes in several forms, which can perhaps best be summarized in the statement that the intervention was, or has become, 'excessive' relative to the achievement. It should be clear, therefore, why Sri Lanka is seen as a test case—a verdict on whether or not intervention was excessive in that country will have implications for other countries deciding on levels of intervention. The intensity of debate on Sri Lanka as a test case has been further heightened by the fact that in 1977 the government explicitly introduced changes which were seen as a retreat on intervention. The post-1977 experience in Sri Lanka is thus also of great importance to the 'intervention and achievement' debate.

The object of this chapter is to examine the role of public policy in basic

* An earlier version of this paper was presented at a seminar at WIDER, Helsinki, in Aug. 1986. We are grateful to Saman Kelegama and Madhura Swaminathan for research assistance, and to Jean Drèze, Keith Griffin, Lal Jayawardena, Heather Milne, Martin Ravallion, Abhijit Sen, and Amartya Sen for comments.

needs provision in Sri Lanka. How much does Sri Lanka's enviable record owe to direct intervention by the state? The next section provides an overview of the historical development of public policy and intervention in the areas of health, education, and food, taking in both the pre-independence and post-independence periods. It also considers long-term trends in Sri Lanka's health and education indicators, and recent developments in indicators related to food intake. Section 6.3 moves from the descriptive to the econometric method. We assess the recent literature on linking intervention and achievement in the area of basic needs, which is based on evidence from a cross-section of countries. After a critique of some aspects of this literature, we move to a direct analysis of intervention and achievement using time-series evidence for Sri Lanka for the post-independence period. Section 6.4 concludes the chapter.

6.2. *Intervention and achievement: historical overview*

Sri Lanka has a long record of government intervention in the field of social welfare. The record includes intervention in health, education, and other social services, as well as in the area of food subsidies. In most areas intervention predates independence in 1948; in some areas it even predates the granting of universal adult franchise in 1931. The origins of intervention in Sri Lanka lie in legislation to regulate the living conditions of Indian immigrant workers on the estates, with the pressure for these regulations coming from the (colonial) Government of India. Tinker (1974) has analysed the role of the Government of India in regulating the process of indentured labour migration to Ceylon and to other areas of the British Empire, including the West Indies, Mauritius, and Malaya. He documents the conflicting concerns of the government in balancing the requirements of employers for cheap labour, its own perception that such migration was a useful way of easing population pressure in India, and its self-perceived duty to protect its citizens' conditions of passage and work. Revelations of the appalling treatment of indentured labour *en route* to estates and plantations led to the establishment of inspectorates at ports of origin and destination.

Further requirements, e.g. on working conditions, were often seen as an intrusion into the internal affairs of the colonies concerned, and Tinker gives a fascinating account of how the India Office and the Colonial Office in London mediated these conflicts. However, the demand for labour was such that the employers usually gave way. It would be beyond the scope of this chapter to document in detail this intricate bargaining process in the case of labour migration to Ceylon. But Orde Browne (1943: 20–1) summarizes the process well:

Conditions of service had begun to receive the attention of the Legislature far back in the last century (the Ordinance on Contracts for Hire and Service dates from 1866), but the main impetus to improve living conditions came from the gradually increasing requirements of the Government of India. (The Ordinance relating to Estate Labour (Indian) was passed in 1889 and amended in 1890, 1909, 1921, 1927, 1932, and 1941.) Early improvements were chiefly connected with housing and medical attention, but the standard and scope of requirements grew, until employers were called upon to provide hospitals, schools, maternity arrangements, creches, and various other amenities, representing, as a whole, considerable responsibility and expense . . .

While the employer's responsibility for the welfare of his work-people may be fully admitted, there is something anomalous about an arrangement whereby the supervision and management of such institutions as a school or a hospital must be undertaken by an estate manager . . . Consequently, the existing waste of money, effort, and efficiency in maintaining numerous small schools and hospitals could largely be eliminated by grouping these around central institutions, which would admit a higher standard of inspection and supervision by the appropriate Government Officers.

Orde Browne thus hints at the next logical stage in the process, a shift in responsibility from the employers to the Government of Ceylon—a transition in which the employers themselves had no small interest and which had in any case already begun, as we shall see. The main point of interest for us is that the provision of 'basic needs' goes back a long way in Sri Lanka and began with immigrant workers on the estates, i.e. among workers who are today the least well off in terms of satisfaction of basic needs. While the process of indentured labour migration may only be a part of the explanation (for instance it cannot explain the different developments in the former colonies during the post-independence period), it nevertheless provides a backdrop to the consistent intervention of government in basic needs provision in the modern period.

In what follows we will examine in greater detail the historical record of intervention and achievement under the headings of health, education, and food subsidies.

(a)   Health

Table 6.1 provides some indicators for the health sector from 1926 onwards. As Alailima (1985) notes, the date 1926 is significant for the fact that the first Health Unit in Sri Lanka was established in this year, providing primary health care, including control of infectious diseases.[1] Before this date the network of hospitals was in the main restricted to the estate sector and the urban areas. In 1926 a total of 98 hospitals in Sri Lanka served the entire population, implying a figure of around 50,000 persons per hospital, and 605 persons per bed. There were 285 doctors for the then population of 4.9 million. The formal training of doctors had started in 1870 and that of nurses in 1878. By 1926 there were 437 nurses—one per 11,213 persons.

While we have figures for nominal government expenditure on health from

---

[1] Perera (1985) gives an intriguing historical account of health care systems in Sri Lanka from 300 BC to the present. A detailed overview of health and development in Sri Lanka in the modern period is provided by Gunatilleke (1985).

Table 6.1 Selected statistics for the health sector in Sri Lanka, 1926–1984

Year	Total no. of hospitals[a]	Persons per hospital	Persons per bed	No. of doctors	Persons per doctor	Total no. of nurses	Persons per nurse
1926	98	50,000	605	285	17,193	437	11,213
1927	98	51,020	599	308	16,234	499	10,020
1928	107	47,664	592	321	15,888	545	9,358
1929	108	48,148	575	337	15,302	569	9,139
1930	112	46,429	549	341	15,249	605	8,595
1931	112	47,321	562	341	15,543	612	8,660
1932	113	47,788	566	339	15,929	611	8,838
1933	112	48,214	572	338	15,976	613	8,809
1934	111	50,451	600	333	16,817	613	9,135
1935	112	50,000	471	339	16,519	618	9,061
1936	112	50,000	478	342	16,374	632	8,861
1937	114	50,000	473	367	15,531	688	7,884
1938	115	50,435	564	366	15,847	723	8,022
1939	120	49,167	482	403	14,640	730	8,083
1940	126	47,619	490	404	14,851	744	8,065
1941	129	48,062	507	426	14,554	791	7,838
1942	132	46,970	507	455	13,626	848	7,311
1943	134	47,015	515	450	14,000	895	7,039
1944	141	45,390	514	459	13,943	n/a	n/a
1945	153	43,137	425	514	12,938	769	8,583
1946	189	35,979	408	559	12,261	n/a	n/a
1947	223	31,390	385	n/a	n/a	n/a	n/a
1948	246	29,268	381	689	10,334	948	7,595
1949	256	28,906	376	643	11,594	1,124	6,584
1950	263	29,278	385	674	11,392	1,165	6,609
1951	266	29,699	388	752	10,529	1,762	4,484
1952	268	30,224	388	768	10,486	1,729	4,685
1953	268	30,970	388	773	10,724	1,938	4,283
1954	270	31,555	368	814	10,447	2,105	4,038
1955	274	31,835	358	952	9,163	2,210	3,936
1956	278	32,118	350	984	9,074	2,304	3,863
1957	279	32,849	347	947	9,678	2,587	3,556
1958	282	33,290	341	1,128	8,323	2,767	3,397
1959	283	34,010	345	1,172	8,212	3,129	3,068
1960	289	34,242	332	1,173	8,436	3,232	3,063
1961	291	34,941	340	1,236	8,226	3,547	2,848
1962	292	35,763	318	1,345	7,764	3,270	3,180
1963	295	36,088	329	1,436	7,413	4,420	2,398
1964	294	37,085	329	1,454	7,498	3,435	3,086
1965	296	37,716	330	1,494	7,472	3,642	2,993
1966	297	38,515	342	1,512	7,565	3,499	3,258
1967	298	39,271	328	1,598	7,323	3,999	2,926

1968	302	39,708	332	1,613	7,434	4,382	2,738
1969	310	39,522	332	1,841	6,655	4,734	2,577
1970	455	27,503	320	1,932	6,477	5,542	2,256
1971	450	27,617	320	1,983	8,840	5,003	2,518
1972	457	28,490	325	2,038	6,388	4,955	2,603
1973	456	29,055	329	2,089	6,342	6,234	2,101
1974	451	29,067	332	2,127	6,295	5,288	2,496
1975	458	29,506	332	2,138	6,356	5,653	2,388
1976	460	29,848	334	2,248	6,108	5,640	2,429
1977	469	29,723	340	2,168	6,429	6,266	2,234
1978	484	29,326	352	2,258	6,286	6,169	2,286
1979	480	29,961	342	2,263	6,394	6,673	2,173
1980	480	30,704	340	2,051	7,186	6,227	2,361
1981	488	30,713	340	2,233	6,712	6,805	2,204
1982	479	31,710	350	2,036	7,460	6,931	2,193
1983	483	31,917	350	1,951	7,902	7,114	2,165
1984	484	32,229	n/a	2,822	5,528	7,216	2,162

Notes: *a* Includes maternity homes.
         n/a denotes not available.
Source: Rasaputra (1986: Statistical Appendix, table 11).

1926 onwards (Rasaputra 1986: Statistical Appendix, table 11), the problem is that we do not have an adequate deflator to express these in real terms before 1951. Intertemporal comparisons and trend calculations are therefore not possible between 1926 and 1950 in so far as *real* expenditure is concerned. However, an indication that this must have risen is provided by the large increase in the number of hospitals (from 98 to 263), doctors (from 285 to 674), and nurses (from 437 to 1,165). Sri Lanka's population was also rising over this period, of course, but the population per hospital bed, for example, fell from 605 to 385, while the population per nurse fell from 11,213 to 6,609.

A major feature of the 1926–50 period was the campaign against malaria. In terms of expenditure this was reflected in a substantial increase in *nominal* per capita expenditure on health after the mid-1930s—from Rs. 3.49 in 1935 to Rs. 8.34 in 1950 (Rasaputra 1986: Statistical Appendix, table 11). While these nominal figures do not allow for price changes, they do reflect institutional evidence of the concerted effort to combat malaria after the 1935 epidemic, when deaths from malaria were responsible for 23 per cent of all deaths. The system of health units was also expanded, and in the later 1940s DDT was used. The results were dramatic. The mortality rate from malaria fell from 187.3 per 100,000 of the population in 1946 to 66.1 in 1947, and then to 32.8 in 1949 and 20.6 in 1953.[2] The morbidity rate similarly fell from 41,200 per

[2] In his review of health and development in Sri Lanka, Gunatilleke (1985: 112) notes that 'The year 1947 marks a very significant turning point. The infant mortality rate dropped steeply from 141 per thousand to 101 and the crude death rate from 19.8 to 14. This steep decline in mortality recorded in the period of one year was described by WHO as "an unparalleled achievement in world demography".'

100,000 of the population in 1946 to 19,600 in 1947, 9,900 in 1949, and 5,800 in 1951 (Rasaputra 1986: table 22, p. 62). By 1960 malaria had become insignificant as a cause of morbidity and mortality. The campaign against tuberculosis also showed success. From a level of 62 per 100,000 in 1940, the mortality rate from this disease fell to 57 in 1948; by 1960 it had reached a figure of 16 (Rasaputra 1986: 63). These specific campaigns had a major effect on overall mortality rates. As Table 6.2 shows, the crude death rate fell from 22.9 per 1,000 in 1934 to 21.8 in 1936 (during the malaria epidemic of 1935 it reached a high of 36.6). By 1946–50 it averaged 14.6, and in the late 1950s it had fallen to below 10.

Thus despite certain shortcomings in the data, primarily the lack of a series on real health expenditures, the link between intervention and achievement can be documented with some confidence for the two decades before independence. From 1951 onwards, we can use the GDP deflator to calculate year-to-year movements in real health expenditure, and indeed real values of other categories of social expenditure. Table 6.3, based on Alailima (1985: table 8), shows real per capita expenditure from 1950/1 to 1982 on different categories of social services—health, education, food, and other. For the same period, Table 6.4 expresses these categories of expenditure, as well as total social expenditure, as a percentage of GNP. These figures provide a picture of the evolution of the level and pattern of social expenditure in Sri Lanka in the 1950s, 1960s, and 1970s. We turn now to a detailed examination of the record on health over these three decades.

After 1950 real social expenditure per capita on health continued to increase from a figure of Rs. 8.80 in 1950/1 to Rs. 15.86 in 1960/1 (except for very small declines between 1953/4 and 1954/5, and between 1958/9 and 1959/60). After that a decline set in, and real expenditure did not overtake the 1960/1 level until the turn of the decade, when it reached just over Rs. 16. There was again a sharp decline till the trough of 1974 (Rs. 11.63) and then a rise to the all-time peak of Rs. 16.54 in 1979. However, while the 1979 figure is the highest per capita real expenditure on health in the three decades between 1950/1 and 1982, the figures in table 6.4 indicate that expenditure on health has *not* risen as fast as GNP. From the mid-1950s to the end of the 1960s, health expenditure was equal to or exceeded 2 per cent of GNP. After this it hovered around 1.5 per cent in the mid-1970s and fell to 1.3 per cent in 1982.

It is particularly interesting to note that in the 'post-liberalization' years after 1977, real health expenditure per capita did *not* fall. If anything, it increased relative to the immediate pre-liberalization years. Average real health expenditure per capita for the five years 1973–7 was Rs. 13.16 while the average for the next five years 1978–82 was Rs. 15.48—some 17 per cent higher. Similarly, as a fraction of GNP, health expenditure averaged 1.44 per cent during 1973–7, and fell only to 1.38 per cent during 1978–82. Whatever the implications of the post-1977 period of adjustment for other items of social expenditure, it does seem as though health expenditure was protected in real terms.

We have already noted the dramatic improvements in health-related indicators during the quarter-century before 1950. These improvements were consolidated during the next three decades. Between 1952 and 1981 the death rate declined at an average annual rate of 1.60 per cent (see Table 6.5). In fact, the bulk of the improvement appears to have come in the early part of this period, which suggests a link with the rapid increases in health expenditure in the 1950s. If we consider just the subperiod 1952–60, the rate of decline is 3.12 per cent per annum (not shown in Table 6.5), compared with 1.60 per cent per annum for the full period. Similarly, the infant mortality rate (IMR) declined at an average annual rate of 3.57 per cent in the earlier period (not shown in Table 6.5), compared with a rate of decline over the whole period of 2.50 per cent per annum.

To suggest further the link between intervention and achievement, we note that these declines in mortality rates were underpinned by a steady improvement in the indicator of persons per doctor, which stood at 10,486 in 1952 and at 6,712 in 1981 (see Table 6.1). While the ratio has fluctuated somewhat from year to year, this long-run fall of 35 per cent over three decades must indicate a significant improvement in the provision of medical services to the population, especially when added to the fact that the number of persons per nurse fell from 4,685 to 2,204 over this period (an improvement of more than 50 per cent). A Ministry of Plan Implementation report (1985: 21) gives some indication of the quality of treatment when it notes that deaths in government hospitals fell from 229.1 per 100,000 population in 1965 to 174.1 in 1983. Of course, such figures have to be treated with caution as indicators of quality, since the deaths could instead have been occurring outside government hospitals if the system was contracting; but we know that the system was not contracting. The same report gives figures for hospital morbidity: the cases discharged from government hospitals per 100,000 population increased from 14,773.9 in 1965 to 15,471.9 in 1983. Again, this has to be seen in the context of an expanding service, where it can be interpreted as reaching out to more people, rather than as increased morbidity *per se*.

We end, however, with a note of caution. While the achievements in health at the all-island level have been remarkable, the picture is by no means uniform. Although the crude death rate and the infant mortality rate have come down for Sri Lanka as a whole, the rates are much higher for the estates than for the rest of the island. Thus, in 1970, the estate sector mortality rate was 11.9 per 1,000 while the all-island rate was 7.5 (Gunatilleke 1985: table 4). In 1980, the all-island death rate had fallen to 6.1 while the estate sector rate was still 11.4. Similarly, in the estate sector, infant mortality rates persisted at above 100 per 1,000 live births throughout the 1950s and 1960s, and were about 85 in the 1970s; for Sri Lanka as a whole they were already below 50 in the 1970s, and down to 38 by 1979 (see Table 6.2 and Funatilleke 1985: table 4). An interesting cross-district regression analysis of infant mortality rates in 1953, 1963, and 1971 is reported in Fernando (1985: table 9). Fernando

Table 6.2 Population, crude birth and death rates, infant mortality rate, and life expectancy, Sri Lanka, 1900–1984

Year	Population (mid-year) (m.)	Crude birth rate (per 1,000)	Crude death rate (per 1,000)	Rate of natural increase (%)	Infant mortality rate (per 1,000 live births)	Life expectancy at birth	
						Male	Female
1900	3.9	38.6	28.7	1.0	178	n/a	n/a
1901	4.0	37.5	27.6	1.0	170	n/a	n/a
1902	4.1	39.1	27.5	1.2	173	n/a	n/a
1903	4.1	40.0	25.9	1.4	164	n/a	n/a
1904	4.2	38.6	24.9	1.4	174	n/a	n/a
1905	4.3	38.6	27.7	1.1	176	n/a	n/a
1906	4.4	36.5	35.1	0.1	198	n/a	n/a
1907	4.5	33.6	30.7	0.3	186	n/a	n/a
1908	4.5	40.8	30.1	1.1	183	n/a	n/a
1909	4.5	37.5	31.0	0.7	202	n/a	n/a
1910	4.6	39.0	27.3	1.2	176	n/a	n/a
1911	4.7	38.0	34.8	0.3	218	n/a	n/a
1912	4.8	33.3	32.4	0.1	215	n/a	n/a
1913	4.8	38.6	28.4	1.0	189	n/a	n/a
1914	4.8	38.2	32.2	0.6	213	n/a	n/a
1915	4.9	37.0	25.2	1.2	171	n/a	n/a
1916	5.0	39.0	26.8	1.2	184	n/a	n/a
1917	5.0	40.1	24.7	1.5	174	n/a	n/a
1918	5.1	39.2	31.9	0.7	188	n/a	n/a
1919	5.2	36.0	37.6	−0.2	223	n/a	n/a
1920	5.2	36.5	29.6	0.7	182	n/a	n/a
1921	5.3	40.7	31.1	1.0	192	n/a	n/a
1922	5.4	39.1	27.6	1.2	188	n/a	n/a
1923	5.4	38.7	30.3	0.8	212	n/a	n/a
1924	5.4	37.5	25.8	1.2	186	n/a	n/a
1925	5.5	39.9	24.3	1.6	172	n/a	n/a
1926	4.9	42.0	25.3	1.8	174	n/a	n/a
1927	5.0	41.0	22.6	1.8	160	n/a	n/a
1928	5.1	41.9	26.0	1.6	177	n/a	n/a
1929	5.2	38.3	26.1	1.2	187	n/a	n/a
1930	5.2	39.0	25.4	1.4	175	n/a	n/a
1931	5.3	37.4	22.1	1.5	158	n/a	n/a
1932	5.4	37.0	20.5	1.7	162	n/a	n/a
1933	5.4	38.6	21.2	1.7	157	n/a	n/a
1934	5.6	37.2	22.9	1.4	173	n/a	n/a
1935	5.6	34.4	36.6	−0.2	263	n/a	n/a
1936	5.6	34.1	21.8	1.2	166	n/a	n/a
1937	5.7	37.8	21.7	1.6	158	n/a	n/a
1938	5.8	35.9	20.2	1.6	161	n/a	n/a

1939	5.9	36.0	20.9	1.5	166	n/a	n/a
1940	6.0	35.8	19.9	1.6	149	n/a	n/a
1941	6.2	36.5	18.3	1.8	129	n/a	n/a
1942	6.2	36.7	18.5	1.8	120	n/a	n/a
1943	6.3	40.6	21.3	1.9	132	n/a	n/a
1944	6.4	37.1	21.0	1.6	135	n/a	n/a
1945	6.6	36.7	21.4	1.5	139	47.2	42.5
1946	6.8	38.4	19.6	1.9	141	43.8	41.5
1947	7.0	39.4	13.8	2.6	101	52.7	51.0
1948	7.2	40.6	12.7	2.8	92	54.9	53.0
1949	7.4	39.0	12.6	2.6	87	56.1	54.8
1950	7.7	39.6	12.6	2.7	82	56.4	54.8
1951	7.9	39.8	12.9	2.7	82	56.1	54.0
1952	8.1	38.8	12.0	2.7	78	57.6	55.5
1953	8.3	38.7	10.1	2.9	71	58.8	57.5
1954	8.5	35.7	10.4	2.5	72	60.3	59.4
1955	8.7	37.3	11.0	2.6	71	58.1	57.1
1956	8.9	36.3	9.8	2.7	67	59.9	58.7
1957	9.2	36.4	10.1	2.6	68	59.1	57.9
1958	9.4	35.8	9.7	2.6	64	59.8	58.8
1959	9.6	37.0	9.1	2.8	58	60.9	60.1
1960	9.9	36.6	8.6	2.8	57	61.9	61.4
1961	10.1	35.8	8.0	2.8	52	63.0	62.4
1962	10.4	35.5	8.5	2.8	53	61.9	61.4
1963	10.6	34.1	8.5	2.6	56	62.8	63.0
1964	10.6	33.2	8.7	2.5	55	63.0	63.6
1965	10.9	33.1	8.2	2.5	53	63.7	65.0
1966	11.4	32.3	8.3	2.4	54	63.6	65.0
1967	11.7	31.6	7.5	2.4	48	64.8	66.9
1968	12.0	32.0	7.8	2.4	50	64.0	66.8
1969	12.2	30.4	8.0	2.2	53	n/a	n/a
1970	12.5	29.4	7.5	2.2	47	n/a	n/a
1971	12.6	32.7	8.2	2.4	45	64.0	66.9
1972	12.9	30.0	8.1	2.2	46	n/a	n/a
1973	13.1	28.0	8.7	1.9	46	n/a	n/a
1974	13.2	27.5	9.0	1.9	51	n/a	n/a
1975	13.5	27.8	8.5	1.9	45	n/a	n/a
1976	13.7	27.8	7.8	2.0	44	n/a	n/a
1977	14.0	27.9	7.4	2.1	42	n/a	n/a
1978	14.1	28.5	6.6	2.2	37	67.1	71.2
1979	14.5	28.7	6.5	2.2	38	67.2	71.2
1980	14.7	27.6	6.1	2.2	34	67.0	71.2
1981	15.0	28.0	6.0	2.2	29.5	n/a	n/a
1982	15.2	26.8	6.1	2.1	n/a	n/a	n/a
1983	15.4	26.2	6.1	2.0	n/a	n/a	n/a
1984	15.6	24.8	6.5	1.8	n/a	n/a	n/a

Source: Rasaputra (1986: Statistical Appendix, table 10).

Table 6.3 Real GDP per capita and real public expenditure per capita on social services, Sri Lanka, 1950/1–1982 (Rs. at 1959 prices)

Year	GDP per capita	Education expenditure per capita	Health expenditure per capita	Food subsidy expenditure per capita	Other social welfare expenditure per capita
1950/1	617.59	14.60	8.80	n/a	2.05
1951/2	629.63	16.47	10.51	31.38	2.30
1952/3	619.40	16.96	10.78	15.73	2.54
1953/4	623.65	15.96	10.84	1.45	2.34
1954/5	648.85	16.51	10.67	4.23	2.32
1955/6	634.94	17.84	11.40	9.50	2.60
1956/7	622.72	19.88	11.87	11.76	2.70
1957/8	619.15	22.09	12.90	12.22	3.26
1958/9	617.71	24.84	14.72	15.55	3.55
1959/60	641.41	24.14	14.28	20.25	3.81
1960/1	646.34	29.64	15.86	25.57	4.17
1961/2	649.81	30.31	14.56	23.56	4.57
1962/3	655.75	31.44	14.77	23.99	4.31
1963/4	697.83	32.27	13.82	34.28	4.17
1964/5	694.04	33.38	13.98	25.01	4.04
1965/6	688.95	32.49	14.45	24.44	4.04
1966/7	705.56	30.53	14.38	16.13	3.65
1967/8	744.75	30.13	14.74	22.23	3.41
1968/9	767.87	32.26	15.99	23.15	3.16
1969/70	786.16	35.53	16.10	21.96	3.10
1970/1	780.63	32.42	16.16	34.19	3.08
1971/2	786.43	33.67	15.62	31.42	3.79
1973	802.60	31.03	13.80	34.25	2.35
1974	825.15	24.44	11.63	35.72	2.03
1975	883.11	25.89	12.63	44.18	3.33
1976	842.48	28.66	14.28	31.05	7.29
1977	860.07	25.17	13.45	39.51	4.47
1978	924.96	25.25	15.42	54.46	3.51
1979	956.14	29.78	16.54	62.29	0.62
1980	997.82	32.29	15.84	34.38	2.92
1981	1,034.60	30.93	14.08	24.31	2.77
1982	1,073.03	33.97	15.54	20.72	5.02

Note: Before 1973 the financial year covered the period from 1 Oct. to 30 Sept. With effect from 1973 the financial year was changed to coincide with the calendar year. All the estimates in this table refer to a period of 12 months. (This has been accomplished by multiplying the expenditure figures for the 15-month period from 1 Oct. 1971 to 31 Dec. 1972 by the factor 12/15.)

Sources: The GDP per capita figures are calculated from Rasaputra (1986: Statistical Appendix, table 1), which gives GDP at 1959 factor costs, and the mid-year population estimates in our Table 6.2. The social expenditure figures are taken from Alailima (1985: table 8).

Table 6.4 Social expenditure as a percentage of GNP, Sri Lanka, 1950/1–1982

Year	Education	Health	Food subsidies	Other social welfare	Total social expenditure
1950/1	2.5	1.5	n/a	0.3	n/a
1951/2	3.0	1.9	5.3	0.4	10.6
1952/3	3.1	2.0	2.8	0.5	8.4
1953/4	2.9	1.9	0.3	0.4	5.5
1954/5	2.7	1.8	0.8	0.4	5.7
1955/6	3.2	2.0	1.5	0.5	7.2
1956/7	3.5	2.1	2.1	0.5	8.2
1957/8	3.8	2.2	2.2	0.6	8.8
1958/9	4.1	2.4	2.6	0.6	9.7
1959/60	3.8	2.2	3.1	0.6	9.7
1960/1	4.7	2.5	3.9	0.7	11.8
1961/2	4.7	2.2	3.5	0.7	11.1
1962/3	4.7	2.2	5.1	0.6	11.0
1963/4	4.8	2.0	5.1	0.6	12.5
1964/5	4.9	2.1	3.6	0.6	11.2
1965/6	4.7	2.1	3.6	0.6	11.0
1966/7	4.6	2.2	2.4	0.6	9.8
1967/8	4.1	2.0	3.0	0.5	9.6
1968/9	4.3	2.1	3.1	0.4	9.9
1969/70	4.6	2.1	2.8	0.4	9.9
1970/1	4.3	2.1	4.5	0.4	11.3
1971/2[a]	4.4	2.6	4.1	0.5	11.6
1973	3.5	1.5	3.8	0.3	9.1
1974	2.8	1.3	4.0	0.2	9.3
1975	2.8	1.4	4.8	0.4	9.4
1976	3.1	1.6	3.4	0.8	8.9
1977	2.7	1.4	4.1	0.5	8.7
1978	2.7	1.5	5.3	0.3	9.8
1979	2.7	1.5	5.7	0.1	10.0
1980	2.9	1.4	3.1	0.3	7.7
1981	2.7	1.2	2.1	0.2	6.2
1982	2.9	1.3	1.8	0.4	6.4

Notes: GNP for 1951–6 obtained from National Accounts of the Department of Census and Statistics. GNP for 1956 onwards obtained from Central Bank Annual Reports.
    Expenditure figures obtained from Treasury Estimates.
[a] Estimated from 15 months' expenditure and GNP figures.

Source: Alailima (1985: table 7).

Table 6.5 Average annual rate of change in infant mortality rate, death rate, and birth rate, Sri Lanka, 1952–1981

Indicator	Annual rate of change 1960–78 (%)	Annual rate of change 1952–81 (%)
Infant mortality rate (IMR)	−1.72	−2.50
Death rate (DR)	−0.55	−1.60
Birth rate (BR)	−1.58	−1.28

Note: For each time period, the annual rates of change reported in this table have been estimated by means of a semi-logarithmic regression of the variable in question on time. The data on IMR, DR, and BR are from Table 6.2.

(1985: 83) also reports the results of another study relating to 1971 which shows that 83 per cent of the interdistrict variation in IMR is accounted for by the following variables: the proportion of the district population that is Indian Tamil, the proportion of employed females, and the proportion of females aged 15–19 with more than five years of education. The last of these highlights another factor which may be important in determining the course of IMR —education—and it is to this factor that we now turn.

(b) Education

As with health, government intervention in education in Sri Lanka predates independence. Education became the responsibility of central government with Education Ordinance No. 1 in 1920. This was the culmination of a process which began with the disclosure in the Census Report of 1901 that only 218,479 children out of a total of 867,103 between the ages of 5 and 14 years were actually receiving formal education (Alailima 1985: 6). The period after 1920 saw a steady increase of government responsibility in the field of education, and a corresponding increase in expenditure. In 1926, the expenditure on education was only 0.5 per cent of GNP; thereafter, the ratio rose to 1.5 per cent in 1946 following the adoption of free education (calculated from Rasaputra 1986: Statistical Appendix, tables 1 and 7).

Selected educational indicators for Sri Lanka are provided in Table 6.6. Between 1926 and 1950 the number of pupils in the country rose from 10.1 per cent of the population to 17.7 per cent (calculated from Tables 6.2 and 6.6). Of course, these figures have to be interpreted with care—there are other reasons why this number may increase than an expansion of education to the previously uncovered population. However, the institutional details of the development of education in Sri Lanka corroborate these figures. As Alailima (1985: 8) notes:

In 1931 universal adult suffrage was granted and under the new Constitution there was provision for an elected Minister of Education. For the first time a man who was from the people and knew their problems was put in charge of the education of their children. The electorate was transformed from a restricted literate and property owning minority and the Minister and his Executive Committee of elected representatives had to be responsive to their needs. This change had an immediate effect on the sphere of education. After the General Elections of 1931 and 1936 (the first conducted under the new Constitution) the state assumed much greater responsibility for the provision of education. Enrollment in government schools increased from 216,067 (39% of total enrollment) in 1931 to 378,861 (44%) in 1945 and the number of government schools almost doubled from 1,341 to 2,391 over this period . . . Due to the inability of some private schools to pay their teachers during the depression, the state also took on the direct payment of these teachers.

While we have figures for nominal expenditures on education before 1950 (Rasaputra 1986: Statistical Appendix, table 7), we do not—as noted in the previous section—have an appropriate index to account for price changes during this period. After 1950 the GDP deflator can be used to convert nominal figures to real magnitudes, and these are shown in our Table 6.3. We turn to a discussion of the post-1950 period.

An examination of the movements of real per capita expenditure on education in the post-independence period shows that there was a doubling of such expenditure in the decade of the 1950s, followed by a gradual increase in the 1960s until a peak was reached in 1969/70 (Table 6.3). Thus, real per capita expenditure on education rose from Rs. 14.60 in 1950/1 to Rs. 29.64 in 1960/1, and reached Rs. 35.53 in 1969/70. There was a sharp decline of over 20 per cent between 1973 and 1974, and real per capita expenditure did not recover its 1971/2 value until 1982. The five-year average for 1973–7 was Rs. 27.04 while that for 1978–82 was Rs. 30.44. As in the case of health, real educational expenditure per capita seems to have been protected in the post-1977 reform period.

In the thirty years from 1952 to 1981, the number of pupils more than doubled (Table 6.6). In light of this increase, the decrease in the pupil–teacher ratio from an average of 33.3 in the 1950s to an average of 25.6 during 1980–4 can perhaps be seen as an indicator of improved quality of education. The problem with this interpretation, as with interpretations of other educational indicators, is that such indicators should really be viewed as 'inputs' rather than 'outputs'. The problem lies in specifying an appropriate 'output' of the educational system beyond such obvious indicators as literacy rates. In fact, as Table 6.7 shows, literacy rates have improved dramatically in Sri Lanka since the turn of the century. They increased from 26.4 per cent in 1901 to 39.9 per cent in 1921, and by 1953—the start of our three-decade modern period—the literacy rate was already 65.4 per cent. By 1981, it was as high as 86.5 per cent.

Of course, since the maximum literacy rate is 100 per cent it is inappropriate to compare percentage changes over time—it is easier to get large percentage

Table 6.6 Number of schools, teachers, and pupils, Sri Lanka, 1926–1984

Year	Total no. of schools	Total no. of teachers	Total no. of pupils	Pupil–teacher ratio
1926	4,523	16,606	494,004	29.7
1927	4,512	17,787	515,221	29.0
1928	4,741	19,162	532,894	27.8
1929	4,941	18,571	562,550	30.3
1930	5,219	17,934	578,999	32.3
1931	5,304	18,242	593,437	32.5
1932	5,183	17,947	613,210	34.2
1933	5,145	18,131	631,122	34.8
1934	5,327	18,516	653,509	35.3
1935	5,351	19,243	717,287	37.3
1936	5,749	20,019	726,502	36.3
1937	6,029	20,553	783,905	38.1
1938	6,151	20,628	802,853	38.9
1939	6,100	21,570	828,090	38.4
1940	n/a	n/a	n/a	n/a
1941	n/a	n/a	n/a	n/a
1942	5,746	22,163	606,051	27.3
1943	5,568	22,698	611,529	26.9
1944	5,686	24,308	833,670	34.3
1945	5,726	25,281	867,309	33.9
1946	5,945	27,693	944,508	34.1
1947	6,097	28,977	1,036,134	35.8
1948	6,409	33,668	1,192,423	35.4
1949	6,447	35,084	1,260,667	35.9
1950	6,487	39,256	1,366,742	34.8
1951	6,708	42,558	1,454,773	34.2
1952	6,636	45,508	1,502,107	33.0
1953	6,731	47,426	1,578,349	33.3
1954	6,894	49,283	1,625,742	33.0
1955	6,755	48,342	1,637,008	33.8
1956	6,844	50,186	1,693,879	33.7
1957	7,119	55,410	1,833,074	33.0
1958	7,406	59,679	1,962,243	32.8
1959	7,586	66,113	2,098,941	31.7
1960	7,860	69,658	2,192,379	31.4
1961	8,434	69,859	2,140,698	30.6
1962	8,765	76,353	2,267,564	29.6
1963	9,327	81,109	2,482,613	30.6
1964	9,434	95,137	2,540,913	26.7
1965	9,550	91,981	2,556,191	27.7
1966	9,560	90,515	2,565,891	28.3
1967	9,585	93,673	2,588,502	27.6
1968	9,801	92,982	2,633,637	28.3
1969	9,955	95,117	2,670,099	28.0

1970	9,931	96,426	2,716,187	28.1
1971	9,502	93,539	2,717,719	29.0
1972	9,417	95,281	2,265,241	26.9
1973	8,952	102,649	2,698,854	26.3
1974	9,645	102,656	2,622,424	25.1
1975	9,629	104,043	2,543,641	24.6
1976	9,683	110,563	2,571,984	23.2
1977	9,701	117,735	2,566,381	21.7
1978	9,726	n/a	3,083,725	25.0
1979	9,626	142,207	3,208,191	22.5
1980	9,794	141,185	3,389,776	24.0
1981	9,789	135,869	3,451,358	25.6
1982	9,901	133,802	3,484,661	26.0
1983	9,947	134,299	3,553,027	26.5
1984	9,914	140,190	3,625,897	25.9

Source: Rasaputra (1986: Statistical Appendix, table 7).

Table 6.7 Literacy rate for population over 10 years of age, Sri Lanka, 1901–1981 (%)

Year	Female	Male	All
1901	8.5	42.0	26.4
1911	12.5	47.2	31.0
1921	21.2	56.4	39.9
1946	43.8	70.1	57.8
1953	53.6	75.9	65.4
1963	63.2	79.3	71.6
1971	70.9	85.6	78.5
1981	82.4	90.5	86.5

Source: Alailima (1985: table 4).

increases when the absolute level is low. Rather, we can ask what percentage of the *shortfall* between the base value of the literacy rate and the upper bound of 100 per cent is made up in any period (Sen 1981: 292). Using this measure for the period 1921–53, the shortfall of 60.1 per cent in 1921 was reduced to a shortfall of 34.6 per cent in 1953, i.e. a proportionate decline of 42.4 per cent over the 32-year period, or 1.7 per cent a year. Between 1953 and 1981 the shortfall was reduced further to 13.5 per cent, which was a decrease of 61.0 per cent over the 28-year period, or 3.3 per cent a year. Viewed in this way, the improvements in the literacy rate are seen as being much faster in the post-independence period, although of course the movement had gathered some momentum by the time independence came.

In the case of mortality rates in the post-independence period, we saw that declines were much faster in the 1950s than in the 1960s and 1970s. Is the same true of the improvement in the literacy rate? We know that in 1963 the average literacy rate stood at 71.6 per cent. Thus, in the 10-year period 1953–63 the literacy shortfall was reduced from 34.6 per cent to 28.4 per cent—a proportionate decline of 17.9 per cent, or 2.0 per cent a year. In the 18-year period 1963–81 the shortfall decreased from 28.4 per cent to 13.5 per cent, a proportionate decline of 52.5 per cent, or 4.0 per cent a year. It does seem, then, as if the momentum towards greater literacy was not only maintained but intensified in the later post-independence period. In contrast to the behaviour of health indicators, the improvement in literacy is much faster during the 1960s and 1970s.

As with health indicators, the overall satisfactory level of all-island literacy rates masks important sectoral differences. From Rasaputra (1986: table 18, p. 54) it is clear that literacy rates in the estate sector are much lower than those in other parts of the island. Moreover, most of the improvement in literacy rates seems to have come about in the non-estate sectors, with the estate sector in fact registering a slight worsening in literacy.

(c)   Food subsidies

Food subsidies in Sri Lanka were first introduced as the food ration scheme in 1942, a wartime relief measure. The scheme guaranteed the supply of basic food items at low prices. Rice was the most important component of this scheme and in what follows we will concentrate on rice. After a description of the rice ration schemes in the post-war period, we will discuss food subsidy expenditure. Having established the nature of the intervention, we will then proceed to a consideration of the achievements, in so far as the data permit us to do so.

A brief history of rice subsidies is provided in Tables 6.8 and 6.9. Before 1954 the rationed quantity varied between adults, children, and infants. In 1954 all individuals became entitled to two measures of rationed rice per week at a low price (a measure is equal to two pounds avoirdupois). In June 1959 a price differential was introduced between the two measures allowed under the ration—the first measure was priced at Rs. 0.25 while the second was priced at Rs. 0.45. In April 1960 *both* measures were priced at Rs. 0.25. This price remained constant until December 1966.

In December 1966 the scheme was changed again. The rationed quantity was halved to only one measure, but this measure was provided *free*. The rest of an individual's or a household's consumption could be made up in the open market. In 1970 there was a shift back to the June 1959 pattern of differential pricing—the first measure was still free but the second measure now cost Rs. 0.75. In December 1972 a very important distinction of principle was introduced, that between income tax payers and non-income tax payers. The argument for 'targeting' was therefore accepted in principle. While non-income tax payers still received their basic ration of one measure free, the income tax payers had to pay Rs. 1.00 for this measure. The additional ration of

Table 6.8 Rice ration distribution, Sri Lanka, 1950–1966

	Ration quantity (measures per week)					Price (Rs. per measure)
	Adults	Children	Infants	Manual workers	Income tax payers	
Dec. 1950–	1.25	1.00	0.75	1.25	1.25	0.25
Sept. 1952–	1.00	0.75	0.50	1.25	1.00	0.25
July 1953–	1.25	1.00	0.75	2.00	1.25	0.70
Oct. 1953–	1.25	1.00	0.75	2.00	1.25	0.55
Nov. 1954–	2.00	2.00	2.00	2.00	2.00	0.55
May 1955–	2.00	2.00	2.00	2.00	2.00	0.50
May 1956–	2.00	2.00	2.00	2.00	2.00	0.40
June 1958–	2.00	2.00	2.00	2.00	2.00	0.35
June 1959–	2.00	2.00	2.00	2.00	2.00	0.25 (1st measure) 0.45 (2nd measure)
Apr. 1960– Dec. 1966	2.00	2.00	2.00	2.00	2.00	0.25 (1st measure) 0.25 (2nd measure)

Note: A measure is equal to two pounds avoirdupois.

Source: Rasaputra (1986: Appendix A, table A-6).

one measure cost both groups of people Rs. 1.00.[3] This basic structure was maintained, with changes in ration quantities and prices, until after the major reforms of 1977—and it is to these that we now turn.

As discussed in Anand and Sen (1984) (see also Jayawardena *et al.* 1987 and Kelegama 1990) the newly elected government of July 1977 began to introduce a programme of liberalization and adjustment. A devaluation of currency took place and this immediately increased the cost of imported food, and hence the cost of the food subsidy, measured in local currency terms. Over the next two years the subsidy was modified fundamentally by a series of policy changes. In April 1977, before the changes, the basic ration was half a measure per week, which was free to non-income tax payers and cost Rs. 2.00 per measure to income tax payers. The additional ration was 1½ measures a week at Rs. 2.00 per measure for everyone. In February 1978, the ration was restricted to households with an income of less than Rs. 300 per month. Some adjustments were made to allow for household size: for households with more than five members, each additional member increased the income ceiling by Rs. 60, subject to a maximum of Rs. 750 per month. These new rules are estimated to have restricted the recipients of rationed rice to 7.6 million persons, around half the population (Ministry of Plan Implementation 1982).

[3] See Gavan and Chandrasekera (1979: 27–9) for details of changes in the food subsidy scheme between 1952 and 1977.

Table 6.9 Rice ration distribution, Sri Lanka 1966–1979

	Basic ration			Additional ration	
	Quantity (measures per week)	Price (Rs. per measure)		Quantity (measures per week)	Price (Rs. per measure)
		Non-income tax payers	Income tax payers		
19 Dec. 1966–	1.00	Free	Free	—	—
26 Sept. 1970–	1.00	Free	Free	1.00	0.75
10 Nov. 1971–	1.00	Free	Free	1.00	1.00
4 Dec. 1972–	1.00	Free	1.00	1.00	1.00
19 Feb. 1973–	1.00	Free	1.60	1.00	1.60
12 Mar. 1973–	1.00	Free	1.40	1.00	1.40
1 Oct. 1973–	0.50	Free	2.00	—	—
29 Oct. 1973–	0.50	Free	2.00	0.50	2.00
11 Nov. 1973–	0.50	Free	2.00	—	—
10 Dec. 1973–	0.50	Free	2.00	0.50	2.00
1 Feb. 1974–	0.50	Free	2.00	—	—
18 Feb. 1974–	0.50	Free	2.00	0.50[a]	2.00
18 Mar. 1974–	0.50	Free	2.00	1.00	2.00
15 Apr. 1974–	0.50	Free	2.30	1.00	2.30
29 Apr. 1974–	0.50	Free	2.30	0.50	2.30
6 May 1974–	0.50	Free	2.30	1.00[b]	2.30
15 July 1974–	0.50	Free	1.50	1.00[b]	2.50
5 Aug. 1974–	0.50	Free	2.20	1.00[b]	2.20
6 Nov. 1975–	0.50	Free	2.00	1.00[b]	2.00
4 Apr. 1977–	0.50	Free	2.00	1.50	2.00
May 1977–	0.50	Free	2.00	2.00	2.00
Feb. 1978[c]–	1.00	Free	—	1.50	2.00
May 1978[c] – Sept. 1979	0.50	Free	—	1.50	2.00

Notes: A measure is equal to two pounds avoirdupois.
[a] Colombo and suburbs only.
[b] In 21 deficit districts. Additional ration was half a measure for the rest of the country.
[c] Restricted to households with income less than Rs. 300 per month; some adjustment made for households of size greater than five.

Source: Rasaputra (1986: Appendix A, table A-7).

In September 1979, the government introduced a food stamp scheme to replace the rationing system which had been in operation in Sri Lanka since 1942. Those families receiving income of Rs. 300 or less per month (excluding the income support of Rs. 50 per month given to the unemployed) were eligible for food stamps, which could be used to purchase a specified basket of goods. Families in receipt of an income in excess of Rs. 300 but less than Rs. 750 per month were also eligible for food stamps, the number of people eligible depending on the income and size of the family and the value of stamps received depending on the age-composition of the family (Ministry of Plan Implementation 1982).

In the final phase of the post-1977 reforms beginning in 1980, price subsidies on rice, flour, and sugar were removed and their prices raised to reflect costs. The most striking feature of the new food stamp scheme was that the value of stamps received was not indexed to inflation. A total of Rs. 1,800 million, fixed in nominal terms, was allocated from the annual budget to meet the cost of food (and kerosene) stamps. It has been estimated that by 1984 the real value of this expenditure had been eroded by inflation to such an extent that a nominal expenditure of Rs. 3,200 million (nearly 7 per cent of the government budget) would have been required in that year to maintain the real value.

What seems to have happened, then, is that a major component of savings for the government budget in the post-1977 period has come not from retargeting but from the post-1979 erosion of real expenditure on food stamps. The strain on the budget has, of course, been a major theme of discussions on food subsidy policy ever since the first rationing scheme was introduced over four decades ago. Tables 6.3 and 6.4 show the real value of food subsidy expenditure per capita, and food subsidies as a percentage of GNP, respectively. As can be seen, the early period is characterized by a sharp fall in real food subsidy expenditure per capita from a high of Rs. 31.38 in 1951/2 to Rs. 1.45 in 1953/4 (at 1959 prices). The high values were the result of increases in the price of imported rice as a consequence of the Korean War. The low value was the result of a policy decision effectively to end all subsidies on food. The decision led to 'food riots', and the government changed. The new government reversed the policy, and real expenditure on food subsidies began a steady increase to Rs. 34.28 in 1963/4, which was more than its 1951/2 value. The rise during the ten-year period from 1953/4 to 1963/4 was the longest sustained increase or decrease in the post-independence period. After the peak of 1963/4, real expenditure per capita fluctuated with a three- or even two-year cycle —troughs in 1966/7, 1969/70, 1971/2, and 1976, and peaks in 1968/9, 1970/1, 1975, and 1979. By 1982 real per capita expenditure on food subsidies had fallen to Rs. 20.72, a value comparable with that of the late 1950s (in the middle of the long period of sustained increase).

This brief account shows that government intervention in the area of food subsidy has been extensive. What have been its achievements? Fairly clearly, the record in achievements in the area of food has to be seen in terms of the extent to which food consumption—on average and for the poor—has changed over the years. We can consider real food consumption in aggregate, or the consumption of particular commodities. More directly, we can analyse how the nutritional status of the population—measured in terms of its calorie intake for example—has changed over time. A particularly serious problem is faced if we are interested in measuring intertemporal variations of the nutritional status of the *poor* in the country. For this we would need data on the joint distribution of food consumption and the variable with respect to which poverty is defined. To match the annual figures for food subsidy expenditure, we would require corresponding distributional data for each year during the past three decades. Such data are simply not available for Sri Lanka.

What we have are a small number of surveys, undertaken at different points in time over the previous twenty years. There are the Consumer Finance Surveys (CFSs) conducted by the Central Bank of Ceylon for 1953, 1963, 1973, 1978/79, and 1981/82. Other surveys that have been used in the literature are the 1969/70 and 1980/81 Socio-Economic Surveys conducted by the Department of Census and Statistics. The major problem that arises in using these surveys as seven observations spanning the post-independence period is their comparability. As Pyatt (1987: 518) notes, the Socio-Economic Surveys differ from the Consumer Finance Surveys in a number of respects which make comparisons difficult. Moreover, even if we stick to the Consumer Finance Surveys, for example, there is some question about comparability of the later surveys with the 1953 and 1963 ones, and about the quality of the data in the earlier period (see Anand and Harris 1985).

Given these problems, we will restrict ourselves to a comparison of the results of the 1973, 1978/79, and 1981/82 Consumer Finance Surveys. Anand and Harris (1985: 53–82) have argued for the comparability of these surveys in terms of their income and expenditure concepts, definition of unit of enumeration, continuity of Central Bank staff participation, etc. The 1978/79 and 1981/82 surveys also span the major food policy change in Sri Lanka—the removal of the generalized food subsidy scheme and its replacement by a targeted food stamp scheme. As discussed above, the change in structure was accompanied by a sharp decline in the real value of transfers to the poor accomplished through the scheme. We will, first of all, examine the changes in real food consumption and calorie intake between these two years, and then move on to a comparison with 1973.

Anand and Harris (1985) have constructed food price indices based on detailed food price and quantity data from the 1978/79 and 1981/82 surveys. Using these, they show that real food consumption per capita increased by 2.2 per cent for Sri Lanka as a whole between the survey years. But this aggregate increase hides major sectoral differences. While the urban sector increased its real food consumption per capita by 5.5 per cent, and the rural sector by 3.2 per cent, the estate sector experienced a fall of 8.7 per cent. A possible explanation is that while urban workers were protected from the decrease in food subsidy through cost-of-living related wage increases, and the rural sector benefited from higher paddy prices, the estate sector lost out in the changeover from the ration to the food stamp scheme (perhaps because of relatively easy to monitor money incomes from estates' wage registers).

So much for change in average real food consumption per capita. What happened at the lower end of the food consumption distribution? Anand and Harris (1985) calculate the incidence of food poverty for two poverty lines —monthly food expenditure per capita in 1978/79 of Rs. 70 and Rs. 60, respectively. (These poverty lines are adjusted to take account of both *intersectoral* and *intertemporal* price differences.) Taking first the higher of the two poverty lines, they find that the incidence of poverty fell from 22.7 per cent to 21.9 per cent for Sri Lanka as a whole. Again, this overall small improvement conceals a significant improvement in the urban sector (24.4 per cent to 19.6 per cent), a minor improvement in the rural sector (23.8 per cent to 23.2 per cent), and a major deterioration in the estate sector (8.9 per cent to 13.8 per cent).

The above results are perhaps to be expected given the movements in average real food consumption per capita for Sri Lanka as a whole and for the sectors taken separately. However, results for the *lower* poverty line indicate some interesting changes at the bottom end of the distribution. With the Rs. 60 poverty line, the incidence of food poverty in Sri Lanka goes *up* from 12.9 per cent to 13.3 per cent. This increase in all-island incidence is driven largely by an increase in rural sector incidence from 12.8 per cent to 13.6 per cent; a small positive contribution is also made by the rise in estate sector incidence from 3.6 to 5.8 per cent, but this is more than offset by the fall in urban incidence from 14.3 to 12.4 per cent.

The results for real food consumption are supported by Sahn's (1987) calculation of the percentage of individuals with a calorie intake per adult equivalent below certain levels. (Household calorie intake was derived from the CFSs by converting food quantities into calorie equivalents using food composition factors estimated by the Medical Research Institute of Sri Lanka.) Sahn (1987: table 5, p. 818) shows that between 1978/79 and 1981/82 the percentage of individuals who belong to households with a daily intake per adult equivalent below 2,200 calories stayed constant at 31.1 per cent. But there was an increase in the percentage of individuals with an intake below 2,000 calories per day from 20.8 to 22.7 per cent. The percentage with an intake below 1,800 calories rose more sharply between 1978/79 and 1981/82, from 12.6 to 15.5 per cent. However, if an even lower cut-off of 1,600 calories per day is used, the increase (from 7.0 to 10.2 per cent) is even more pronounced—the incidence of undernutrition goes up by 45 per cent.

An indirect method of looking at the distribution of calorie intake is to consider the calorie intake of those who are poor in terms of income or total expenditure. This is the strategy followed by Edirisinghe (1987: tables 22 and 23, pp. 38–9) in his analysis of the CFS 1978/79 and 1981/82 data. His table 22 shows that between 1978/79 and 1981/82 mean calorie consumption in the island as a whole—and in the urban and estate sectors—fell, while in the rural sector it rose. Furthermore, his table 23 shows that the mean calorie consumption of the bottom three all-island deciles fell between the survey years. A recent paper by Anand and Harris (1987) also estimates changes in nutrition in Sri Lanka between 1978/79 and 1981/82. Although critical of the methodology used—and the cleaning of CFS data—by Edirisinghe (1987), it nevertheless confirms the decline in per capita calorie intake by the lowest 30 per cent of the all-island population.[4] At the sectoral level, however, the findings of Anand and Harris (1987) are significantly different: they find an increase in per capita calorie intake in the urban and rural sectors—and in the island as a whole —and a decrease only in the estate sector.[5]

Between 1979 and 1982 real government expenditure per capita on food subsidies fell from Rs. 62.29 to Rs. 20.72 (Table 6.3). While it would be difficult, given the other forces at play and the nature of the available data, to establish a clear and unambiguous link between this cut and food consumption of the population—the results are at the very least suggestive. The food stamp scheme replaced the earlier ration scheme in September 1979 and, despite leakages, the burden of real cuts in the food subsidy budget is likely to have fallen disproportionately on the poor. The increase in food poverty using the Anand and Harris (1985) low poverty line corroborates this suggestion, as does the increase in the percentage of individuals with calorie intake below a low cut-off.

In order to investigate further the link between food subsidy expenditure and poverty, it would be instructive to compare 1979 with an earlier period. This is possible using the CFS 1973 data. Although there are no distributions of calorie intake available for that year,[6] Anand and Harris (1985) have calculated the change in food poverty between 1973 and 1978/79. Using the poverty line of Rs. 70 (at 1978/79 prices), there was a fall in the incidence of poverty from 27.6 per cent to 22.7 per cent. The same trend is seen with the Rs. 60 (at 1978/79 prices) poverty line—the incidence of poverty fell from 15.0 per cent in 1973 to 12.3 per cent in 1978/79. Given that real food subsidy

---

[4] Another indication of the deteriorating nutritional status of the population emerges from the anthropometric data collected in two surveys on pre-school children undertaken in 1975/76 and 1980/82. The 1975/76 survey was conducted by the Ministry of Health in Sri Lanka, with technical assistance from the US Center for Disease Control in Atlanta, Georgia. The 1980/82 survey was conducted by the Food and Nutrition Policy Planning Division of the Ministry of Plan Implementation, Sri Lanka. The findings of these surveys have been reviewed in, *inter alia*, Ministry of Plan Implementation (1983?: ch. II), Ratnayake (1985), and Sahn (1987). The conclusion of Sahn (1987: 813) is that 'The percentage of children suffering from acute malnutrition was higher in 1980/82 than in 1975/76. Overall, there was a 64 per cent increase in wasting in the rural sector from one survey to the next. The increase was especially high among the 6–11 month old age cohort. This undoubtedly reflects a combination of a decline in dietary intake, more episodes of infection, and less favourable birth outcomes conditioned by the mother's health and nutritional status. The prevalence of concurrent wasting and stunting is also higher in 1980/82 than in 1975/76 . . .'

[5] Anand and Harris (1987) identify several problems with the Edirisinghe (1987) methodology for estimating mean calorie consumption by decile and sector. (These are apart from problems with his cleaning of the CFS 1978/79 and CFS 1981/82 food quantity files, and with ensuring the comparability of food items between the two surveys.) For example, Edirisinghe (1987: 37–9) estimates per capita daily calorie consumption as an *unweighted* mean across households of household per capita calorie consumption. Obviously this is *not* a meaningful average of *individual* calorie intakes. For details of the biases caused by this and other problems with the Edirisinghe methodology, see Anand and Harris (1987).

[6] As noted in Anand and Harris (1985), the detailed food quantities file of the CFS 1973 data is unfortunately no longer available.

expenditure per capita increased from Rs. 34.25 in 1973 to Rs. 62.29 in 1979 (see Table 6.3), this would tend to confirm the link between intervention and achievement. However, before entertaining such a conclusion, we should note that both estate and urban sector poverty increased during this period, no matter which poverty line is chosen. The causes of poverty are manifold, and without further detailed investigation of the pattern of food subsidy distribution, we cannot so easily draw a firm connection between food subsidy expenditure and poverty. Nevertheless, we would argue that there is a prima-facie case for the link between intervention and achievement given this description of the historical record in Sri Lanka.

6.3. *Intervention and achievement: an econometric analysis*

The previous section has provided a historical overview of intervention and achievement in Sri Lanka. The discussion is suggestive of the link between intervention and achievement. It cannot be more than suggestive as we have not established a statistically significant relationship between them. This is where econometric analysis comes in. While such an analysis cannot do justice to the institutional detail of the historical development, it does provide a framework for testing relationships between variables in a stochastic setting.

Given the importance of Sri Lanka as a test case, it should not be surprising that much is written about the country in the applied econometric literature. In a series of papers, Isenman (1980, 1987), Sen (1981, 1988), Bhalla and Glewwe (1986), Glewwe and Bhalla (1987), Pyatt (1987), Ravallion (1987), and Bhalla (1988a, 1988b) have all contributed to a debate on whether Sri Lanka's achievements are exceptional, and the links of these achievements to intervention. A characteristic feature of this literature is that it is based on econometric analysis of a cross-section of countries, Sri Lanka being one of them. The debate centres around establishing Sri Lanka as an 'outlier' in the sample, and around the interpretation of its outlier status.[7]

Our major concern in this chapter is with examining intervention and achievement in Sri Lanka over time. Accordingly, we wish to investigate the link by means of econometric analysis of *time-series* data for Sri Lanka. In doing so we circumvent many of the problems that are peculiar to the cross-section framework. Section 6.3(a) provides a brief review of the cross-section evidence, focusing on why a time-series approach is more appropriate. Section 6.3(b) proceeds to the time-series analysis.

---

[7] A non-econometric but nevertheless 'cross-country' approach is also employed by Caldwell (1986). Using World Bank data he shows that 'some countries reach health levels far above those that would be dictated by their economies and others fall far below. Thus the superior health achievers are characterized by average per capita income levels one-ninth of those of the poor health achievers, but, nevertheless, record half the infant mortality level and an expectation of life at birth ten years higher.' (Caldwell 1986: 173)

(a) A critique of the cross-section literature

In our brief excursion into the cross-section literature, we will adopt the basic notation used by Bhalla and Glewwe (1986: equation (4), p. 39). They posit the following model to explain some measure of living standard, H_{it}, for country i at time t:

$$H_{it} = \alpha_t + \beta Y_{it} + \delta E_{it} + \lambda_i + u_{it}'' \tag{6.1}$$

where Y_{it} is per capita income; E_{it} is social welfare expenditure; α_t is a time-specific but country-invariant effect assumed to reflect technological advances (e.g. disease eradication techniques); λ_i is a country-specific and time-invariant 'fixed effect'; δ is the marginal impact of social expenditure on living standards; and u_{it}'' is a random error term.[8]

If we had data on all the variables of (6.1), then of course we could estimate the equation directly. However, data on E_{it} and λ_i are typically not available for a cross-section of countries, and Isenman (1980), Sen (1981), and others usually estimate

$$H_{it} = \alpha_t + \beta Y_{it} + e_{it} \tag{6.2}$$

for a cross-section of countries at a given point in time. They find that Sri Lanka is an outlier, having much higher values of H than predicted by the estimated relationship. This they attribute to Sri Lanka's record in intervention on basic needs. Comparing (6.1) and (6.2) we see that

$$e_{it} = \delta E_{it} + \lambda_i + u_{it}'' \tag{6.3}$$

so that a large positive residual for a country could be attributed either to a large E_{it} (assuming $\delta > 0$) or to a large λ_i, or to some combination of the two. This is the crux of the Bhalla and Glewwe (1986) and Bhalla (1988a, 1988b) criticism of the Isenman–Sen analysis. Of course, a large λ_i may itself be due to past expenditures on social welfare, but presumably the focus is on the period in question.

In order to control for the effect of λ_i, Bhalla and Glewwe (1986: equation (5), p. 39) suggest the first-difference model

$$\Delta H_{it} = \Delta \alpha_t + \beta \Delta Y_{it} + u^* \tag{6.4}$$

where, for a variable x, Δx_t is defined as

$$\Delta x_t = x_{t+1} - x_t.$$

---

[8] It should be stated at the outset that this specification has a number of problems other than the ones which we deal with below. For example, the distribution of income as well as its average level may be expected to influence social indicators; and there may be *interaction* effects between Y and E. Furthermore, dynamic considerations and the role of the 'stock' of E, as opposed to its flow, may also be important. These shortcomings are recognized in the literature, but the bulk of the discussion is organized around the Bhalla–Glewwe specification given in equation (6.1). A major problem with the more complete specification is that the data requirements—e.g. on the distribution of income and the stock of E—are greater.

A comparison of (6.1) and (6.4) shows that

$$u^* = \delta\Delta E_{it} + \Delta u''_{it}. \tag{6.5}$$

Bhalla and Glewwe (1986: 40) argue that 'It is the residual of equation [6.4], and not the residual of equation [6.2], that may be useful in assessing country performance over time'. They estimate equation (6.4) for a cross-section of countries, with $t = 1960$ and $t + 1 = 1978$. They argue that for *this* regression Sri Lanka is no longer an outlier.

Let us return to the basic model in (6.1). We are interested in the sign and magnitude of the coefficient δ, and also its magnitude relative to the coefficient β. It is this comparison which allows us to comment on the efficacy or otherwise of the direct and indirect (i.e. income-growth) route to improving living standards. If we do not have data on E_{it} and estimate (6.2), can we nevertheless infer the sign and magnitude of δ from the residual of the cross-section regression?

If the regression is as in (6.2), and we denote the estimated value of the residual as $\hat{e}_{it}$, then

$$E(\hat{e}_i) = (Y_i - \bar{Y})(\beta - E(\hat{\beta})) + \delta(E_i - \bar{E}) + (\lambda_i - \bar{\lambda}) \tag{6.6}$$

where the t-subscript has been suppressed because the regression is cross-section, $\hat{\beta}$ is the ordinary least squares (OLS) estimate of β, and a bar over a variable indicates its sample mean.[9] As can be seen from (2.6) it is more likely that the residual for a country i will be large and positive in expectation if: (1) $\delta > 0$ and $E_i > \bar{E}$, which is the Isenman–Sen argument; or (2) $\lambda_i > \bar{\lambda}$, which is the Bhalla–Glewwe critique; or (3) $(Y_i - \bar{Y})(\beta - E(\hat{\beta})) > 0$, a possibility which is not entertained to any great extent by either Isenman–Sen or Bhalla–Glewwe. It is easy to show that in the OLS estimate $\hat{\beta}$ of β in (6.2) the bias arising from the omitted variables (E_i and λ_i) is

$$\beta - E(\hat{\beta}) = -\delta \frac{\Sigma_i(Y_i - \bar{Y})(E_i - \bar{E})}{\Sigma_i(Y_i - \bar{Y})^2} - \frac{\Sigma_i(Y_i - \bar{Y})(\lambda_i - \bar{\lambda})}{\Sigma_i(Y_i - \bar{Y})^2}.$$

Assume for the moment that the correlation between λ_i and Y_i is zero; we have little reason to suppose otherwise. Then if $\delta > 0$ and E_i and Y_i are positively

---

[9] Dropping the t-subscript, the OLS regression of (6.2) yields the residual

$$\hat{e}_i = H_i - \hat{H}_i$$
$$= \alpha + \beta Y_i + \delta E_i + \lambda_i + u''_i - \hat{\alpha} - \hat{\beta}Y_i$$

using (6.1) and $\hat{H}_i = \hat{\alpha} + \hat{\beta}Y_i$. But since the OLS regression passes through the sample means $\bar{Y}$, $\bar{H}$, we have

$$\hat{\alpha} = \bar{H} - \hat{\beta}\bar{Y}$$
$$= \alpha + \beta\bar{Y} + \delta\bar{E} + \bar{\lambda} + \bar{u}'' - \hat{\beta}\bar{Y}$$

using (6.1). Substituting in the equation above for $\hat{e}_i$, and taking expectations, gives the expression (6.6) for $E(\hat{e}_i)$.

correlated,[10] we have $\beta - E(\hat{\beta}) < 0$. Now from (6.6), if $Y_i < \bar{Y}$ (country i's income is less than the sample average) then we will get an upward bias in the residual $\hat{e}_i$. Of course, a non-zero correlation between λ_i and Y_i will also confound the inference that can be drawn from the residual $\hat{e}_i$.

What if we estimate the Bhalla–Glewwe first-difference model (6.4)? What can be inferred from *its* estimated residual $\hat{u}^*$? Analogously to (6.6), we get

$$E(\hat{u}^*) = (\Delta Y_i - \overline{\Delta Y})(\beta - E(\hat{\beta})) + \delta(\Delta E_i - \overline{\Delta E}) \qquad (6.7)$$

where $\hat{\beta}$ is now the OLS estimate of β in (6.4) and the bias depends on the correlation between ΔE_i and ΔY_i. As can be seen from (6.7), even though there is no $(\lambda_i - \bar{\lambda})$ term, an insignificant value of $\hat{u}^*$ does *not* necessarily imply that δ is zero. A zero value for $E(\hat{u}^*)$ is quite consistent with a positive value for δ. For example, if there is no bias in $\hat{\beta}$, i.e. $\beta = E(\hat{\beta})$, then $\Delta E_i = \overline{\Delta E}$ will give a zero value for $E(\hat{u}^*)$ even with $\delta > 0$, and this is indeed a line of defence adopted by Sen (1988: 550–2).

Sen argues that during the period under consideration (1960–78), the increment in social welfare expenditure in Sri Lanka was not exceptional relative to the sample; thus, it is not surprising that the increment in H is not exceptional. In order to adjudicate on this issue we would need fuller data on ΔE_i in the sample, and this is indeed the problem—if we had those data we could estimate the relationship directly and not have to rely on the residual method to give us an indication of the value of δ.

Thus, our conclusion is that while the Isenman–Sen method may be open to certain criticisms, the Bhalla–Glewwe alternative *cannot* resolve the basic question of the relative magnitudes of δ and β. Given the lack of cross-section data on social welfare expenditures it is difficult to see how it could, in fact, be resolved. However, with time-series data for a particular country, we can obtain estimates of δ and β directly for that country. It so happens that Sri Lanka is indeed a country for which such data are available. In the next section we proceed to utilize these data in an econometric analysis of the relationship between intervention and achievement. This corresponds to the 'explicit approach' of Sen (1988: 550):

The common wisdom of the approach is based on the idea that we cannot really measure the impact of a policy of social welfare programs without explicitly incorporating it as a variable in a causal framework and testing its effect.

(b)   Time-series evidence for Sri Lanka

For our time-series investigation, we retain the Bhalla–Glewwe (1986) specification given in equation (6.1). We focus attention on Sri Lanka for the Bhalla–Glewwe period 1960–78, but also discuss the longest time period for

[10] In fact, Bhalla seems committed to such a positive correlation between E_i and Y_i. In the course of formulating his living standards model, Bhalla (1988a: 101) specifies the relationship $E_{it} = \beta' Y_{it} + e'_{it}$, which with $\beta' > 0$ will in general imply a positive correlation between E_i and Y_i. By contrast, Isenman (1980; 1987) and Sen (1981; 1988) are not committed to any such correlation.

which a consistent series is available, namely 1952–81. Relevant measures of social expenditure E_{it} are explicitly included for each year.

Our data for this purpose are drawn almost exclusively from the paper by Alailima (1985), 'Evolution of Government Policies and Expenditure on Social Welfare in Sri Lanka during the 20th Century', which is extensively referred to and used by Bhalla–Glewwe (1986) and Bhalla (1988a, 1988b). Alailima's table 8, on which our Table 6.3 is based, gives a 32-year series from 1950/1 to 1982 for real per capita expenditure on social services (separately for education, health, food subsidies, and other social welfare).

Alailima (1985: table 8) calculates real expenditures by using the GDP deflator, which includes social welfare expenditure as a component. She calculates per capita expenditure by using population estimates from the Department of Census and Statistics. Finally, her table 3 presents vital statistics data from the same source for the period 1900 to 1981. This series consists of estimates of the crude birth rate, the crude death rate, and the infant mortality rate. The same information is available, but up to 1984, in Rasaputra (1986: Statistical Appendix, table 10), and this is reproduced in our Table 6.2). Rasaputra's paper (1986: Statistical Appendix, table 1) also contains a *consistent* series for real GDP at factor cost from 1950 onwards, using the same GDP deflator (with 1959 = 100) as Alailima does for her series on real social welfare expenditures. It is important to use this *comparable* income series for GDP at factor cost because, as is well known, the GNP series in Sri Lanka has been revised twice—in 1958 and 1970—and the new series is not consistent with the old one. Real GDP per capita has been calculated by us using the same mid-year population figures (Table 6.2) as Alailima (1985: table 8) uses to calculate her per capita social expenditures. These real GDP per capita estimates are shown in our Table 6.3.

We are now ready to estimate the Bhalla–Glewwe specification of the living standards relationship

$$H_{it} = \lambda_i + \alpha_t + \beta Y_{it} + \delta E_{it} + u''_{it} \qquad (6.1)$$

where

country i = Sri Lanka, fixed in the sample
  H_{it} = some measure of living standard such as infant mortality rate (IMR), death rate (DR), or birth rate (BR) in year t
  λ_i = country-specific intercept term for Sri Lanka
  α_t = technical progress term, specified simply as $\alpha.t$ (with α constant)
  Y_{it} = real GDP per capita in year t
  E_{it} = real social expenditure per capita in year t (separately for health, education, and food).

In their cross-section analysis, Bhalla–Glewwe (1986) and Bhalla (1988a) consider six indicators of living standard—life expectancy, primary school enrolment, adult literacy rate, infant mortality rate, death rate, and total fertility rate. Given the time-series data available to us, we are obliged to restrict attention to the infant mortality rate (IMR), the death rate (DR), and the birth rate (BR). Since the H_{it} variables are bounded below by zero, we use them in logarithmic form—as ln H—so that the dependent variable in equation (6.1) can be negative (to minus infinity) for negative realizations of the right-hand side. Since the H_{it} variables are also bounded *above* by 1,000 (IMR, DR, and BR are all measured per 1,000 population), we can allow unbounded variation upwards (to plus infinity) of the dependent variable by *subtracting* ln (1,000 − H) from ln H, i.e. by using H_{it} in the *logistic form* ln [$H/(1,000 − H)$]. We have not done this here because the sample values of H_{it} occur in a region much closer to zero than to 1,000; hence the further transformation is unlikely to affect significantly the estimates of the coefficients of the independent variables (excepting, of course, the intercept term). In any case, this has been confirmed by doing the regressions in logistic form (not reported here).

Table 6.10 presents the results of our time-series regressions. The right-hand side independent variables (except t) have been entered in both *linear* (non-log) and *logarithmic* form; t is always entered in *linear* form. The 'A' and 'B' equations in Table 6.10 refer respectively to these forms. First we report results for the Bhalla–Glewwe period 1960–78, for which the authors claim that Sri Lanka is *not* an outlier. This is followed by results for the full three-decade period 1952–81 for which a consistent time series was available. We have entered the real per capita health and food subsidy expenditures separately—as the variables HEXP and FEXP. There are two interrelated reasons for doing this. First, the impact of health and food subsidy expenditures may be expected to be different from one another. Secondly, the food subsidy accounts for a relatively small proportion of total food consumption, so that variations in it will not reflect corresponding variations in the total food consumed by the population. By contrast, the coverage of health is more nearly universal, so that variations in health expenditure will more closely track health provision for the population. Current and capital expenditures on health have been aggregated in the variable HEXP. A similar procedure is followed for real per capita education expenditure, EEXP, which is also introduced into the regressions separately to allow for possible differential effects.

For the period 1960–78, the results (equations (1A) and (1B) in Table 6.10) show that health expenditure HEXP has a very significant negative effect on IMR, but that FEXP, EEXP, and PCY (real GDP per capita) are insignificant.[11] What is important about the results is that direct intervention, as reflected in government health expenditure, has a statistically significant beneficial impact on IMR. Note that our procedure based on time-series data

---

[11] The significance level chosen for the discussion here is 5%.

Table 6.10 Time-series estimates of living standard equations, Sri Lanka, 1960–1978 and 1952–1981

Dependent variable	Equation number	Time period	Intercept	HEXP	FEXP	EEXP	PCY	t (year)	F-statistic	SEE	Mean of dependent variable	R^2	Log of likelihood function
Ln IMR	(1A)	1960–78	44.54 (2.14)	−0.0381 (−3.21)	−0.002900 (−1.33)	0.00599 (1.33)	0.000412 (0.52)	−0.02060 (−1.90)	17.84	0.0471	3.89	0.873	34.72
		1952–81	24.27 (2.30)	−0.0322 (−2.79)	0.001970 (1.63)	−0.00117 (−0.28)	−0.000982 (−3.01)	−0.00975 (−1.77)	90.16	0.0572	3.94	0.949	46.63
	(1B)	1960–78	44.99 (2.46)	−0.5620 (−3.36)	−0.054400 (−0.91)	0.20200 (1.62)	0.274000 (0.47)	−0.02130 (−1.91)	17.20	0.0478	3.89	0.869	34.42
		1952–81	25.97 (2.18)	−0.4300 (−2.42)	0.018300 (0.82)	−0.04260 (−0.35)	−0.764000 (−2.22)	−0.00802 (−1.10)	75.35	0.0622	3.94	0.940	44.08
Ln DR	(2A)	1960–78	11.43 (0.46)	−0.0460 (−3.23)	0.001380 (0.53)	0.00795 (1.47)	−0.000229 (−0.24)	−0.00446 (−0.34)	3.52	0.0565	2.09	0.575	31.24
		1952–81	8.53 (0.79)	−0.0482 (−4.10)	0.002420 (1.96)	0.00063 (0.15)	−0.000787 (−2.37)	−0.00266 (−0.47)	40.84	0.0582	2.13	0.895	46.11
	(2B)	1960–78	17.32 (0.85)	−0.6630 (−3.56)	0.072000 (1.08)	0.25400 (1.83)	−0.095700 (−0.15)	−0.00708 (−0.57)	4.30	0.0532	2.09	0.623	32.38
		1952–81	9.61 (0.82)	−0.6450 (−3.68)	0.030100 (1.37)	−0.00733 (−0.06)	−0.613000 (−1.80)	−0.00092 (−0.13)	36.03	0.0615	2.13	0.882	44.44
Ln BR	(3A)	1960–78	19.59 (1.98)	0.0232 (4.10)	0.002720 (2.62)	−0.00520 (−2.43)	−0.000733 (−1.95)	−0.00805 (−1.56)	61.51	0.0224	3.44	0.959	48.80
		1952–81	39.13 (7.54)	0.0191 (3.37)	0.000487 (0.82)	−0.00176 (−0.88)	0.000258 (1.61)	−0.01830 (−6.77)	96.58	0.0281	3.47	0.953	67.96
	(3B)	1960–78	24.20 (2.75)	0.3290 (4.09)	0.068300 (2.37)	−0.15000 (−2.50)	−0.451000 (−1.60)	−0.00933 (−1.74)	58.46	0.0230	3.44	0.957	48.34
		1952–81	37.88 (7.21)	0.2810 (3.58)	0.016900 (1.72)	−0.07630 (−1.43)	0.200000 (1.32)	−0.01840 (−5.75)	100.90	0.0275	3.47	0.955	68.59

Notes: The coefficients of the 'A' equations refer to the independent variables entered in *linear* (non-log) form; those for the 'B' equations refer to the independent variables (except for year *t*) entered in *logarithmic* form. Year *t* is entered in *linear* form in *both* the 'A' and the 'B' equations. Thus, the estimated equation (1A) for the time period 1960–78 is:

Ln IMR = 44.54 − 0.0381 HEXP − 0.002900 FEXP + 0.00599 EEXP + 0.000412 PCY − 0.02060 *t*.

The estimated equation (1B) for the time period 1960–78 is:

Ln IMR = 44.99 − 0.5620 ln HEXP − 0.054400 ln FEXP + 0.20200 ln EEXP + 0.274000 ln PCY − 0.02130 *t*.

t statistics are shown in parentheses below the coefficient estimates.

has allowed a *direct* test of this relationship, and is not open to the problems of the cross-section approach (mentioned in Section 6.3(*a*)).

For the full period 1952–81, the results show that HEXP remains significant in reducing IMR: government intervention continues to matter. For this longer period, in contrast, the coefficient on the income term, PCY, becomes significant.

These results shed some light on the role of direct intervention versus an indirect, income-growth strategy in reducing the infant mortality rate. According to our results for the Bhalla–Glewwe period 1960–78, income growth did not matter at all. This is a rather striking finding because not only is it the case that direct intervention has worked—a claim which is at the heart of the Bhalla–Glewwe versus Isenman–Sen controversy—but the estimates suggest that reliance on an income-growth strategy would *not* have worked during 1960–78.

For the full period 1952–81, the estimates do show a significant income effect, but this effect is small. A rupee of government health expenditure diverted to income in the hands of the population would have led to an immediate rise in the infant mortality rate. Comparing the coefficient (−0.0322) on HEXP with that (−0.000982) on PCY in equation (1A), the former is larger than the latter by a factor of 33 in absolute terms. This implies that to redress the effect on IMR of a Rs. 1 decrease in health expenditure would require, *ceteris paribus*, a Rs. 33 increase in equivalent income—a manifestly adverse trade-off for the income-growth strategy.

For both the periods 1960–78 and 1952–81, the results for IMR appear to be well determined and robust with respect to the functional form (various diagnostic tests not reported here support this conclusion). Thus in Table 6.10 the picture for equation (1B) turns out to be very similar to that for equation (1A). When the independent variables are entered in logarithmic instead of linear form, hardly any difference is made to the significance of the coefficients, though obviously their magnitude changes.[12]

In the next set of equations the dependent variable is the logarithm of the death rate, ln DR. For the period 1960–78, the results in equation (2A) are again very striking with real health expenditure per capita being highly significant in reducing the death rate. No other variable is significant. For 1960–78 the results in equation (2B) show the same pattern as in (2A) and, as before, the functional form does not seem to make any qualitative difference to the findings.

---

[12] For the sample period 1952–81 the absolute value of the coefficient on ln PCY is greater than that on ln HEXP. However, these coefficients, unlike those in the equations in non-log form, are elasticities: they indicate the impact of a *proportionate* change in the independent variable. A 1% decrease in HEXP will only allow an increase of approximately 0.019% in income in the hands of the population, since the average ratio of HEXP to PCY over the sample period is 0.019 (see Table 6.4). Hence the relevant comparison (in terms of 'bang-for-a-buck') is between the coefficient (−0.4300) on ln HEXP and 0.019 times the coefficient (−0.764000) on ln PCY—which implies a factor of 30 for the trade-off.

For the full period 1952–81, the estimates in equations (2A) and (2B) do display a degree of sensitivity to the functional form chosen. In equation (2B) the income variable ln PCY is not significant while in equation (2A) the income variable PCY is indeed significant (but again with very small coefficient). Whereas in equation (2A) the food subsidy variable FEXP is significant (and with positive coefficient), in equation (2B) ln FEXP is not significant. The education expenditure variable EEXP is insignificant in both functional forms. The only robust inference for the 1952–81 ln DR regressions seems to be that health expenditure HEXP has a very significant beneficial impact in reducing the death rate.

The final demographic indicator considered is the birth rate (BR), for which the regression results are shown in equations (3A) and (3B). At the outset, it should be emphasized that this is arguable as a living standard indicator, but we include it here only to correspond to Bhalla and Glewwe's total fertility rate.[13] Over the period 1960–78, the birth rate turns out to be positively related to both health and food expenditure by government, and negatively related to educational expenditure—all significant at the 5 per cent level. In the non-log form, the coefficient on income is negative and (almost) significant; in the log form the income coefficient is insignificant but still negative.

The coefficients on educational expenditure and on average (across-the-board) income are not difficult to rationalize, and may be considered to be of the expected sign. But how are we to interpret the positive coefficients on health and food expenditure? One possibility is that larger health and food subsidies lead to better antenatal care (including nutrition) of mothers, especially at the lower end of the income distribution. This might help more pregnancies to come to term and to avoid miscarriages. To test this hypothesis directly, however, we need more disaggregate data on the composition of health expenditures and on birth rate by income group (*who* is having more children?).

For the full period 1952–81, the relationship seems to be quite different, except in the respect that health expenditure continues to be significant and positive. Otherwise, the coefficients on food expenditure and educational expenditure become insignificant, the coefficient on income turns from negative to positive (but becomes decidedly insignificant), and a strong negative time trend emerges. Our worries about the use of the birth rate as an appropriate living standard indicator are compounded by this non-robustness in the face of sample period variation.

To conclude, then, we note that this first attempt at a time-series analysis of intervention and achievement does provide econometric support for the hypothesis of a link between the two. The results for the infant mortality rate will perhaps bear emphasizing. Over the period 1960–78, and for the full

---

[13] See e.g. Basu (1991: n. 6) who argues that the birth rate should *not* be included as a living standard indicator.

period 1952–81, health expenditure has a very significant effect as an explanatory variable for IMR. Moreover, the estimates for the period 1960–78 indicate that income would have had an insignificant effect on IMR. The estimates for the full period 1952–81 do show a significant effect for income, but this effect is very small. In this context, at least, reliance on income growth alone can be questioned.

We view our results as cautionary rather than definitive. A large and sustained increase in income over a long period might well have an impact on social indicators. Over the short- to medium-run planning horizon, however, developing countries do face real choices between social expenditure and capital investment. Our results would tend to support those who argue for greater benefits at the margin from targeted social expenditure.

6.4. *Conclusion*

The object of this chapter has been to consider Sri Lanka's record of intervention and achievement in some areas of basic needs provision. We have used two methods of analysis. First, we have provided a descriptive account of intervention over the long run of historical developments this century, and have tried to relate this intervention to achievement by an accompanying narrative of the achievement. This discussion is strongly suggestive that purposive and directed intervention has had remarkable effects on health and education standards both in the early part of the century and in the period after independence.

Complementary to the descriptive approach is our second method of econometric analysis. We have reviewed the current literature on establishing and interpreting Sri Lanka's position as an outlier in a cross-section of countries. We argue that in the absence of direct information on intervention for countries in the sample, such cross-section analysis can be problematic. We propose instead that time-series data for Sri Lanka be used to conduct a more direct investigation of the issues. We have presented a first attempt at such an analysis using data for the 1952–81 period. While our results need to be confirmed by further research, they do suggest that income growth alone would not have achieved for Sri Lanka its enviable basic needs record—the role of direct intervention has been significant.

We are not alone in reaching this conclusion. The central finding of Caldwell (1986: 204), who uses a combination of comparative and intertemporal methods, is that 'the provision of health services (and, better still, its accompaniment by the establishment of a nutritional floor and perhaps a family planning program) can markedly reduce mortality'. His findings and ours suggest, therefore, that attention should now shift from the question of *whether* intervention can have a positive impact on basic needs to the more important question of the best patterns and combinations of social welfare expenditure to achieve the *maximum* impact on basic needs.

References

ALAILIMA, P. (1985), 'Evolution of Government Policies and Expenditure on Social Welfare in Sri Lanka during the 20th Century', mimeo (Colombo: Ministry of Finance and Planning).

ANAND, S., and HARRIS, C. J. (1985), 'Living Standards in Sri Lanka, 1973–1981/82: An Analysis of Consumer Finance Survey Data', mimeo (Oxford).

——(1987), 'Changes in Nutrition in Sri Lanka, 1978/79–1981/82', mimeo (Helsinki: WIDER).

—— and SEN, ABHIJIT (1984), 'The Macroeconomy of Sri Lanka after Liberalization', mimeo (Oxford: St Catherine's College).

BASU, K. (1991), 'The Elimination of Endemic Poverty in South Asia: Some Policy Options', this volume.

BHALLA, S. S. (1988a), 'Is Sri Lanka an Exception? A Comparative Study of Living Standards', in Srinivasan and Bardhan (1988).

——(1988b), 'Sri Lanka's Achievements: Fact and Fancy', in Srinivasan and Bardhan (1988).

—— and GLEWWE, P. (1986), 'Growth and Equity in Developing Countries: A Reinterpretation of the Sri Lankan Experience', *World Bank Economic Review*, 1.

CALDWELL, J. C. (1986), 'Routes to Low Mortality in Poor Countries', *Population and Development Review*, 12.

EDIRISINGHE, N. (1987), *The Food Stamp Scheme in Sri Lanka: Costs, Benefits and Options for Modification*, Research Report 58 (Washington, DC: IFPRI).

FERNANDO, D. F. S. (1985), 'Health Statistics in Sri Lanka, 1921–80', in Halstead *et al.* (1985).

GAVAN, J. D., and CHANDRASEKERA, I. S. (1979), *The Impact of Public Foodgrain Distribution on Food Consumption and Welfare in Sri Lanka*, Research Report 13 (Washington, DC: IFPRI).

GLEWWE, P., and BHALLA, S. S. (1987), 'A Response to Comments by Graham Pyatt and Paul Isenman', *World Bank Economic Review*, 1.

GUNATILLEKE, G. (ed.) (1984), *Intersectoral Linkages and Health Development: Case Studies in India (Kerala State), Jamaica, Norway, Sri Lanka, and Thailand*, WHO Offset Publication No. 83 (Geneva: WHO).

—— (1985), 'Health and Development in Sri Lanka: An Overview', in Halstead *et al.* (1985).

HALSTEAD, S. B., WALSH, J. A., and WARREN, K. S. (eds.) (1985), *Good Health at Low Cost*, Proceedings of a Conference held at the Bellagio Conference Centre, Bellagio, Italy, 29 Apr.–2 May (New York: Rockefeller Foundation).

ISENMAN, P. (1980), 'Basic Needs: The Case of Sri Lanka', *World Development*, 8.

——(1987), 'A Comment on "Growth and Equity in Developing Countries: A Reinterpretation of the Sri Lankan Experience," by Bhalla and Glewwe', *World Bank Economic Review*, 1.

JAYAWARDENA, L. R., MAASLAND, A., and RADHAKRISHNAN, P. N. (1987), 'Sri Lanka', Country Study 15, WIDER Series on Stabilization and Adjustment Policies and Programmes (Helsinki: WIDER).

KELEGAMA, S. B. (1990), 'The Consequences of Economic Liberalization in Sri Lanka', unpublished D.Phil. thesis, University of Oxford.

Marga Institute (1984), *Intersectoral Action for Health: Sri Lanka Study* (Colombo: Sri Lanka Centre for Development Studies).

Ministry of Plan Implementation (1982), *Evaluation Report on the Food Stamp Scheme*, Publication No. 7 (Colombo: Food and Nutrition Policy Planning Division).

——(1983?), *Nutritional Status: Its Determinants and Intervention Programmes*, Final Report (Colombo: Food and Nutrition Policy Planning Division).

——(1984), *Nutrition Strategy* (Colombo).

——(1985), *Health and Nutrition Sector Report*, National Science and Technology Policy for Sri Lanka, vol. vii (Colombo).

ORDE BROWNE, G. St J. (1943), *Labour Conditions in Ceylon, Mauritius, and Malaya*, Cmd. 6423 (London: HMSO).

PERERA, P. D. A. (1985), 'Health Care Systems of Sri Lanka', in Halstead *et al.* (1985).

PYATT, F. G. (1987), 'A Comment on "Growth and Equity in Developing Countries: A Reinterpretation of the Sri Lankan Experience," by Bhalla and Glewwe', *World Bank Economic Review*, 1.

RASAPUTRA, W. (1986), 'Public Policy: An Assessment of the Sri Lanka Experience', mimeo (Colombo: Central Bank of Ceylon; and Helsinki: WIDER).

RATNAYAKE, R. M. K. (1985), 'A Survey Paper on Nutrition Situation in Sri Lanka', mimeo (Colombo: Food and Nutrition Policy Planning Division, Ministry of Plan Implementation).

RAVALLION, M. S. (1987), 'Growth and Equity in Sri Lanka: A Comment', mimeo (Canberra: Australian National University).

SAHN, D. E. (1987), 'Changes in the Living Standards of the Poor in Sri Lanka during a Period of Macroeconomic Restructuring', *World Development*, 15.

SEN, A. K. (1981), 'Public Action and the Quality of Life in Developing Countries', *Oxford Bulletin of Economics and Statistics*, 43.

——(1988), 'Sri Lanka's Achievements: How and When?', in Srinivasan and Bardhan (1988).

SRINIVASAN, T. N., and BARDHAN, P. K. (eds.) (1988), *Rural Poverty in South Asia* (New York: Columbia University Press).

TINKER, H. (1974), *A New System of Slavery: The Export of Indian Labour Overseas, 1830–1920* (London: Oxford University Press).

7

The Food Problems of Bangladesh

S. R. Osmani

7.1. *Introduction*

When hunger is as pervasive and as persistently so as in Bangladesh, the food problem ceases to be just one aspect of the economic problem. It becomes indistinguishable from the totality of the development problem itself. While an analysis of this totality is beyond the scope of a single paper, we shall at least try to highlight the major forces impinging on the problem of hunger—both in the past and in the future. Moreover, in an attempt to bring some kind of order to the diversity of the issues involved, we shall organize the discussion around two themes.

The first theme relates to the long-term process of the genesis of hunger and its persistence. We shall attempt to identify the structural forces determining the long-term trend of hunger and the changes therein. An interesting issue in this context is the relationship between persistent hunger and famine. It has been observed, and rightly so, that while famine has of late become a recurrent feature in some parts of Africa, Bangladesh has successfully avoided a recurrence of famine since 1974, despite a couple of close calls. Does this success indicate an improvement in the underlying trend of persistent hunger? If not, how does one explain the avoidance of famine, particularly in the years 1979 and 1984 when crop damage was comparable to that of 1974? In trying to answer these questions, we hope to be able to shed some light not only on the question of what is happening to persistent hunger in Bangladesh, but also on whether the country is becoming increasingly or decreasingly susceptible to famine.

The second theme relates to the future—how is the future likely to be shaped by the policies being implemented at present. Of particular interest here is a decisive shift that has occurred in the recent past in the orientation of food policy in particular and development strategy in general—away from government control and towards a greater reliance on market forces. We shall critically examine the implications of this shift in strategy *vis-à-vis* alternative policy options.

But we begin by giving a brief account of the incidence of hunger in Bangladesh.

I am grateful to Iftikhar Hossain and two anonymous referees for extremely helpful comments on an earlier draft, and to Matiur Rahman for his generous permission to use unpublished material from his Ph.D. dissertation.

7.1. *Magnitude and distribution of hunger in Bangladesh*

The most common method of estimating the magnitude of hunger is to calculate the percentage of people with a calorie-deficient diet. Using this method and taking FAO recommendations as the standard of calorie requirement, a recent Nutrition Survey has found that 76 per cent of the rural population of Bangladesh are unable to consume enough calories (INFS 1981/2). This survey was based on actual measurement of food consumed within a household. Another survey, using the same FAO norms but based on information on household expenditure on food, has estimated that 79 per cent of the rural households did not have enough income in 1981 to afford a calorie-adequate diet (Table 7.1).

Since rural population constitutes over 90 per cent of the total population, the above figures clearly indicate the pervasiveness of hunger in Bangladesh. But it is by no means confined to rural areas only. An occupation-wise breakdown of per capita calorie intake in 1976/7 shows that the urban informal sector, which constitutes 60 per cent of urban population, has a per capita calorie intake 15 per cent below the FAO norm (Table 7.2). Even the urban formal sector is not free from hunger, although per capita calorie intake of this group is above the FAO norm. As the Nutrition Survey of 1981/2 has found, the average calorie intake of industrial workers, who constitute a sizeable part of the urban formal sector, was only 74 per cent of requirement.

Table 7.1 Distribution of hunger by occupation in rural Bangladesh, 1981

Occupation group	% of households with inadequate food (1)	Share of the group in total rural households (%) (2)	Share of the group in inadequately fed rural households (%) (3)
Farming	72.5	40.7	37.2
Service	77.4	6.3	6.2
Business	60.9	16.6	12.7
Agricultural wage labour	96.6	25.6	31.3
Non-agricultural wage labour	95.5	9.3	11.2
Others	71.7	1.5	1.4
ALL	79.3	100.0	100.0

Source: This table has been drawn from the first draft of an ongoing Ph.D. dissertation by M. Rahman (forthcoming). It is based on an expenditure survey of over 4,000 rural households drawn from different parts of Bangladesh.

Table 7.2 Foodgrains and calorie intake by socio-economic class, Bangladesh, 1976/7

Class	% of population	Average income per month (Tk)	Calories (day/capita)	% of calories from foodgrain
Landless farm workers	21	897	1,519	92
Small farmers	12	894	1,638	92
Medium farmers (mainly tenants)	12	1,119	1,764	91
Medium farmers (mainly owners)	13	1,285	1,956	90
Large farmers	10	1,659	2,150	89
Very large farmers	4	2,789	2,087	87
Rural informal non-farmers	11	850	1,482	91
Rural formal non-farmers	7	1,840	2,118	88
Urban informal	6	1,039	1,708	90
Urban formal	4	2,612	2,080	82
Average for all classes	100	1,281	1,782	90

Note: Calorie requirement (day/capita): 2,020
Source: World Bank (1985a: table 1, p. 4).

Before proceeding further, however, several limitations of these estimates need to be pointed out.

First, the estimates depend crucially on the norm of calorie requirement. The difficulties of determining this norm are well known and the traditional approach (as embodied in the FAO recommendations) has come under severe criticism recently. But unfortunately the debate has not yet resolved any of the difficult issues and it seems that the use of a cut-off norm is bound to involve some amount of ambiguity.[1] Definitive estimates of hunger are thus difficult to provide, even leaving aside the problem of data reliability. Nevertheless, one may note that the qualitative conclusion regarding the severity of hunger in Bangladesh is not substantially changed under alternative methodologies, such as taking a cut-off point at 80 per cent of average requirement, a popular way of correcting for the criticism that the average norm does not allow for inter-personal and intrapersonal variation in requirement. It may be seen from Table 7.2 that landless agricultural workers, small farmers, and rural informal workers in the non-farm sector, who together constitute nearly 50 per cent of

[1] A review of this debate can be found, *inter alia*, in Osmani (1984) and Srinivasan (1983).

rural population, have an average calorie intake which is either below or close to the lower cut-off point (i.e. 80 per cent of average requirement).

Secondly, while the estimation of calorie deficit implies measurement of hunger from the input side, it may be argued that measuring the outcome directly in terms of physical undernutrition may be more appropriate. Not only will this help to avoid the troublesome issue of specifying requirement; but conceptually the more important point is that the food problem, in so far as it is a problem, consists after all in the harm it does to the 'functioning' and 'capabilities' of a person; and the measures of undernutrition can be taken as a measure of such 'functioning'.[2] Unfortunately, however, the scientific status of the traditional (anthropometric) measures of undernutrition as an index of 'functioning' is no less in doubt today than the concept of calorie requirement itself.[3] Yet, for whatever they are worth, these traditional measures too confirm the pervasiveness of the food problem in Bangladesh. Food deficit has a most immediate and visible impact on the nutritional status of children; and the Nutrition Survey of 1981/2 shows that over 60 per cent of rural children in the under-5 age group suffer from second- or third-degree malnutrition (INFS 1981/2).[4] Mortality is also very high in this age group; it is estimated that nearly 50 per cent of all mortality in Bangladesh occurs in this cohort. The severity of malnutrition (in terms of weight for height measures) subsides in the age group of 5–14 years; but the prevalence of stunting persists among three-quarters of these children due to the cumulative effects of long-term nutritional deprivation.[5]

Thirdly, even as an input-based measure, calorie deficit is an incomplete guide to the severity of the food problem. At best, calorie deficit indicates the 'quantity' of the food problem; but no less important is 'quality', i.e. the ability of the diets to provide all nutrients in the right amounts. It has been estimated that of all the occupational groups enumerated in Table 7.2, only the urban formal group, comprising a tiny 4 per cent of the population of the country, consume diets which are adequate in both quantity and quality. This they are able to achieve by virtue of their relatively diversified diet which consists of both cereals and non-cereals in the right proportion. On the other hand, large farmers and other rich people in the rural areas who on the average consume adequate calories in terms of quantity tend to derive an excessive proportion of

---

[2] For a welfare-theoretic justification of the 'capabilities' approach, see Sen (1985).

[3] See Beaton (1983) for a critical view of excessive reliance on anthropometry as a measure of undernutrition.

[4] A similar incidence of malnutrition is reported by UNICEF/FREPD (1981).

[5] It is of course well recognized that inadequate intake of calories is not the only and sometimes not even the most important cause of physical undernutrition. Diseases related to environmental health conditions such as sanitation and the quality of drinking water are also a major determining factor of malnutrition in the developing countries. But it is also true that lack of food accentuates the effects of such disease-induced malnutrition. As a result, those with a poorer entitlement to food are more vulnerable to physical malnutrition. See World Bank (1985a) for a review of studies showing positive association between malnutrition and economic status in Bangladesh.

their calories from cereals which are poor in micronutrients and minerals. As a result, their diet tends to be qualitatively inadequate (World Bank 1985*a*). However, it has also been noted that, given the dietary pattern in Bangladesh, those who consume adequate calories also in general consume adequate protein (Osmani 1982). Thus a focus on quantity serves at least to cover the two most important nutrients.[6]

One other aspect of the food problem, which is of great importance but cannot be covered in this chapter, is the problem of intrafamily distribution of food. There is some evidence of systematic bias against females in the distribution of food within the family (Chen *et al.* 1981). The effect of this bias is also reflected in the outcome, i.e. in the relative nutritional status of males and females. The Nutrition Survey of 1981/2 has noted for example that in both the preschool and school-age cohorts, female children suffer from a greater degree of chronic and acute malnutrition than male children (INFS 1981/2). Limitation of space prevents us from exploring the socio-economic basis of this sex bias in the distribution of food.

We shall however have a good deal more to say on another kind of distribution—the occupational distribution of hunger. One can see from Tables 7.1 and 7.2 that rural wage labourers, both in farm and non-farm sectors, are the most severely deprived among all socio-economic groups. But food deprivation is not confined to these groups only; it is widely distributed among both wage labourers and the self-employed, and similarly among both producers and non-producers of food.

The phenomenon of food deprivation thus encompasses different segments of the labour force who have very different modes of acquiring entitlement on food. As column 3 of Table 7.1 shows, just over one-third of all those who cannot afford an adequate diet in the rural areas comprises direct producers of food, i.e. the farmers. Another one-third, though being involved in the production of food as agricultural labourers, do not acquire food through the production process, but from the market. The other one-third, who are primarily engaged in the non-farm sector, also have to rely mainly on the market to realize their food entitlement. Thus market exchange plays a crucial role in determining the food entitlement of nearly two-thirds of the underfed people in the rural areas.

It may be noted that even the farmers among the underfed are not entirely independent of the market. It has been estimated that as many as 50 per cent of the farmers have a net deficit even in a normal crop year (Ahmed 1981). They are perforce compelled to buy food from the market in the lean season. Part of the money to buy this food comes from wage labour which is known to account for almost half the family income of small farmers. Thus both the wage rate and the price of food turn out to be crucial market variables in determining the food entitlement of the farmers as well.

[6] For a discussion of the issues and evidence related to the deficiency of other nutrients in Bangladesh, see World Bank (1985*a*).

This simple analysis already reveals the great complexity of the problem of food entitlement in Bangladesh. Three rural groups—small farmers, wage labourers, and a large part of the non-farm sector—are severely afflicted by food deprivation, but each has a different acquisition problem. As a result, the structural forces as well as various policies and programmes operating in the economy may affect them differently through different channels. Identification of these channels and their operation over time is of crucial importance in understanding the long-term process of persistent hunger, to which we now turn.

7.3. Trend of persistent hunger: the long-term process of entitlement contraction

The statistics of persistent hunger

We may begin by looking at the aggregate picture of foodgrain production and its availability. It may be seen from Table 7.3 that between 1960/1 and 1983/4 total production of cereals expanded at the rate of 2.3 per cent, while population grew in the same period at the somewhat higher rate of 2.7 per cent. Per capita production has thus declined over time. However, when production is combined with imports (and adjusted for changes in government stocks), per capita *availability* is seen to be not very different in the early 1980s (if anything, slightly higher) compared to what it was two decades ago (Table 7.4).

Table 7.3 Comparative rates of growth of cereal production and population, Bangladesh (% p.a.)

Period	Foodgrain	Population
1960/1–1983/4	2.3	2.7
1960/1–1969/70	3.7	3.1
1975/6–1983/4	3.0	2.4

Notes: Cereal includes both rice and wheat.
  Rate of growth of foodgrain production refers to trend rate of growth.

Source: Statistical Yearbook of Bangladesh, various years.

Table 7.4 Production and availability of cereals in Bangladesh (yearly average for different time periods)

Period	Production (m. tons)	Availability (lbs/capita/day)
1960/1–1964/5	8.76	0.984
1965/6–1969/70	9.72	0.958
1972/3–1977/8	10.38	0.948
1977/8–1980/1	12.22	0.958
1981/2–1984/5	13.70	1.008

Source: MOF (1986: tables A2.1 and A2.2).

Cereals of course give only a part of the picture, albeit by far the major part (around 90 per cent of total calorie intake at present). The other part, relating to non-cereal food crops, presents a particularly grim picture. While per capita availability of cereals has not changed much, taking the last two decades as a whole, per capita production and availability of the major non-cereal food crops (such as pulses, oilseeds, and sugar) has declined drastically over this period (Hossain 1985c). The result, as revealed by the Nutrition Surveys, is an overall decline in per capita calorie intake in the rural areas—from 2,251 calories per day in 1962/4 to 1,943 calories in 1981/2 (INFS 1981/2).

The trend for the overall period, however, gives a somewhat misleading picture of the race between food and mouth. The race was lost only during the years immediately following the War of Liberation in 1971 when production was seriously disrupted by the accumulated effect of political turmoil and a series of natural disasters. In order to get a better appreciation of the underlying trend, it is therefore necessary to exclude these turbulent years and look separately at the 1960s and the period since the mid-1970s. This is done for cereals in Table 7.3, and it may be seen that the production of cereals has been able to keep ahead of population growth in both the subperiods. Not just production; per capita availability too has been moving on a rising trend in the 1970s (Table 7.4). As for non-cereal food crops, one finds a somewhat mixed picture—with the per capita availability of pulses continuing to decline but that of potato and sugar either rising or stagnating (Hossain 1984b).

What then is the overall trend of per capita calorie availability in the recent subperiod, i.e. during the period since the mid-1970s? On this there is a bit of conflicting evidence. According to two Nutrition Surveys, per capita calorie intake in rural Bangladesh has declined from 2,094 calories per day in 1975/6 to 1,943 calories in 1981/2 (INFS 1981/2). However, the picture is reversed if instead of using the Nutrition Survey of 1975/6 one uses the Household Expenditure Survey of 1976/7 as the base, which shows rural per capita calorie intake to be only 1,768 calories per day (World Bank 1985a: table 1). There is of course a problem of comparability between the two kinds of surveys;[7] yet the main reason behind the difference between the figures for 1975/6 and 1976/7 would appear to lie in random fluctuations in agricultural production—1975/6 was a year of bumper crop, while 1976/7 was a below average year when viewed against the overall trend. If, as a rough compromise, one takes the average of the estimates for the two years as representing the picture in the mid-1970s, one finds very little change in per capita calorie intake between then (1,931 calories) and 1981/2 (1,943 calories).

When this finding is combined with the evidence presented earlier on the rising trend of per capita cereal availability and mixed performance of non-

[7] The Household Expenditure Surveys are much bigger in scale and are hence subject to a lower sampling error. But the Nutrition Surveys probably contain fewer measurement errors, as they estimate calorie intake from direct measurement of food consumed within a household, whereas the Expenditure Surveys rely on memory recall by the respondents.

cereal food crops, one feels inclined to take the view that per capita calorie availability has probably not declined in the post-Liberation period. Whether it has improved, one cannot say for sure given the available data.

If these statistics of aggregate availability appear a bit shaky, they are at least on firmer grounds than those on the long-term trend of hunger. The latter requires quite detailed information on the distribution of food intake, which is available only for a few points in time. Analysis of changes in hunger and poverty has usually involved comparison between pairs of some of these points in time. One may of course try to deduce the long-term trend by piecing together these point-to-point comparisons. But there are two difficulties here that one must guard against.

First, the data sets of different studies are not always comparable. For instance, for the 1960s and up to the mid-1970s one could use nationally representative large-scale surveys of household income and expenditure. The last such survey for which results are available in sufficient detail relates to 1976/7. For the period since then, one has to rely on much smaller surveys such as the Nutrition Survey of 1981/2 or some village survey, of which there are plenty but most of which are too small to represent the national picture (we have used one of the largest of such surveys in constructing Table 7.1). The second difficulty is that the various point-to-point comparisons often use different methodologies, including different requirement norms. As a consequence of such discrepancies in data sets as well as methodology, the numbers thrown up by different studies are not often comparable.

However, one can still make some progress by piecing together information on the direction in which the level of hunger has changed. In other words, we are assuming that the findings about the *direction* of change are much more robust than the *numbers* themselves. As a result, if hunger is seen to have increased between time periods A and B according to one study, and increased again between B and C according to another, we hope to be able to say that hunger has increased between A and C, although we shall not know by how much.

Following this procedure, it is possible to conclude that the long-term trend of hunger in Bangladesh is one of persistent deterioration. According to a comparative study of the time periods 1963/4 and 1973/4, the magnitude of food deprivation (as measured by the Sen index of poverty) increased over time in rural Bangladesh (Osmani 1982). A subsequent study on income distribution showed that rural inequality had worsened between 1973/4 and 1976/7 while per capita income had also declined a little, indicating that the poorer segments faced an absolute decline in their living standards (Osmani and Rahman 1984). In fact, taking the longer period from 1963/4 to 1976/7, the same study also noted that while per capita income in real terms actually declined over this period, the richest 10 to 15 per cent of the population enjoyed an increase in their absolute real income. It implies that the poorest 85 per cent of the population not only bore the entire brunt of the overall reduction of per capita income, they were also forced into a perverse redistribution of income towards the rich. Although this study did not go on to estimate the magnitude of hunger, it is easy to infer from the above findings that absolute hunger increased over this period. One other study which did go into this estimation confirms this inference (Ahmad and Hossain 1985).

The picture since the mid-1970s is rather sketchy, mainly because results of large-scale household surveys have not been available in sufficient detail since then. However, as our subsequent analysis of structural changes will show, all the pointers are strongly towards further deterioration. For the moment we may note that two Nutrition Surveys in 1975/6 and 1981/2 found the food consumption of the rural poor to have declined over this period (INFS 1975/6 and INFS 1981/2). Although these surveys did not find a corresponding decline in the physical nutritional status of the poor, yet another Nutritional Survey of 1981 (UNICEF/FREPD 1981) shows marked deterioration in the nutritional status of children when compared with the findings of INFS (1975/6). Finally, the Nutrition Survey of 1981/2 found that when compared with the findings of an earlier survey of comparable methodology (USDH 1962–6), the proportion of rural households with inadequate food seemed to have increased substantially (from 59 to 76 per cent) from the early 1960s to the early 1980s.

The forces of entitlement contraction

The preceding evidence of course relates to overall hunger and does not say anything about how the different occupational groups have been doing over time. There is unfortunately no concrete information on the trend of occupational or any other distribution of hunger. We shall however try to deduce the picture by examining the structural forces operating on the economic environment facing each of the major food-deprived groups (namely the small farmers, rural wage labourers, and the poorer segment of the rural non-farm sector).

In order to choose an appropriate analytical framework for such a structural analysis, it is first necessary to have an understanding of the relationship between production and entitlement of food. One obvious linkage between production and entitlement is of course through the price of food and hence the exchange entitlement of those who rely heavily on market purchase to meet their food requirement. But there are also other, no less important, linkages whose significance emanates from the fact that food occupies a pre-eminent position in the production structure of Bangladesh agriculture. Production of food crops (cereals and non-cereals together) accounted for over 90 per cent of the total value of crop production in the 1980s, rising from about 83 per cent in the middle of this century. The share of cereals (rice and wheat) alone has risen from 73 per cent to 85 per cent during the same period (Hossain 1985c).

Given this overwhelming importance of food in the production structure, it is natural that food production should have a decisive impact on the level of economic activity in general and hence on the incomes and entitlements of almost all groups of people.

In the first place, food production has an immediate relevance for the entitlement of farmers who try to acquire as much food as possible from the production process itself, i.e. by growing food on their own land.

Secondly, because of its pre-eminence, food production exerts a preponderant influence on the demand for wage labour in agriculture. The consequent impacts on wage and employment are crucial factors in determining the entitlement of agricultural wage labourers.

The same pre-eminence of food also ensures that, through the linkages between farm and non-farm sectors, the ripples of its production effect will spread strongly to the non-farm sector as well. One such linkage is the trading in food crops. A recent evaluation of a credit programme for the poor in the non-farm sector has shown that trading is the most popular non-farm activity among the poor and that loans for trading in crops and vegetables account for nearly half the loans taken for trading purposes (Hossain 1984c). Obviously, then, food production has a lot to do with the trading income of a lot of non-farm poor. But perhaps the most significant linkage operates on the demand side—the line of causation running from food production to farm income to the demand for non-farm products. At the current low levels of income, a huge proportion of a rural household's budget is spent on basic food items, produced mostly in the farm sector, leaving very little room for non-farm products. For instance, a recent survey of rural expenditure pattern has found that an average rural household spends around 80 per cent of its budget on food alone (Osmani and Deb 1984). Of course some of the food items are produced or processed in the rural industrial sector; but even the combined food and non-food products of rural industry account for only 13 per cent of the average budget. While the total size of the market is thus severely limited by existing levels of income, it can however expand quite rapidly with the rise in rural income, since the income elasticity of demand for most of these products happens to lie above or close to unity (Osmani and Deb 1984). The same is true also about most kinds of non-farm products in general (Hossain 1984c). These estimates of budget-shares and elasticities clearly indicate that the growth of demand for non-farm products depends crucially on the growth in rural income. But the bulk of rural income is generated by the production, processing, and trading of agricultural products in general and food crops in particular; hence the importance of food production for the expansion of the non-farm sector, and for the incomes and entitlements of those engaged in this sector.

There is thus ample reason to believe that all three major rural groups afflicted by severe hunger have much at stake in the growth of food production. This point is perhaps worth emphasizing a little. Although production and entitlement are conceptually distinct categories and it has been rightly demonstrated that changes in one do not necessarily correlate with changes in the other (Sen 1981), the causal nexus between them seems strong enough in rural Bangladesh to entail a close positive association between the two. This closeness of association derives simply from the overwhelming importance of foodcrops in agriculture and from the importance of agriculture in turn in the rural economy of Bangladesh. It is of course possible that even in the case of Bangladesh, the nexus may not appear to be a strong one in the event of a sudden collapse of entitlement, as has indeed been shown to have been the case during the famine of 1974 (Sen 1981). But as far as the long-term evolution of entitlement is concerned, development on the front of food production can certainly be expected to play a decisive role in an economy with a food-dominated production structure.

Yet, as we have noted, the growth of food production, despite surpassing the rate of population growth in the post-Liberation era, does not seem to have been able to reduce the incidence of hunger. An understanding of the reason for this discordance between growth and hunger is crucial for identifying the structural forces of persistent hunger.

One can think of three alternative hypotheses to explain this observed discordance: (1) hunger expanded 'regardless of' growth, because the benefits of growth did not reach the poor, (2) hunger increased 'because of' growth, since the very process of growth created or strengthened the forces of hunger, and (3) hunger expanded 'in spite of' growth, because growth was inadequate to overcome some underlying force of hunger.

We shall argue that the particular empirical reality of Bangladesh suggests the third hypothesis to be the most plausible one.

The first hypothesis is valid when growth takes place in a lopsided manner, confining all the productivity gains to the lands of the large farmers and bypassing the smaller ones. This is indeed believed to be a characteristic of the so-called 'Green Revolution' in many parts of the world. It is well known that the seed-fertilizer-water technology of modern agriculture raises the working capital requirement well beyond the level obtaining in traditional agriculture. Unless special measures are taken to meet this enhanced requirement for working capital the small farmers are likely to remain outside the orbit of new technology, and the large farmers will reap all the gains. While this explanation is internally consistent,[8] it does not square with the actual observations on the pattern of growth in Bangladesh. Numerous field surveys have shown that the diffusion of modern technology has not remained disproportionately confined to the large farmers. For example, the results of a fairly large-scale survey of this kind are shown in Table 7.5.[9] The small farmers are seen to have

[8] But note that the argument, as presented, is not quite complete. If productivity gains are concentrated on the lands of the larger farmers, it only explains why relative inequality will increase over time; it does not explain why absolute hunger should deteriorate for those not blessed with improved productivity. It can nevertheless be shown that absolute hunger will increase, by bringing in the notion of an underlying immiserizing force which we discuss in the context of the third hypothesis.

[9] Evidence from several other studies is discussed in Osmani and Rahman (1984).

Table 7.5 Shares of different farm-size groups in the consumption of modern inputs, Bangladesh, 1981/2

Size of farm (acres)	% of farms	% of land operated	Share of fertilizer (%)	Share of irrigated land (%)	Share of institutional credit (%)
Up to 1.00	31.5	12.6	15.6	16.7	3.2
1.01–2.50	32.8	22.0	23.2	25.1	21.9
2.51–5.00	21.9	27.5	28.8	27.9	35.7
Above 5.00	13.8	37.9	32.4	30.2	39.2

Source: Abdullah (1985).

participated equally in the adoption of modern seed-fertilizer-water technology, if anything slightly more than in proportion to their share of land. This pattern, we believe, is owed mainly to the policy of heavy subsidization of agricultural inputs which the government has pursued until recently, thus enabling the small farmers to overcome the working capital constraint.[10]

Turning now to the second hypothesis, one can think of several ways in which hunger can expand 'because of' growth, i.e. through the process of growth itself. For instance, the growth-augmenting technology may be a labour-displacing one, as it is the case when mechanization spreads along with the seed-fertilizer-water technology. By reducing demand for labour, such growth can indeed accentuate the hunger of agricultural labourers. Even the small farmers can be harmed. This will happen if the profitability of new technology induces the landowners to bring back land from the share-croppers for cultivation under their own management. There are also other possibilities. While the share-croppers receive only half of the increased yield, they typically have to bear the entire burden of the increased cost of cultivation. This may conceivably lead to a situation where the net return to share-croppers' labour actually goes down with the adoption of new technology.

While all these are theoretical possibilities and some of these tendencies have actually been observed in different parts of the world where a Green Revolution has occurred, they do not seem to have a great deal of empirical relevance for Bangladesh agriculture. In the first place, mechanization of Bangladesh agriculture is still of a very minuscule order of magnitude—less than 1 per cent of farms use tractors or power tillers, according to the Agricultural Census of 1977. On the eviction of share-croppers, it is well known that this does happen at times, but there is no quantitative estimate of its degree of occurrence. However, from what is known about the size of the tenancy market and its changes over time, it does not appear that eviction could have been a

---

[10] The question of subsidies and credit constraint is discussed further in the final section of the chapter.

quantitatively significant phenomenon; according to the Agricultural Censuses of 1960 and 1977, the proportion of tenant farmers among all farm
households rose from 39 per cent to 42 per cent during the intercensal period
and the proportion of total land under tenancy fell marginally from 18 per cent
to 17 per cent during the same period. Finally, it is also well known that the
share-croppers in Bangladesh do typically incur all the increased cost of new
technology; yet empirical estimates show that net return to their labour from
the cultivation of HYV crops is considerably higher than what the traditional
crops typically offer.[11] Thus none of the channels through which the process of
growth can plausibly lead to a squeeze of the entitlement of the poor seems to fit
the empirical reality of Bangladesh.[12]

We are thus left with the hypothesis of 'inadequate growth' to explain the
observed discordance between growth and hunger. Before going into the
empirics of this explanation, let us first spell out the logic of the hypothesis.
The essence of the argument is that the combination of private property
relations and intense demographic pressure obtaining in rural Bangladesh is
constantly generating an 'immiserizing' force which growth will have to
overcome before it can begin to reduce the incidence of hunger. The way this
force works can be seen most simply by assuming a 'no growth' scenario. It is
also convenient to begin the story with the case of small farmers.

A high rate of population growth from an already high base of population
density combines with the Muslim law of inheritance to lead to a progressive
reduction in the average size of farm over the years. It has indeed declined from
3.5 acres in 1960 to 2.4 acres in 1982. With reduced landholding, the small and
marginal farmers can only maintain their standard of living if corresponding
gains can be made in land productivity. In the absence of such productivity
growth, demographic pressure leads inevitably to a continual increase in the
number of economically unviable holdings. The resulting marginalization of
the peasantry is the beginning of the process of overall impoverishment. Under
constant economic pressure, the marginalized peasantry eventually becomes
alienated from land and swells the rank of landless labourers whose own stock

[11] It has been estimated for instance that whereas the return to share-croppers' labour in the
cultivation of traditional crops is often less than the agricultural wage rate, in the case of
high-yielding varieties it is clearly higher, although not as much as in the case of owner-farmers.
See the discussion in Hossain (1981: 77).

[12] There is one other channel which is sometimes mentioned, but not with enough theoretical
justification in our view. It is suggested that by increasing the income of large farmers, Green
Revolution enhances their ability to buy the land of marginal farmers, thus accentuating the
process of rural landlessness. This argument ignores the point that since most land sales by the
poor are in the nature of 'distress sale' intended to meet some given cash needs, they will tend to sell
less if the price of land goes up (because the same cash needs can now be met by selling a smaller
piece of land). Therefore, higher income of the rural rich, by raising the demand price of land,
should if anything reduce the volume of distress sales, other things remaining the same. If
landlessness is nevertheless seen to have gone up, as it indeed has in Bangladesh, then obviously
the other things did not remain the same, and this is where the analysis should turn. We take up
this analysis in the context of the third hypothesis.

has also been growing at a rapid pace due to the same demographic pressure. While the supply of wage labour is thus being doubly augmented, demand for labour cannot obviously rise in the absence of productivity growth. The consequent decline in real wage and employment leads to persistent contraction in the entitlement of the wage-labour class. Many of them pour into the non-farm sector in search of alternative employment. But this only adds to the misery of the non-farm population whose real income cannot expand (because the demand for their products does not expand) in the absence of agricultural growth.

This tendency towards pervasive impoverishment can be overcome if the growth in productivity is strong enough to arrest the marginalization of the peasantry, to raise the demand for wage labour ahead of expanding supply, and to strengthen the demand for non-farm products. It is thus apparent how growth can occur and hunger can spread at the same time because growth is inadequate to outweigh the underlying force of immiserization.[13]

Turning now to the actual record of growth, it has to be first noted that, given very limited possibility of augmenting the size of cultivable land, growth in Bangladesh agriculture must occur mainly through the diffusion of yield-augmenting technology. It is of course true that the use of high-yielding variety (HYV) seeds has expanded rapidly in the 1970s starting from a meagre 2.5 per cent of total cereal acreage in 1969/70; but even by 1983/4, nearly three-quarters of all cereal acreage remained under the low-yielding traditional seeds. Irrigation facilities, which are crucial for the adoption of HYVs, have also expanded rapidly; yet by 1982/3, four-fifths of all cultivated land remained outside the ambit of controlled irrigation. Chemical fertilizers, which are most productive when used with HYVs but can also improve the yield of traditional seeds, have achieved the fastest rate of expansion; yet field surveys indicate that over 40 per cent of all cereal lands are not treated with fertilizer at all. Even when fertilizer is applied, the rate of application is well below the recommended dose. Moreover, almost half the fertilizer is applied on rainfed land where its return is both low and insecure.[14]

Thus although modern technology has made a significant inroad and the small farmers too seem to have participated in this process, Bangladesh agriculture still remains dominated by the moribund technology of yesteryear. It is in the light of this inadequate technological diffusion, and hence inadequate growth, that we shall now analyse the available empirical evidence on the structural forces operating on the entitlement of the rural poor.

[13] This argument assumes that the existing system of private property relations and the associated system of entitlements remain intact. Under a more egalitarian system of ownership and entitlements, the 'warranted' rate of growth, i.e. the rate of growth required to neutralize the underlying immiserizing force, would be lower, and could conceivably be even lower than the observed rate of growth.

[14] For more detailed information on the diffusion of modern technology in Bangladesh agriculture, see Hossain (1984*b*) and Osmani and Quasem (1985: ch. II).

We shall begin with the situation of the small farmers. Table 7.6 shows the change in the distribution of landholding that has taken place over the last two decades. It shows how demographic forces have exerted a downward pressure on the overall distribution of landholding, reducing the proportion of large farms and increasing the proportion of smaller ones. This downward pressure has pushed many small farms out of the farming occupation altogether by making their subdivided plots too small to be economic. This is evidenced by the fact that the total number of farms increased at the rate of only 1.3 per cent a year, while population increased at the rate of 2.7 per cent. Assuming that the number of households grew at the same rate as population, the number of farms should also have grown at the same rate if all the farms created through subdivision remained in business.[15] This obviously did not happen; the number of farms grew only at half the rate, which means a great many farms were thrown out of business, the small plots of land being sold or leased out to the larger farmers. Whatever technological improvement has occurred has not obviously been able to prevent many small farms from becoming uneconomic. The resulting process of land alienation has been confirmed by a number of field surveys.[16] A general finding of these studies is that the sale of land occurs predominantly at the bottom end of the scale and it is the medium farmers who buy up most of the land on offer. Supportive evidence of this phenomenon at the national level is offered by Table 7.6 which shows that the medium farmers (2.5 to 7.5 acres) hold an increasing share of land, despite going down in numbers in both relative and absolute terms.[17]

The long term effect of this process of land transfer is reflected in generational transition from one occupation group to another. Table 7.7, which shows the occupation of predecessors of a cross-section of the rural population, tells the story poignantly. Nearly 75 per cent of the landless labourers are seen to have come from families which as recently as their father's or grandfather's time had farming as the principal occupation.

By all accounts, the process of land transfer has continued unabated leading to an increase in the proportion of landless rural people. Combining information from various censuses and surveys, Hossain (1985a) has estimated that between 1960 and 1982 the number of landless households grew much faster

---

[15] This argument is premissed on the prevailing law of inheritance which entitles every son (and to a lesser extent every daughter) to a piece of his father's land.

[16] The relevant evidence has been collated by Khan (1976) and Osmani and Rahman (1984), among others.

[17] Note that the small farmers' share of total holdings has also gone up, but this is to be expected because, unlike in the case of medium farmers, the proportion of small farmers has gone up too. It is true that their share of land has gone up at a faster rate than their share of farm households; but it does not mean that the small farmers are actually gaining land! All it means is probably that those erstwhile small farmers who have now become landless and do not therefore figure in Table 7.6 under the column of the year 1982 had a smaller average size of land than that which the new entrants to the category of small farmers have brought from their erstwhile status of medium–large farmers through the process of land subdivision.

Table 7.6 Changes in the distribution of landholdings, Bangladesh, 1960–1982

Size of farm (acres)	% of farms		% share of holding	
	1960	1982	1960	1982
Up to 1.00	24.3	34.0	3.2	7.1
1.01–2.50	27.3	33.5	12.9	22.3
2.51–7.50	37.7	27.6	45.7	47.0
Above 7.50	10.7	4.9	38.1	23.6
All farms	100.0	100.0	100.0	100.0

Notes: Number of farms: 1960: 6,139,000; 1982: 8,124,000.
  Average size of farm: 1960: 3.5 acres; 1982: 2.4 acres.

Source: Compiled from Agriculture Census of 1960 and the Pilot Agriculture Census of 1982.

Table 7.7 Transition towards impoverishment through generations in rural Bangladesh

Occupation of predecessors	Owner-farmers	Share-croppers	Landless labourers	Beggars
Grandfather: farmer Father: farmer	95.1	84.8	60.2	59.8
Grandfather: farmer Father: labourer	0.4	1.6	12.7	9.9
Grandfather: labourer Father: farmer	0.4	2.5	1.5	0.9
Grandfather: labourer Father: labourer	0.3	2.2	16.6	12.3
Others	3.8	8.9	9.0	17.1
ALL	100.0	100.0	100.0	100.0

Source: Quoted from Muqtada and Alam (1983). The findings are based on *IRDP Benchmark Survey of Rural Bangladesh*, 1973/4.

than both rural households in general and farm households in particular. It is however worth pointing out that such estimates based on census of rural areas at two points in time are likely to underestimate the growth in landlessness, since many landless choose over time to migrate to the urban areas rather than stay in the village.

Despite such underestimation, Hossain found that the proportion of completely landless households increased from 33 per cent in 1960 to 37 per cent in 1982, and the proportion of functionally landless households (with less than 0.5 acres of land) rose from 42 per cent to 47 per cent.

Alienation from land is of course the last desperate act of an impoverished farmer who likes to cling to his land for as long as he can. Growing landlessness thus clearly implies growing impoverishment of the peasantry. As we have argued, the principal reason for this is the slow rate of technological improvement and the resulting slow growth in production.

The long-term evolution in the entitlement of wage labourers can be explained in terms of the same set of forces. It is possible to argue that inadequate growth of production has adversely affected their wage and employment, by augmenting an already existing imbalance between supply and demand for wage labour. How this imbalance has developed can be seen most clearly by tracing the effect of slow growth on both supply and demand sides of the labour market and relating the growth of supply and demand to the rate of population growth as a common reference for comparison.

On the supply side, slow growth has augmented the natural increase in labour force by helping to create a marginalized peasantry who would seek employment in the labour market not only when they became landless, but even as they remained peasants. As the Pilot Agricultural Census of 1982 shows, 33 per cent of all farm households and 60 per cent of all households with less than one acre of land depend upon wage labour in agriculture as their *main* source of income. Because of this forced augmentation of the labour market, the supply of wage labour has naturally grown faster than the rate of population growth.

On the other hand, there is reason to believe that the demand for wage labour has grown at a slower rate than that of population growth. Once again inadequate growth of food production has played its part. While production itself has grown at about the same rate as the rural labour force (around 3 per cent), employment opportunities have grown a lot slower, since the employment elasticity of productivity growth is known to be substantially less than unity in Bangladesh agriculture.[18] Moreover, a part of the increased employment must have been taken up by the hitherto underemployed family labour. The residual increase in the demand for wage labour must therefore have been less than the growth of employment opportunities and hence less than the rate of population growth.

Since demand for wage labour is thus seen to have grown slower than population, while supply is seen to have grown faster, there obviously developed a growing imbalance between supply and demand for labour. The resulting depression of real wages of agricultural labourers has been well documented for the period of the 1960s and early 1970s (Khan 1976). The picture since the mid-1970s is given in Table 7.8. Although there is no clear trend for this period, the rice exchange rate of wages is seen to have remained generally below the pre-Liberation level. Of course to the extent that the rural labour market does not completely clear, as is generally believed to be the case, the fall in real wage may not fully reflect the magnitude of excess supply. In that case a part of excess supply will be resolved through employment rationing,

---

[18] Clay and Khan (1977) conclude after a careful review of available evidence that the yield elasticity of employment would vary between 0.2 and 0.5 for various types of yield-increasing operations, including the shift from traditional varieties to the HYVs.

Table 7.8 Rice exchange rate of agricultural wages in Bangladesh, 1969/70–1982/3

Year	Index of nominal wage	Index of retail price of rice	Index of rice exchange rate of wages
1969/70	100	100	100
1976/7	301	293	103
1977/8	317	360	88
1978/9	366	407	90
1979/80	421	548	77
1980/1	473	471	100
1981/2	520	583	89
1982/3	576	628	92

Source: Constructed from World Bank (1984: tables 9.5, 9.7, 9.10).

which will imply a reduction in per capita employment. It is difficult to tell exactly in what proportion the excess supply has in fact been resolved through the two channels. But it does not really matter for the present analysis, since whichever channel it takes, the effect is to contract the entitlement of wage labourers.

Turning now to the non-farm sector of the rural population, we find precious little that can be presented by way of concrete evidence on the long-term trend of their entitlement. Some inference however can still be drawn by putting together indirect evidence of various kinds.

The first point to note is the growing size of the non-farm sector. According to census data, the labour force engaged primarily in non-farm activities has expanded from 19 per cent in 1974 to 39 per cent in 1981.[19] The rise in the relative share of the non-farm labour force is not surprising in view of the evidence presented earlier that employment opportunities in the farm sector have grown more slowly than the rural labour force. Unable to find sustained employment in the farm sector, many among the landless people must have turned to the non-farm sector. From the findings of some recent surveys of occupational distribution in rural Bangladesh, it can be roughly estimated that not less than 60 per cent of the functionally landless people (owning less than 0.5 acres of land) are primarily engaged in the non-farm sector, while no more than one-third have agricultural wage labour as their primary occupation.[20]

Does this preponderance of non-farm activities among the poor indicate a dynamism in the non-farm sector which attracts the labour force, or does it merely imply that this sector acts as a residual absorber of those impoverished

[19] Several other studies also confirm that the present size of the non-farm labour force would be about 40–5% of the total. See BIDS (1981), Hossain (1984c).

[20] Findings of these surveys are discussed in Hossain (1984c, 1984d).

agricultural workers who cannot make a living out of agriculture any more? The answer to this question will provide at least some indirect evidence on what has been happening to the income and entitlement of the non-farm population.

Unfortunately, it is not possible to give a very definitive answer to this question. But there is some evidence to suggest that the returns from non-farm activities, especially where the poor are mainly involved, are simply not attractive enough to divert labour away from agriculture. For instance, a recent study has found that nearly one-third of the rural industrial workforce, usually the poorer ones, are engaged in industries where return to family labour is lower than the agricultural wage rate. Average labour productivity in rural industries in general is of course higher than agricultural wages. But productivity is found to depend mostly on capital intensity; and the poorer among the workforce cannot afford to undertake the relatively high-yielding capital intensive activities. As a result, the landless and near landless families are found to be engaged mostly in the low-yielding activities (Hossain 1984a). This is not a characteristic of rural industries alone, but of non-farm activities in general. For instance, Muqtada and Alam (1983) have found in a survey of the rural labour market that income from non-farm activities is positively correlated with the amount of land owned. Obviously, those with more land have greater access to resources in general and hence can afford to take up those activities which yield higher returns through the use of more capital. The landless and the near-landless can use little more than their physical labour and, when they do that, return is usually lower than the agricultural wage. For instance, in 10 out of 14 major cottage industries, the wage rate for hired labour was found to be less than the wage rate for unskilled labour in agriculture (Hossain 1984e).

Non-farm activities do not therefore seem to provide a haven where the poor in the farm sector would have found a more rewarding employment.[21] One cannot thus explain the growth of the non-farm sector as a 'pull-effect' of its attractiveness *vis-à-vis* the farm sector.[22] The explanation must rather lie in the 'push-effect' of entitlement contraction that has occurred in the farm sector.

[21] This is not to deny that more rewarding employment can be found in the non-farm sector if opportunities are created. The crucial factor is to help the poor with credit so that they can avail themselves of the opportunities which remain otherwise open to the richer stratum only. The celebrated Grameen Bank experiment in Bangladesh has shown that a well-executed credit programme for the poor in the non-farm sector can indeed raise their earnings well above the agricultural wage rate, especially in trading and livestock activities and some types of cottage industries (Hossain 1984c). But this experiment is very recent and by now it has covered only about 15% of all villages in the country. Its effects are therefore unlikely to have been significant enough to invalidate the broad historical generalization we have made about the relative unattractiveness of the non-farm sector from the point of view of the poor.

[22] This argument is based on the premise that the labour market does not clear in the farm sector and excess supply is taken care of by some form of employment rationing, so that many among the farm sector labour force come over to the non-farm sector despite the prospect of a lower rate of return on their labour.

The most probable consequence of this scenario is an increasing degree of work and income sharing in the non-farm sector, hence a contraction in per capita entitlement, especially among the poorer group.

The preceding analysis thus suggests that all three rural groups with severe problems of hunger have probably been experiencing a secular contraction in their entitlement to food. As is to be expected, their fates are closely related to each other. Impoverishment of the small farmers has a spill-over effect on the income of agricultural wage labourers. These two classes in turn tend to drag the non-farm poor along with them, when they are themselves sliding down the slippery road to hunger. It is therefore not surprising that the same set of forces can explain their common predicament. As argued before, these forces consist of an underlying immiserizing tendency emanating from intense demographic pressure and private property relations, a tendency that can in theory be neutralized by strong enough growth (in food production in particular and agricultural production in general); but what growth has actually occurred has obviously not been strong enough to neutralize this tendency. It is important to realize that a rate of growth that is arithmetically higher than the rate of population growth may still be qualitatively weaker than the immiserizing force of demographic pressure.

This brings us to the fundamental question of why production has not been able to grow any faster. The reason certainly does not lie in the limiting constraint of known technology. It has been estimated, for instance, that only about a third of the suitable land is currently being planted with HYV crops, and not more than half of the potentially irrigable land is actually being irrigated. Capacity utilization of the existing irrigation facility is also well below the true potential. The technologically feasible maximal growth rate is therefore considerably higher than what has been achieved so far.[23]

However, a more rapid diffusion of technology would have called for increased investment in water control in the rainy season and irrigation in the dry season. Investment would thus appear to have been the limiting factor. The reason however does not lie in the lack of investible resources, for there are reasons to believe that both private and public investment in agriculture have remained well below the potential. A number of field surveys have shown for instance that the large farmers devote only a small proportion of their surplus (over essential consumption) to agricultural investment.[24] Also a rather negligible proportion of this surplus is siphoned off by the state machinery through its fiscal system (Hossain et al. 1985), which is a crucial factor in limiting the size of public investment. Even within the limits of total resources

---

[23] For further details on the gap between potential and realized technological achievement, see Osmani and Quasem (1985: ch. II).

[24] Rahman (1979) reports from a field survey that the large farmers devote only 15–20% of their savings to agricultural investment. Yet another survey found the ratio to vary from 10 to 16% (CSS 1980). Note that these figures are expressed as proportions of *savings*: as proportions of *surplus* (income minus essential consumption), the figures would be even lower.

available for public investment it cannot be said that agriculture has received resources commensurate with its importance. The importance of agriculture does not consist simply in the fact that it generates more than half the national income; we have demonstrated that the entitlement of all the rural poor depends directly or indirectly on the progress of agricultural production in general and food production in particular. Yet agriculture has historically received no more than a third of public investment funds; and the share is showing an ominously declining trend in recent years.

Why has the bulk of private surplus shied away from agricultural investment, why has so little of the surplus been siphoned into public investment, and why has resource allocation in the public sector failed to give agriculture its due? These are some of the crucial questions that must be answered in order to understand why food production has remained well below the technological frontier and thus failed to make a dent into the problem of persistent hunger. This enquiry would however lead to all the complex issues of the political economy of underdevelopment in Bangladesh, a task that cannot obviously be attempted, let alone be accomplished, in this short chapter. The limited objective of this section was merely to demonstrate that lack of growth rather than the nature of growth has historically been responsible for persistent contraction of food entitlement in rural Bangladesh. How the future is likely to emerge in view of recent policy changes is the subject matter for the final part of the chapter. But before that, we turn briefly to the issue of famines and their relationship, if any, with the trend of persistent hunger.

7.4. *Persistent hunger* vis-à-vis *famine*

The grip of persistent hunger may be tightening in rural Bangladesh, but at least there has been no famine since 1974. There were however famine scares on two occasions—once in 1979 and again in 1984. On both occasions the scare arose from genuine enough reasons. In 1979 successive crops were damaged by severe drought. Actual loss was less than feared, but the crop was still down by 4.8 per cent from the previous year. More significantly, per capita systemic availability (production plus imports) was in fact lower than in the famine year of 1974. In 1984, there were several rounds of severe flooding causing extensive crop damage. In the event, production was only 1 per cent less than in the previous year; but the important point is that the floods were even more severe than those of 1974 and production declined, while in 1974 production had actually risen despite the flood.

In spite of all this and in spite of the fact that, according to our analysis, endemic hunger has worsened over time, famine did not occur in either year. This observation raises a number of interesting issues. Does it imply that just as aggregate food availability has no necessary correlation with the occurrence of famine, so the secular contraction of food entitlement does not imply greater susceptibility to catastrophic breakdown in entitlement? Or does it raise doubts about the thesis of worsening hunger itself? Or does it merely mean that the authorities have learnt some secret trick of averting famine, which they did not know in 1974? We shall try to answer these questions by comparing the situations obtaining in each of the three years 1974, 1979, and 1984.[25]

As several analyses of the 1974 famine have shown, the most vulnerable groups are those who sell their labour for wages and buy food from the market (Alamgir 1980; Sen 1981). What happens to their employment and to the rice exchange equivalent of their wage are the two crucial variables that determine whether there is going to be a famine or not.

Loss of employment due to flooding clearly played its part in the 1974 famine. Especially significant was the damage to the jute crop, whose produc- tion declined by a massive 42 per cent. Jute is one of the most labour intensive crops of Bangladesh agriculture and wage income from its production provides the principal cushion for surviving through the lean season of July–October in the jute-growing areas. Loss of this cushion was no doubt a crucial factor in precipitating the famine that struck in the lean season.[26]

In contrast, the 1979 jute output suffered a relatively modest decline of only 8 per cent. But one must set against this the fact that foodgrain production in this year fell by 4.8 per cent due to severe drought, whereas 1974 saw an increase in output. As a result, loss of employment in the foodgrain sector must have been much more extensive in 1979. In view of the fact that foodgrain acreage was more than twelve times that of jute (in 1979), it is not altogether improbable that overall loss of employment was no less severe in 1979 than in 1974, although it is difficult to be very precise about this.

In 1984, the damage to the jute crop (18 per cent decline) was much more extensive than in 1979, though not quite as bad as in 1974. On the foodgrain front, however, output declined by about 1 per cent, as against an increase in 1974. Moreover, as in 1974, there was extensive inundation of the acreage devoted to the winter crop whose output becomes available in the following year but whose employment effects are felt here and now.

Thus, on the whole, employment does not seem to have been the crucial difference in the three years in question. The difference in fact lies in the contrasting movements in the purchasing power of labour. In the crucial famine months (August–November) of 1974, the rice exchange rate of the agricultural wage fell by almost 40 per cent compared to the same period in the preceding year, as against a 30 per cent decline in 1979. But more importantly, while the exchange rate continuously fell during the famine period of 1974, it improved steadily throughout August–November of 1979. Finally, the exchange rate in this period remained 50 per cent higher in 1979 than in 1974.

[25] The comparative analysis for the years 1974 and 1979 draws heavily on Ahmad (1985). The chief source of data for 1984 is World Bank (1985b). For 1974, heavy use has also been made of the information and analyses contained in Sobhan (1979), Alamgir (1980), Sen (1981).

[26] It is significant that two of the three worst famine-hit districts (namely Mymemsingh and Rangpur) are also the two most important jute-growing areas of Bangladesh.

The key of this difference is the movement in the price of rice. While the price of rice in the famine months of 1974 was about 250 per cent higher than in the same period of the preceding year, the corresponding increase was only 54 per cent in 1979 and a meagre 11 per cent in 1984. Moreover, while the price kept on rising throughout the famine period of 1974 at the rate of 20 per cent a month, it had a declining trend during the corresponding lean months of 1979 and rose at the modest rate of only 1 per cent a month in 1984. On the whole, the price of foodgrain rose by more than 100 per cent in 1974 over the preceding year, whereas the average rise in 1979 was only about 35 per cent. In 1984, the price increase was even more modest—just about 10 per cent, nothing more than the normal rate of inflation.

What explains such disparate movements in the price of foodgrain? Certainly not the size of its availability. As mentioned before, per capita systemic availability was in fact lower in 1979 than in 1974. While it was somewhat higher in 1984, that alone cannot explain the difference between a 100 per cent and a 10 per cent increase in price. Nor can it be explained by general inflationary forces such as expansion of money supply, as has been demonstrated in the case of the 1974 famine by Ravallion (1985) and Ahmad (1985). Ravallion (1985) has also shown that the dramatic price increase of 1974 can be neatly explained by the speculative behaviour of rice traders. Exaggerated reports of crop damage led the traders to overestimate future scarcity. The resulting overshooting of future price expectations caused 'excessive hoarding' and hence the abnormal increase in current price.

While this story fits very well with the experience of 1974, it runs into some difficulty in 1979 and 1984. Exaggerated fear of crop loss was also a characteristic of both these years. At the peak of drought in 1978, the Bangladesh Ministry of Agriculture had estimated that the 1979 *aman* crop (the main rice crop) would be 20–25 per cent below normal. In reality, output turned out to be marginally higher than that of the preceding *aman* crop. But the important point is that the fears persisted until the harvests actually came in. Meanwhile, however, the drought continued and threatened to damage the two subsequent crops, which it partly did. As a result of this prolonged drought a famine scare persisted throughout the year. Yet, as we have noted, there was no extraordinary rise in the price of rice. In 1984, the scare was even greater, with several rounds of flooding damaging and threatening to damage four successive crops, an unprecedented mishap in the recent history of the country. In the end, loss of output turned out to be quite modest, thanks largely to an unexpected improvement in yield (World Bank 1985b). But this was an *ex post* achievement which could do nothing to diminish the *ex ante* scare. Yet the price of rice rose very modestly.

Obviously, something more than mere overestimation of crop damage is involved. Ravallion (1985) seems to be aware of the missing link and speculates correctly in his concluding observation, 'The most plausible conclusion is that the stock-holders' over-optimistic price expectations and/or anticipations of future rationing during the 1974 famine were premised on a belief that the Government would be unable to implement a suitable stabilising response to the reported damage to the future crop' (p. 28). Belief in the ability of the government's public food distribution system (PFDS) to deal with an emerging crisis seems indeed to be crucial. An analysis of PFDS in the famine *vis-à-vis* non-famine years brings out the point quite clearly.

It has been well documented that the public stock of foodgrain was very low in 1974 and the government's capacity to import was also very limited due to an unfavourable aid climate on the one hand and dwindling foreign exchange reserves on the other (Alamgir 1980; Sen 1981; Ahmad 1985). This was no secret and the speculators were obviously aware of the predicament. They were quite right in thinking that PFDS was in no position to redress the emerging crisis. But this was not the case in 1979 or 1984. As soon as the crisis bell rang in 1979, the government lined up imports on both aid and commercial bases. The same happened in 1984 and foodgrain import in that year reached an all-time peak. In each of these two later years, monthly stock and distribution were substantially higher than in 1974.[27] What this distribution did to bolster aggregate availability is not the important part of the story. What is important is the effect it seems to have had on the speculators. By pursuing a vigorous import and distribution policy, the authorities succeeded in softening future price expectations. The resulting containment of current price level was an additional and by far the more important effect of PFDS on top of whatever it did to affect the current balance of supply and demand.

It is of course true that apart from containing the speculative price spiral, the PFDS in 1979 and 1984 also achieved much more than in 1974 by way of directly relieving the distress of the immediate victims of drought and flood. The quantity of foodgrain supplied to the rural poor through rationing, food-for-work, and relief in 1979/80 was higher than in any other year during 1973/4–1980/1. Also, during the crucial months of May to November 1984, the amount of relief distributed per month was three times the typical levels of the preceding years. These measures undoubtedly helped in alleviating human misery in the worst affected areas. But they do not by themselves explain why localized crisis did not turn into generalized disaster through a spiralling price increase, as it did in 1974; for, as we have already noted, despite a much higher level of public distribution, total (systemic) availability of foodgrain was no higher in 1979 than in 1974 and was only marginally higher in 1984. This is

[27] Average monthly distribution of foodgrain during the famine months of 1974 was 170,000 tons, as against 250,000 and 230,000 tons in the corresponding months of 1979 and 1984 respectively. More striking is the difference in the level of stocks: the average month-end stock of foodgrains in government stores was only about 140,000 tons in the famine months of 1974, as against 700,000 and 650,000 tons in 1979 and 1984 (corresponding months) respectively. Thus although the difference in terms of offtake is not all that dramatic, the difference in stock would indicate that the government's ability to tackle a crisis was much higher in 1979 and 1984 than in 1974. It also has to be remembered that the level of offtake improved in 1974 only towards the end of the famine. In the earlier period, when speculative pressure was gradually building up, both stock and offtake were much lower than during the famine months.

where the role of PFDS in containing speculative price increase comes in. The price spiral of 1974 was a direct consequence of speculative market withdrawal encouraged by a perceived inability of the PFDS to deal with future scarcity. In contrast, the health of PFDS in 1979 and 1984 in all its aspects (namely import, stocks, and distribution) signalled the futility of speculating on future scarcity. This had an obvious softening effect on market withdrawal and the consequent rise in the current price of foodgrain. The limitations of PFDS in 1974 and its vitality in the two later years should therefore constitute the key explanation of why famine occurred in one case and not in the others.[28]

The time has now come to answer the questions posed at the beginning of this section. Note first that while the authorities were highly successful in checking speculative price increase in both 1979 and 1984, they were also helped in this effort by a couple of fortunate circumstances. On both occasions, the government found itself blessed with a healthy foreign exchange reserve, a rare phenomenon in a country with a chronic balance-of-payments problem. The situation in 1984 was particularly fortuitous, as the reserves actually represented the 'unwelcome' consequence of a recession in the preceding years which had depressed imports to disconcertingly low levels. But it turned out to be a boon in disguise when the floods came, and helped to procure a record level of imports on a commercial basis. In fact, in both 1979 and 1984, commercial imports accounted for over half of total imports, while usually food aid accounts for more than two-thirds of imports in normal years. Commercial imports on such a scale were a dream in 1974, as foreign exchange reserves had already been drawn down to precariously low levels when the real crunch came.

The second fortunate circumstance was the highly favourable aid climate obtaining at the time, particularly in 1979. Not only were the donors generous and prompt in their response, even the IMF was very understanding! The country was under a stand-by agreement with the IMF in that year and there was, inevitably, an agreed ceiling on government borrowing. That ceiling was breached as the government borrowed heavily from the Central Bank in order to finance its commercial imports, but the IMF did not raise any fuss.[29] The donors were somewhat less forthcoming in 1984, but nowhere near as niggardly as in 1974.[30]

---

[28] It would appear that Sen (1981) has underestimated the role of a weakened public food distribution system in precipitating the famine of 1974. He recognizes its importance in constraining the relief operations of the government once the famine had struck, but does not attach any *causal* significance to it. This he does by ignoring the effect of PFDS on speculative price increase and concentrating merely on its effect on the current availability of foodgrains.

[29] However the very next year, in 1980, when the government broke its credit ceiling again, this time to replenish its depleted food stock through a massive drive for domestic procurement out of a bumper harvest, the IMF responded by cancelling a newly contracted Extended Fund Facility programme. For a critical review of these incidents see Matin (1986).

[30] For information on donors' response in 1984, see World Bank (1985b). The story of 1974 is told most vividly by McHenry and Bird (1977).

Thus the episodes of 1979 and 1984 do not really testify to any systemic improvement on the front of short-term food security. Aid climate, one of the favourable factors, is essentially an exogenous variable. The other factor, namely a healthy foreign exchange reserve, is in principle a control variable, and there has been a lot of discussion about holding such reserves in lieu of or as a supplement to a buffer stock of food. But the government has not been able to pursue any consistent policy in this regard, hard-pressed as it is to provide foreign exchange for much-needed imports. Accumulation of reserves has always been a consequence of unforeseen shortfall in the import programme. The two years in question were no exception. Therefore, the hypothesis that the government has acquired a greater capability of dealing with famine threats remains untested, at best, and in considerable doubt, to be more realistic.

The fortuitous manner in which famine was averted in 1979 and 1984 also gives no comfort to the thought that the structure of Bangladesh economy has acquired a greater resilience over time against threats of dramatic entitlement failures. Nor does it negate the thesis of secular deterioration in the trend of endemic hunger.

Finally, what can one say about the relationship between 'persistent entitlement contraction' and 'sudden entitlement failures'? The experience of the recent years of course shows that, despite entitlement contraction, catastrophic failures of entitlement can be avoided if fortune smiles. But that is not saying much. One would suspect on a priori grounds that the probability of 'failure' would increase with the intensification of 'contraction'. Indeed it is possible to argue that entitlement failure in 1974 turned out to be as precipitous as it was mainly because of severe entitlement contraction that had occurred in the preceding years, partly through natural calamities and partly through the destructions and dislocations caused by a prolonged war of liberation. The destruction of assets (houses, cattle, etc.) caused by these events was a direct dent in the 'endowment set', especially for the rural people. Endowment contractions of this kind must have accentuated the gravity of the famine. These contractions of entitlement of course occurred under exceptional circumstances, in a relatively rapid manner. But persistent contractions can also produce qualitatively similar results. There is therefore hardly any ground for feeling confident that the Bangladesh economy has acquired a greater immunity from famine in recent years.[31]

---

[31] It ought to be recognized, however, that the production structure of Bangladesh agriculture has probably acquired a somewhat greater degree of resilience against the destructive effects of natural disasters such as flooding. But for the recent advances in dry-season cultivation through modern irrigation and spread of HYVs in the rainfed winter crop, the effect of the 1984 floods would have been much more devastating, making it harder to contain a potentially dangerous price spiral. On this, see World Bank (1985b). It should also be noted that the necessary physical infrastructure for the storage and distribution of foodgrains is much better now than it was in 1974. It means that, if the necessary foodgrains can somehow be acquired at the right time, the authorities can now deal with a crisis more effectively than before. But the crucial 'acquisition' problem remains as uncertain as ever.

7.5. *Elements of food strategy*

We have analysed the structural forces governing the evolution of entitlement over time and also tried to judge the prospect of dramatic failures in entitlement. The analysis reveals a rather grim picture. It is now necessary to move on to the level of policy, to see if the policies being pursued have the potential to change the course of structural evolution.

While policies with long-term structural effects are our primary interest here, it should also be recognized that a comprehensive food strategy ought to incorporate short-term elements as well. These short-term policies can be broadly classified into two groups—those in the nature of 'palliatives' and those meant for 'crisis management'. The two are often merged under the common rubric of short-term 'food security'; but they perform two separate functions and it seems analytically more helpful to recognize the distinction. Since hunger is going to persist for some time yet no matter what long-term measures are adopted, 'palliatives' are required to redress the more extreme cases of misery. Policies of 'crisis management' on the other hand are meant to prevent calamitous failures of entitlement and to minimize the effect of such failures, if they occur. Although conceptually distinct, the two objectives can often be pursued through the same set of policies. This is indeed the case in Bangladesh: The Public Foodgrain Distribution System (PFDS) is meant to provide both the palliatives and the instruments of crisis management. We shall have a brief look at it before turning to the long-term issues.

Foodgrain distributed through PFDS has expanded over time both in absolute terms and in relation to total availability.[32] The offtake–availability ratio has risen from an average of 8 per cent in the 1960s to about 14 per cent in the decade and a half since Liberation. There has also occurred a significant shift in the relative shares of different channels of distribution. Modified rationing (MR), which distributes subsidized foodgrain to the rural poor, used to account for about 55 per cent of total offtake in the 1960s. In the early years of the 1970s, its share came down to 30–40 per cent, dropping further to only 18 per cent in the 1980s. Statutory urban rationing (SR), which supplies subsidized foodgrain to the residents of certain important urban areas, has also faced a relative decline, but not to the same extent as MR. Its share remained at around 23 per cent throughout the 1960s and 1970s, but fell rather sharply to 15 per cent in the 1980s. The channels which have gained in relative share are mainly three: (1) other priorities (OP), which supplies subsidized foodgrain to certain priority groups (mainly urban), (2) food-for-work programme (FFW), which serves the rural labourers by paying them in kind in return for work, and (3) open market sales (OMS) plus marketing operations (MO), both of which are designed to augment market supply for the general benefit of all consumers rather than for any particular target group.

[32] For a recent in-depth study of the operation and effectiveness of PFDS, see MOF (1986). The following statistics are derived from this source.

Among all the shifts that have taken place, the most remarkable one is the dramatic decline in the share of MR from the 1960s to the 1980s. It is also apparently the most perverse one, when viewed in the light of our earlier analysis of widening rural hunger. Recent policy disposition appears to be one of going further ahead in the direction of phasing out MR, and replacing it by market augmentation in the rural area. It is not at all obvious, however, how the strategy of leaving the poor entirely at the mercy of the market is going to improve their food security. To the extent that market augmentation helps to stabilize prices, the cause of food security will indeed be served to some extent. But it is not clear that the resulting 'price security' will be more effective than the assured 'quantity security' for those living at the edge of subsistence.

When the foodgrain distributed through the food-for-work programme is added to MR, the share of rural poor does not appear quite as bad, but it is still less than used to be the case in the 1960s. The expansion of the FFW programme is on the whole a welcome phenomenon, as recent studies of its impact appear to indicate.[33] But equally unwelcome is the contraction of modified rationing. A recent survey of MR beneficiaries has shown that about 95 per cent of them actually belong to the target group (MOF 1986). Many of the eligible households are of course left out and even those who receive the ration only gain a small increase in real income (2 per cent); but that is a consequence of the small size of the whole operation. It has at least the potential to make a bigger contribution to the real income of rural poor if the scale of operation is expanded.[34]

There are however serious problems with urban statutory rationing (SR) as it is currently practised. It has been found that the average income of SR beneficiaries is considerably higher than that of an average urban household, and per capita calorie intake comfortably above the national average (MOF 1986). Thus, unlike in the case of modified rationing, the contraction of statutory rationing did not imply a great loss for the urban poor, since they did not receive much benefit from it anyway. This does not however mean that urban rationing should therefore be abandoned, though that again is the current trend of policy. But it does mean that a method has to be found for reaching the urban poor.

On the whole, then, with the exception of its FFW component, PFDS in its

---

[33] The short-run impacts of the FFW programme are analysed in Osmani and Chowdhury (1983). The long-term effects are studied in BIDS/IFPRI (1985).

[34] In so far as both MR and FFW are 'targeted' to the rural poor, there may be an inclination to treat them as substitutes and to take a lenient view of the contraction of MR in view of the fact that FFW has expanded so rapidly. But it will be wrong to take such a view in our judgement. The two should really be treated as complements rather than substitutes because, first, MR can reach those who are not capable of the physical rigour demanded by FFW, and, secondly, MR can operate throughout the year while FFW is necessarily constrained to the short intersection between the dry season and the lean period of agricultural operations. However, in so far as FFW has the additional benefit of creating potentially useful rural intrastructure, there is indeed a case for giving it preference when seasonality permits.

present shape does not appear to be particularly effective as a short-term palliative for persistent hunger. However, as we have noted earlier in the context of the events of 1979 and 1984, it has been a good deal more effective as an instrument of crisis management.

7.6. *The long-range strategy*

While the importance of a properly targeted public food distribution system can hardly be questioned, especially as a short-term palliative for extreme cases of poverty, its limitations as a strategy for solving the long-term problem of hunger are also pretty obvious. The sheer magnitude of the problem of food deprivation rules out public distribution as an effective long-term strategy. The administrative problem of targeting food distribution to nearly three-quarters of the total population is one of the reasons for doubting its effectiveness, but by no means the most important one. An even bigger problem is the limited amount of food available for distribution. Of course, if the total available food were to be distributed according to one's requirement, the currently available calories might be just enough to satisfy everyone's need.[35] However, one does not have to be a cynic to rule out the feasibility of such an ideal distribution.

Higher levels of production are therefore an obvious necessity; but not so much because it will provide a larger base for public distribution, as because the dynamics of production will help improve the entitlement of all the rural groups through the structural processes described earlier. However, a couple of qualifications to this statement should be noted before proceeding further.

First, it is easy to show that, even with a considerable increase in the rate of food production, the incomes of the poor may not rise enough to eliminate hunger. Khan (1985) has recently given a quantitative demonstration of this argument through an empirical model linking production with income distribution. It is indeed clear that, given the existing endowment distribution and continued demographic pressure, no 'feasible' rates of food production can eliminate hunger in the near future. This naturally turns one's attention to the need for changing the 'endowment distribution' as well as for containing the rate of population growth. But this does not obviate the need for stepping up the rate of food production. A higher rate of growth may not be *sufficient* to *eliminate* hunger, but will at least be *necessary* to *reduce* it.[36]

[35] Note that per capita calorie intake was estimated to be 1,943 calories per day in 1981/2 (INFS 1981/2) while per capita requirement according to one estimate is 2,020 calories (World Bank 1985a). Given the margin of error that is likely to be involved in both these estimates, it is perhaps fair to conclude that requirement and availability match each other reasonably well at the aggregate level.

[36] It follows from this observation that any comprehensive discussion of the strategies for eliminating hunger should also involve discussion of the political strategy for bringing about changes in 'endowment distributions'. Lack of competence on the part of the author is the principal reason for not venturing into this field.

But will it be *sufficient* to *reduce* hunger? This is where the second set of qualifications come in. We have pointed out earlier that growth can certainly occur in a manner which will not only fail to reduce hunger, but may even accentuate it. If, for instance, all the growth is concentrated on the lands of large farmers who decide to switch over to mechanized cultivation, then both small peasants and wage labourers may experience increasing hunger. Mechanization however is very unlikely to be adopted extensively in Bangladesh agriculture, given the cheap labour and fragmented holdings prevailing there. But the possibility of large-farmer bias in the pattern of growth cannot be ruled out. We have seen earlier that the past history of technological transformation in Bangladesh agriculture does not indicate any such bias. But whether the past pattern will continue into the future is very largely a function of present policy. It is in this light that we intend to review the present orientation of long-range food strategy in Bangladesh.

In the past, the diffusion of modern technology has been brought about largely through heavy subsidization of two crucial inputs, fertilizer and irrigation, combined with extensive government control in the distribution of these inputs. In contrast, price support for farm output has played a negligible role. A foodgrain procurement system has of course been in operation for a long time, but it was geared essentially to meeting the needs of a subsidized public foodgrain distribution system (PFDS). Accordingly, the objective was to procure a target quantity of foodgrain at a price which would be low enough to avoid an excessive fiscal burden on account of PFDS. Whether that price would provide an incentive to the producers to expand production was not a matter of explicit concern. One other element of policy was government ownership of the major irrigation assets such as large-scale river-control projects as well as power pumps and deep tubewells. Only the small irrigation equipment such as shallow tubewells and hand tubewells was sold to the private sector. The publicly owned irrigation equipment used to be rented out to groups of farmers at a subsidized fee.

All these policies have recently undergone an almost complete reversal, beginning in the late 1970s and gaining momentum in the 1980s. The emerging policy regime can be characterized by the following features: (1) withdrawal of input subsidies, (2) instituting a compensating price support programme, (3) a relatively free market for determining both input price and consumer price of foodgrain, (4) distribution of fertilizer through private traders, and (5) private ownership of irrigation equipment (all kinds of tubewells and power pumps), with large-scale irrigation projects being financed and executed by the public sector.

How is this strategy going to affect the growth and pattern of foodgrain production and, through it, the evolution of food entitlement? Let us begin by looking at the implications of the policy of withdrawing input subsidy.

We have argued elsewhere that the main rationale for providing input subsidy in Bangladesh agriculture lies in the fact that it helps to ease the credit constraint faced by the small farmers (Osmani and Quasem 1985). The adoption of HYV technology raises the working capital requirements for cultivation as the farmers have to pay for fertilizers and irrigation charges before they reap the harvest. This cost however cannot usually be covered through institutional credit to which they have very little access (Table 9.5). It has been estimated for instance that no more than 10 per cent of the fertilizer cost of small farmers is financed out of institutional credit (Hossain 1985c).

Under the circumstances, the small farmers are left with the option of either borrowing from the informal credit market or drawing upon their own meagre resources. In the first case, they are usually forced to pay an exorbitant rate of interest and in the second they apply high subjective rates of discount on future income in view of their subsistence level of present consumption. In either case, both equity and efficiency are adversely affected. An interesting piece of evidence in this regard is provided by a recent survey (Hossain 1985b). It shows that at the current level of fertilizer application, the marginal value product (MVP) of fertilizer is considerably higher than its price, in fact much higher than can be accounted for as the interest cost at the official rate of interest. There are several alternative ways in which such a differential could conceivably arise.[37] In the first place, there could have been a binding constraint of fertilizer supply which would force the farmers off their demand curve. But it has been shown by Quasem (1985) through an analysis of the stocks and sales of the fertilizer-distributing agency (BADC) that supply of fertilizer was not generally short of demand (barring some occasional localized shortages) in the recent years, including the period to which the above survey results relate. Secondly, the observed divergence could be a consequence of farmers' risk aversion in a situation of uncertainty. In fact, the uncertainty involved in the use of an unfamiliar input, and the resulting divergence between its MVP and price, has been the traditional argument for subsidizing an input in the early stage of adoption. The proponents of 'subsidy withdrawal' however argue that after two decades of experience with modern technology, the farmers are now well aware of its benefits and do not need subsidy any more.[38] If this argument is accepted, then the only other plausible explanation of the observed divergence would be in credit constraint.[39] Under the usual maximizing assumptions, the divergence would then imply either that the effective cost of fertilizer is very high (because the farmers have to borrow from the informal credit market) or that the effective MVP is low (because the small farmers draw upon

[37] Note that price here refers to the actual market price paid by the farmers and not the official subsidized price. The divergence is therefore a real one and not a consequence of using the wrong prices.

[38] Arguments of this kind frequently appear in various World Bank documents urging the government of Bangladesh to withdraw input subsidy. For a comprehensive documentation of the World Bank view and its arguments, see Osmani and Quasem (1985).

[39] The other possibility, namely the uncertainty due to the vagaries of nature, is not particularly relevant in the case of HYVs which are grown mostly under controlled irrigated condition.

their own resources and hence apply a high subjective rate of discount). It will then be necessary on the ground of economic efficiency to remove the credit constraint so that the price of input can be equated with its nominal MVP. One way of doing it is to provide input subsidy which will ease the credit constraint by the simple expedient of reducing the need for credit.[40]

However, it may be argued that the best answer to the credit problem is to solve it directly by providing more credit to the small farmer instead of going through the roundabout way of subsidizing inputs. That is indeed true, in principle; but in reality credit programmes for small farmers have proved notoriously unsuccessful almost everywhere in the developing world. Until an institutional mechanism can be found for successful targeting of credit to the small farmers, input subsidy is necessary to deal with the credit constraint, albeit as a second-best strategy.[41]

We have already noted that the high levels of input subsidy offered at the early stage of 'Green Revolution' in Bangladesh probably explain why the small farmers could participate at least proportionately in the adoption of new technology. But the subsidies have been reduced at a rapid rate in recent years.[42] It is sometimes argued that the withdrawal of subsidy would not affect the farmers since they, especially the small farmers, do not receive the benefit of subsidy anyway. The basis of the argument is that the farmers usually buy their fertilizer not directly from the official distributing agency but from private dealers who lift fertilizer at the subsidized price and allegedly sell to the farmers at a higher price as dictated by supply and demand.[43] But this is really

[40] If uncertainty due to the use of an unfamiliar input is thought to persist and contribute to the divergence between price and MVP, then of course the case for subsidy is further strengthened.

[41] It may be mentioned in this context that the Grameen Bank experiment (see n. 21 above) seems to have found an effective institutional method of reaching the poor in the non-farm sector. One might naturally ask why this method cannot be extended to the farm sector as well. The Grameen Bank has already made a beginning in this direction, but it is still too early to assess the results. There would however appear to be some intrinsic problems of agricultural credit which the Grameen Bank approach might come up against. It is well known that one of the keys to the success of the Grameen Bank is the system of weekly repayment of loans. The poor people, who are under the constant pressure of immediate consumption, find it so much more convenient to repay their loans if they are to repay in small instalments over an extended period of time. This process is facilitated if they also have a continuous flow of income. Repayments can then be made regularly out of current income, obviating the need for first accumulating and then drawing down a savings balance. Most of the activities in the non-farm sector are in fact of this 'point-input continuous-output' type. In contrast, agricultural operations are more akin to 'point-input point-output' type. Output is harvested at a point in time; and the small farmers are hardly capable of converting a 'point output' into a 'continuous income' by phasing out the sale of crops over an extended period. The discipline of weekly repayment in this case is likely to come up against a very strong time preference for current consumption.

[42] For instance, urea, the most widely used fertilizer in Bangladesh agriculture, used to enjoy a subsidy of 58% in the late 1960s; and even as late as 1975/6, the rate was 52%, but it fell to a mere 4% in 1982/3.

[43] Field information on actual prices paid by the farmers reveals that they do generally pay a premium over the official price, but a fairly small one. It is also found that the small farmers sometimes pay more than the large farmers, but again the difference is not a striking one. For details of the evidence, see Osmani and Quasem (1985).

a non-argument; it represents a confusion over the relevant concept of subsidy. The market price, as determined by supply and demand, may of course be regarded as one notion of unsubsidized price, and by that criterion the farmers may not be receiving any subsidy. But when the government of Bangladesh and its advisers propose to withdraw subsidy, they take the cost of procurement as the unsubsidized price; and it turns out that actual market prices have always remained far below the cost of procurement (Osmani and Quasem 1985).

In other words, the scarcity premium reaped by the dealers was lower than the rate of subsidy and to that extent the farmers have indeed shared the benefit of subsidy. One implication of this fact is that if the subsidy is removed and the official price is set at the cost of procurement, the resulting price increase will be too high to be absorbed into the scarcity margin. Consequently, the market price will have to rise and, as indicated by some recent estimates of elasticity,[44] this will have a substantial dampening effect on the demand for fertilizer.

Of course, the net effect will depend also on what has been happening to the other determinants of fertilizer demand, one of them being the price of food crop. As it happens, however, the price of crop has failed completely to keep pace with the rising price of fertilizer. As a result, the fertilizer–paddy price ratio has trebled from 0.74 in 1971/2 to 2.03 in 1983/4. The growth-retarding effect of this price disincentive has recently been demonstrated by Osmani and Quasem (1985). The subsidies have been reduced most drastically in the second half of the post-Liberation period and it is in this half that the intensity of fertilizer application on individual crop varieties has come to a standstill after exhibiting a rapid growth in the preceding years. It is also in this subperiod that yield improvement in individual crop varieties has made a negative contribution to the overall growth of foodgrain production, while it had made the biggest contribution to growth in the earlier period.

Growth of course has still occurred and the average application of fertilizer per unit of land has still risen as irrigation facilities have made it possible to shift from local to improved varieties of seeds which are more intensive in the use of fertilizer and have a higher level of yield.

But even this process is now being threatened by the policy of privatization and subsidy reduction that is being followed in the irrigation sector. There is ample evidence that privatization of irrigation equipment has added to the cost of irrigation on top of the effect of subsidy reduction.[45] Private owners of irrigation equipment charge a higher rate to its users than that generally paid by the groups renting publicly owned equipment and the area irrigated per machine is correspondingly lower for the privately owned ones. At the same time, the sale of irrigation equipment is also facing increasing difficulty. After

[44] These estimates seem to lie between −0.7 and −0.8. For details of estimation procedures, see Hossain (1985b) and Osmani and Quasem (1985).

[45] For substantiation of the empirical statements made in this paragraph, see Osmani and Quasem (1985).

the initial burst of privatization, the market for new equipment seems to have shrunk considerably. This is quite understandable when one realizes that after the initial purchase by larger farmers (of whom there are not very many), the smaller ones are finding it harder to pay the price, especially as the rate of subsidy is being scaled down.

Clearly, all these developments have a potentially restrictive effect on both overall production and the small farmers' participation in it. However, one may recall that the current policy package does at least in principle provide an antidote to all this in the form of a compensating price support programme. The foodgrain procurement system is being increasingly reorganized as a price support programme, as the procurement price is now being consciously set at a level that is expected to cover the cost of production and also leave a margin of profit. If effective, this should in principle be able to neutralize the accentuation of credit constraint caused by the happenings on the input side. This it will achieve by ensuring a higher price for the marketed surplus and thus offsetting the effect of a high rate of interest or subjective discount.

But there are serious limitations to this policy: it is simply irrelevant for subsistence farmers who do not have any marketable surplus and positively harmful to the deficit farmers who are net buyers in the market. According to some calculations, no more than 30 per cent of the farmers will derive any substantial benefits from an output price support programme (Ahmed 1981). The rest will not only fail to derive any benefit, they will in fact be worse off as the credit constraint gets tightened by the policies on the input side such as withdrawal of subsidy and privatization of irrigation equipment. Further diffusion of HYV technology will then be concentrated on the lands of the rich peasants, while the poor peasants become increasingly marginalized and eventually alienated from land. Man-made policies will thus combine with underlying structural forces to hasten the proletarianization of an already marginalized peasantry.

The stage is thus being set for a neatly polarized agrarian structure by concentrating incentive in the sphere of large farmers and driving the small peasants out of the production nexus. In the mean time, privatization of fertilizer trade and creation of irrigation entrepreneurs will help in the process of primitive capital accumulation. Thus the various components of the prevailing long-range food strategy appear to derive their unifying logic from an underlying development strategy that aims at the capitalist transformation of Bangladesh agriculture.

All the issues that are raised by the prospect of such a transformation cannot obviously be discussed within the confines of this chapter. But at least its implications for the evolution of food entitlement ought to be mentioned.

It is immediately obvious that the small peasants, marginalized and eventually driven out of land, will suffer a decline in food entitlement unless alternative employment opportunities are opened up. But the prospects of such alternative opportunities are not very bright either. It has been estimated that during the rest of the century the rural labour force will grow at the rate of around 3 per cent a year. Even with a 3.7 per cent growth in production, a rate that has not on average been achieved in recent years, agriculture can absorb no more than a quarter of the additional labour force (World Bank 1983). There is therefore already a strong tendency to aggravate the excess supply of agricultural labour. If the proletarianization of the peasantry adds to this natural increase in labour supply, there can only be an all-round reduction in wage and employment per person, with its obvious implications for food entitlement.

Nor does non-farm employment opportunity hold out any better hope. We have noted earlier that the non-farm sector is already severely stretched to provide residual employment for those being thrown out of the agricultural sector. An exodus into this sector will only serve to bring down further the entitlement of the poor engaged in this sector. Such an all-round impoverishment and the resulting shrinkage of effective demand may even constrain the process of capitalist growth itself, unless of course the 'capitalist dynamism' is sustained by exporting food while people within the country go hungry.

7.7. *Summary and concluding remarks*

Our aim in this chapter was to seek illumination on three questions pertaining to the food problems of Bangladesh: first, what are the processes perpetuating the food deprivation of the great majority of the masses; secondly, has Bangladesh achieved over time a greater degree of immunity from the sudden failures of food entitlement leading to famines; and finally, what hopes do the current food policies hold out for the elimination of endemic hunger?

On the first question, we started with the premise that, in a food-dominated production structure, as happens to obtain in rural Bangladesh, the long-term food entitlement of all sections of people depends crucially on the pace and pattern of food production. Yet one finds that, despite positive growth in per capita food production, the food entitlement of a great majority shows no visible signs of improvement during the post-Liberation period. Various alternative hypotheses were considered to explain this phenomenon. In particular, we tried to investigate whether the very pattern of growth was immiserizing, or whether the rate of growth was inadequate to offset the immiserizing force of demographic pressure operating within a system of private property ownership. The available empirical evidence seems to support the latter hypothesis. It is the slow rate of growth rather than a 'distorted' pattern of growth in food production that has been historically responsible for persistent contraction in the food entitlement of the masses. Also, it was argued that the proximate cause of slow growth was sluggish investment in agriculture and the resulting failure to convert a huge pool of surplus manpower into productive farmland capital. No attempt was made however to go beyond the proximate cause and to explore how the rate of investment has in fact been constrained by various factors such as the prevailing social structure, incentive systems, and the political economy of public sector decision making. Consideration of these issues, vital as they are, would have broadened the scope far beyond the limitations of a single chapter.

On the issue of vulnerability to famines, it was noted that, since the famine of 1974, the country has successfully avoided similar disasters despite the recurrence of potential threats, especially in 1979 and 1984. We have argued however that this success does not unfortunately indicate any inherent improvement in the country's immunity from famines. The proximate reason why famine did not occur in 1979 and 1984 was that anticipated loss of food crops could not generate a speculative price spiral, as it did in 1974. Strong government intervention through the public foodgrain distribution system served to dampen the speculative hoarding of foodgrain, whereas in the famine year of 1974 speculation was in fact fuelled by a thoroughly inadequate and unreliable public intervention. But it is important to note that intervention was made possible in 1979 and 1984 only by the existence of two fortuitous circumstances. One was a congenial aid atmosphere and the other was an unexpectedly large foreign exchange reserve which together made it possible to import a record amount of foodgrain to feed the public distribution system. Since neither of these factors can be relied upon to prevail every time a crisis occurs, there is no ground for inferring from the recent success stories that the economy has acquired any genuine resilience against the threats of famine.

The final issue we addressed was the implication of prevailing food policies for the evolution of food entitlement in the future. The focus was on the likely impact of these policies on the pace and pattern of growth in food production. It was of course recognized that, in the absence of fundamental changes in endowment distribution, no feasible rate or pattern of growth can possibly eliminate the scourge of hunger in the face of an increasingly adverse land–man ratio. Accordingly, the focus was on the role of food policies in containing rather than eliminating long-term hunger. Our analysis shows that even the limited goal of containing long-term hunger is unlikely to be accomplished by the pursuit of food policies currently being implemented. The various components of the existing food strategy mutually reinforce each other to concentrate incentives and opportunities among the relatively well-off farmers. This is likely to alter the historical pattern of a fairly equitable diffusion of modern technology, making it increasingly difficult for the small farmers to benefit from further gains in productivity. In the face of unabated demographic pressure, the failure to improve the productivity of land will hasten the impoverishment of small farmers and quicken the pace of landlessness. As they swell the ranks of agricultural labour and non-farm workers, adding to the natural increase of labour supply in these sectors, there is likely to occur an all-round contraction in the entitlement of the rural poor.

If the food policies are to contain rather than accentuate the process of entitlement contraction, a minimal requirement is to ensure an equitable diffusion of modern technology so that the proletarianization of the peasantry can at least be retarded. A chief obstacle to be overcome in this regard is the credit constraint faced by the small farmers. Input subsidies and public provision of capital assets should form essential ingredients of any food strategy aimed at overcoming this constraint.[46]

[46] For a fuller account of the author's views on the appropriate strategies for both farm and non-farm sectors in rural Bangladesh, see Osmani (1985).

References

ABDULLAH, A. A. (1985), 'Three Notes on Fertilizer Subsidy Removal in Bangladesh' (revised), mimeo (Dhaka: Bangladesh Institute of Development Studies).

AHMAD, Q. K. (1985), 'Food Shortages and Food Entitlements in Bangladesh: An Indepth Enquiry in Respect of Selected Years', mimeo (Rome: FAO).

——and HOSSAIN, M. (1985), 'An Evaluation of Selected Policies and Programmes for the Alleviation of Rural Poverty in Bangladesh', in Islam, R. (ed.), *Strategies for Alleviating Poverty in Rural Asia* (Dhaka: Bangladesh Institute of Development Studies; Bangkok: ILO/ARTEP).

AHMED, R. (1981), 'Agricultural Price Policies under Complex Socioeconomic and Natural Constraints: The Case of Bangladesh', Research Report 27 (Washington, DC: IFPRI).

ALAMGIR, M. (1980), *Famine in South Asia: Political Economy of Mass Starvation in Bangladesh* (Cambridge, Mass.: Oelgeschlager, Gunn & Hain).

BEATON, C. H. (1983), 'Energy in Human Nutrition', *Nutrition Today*, 18.

BIDS (1981), 'Rural Industries Study Project: Final Report', mimeo (Dhaka: Bangladesh Institute of Development Studies).

——and IFPRI (1985), *Development impact of the Food-for-Work Program in Bangladesh: Summary* (Dhaka: Bangladesh Institute of Development Studies; Washington, DC: IFPRI).

CHEN, L. C., HUQ, E., and D'SOUZA, S. (1981), 'Sex Bias in the Family Allocation of Food and Health Care in Rural Bangladesh', *Population and Development Review*, 7.

CLAY, E. J., and KHAN, M. S. (1977), 'Agricultural Employment and Unemployment in Bangladesh: The Next Decade', mimeo (Dhaka: Bangladesh Agricultural Research Council).

CSS (1980), 'Report on Barisal Area III Project: Agrarian Structure and Trends', mimeo (Dhaka: Centre for Social Studies, University of Dhaka).

HOSSAIN, M. (1981), 'Land Tenure and Agricultural Development in Bangladesh', VRF Series No. 85 (Tokyo: Institute of Developing Economies).

——(1984a), 'Employment and Labour in Bangladesh Rural Industries', *Bangladesh Development Studies*, 12.

——(1984b), 'Increasing Food Availability in Bangladesh: Constraints and Possibilities', Technical Paper 'A', Food Strategy Review Exercise, mimeo (Dhaka: Ministry of Agriculture, Government of Bangladesh).

——(1984c), 'Credit for the Rural Poor: The Grameen Bank of Bangladesh', Research Monograph No. 4 (Dhaka: Bangladesh Institute of Development Studies).

——(1984d), 'Productivity and Profitability in Bangladesh Rural Industries', *Bangladesh Development Studies*, 12.

——(1984e), *Employment Generation through Cottage Industries: Potential and Constraints* (Bangkok: ILO/ARTEP).

——(1985a), 'A Note on the Trend of Landlessness in Bangladesh', mimeo (Dhaka: Bangladesh Institute of Development Studies).

——(1985b), 'Fertilizer Consumption, Pricing and Foodgrain Consumption in Bangladesh', in BIDS/IFPRI, *Fertilizer Pricing Policy and Foodgrain Production Strategy in Bangladesh*, vol. ii (Dhaka: BIDS; Washington, DC: IFPRI).

——(1985c), 'Agricultural Development in Bangladesh: A Historical Perspective', paper presented at a joint seminar of Bangladesh Economic Association and the International Food Policy Research Institute held in Dhaka.

——RAHMAN, A., and AKASH, M. M. (1985), 'Agricultural Taxation in Bangladesh: Potential and Policies', Research Report No. 42 (Dhaka: Bangladesh Institute of Development Studies).

INFS (1975/6), *Nutrition Survey of Rural Bangladesh 1975–76* (Dhaka: Institute of Nutrition and Food Science, University of Dhaka).

——(1981/2), *Nutrition Survey of Rural Bangladesh 1981–82*, (Dhaka: Institute of Nutrition and Food Science, University of Dhaka).

KHAN, A. R. (1976), 'Poverty and Inequality in Rural Bangladesh', Working Paper (Geneva: ILO).

KHAN, Q. M. (1985), 'A Model of Endowment-Constrained Demand for Food in an Agricultural Economy with Empirical Applications to Bangladesh', *World Development*, 13.

MATIN, K. M. (1986), 'Bangladesh and the IMF: An Exploratory Study', Research Monograph No. 5 (Dhaka: Bangladesh Institute of Development Studies).

MCHENRY, D. F., and BIRD, K. (1977), 'Food Bungle in Bangladesh', *Foreign Policy*, 27.

MOF (1986), 'The Existing System of Public Foodgrain Distribution in Bangladesh and Proposal for Restructuring', Draft Report, prepared by Beacon Consultants for the Ministry of Food, Government of Bangladesh, mimeo (Dhaka).

MUQTADA, M., and ALAM, M. M. (1983), *Hired Labour and Rural Labour Market in Bangladesh* (Bangkok: ILO/ARTEP).

OSMANI, S. R. (1982), *Economic Inequality and Group Welfare* (Oxford: Oxford University Press).

——(1984), *Food and the Nutrition Problem: Methodology of Global Estimation* (Rome: FAO).

—— (1985), 'Planning for Distributive Justice in Bangladesh', paper presented at the biennial conference of the Bangladesh Economic Association, Dec., Dhaka.

——and CHOWDHURY, O. H. (1983), 'Short Run Impacts of Food for Work Programme in Bangladesh', *Bangladesh Development Studies*, 11.

——and DEB, N. C. (1984), 'Demand for Rural Industry Products in Bangladesh', mimeo (Dhaka: Bangladesh Institute of Development Studies; Bangkok: ILO/ARTEP).

—— and QUASEM, M. A. (1985), 'Pricing and Subsidy Policies for Bangladesh Agriculture', mimeo (Dhaka: Bangladesh Institute of Development Studies).

——and RAHMAN, A. (1984), *A Study on Income Distribution in Bangladesh* (New York: Department of International Economic and Social Affairs of the United Nations Secretariat).

QUASEM, M. A. (1985), 'Supply and Distribution of Fertilizers in Bangladesh', in BIDS/IFPRI, *Fertilizer Pricing Policy and Foodgrain Production Strategy in Bangladesh* (Dhaka: BIDS; Washington, DC: IFPRI).

RAHMAN, A. (1979), 'Agrarian Structure and Capital Formation: A Study of Bangladesh Agriculture', unpublished Ph.D. dissertation, University of Cambridge.

RAHMAN, M. (forthcoming), 'Socio-economic Determinants of Poverty in Rural Bangladesh', ongoing Ph.D. dissertation, Institute of Statistical Research and Training, University of Dhaka.

RAVALLION, M. (1985), 'The Performance of Rice Markets in Bangladesh during the 1974 Famine', *Economic Journal*, 95.

SEN, A. K. (1981), *Poverty and Famines: An Essay on Entitlement and Deprivation* (Oxford: Oxford University Press).

——(1985), *Commodities and Capabilities* (Amsterdam: North-Holland).

SOBHAN, R. (1979), 'Politics of Food and Famine in Bangladesh', *Economic and Political Weekly*, 48.

SRINIVASAN, T. N. (1983), *Malnutrition in Developing Countries: The State of Knowledge of the Extent of its Prevalence, its Causes and its Consequences* (Rome: FAO).

UNICEF/FREPD (1981), *The Situation of Children in Bangladesh* (Dhaka: University of Dhaka).

USDH (1962–6), *Nutrition Survey of East Pakistan* (Washington, DC: Department of Health, Education and Welfare).

World Bank (1983), *Bangladesh: Selected Issues in Rural Employment* (Washington, DC: World Bank).

——(1984), *Bangladesh: Economic Trends and Development Administration*, vol. ii: *Statistical Appendix* (Washington, DC: World Bank).

——(1985a), *Bangladesh: Food and Nutrition Sector Review* (Washington, DC: World Bank).

——(1985b), *Bangladesh: Economic and Social Development Prospects* (Washington, DC: World Bank).

8

The Elimination of Endemic Poverty in South Asia: Some Policy Options

Kaushik Basu

8.1. *Introduction*

In this age of mammoth scientific achievements we have the necessary technology, raw material, and skills to grow all the food we need. We also have a transport system—or at least the capacity to build up the transport system —which will carry the food to everybody. Nevertheless we have failed to do so, and persistent mass poverty is a part of twentieth-century life. That this appears shocking to most of us shows that we have an inherent tendency to underestimate the complexities of social and political engineering. The oft-heard view that removing poverty is not difficult at all and our failure is merely because of vested interests or lack of willingness among powerful people reflects a misunderstanding of the word 'difficult'. Given that vested interests are a part of the world, as also are powerful and uncaring people, it is indeed a difficult task. In designing policies, it is important to recognize this.

This work is a contribution to the problem of formulating policies to combat persistent poverty, while recognizing that there are interests and incentive structures which need to be overcome or tiptoed past. The context of almost all the analysis will be South Asia, in particular, Bangladesh, India, and Sri Lanka.

The study begins by considering the issue of basic needs provision.[1] In order to improve the standard of living of the masses, do we have to wait for the

I am grateful to T. C. A. Anant, Elias Dinopoulos, Jean Drèze, Keith Griffin, Subbiah Kannappan, Sunil Sengupta, and Susan Watkins for discussions. I thank Surjit Bhalla for the unpublished papers and monographs on Sri Lanka he has sent me, though I am sure he will disapprove of the use to which these have been put. This work was done at the Institute for Advanced Study, Princeton. It would have been difficult to complete it without the excellent support provided by the Institute.

[1] The definition of 'basic needs' can be controversial. As Streeten (1984: 973–4) notes, 'The ILO considers employment a basic need; Sidney Webb included leisure. High on the list, as China recognized in the six guarantees, is a decent funeral . . .' In common parlance basic needs or standard of living is taken to mean the availability of basic economic necessities (food, shelter, clothing, etc.) and minimum standards of health and medical facilities (captured by demographic data on nutrition, life expectancy, etc.). I take advantage of these conventions and escape having to provide exact measures and definitions. It is arguable that 'basic needs' should also include indices of political and social ethos. However, the absence of commonly accepted statistics on these makes them too difficult for use in any meaningful discussion. For those who are overly enthusiastic about introducing indices of political and social climate to evaluate 'basic needs' policies, a reading of how such indices are computed could be sobering: see Taylor and Hudson (1972).

benefits of growth to trickle down or could we adopt 'direct action'? This is the subject matter of Section 8.2.

Section 8.3 is a detailed consideration of one aspect of basic needs: the removal of poverty and hunger. South Asia has experimented with myriad schemes for supporting the poorest sections and providing employment to the rural landless labourers, for example, the food-for-work programme and the Employment Guarantee Scheme. These are surveyed briefly and suggestions are made for making them more effective.

Even if we accept the desirability of direct action and also know what programmes and schemes to adopt, the actual implementation of such a policy may be hindered because of political constraints. The subject of political constraints is a difficult one and Section 8.4 makes a few preliminary comments on it.

8.2. On direct action and 'trickle-down'

It is an old debate as to whether, in a nation's fight against poverty and deprivation, the aim should be to undertake direct action against these or to strengthen the forces of growth and let the poor benefit from the trickle-down effect. Not only does this debate have important policy-consequences for South Asia, but the varied experience of regions in South Asia provides useful evidence for designing effective policy. From our point of view the most remarkable evidence comes from Sri Lanka and the State of Kerala in India. In terms of economic performance, especially growth rates and per capita incomes, these are backward regions; but their achievements in terms of basic needs and standards of living, captured mainly by health and social statistics, are outstanding.[2] Not surprisingly, the role of direct action in these areas has been extensively written about and debated.[3]

I shall begin by commenting on the Sri Lanka debate, comments on Kerala being reserved for later. The Sri Lankan 'paradox' is well known. In terms of the economic criterion that receives most attention, to wit, the per capita real income, Sri Lanka is a very poor country. But its social statistics—variables which indicate the standard of living or quality of life—are very close to those of advanced industrialized countries.[4] As far as per capita income goes, Sri Lanka ranked exactly on par with only one other country in 1983: Sierra Leone. Both these countries had a GNP per capita of $330 in that year.

---

[2] There are other such examples outside South Asia. These include Costa Rica, Cuba, and China.

[3] See Centre for Development Studies (1975), Fields (1980), Isenman (1980), Richards and Gooneratne (1980), Sen (1981a, 1985), Nag (1983), Bhalla and Glewwe (1986), Morrison and Waxler (1986).

[4] All the data cited in this and the next two paragraphs, as well as some additional ones, are presented in Table 8.1. All these statistics, except where specified to the contrary, refer to 1983.

Table 8.1 Inter-country social statistics, *c.*1983

	GNP per capita, 1983 ($US)	Life expectancy at birth, 1983 (years)	Infant mortality rate, 1983 (per 1,000 live births)	Number enrolled in secondary school as % of age group, 1982
Mexico	2,240	66	52	54
Korea, Rep. of	2,010	67	29	89
Pakistan	390	50	119	14
Sierra Leone	330	38	198	12
Sri Lanka	330	69	37	54
China	300	67	38	35
India	260	55	93	30
Bangladesh	130	50	132	15

Source: World Bank (1985).

However, in Sri Lanka life expectancy at birth was 69 years, whereas in Sierra Leone it was 38.

Turning to the geographic area being studied in this paper, which also happens to be culturally comparable to Sri Lanka, we find a similar contrast. In India and Bangladesh, life expectancy in 1983 was 55 and 50 years respectively. In Pakistan, where per capita income at $390 is higher than that of Sri Lanka, life expectancy was only 50. Infant mortality in Sri Lanka was 37 (per 1,000 live births), whereas in India it was 93 and in Bangladesh 132. In terms of the percentage of children of the relevant age group attending secondary school,[5] Sri Lanka with a score of 54 is ahead of India (30), Bangladesh (15), and even China (35). In fact, the only country with a comparable per capita income and with similar standard-of-living indicators is China.

It is possible to find countries with six or seven times Sri Lanka's income with standards of living not markedly different from it. Examples include South Korea, with a per capita GNP of $2,010, and Mexico with $2,240. In all the three standard-of-living indicators discussed so far,[6] Mexico does equally

---

[5] The reason I have chosen secondary school registration data is because this indicates completion of at least the primary level of education. Primary school registration on the other hand may not be sufficiently informative because of high drop-out rates. For example, in UP initial school enrolment in 1965–6 was much higher than in Kerala whereas towards the end of primary school the situation was completely reversed (Centre for Development Studies, 1975: 122).

[6] One variable which is often taken to indicate living standards and is omitted here is fertility. The usual presumption is that in a poor country a drop in fertility rates reflects improved living standards. A careful scrutiny of Kerala's demographic data, however, seems to jeopardize this presumption. It has been shown (A. M. Basu 1986) that the sharper drop in fertility rates in Kerala has occurred among the landless labourers, suggesting that poverty is sometimes as likely to induce fertility declines as are improved living standards.

well or marginally worse than Sri Lanka. In short, a comparison across countries shows Sri Lanka as an 'outlier': In terms of most social and health indicators, Sri Lanka's actual figures are substantially superior to what we would 'predict' on the basis of its per capita income.[7] For these reasons Sri Lanka is often held up as exemplary for other poor countries and also as proof of the fact that 'public action' can lead to the provision of basic needs and, therefore, to an improvement in the quality of life (see e.g. Jayawardena 1974; Fields 1980; Isenman 1980; Sen 1981a; Caldwell 1986).

This very broad thesis has recently been subjected to a detailed econometric scrutiny and has been the source of much controversy and debate (Bhalla 1988a, 1988b; Bhalla and Glewwe 1986; Sen 1988). Bhalla and Glewwe argued that the existing studies, in particular Fields (1980), Isenman (1980), and Sen (1981a), were flawed because they were based on a comparison across countries at a point of time. This, they showed, led to the 'initial conditions' getting omitted. So they set out to examine Sri Lanka's performance over the period 1960 to 1977. As I have already argued and is clear from Table 8.1, if we look at Sri Lanka's ratio of social indicators to per capita income, it is markedly better than that of almost all other countries. Now in order to net out the effect of 'initial conditions' what needs to be done is this: construct a table similar to my Table 8.1, but replace column 1, which shows per capita income at a point of time, with a column showing changes in per capita income between 1960 and 1978; and similarly replace the other columns with 'changes' in variables from the existing 'values at a point of time'. Does Sri Lanka continue to stand out as a country which has done exceedingly well in improving living standards compared to other countries whose change in per capita incomes is similar to that of Sri Lanka? This is the question that Bhalla (1988a, 1988b) and Bhalla and Glewwe (1986) examine meticulously, and they come out with a clear answer: No. On this they are completely convincing; where they err is in drawing inferences from their finding.

For instance, they treat their finding as evidence that a larger social expenditure need not lead to higher living standards. But to maintain this on the basis of a regression analysis of the kind conducted by Bhalla and Glewwe, it is clearly necessary to have comparative data on *changes* in social welfare expenditure in all the countries appearing in the analysis.[8] Without this we cannot jump to any conclusion about the impact of social welfare expenditure based on the finding that in terms of 'changes' between 1960 and 1978 Sri Lanka is not an outlier. Consequently, the basis of their claim gives way when,

---

[7] Though I used only a few countries and a few variables to demonstrate this, there are more systematic studies which have established it (Isenman 1980; Sen 1981a).

[8] In the absence of this a second-best option is to confine the study to the early 1960s (instead of 1960–78) because there is some evidence that welfare expenditure was increasing in Sri Lanka in the late 1950s. We could therefore argue that the economy in the early 1960s reflected this increase (which we may suppose was sharper in Sri Lanka than in other countries).

after conducting their econometric exercises, Bhalla and Glewwe announce that they do not have these crucial data on welfare expenditures.

As a matter of fact, the proposition that large social expenditures do not necessarily lead to better standards of living is obvious enough not to require any formal econometric study. This is because money is easy to fritter away. One region with a small expenditure can achieve what another region with a large expenditure fails to because of differences in efficiency or methods of disbursement. Thus in Kerala and West Bengal the volume of medical facilities available is comparable, but utilization is much higher in Kerala (Nag 1983); not surprisingly Kerala performs much better than West Bengal in terms of health statistics. So it is easy to concede that while a certain volume of social expenditure is necessary to improve living standards, it is not a sufficient condition.

The other important question that emerges from this debate is: can basic needs be provided directly or do we have to wait for the trickle-down effects of growth? Bhalla and Glewwe treat their findings as implying that reliance on growth rather than direct action is essential. But to answer the above question we have simply to seek examples where income is low but living standards are high, i.e. do the kind of exercise that Isenman (1980) and Sen (1981a) have done. This, as we have just shown, is the case with Sri Lanka, and, as I show below, is also partly the case with Kerala. Hence, whatever it is that Sri Lanka did has led to its achieving very high levels of provision of basic needs. Clearly this is all we need to show that we do not *have to* rely on growth to mitigate poverty and provide basic needs. To assert that something works, but direct action does not, implies a semantic misunderstanding of the term 'direct action'.

It is possible to argue that the cause of the misunderstanding is that many analysts have labelled whatever the Sri Lanka Freedom Party (the one associated with the Bandarnaikes) did as 'direct action' and have taken the failure of those policies to mean a failure of direct action. I will argue later that despite the equity orientation of the Bandarnaike government its policies were often inappropriate.

Given that direct action is possible, the next question is: what is the appropriate direct action for South Asian countries? Before delving into this general subject, let us take a look at the causes of Sri Lanka's—and later I comment on Kerala—exceptional performance. The main contribution of Bhalla's work is to shift our attention to the period before the 1970s. As it turns out, there is clear evidence of governmental action. In particular, three policies which played important roles are: provision of health facilities, free and compulsory education, and free or subsidized food rations.

Sri Lanka's record in terms of health facilities is good. Richards and Gooneratne (1980) have documented some of these and I note here only a few salient features. It is well known that Sri Lanka's excellent mortality figures owe a lot to the malaria eradication programme of 1946. In one year, between

1946 and 1947, the death rate fell from 20 to 14. As one would expect, there were sharp improvements in infant mortality and life expectancy around the same time. Clearly a malaria eradication programme is a direct welfare activity of the government. More generally, the ratio of doctors and nurses to the total population in Sri Lanka has been high relative to the South Asian experience. In the early 1970s the nurse–population ratio was four times that of India. From the mid-1950s to the early 1970s real expenditure on health services rose steadily.[9]

Despite all this, for a health programme to succeed, it is essential that the people accept what the government offers. It is not sufficient to have a large family planning programme if people are not willing to listen, or a large vaccination centre if people view it as a torture cell. So for a health programme to succeed it is important that people have some education. Isenman's regression analysis confirms the crucial role of literacy in improving life expectancy and infant mortality.[10] Demographers have often stressed the positive relation between literacy among women and infant mortality. Some data suggesting this relation can be found in the Survey on Infant and Child Mortality 1979, conducted by the Office of the Registrar-General in India. This is presented in Table 8.2. The table suggests not only a relation between health and the 0–1 concept of literacy but a monotonic relation, with increasing education resulting in lower mortality.

Table 8.2 Mortality and the education of women in India, 1978

Education of mother	Infant mortality	
	Rural	Urban
Illiterate	145	88
Literate but below primary	101	57
Primary and above	71	47

Source: Office of the Registrar-General of India (1981*a*).

Given that Sri Lanka has had a long history of free education—dating back to its pre-independence period—it is not surprising that its health programme has been successful. Its education programme is an example of meaningful social expenditure. As Isenman (1980: 239) notes, 'As a result of high expenditures and high enrolment rates at all levels of education, adult literacy increased from 58% in 1946 to 78% in 1971.'

Finally, Sri Lanka has had a comprehensive system of free food rations for

[9] Richards and Gooneratne (1980).

[10] It also probably influences fertility. The World Development Report, 1985, notes that the percentage of married women of child-bearing age using contraceptives in Sri Lanka in 1982 was 55. This compares favourably not only to Bangladesh's 25 but to India's 32.

about 40 years.[11] This has taken the form of providing a certain amount of free rice (and, on occasions, wheat) and some additional rations at a subsidized price. What is unusual about Sri Lanka's rationing system is its comprehensive coverage of the entire population, including the urban *and rural* areas. This is in sharp contrast to India and Bangladesh. It will be argued later that Sri Lanka would have done better to cover a target population, namely those in poverty. Nevertheless, Sri Lanka's system of *total* coverage was better than having a system where only the urban sector has access to rationed foods. There has been a tendency for this to happen in some countries and its deleterious consequence was clearly evident during the Bangladesh famine of 1974. The urban sector, being covered by a rationing scheme, could ensure that a substantial part of the food would be diverted to it. The rural entitlement crisis was thus heightened by the very fact of the rationing scheme (McHenry and Bird 1977; Sen 1981*b*).

Not surprisingly, Sri Lanka's daily calorie intake is much higher than that of India or Bangladesh. Coupled with the fact that poverty in Sri Lanka is less, this suggests that the calorie intake of the poor is superior. The Sri Lankan food ration and subsidy scheme has been noted by several authors as the cause of its greater equality and better nutrition (Jayawardena 1974; Sen 1981*a*). The change in inequality in Sri Lanka over time is a much more controversial subject.[12] In fact, the whole question of changes in economic conditions in the 1960s and 1970s and their connections with the politics of the nation is an interesting and much misunderstood subject. But before going on to that I want to dwell briefly on the other striking example in South Asia of a poor region attaining a high standard of living—the State of Kerala.

The status of Sri Lanka among nations and that of Kerala among the Indian States bear striking resemblances. Kerala is one of the poorer States in India in terms of per capita income and also per capita nutrition (see Centre for Development Studies 1975; Dholakia and Dholakia 1980; Bardhan 1984*a*) —though its nutritional status is probably much better than a direct reading of the data suggests (Centre for Development Studies 1975: ch. 1). In terms of standard-of-living indicators, however, Kerala is markedly ahead of other States and in some ways quite close to advanced industrialized countries. In 1978 literacy in Kerala was 72 per cent as compared to the all-India figure of 39 and Punjab's 47. Infant mortality in Kerala was 39 compared to the all-India

---

[11] This has been largely dismantled in recent years, a point that is discussed later.

[12] It is commonly believed that Sri Lanka's income distribution in 1973 was more equitable than the ones in 1963 or 1953. It has in fact been shown (Fields 1980: 198) that the distribution in 1973 Lorenz-dominates the earlier ones. These facts run into controversy once we look at consumer expenditure data. It can be shown that in terms of this the share of income accruing to the bottom one-fifth of the population fell and the share going to the highest one-fifth rose between 1963 and 1973 (Lee 1977). Lee has argued convincingly that because of sharp relative price changes and a consequent index-number problem, the income data is rendered a less accurate indicator of what happened between 1963 and 1973 than the expenditure data.

Table 8.3 Inter-state social statistics in India, 1978

	Literacy (%)	Male literacy (%)	Female literacy (%)	Infant mortality (per 1,000 live births)
All India	39	50	27	126
Kerala	72	77	66	39
Punjab	47	54	39	103
Uttar Pradesh	33	46	19	167
West Bengal	47	56	35	78 (approx.)

Source: Office of the Registrar-General of India (1981*a*).

average of 126 and Punjab's 103. These statistics and more are presented in Table 8.3.

As in the case of Sri Lanka, Kerala demonstrates that improvement in the standard of living does not have to come via growth. Also, as we look into the factors behind Kerala's remarkable achievement, a lot of the same factors stand out here as in the case of Sri Lanka.

Kerala's educational performance is a direct consequence of progressive government policies. The State has had a long tradition of free primary schooling which has led to high enrolment rates and, more importantly, low drop-out rates. These tendencies have been strengthened by the provision of free meals at schools to some categories of students (CDS 1975).[13] Compared to other States, Kerala's performance in terms of *female* literacy is particularly striking, as Table 8.3 shows. This, as argued earlier, helps in the attainment of a better health status.

It seems generally accepted that health facilities are better distributed in Kerala.[14] The State's progressive health policies go far back into history, to the policies of the princely State of Travancore (Panikar and Soman 1984).

A major factor behind Kerala's health statistics is its food rationing scheme. As in the rest of India, subsidized foodgrains are sold in limited quantities to individuals through ration shops. However, whereas, all over India, food rations are essentially an urban feature, in Kerala the coverage is comprehensive, including urban and rural areas. This is again a striking similarity with Sri

[13] The Keralite's general penchant for education is also well known. This partially explains the recent mushrooming of private English-medium schools in Kerala. As a cynical bureaucrat noted, in Kerala you have to simply put up the label 'English Medium', think of a good English name, like John or Mary, prefix it with a 'Saint', and you are in business.

[14] The percentage of population within two kilometres of medical facilities in 1978 is 64 for Kerala compared to the Indian average of 35 (Office of Registrar-General 1981*a*). Percentage of live births unattended by trained medical practitioners in 1978 in Kerala is 38% in the rural sector and 25% in the urban sector. The all-India figures for the same are 42 and 33 (Office of Registrar-General 1981*b*).

Lanka. In Kerala the public distribution scheme reaches 97 per cent of the population; in Sri Lanka, before 1978, 93 per cent of the population was covered. Detailed studies of Kerala (Kumar 1979; George 1979) seem to establish the important contribution of the public distribution system to the citizens' nutrition and health. This is particularly true of the poorer classes.

State-wide data on social expenditure are difficult to get and what little is available presents problems of interpretation. Hence, it is difficult to judge whether social expenditure was high in the case of Kerala. This, however, as argued earlier, is not the crucial question. Clearly the expenditure must have been above a certain level since the provision of free education, subsidized health facilities, and rationed food entails this. Apart from this it is not clear whether Kerala spent little on social expenditure very efficiently or a lot inefficiently. The important point is that Kerala undertook direct action in government activities and this resulted in a relatively higher standard of living than one would expect from its general economic indicators.

What then is the basis of the view that direct redistributive and equity-oriented policies cannot work? One reason must be that policies come in bundles and it is difficult for us to sort out which is the cause of success and which of failure. We have some broad stereotypical notions of different governments: South Korea and Taiwan are *laissez-faire* economies, so if they succeed it is a success of non-intervention. China is a socialist country, so its success indicates the effectiveness of intervention. Reality can be different. For instance, in the case of South Korea and Taiwan, some policies that have been followed by their governments (e.g. land reform) are more radical than those any South Asian government has tried.[15] Given the scope of this essay, I shall concentrate on South Asia and illustrate this point with the example of Sri Lankan politics.

For all practical purposes, Sri Lanka has had a two-party system: the Sri Lanka Freedom Party (SLFP) associated with the Bandarnaikes, and the United National Party (UNP) associated with Senanayake and now Jayawardena.[16] The SLFP is considered the left-of-centre party and the UNP the right. The Sri Lankan electorate is volatile and responsive and regular changes in government have been seen, as follows: 1947–56, UNP in power; 1956–65, SLFP;[17] 1965–70, UNP; 1970–7, SLFP; 1977 onwards, UNP.

Economists, implicitly or explicitly, have taken 1956–65 and 1970–7 (because these were the times when the SLFP was in power) as the periods when 'direct action' was at its peak; failures during these periods have been taken to

[15] See Lee (1981) and in particular Datta Chaudhuri's (1981) essay in that collection. For a very interesting analysis contrasting South Korea and Taiwan, see Scitovsky (1985).

[16] There are several other parties of varying importance and governments have generally been coalitions, but such details are being ignored here.

[17] This is so excepting for a brief period in 1960 when, after a general election in which there were no clear victors, Dudley Senanayake of the UNP was appointed Prime Minister.

be failures of direct governmental action. But politics is a more complex game. A country which espouses socialism within its boundaries may follow a foreign policy of supporting right-wing regimes. Even in a party's domestic policy one can find unexpected mixtures which render easy labelling hazardous.

Note first that Sri Lanka's welfare programmes concerning education, health, and food were in effect during the first UNP government. Also, in 1978 it was the UNP government that made the food rationing scheme more equitable by ruling that only families whose annual income fell below Rs 3,600 would be eligible for free rations.[18] With this progressive move, the total number of beneficiaries fell from 93 per cent of the population to 54 per cent.[19] In retrospect it is clear that this progressive move was but a first step towards dismantling most of the public distribution schemes Sri Lanka had had. In 1979 the Jayawardena government abolished the rice rations and introduced a food stamp programme in its place. But the value of the food stamp programme was fixed in nominal terms and its real value has unfortunately declined rapidly because of inflation.[20]

As far as the SLFP is concerned, it is vital to distinguish between its two periods of government. During its first reign, that is, 1956–65, it stepped up social expenditure sharply—from about 5.3 per cent of GNP to 12.8.[21] It passed the Paddy Lands Act (1958), to increase security of tenure, and undertook many other domestic measures.

The second period, 1970–7, was very different.[22] The government's foreign policy was now more radical (e.g. it established diplomatic relations with several Communist countries), but its domestic rule was inefficient and inequitable. There was first of all considerable instability, including that stemming from the Communist insurgency of 1971, which the Prime Minister, Mrs Bandarnaike, put down ruthlessly. Unemployment was on the increase and money wages began to slip behind the price index. The real downturn came in 1973–4 with a severe failure of food crops and also as a consequence of the general international slump. Calorie intakes fell and health indicators deteriorated slightly. In addition, welfare expenditures were on the decline. Real expenditure on health programmes was probably falling, but, more

[18] Marginal adjustments were made for family size (Edirisinghe 1986).

[19] From full coverage of the population, in 1972 Mrs Bandarnaike ruled that income tax payers would not get rationed food. The effect of this was negligible (Edirisinghe 1986).

[20] The full consequence of this cannot as yet be judged but, based on some preliminary evidence, Jayanntha (1985: 47) has noted in his lucid monograph on Sri Lankan politics, 'Available evidence suggests that the nutritional status especially of infants and children under two years has deteriorated significantly.' Regarding why this did not erode the popularity of the UNP government (judging by some by-election results), he observes, 'These groups though vulnerable are not articulate or politically organized. Moreover malnutrition is often not recognized by the mother . . . Thus increased malnutrition alone . . . may not be translated into overt forms of political discontent.'

[21] Bhalla (1988a).

[22] See Jayanntha (1985) for an excellent account.

importantly, the size of the population per doctor or assistant medical practitioner was rising: from 3,800 in 1971 to 4,250 in 1976.[23] As Richards and Gooneratne (1980: 152) note, 'This coupled with drug scarcities and rising costs must indicate a recent deterioration in levels of medical care.' Government expenditure on education as a percentage of GNP also fell, from 4.3 in 1970 to 2.7 in 1977.[24] It is not surprising, therefore, that a study of change during the 1970s does not show up Sri Lanka in a particularly favourable light.

The final issue that I want to discuss in this section is the larger macroeconomic one of the alleged trade-off between growth and equity. If we do go in for the kind of basic needs policy discussed above, do we have to sacrifice growth? A lot of traditional thinking presupposes the existence of such a trade-off, though several authors have challenged this presupposition (a particularly vehement and clear case was made by Myrdal 1970).[25] There are two reasons why a simplistic view of a growth–equity trade-off may be wrong. First, it is reasonable to assert that, even if there is a relation between growth and equity, it is not a 'functional' one but in the nature of a 'correspondence', whereby a set of values of growth is compatible with each level of equity. Though in this case there may be a *potential* trade-off, this may not be of any immediate concern to the economy. This would be true of an economy which is functioning below its 'possibility frontier' in the growth–equity space. This is the view that I take here: in most LDCs there is sufficient slack for them to have more of both equity and growth.

A second and more fundamental criticism (one which is not pursued here) is to deny any relation between growth and equity in an economy. The absence of any relation between two variables may at first sight seem difficult to imagine but there are plenty of examples of this in economics. For example, it is meaningless to talk of the relation between price and supply in a traditional monopoly. If this happened to be true of growth and equity, then we would not be able to talk of a trade-off, immediate or potential. There can be other, more philosophical problems. For instance, one could argue that the only growth–equity combination that *can* occur in a country is the one that actually *does* occur. The question of what rates of growth are compatible with a different level of equity may then be meaningless because a different level of equity may be logically inconsistent with the other given features of the country.

One reason for the widespread belief in a trade-off is that policies often come in bundles: the government that enhances controls (an act which often has a negative impact on growth) is the one that has a more radical poverty-removal programme (which brings about greater equity). On the other hand a government like the one formed by Jayawardena tends to cut controls and minimize expenditure on basic needs programmes.[26] It is this policy bundling which

---

[23] Richards and Gooneratne (1980).   [24] Bhalla (1988a).   [25] See also Sen (1981a).

[26] There are important exceptions to this, as just discussed in terms of Sri Lanka's experience between 1971 and 1977.

may give us an exaggerated view of trade-offs, in particular the false view that an increased social spending must result in sluggishness of growth.

The amount of slack in most LDCs is large. The fact that a country takes up an activity x with zeal therefore does not mean that there will be less of activity y.[27] (Of course, we may nevertheless lament that the zeal is for x and not for y.) Parents who curb a child's zeal for sports, in the belief that this will help him become a scientist, will usually be disappointed. A better strategy for the parents would be to try to develop the child's enthusiasm for science.

Given the political structure of South Asian governments, there is an inherent tendency for them to indulge in controlling activities: licensing, price-setting, and fixing trade tariffs and quotas. These often encourage inefficiencies and curb growth, but the established domestic businesses have a vested interest in this structure of controls which makes it very difficult to dismantle it. Every time some import restriction is removed and consumers find they can buy some product cheaper and of better quality, one hears cries of dumping and 'foul'. There is much to be gained on the growth front by lowering trade restrictions and allowing prices to play a more important role;[28] and these policies need not be a curb on basic needs policies. In fact in the long run basic needs policies may actually be helped by these.

Bhagwati (1985) has argued that the problem with a large basic needs programme is not that in itself we cannot have it or it will not be beneficial; but simply that we may not be able to sustain such a programme for long. Indeed Sri Lanka was under severe fiscal strain in the 1970s. To ensure the sustenance of poverty alleviation programmes, we need some concomitant policies. We need to bolster growth so that the government has adequate resources for its programmes. What I have just been arguing is that it is not necessary to prune the poverty alleviation projects in order to have growth. Growth can be bolstered through a different set of policy instruments while continuing with the same basic needs policies. Of course, we may have to try to restrict the recipients of government support to the really needy.[29] This, as we have seen in the case of Sri Lanka, is a difficult task; but it is essential for keeping the fiscal burden manageable. This subject is discussed in the next section. Thirdly, what can be implemented or sustained depends on the political climate of a nation. This is discussed in Section 8.4.

In the next section I narrow the focus from basic needs policy in general to a part of it: the provision of food and the combating of poverty. This narrowing

[27] Scitovsky's (1985) study shows that Taiwan is ahead of Korea in terms not only of equity and standards of living but also (albeit marginally) of growth and economic performance. What comes out of this study is that Taiwan's growth rate instead of having been curtailed by its greater equity was probably aided by it. For a detailed cross-country study of growth and equity, see Ahluwalia (1976).

[28] I have discussed some of these issues in several short articles in the *Indian Express* and in a longer essay in the *Statesman* of 5 Nov. 1985.

[29] As Ahluwalia (1974) emphasizes, the very purpose of a support programme is to exercise selectivity.

down reflects the scope of this chapter and is not meant to suggest the unimportance of the other features of a basic needs programme.

8.3. *Poverty alleviation programmes*

South Asia has seen a plethora of schemes for alleviating poverty and acronyms have multiplied faster than one can count. Popular programmes include: food-for-work (FFW); Employment Guarantee Scheme (EGS); food ration and subsidy schemes; food stamps; nutrition programmes like Tamil Nadu's noon-meal scheme; Integrated Rural Development Programme (IRDP); credit support schemes like the Grameen Bank in Bangladesh. Of these, the IRDP and Grameen Bank, while very different from each other, are also very different from the other schemes and on these I offer only a few remarks. Programmes like FFW and food rations are more directly concerned with attacking the problem of food entitlement and unemployment and these are of central interest in this section.[30] I shall however begin with a few comments on programmes which provide some credit support.

IRDP is an important programme in Bangladesh and India. In India 15 million people were meant to be assisted by it during the Sixth Five Year Plan.[31] The motivation for the programme arose out of a feeling that the earlier anti-poverty policies were piecemeal and needed consolidation and that they were working mainly as subsidy schemes on which the poor were likely to get chronically dependent. The aim of IRDP was, therefore, to offer a combination of subsidies and credit to poor households so as to bolster their asset position and enable them to have a higher income and become self-sufficient. The scheme was supposed to help the poorest sections of the rural sector. 'Poor' was now being defined differently from what was conventional. First, the household, instead of each individual, was being treated as a unit. Secondly, poverty was not defined in terms of landholdings, but in terms of the family's income from all sources. If this was below a certain level the family was considered eligible for support from IRDP. While this is, in principle, a better criterion for selecting the needy, it is also one which makes the problem of identifying the beneficiaries more acute.

Studies of the functioning of IRDP in India so far reveal that it has been very successful in terms of the target number of beneficiaries. But the average amount of investment that each beneficiary received was only about half of the planned investment of Rs 3,000 per family at 1979–80 prices. Also, in terms of

---

[30] Also omitted from the purview of the present paper are more structural reforms like land redistribution. Programmes like the EGS and FFW do not usually require structural changes and, as Herring and Edwards (1983) rightly observe, they may even help ossify existing structures.

[31] For critical assessments, see Sundaram and Tendulkar (1985*a*, 1985*b*) and Bandyopadhyay (1985). A general survey of poverty programmes in South Asia is contained in Islam and Lee (1985).

the objective of reaching the poorest people, the achievement of IRDP is doubtful, though no definitive study on this is available.

The targeting problem was, to a certain extent, preordained because of some inconsistencies in the planned objectives of the project. While (1) it was supposed to benefit the poorest, (2) it was also expected to assist families so as to push them above the poverty line. There is some ambiguity about objective (2). Two alternative elucidations of (2) are: (*a*) the number of families that cross the poverty line should be maximized. (*b*) A family which is assisted ought to be assisted sufficiently to cross the poverty line. Under both interpretations (2) conflicts with (1). With (*b*) the conflict is indirect and stems from the fact that during the process (over time) of assisting a family, it may cease to be the poorest. The conflict between (1) and the first interpretation is direct. If we want to maximize the number of families that cross the poverty line, we should choose as beneficiaries families which are close to the poverty line. This would, of course, conflict with objective (1). The incompatibility between (1) and (2) is very marked in practice. Sundaram and Tendulkar (1985*a*) have shown that, given some assumptions, if the average amount of benefit per family disbursed during the first three years of the Sixth Five Year Plan had gone to the poorest 30 per cent of the rural population, then none of the IRDP beneficiary households would have crossed the poverty line, that is, objective (2) would have remained completely unsatisfied.

Though we have to wait for more detailed empirical research, there are some grounds for maintaining that the poorest people were not reached. For one, there were other objectives which militated against this happening. For instance, the so-called 'cluster approach' which was adopted by IRDP meant that its assistance would go to areas where credit institutions existed and there was 'the capacity to absorb credit to the extent envisaged' (Sundaram and Tendulkar 1985*b*: 209). Further, since a part of the IRDP package consists of assistance with credit, it would face the difficulties which credit support policies face in general in trying to reach the very poor.[32] I am in sympathy with Rath's (1985) argument that, though credit and subsidy for self-employment are important, we cannot ignore the need for massive programmes for creating public and private employment (see also Dantwala 1985 and Hirway 1985). Consequently, the waning of official interest in India for such schemes (see Rath 1985) is unfortunate. A similar sentiment is expressed by Dandekar (1986: A-100): 'while the possibilities of creating self-employment should be explored, the main reliance will have to be on offering wage-employment'. He rightly observes that this does not mean a perennial dependence because the 'more thrifty, provident, and enterprising' among the beneficiaries of an

---

[32] In general the 'very poor' tend to raise problems quite distinct from the ones associated with the poor. Can the very poor be helped so as to become permanently self-sufficient? Are they in a position to avail themselves of the benefits provided for the poor? Such questions need investigation (see Lipton 1983).

employment scheme are likely to 'set themselves up' in the long run and become independent.

Before turning to employment programmes, let us take a brief look at pure credit support policies which have also been tried over a long period in South Asia. In India, the coverage provided by institutional credit has steadily increased (thereby hopefully diminishing the hold of the legendary rural money-lender). But nevertheless the credit policy has been far from a success. The main reason is that institutional credit has failed to reach the poorest people, who have by and large remained dependent on the unorganized sector, i.e. on private money-lenders.[33] Hence it is possible that institutional credit, instead of having alleviated the condition of the poorest, has merely bolstered the position of the not-so-poor. The reason for this is sufficiently deep as to imply that it cannot be corrected by merely doctoring the credit programmes. The main problem of providing organized credit to the poor is the recovery of loans. The village money-lender has a variety of methods for ensuring repayment[34] which are not open to the manager of the bank sent from the nearest city to provide rural credit. Apart from the problem of absconding from repaying, there is the genuine problem of bankruptcy. The very poor who borrow to survive may well find themselves with no liquidity at the time of repayment. The private money-lender may then 'bond' them, that is, acquire a right over their labour for a long enough period to recover the loan.[35] It is this knowledge which gives the money-lender the confidence to lend to the poor. Clearly this option is not open to government-run banks. Moreover, the rich and influential have the ability to divert to themselves the organized-sector low-interest credit; and even if their repayment record is poor they continue to get loans (see e.g. Bhende 1986). It is for these reasons that a credit scheme is very unlikely to be able to confer benefits on the poorest sections.

The Grameen Bank of Bangladesh however seems to provide a counter-example. Established in 1983, it is a successor to the Grameen Bank Project which was launched in 1976 by Muhammed Yunus, an economics professor at Chittagong University. It is considered one of the most successful rural credit schemes in South Asia. The Grameen Bank is a public sector credit institution and its aim is to provide loans to the poor on reasonable terms, the idea being that of enabling the poor to become self-sufficient. A member of any household owning less than half an acre of cultivable land can avail himself of the services of the Grameen Bank. The workers of the bank actually search for poor people who need financial support but are too ignorant or diffident actively to seek credit. Paradoxically it has done well exactly where other schemes have

[33] The problem seems to be similar for Bangladesh (Khan 1972; Rahman 1979).

[34] The use of personalized relationship and collateral has been discussed in Bhaduri (1977) and Basu (1984a, 1984b).

[35] This, as is well known, may be long enough to cover the lifetime of the borrower and may even spill over to his children who would then be born into bondage.

floundered. Its repayment record is excellent. Studies done in the early 1980s show that only 1 or 2 per cent of all outstanding loans were overdue (Siddiqui 1985; see also Ahmad and Hossain 1985). Secondly, its targeting has been quite good. According to a 1983 survey, a vast majority of loanees owned no agricultural land (for detailed tables, see Siddiqui 1985: 175). Another striking feature of the Grameen Bank is the prominence of women among the borrowers. In 1980, 39 per cent of the borrowers were women and by late 1984 the figure had risen to 54 per cent (Hossain 1985: 12).

A part of the Grameen Bank's success lies in its organizational structure. For example, the manager of a new branch has to survey the concerned villages for two months without subordinates. This ensures first-hand knowledge and direct involvement. The Grameen Bank is, in part, a co-operative. It organizes credit recipients into groups and helps them build up their own savings for emergencies. The group is useful in preventing defaults by applying 'social' pressure on individuals to stick to schedules. This co-operative aspect of the bank may have had other indirect benefits. It has, for instance, been found that an increasing amount of credit is being taken from the bank for co-operative ventures like purchasing equipment for irrigation which would benefit a group or buying rice hullers or even leasing market-places (Ahmad and Hossain 1985). According to Hossain (1985: 12–13), among the main causes of the Bank's good record are the 'close supervision of the activities in the field by the managing director' and the dedication of the bank workers, 'most of whom have taken the job as providing services to the poor rather than simply as an income earning opportunity'. In the context of the present chapter the important question is: to what extent can such a credit programme be replicated elsewhere?

In the early 1980s the Grameen Bank was a small project with plans for vast expansion through the 1980s. In May 1980 the bank had 24 branches. By February 1987 this had grown to 298 and loans had been disbursed to about 250,000 households. The plan was to keep up the expansion for some more years.[36] With such expansion it will of course lose the personal touch; and the robustness of its organization and its relevance for large countries, like India, will only then be fully tested. However, its success thus far is good reason for other South Asian countries to examine the viability of such a credit programme.

More direct methods of enhancing the food entitlements of the poor are the EGS or FFW and food rations or food stamps. These have had a fair measure of success in the Indian subcontinent. Food-for-work in Bangladesh was begun in the wake of the 1974 famine. The programme has run mainly on food received as aid—primarily from the US. In the first year of the programme,

---

[36] See Ahmed (1986) for a discussion of the prospects of the Grameen Bank and the impact of credit availability on employment. He argues that in the long run technology upgradation will be necessary for fully realizing the benefits of a credit programme.

32,000 tons of wheat were disbursed through the programme and 8.6 million man days of work were created. In 1982–3, approximately 371,000 tons of wheat were used to create 101 million man days of work. The FFW programme is computed to have created jobs equivalent to only 2–3 per cent of the total annual unemployed labour time in Bangladesh. Also, it has been estimated that 30 per cent of the workers came from households owning more than half an acre of land (Ahmad and Hossain 1985).

In India FFW (which was subsequently renamed the National Rural Employment Programme, NREP) was begun in April 1977, with the objective of creating jobs, creating durable infrastructure, and using up the surplus grain which had accumulated with the government.[37] In this respect India differed from other countries; its programme was not based on food received as aid.[38] In 1978, 12 lakh tonnes of wheat were used and 286 million man days of jobs were created.[39] Though the programme was running fairly successfully it got mired in political controversy and was somewhat tarnished. First of all the programme caused a certain amount of alarm because it was having the sort of impact it was intended to have: a study of the Planning Commission found that, of the twenty Districts surveyed, six had experienced a significant upward movement of wages. This was undesirable from the point of view of rich landlords and may have been a factor behind the loss of official enthusiasm for FFW. Secondly, FFW became the source of Centre–State conflicts and this resulted in a curb on foodgrain supplies to several States, including West Bengal (for a discussion, see Basu 1982).[40] In terms of economic efficiency, where the programme has really floundered is in its effort at creating infrastructure. While it did create a certain amount of employment, it was usually unproductive. But indeed the sheer fact of doling out food may be of value.

The rice ration scheme or the provision of food stamps[41] are methods of

[37] Contrary to the official proclamation, this last 'objective' is not really an objective. The availability of surplus grain simply makes it easier to fulfil the real objectives of employment and income transfer and production.

[38] FFW or some variant of it has been used in several LDCs, e.g. Tunisia, Morocco, and Egypt. Tunisia is also one of the few countries where FFW began without foreign support, though within a few years food shortages developed and it had to use US wheat.

[39] India's FFW had an important precursor in the EGS which had been in operation since 1972 in Maharashtra. It was merged with the FFW programme when the latter was started. For a study of the EGS, see Dandekar (1983).

[40] The original organization structure of the FFW was as follows. The Centre supplied foodgrains to the State governments, which were responsible for setting up labour intensive projects in the rural regions. The States had considerable freedom in terms of the actual execution of projects. They could, for instance, pay wages purely in terms of foodgrain or pay partly in foodgrains and partly in cash.

[41] The food stamp programme, as implemented in Sri Lanka, is something in between a free rice ration scheme and a negative income tax. A recipient of food stamps can exchange them for a certain range of food items, including rice. Members of households which earn less than Rs 300 per month were eligible. Adults received stamps worth Rs 15 per month and children a little more (see Edirisinghe 1986).

doling out food and, as I have argued in the previous section, they have played an important role in raising living standards in Sri Lanka and Kerala. Ideally FFW and rice rations should be used as complementary schemes because their points of strength are very different. FFW, properly executed, can provide a self-selection device for picking out the poor and also it has the advantage of being productive. Its main disadvantage *vis-à-vis* a rice ration scheme is that it discriminates against the old and the disabled. Since the old and disabled are easier to identify, one possibility is to have free rations restricted to them and an FFW open to all and hopefully, because of its self-selection property, utilized only by the poor.

For countries as large as India and Bangladesh, the problem of selecting the poor is so important that reliance on FFW seems natural. If too many non-deserving people rely on such governmental support, the burden on the exchequer may be unbearable. To get the full advantage of an FFW we need to organize it very skilfully. To bring out the salient features of FFW, I present some simple analytics.

The difference between an FFW and a food ration scheme is that they alter entitlements differently. Suppose a person earns z rupees from a day's labour;[42] and that his daily non-labour income is Rs v. Let y denote his total income. Thus

$$y = z + v$$

Let p be the price of the foodgrain in the open market. In the absence of a price support scheme, his budget set is given by $y0A$ in Fig. 8.1. Now let us consider two alternative support programmes.

Food ration scheme: let us suppose that a free rice ration of R units is given. Then this person's budget set becomes $0yCB$. Here and below I assume that the transaction cost of reselling food is prohibitive.

Food-for-work: now suppose that instead of a food ration scheme food-for-work is started where foodgrains worth G units are given in exchange for a day's labour. Then his budget set is $0vDE$.

So what these schemes do is alter the entitlements of individuals. The interesting feature of FFW is that z will vary between individuals. If for a person z is sufficiently high, then his food-for-work budget set becomes a subset of oyA (see Fig. 8.1) and he would prefer not to avail himself of the opportunity of FFW. It is easy to check that the FFW budget set is subsumed in the normal budget set if

$$G < z/p. \tag{8.1}$$

Hence a person will certainly not work for FFW if condition (8.1) is true. (If 8.1 is false he may or may not work.) It is clear therefore that those who have

---

[42] I am assuming that a day's labour is an indivisible unit. That is, a worker does not face a choice between hours of leisure each day and daily income.

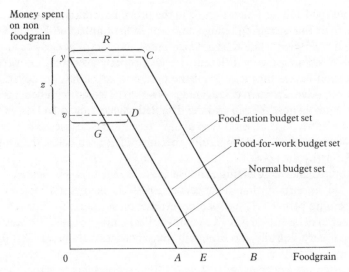

Fig. 8.1. Food for work and food ration

access to a well-paid labour market or high productivity in their own farms (basically a high z) will not participate in FFW projects. This is the self-selection property of FFW.

There is one problem. A person with a high non-labour income, but low z, may nevertheless come to work for FFW and clearly we would not like to have such people. There are two mitigating factors. First, manual labour is considered demeaning for anybody who has access to other income, especially a large non-labour income. Thus for reasons of status, those with a sufficiently high v are unlikely to come. Secondly, it is quite possible that v and z are positively correlated: it is the richer people who have access to well-paid labour markets. This may be briefly captured by asserting

$$z = z(v), z'(v) > 0.$$

In that case it is clear that if a person's v is large, (10.1) will be satisfied and the FFW programme will be spared the labours of such a person.

A controversial matter concerning FFW is the level of wages that ought to be paid to the labourers.[43] It is a widely held view that the wages paid on FFW ought to be higher. It will, however, be argued here that both on grounds of keeping the self-selection property sharp and *also for ethical reasons* the wage paid at FFW sites, i.e. G, should be kept as low as possible (in a sense made clear below).[44]

This seems to be a surprising recommendation if our objective is to remove

[43] Dandekar and Sathe (1980); Basu (1981, 1982); Panda (1981).

[44] I argued this in Basu (1981) and the next few paragraphs draw heavily on that paper.

poverty. But such a feeling of surprise arises from an implicit 'headcount' view of poverty. This comes out clearly from Dandekar and Sathe's (1980) study of FFW and EGS in Maharashtra. They found that 90 per cent of the people working on this scheme continue to be below the poverty line despite such work. From this they went on to conclude that wages should be raised. In the case of Bangladesh, Ahmad and Hossain (1985: 80) observed that wages paid to FFW workers were substantially below the officially stipulated wage rate. 'It has been shown that about 56 per cent of the workers did not know about the stipulated wage rate. Those who know do not bargain lest they do not get the jobs at all as *there are many others who are unemployed and would be too willing to take them up on the offered terms and conditions*' (my italics).[45] It is the italicized part which suggests why underpayment need not be unethical, since that will make it possible to employ a larger number of people who are needy enough to be willing to work for a low wage.

Suppose we subscribe to a headcount view of poverty[46] and try to minimize this. Then, given a total stock of foodgrain X, which is to be disbursed through the FFW, we would try to heap it on people so as to ensure that the maximum number of people cross the poverty line. But clearly our more intuitive normative penchant (as opposed to one formally derived from trying to minimize the headcount index) would be to spread out X over the poorest people, even if that leaves the numbers on the two sides of the poverty line the same. Fortunately, according to some more sophisticated measures, this will register a decline in poverty.

To formalize this argument suppose X is the total amount of grain available for giving out as wages in a FFW. For simplicity I am assuming that wages are paid entirely in terms of food grain. Let L be the number of labourers supplying their labour to FFW. As usual, we assume

$$L = L(G), L'(G) > 0 \qquad\qquad (8.2)$$

This supply curve of labour is depicted in Fig. 8.2.

Given a wage of G, the maximum number that can be employed, which may be labelled 'potential employment', is given by X/G. The relation between G and potential employment is depicted in Fig. 8.2. Clearly this is a rectangular hyperbola. What is being recommended here is that G should be minimized subject to $L(G) > X/G$. Let the solution of this be defined by G^*. This is easily seen to be given by the point of intersection of the two curves in Fig. 8.2. G^*, it is being argued here, is the wage that we should aim to offer.[47]

---

[45] See Bandyopadhyay (1985: 137) concerning underpayment in FFW in India.

[46] For a critique of such a view of poverty see Sen (1988: ch. 3 and Appendix C).

[47] The actual execution of this may not be as easy as it appears. In Afghanistan, wages were set so low, in an effort to maximize the spread, that the projects were perennially short of labour. In Lesotho the wage was set so high that landowners were quitting working on their own land to work at FFW sites.

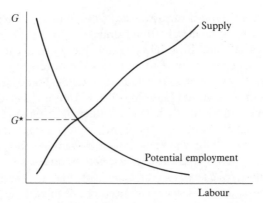

Fig. 8.2. Employment and optimal wage

As I have argued in Basu (1981) on the basis of some Planning Commission data (Project Evaluation Organization 1979) it seems likely that the wage that has been paid in India is above G^*. A similar claim seems to be possible for Bangladesh on the basis of Ahmad and Hossain's paper.

It has already been argued that G^* is more equitable (in the sense of ameliorating poverty) than a higher wage. G^* has another advantage. It sharpens the self-selection property of FFW since from (8.1) it follows that, as G becomes smaller, the wealthier (in terms of labour income) will be less inclined to come for FFW jobs, thereby paving the way for the poor to take these up.

The above analysis implies that there are three ways of raising the wage: (1) by improving the opportunities open to the labourers (by, for example, having infrastructural investments in the rural sector. This would raise the supply curve in Fig. 8.2). (2) By assigning a larger food stock for distribution through FFW. This raises the 'potential employment' curve. (3) By simply deciding to set G above G^* and maintaining an excess supply of labour. What I have argued above is that we should raise wages via methods (1) and (2); option (3) ought not to be normally used. It may be used only if we can devise some additional selection criterion whereby the poorest among the job applicants are selected. Here and elsewhere it ought to be kept in mind however that accurate targeting of benefits may itself be an expensive exercise and there may be times when it is suboptimal to perfect one's marksmanship in this respect.[48]

Finally, I make some brief comments on the form of wage payment. Should this be paid in cash or kind? In other words, should we have an FFW programme or a cash-for-work programme? I do not want to give a firm answer

---

[48] Reutlinger (1984) has suggested a method of computing the relative efficiency of giving aid in the form of different goods, which takes into account the delivery cost. A similar exercise should be possible whereby the efficiency of transferring income to the poor via different schemes is computed, taking into account the cost of organizing the schemes.

here but merely point out the pros and cons. The popular argument for paying in food grains is to encourage the poor to have better nourishment even if that is not what they would do with the same amount of income. The ethical strength or weakness of this will not be discussed here. I will simply evaluate the positive argument that underlies this prescription, namely, that payment in foodgrains ensures that people will not fritter away their income on 'useless' consumption.

The weakness of this proposition becomes apparent as soon as we recognize that money is fungible. To make the proposition as strong as possible before attacking it let me assume that people cannot sell off foodgrains earned as wages (perhaps because of the high transaction costs of selling such small quantities). Nevertheless, as soon as we grant that most people will have some income from other sources (i.e. other than what they earn from FFW), it follows that the portion of that other income which they would have spent on food they can now spend on other things given that their food supply now comes from the FFW project. In other words, the fact of paying wages in food does not mean that food consumption will go up by that amount and it may not in fact go up at all. A little calculation shows that, given the actual facts of FFW in India (see Basu 1981, it is the case that the *form* of payment is unlikely to affect the volume of consumption of food. The evidence from Bangladesh suggests that payment in wheat does not affect significantly the *volume* of foodgrain consumption, but it does tilt its *composition* in favour of wheat (Osmani and Chowdhury 1983).

An important case for payment in food stems from the recognition of some political constraints, which apply especially to India. In the Indian economy, thanks to several compulsions including those emanating from the agrarian lobby, it seems likely that the food procurement policies of the government will continue for some time. If wages are paid in foodgrain at rural works programmes then the procured grain—or at least a part of it—will get earmarked for use in FFW. If, on the other hand, wages are paid in cash, the government will soon be looking for avenues for selling this grain. Once the grain gets converted into cash, it is unlikely that it will be used for the poor. Given the forces around government—and this is the central point of Griffin's paper (Griffin 1985)—it is more likely to get spent on amenities for the urban middle class. One may object here that if a government is inclined to do so, it will do so anyway. But the logic of large organizations like government does not work that way. The same 'end' may be infeasible by one route but by another route it may just be possible to tiptoe past vested interests.

The subject of political constraints has been mentioned several times, but in passing. It is an important issue in food policy but also a difficult one to write about; and so I reserve only a brief section for it.

8.4. *Optimal policies and political constraints*

Keith Griffin (1985) has pointed out in a lucid essay on the state of poverty in Asia that the problem of poverty can be largely eliminated through 'purposeful government intervention'; but 'given the class basis of the state, a question arises about the possibility of effective action'. He argued correctly that, in most South Asian countries, governments are closely in alliance with the wealthier sections of society. These people therefore guide policy to their advantage. The government's rhetoric is meant for the poor who are not near enough to see the actual policies, and the actual policies are inclined to help the already wealthy who keep a close watch on them. More disturbing is Gunnar Myrdal's (1970) accurate observation that not only policies but even the perception of truth can deviate in favour of the dominant classes.

There is a danger in pushing this kind of an argument too far. Though such a charge cannot be levelled against Griffin or Myrdal, several radical and conservative writers have been *too* successful in explaining the backwardness of LDCs, in the sense that their models leave no chinks for changing the situation. If such an all-encompassing explanation was valid, then there would be no point in making policy recommendations.

More formally, what I am claiming is that if a model of an economy is constructed in which every agent knows what is in his own interest and acts to achieve it, then 'advice' can have no role in affecting the 'outcome' of such an economy. This is the case with the Arrow–Debreu model of general equilibrium. There is no provision here for 'advice' to change any agent's behaviour. Let us call an agent whose actions can be altered by *some* advice an 'open end' of a model. If we want to construct a model and make recommendations, the model must be one which has open ends. In some conventional models the government is treated as an open end. If however we treat the government as either completely subservient to certain class interests or comprising of fully informed individuals with well-defined objectives, we lose the open end and policy advice becomes redundant again. In reality there is scope, however slender, for influencing the outcomes of economies.

First note that people do not always act selfishly and our hope for more equitable policies lies in the fact that altruism, anger, envy, or the influence of writings can lead us to work against our own interest. Secondly, the rich constitute a group. Consequently, even though a particular policy may be in their own interest, they may fail to implement it because their individual rationality may be incompatible with their group rational behaviour. In short, within their own class they may interact as in the Prisoner's Dilemma.

Finally, even though governments do exhibit class bias, there are chinks in the system, which can be exploited to divert resources to the poor. A government or a Minister chooses his policy bundle subject to several constraints. Some of these are, however, unusual constraints in that they may be political in character: certain powerful lobbies could make some policies impossible to implement. How much of a government's preference or ideology is revealed in its choice of policies depends on how restrictive these constraints are. Given the several lobbies that surround South Asian governments[49] the room for manœuvre must indeed be small. Hence two Finance Ministers with very different ideologies would draft budgets which are not too different (otherwise at least one of them would cease to be Finance Minister). In brief, South Asian economies are Finance Minister neutral—or almost so. This makes it clear that if government policies are to be influenced, instead of trying to alter the government's preference, our aim should be to alter the constraints. The poorer sections have to be made more demanding and more conscious of their rights.

There is an interesting self-referential reason why some downtrodden groups are so dormant. Note first that if all members of a group, H, consider it unreasonable to demand a larger share of the cake then, given that a government is always under severe pressure to make concessions to different groups lobbying for more, it will indeed be reasonable not to give H a larger cut. After all H is not pressing for more and others are. Hence each individual member of H will be right in supposing that it is unreasonable to ask for a larger share. If however each member of H chooses to be unreasonable and demands more, the government may find it in its own interest to concede to the group's demand. Also, the government would be able to persuade the other lobbies that it *has* to concede to H, because of its large 'voice'. In other words, it would no longer be an unreasonable demand to ask for more.[50] This is where the media can play a major role. They can influence our view of what is acceptable. And, as has just been argued, what is acceptable depends, at least in part, on what we consider to be acceptable.

8.5. *Concluding remarks*

The aim of this chapter was to evaluate policies for combating persistent and mass poverty in South Asia. In so doing it was necessary to go into some general analytical questions and to comment on existing debates. Though most of the empirical discussions were based on India and Sri Lanka, it is hoped that the analysis and policy suggestions which emerged will be of interest for the larger problem of poverty in the Third World.

The chapter began with the question as to whether 'direct action' for mitigating the poverty problem could be fruitful or would it be necessary to wait for the benefits of growth to 'trickle down'. It was argued that direct action

---

[49] Bardhan (1984*b*) has argued that Indian policy making is a compromise of the interests of three dominant classes: the industrial bourgeoisie, wealthy farmers, and the bureaucracy.

[50] Using the idea of self-fulfilling conjectures I have tried to show in a different context (Basu 1986) how certain unwanted political power structures could be sustained by a web of reinforcing beliefs among individuals.

was possible and desirable. To pursue this objective it was not necessary to sacrifice growth. Different policy instruments are available for achieving higher growth and greater equity. Given the enormity of this problem my comments were, perforce, in the nature of an overview. Several subthemes would have to be the subject of much more detailed research. The present chapter pursued in greater depth one particular subtheme—that of poverty alleviation programmes in rural South Asia.

Several schemes, for example, food-for-work and the Integrated Rural Development Programme, were commented on. However, it ought to be mentioned that, while I have analysed the schemes separately, in designing a full anti-poverty policy it will be essential to evaluate the whole package together. This is because poverty has many dimensions[51] and it will be necessary to use more than one programme to mitigate poverty,[52] and the value of one particular programme may depend on what else is being implemented. Some complementarities, for example, that between food-for-work and food rationing, were discussed in this chapter but a more systematic evaluation of *packages* will have to be undertaken in future.

The last part of the chapter was devoted to the politics of anti-poverty programmes. The brevity of Section 8.4 reflects the difficulty of the subject, not its unimportance. Political constraints do not necessarily arise out of the wilful machinations of groups and lobbies but could be the inadvertent consequence of a multitude of individuals, each acting atomistically and in his own interest. This makes political constraints difficult not only to overcome but even to understand; and this subject must loom large in any agenda for research on poverty.

[51] See Rodgers (1976) for a discussion of the concept of poverty viewed as a 'multivariate phenomenon'.

[52] There is a semantic problem here in that we may think of a combination of programmes as yet another programme. This would render the claim that *one* programme can never be sufficient erroneous. The defence against this criticism is that the expression (one programme) is being used here to describe one member of the existing menu of anti-poverty schemes.

References

AHLUWALIA, M. S. (1974), 'The Scope for Policy Intervention', in Chenery *et al.* (1974).

——(1976), 'Inequality, Poverty and Development', *Journal of Development Economics*, 3.

AHMAD, A. K., and HOSSAIN, M. (1985), 'An Evaluation of Selected Policies and Programmes for the Alleviation of Rural Poverty in Bangladesh', in Islam (1985).

AHMED, H. (1986), 'Rural Landless in Bangladesh: An Enquiry into the Economic Results of Grameen Bank', mimeo (Oslo: Institute of Economics).

BANDYOPADHYAY, D. (1985), 'An Evaluation of Policies and Programmes for the Alleviation of Rural Poverty in India', in Islam (1985).

BARDHAN, P. K. (1984a), *Land, Labour and Rural Poverty: Essays in Development Economics* (New York: Columbia University Press).

——(1984b), *The Political Economy of Development in India* (Oxford: Basil Blackwell).

BASU, A. M. (1986), 'Birth Control by Assetless Workers in Kerala: The Possibility of a Poverty-Induced Fertility Transition', *Development and Change*, 17.

BASU, K. (1981), 'Food for Work Programmes: Beyond Roads that Get Washed Away', *Economic and Political Weekly*, 16.

——(1982), 'Food for Work: Some Economic and Political Consequences', *Economic and Political Weekly, Review of Agriculture*, 17.

——(1984a), *The Less Developed Economy: A Critique of Contemporary Theory* (Oxford: Basil Blackwell).

——(1984b), 'Implicit Interest Rates, Usury and Isolation in Backward Agriculture', *Cambridge Journal of Economics*, 8.

——(1986), 'One Kind of Power', *Oxford Economic Papers*, 38.

BHADURI, A. (1977), 'On the Formation of Usurious Interest Rates in Backward Agriculture', *Cambridge Journal of Economics*, 1.

BHAGWATI, J. N. (1985), 'Growth and Poverty', Occasional Paper No. 9 (East Lansing, Mich.: Center for Advanced Study of International Development, Michigan State University).

BHALLA, S. S. (1988a), 'Is Sri Lanka an Exception? A Comparative Study in Living Standards', in Srinivasan and Bardhan (1988).

——(1988b), 'Sri Lanka's Achievements: Fact and Fancy', in Srinivasan and Bardhan (1988).

—— and GLEWWE P. (1986), 'Growth and Equity in Developing Countries: A Reinterpretation of the Sri Lankan Experience', *World Bank Economic Review*, 1.

BHENDE, M. J. (1986), 'Credit Markets in Rural South India', *Economic and Political Weekly*, Review of Agriculture, 21.

CALDWELL, J. C. (1986), 'Routes to Low Mortality in Poor Countries', *Population and Development Review*, 12.

Centre for Development Studies, Trivandrum (1975), *Poverty, Unemployment and Development Policy: A Case Study of Selected Issues with Reference to Kerala* (New York: United Nations ST/ESA/29).

CHENERY, H., AHLUWALIA, M. S., BELL, C. L. G., DULOY, J. H., and JOLLY, R. (1974), *Redistribution with Growth* (Oxford: Oxford University Press).

DANDEKAR, K. (1983), *Employment Guarantee Scheme: An Employment Opportunity for Women* (Bombay: Orient Longman).

—— and SATHE, M. (1980), 'Employment Guaranteee Scheme and Food-for-Work Program', *Economic and Political Weekly*, 15.

DANDEKAR, V. M. (1986), 'Agriculture, Employment and Poverty', *Economic and Political Weekly, Review of Agriculture*, 21.

DANTWALA, M. L. (1985), '"Garibi Hatao": Strategy Options', *Economic and Political Weekly*, 20.

DATTA CHAUDHURI, M. K. (1981), 'Industrialization and Foreign Trade: The Development Experiences of South Korea and the Philippines', in Lee (1981).

DHOLAKIA, B., and DHOLAKIA, R. (1980), 'State Income Inequalities and Inter-state Variations in Growth of Real Capital Stock', *Economic and Political Weekly*, 15.

EDIRISINGHE, N. (1986), 'The Food Stamp Program in Sri Lanka: Costs, Benefits and Policy Options' (Washington, DC: IFPRI).

FIELDS, G. S. (1980), *Poverty, Inequality and Development* (Cambridge: Cambridge University Press).

GEORGE, P. S. (1979), 'Public Distribution of Foodgrains in Kerala: Income Distribution Implications and Effectiveness' (Washington, DC: IFPRI).

GRIFFIN, K. (1985), 'Rural Poverty in Asia: Analysis and Policy Alternatives', in Islam (1985).

HERRING, R. J., and EDWARDS, R. M. (1983), 'Guaranteeing Employment to the Rural Poor: Social Functions and Class Interests in the Employment Guarantee Scheme in Western India', *World Development*, 11.

HIRWAY, I. (1985), '"Garibi Hatao": Can IRDP Do It?', *Economic and Political Weekly*, 20.

HOSSAIN, M. (1985), 'Institutional Credit for Rural Development: An Overview of the Bangladesh Case', *Bangladesh Journal of Agricultural Economics*, 8.

ISENMAN, P. (1980), 'Basic Needs: The Case of Sri Lanka', *World Development*, 8.

ISLAM, R. (ed.) (1985), *Strategies for Alleviating Poverty in Rural Asia* (Bangkok: ILO).

—— and LEE, E. (1985), 'Strategies for Alleviating Poverty in Rural Asia', in Islam (1985).

JAYANNTHA, D. (1985), 'Sri Lanka: The Political Framework (1947–84)', mimeo (Washington, DC: World Bank).

JAYAWARDENA, L. (1974), 'Redistribution with Growth: Some Country Experience —Sri Lanka', in Chenery *et al.* (1974).

KHAN, A. R. (1972), *The Economy of Bangladesh* (London: Macmillan).

KUMAR S. K. (1979), 'Impact of Subsidized Rice on Food Consumption in Kerala' (Washington, DC: IFPRI).

LEE, E. (ed.) (1981), *Export Led Industrialization and Development* (Bangkok: ILO).

LEE, E. L. H. (1977), 'Rural Poverty in Sri Lanka, 1963–73', in International Labour Organization, *Poverty and Landlessness in Rural Asia* (Geneva: ILO).

LIPTON, M. (1983), 'Poverty, Undernutrition and Hunger', World Bank Staff Working Paper No. 597 (Washington, DC: World Bank).

MCHENRY, D. F., and BIRD K. (1977), 'Food Bungle in Bangladesh', *Foreign Policy*, 27.

MORRISON, B. M., and WAXLER, N. E. (1986), 'Three Patterns of Basic Needs Distribution within Sri Lanka: 1971–73', *World Development*, 14. ,

MUKHOPADHYAY, S. (ed.) (1985*a*), *The Poor in Asia: Productivity-Raising Programmes and Strategies* (Kuala Lumpur: Asian and Pacific Development Centre).

—— (ed.) (1985*b*), *Case Studies on Poverty Programmes in Asia* (Kuala Lumpur: Asian and Pacific Development Centre).

MYRDAL, G. (1970), *The Challenge of World Poverty* (London: Allen Lane).

NAG, M. (1983), 'Impact of Social and Economic Development on Mortality: Comparative Study of Kerala and West Bengal', *Economic and Political Weekly*, 28.

Office of the Registrar-General of India (1981*a*), *Survey on Infant and Child Mortality 1979* (New Delhi: Government of India).

—— (1981*b*), *Levels, Trends and Differentials in Fertility 1979* (New Delhi: Government of India).

OSMANI, S. R., and CHOWDHURY, O. H. (1983), 'Short Run Impacts of Food For Work Programme in Bangladesh', *Bangladesh Development Studies*, 11.

PANDA, M. K. (1981), 'Productivity Aspects of Wages in Food for Work Programme', *Economic and Political Weekly*, 16.

PANIKAR, P. G. K., and SOMAN, C. R. (1984), *Health Status of Kerala* (Trivandrum: Centre for Development Studies).

Project Evaluation Organization, Planning Commission (1979), *A Quick Evaluation Study of Food for Work Programmes* (New Delhi: Government of India).

RAHMAN, A. (1979), 'Usury Capital and Credit Relations in Bangladesh Agriculture: Some Implications for Capital Formation and Capitalist Growth', *Bangladesh Development Studies*, 7.

RATH, N. (1985), '"Garibi Hatao": Can IRDP Do It?', *Economic and Political Weekly*, 20.

REUTLINGER, S. (1984), 'Project Food Aid and Equitable Growth: Income Transfer Efficiency First!', *World Development*, 12.

RICHARDS, P., and GOONERATNE, W. (1980), *Basic Needs, Poverty and Government Policies in Sri Lanka* (Geneva: International Labour Office).

RODGERS, G. B. (1976), 'A Conceptualisation of Poverty in Rural India', *World Development*, 4.

SCITOVSKY, T. (1985), 'Economic Development in Taiwan and South Korea: 1965–81', *Food Research Institute Studies*, 19.

SEN, A. K. (1981*a*), 'Public Action and the Quality of Life in Developing Countries', *Oxford Bulletin of Economics and Statistics*, 43.

—— (1981*b*), *Poverty and Famines: An Essay on Entitlement and Deprivation* (Oxford: Oxford University Press).

—— (1985), *Commodities and Capabilities* (Amsterdam: North-Holland).

—— (1988), 'Sri Lanka's Achievements: How and When?', in Srinivasan and Bardhan (1988).

SIDDIQUI, K. (1985), 'An Evaluation of Grameen Bank Operations', in Mukhopadhyay (1985*b*).

SRINIVASAN, T. N., and BARDHAN, P. K. (ed.) (1988), *Rural Poverty in South Asia* (New York: Columbia University Press).

STREETEN, P. (1984), 'Basic Needs: Some Unsettled Questions', *World Development*, 12.

SUNDARAM, K., and TENDULKAR, S. D. (1985*a*), 'Anti-poverty Programmes in India: An Assessment', in Mukhopadhyay (1985*a*).

SUNDARAM, K., and TENDULKAR, S. D., (1985*b*), 'Integrated Rural Development Programme in India: A Case Study of a Poverty Eradication Programme', in Mukhopadhyay (1985*b*).

TAYLOR, C. L., and HUDSON, M. C. (1972), *World Handbook of Political and Social Indicators* (New Haven, Conn., and London: Yale University Press).

World Bank (1985), *World Development Report* (New York: Oxford University Press).

9

Feeding China: The Experience since 1949

Carl Riskin

China's approach to feeding its 22 per cent of the world population has varied considerably during the thirty-six years of the People's Republic, as have the results. In the late 1970s its leadership began repudiating much of the country's earlier experience. While food policy since 1978 has moved along new paths, there are nevertheless close links between recent accomplishments and the earlier record.

The purpose of this chapter is to survey the experience of food policy under the People's Republic in a comprehensive manner and in historical context. The first two sections present background information on China's agricultural economy and a chronology of important institutional developments since 1949. Section 9.3 then discusses food supply and nutrition in terms of national averages. The fourth section takes up in some detail the famine of 1959–62, and this is followed in Section 9.5 by a general discussion of food policy problems before the reforms that began in the late 1970s. Issues of regional and personal distribution of food are examined in the sixth section. Finally, there is a brief summary and conclusion.

9.1. Background features

The central fact of the Chinese food supply situation is the relative scarcity of arable land. John Lossing Buck (1956: 165) estimated in the 1930s that about 362,000 square miles were under cultivation in the main agricultural areas of China, which would make the cultivated area only about 10 per cent of a gross land area of about 3.7 million square miles. Dominated by arid grasslands in the north-west, high plateaux and massive mountain ranges in the west, and uneven hills in the south and south-west, the topography of China begrudges its people good farm land.

What there is of it is limited almost entirely to five specific areas (*Geography of China* 1972: 6–9): (1) the North-East or Heilongjiang Plain, which is China's principal producer of *gaoliang* (sorghum) and soybeans: (2) the North China Plain, earliest and largest of China's farm regions, dominated by the Yellow River and producing winter wheat, *gaoliang*, maize, and cotton; (3) the Middle

I would like to thank Thomas P. Bernstein, Jean Drèze, Keith Griffin, Mark Selden, and an anonymous referee for valuable comments on an earlier draft of this chapter. I alone am responsible for remaining errors as well as for interpretations of the data.

and Lower Changjiang (Yangtse) Plain, a major rice area; (4) the Chengdu Plain, a fertile rice-growing basin in western Sichuan; and (5) various south China valleys (especially the Pearl River Delta of southern Guangdong) that are ribbons of rice and subtropical cultivation amidst the prevailing hills.

This physical geography explains why 90 per cent of China's population lives on only one-sixth of the total land area. In fact, the last four of these regions account for about three-quarters of the population.

Official figures for cultivated acreage indicate a reduction from 108 million hectares in 1952 to 99.5 million in 1979 (Xue Muqiao 1981/2: vi–9).[1] The downward trend is explained by the fact that the 17 million hectares known to have been reclaimed between the late 1950s and late 1970s were more than offset by some 27 million hectares abandoned to new housing, factories, and road construction (Lardy 1983a: 3). Moreover, the lost acreage was on average more fertile than the marginal land brought under cultivation.

Arable land per capita thus declined by half between the early years of the PRC and the late 1970s, when it came to 0.1 hectares. Table 9.1 shows China's arable land–population ratio in comparison with that of several other countries. It is evident that China ranks lower in the amount of land available to its farm population than in its overall land availability.

Tables 9.2 and 9.3 look somewhat more closely at physical conditions. From the former it can be seen that the ratio of sown to cultivated area yields a multiple cropping index of about 1.5. This was pushed past the point of negative marginal returns in some areas in the late 1960s and early 1970s; it subsequently declined slightly. About 45 per cent of China's farmland is irrigated (Table 9.3), half of this by power machinery. The major increases in irrigated area occurred before 1975. Since 1978 neither total nor power irrigated area has increased (State Statistical Bureau 1984b: 26).

Table 9.1 Arable land per capita, mid-1970s:
international comparison

	Arable land per capita (ha)	Arable land per farm population (ha)
China	0.10	0.12
World	0.38	1.82
Asia (exc. China)	0.24	0.44
S. Korea	0.07	0.15
India	0.27	0.44
Japan	0.05	0.27
US	0.97	27.50

Source: Perkins and Yusuf (1984: 52).

[1] The statistical authorities warn that actual cultivated acreage in the early 1980s probably exceeded official estimates by as much as one-quarter to one-third. See World Bank (1985: 28).

Table 9.2 Relation between land, population, and labour force, China, 1952–1987

	Population (m.)	Agricultural labour force (m.)	Arable land (m. ha)	Sown area (m. ha)	Multiple cropping index	Arable land per capita (ha)	Arable land per agricultural worker (ha)
1952	575	173	107.9	141.3	1.3	0.19	0.62
1957	647	193	111.8	157.2	1.4	0.17	0.58
1965	725	234	103.6	143.3	1.4	0.14	0.44
1975	920	295	99.7	149.5	1.5	0.11	0.34
1984	1,035	309	98.4[a]	144.2	1.5	0.10	0.32
1987	1,081	317	95.9	144.9	1.5	0.09	0.30

[a] Estimate for 1983. But see n. 1 above.

Sources: Lardy (1983a: 4, 5); State Statistical Bureau 1984b, 1985c, 1988). World Bank (1985: 30).

Table 9.3 Irrigated area, China, 1952–1987

	Irrigated area (m. ha)		Irrigated area as % of cultivated area
	Total	% power irrigated	
1952	19.96	1.6	18.5
1957	27.34	4.4	24.4
1965	33.06	24.5	31.9
1975	43.30	n/a	43.4
1979	45.00	56.3	45.2
1984	44.45	56.4	45.2
1987	44.40	55.9	46.3

Source: Perkins and Yusuf (1984: 52); World Bank (1985: 30); State Statistical Bureau (1985c: 41; 1988: 233).

9.1. *The institutional framework*

Most of China's agriculture consisted of peasant smallholdings until 1955. Land reform, which lasted from the late 1940s to 1952, resulted in a fairly even distribution of land holdings. Nevertheless, remaining inequality, together with the great density of farm population, left less than half an acre of farm land per capita for the poorest three deciles of the rural population. The average 'poor peasant' farm of 1½ acres in southern Jiangsu Province could provide its owners with only about 1,500 kilocalories per day each (Ash 1976: 529). Some leaders, notably Mao Zedong, feared that the evident unviability of poor peasant farms implied that repolarization was inevitable. For that reason, as well as to make surplus extraction easier and to substitute large-scale organization of labour for capital investment, Mao moved quickly in the mid-1950s to collectivize agriculture. Between 1954 and 1956 virtually all of China's more than 100 million farm households joined collectives.[2] After a breathing period in 1957, the trend of rapid institutional change resumed in 1958 with the 'Great Leap Forward' and the formation of 'rural people's communes'.

The commune underwent several years of adjustment under the trying circumstances of the famine that ended the 'Leap'. By 1962 it had attained the form that, in large part, was to last almost two decades. It consisted of three levels of formal organization—the commune level at the top, the production team at the bottom, and between them the production brigade—plus the household economy below. The team consisted of 20 to 30 households and was the 'basic accounting unit', meaning that it organized ordinary farm labour and

---

[2] At the autumn harvest of 1954 only 2% of farm households were in small lower-stage co-operatives (in which land was still owned privately and yielded rent to its owners). By late 1956, 88% of households were in larger collectives and private ownership had been abolished. Despite the rapidity of this transition, the myth persists of a golden age of gradual, voluntary formation of co-operatives up to mid-1955.

distributed its net income among its members. The brigade distributed important inputs to the teams, including power, irrigation water, and the use of larger machines, and ran social services such as health clinics and primary schools. It was composed of an average of 7 or 8 teams. Brigades also had militia units, which were often thrown into construction projects.

The commune level, made up of 8–12 brigades, ran larger-scale enterprises, including small industries, and some operated hospitals and secondary schools. The commune was the basic level of state government in the country-side and it accordingly had governmental institutions such as People's Bank branches, tax collection and grain management offices, and supply and marketing co-operatives.

The household economy remained a crucial part of agricultural organization for most of the duration of the commune. Private plots and family sideline production provided a large share of cash income and of vegetables and other subsidiary foods.

This quadripartite division of labour was convenient for organizing produc-tion and capital construction work (such as water conservancy projects) at whichever level was called for by the required scale of work. It also facilitated the transmission of technological innovations from central research institutes to the villages.

Income was distributed in this system according to the number of 'work-points' earned in labour. Two basic methods of workpoint assignment were used: one based on evaluating the worker, the other the task. In the first, the individual was given a workpoint rating based on strength and skill (and later, on political 'attitude') and then earned that rating by putting in a full day's work. In the second, each task was rated and workers earned points by carrying out tasks. When the harvest was in, the team's net income—after deductions of anticipated production costs, agricultural tax, and contributions to an accumulation fund for capital purchases and a welfare fund to help indigent members—was divided by the total number of workpoints accumulated to derive the money value of a workpoint, and income was distributed accord-ingly. During the year, grain was usually made available on a per capita basis to member households; the money value of this grain was deducted at the time of distribution. This was an important factor in bringing about a relatively equal income distribution within individual teams and in putting a floor under rural income (see Section 9.6 below).

Neither workpoint system replicated the incentive furnished by the problem of survival itself in private farming. Both presented problems of allocative efficiency, for there was no immediate individual payoff for doing the right thing at the right time (as opposed to doing the task that brought the highest workpoints). Both also presented incentive problems *per se*, for they lengthened considerably the link between work and income, while putting a big premium on the values of co-operation and collective solidarity. The effectiveness of both systems thus depended heavily upon the strength of these values in a particular team, which in turn depended on the quality of team leadership and on the general social and political environment that shaped and limited team operations. In retrospect, the deterioration of that environment in the decade beginning with the Cultural Revolution (1966–9) doomed whatever chance the Chinese form of collective farming might have had to take advantage of its inherent strengths (e.g. in 'farmland capital construction') and achieve a high per capita rate of growth.

From the viewpoint of the reform government that came to power after 1978, the commune system suffered from a fatal flaw: because the commune itself was both the lowest level of state administration and the highest level of collective organization, it lent itself to government dictation to the farmers as if the production teams were state farms. Autocratic and sometimes corrupt behaviour by shielded state cadres, as well as compromise of the teams' collective autonomy in matters of production (e.g. decisions about what to plant) and distribution (e.g. putting arbitrary caps on distributed income), were quite common and are blamed for destroying the initiative of the farmers under the commune system. The egalitarian quality of intrateam distribution is also faulted, but it is difficult to know what to make of this criticism in view of the obvious link between the incentive implications of a given distribution and the fairness of the surrounding environment.

Starting about 1978 the government encouraged and then required the dissolution of the commune system in favour of a 'household responsibility system' (HRS), in which land was contracted out to individual households. The system of HRS that came to predominate allowed the household to keep all produce above an amount due to the 'collective' for meeting its tax and quota sales obligations and contributing to its accumulation and welfare fund. Workpoints were thus abolished, as was collective organization of much ordinary farm work. Some farm tasks, however, such as planting and harvesting, are often still done collectively (Bernstein 1986), as are capital construction projects, irrigation management, and other infrastructural work.[3]

The term 'quota sales' in the preceding paragraph refers to an essential institution in China's food supply system from the mid-1950s until 1985. Farmers or their collectives in areas producing more than their subsistence needs of grains and some other crops were obligated to sell a portion of the surplus to the state at below-market 'quota prices'. The sales obligation was calculated as a fraction of 'normal yield' and was kept constant for several years as an incentive to improve yields. The treatment of above-quota output varied over time; in recent years it was divided into two categories, one of which would bring 'above-quota' prices and the other still higher 'negotiated' prices from the state. The state also undertook to resell grain at quota prices to grain-deficient areas. Standards for rural grain distribution varied by region.

[3] On the post-1978 reforms see, *inter alia*, Bernstein (1984*b*, 1986); Domes (1982); Khan and Lee (1983); Lin (1983); Shue (1984); Watson (1983); Zweig (1982).

In the cities, however, grain was strictly rationed; besides stretching tight supplies, urban rationing was a crucial element in the control of rural–urban migration.

In 1985 the state abolished the mandatory quota system. Now farmers contract their sales to the state and sell surplus on the open market. This change was carried out under conditions of relative grain abundance. Total grain purchases had risen more than proportionally with the rapid post-reform increases in output, going from 51 MMT in 1978 to 117 MMT in 1984 (State Statistical Bureau 1985a: 480).[4] Since the state makes losses on its grain trade as a means of subsidizing urban consumption, this development entailed a growing financial burden (see Section 9.6 below).

The immediate effect of the shift from mandatory quotas to contract purchases was to lighten this burden by relieving the state of the obligation to purchase at premium prices all above-quota grain offered to it. In 1985 the state purchased only 75 MMT of rice, wheat, and corn (Erisman 1986: 20). Peasants must now dispose of extra grain on the open market and the state will intervene only if the market price falls below a set trigger level. Grain production responded in 1985 with the first decline in several years, a sharp fall of 28 MMT, or 7 per cent.[5]

Aside from lightening the state's burden, it seems that the contract system as now practised differs little from the previous quota system. Local cadres often assign 'contractual obligations' as they once assigned quotas, although in some cases more genuine negotiations occur (Oi 1986). Since the state continues to set 'quota' and 'above-quota' prices (70 per cent of contract sales are supposed to take place at the latter price) and purchase targets, the system clearly embodies a mix of plan and market elements.

9.3. *National food supply and nutrition*

Since 1950 foodgrains (which in Chinese statistics include soybeans, tubers at 5 : 1 weight ratio, and pulses) have supplied some 86–89 per cent of available energy and 80–85 per cent of available protein (Piazza 1983: 17–18). The grain harvest has thus been a major determinant of the overall food situation.

---

[4] Data are in 'trade grain', i.e. rice and millet are measured in husked form, other grains in unprocessed form.

[5] While bad weather also affected the grain crop in 1985, policies, including the sudden disappearance of market security for grain producers and a structure of relative prices that distinctly favours industry, trade, and sideline activity over crop growing, probably played a major role. CIA analysts argue that 'much of the decrease in grain production in 1985 probably can be attributed to the new rural policies' (US Central Intelligence Agency 1986: 9). However, given severe storage and disposal problems that occurred in 1984 and the underdevelopment of a grain-using animal husbandry industry, reducing grain production was quite a rational course of action for the farmers to take.

Table 9.4 Aggregate and per capita foodgrain
production, China, 1952–1985

Year	Aggregate output (MMT)	Per capita output (kg)
1952	163.92	288.00
1953	166.83	287.00
1954	169.52	285.00
1955	183.94	302.00
1956	192.75	310.00
1957	195.05	306.00
1958	200.00	306.00
1959	170.00	255.00
1960	143.50	215.00
1961	147.50	223.00
1962	160.00	240.50
1963	170.00	249.00
1964	187.50	269.00
1965	194.53	272.00
1966	214.00	291.00
1967	217.82	289.00
1968	209.06	270.00
1969	210.97	265.00
1970	239.96	293.00
1971	250.14	297.00
1972	240.48	279.00
1973	264.94	300.50
1974	275.27	305.50
1975	284.52	310.50
1976	286.31	307.50
1977	282.73	299.50
1978	304.77	318.50
1979	332.12	342.50
1980	320.56	326.50
1981	325.02	327.00
1982	354.50	351.50
1983	387.28	379.50
1984	407.31	395.50
1985	378.98	362.18

Sources: State Statistical Bureau (1983*a*; 1985*a*; 1986*a*: 27,
33).

Foodgrain output from 1952 to 1985 is shown in Table 9.4.[6] Over the entire period aggregate grain production increased about 1½ times, for an average annual growth rate of 2.8 per cent. From 1957 to 1977, however, the growth rate was only 1.8 per cent, while it rose to 3.9 per cent during 1978–85. On a per capita basis, food production averaged 0.9 per cent growth over the entire period. The two decades 1956–77 saw only a 0.2 per cent growth rate, but since 1978 it has averaged 2.6 per cent. Both production and consumption per capita fluctuated substantially from year to year, although the use of stocks and imports and the treatment of commercial uses of foodgrain as a residual reduced fluctuations in consumption relative to those in production (see Fig. 9.1). It is also apparent that annual variability in consumption was greater during 1958–73 than in the years of relative normalcy that preceded and followed that turbulent period.

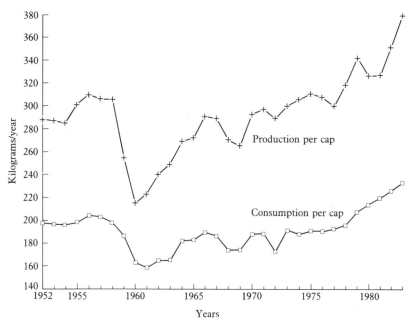

Fig. 9.1 Cereal production and consumption per capita, China, 1952–1984

6 A word needs to be said about the accuracy of Chinese official statistics. Checks of internal consistency and other considerations have convinced most independent scholars that government statistics during most of the post-1949 years have been accurate expressions of what the Chinese government believed to be true. The community of foreign scholars has generally found them usable on this basis (see Eckstein 1980). The government has often not released information available to it; there have been periods, especially during the Great Leap Forward, when politically motivated distortion of information has occurred; the bases and/or definitions of statistics are frequently not made clear; capacity to collect and process accurate information has fluctuated quite sharply, and methods (e.g. sampling methods) are sometimes flawed. Thus, to say that deliberate falsification has rarely occurred is not to confirm the accuracy of official information. The problems of using such information, however, and the need for suitable caution are generally well known and accepted by students of the Chinese economy.

Table 9.5 Daily per capita availability of energy, protein, and fat,
China, 1952–1982

Year	Total energy (Kcal)	Annual change in energy (%)	Total protein (g)	Total fat (g)
1952	1,861		51	24
1953	1,879	1.0	50	23
1954	1,895	0.9	50	24
1955	2,005	5.8	53	25
1956	2,051	2.3	53	24
1957	2,045	−0.3	55	24
1958	2,053	0.4	54	26
1959	1,722	−16.1	46	22
1960	1,453 (1,875)	−15.6	39	16
1961	1,558	7.2	43	16
1962	1,660	6.5	45	17
1963	1,776	7.0	46	19
1964	1,934	8.9	50	22
1965	1,967	1.7	53	22
1966	2,078	5.6	53	23
1967	2,042	−1.7	52	23
1968	1,931	−5.4	49	22
1969	1,881	−2.6	48	22
1970	2,076 (2,131)	10.4	52	23
1971	2,082	0.3	51	23
1972	2,006	−3.7	49	24
1973	2,160	7.7	53	25
1974	2,194	1.6	54	24
1975	2,210	0.7	55	24
1976	2,220	0.5	56	24
1977	2,236	0.7	56	25
1978	2,360	5.5	58	25
1979	2,562	8.6	65	31
1980	2,487 (2,611)	−2.9	64	32
1981	2,517 (2,650)	1.2	65	33
1982	2,729	8.4	68	38

Note: The source notes that figures in parentheses show estimates of energy availability based only upon a 20% wastage rate for grain, as assumed by the Chinese government. The World Bank estimates are based on commodity-specific deductions for seed, feed, waste, and manufacturing use.

Source: World Bank (1984: 164), based on methodology of Piazza (1983).

Estimates of the average daily per capita availabilities of energy, protein, and fat between 1952 and 1982 are shown in Table 9.5 and Figs. 9.2 and 9.3. Energy availability has trended upward with per capita grain production, and has been subject to similar fluctuations. Estimates have been made of per capita

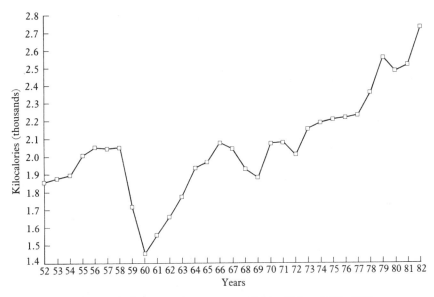

Fig. 9.2 Daily per capita energy available, China, 1952–1982

requirements of energy and protein in China for 1953 and 1979.[7] Energy availability in 1953 fell short of estimated requirements (put at 2,023 Kcal) by 5 per cent. In 1979 availability exceeded the higher requirements of that year (2,185 Kcal) by 18 per cent.

Protein availability appears to have exceeded safe requirements substantially throughout the entire period. However, Piazza (1983: 23–7) provides alternative estimates that take into account protein quality (which determines the degree of absorption and utilization of amino acids). Much protein consumed in China is derived from grain and is of low quality. Accordingly, Piazza's estimates of 'net protein utilization' fall significantly short of requirements in 1950, 1951, and the years 1960–2. Shortfalls might have been greater in those years and might have existed in other years when energy availability did not meet requirements; under such circumstances protein sources may be utilized by the body for energy rather than for protein (Piazza 1983: 23, 27).[8] Lardy (1983a: 156) believes that average protein availability must have been lower in 1976–8 than in 1957 because of the marked decline in per capita soybean production between those two dates; and that this presented a serious nutritional problem in rural areas: 'Widespread anemia among children has been attributed by Chinese medical sources to protein deficiency in the diet,

[7] See World Bank (1984: 169–72). The estimates use WHO/FAO standards and data on age-specific average body weights, age distribution, and assumptions about activity levels.

[8] On the other hand, Piazza's estimates ignore protein complementarity, and thus *understate* to some degree the quality of protein consumption (1983a: 27).

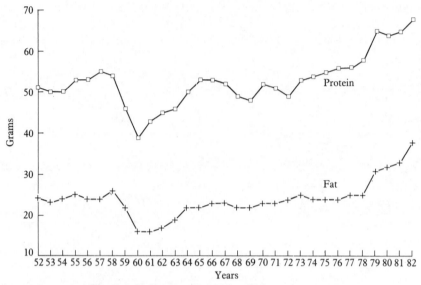

Fig. 9.3 Daily protein and fat, China, 1952–1982

because anemia is widespread except in the traditional soybean-growing areas of the Northeast' (Lardy, 1983a: 156).[9]

Evidence of secular improvements in nutrition up to the early 1980s is limited. One of China's most noteworthy accomplishments, namely the steady rise in estimated life expectancy at birth[10] from 34 years in 1952 to 69 years in 1982 (World Bank 1984: 113), was influenced by many factors besides nutrition. There were marked gains between 1957 and 1977 in height for age of school-age children in some urban and prosperous suburban areas, notably suburban Shanghai, Beijing, and Guangzhou (Canton), but hardly any longitudinal data are available from areas more representative of the conditions of most Chinese (Jamison and Trowbridge 1984; World Bank 1984: 19–20).

Anthropometric surveys from 1975 and 1979 reveal evidence of little malnutrition in urban areas but a continuing problem in rural ones. There is also considerable regional variation in the incidence of malnutrition. The 1979 survey of 16 provinces and centrally administered municipalities found that a national average of 2.6 per cent of urban and 12.7 per cent of rural 7-year-old boys were stunted.[11] Provincial rural rates (not including suburbs of municipalities) ranged up to 37.1 per cent in Sichuan. In seeking to explain these results, World Bank analysts argue that diarrhoeal diseases remain much more

[9] Lardy (1983a) reports an experiment in which the incidence of anaemia among children in one region was rapidly and sharply reduced by adding a small amount of beans to their diet.

[10] This 'steady' rise was interrupted by the famine of 1959–62. Life expectancy fell from 38 years in 1957 to 25 in 1960, according to World Bank estimates, before resuming its upward trend.

[11] However, the rural figure is biased downward because it includes suburban areas of major cities.

prevalent in rural than urban areas, and they also cite urban–rural differences in the quantity and quality of the diet (World Bank 1984: 31). No significant difference in incidence of stunting was found between males and females (World Bank 1984: 30, 32).

As a result of the agricultural reforms beginning in 1978, including rises in farm prices, encouragement of trade and diversification, and long-term household contracting of production, per capita consumption of food began to increase at substantially higher rates, as is shown in Tables 1.6, 1.7. Grain consumption per capita grew by almost 4 per cent between 1977 and 1984, compared with prior long-term rates of well under 1 per cent. Although absolute consumption levels of meat, fish, eggs, and other non-cereals are still

Table 9.6 Per capita consumption, various foods, selected years, China, 1952–1984 (kg)

Year	Grain	Edible oil	Pork	Beef, mutton	Poultry	Fresh eggs	Aquatic products
1952	197.67	2.05	5.92	0.92	0.43	1.02	2.67
1957	203.06	2.42	5.08	1.11	0.50	2.51	2.34
1962	164.63	1.09	2.22	0.79	0.38	1.53	2.96
1965	182.84	1.72	6.29	1.02	0.36	2.84	3.33
1970	187.22	1.61	6.02	0.82	0.32	2.64	2.94
1975	190.52	1.73	7.63	0.72	0.35	3.26	3.26
1976	190.28	1.60	7.38	0.66	0.35	3.52	3.52
1977	192.07	1.56	7.25	0.71	0.36	3.70	3.23
1978	195.46	1.60	7.67	0.75	0.44	3.94	3.50
1979	207.03	1.96	9.66	0.82	0.57	4.15	3.22
1980	213.81	2.30	11.16	0.83	0.80	4.54	3.41
1981	219.18	2.94	11.08	0.85	0.83	4.87	3.57
1982	225.46	3.54	11.76	1.03	1.02	5.05	3.85
1983	232.23	4.03	12.35	1.11	1.18	5.92	4.02
1984	251.34	4.70	13.02	1.25	1.35	7.81	4.36

Note: Grain is measured in 'trade grain'. 'Edible oil' refers to vegetable oil and includes the oil equivalent of oil-bearing crops.

Source: State Statistical Bureau (1985*a*: 576).

Table 9.7 Average annual growth rate of per capita consumption, various foods, selected years, China, 1952–1984 (%)

Years	Grain	Edible oil	Pork	Beef, mutton	Poultry	Fresh eggs	Aquatic products
1952–7	0.5	3.4	−3.0	3.8	0.03	19.7	26.6
1965–77	0.4	−0.8	1.2	−3.0	0.00	2.2	0.0
1977–84	3.9	17.3	8.7	8.6	21.50	11.6	4.5

Source: Table 9.6.

very low, their differentially high growth over recent years offers hope that the Chinese diet can finally begin to escape from its overwhelming dependence on cereals.

9.4. The famine of 1959–1962: extent and measurement

Fluctuations around the trend in food supply have created periods of extreme national shortage. The most serious such event was the famine of 1959–62, perhaps the greatest famine on record in terms of scale of loss of life. After rising by 2.6 per cent in 1958, foodgrain output fell sharply for the following two years to reach a 1960 nadir some 29 per cent below the 1958 peak (Table 9.4). The average per capita level of grain consumption in the countryside fell from 204 kg in 1957 to only 154 kg in 1961 (Table 9.9) and one estimate of national average per capita daily caloric intake in 1960 put it at only 1,453 calories (Table 9.5).[12]

Chinese reports at the time mentioned the existence of malnutrition, 'serious famine', and even 'starvation' (Walker 1977: 559) but did not report the magnitude of loss of life. More recent foreign analyses, based upon newly released mortality and fertility statistics for the years in question (see Table 9.8) as well as the population age distribution emerging from the 1964 and 1982 censuses, suggest an appalling loss (Aird 1980, 1982: Ashton et al. 1984; Coale 1981, 1984; Sun Yefang 1981). The increases in official mortality rates alone during 1959–61 imply deaths above the 'normal' level (defined by the 1957 mortality rate) numbering over 15 million. One estimate, that of Ashton et al. (1984), is almost twice this figure.[13] There remain many unanswered questions about the sources and quality of the statistics, which describe a period in which the statistical system itself was in disarray.[14] At this point no exact estimate of famine mortality can be accepted with confidence, but available information leaves little doubt that it was very large.

Both natural conditions and socio-political factors contributed to the situation, although their relative shares of the blame cannot be assessed with

[12] The method of estimation used by the Chinese government yields a higher calorie intake of 1,875 Kcal for 1960 (see Note to Table 1.5). Ashton et al. (1984: 622) put it at 1,535 Kcal for that year.

[13] This estimate, of 29.5 million premature deaths, also has problems associated with it. It results in part from an unrealistically low estimate of 'normal' deaths obtained by applying normal infant mortality rates to the abnormally small number of births that took place during the crisis. Furthermore, the ratio of child to adult mortality fluctuates in ways that are hard to explain. Unreported deaths are also assumed to fluctuate sharply—from 28 to 47% of actual deaths during the famine years.

[14] The fact that the regime which released these figures had an interest in discrediting its predecessor has led some to discount the figures themselves. My own view is that to have manufactured such enormous mortality statistics in order to attack the previous government would have been political overkill. To say that the figures were unlikely to have been deliberately inflated, however, is not to say that they are necessarily accurate. The fact is, nothing concrete is known about how they were arrived at.

confidence. Natural disasters were widespread, especially in 1960 (Freeberne 1962), but state policy undoubtedly contributed to the shortages, doing both short- and long-run damage to agriculture, as well as complicating and delaying relief measures. Construction of dams and reservoirs without prior assessment of their impact on the water table led to salinization and alkaliniza-tion of the soil. Such damage is not easily reversed and helps to explain why the collective grain output of the three North China Plain provinces of Henan, Hebei, and Shandong did not regain its previous peak level until the late 1960s (Walker 1977: 558). Innovations such as deep ploughing and close planting, promoted by the centre beyond the bounds of rationality, also reduced output, as did the excessive drain of labour out of agriculture and into small-scale industry and transport. The military organization of farm production and confiscation of peasants' personal property, especially in the earlier part of the Leap, the elimination in many places of farmers' private plots, the overcentral-ized and redistributive character of the early communes, and the adoption of a public dining hall system featuring free food all harmed peasant incentives.

Great Leap policies not only helped create the crisis but also caused costly delays in responding to it. The politically motivated exaggeration of harvest size and destruction of objective reporting systems kept the leadership in the dark about real supply conditions: 'Leaders believed in 1959–60 that they had 100 MMT more grain than they actually did' (Bernstein 1984a: 13). Some local cadres, their reputations dependent upon meeting impossibly high output commitments, failed to seek relief or even sealed their localities to keep news of real conditions from getting out.

Table 9.8 Demographic crisis and state procurement of foodgrains, China, 1955–1965

	Crude birth rate	Crude death rate	Natural increase rate	Grain output	State procurement		% of output procured	
					Total	Net	Total	Net
1955	32.60	12.28	20.32	183.9	50.7	36.2	27.6	19.7
1956	31.90	11.40	20.50	192.7	45.4	28.7	23.6	14.9
1957	34.03	10.80	23.23	195.0	48.0	33.9	24.6	17.4
1958	29.22	11.98	17.24	200.0	58.8	41.7	29.4	20.9
1959	24.78	14.59	10.19	170.0	67.4	47.6	39.7	28.0
1960	20.86	25.43	−4.57	143.5	51.1	30.9	35.6	21.5
1961	18.02	14.24	3.78	147.5	40.5	25.8	27.4	17.5
1962	37.01	10.02	26.99	160.0	38.1	25.7	23.8	16.1
1963	43.37	10.04	33.33	170.0	44.0	28.9	25.9	17.0
1964	39.14	11.50	27.64	187.5	47.4	31.8	25.3	17.0
1965	37.88	9.50	28.38	194.5	48.7	33.6	25.0	17.3

Note: 'Net' procurement refers to gross procurement minus resales to deficit areas in the countryside.

Source: State Statistical Bureau (1984c: 83, 370).

Excessive procurement of grain was a prime contributor to shortages in the countryside (Bernstein 1984a; Lardy 1983a). Under the mistaken belief that harvests had broken all records, the government in 1958, 1959, and 1960 procured 22 per cent, 40 per cent, and 6 per cent, respectively, more than in 1957 (Table 9.8). In 1957 gross procurement had come to 24.6 per cent of the harvest; by 1959 it had gone up to 39.7 per cent, and in the year of greatest crisis, 1960, it was 35.6 per cent of output. Even after resales to deficit rural areas it remained a full 10 percentage points higher in 1959 and 4 points higher in 1960 than in 1957. Rural areas were the chief sufferers: as Table 9.9 and Fig. 9.4 show, government efforts to keep the cities adequately supplied succeeded in suppressing rural per capita grain supplies well below urban supplies, where they stayed right up to the 1980s.[15] Substantial grain imports, designed to supply the coastal cities and relieve pressure on the countryside, finally began in 1961, two years late.[16]

Table 9.9 Annual per capita grain
supply and daily food energy,
China, 1957–1964

Year	Annual average per capita consumption of grain (kg)	
	National	(Rural)
1957	203	(204)
1958	198	(201)
1959	187	(183)
1960	164	(156)
1961	159	(154)
1962	165	(161)
1963	165	(160)
1964	182	(178)

Note: Data are in 'trade grain' and labelled 'pingjun meiren shenghuo xiaofei liang' (average per capita amount of consumption).

Source: State Statistical Bureau (1984a: 27).

[15] State Statistical Bureau (1984a: 27). State Statistical Bureau (1983b: 509) shows urban–rural differentials in calorie consumption ranging from 380 to 490 Kcal per day for every year from 1978 to 1982, whereas Fig. 9.4 indicates that rural inhabitants had a growing advantage in grain consumption from 1980 on. It is likely that city dwellers maintained their superiority with respect to non-grain foods, however.

[16] These imports, together with reduced procurement pressure on the countryside and the belated organization of relief measures—including stringent conservation measures, emergency food-growing campaigns, and vigorous redistribution to affected regions—probably provide a sufficient explanation for the fall in mortality after 1960 despite continued low levels of consumption and energy intake through 1963. Note also that the energy (Table 9.5) and per capita grain consumption (Table 9.9) series are from different sources; there is no immediate explanation for the fact that the former rises from 1960 to 1961 while the latter falls.

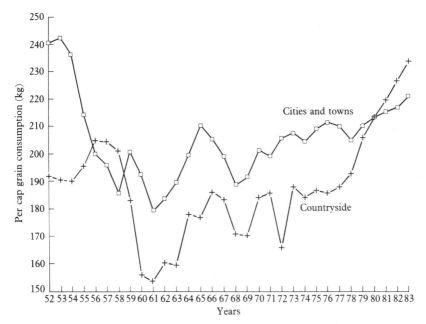

Fig. 9.4 Grain consumption per capita, urban vs. rural areas, China, 1952–1983

Party and government decisions worsened the crisis in more general ways, as well. Thus, Mao was in the process of moderating the policies of the Great Leap in 1959 when the popular Defence Minister and veteran revolutionary Peng Dehuai criticized them and thus indirectly challenged Mao's leadership at a meeting of the Party Central Committee. The purge of Peng Dehuai resulted in a resurrection of the excessive policies he had attacked, which must have deepened and prolonged the famine. Moreover, as Mao himself later acknowledged, preoccupation from late 1959 with the growing polemic with the Soviet Union slowed the leadership's perception of and response to the domestic crisis (Bernstein 1984a: 31; MacFarquhar 1983: parts iii and iv).[17]

In the 1959–61 famine, then, there was a complementarity between short-falls in supply, on the one hand, and deprivation of food entitlements, on the other. Policy was itself partly responsible for the fall in supply, as well as for the allocation of the resulting burden. The process of depriving those affected of their entitlements began with the wrecking of the food production system during the Great Leap Forward, continued with the abandonment of objective statistical reporting, which prevented remedial measures (including imports) from being undertaken until quite late, and ended with the state's overprocure-ment of grain to protect the cities and the leadership's preoccupation with domestic and foreign political matters.

Ordinarily, one would expect that in times of scarcity a greater than normal

[17] Much in the above paragraphs on the famine is taken from Riskin (1987: ch. 6).

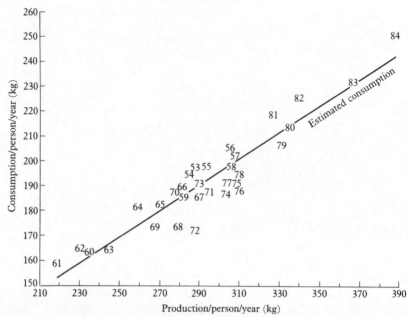

Fig. 9.5 Grain production and consumption, China, 1953–1984

proportion of food output would be eaten, as waste and non-food uses of grain are reduced and stocks consumed. Fig. 9.5 plots the regression of consumption on (half-year lagged) production (both per capita).[18] The bad years, 1960–2, are above the line as expected, but very close to it, while 1959 (probably because of the exceptionally large fraction of waste in the 1958 output) lies virtually on the line. More unexpectedly, other bad years, such as 1968, 1969, 1972, and 1977 (see Fig. 9.1), show consumption well *below* the line.

Part of the explanation may lie in a pronounced downward time trend through the 1970s—not captured in Fig. 9.5—in the fraction of lagged per capita production consumed. Fig. 9.6 shows this trend, and the fluctuations of the annual observations around it. The crisis years now emerge starkly, the fraction of output consumed rising well above the trend line. For subsequent bad years, especially 1968 and 1972, however, the unexpected outcome of Fig. 9.5 is accentuated, for these observations lie well below the trend line.

This suggests that stocks were not used very effectively to even out consumption over the harvest cycle during the chaotic period 1966–76, despite substantial annual food imports. Consumption seems to have been cut back at the first signs of an impending poor harvest. It then recovered whether the next harvest was better or not (in the latter event, 1969 being a case in point,

[18] The regression is of consumption on the average of current and previous year's output (since much of consumption is of the previous year's harvest): $C_t = a + \frac{1}{2}b(P_t + P_{t-1})$, where C = annual foodgrain consumption per capita, P = annual foodgrain production per capita, and t = year. The results are as follows: constant $a = 36.19$; production coefficient $b = 0.53$; $R^2 = 0.89$.

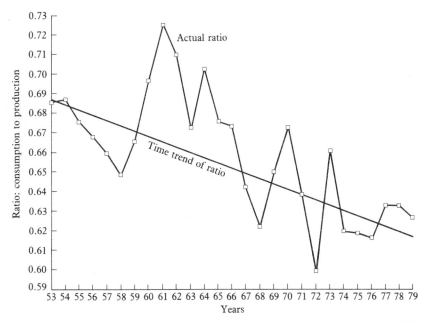

Fig. 9.6 Grain consumption per capita/production per capita, actual and trend, China, 1952–1979

presumably because stocks had been drawn down). We know that the capacity of the government to redistribute food spatially declined over the 1960s and 1970s (see section 1.6 below); it seems that its ability to redistribute temporally may also have suffered.

9.5. *Problems of food policy before the reform*

Chinese statistics show that per capita grain production levels of 1956–8 were not attained again until 1973 (see Table 9.4), and per capita grain 'livelihood consumption'[19] levels of 1956 were equalled again only in 1979 (State Statistical Bureau 1984a: 27). World Bank estimates of per capita calorie consumption find the 1958 level being matched in 1970 (Table 9.5). Although discussion of the standards and criteria that must lie behind evaluation —especially in a comparative context—is beyond the scope of this paper, it is hard to avoid the conclusion that the record of China's food provision up to the end of the 1970s suffered in some respects from deeply flawed policies (and, during the height of the factional strife throughout the 1966–76 decade, from the *absence* of coherent policy).

---

[19] As measured in 'trade grain'. 'Livelihood consumption' probably excludes grain consumed in the form of meat.

This impression is strengthened by the great success of agriculture in the years after 1977. Between that year and 1984, per capita foodgrain output increased by 31 per cent (Table 9.4) while other sectors of agriculture were growing even more quickly. It is widely believed that the basis for this rapid advance was laid in the 1960s and 1970s by such improvements as the extension of irrigated area, the adoption of improved varieties of wheat, rice, and other grains, the development of chemical fertilizer and pesticide industries, and the levelling and terracing of fields via winter 'farmland capital construction' work.

These positive developments of the collective era were prevented from bearing fruit in growing per capita supplies of food by policies that weakened farm incentives. The speed with which output bounded forward when incentives were restored implies that resources already in place were being productively reallocated.

Chief among the negative policies pre-1978 was that of local foodgrain self-sufficiency. Government policy strongly encouraged all regions to be self-sufficient in grains, including those with a long history of specialization in raising economic crops or livestock or in other non-grain activities. Because the state monopolized the grain trade and could withhold grain from areas that resisted abandoning their specialities, the localities had no choice but to comply. The result was that grain basket areas were deprived of their markets, while non-grain regions produced grain inefficiently.

Both objective circumstance and ideological predilection contributed to the policy of foodgrain self-sufficiency. Through much of the period in question, China's leaders felt threatened, first from the US, which was at war with Vietnam on China's border, then from the USSR. Local self-sufficiency was seen as part of a strategy of defence in depth against a threat from abroad. In addition, however, it seems that Mao Zedong and his followers in the leadership were intent on developing a form of economic organization that would minimize the bureaucratic hierarchies and rigidities associated with central administrative planning, yet without developing the role of the market as a substitute. As part of this quest, Mao had waged political war on the planning system and its upholders in the party and government, largely disabling it by the 1970s. The state in the end had neither the capacity nor the will to implement the complex redistribution of goods that would have been necessary had regional specialization and division of labour been encouraged. Local food self-sufficiency was, in the end, a principle dictated by necessity.[20]

The maintenance of low purchase prices for farm products was another policy that hurt production incentives. Table 9.10 shows official estimates of the commodity terms of trade between agriculture and industry from the 1930s until 1979. It is acknowledged in China that a 'scissors gap' has existed since the early days of the PRC and has functioned as a virtual tax on agriculture (the

[20] This thesis is argued in detail in Riskin (1987).

Table 9.10 Terms of trade between agriculture and industry, China, 1930–1936 to 1979 (official estimates)

Year	1950 = 100			Terms of trade (1936 = 100)
	Agricultural prices (1)	Industrial prices (2)	Terms of trade (1)/(2)	
1930–6 (av.)	49.6	37.6	131.9	100.0
1944	—	—	50.1	38.0
1948	—	—	79.1	60.0
1951	119.6	110.2	108.5	82.3
1952	121.6	109.7	110.8	84.0
1957	146.2	112.1	130.4	98.9
1962	193.4	126.6	152.8	115.8
1965	185.1	118.4	156.3	118.5
1975	208.7	109.6	190.4	144.4
1978	207.3	109.8	188.8	143.1
1979	265.5	109.9	241.6	183.1

Notes: Reprinted from Riskin (1987: table 10.11), where sources are given. 'Agricultural prices' are 'purchase prices of agricultural and subsidiary products' and 'industrial prices' are 'retail prices of industrial goods in the countryside'.

actual tax having declined in importance since the early 1950s). Table 9.10 appears to show the gap narrowing substantially between the 1950s and late 1970s. Yet, despite the fact that one yuan of agricultural earnings apparently purchased 74 per cent more industrial goods in 1978 than in 1951, there were renewed complaints in the late 1970s that the scissors gap remained wide, and some even claimed it had widened, creating difficulties for the farmers and depressing their living standards.

The explanation for this apparent anomaly may lie in flaws in the price indices used in Table 9.10. The industrial index seems to be composed of the prices of traditional goods, such as kerosene, salt, sugar, and matches, and to omit highly priced modern producer goods, such as farm chemicals and machinery (Yang and Li 1980: 207). Prices of the latter kinds of goods were very high in China relative to their international levels. A kilogram of rice exchanged in China for less than half the amount of fertilizer it could command on the world market, and it took five or six times as much rice to purchase a tractor of given horsepower in China as in Japan (ibid.). These prices imposed heavy burdens on farmers who were increasingly dependent on modern inputs to overcome diminishing returns to scarce land. A national survey found that, between 1962 and 1976, production costs per hectare for six grain crops grew by 305 yuan, exceeding the gain in output value per hectare of Y249, and causing net income per hectare to fall (Yang and Li 1980: 207–8).

Farm prices also fared poorly against those of industrial consumer goods. A sample of the low exchange rate of rice against various consumer goods, relative to Hong Kong prices, is given in Table 9.11. Low farm prices not only hurt production incentives; they also contributed to the urban–rural gap in income and entitlement to food over much of the period (Fig. 9.4).

Table 9.11 Terms of trade between rice and selected industrial goods, Guangzhou and Hong Kong, mid-1970s

	No. of kg of husked, polished rice required to buy one unit in		Ratio: Guangzhou–Hong Kong
	Guangzhou	Hong Kong	
Portable radio (Guangzhou)	14.0	6.0	2.3
Thermos bottle (Guangzhou)	15.5	3.5	4.4
Sewing machine (Shanghai)	616.5	124.0	5.0
Bicycle (Shanghai)	582.0	110.5	5.3
Camera (Shanghai)	462.5	59.0	7.8
Alarm clock (Shanghai)	75.5	7.5	10.1

Note: Cities in parentheses indicate place of manufacture. Data refer to identical brands sold in Guangzhou and Hong Kong.
Source: Liu (1980: 5–6).

In 1978, the Central Committee raised farm prices sharply. Grain quota purchase prices were increased by 20 per cent, beginning with the summer harvest of 1979, and an additional 50 per cent premium was set for above-quota sales. Purchase prices of cotton, oil-bearing crops, sugar, and other farm and sideline products were also raised. The average price increase for all agricultural purchases was about 22 per cent (Cheng Zhiping 1983: 19). Smaller price hikes followed in subsequent years, and the proportion of state purchases at above-quota and negotiated prices also rose from negligible levels in 1977 to reach 60 per cent in 1981 (Travers 1984: 242). The resulting average purchase price increases in the years 1980–4 for farm and subsidiary goods were as follows (State Statistical Bureau 1986b: 623):

1980	7.1%
1981	5.9%
1982	2.2%
1983	4.4%
1984	4.0%

However, industrial prices also rose during the first half of the 1980s (Lardy 1983a: 192); agricultural means of production sold by state commercial organs rose 18 per cent between 1978 and 1984 (State Statistical Bureau 1985a: 533). It is thus unclear in what direction the commodity terms of trade moved after 1980.

However, farm purchasing power might be better gauged by either the single factoral or the income terms of trade.[21] Farm output and labour productivity both grew rapidly between 1978 and 1984. Their growth must have outpaced any conceivable decline in agriculture's commodity terms of trade, as farmers used their new freedom to select more profitable output mixes, and as the new incentives spurred them to greater effort and efficiency. Agriculture's income and single factoral terms of trade must therefore have improved, and with them farmers' access to industrial goods.[22]

Linked to the abandoned policies of grain self-sufficiency and low farm prices was that of state dictation to the communes. Nominally, the communes and their subunits were collectively owned, and policy should have been made by their members. The team leaders, in particular, were not state cadres but were paid out of team income. Like other commune cadres but more so, they owed their success not only to the ability to satisfy higher authorities, but also to their rapport with the villagers. The degree to which rural leaders exercised development initiative and also protected their constituents from the more arbitrary demands of the higher levels has probably been underestimated in recent indictments of the commune system.

However, it is also true that the ambiguous identity of the commune, which was the lowest level of state administration as well as a collective economic organization, facilitated the practice of the government issuing direct orders to the farmers. In the 1960s and 1970s this became common. Cropping patterns, technological choices, and income distribution all became subject to government determination. Not only did the workpoint system tend to produce a highly even intravillage distribution to minimize the social friction that differentiation would produce, but caps were put on personal income as a matter of state policy. Thus, even solidary collectives with relatively equal distribution could not hope to raise personal incomes commensurately with productivity.

Rhetorically, the post-1978 reforms were committed to respecting peasant and collective autonomy. The abandonment of the commune institution was justified because it removed the state from direct political control of farm production activities. The substitute *xiang* or township government is a purely political body. The death of the commune also meant the weakening of the structures of egalitarian distribution in the countryside. Individual household farming, under the encouragement of state policy favouring 'letting some get rich first', has encouraged those with superior skills, labour power, or political access to forge ahead of their less well-endowed neighbours. Collective

[21] The commodity terms of trade index N is here simply P_a/P_i (where P_a and P_i are price indexes for agricultural and industrial goods). The single factoral terms of trade, here $N \times Z_a$ (where Z_a is an index of farm labour productivity), measure changes in the command over industrial goods of a unit of agricultural labour. The income terms of trade, here $N \times Q_a$ (where Q_a is an index of agricultural output), measure changes in agriculture's overall access to industrial goods.

[22] I am indebted to Keith Griffin for this point.

autonomy and individual differentiation are two quite separate issues; China seems to have moved between the extremes of state-controlled collectives and family farms, bypassing autonomous collectives.[23]

9.6. *Distribution of food*

Rationing, an ethic of relative equality as well as frugality, and powerful state organization have been credited with stretching meagre food supplies over China's enormous population so that the most extreme deprivation to be found in many other poor countries was on the whole avoided most of the time (the major exception, of course, being 1959–1961). Impressive statistics on life expectancy and infant mortality are consistent with this picture, and it is not contradicted by the observations of international observers.

The subject of food distribution is a good deal more complex than this, however, and the record has also varied substantially over time. The question of urban–rural differentials in food availability has already been touched on. This section will discuss the interprovincial and interpersonal dimensions of the Chinese approach to distribution.

(a) *Variations by province*

Published reports in China in the late 1970s and early 1980s stated that in 1978 100 million peasants had yearly per capita grain rations of less than 150 kg (Jiang *et al*. 1980: 53); if ration is interpreted to mean consumption (it is probably lower than consumption),[24] this implies a daily intake of only 1,500 calories (Lardy 1982*a*: 161 n. 9). Such widespread want of food is not known to have existed in the 1950s. If in fact it was a new phenomenon, food distribution must have become more erratic[25] between that decade and the 1970s, since average per capita food availability (i.e. output plus imports) did not decrease. Indeed, the state's capacity to redistribute grain, especially between surplus and deficit provinces, may well have declined.

Interprovincial transfers of food are in the first instance a function of the overall 'commercialization rate', meaning the fraction of total output extracted from the producer by means of tax, quota sales, or market sales. Of this fraction, most is redistributed within the province of origin, but a portion

[23] This sentence oversimplifies a complex situation. Bernstein (1986: 2) brought back from his field study of rural structural reform a dominant impression that 'party, government and collective economic organizations continue to play a major role in the rural economy and indeed, in the ongoing reform process'.

[24] The term 'rations' (*kouliang*) is used in the source. 'Rations' are usually lower than total grain consumption (see Walker 1982: 578–82). The calorie figure in the text might thus underestimate actual consumption in the affected regions.

[25] Not necessarily more unequal. Declining ability to supply enough food to particular deficit regions can be compatible with growing average equality (as measured, e.g., by the coefficient of variation of provincial per capita consumption). This indeed is what seems to have happened, as the text below argues.

crosses provincial boundaries to feed major cities and deficit provinces and for export abroad.

Free market sales of basic foodgrains were illegal from the mid-1950s until the late 1970s; during that period virtually all 'marketed' grain (except an indeterminate amount that entered the black market) was procured by the government through tax and purchase quotas. From the late 1970s on, however, grain was increasingly available on the free market. Total purchases (including tax extraction, and measured in trade grain) rose from 51 million metric tons in calendar 1978 to 117 MMT in 1984 (State Statistical Bureau 1985a: 480); although a growing portion of this took the form of direct sales by farmers to the non-agricultural population,[26] the great bulk was bought by the state, which was accordingly subject to a growing financial and logistical burden. In 1985, the state shed its role of guaranteed buyer of last resort, limiting its purchase to 75 MMT of rice, wheat, and corn, and the rest of the surplus was sold on the market (Erisman 1986: 20).

The declining role of the state in redistributing foodgrain is pictured in Table 9.12. Total tax plus purchases declined as a fraction of grain output from 25–30 per cent in the 1950s to only 20–1 per cent in the 1970s (col. 5). Out of this, an average of 18 per cent of total output was kept during the First Plan period of 1953–7 to feed the cities and build up stocks. This category had slipped to about 16 per cent during the 1962–77 period (col. 6). The last column shows what was resold to deficit areas of the countryside. Never a large share of output, it nevertheless fell from an average of 8.6 per cent during the First Plan period to 5.7 per cent during the years 1966–76. If indeed 100 to 150 million people were unable to provide themselves with sufficient food, the small fractions of the harvest available for state relief would not seem to have been enough to meet the need.

In the 1950s, vigorous government commerce in grain played a role in evening out provincial consumption. Table 9.13 gives K. Walker's estimates of the provincial distributions of per capita net output and consumption for the First Plan period. Output varied from Hebei's 195 kg to Heilongjiang's 756, a range of 3.9. The coefficient of variation was 35 per cent. After state redistribution, the range for consumption was reduced to 2.2 and the coefficient of variation to 20 per cent.

Table 9.14, columns 1 and 2, presents the provincial distributions for 1979 of per capita 'availabilities' of grain and total energy. Unfortunately, these estimates unlike Walker's do not take into account interprovincial (or international) trade; to the degree that trade redistributed food among provinces, therefore, the term 'availability' is a misnomer.

Grain imports (shown in Table 9.15 and Fig. 9.7, along with exports) have

[26] Chinese grain trade statistics are ambiguous as to coverage. They explicitly include the agricultural tax, purchases by state commercial, industrial, and other departments, and direct purchases by the non-agricultural population from peasants. They appear to exclude direct market transactions within agriculture, e.g. market purchases by non-grain-growing farmers.

Table 9.12 Foodgrain procurement (unprocessed grain), China, 1952–1984

| Grain year[a] | Output (MMT) | Marketing[b] | | Annual increase in marketing | Gross marketing ratio | Net marketing ratio | Proportion of output resold to countryside (5) − (6) |
| | | Total (MMT) | Net[c] (MMT) | | (2)/(1) | (3)/(1) | |
	(1)	(2)	(3)	(4)	(5)	(6)	(7)
1952	163.92	33.3	28.19		0.20	0.17	0.03
1953	166.83	47.5	35.89	42.7	0.28	0.22	0.07
1954	169.52	51.8	31.59	9.2	0.31	0.19	0.12
1955	183.94	50.7	36.18	−2.1	0.28	0.20	0.08
1956	192.75	45.4	28.70	10.5	0.24	0.15	0.09
1957	195.05	48.0	33.87	5.7	0.25	0.17	0.07
1958	200.00	58.8	41.73	22.3	0.29	0.21	0.09
1959	170.00	67.4	47.57	14.7	0.40	0.28	0.12
1960	143.50	51.1	30.90	−24.3	0.36	0.22	0.14
1961	147.50	40.5	25.81	−20.7	0.27	0.17	0.10
1962	160.00	38.2	25.72	−5.7	0.24	0.16	0.08
1963	170.00	44.0	28.92	15.2	0.26	0.17	0.09
1964	187.50	47.4	31.85	7.9	0.25	0.17	0.08
1965	194.53	48.7	33.60	2.7	0.25	0.17	0.08
1966	214.00	51.6	38.24	5.9	0.24	0.18	0.06
1967	217.82	49.4	37.74	−4.3	0.23	0.17	0.05
1968	209.06	48.7	37.87	−1.4	0.23	0.18	0.05
1969	210.97	46.7	33.83	−4.1	0.22	0.16	0.06
1970	239.96	54.4	42.02	16.6	0.23	0.18	0.05
1971	250.14	53.0	39.82	−2.6	0.21	0.16	0.05
1972	240.48	48.3	33.92	−8.9	0.20	0.14	0.06
1973	264.94	56.1	41.01	16.2	0.21	0.15	0.06
1974	275.27	58.1	43.98	3.5	0.21	0.16	0.05
1975	284.52	60.9	43.98	4.8	0.21	0.15	0.06
1976	286.31	58.3	40.72	−4.3	0.20	0.14	0.06
1977	282.73	56.6	37.56	−2.8	0.20	0.13	0.07
1978	304.77	61.7	42.71	9.1	0.20	0.14	0.06
1979	332.12	72.0	51.70	16.6	0.22	0.16	0.06
1980	320.56	73.0	47.97	1.4	0.23	0.15	0.08
1981	325.02	78.5	48.77	7.5	0.24	0.15	0.09
1982	354.50	91.9	52.02	17.0	0.26	0.15	0.11
1983	387.28	119.9	85.27	30.5	0.31	0.22	0.09
1984	407.31	141.7	94.61	18.2	0.35	0.23	0.12

[a] The grain year runs from 1 Apr. to the following 31 Mar.
[b] 'Marketing' includes tax procurements, state quota purchases and above-quota purchases, and free market sales.
[c] 'Net' refers to total marketing less state resales to the countryside.

Source: State Statistical Bureau (1983b: 393; 1985a: 482).

Table 9.13 Walker's estimates of provincial rural per capita net grain production and consumption in China (averages for 1953–1957)

	Net output per capita (kg)	Grain consumption per capita (kg)
North-east		
Liaoning	348	297
Jilin	562	355
Heilongjiang	756	424
North		
Hebei	195	195
Shanxi	254	196
Inner Mongolia	433	249
East		
Jiangsu	291	230
Zhejiang	338	271
Anhui	313	262
Fujian	307	259
Jiangxi	375	278
Shandong	233	210
Central south		
Henan	233	204
Hubei	343	297
Hunan	307	258
Guangdong	327	276
Guangxi	294	254
South-west		
Sichuan	294	240
Guizhou	277	213
Yunnan	296	247
North-west		
Shaanxi	282	229
Gansu	269	217
Qinghai	267	233
Xinjiang	271	227
Average	327.71	255.04
Range	3.9	2.2
Coefficient of variation	35%	20%

Notes: Estimates of consumption are based on production and procurement data, and are net of estimated seed and livestock feed uses as well as of loss from storage. Tibet is omitted.

Source: Walker (1984*b*: 107).

Table 9.14 Per capita food supply by province, China, 1979 and 1984

	1979			1984		
	Grain 'availability' (kg) (1)	Energy (Kcal) (2)	Grain output per capita (kg) (3)	Total output of grains (MMT) (4)	Population (m.) (5)	Grain output per capita (kg) (6)
North-east						
Liaoning	186.11	2,139	338	14.26	36.55	390.15
Jilin	222.69	2,476	408	16.34	22.84	715.41
Heilongjiang	259.59	2,888	462	17.57	32.95	533.23
North						
Hebei	206.38	2,313	325	18.70	54.87	340.81
Shanxi	184.40	2,041	294	8.72	26.00	335.38
Inner Mongolia	159.00	1,882	253	5.95	19.85	299.50
East						
Jiangsu	255.38	2,888	402	33.54	61.71	543.43
Zhejiang	249.22	2,863	393	18.17	39.93	455.05
Anhui	205.62	2,394	315	22.03	51.03	431.61
Fujian	182.96	2,318	308	8.51	26.77	317.71
Jiangxi	241.90	2,735	379	15.49	34.21	452.79
Shandong	203.91	2,549	330	30.40	76.37	398.06
Central south						
Henan	182.33	2,106	292	28.94	76.46	378.43
Hubei	243.25	2,758	368	22.63	48.76	464.11
Hunan	254.76	2,906	411	26.13	55.61	469.88
Guangdong	183.55	2,313	303	19.73	61.66	319.90
Guangxi	202.93	2,434	331	12.13	38.06	318.71

	Col. 1	Col. 2	Col. 3	Col. 4	Col. 5	Col. 6
South-west						
Sichuan	194.85	2,364	321	40.80	101.12	403.43
Guizhou	134.05	1,577	234	7.58	29.32	258.53
Yunnan	149.95	1,758	269	10.05	33.62	298.93
Tibet	154.45	1,926	232	0.50	1.97	251.27
North-west						
Shaanxi	197.22	2,190	293	10.24	29.66	345.08
Gansu	152.21	1,722	251	5.40	20.16	267.61
Qinghai	147.04	1,865	238	1.01	4.02	251.24
Ningxia	181.13	1,995	315	1.54	4.06	379.31
Xinjiang	197.45	2,228	306	4.97	13.44	369.79
Central cities						
Beijing				2.18	9.47	229.67
Shanghai				2.53	12.05	209.54
Tianjin				1.32	7.99	164.58
Average	197.40	2,293.38	321.96		38.50	384.21
Standard deviation	35.90	381.97	59.19			104.08
Coefficient of variation	18.2%	16.7%	18.4%			27.1%
Maximum	259.59	2,906	462			715.41
Minimum	134.05	1,577	232			251.24
Range	1.94	1.84	1.99			2.85

Notes: Col. 1: Piazza (1983: 115). Provincial grain output net of processing, waste, seed use, and other non-human food end uses. Figures exclude interprovincial and international trade in grains.

Col. 2: World Bank (1984b: 166). Figures exclude interprovincial and international trade.

Col. 3: Walker (1984b: 169). Refers to average for 1978–80. Figure for Tibet estimated from output given in Chang Zizhong and Luo Hanxian (1982: 55) and provincial population given in Hu Qiaomu (1980: 114).

Cols. 4–5: State Statistical Bureau (1985b: 19, 38).

Col. 6: col. 4 divided by col. 5.

Table 9.15 Foodgrain imports and exports,
China, 1952–1984 (m. metric tons)

Year	Imports	Exports
1950	0.06	1.23
1951	0.00	1.97
1952	0.00	1.53
1953	0.01	1.83
1954	0.03	1.71
1955	0.18	2.23
1956	0.15	2.67
1957	0.17	2.09
1958	0.22	2.88
1959	0.00	4.16
1960	0.07	2.72
1961	5.81	1.35
1962	4.92	1.03
1963	5.95	1.49
1964	6.57	1.82
1965	6.41	2.42
1966	6.44	2.89
1967	4.70	2.99
1968	4.60	2.60
1969	3.79	2.24
1970	5.36	2.12
1971	3.17	2.62
1972	4.76	2.93
1973	8.13	3.89
1974	8.12	3.64
1975	3.74	2.81
1976	2.37	1.76
1977	7.34	1.67
1978	8.83	1.88
1979	12.36	1.65
1980	13.43	1.62
1981	14.81	1.26
1982	16.12	1.25
1983	13.44	1.96
1984	10.45	3.57
1985	5.97	9.33

Source: State Statistical Bureau (1983b: 422, 438; 1985a:
510, 517; 1986b: 569, 572).

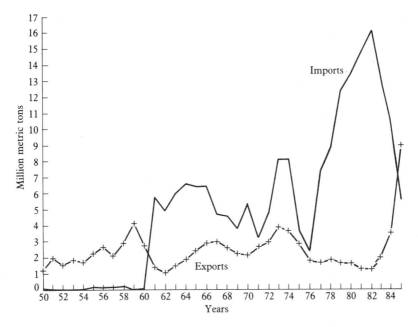

Fig. 9.7 Foodgrain imports and exports by volume, China, 1950–1984

gone chiefly to feed the coastal cities, especially Beijing, Tianjin, and Shanghai.[27] Their omission therefore has minor impact on the distribution. As for interprovincial trade, this has been declining since the 1950s. The number of provinces that shipped grain out declined from 15 in 1965 to 8 in 1978 (Piazza 1983: 41). Interprovincial cereal exports appear to have dropped from 7.85 MMT in 1953 (5.5 per cent of national output) to 4.7 MMT in 1965 (2.8 per cent of output); in 1978 they were only 2.05 MMT (less than 1 per cent of output), of which all but about 0.325 MMT were destined for export abroad (Lardy 1982b). This trend was closely connected to the grain self-sufficiency policy, the reasons for which were discussed in section 1.5 above. In short, for both ideological and practical reasons, and because Mao's assault on the central planning structure effectively disabled it, the central government largely abandoned the business of shipping grain between provinces.

If the state had only a minimal effect on the provincial distribution of grain in 1979, then the range (1.94) and coefficient of variation (18.2 per cent) of provincial grain 'availability' shown in Table 9.14 represent fairly well the distribution of provincial per capita consumption even after state

[27] Omitting the effects of trade, therefore, causes consumption in these cities to be grossly underestimated; they have therefore been left out of Table 9.14. These three municipalities have the status of provinces. They are therefore not part of other provinces and their omission does not distort the other figures.

intervention.[28] Both of these measures are slightly below their 1950s level for grain consumption (Table 9.13).

On average, then, it seems that the interprovincial grain distribution became more equal.[29] But this was due not to improved mechanisms for state distribution of output but rather to the levelling of provincial per capita output itself: while average output was about the same in 1979 as in the 1950s, the coefficient of variation declined by almost a half between the two periods (Tables 9.13 and 9.14). In this case, the levelling was mostly downward, with high producers, such as Heilongjiang, Jilin, and Inner Mongolia, declining and no provinces rising to take their place. The net result of increasingly equal provincial per capita output, on the one hand, and declining state involvement with interprovincial distribution, on the other, was a somewhat greater equality of provincial per capita consumption. Such a rise in equality, however, was not necessarily inconsistent with the growth of underfed regional populations, as claimed by the government in the late 1970s.

In 1979, to increase per capita energy availability to Piazza's standard of sufficiency (2,160 Kcal per day) in the 10 provinces which fell short of that standard (Table 9.14, col. 2), and to bring Beijing, Shanghai, and Tianjin up to the national average of 2,600 Kcal from their own production of foodgrain, would have required a total of 10 MMT of unprocessed wheat (Piazza 1983: 43). This amount is approximately equal to China's net grain import in 1979. Even without interprovincial redistribution, therefore, China could have met minimum standards in all provinces (disregarding problems of intraprovincial distribution) on the basis of local production plus imports. It is likely, however, that imports served rather to raise urban standards well above the national average, and that poor provinces such as Guizhou, Gansu, Yunnan, and Qinghai were left short.

The picture changed greatly in 1984 (Table 9.14, col. 6). The average provincial output per capita was substantially above that of the 1950s. While the coefficient of variation rose above that of 1979, it remained below the 1950s level; moreover, every province but one (Guangxi) experienced growth in per capita output between 1979 and 1984. In addition, the proportion of the much larger harvest resold to deficit areas of the countryside also rose—from 7 per cent of national output in 1979 to 12 per cent in 1984 (Table 9.12, col. 7). Thus, the increase in provincial inequality in per capita production would seem to be a small price to pay for advance along a wide front and the redistribution of greater surpluses. Indeed, if a combination of state commercial organs and the market can handle the task of supplying grain-deficit regions, then the goal of

[28] Table 9.14 also gives provincial figures for per capita energy availability and grain output. As can be seen, the magnitudes of relative variation are closely similar for all three variables.

[29] This conclusion is tentative because the data for the two periods are not strictly comparable, while the differences between the two ranges and coefficients of variation may be too small to be of much significance.

provincial specialization and division of labour would seem more effective in feeding China than that of provincial grain self-sufficiency.

(b) Personal distribution

There are no published data on personal distribution of food, or of cereal, as far as I am aware. Income data have been used by the World Bank to construct estimates of the distribution of personal income in urban and in rural China. Their estimate of the Gini coefficient for the rural income distribution in 1982 is 0.225, well below the Ginis of other South Asian countries (0.30–0.35). Substantial remaining inequality is largely interregional. The Bank characterizes urban inequality as 'uniquely low . . . with virtually no extreme poverty in urban areas' (World Bank 1985: Main Report, p. 29); the estimated Gini coefficient for 1981 is 0.16 (World Bank 1981: 59).[30] One can infer similar degrees of equality in distribution of food entitlements, but direct data are lacking.

This discussion is therefore confined to the changing methods, with their implications for the personal distribution, by which individuals have gained entitlement to food. In the villages, before the return of family farming (practices after the reforms are discussed below), peasants received rations in two basic ways (see below). They paid an agricultural tax, largely in grain, and were obliged to sell to the state quotas (and above-quota amounts) that were calculated on output above a subsistence ration. The state undertook to resell grain at quota prices to food-deficit localities. Because most redistribution in recent years has been *intra*provincial (and of this much may have been confined within smaller administrative units, such as the district), the guaranteed minimum consumption standard has varied geographically, a common figure being 200 unprocessed kg in rice regions (providing about 1,400 Kcal and 25 grams of protein) and 150 kg elsewhere (if wheat this would provide about 1,250 Kcal and 35 grams of protein) (World Bank 1984: 80).

Land reform and collectivization in the 1950s probably resulted in a marked gain in equality of food distribution in rural areas, both among regions and among individuals within a locality, because these institutional changes eliminated property income, the largest source of intraregional income inequality, and established institutions for food redistribution. The policies of the 1960s and 1970s, on the other hand, may have increased disparities among localities[31] while maintaining (and possibly increasing) equality of distribution *within* localities.

There were two basic methods of grain distribution to members of a production team. First, grain was distributed on a per capita basis according to the age and sex of each family member. This grain (called 'basic grain') was

---

[30] China's overall distribution is less impressive than that of either of these components, however, because of the remaining sizeable urban–rural gap.

[31] However, the discussion of Section 9.6*a* above concluded that disparities among *provinces* seem to have further narrowed on average, but not to the benefit of at least some poor regions.

debited to the family's account with the collective, and in principle had to be paid for at the post-harvest settling of accounts. Second, grain distribution was tied to workpoint earnings, and thus to earning power. A small amount of grain might also be distributed in exchange for household manure.

The relative importance of basic grain and workpoint grain in total grain distribution varied greatly among localities. Villages stressing basic grain tended to have more equal food distribution and greater security for their poor members. In practice, going into debt to the collective for basic grain and postponing repayment was one method by which families in difficult circumstances could survive. Villages where workpoint grain was stressed in order to promote work incentives tended to have less equal distribution. 'The proportion of basic or work-point grain is then a matter of intense and volatile debate, with local systems changing with the current political wind and with the changing needs and desires of team members and their leaders' (Parish and Whyte 1978: 66).[32] The Cultural Revolution of the late 1960s brought about a move to equal distribution, the reaction of the early 1970s a return to more workpoint grain. Parish and Whyte (1978: 69–70) found a link between village affluence and reliance on 'basic grain'. In their sample of villages, higher income, consumption, and land–labour ratios were associated with greater willingness to share food equally.

Basic and workpoint grain seem to have disappeared as a result of the reforms. Now, grain-growing households keep the excess of their output above what is due in tax, contracted sales (formerly quota sales), and contribution to the collective accumulation and welfare funds. Non-grain-growing households commonly are allotted 'ration land' (kouliang tian), on which to grow food for their own needs, in addition to their contract land (Bernstein 1986). Presumably, households unable to grow enough food must buy it with their earnings on the open market, unless they are 'five-guarantee' or 'hardship' households that qualify for public assistance.

The rural elderly do not have access to a government pension system, as do full-status workers and staff in state enterprises. In the villages grown children (sons, in practice, since daughters marry out of the village) are expected to care for their aged parents. Those without grown sons to support them may become 'five-guarantee households' (guaranteed food, clothing, housing, medical care, and burial expenses by their collective). The collective usually tries to provide them with sideline employment and a plot of land as a means of supplementing their incomes.

In the 37 Guangdong production teams studied by Parish and Whyte in the 1970s, only 1.24 persons per team, or 6 per cent of all people over age 60, received five-guarantee help. This system persists into the post-reform era: a

---

[32] This discussion of rural distribution depends heavily on Parish and Whyte (1978) in its depiction of the pre-1978 situation. See below for discussion of the changes brought about by household contracting.

Shandong village of 283 households visited in 1985 by T. Bernstein had three five-guarantee households. Each got 200 kg of grain, 200 yuan in cash, free medical care, and 500 yuan for funeral expenses (Bernstein 1986: 16).

Assistance has been available through various channels to ordinary households in difficulty because of injury, illness, or simply lack of labour power. The team or village might provide extra employment to the children or elderly in the family, make available low-cost loans or direct grants, or permit a household to overdraw indefinitely on its grain account. Much help has also taken the more traditional form of informal assistance based on kinship (Parish and Whyte 1978: 76–7).

With the transformation of the old commune system and the adoption of household farming, collective welfare services broke down in some places. Beggars, some of them peasant migrants, again appeared at railway stations and thoroughfares. The government has put renewed stress on helping poor areas and households. Bernstein (1986: 16) was told that 5 to 6 per cent of households in Anhui Province were classified as hardship cases eligible to receive assistance. The approach taken was to help such households achieve self-sufficiency and avoid long-term dependence on welfare. Policies include reduction or remittance of taxes, provision of low-interest loans, priority in purchasing output and in supplying improved seed and other farm inputs, subsidies to buy such inputs, and provision of technical education and advice (FBIS, 7 Jan. 1985: K17).[33] Cadres in some areas have taken it upon themselves to help indigent families work out plans to overcome their problems (Hinton 1983: 22; Beijing Review, 3 (1981) and 5 (1982); Jing Wei 1983: 20–1). A good deal of pressure seems to have been put on the new village entrepreneurs to develop their philanthropic impulses, and stories abound of the emerging élite privately building old-age homes, establishing local schools, or subsidizing the electrification of their village.[34] Chinese commentators point out that, even amidst the general advance of recent years, 'comparatively speaking, poverty-stricken "pockets" exist everywhere. In the whole nation, there are tens of millions of people whose problems regarding food and clothing have not been completely solved' (Renmin Ribao, 8 Feb. 1986, trans.

[33] Curiously, the Minister of Civil Affairs, discussing aid to the poor in Jan. 1985, 'pledged' that 'his ministry would continue to raise money to support the poorer peasants', making it sound more like a private charitable organization than one funded by the state budget.

[34] A recent article on combating poverty in China's richest county, Wuxi (Jiangsu Province), captures the flavour of current policy: 'In the work to help poor households, the county adopted a method of state subsidies, collective assistance, and mutual help among the masses in order to collect funds through various channels. . . . The county's civil affairs, grain, and supply and marketing departments also did what they could to make things easy for this work in financial affairs and material supply as well as in production and sales . . . (V)arious areas have . . . adopted various measures such as giving priority to poor households to work in the town and township enterprises or in initiating social welfare work. . . . At the same time, they also enthusiastically encourage all kinds of specialized households to encourage poor households and to let the rich help the poor' (Guangming Ribao (Beijing), 8 Feb. 1986, trans. FBIS, 24 Feb. 1986, p. K17).

Table 9.16 Grain rations, Chengdu, 1982 (kg/month)

Category	Ration
Age	
Below 1 year	4.0
1 year	5.5
2 years	6.5
3 years	7.5
4 years	8.5
5 years	9.0
6 years	10.0
7 years	10.5
8 years	11.0
9 years	12.0
10 years	12.5
Senior middle school students	16.0
University students	17.2
'Ordinary persons'	13.5
Office worker	14.0
Manual labourer	22.5–25

Note: Rations vary somewhat by location. Thus, a male office worker in Beijing was entitled to 17 kg rather than 14, a female office worker to 15 rather than 14. The vegetable oil and sugar rations in all three locations noted by the World Bank were 0.25 kg each.

Source: World Bank (1984: 168).

FBIS, 24 Feb. 1986, p. K16).[35] But detailed statistics on the extent of the problem have not been published.

In urban areas, formal rationing of cereals and edible vegetable oils has existed since 1955. A grain ration schedule from Chengdu, in Sichuan Province, is given in Table 9.16. Rationing has undoubtedly served to equalize food distribution within urban areas. With grain relatively scarce during much of China's recent history, urban rationing also served to assure a stable and equitable supply for city residents. Under more recent conditions of relative grain abundance and a growing free market in grain, and given the unusual degree of income equality in urban China, urban rationing may have lost much of its rationale. It may also have contributed to exacerbating the urban–rural gap by safeguarding the urban population's access to relatively stable supplies of cheap grain while giving rise to wider annual fluctuations in per capita supplies in the countryside.

Certainly, the state subsidy of urban grain consumption, occasioned by the rising spread between state purchase and sales prices since the mid-1960s, has

---

[35] There is some evidence that recent policy has in fact exacerbated the situation of many rural poor by eliminating collective food supports and in various other ways rendering their economic position more precarious. See Unger and Xiong (1990).

been a significant contributor to the urban–rural income differential. State losses from this spread averaged 4 billion yuan per year between 1974 and 1978. They came to almost 2 per cent of national income in the latter year or over 179 yuan per state employee (almost 30 per cent of the average annual wage) (Lardy 1983*b*: 193). Moreover, as farm procurement prices were raised after 1978 and the state bought increasing percentages of the harvest at above-quota and high negotiated prices, the subsidy of urban consumption grew rapidly. Lardy estimates that all urban food subsidies in 1981 (including those on imported grain and on non-staple foods) amounted to 6.4 per cent of official national income (roughly net domestic material product), or 30.5 per cent of the total wage bill of state workers, or one quarter of revenue of all levels of government (1983*b*: 194–5). These large subsidies were available to only 16–17 per cent of the population. Their contribution to government budget deficits in the late 1970s and early 1980s was a principal reason for the decontrol of non-staple food prices in 1985 and the switch from mandatory quotas to contract purchases from the peasants.

9.7. *Conclusion*

Certain points in this broad survey deserve a summary reprise.

1. The discussion of institutional development found that the rural collective institutions in place until the end of the 1970s played a role in bringing about the growth of food production and, through relatively egalitarian distribution methods *within* collectives, in ensuring the adequacy of food consumption of poor members. However, the 'workpoint' system of distribution was bound to lose its motivational efficacy as the national political atmosphere became fractious and national policies toward the countryside became increasingly inequitable. Rural communes also suffered from the propensity of the party and government to administer them as if they were state institutions, and to adopt policies, such as those of low farm prices and local foodgrain self-sufficiency, that imposed hardships on both advanced and backward regions.

2. Average per capita food energy availability fluctuated around a flat trend for two decades after 1952, then began rising. China did not exceed the peak 1950s level of average calorie consumption until the early 1970s. Foodgrain production per capita exceeded the 1956–8 level only in 1973. From 1978 to 1984, grain consumption per capita grew quite rapidly, and the diet began to diversify as a result of differentially high growth rates of meat, dairy, and aquatic products.

3. Available evidence indicates that the famine which occurred in 1959–61 was of calamitous proportions. Official government mortality statistics imply a total excess mortality of more than 15 million during those years, and some Western estimates run considerably higher. However, many questions remain about the famine itself and the statistics concerning it, and no precise estimate of mortality can be made with confidence. State policy contributed to the

severity and duration of the crisis in both direct and indirect ways. In this famine, the deprivation of food entitlements began with the destructive effects of state policy on food production itself; later, mistaken distribution policies (such as overprocurement of grain from the peasants) contributed to the disaster.

4. The rapid advances in food production and consumption after 1978 owed much to the elimination of negative incentive policies in place earlier, and of the institutional framework supporting such policies. At the same time, these advances were also due to infrastructural developments and the equalization of access to land that occurred during the era of collective agriculture.

5. Malnutrition appears to be only a slight problem in urban China, but may be a much more substantial one in the countryside, where it is also subject to great regional variation.

6. Food distribution has developed differently, according to which of its several dimensions is examined. Average variation among provinces in per capita grain consumption declined between the 1950s and the 1970s, but in a manner that apparently permitted the growth of large underfed regional populations—not a happy result of greater equality. Conversely, general but differentially rapid growth from 1978 to 1984, together with a more vigorous government redistributive role, seems to have significantly reduced regional insufficiency of food supply.

With respect to the personal distribution of food, very low Gini coefficients in the early 1980s for urban and rural income distributions, taken separately, may imply similarly great equality in food availability, but direct data are lacking. The elimination of the collective system of distribution in the countryside, and the erosion of collective welfare institutions that accompanied the reversion to household farming, created new hardships for some households ill equipped to cope with the new conditions. The Chinese government has stressed the need to provide aid in such cases, but the extent and degree of success of its assistance programmes is not yet known.

Space does not permit an exploration of many other issues relevant to China's food situation, e.g. the record of state investment in agriculture; the government's plans for price reform; the unexpectedly sharp inflation in non-staple food prices brought about by decontrol in 1985; the expressed plan drastically to reduce the fraction of the labour force in agriculture by the end of the century; the intent to adopt and popularize Western types of processing and fast food services. Through these various issues runs the basic and still unresolved question of how to combine planning and state control with family farming and a free market. In the urban industrial sector a viable plan–market mix is even farther from achievement; yet agriculture depends increasingly on industry for inputs and on the cities for markets. Despite the early success of the reforms, China's food problem is far from solved.[36]

[36] Grain output has fallen short of the 1984 peak in all subsequent years up to 1989.

What is notable about China's experience is its extraordinary range. When Mao Zedong was the pre-eminent force in the country, he had and used the authority to implement unprecedented experiments in organization and distribution. At the same time, the existence of major differences within the leadership has meant that economic policy, including food policy, changed dramatically when the balance of power within the party shifted. As a result, a great variety of organizational and institutional forms have been tried in the quest for growth and equity. After early progress there was an extended period in which improvements in the quantity and quality of diet were not forthcoming, and the population at times paid a very high price for ill-considered experiments. The mixed record of the reform years since 1978 leaves very much open the question whether the lessons of almost four decades of experience will be used to devise vigorous yet equitable policies capable of bringing food security to China's people.

References

AIRD, JOHN S. (1980), 'Reconstruction of an Official Data Model of the Population of China' (US Department of Commerce, Bureau of the Census, May).

——(1982), 'Population Studies and Population Policy in China', *Population and Development Review*, 8.

——(1983), 'The Preliminary Results of China's 1982 Census', *China Quarterly*, 96.

——(1984), 'Age Distribution of China's Population', *Beijing Review*, 3.

ASH, ROBERT (1976), 'Economic Aspects of Land Reform in Kiangsu, 1949–52', *China Quarterly*, 66 (June) and 67 (Sept.).

ASHTON, BASIL, HILL, KENNETH, PIAZZA, ALAN, and ZEITZ, ROBIN (1984), 'Famine in China, 1958–61', *Population and Development Review*, 10.

BANISTER, JUDITH (1984a), 'An Analysis of Recent Data on the Population of China', *Population and Development Review*, 10.

——(1984b), 'Population Policy and Trends in China, 1978–83', *China Quarterly*, 100.

BERNSTEIN, THOMAS P. (1984a), 'Stalinism, Famine, and Chinese Peasants', *Theory and Society*, 13.

——(1984b), 'Reforming China's Agriculture', paper prepared for the conference 'To Reform the Chinese Political Order', June 1984, Harwichport, Mass., sponsored by the Joint Committee on Chinese Studies of the ACLS and the SSRC.

——(1986), 'Local Political Authorities and Economic Reform: Observations from Two Counties in Shandong and Anhui, 1985', paper prepared for presentation at the Conference on Market Reforms in China and Eastern Europe, Santa Barbara, Calif. 8–11 May.

BUCK, JOHN LOSSING (1956), *Land Utilization in China* (New York: Paragon Book Reprint Corporation).

CHANG ZIZHONG and LUO HANXIAN (eds.) (1982), *Zhongguo Nongye Nianjian 1980* (Agricultural Yearbook of China), excerpts with tables translated, in Joint Publications Research Service, *China Report, Agriculture*, No. 192, JPRS 80270, Mar.

CHEN KAIGUO (1982), 'A Tentative Inquiry into the Scissors Gap in the Rate of Exchange between Industrial and Agricultural Products', *Social Sciences in China*, 2.

CHEN, S. C., and RIDLEY, CHARLES P. (1969), *The Rural People's Communes in Lien-chiang* (Stanford, Calif.: The Hoover Institution).

CHENG ZHIPING (Director of State Price Bureau) (1983), Interview in *Beijing Review*, 35 (29 Aug.).

COALE, ANSLEY J. (1981), 'Population Trends, Population Policy, and Population Studies in China', *Population and Development Review*, 7/1 (Mar.).

——(1984), *Rapid Population Change in China, 1952–1982*, Report no. 27 (Committee on Population and Demography, Washington, DC: National Academy Press).

'Communiqué of the Third Plenary Session of the 11th Central Committee of the Communist Party of China', *Peking Review*, 52.

Communist Party of China Central Committee (1981), 'Zhonggong zhongyang banfa "guanyu jinyibu jiachiang he wanshan nongye shengchan zerenzhide jige wentide tongzhi"' (Directive of the Central Committee of the Chinese Communist Party on several questions concerning further strengthening and perfecting of the production responsibility system in agriculture), *Zhong Gong Nian Bao* (Yearbook on Chinese Communism) (Taibei).

Communist Party of China Central Committee (1983), 'Some Questions Concerning Current Rural Economic Policies', Document No. 1, 1983, excerpted in Foreign Broadcast Information Service, 13 Apr.

——(1984a), 'Certain Questions Concerning the Current Rural Economic Policy', Document No. 1, 1 Jan. 1984, trans. Foreign Broadcast Information Service, 13 June; also trans. in *China Quarterly*, 101.

——(1984b), Zhonggong zhongyang guanyu yijiubasi nian nongcun gongzuo de tongzhi' (Directive of the Central Committee of the Chinese Communist Party concerning rural work in 1984), *Renmin Ribao*, 12 June.

DELFS, ROBERT (1984), 'Agricultural Yields Rise, but the Boom Cannot Last', FEER, 13 Dec.

DOMES, JURGEN (1982), 'New Policies in the Communes: Notes on Rural Societal Structures in China, 1976–1981', *Journal of Asian Studies*, 41/2.

DONNITHORNE, AUDREY (1970), *China's Grain: Output, Procurement, Transfers and Trade* (Hong Kong: The Chinese University of Hong Kong, Economic Research Centre).

DU RUNSHENG (1985), 'Second-Stage Rural Structural Reform', *Beijing Review*, 25.

ECKSTEIN, ALEXANDER (ed.) (1980), *Quantitative Measures of China's Economic Output* (Ann Arbor, Mich.: University of Michigan Press).

ERISMAN, LEW (1986), 'The Grain Challenge', *China Business Review*, Mar.–Apr.

FREEBERNE, MICHAEL (1962), 'Natural Calamities in China, 1949–1961', *Pacific Viewpoint*, 3.

HINTON, WILLIAM H. (1983), 'A Trip to Fengyang County: Investigating China's New Family Contract System', *Monthly Review*, Nov.

HU QIAOMU (ed.) (1980), *Zhongguo Baike Nianjian* (Annual Encyclopedia of China) (Beijing: China Great Encyclopedia Publishers).

JAMISON, DEAN T., and TROWBRIDGE, F. L. (1984), 'The Nutritional Status of Children in China: A Review of the Anthropometric Evidence' (PHN Technical Note GEN 17), Supplementary Paper No. 8 of World Bank (1984).

JIANG JUNCHEN, ZHOU ZHAOYANG, and SHEN JUN (1980), 'Lun shengchan he shenghuode guanxi wenti' (On the relations between production and livelihood), *Jingji Yanjiu*, 9.

JING PING (1985), 'Contract Purchasing of Grain is a Major Reform', *Red Flag*, 10, trans. JPRS-CRF-85-015, *China Report*, 26 July.

JING WEI (1982), 'Responsibility System Revives Jiangsu Countryside', *Beijing Review*, 48 (28 Nov.).

KHAN, AZIZUR RAHMAN, and LEE, EDDY (1983), *Agrarian Policies and Institutions in China after Mao* (Bangkok: ILO, ARTEP).

LARDY, NICHOLAS R. (1982a), 'Food Consumption in the People's Republic of China', in Barker, Randolph, Sinha, Radha, and Rose, Beth (eds.), *The Chinese Agricultural Economy* (Boulder, Colo.: Westview).

——(1982b), 'Prices, Markets and the Chinese Peasant', Center Discussion Paper No. 428, Yale Economic Growth Center.

——(1983a), *Agriculture in China's Modern Economic Development* (New York and Cambridge: Cambridge University Press).

——(1983b), 'Subsidies', *China Business Review*, 10/6.

——(1984), 'Consumption and Living Standards in China, 1978–83', *China Quarterly*, 100.

Lin Zili (1983), 'The New Situation in the Rural Economy and Its Basic Direction', *Social Sciences in China*, 3.

Liu, Jung-chao (1980), 'A Note on China's Pricing Policies', paper presented to Workshop of the Dept. of Economics, SUNY Binghampton, 19 Mar.

MacFarquhar, Roderick (1983), *Origins of the Cultural Revolution, ii: The Great Leap Forward 1958–1960* (New York: Columbia University Press).

Mao Zedong (1977), 'On the Cooperative Transformation of Agriculture', in Mao, *Selected Works*, v (Beijing: Foreign Languages Press, 1977; originally pub. 1955).

Oi, Jean C. (1986), 'Peasant Grain Marketing and State Procurement: China's Grain Contracting System', *China Quarterly*, 106.

Parish, William F., and Whyte, Martin King (1978), *Village and Family in Contemporary China* (Chicago Ill.: University of Chicago Press).

Perkins, Dwight H. (1969), *Agricultural Development in China, 1368–1968* (Chicago, Ill.: Aldine).

——and Yusuf, Shahid (1984), *Rural Development in China* (Baltimore, Md.: Johns Hopkins).

Piazza, Alan (1983), 'Trends in Food and Nutrient Availability in China, 1950–81', World Bank Staff Working Paper No. 607 (Washington, DC: World Bank).

Policy Research Office (1979), *Zhongguo Nongye Jiben Qingkuang* (Basic situation in Chinese agriculture) (Beijing: Ministry of Agriculture, Nongyechubanshe).

Riskin, Carl (1987), *China's Political Economy: The Quest for Development since 1949* (Oxford: Oxford University Press).

Roll, Charles R. (1974), 'The Distribution of Rural Incomes in China', Ph.D. dissertation, Harvard University, Cambridge, Mass.

Schran, Peter (1969), *The Development of Chinese Agriculture, 1950–1959* (Urbana, Ill.: University of Illinois Press).

Selden, Mark (1981), 'Cooperation and Socialist Transition in China's Countryside', in Selden and Lippit (1981).

——and Lippit, Victor (eds.) (1981), *The Transition to Socialism in China* (Armonk, NY: M. E. Sharpe).

Sen, Amartya (1981), *Poverty and Famines: An Essay on Entitlement and Deprivation* (Oxford: Oxford University Press).

——(1982), 'How is India Doing?', *New York Review of Books*, 16 Dec.

Shue, Vivienne (1984), 'The Fate of the Commune', *Modern China*, 10/3.

State Security Office (1962), 'Nongcun renmin gongshe gongzuo tiaoli (xiuzheng cao'an)' (Work regulations for the rural people's communes (revised draft)) (Taiwan).

State Statistical Bureau (1983a), *Statistical Yearbook of China* (Hong Kong: Economic Information & Agency).

——(1983b), *Zhongguo Tongji Nianjian, 1983* (Statistical Yearbook of China, 1983) (Beijing: Chinese Statistical Publishing House).

——(1983c) *Zhongguo Tongji Zhaiyao* (Statistical Abstract of China) (Beijing: Chinese Statistical Publishing House, repr. with translations of table headings in Joint Publications Research Service 84111).

——(1984a), *Zhongguo Maoyi Wujia Tongji Ziliao, 1952–1983* (Statistics on China's commerce and prices, 1952–1983) (Beijing, Office of Commerce and Price Statistics: Chinese Statistical Publishing House).

——(1984b), *Zhongguo nongyede guanghui chengjiu, 1949–1984* (Brilliant accomplishments of China's agriculture, 1949–1984), Office of Agricultural Statistics, State Statistical Bureau (Beijing: Chinese Statistical Publishing House).

——(1984c), *Zhongguo Tongji Nianjian* (Statistical Yearbook of China) (Beijing: Chinese Statistical Publishing House).

——(1985a), *Statistical Yearbook of China* (Oxford: Oxford University Press).

——(1985b), *Zhongguo Tongji Zhaiyao, 1985* (Statistical Abstract of China, 1985) (Beijing: Chinese Statistical Publishing House).

——(1985c), *Zhongguo Tongji Nianjian* (Statistical Yearbook of China) (Beijing: Chinese Statistical Publishing House).

——(1986a), 'Communiqué on the Statistics of 1985 Economic and Social Development', *Beijing Review*, 12.

——(1986b), *Zhongguo Tongji Nianjian* (Statistical Yearbook of China) (Beijing: Chinese Statistical Publishing House).

——(1988), *Zhongguo Tongji Nianjian* (Statistical Yearbook of China) (Beijing: Chinese Statistical Publishing House).

STAVIS, BENEDICT (1978), *The Politics of Agricultural Mechanization in China* (Ithaca, NY: Cornell University Press).

STONE, BRUCE (1985), 'The Basis for Chinese Agricultural Growth in the 1980s and 1990s: A Comment on Document No. 1, 1984', *China Quarterly*, 101.

STRONG, ANNA LOUISE (1964), *The Chinese People's Communes—and Six Years After* (Peking: New World Press).

SUN YEFANG (1981), 'Jiaqiang tongji gongzuo, gaige tongji zhidu' (Strengthen statistical work, reform the statistical system), *Jingji Guanli*, 2, 15 Feb., trans. Foreign Broadcast Information Service, 26 Mar.

TIAN JIYUN (1985), 'Price System Due for Reform', *Beijing Review*, 4.

TRAVERS, LEE (1982), 'Bias in Chinese Economic Statistics: The Case of the Typical Example Investigation', *China Quarterly*, 91.

——(1984), 'Post-1978 Rural Economic Policy and Peasant Income in China', *China Quarterly*, 98.

UNGER, JONATHAN, and XIONG, JEAN (1990), 'Life in the Chinese Hinterlands under the Rural Economic Reforms', *Bulletin of Concerned Asian Scholars*, 22/2 (Apr.–June).

US Central Intelligence Agency (1986), 'China: Economic Performance in 1985', report presented to the US Congress, Joint Economic Committee, Subcommittee on Economic Resources, Competitiveness, and Security Economics, 17 Mar. (typescript).

US Congress, Joint Economic Committee (1982), *China under the Four Modernizations*, parts i and ii (Washington, DC: US Government Printing Office).

WALKER, KENNETH R. (1965), *Planning in Chinese Agriculture* (Chicago, Ill.: Aldine).

——(1977), 'Grain Self-Sufficiency in North China', *China Quarterly*, 71.

——(1982), 'Interpreting Chinese Grain Consumption Statistics', *China Quarterly*, 92.

——(1984a), 'Chinese Agriculture during the Period of the Readjustment, 1978–83', *China Quarterly*, 100.

——(1984b), *Food Grain Procurement & Consumption in China* (Cambridge: Cambridge University Press).

WAN LI (1985), 'Developing Rural Commodity Production', *Beijing Review*, 9.

WATSON, ANDREW (1983), 'Agriculture Looks for "Shoes that Fit": The Production Responsibility System and Its Implications', *World Development*, 11.

WEI, LIN, and CHAO, ARNOLD (1982), *China's Economic Reforms* (Philadelphia, Penn.: University of Pennsylvania Press).

WIENS, THOMAS (1980), 'Agricultural Statistics in the People's Republic of China', in Eckstein (1980).

World Bank (1983), *China: Socialist Economic Development*, vols. i–iii (Washington, DC: World Bank).

——(1984), *China: The Health Sector* (Washington, DC: World Bank).

——(1985), *China: Long-Term Development Issues and Options* (Baltimore, Md., and London: Johns Hopkins).

WREN, CHRISTOPHER (1984), 'Despite Rural China's Gains, Poverty Grips Some Regions', *New York Times*, 18 Dec.

WU XIANG (1980), 'The Open Road and the Log Bridge: A Preliminary Discussion on the Origins, Advantages and Disadvantages, Nature and Future of the Fixing of Farm Output Quotas for Each Household', *Renmin Ribao*, 5 Nov., trans. Foreign Broadcast Information Service, 7 Nov.

XUE MUQIAO (ed.) (1981/2), *Zhongguo Jingji Nianjian* (Economic Yearbook of China 1981) (Beijing: Jingji guanli chubanshe).

YANG JIANBAI and LI XUEZENG (1980), 'The Relations between Agriculture, Light Industry and Heavy Industry in China', in *Social Sciences in China*, 2.

ZHAO ZIYANG (1985a), 'Loosen Control over the Prices of Farm Products to Promote the Readjustment of the Production Structure in Rural Areas', *Hong Qi*, 3, trans. Foreign Broadcast Information Service, 31 Jan.

——(1985b), 'The Current Economic Situation and the Reform of the Economic Structure', Report on the Work of the Government, 27 Mar., in *Beijing Review*, 16.

ZWEIG, DAVID (1982), 'National Élites, Rural Bureaucrats and Peasants: Limits on Commune Reform', in *The Limits of Reform in China* (Washington, DC: The Wilson Center).

10

The Food Crisis in Africa:
A Comparative Structural Analysis

Jean-Philippe Platteau

A large part of Africa is chronically affected by a severe food crisis which threatens the food security of many of her inhabitants. A peculiarity of this continent is that food production is not only a source of food but also a source of incomes for the numerous smallholder producers who form the most important group exposed to the risk of hunger. Therefore, growing food insecurity is generally associated with a crisis of food production. This chapter is an attempt to analyse various structural factors which underlie this production crisis. It is grounded on the hypothesis that these factors are far more constraining than the inadequate policy mixes which have received so much attention in the economic literature, and that their impact tends to impose serious handicaps on Africa compared to Asia and Latin America.

10.1. *Africa's food crisis in perspective*

(a) *Food security and food self-sufficiency*

There are two striking features or components in the so-called food crisis which faces many developing countries in Asia, Latin America, and Africa: a rapidly increasing number of people who are chronically hungry or malnourished on the one hand, and a quickly rising dependence on food imports on the other hand. While the former problem—that concerned with food security—is especially acute in Asia and (sub-Saharan) Africa, the second problem—that concerned with food self-sufficiency—is typical of all the three continents. It is now a well-known fact that the two problems are not necessarily linked together. In other words, food self-sufficiency does not lead automatically to food security, and vice versa. Indeed, food imports arise whenever domestic supply falls short of demand at the macrolevel, whereas poverty and malnutrition have often to be traced back to a lack of purchasing power among certain vulnerable groups of the population (Sen 1981; Mellor and Desai 1985; Pacey and Payne 1985; World Bank 1986*a*). Thus, it is not difficult to imagine situations in which malnutrition continues unabated although the rate of national food self-sufficiency increases. India and Chile are two cases in point. And it is equally easy to think of situations in which the opposite would

I am greatly indebted to Jean Drèze, Carl Eicher, and Jean-Marie Baland for their helpful comments and criticisms on an earlier version of this paper. Responsibilities for the views expressed remain, however, entirely mine.

occur—decreasing incidence of food hunger and rising dependence on food imports. The example of Taiwan suggests itself as a good illustration of this second possibility.

There is today a growing agreement among economists that the objective of food security should always be given precedence over that of food self-sufficiency. In other words, food security ought to be pursued even at the cost of increased food imports. A good case can however be made for qualifying the above statement. As a matter of fact, if the search for complete food self-sufficiency is a political objective hard to justify in welfare terms except in some peculiar circumstances, there are valid reasons for not letting food dependence develop too far. Uncertainties related to the world food market; shortage of physical facilities to handle large volumes of food imports; foreign exchange constraints; high internal transport costs due to low population densities; low import and capital intensiveness of domestic food production compared with alternative employment opportunities; social, spatial, and environmental considerations; income distribution objectives; all these factors may militate against allowing a decrease in domestic production of staple foods, especially if this decrease is sharp, sudden, or irreversible. The issue of irreversibility deserves to be emphasized since technical progress may cause radical shifts in the structure of comparative advantages and it is practically impossible to recreate a peasantry after having allowed its destruction. Of course, to the extent that the pursuit of food self-reliance threatens food security, the latter ought to be preserved by resorting to compensating measures (like state subsidies).

(b)   The context of Africa's food crisis

An important feature of many African countries is that the bulk of the food output is produced by small family-operated farms whose members form the largest group facing food insecurity. Indeed, if the number of landless people is no doubt rising in Africa, especially so in areas of high population pressure, it still forms a rather low proportion of the agricultural population. In sub-Saharan Africa, more than three-quarters of the population are engaged in smallholder food production (Delgado et al. 1987: 5). In the case of Africa, therefore, the objectives of food security and food self-sufficiency are potentially more compatible than in the countries of Asia and Latin America where the majority of people at risk are net food buyers. Thus, widespread increases in the productivity of agricultural smallholders are likely to lead to both improved food security and diminished dependence on food imports. Furthermore, in so far as such increases can be obtained without entailing a drop in the production of agricultural exportables, the balance-of-payments constraint will be eased, a consideration of the utmost importance in most African countries ridden with serious problems of national economic management.

Conversely, the close link between food security and food self-sufficiency in Africa tends to make the effects of a slowdown in food production more dramatic. This is precisely what has happened during the long period 1960–84 when disappointing agricultural growth performances were widely observed throughout most of the continent. Thus, the trend rate of growth of food output was not only lower than that of consumption but, in addition, it turned out to be significantly less than the rate of population growth. During the years 1960–84, food output per head in sub-Saharan Africa decreased at an alarming rate of about 1 per cent per annum. The situation was even worse during the years 1970–84, not only in sub-Saharan Africa but also in North Africa: food production in the whole of Africa then grew at only half the population growth rate. If a few countries did not conform to this general picture and could increase their food output per head during the period under consideration (e.g. the Ivory Coast, Malawi, Swaziland, Tunisia), the situation was worse still for the not-so-few countries in which total food output actually declined or stagnated during the period 1970–84 (Mellor and Johnston 1984: 534–9; FAO 1985: 32–51; World Bank 1986a: 14; Eicher 1986b: 4; FAO 1986: Appendix I; IFRI 1986: 123; Paulino 1987: 23–38).

In the specific context of Africa, a production crisis of this size could only result in growing food deprivation among the mass of rural small-scale producers and in increasing reliance on food imports. In 1985, about 100 million people, or roughly one-quarter of the African population, were estimated to be hungry and malnourished (Eicher 1985: 84). Too much importance should not be attached to this figure because the reliability of data on poverty in Africa is open to serious question and there is probably a tendency to overestimate it. However, and this is more relevant to our discussion, there are many hints that hunger and undernutrition have increased markedly in quite a number of African countries during the last decades. At the same time, the food import bill of many African states has increased dramatically. In the mid-1980s food import expenditures represented 20 per cent of the total export earnings of Africa, compared to 16 per cent in 1980 and much less in 1970 (FAO 1985: 58 and Marot 1987). In the low-income countries, this proportion was much higher. Food imports therefore contributed significantly to mounting balance-of-payments deficits and, given the bleak prospects of both agricultural and non-agricultural export markets, the drain on foreign exchange which resulted from decreasing food self-sufficiency was particularly harmful. It is also noteworthy that food output grew so slowly in sub-Saharan Africa during 1960–84 that per capita consumption fell despite high growth rates in imports. In other words, had staple food imports not increased dramatically,[1] the per capita consumption of food items would have sunk to intolerable levels (Mellor and Johnston 1984: 538 and FAO 1985: 32–4).

In Asia and Latin America, the 'food crisis' took a different shape. In these two continents, indeed, agricultural growth has usually been quite remarkable

[1] The import content of total calorie consumption for Africa as a whole more than doubled within a decade: from 6% of total calorie supplies in 1969–71 to 13% in 1979–81 (FAO 1985: 34).

during the last two decades (averaging 3 per cent per year), and the production of staple food has increased at a higher rate than population. None the less, with the notable exception of India (and of China during some periods of time), the growth of output has been slower than that of consumption because of regular and significant increases in per capita food consumption. In sharp contrast to the situation observed in Africa, the rapid growth of net food imports has made such increases possible in many Asian and Latin American countries.[2] Provided that the rural masses have an equitable share in the agricultural growth occurring in these countries, there is much reason to expect the rising food imports to be accompanied by a reduction in poverty and malnutrition, at least in the countryside. If this is not the case, attention must obviously be directed to distributive considerations to find the villain of the piece.

Since in Africa food production is not only a source of food but also the main source of incomes for the majority of people facing food insecurity, it is impossible to understand the causes of rising chronic poverty and undernutrition (as well as of increasing food dependence) unless we get a good grasp of the factors responsible for the disappointing growth records of local food production during the last decades. It is the main contention of this chapter that a number of structural factors and constraints act as supply bottlenecks that tend to limit the long-term opportunities for agricultural growth in Africa far more seriously than the inappropriate policy mixes on which economists have focused most of their attention. Furthermore, the hypothesis will be advanced that these structural factors are generally far more constraining in Africa than in Asia and Latin America, so that the former continent suffers from a real handicap in exploiting its agricultural growth potential. It is suggested that the relatively slow growth of African agriculture during the last three decades compared to the performances achieved by the other two continents must be to a large extent ascribed to this structural handicap.

This being said, it would be a mistake to neglect the consumption or demand aspects which have recently been shown to play a crucial role in the food crises of both Asia and Latin America (Mellor and Johnston 1984; Yotopoulos 1985; FAO 1985). As a matter of fact, some demand-related factors have a direct or indirect effect on the smallholders' incentives to produce as well as on the quality of their main productive resource (land). Thus, at least in some areas, rapid population growth creates land pressure with the result that increasingly marginal lands are brought into cultivation and the fertility of existing lands is reduced due to environmental degradation. On the other hand, drastic shifts in consumption patterns towards import-intensive food baskets tend to lower the

---

[2] Bear in mind the exception of India where per capita consumption levels have remained more or less stagnant because increased production has essentially served the purpose of replacing previous food imports (and to build up sizeable stocks of grain). In Chile, during the period 1977–85, the same type of import substitution strategy has created a situation in which average nutrition levels declined while wheat production increased rapidly.

prices of traditional, locally produced, staple foods. Moreover, the rising food import bill following from the above two phenomena—rapid population growth and changes in food consumption patterns—may also constrain agricultural growth in so far as the scarcity of foreign exchange sharply limits the governments' ability to finance imports of modern inputs (fuel, fertilizers, sacks and bags, etc.), capital goods (farm implements, irrigation equipment, etc.), and, perhaps, incentive consumption goods needed to increase agricultural production.

Note that it would be wrong to infer from the above diagnosis that equity issues are non-existent in Africa. In the course of the analysis of some structural growth-inhibiting factors, it will in fact be shown that, in Africa as in Asia and Latin America, there are powerful forces at work that tend to make for discriminatory access to scarce productive resources and for inequitable distribution of growth benefits.

In Section 10.2 below, the role of demand factors in Africa's food crisis will be examined. Section 10.3 will be devoted to a discussion of the 'price-focused' doctrine which ascribes this crisis to distortions of the operations of the market by inadequate agricultural policies. Section 10.4 will form the core of the chapter since it will analyse in some detail the main structural constraints that inhibit agricultural development in Africa. In Section 10.5, the central results of this study will be summarized.

A final remark is in order. It could be objected that, during the years 1986–7, food production has increased notably in a group of sub-Saharan countries, and that in some of them (e.g. Mali, Sudan, Zimbabwe) increases were such as to lead to sizeable grain surpluses. Given that these were generally good years from a climatic viewpoint, it would be premature to conclude that the downward production trend observed during the last decades has come to an end. Repeated observations and an extension of these positive production performances to many more countries (after all, the three aforementioned countries have a relatively good agricultural growth potential) would be needed before one could safely say that the structural thesis put forward in this chapter is not supported by recent empirical evidence.

10.2.   *The role of demand factors*

(a)   *Changes in consumption patterns*

To account for the quickly rising per capita demand for cereals in many Asian and Latin American countries during the last decades, one must be able to explain why the elasticity of demand with respect to income has taken on much higher values than could perhaps be expected on the basis of Engel's law. The answer has to be found in the increased use of cereal as livestock feed (FAO 1985: 43). It is 'the voracious appetite of middle-class consumers for animal protein' that has caused a change in total grain demand significantly over and above the effect of population growth (Yotopoulos 1985: 476). Underlying this disproportionate impact of the (mainly urban) demand for animal protein is a well-known mechanism: the low conversion efficiency of primary (plant) calories to secondary (livestock product) calories. It works in such a way that even a relatively small increase in per capita income, or a moderate shift in consumption patterns towards animal protein diets, or a moderate increase in the size of the (urban) middle classes, can lead to a sizeable increase in indirect cereal consumption, that is in indirect demand for feed use. The income elasticities of demand for feed are actually so high that 'the weighted income elasticity of demand for cereals may well rise to a value larger than the initial value of the elasticity for food use alone' (Mellor and Johnston 1984: 541).

The relationship between the above phenomenon and the food crisis is particularly evident in the case of the trade component. Indeed, since economic growth gives rise to a rapid increase in consumption of livestock products—especially so when most of the income gains accrue to middle classes or when they enable more people to graduate into these classes—the ensuing growth of aggregate demand for foodgrain is likely to outpace that of domestic production, unless the latter increases very fast also. Food imports will then be called for to fill this mounting gap. There may also be a causal link between booming indirect cereal consumption and the incidence of poverty and hunger if food use is crowded out when feed use increases. In other words, as people compete with people for the indirect versus direct consumption of cereals, the distribution of purchasing power between the rich and the poor becomes an important determinant of access to available food supplies (Yotopoulos 1985: 476–9). Note that this human struggle for cereals may take place on a national scale if the domestic food market is sheltered from the forces of international competition. If not, it arises at the world level in which case it is the huge demand of developed countries for feed that is the main claimant on world supplies of cereals.

How does Africa fit in with the above pattern? The declining trend of per capital cereal consumption in this continent could create the impression that the food–feed competition is not at work there. This would be a hasty conclusion, however. As a matter of fact, during the period 1966–80, use of major food crops for animal feed expanded at more than 3 per cent a year, implying that per capita feed use in Africa increased with an income elasticity close to one (Paulino 1987: 31; Yotopoulos 1985: 469).[3] Between 1974–5 and

[3] Africa actually achieved the world's highest rate of growth of total feed use during the years 1966–80, that is 6.2% per year as against 2.9% for food use (Yotopoulos 1985: 468). It is true, however, that this continent started from a very low base, with a share of feed use in total consumption of cereals amounting to 8.3% on an average during the years 1966–70 and reaching 10.3% on average during the years 1976–80. Note that in this respect North Africa is far ahead compared to sub-Saharan Africa: while in the former region, the above proportion was 16.6 and 21.0% during the two periods considered, respectively, it was only 5.6 and 6.1% in the latter region. For all the developing countries (including China) taken together, the share of feed use was 14.1 and 15.7% during the same time periods (adapted from IFPRI 1986). In sub-Saharan Africa, the low share of feed use in total domestic utilization actually reflects the fact that 'livestock feeding in the region is still largely dependent on open range and waste products' (Paulino 1987: 31).

1982–3, the share of livestock products in total agricultural output increased by as much as 17.6 per cent in Africa and that of meat in particular by 13.8 per cent, as against average rates of change of 8.8 and 9.4 per cent, respectively, for the whole developing world (FAO 1985: table 1–19, p. 51). In order to accommodate this increase in consumption of livestock products in conditions of declining per capita supplies of cereals, the direct consumption of cereals, presumably by the lower-income classes, had to be reduced to a much larger extent than would have been necessary if animal protein diets had not expanded among the urban classes. In the words of Yotopoulos, 'a shortfall in per capita supply is not necessarily shared equally by proportional decreases in food and feed' (Yotopoulos 1985: 469–70).

What needs to be stressed is that in the case of Africa the crowding-out effect does not work itself out through an upward pressure on food prices as is apparently suggested by Yotopoulos. On the contrary, a persistent claim made by so many authors and reports about African agriculture is that consumer food prices have been kept at artificially low levels, due to overvaluation of exchange rates, subsidies, international food aid, etc. (see e.g. CILSS 1979: 119–22; World Bank 1981: ch. 5, 1986b: 87–94; IFRI 1986: 143–6; FAO 1986: annex I, ch. 3; Giri 1983: 243–6, 1986: 66–72; Bates 1981; Rose 1985). In Latin America and Asia, many poor people are net buyers of food (urban low-income classes and landless or near landless rural workers) and, as a result, the food–feed competition may affect them directly to the extent that it leads to rising prices on the local food markets. In large parts of sub-Saharan Africa, however, most poor households are net food sellers who suffer from the 'negative pricing policies' followed by their government (Eicher 1984: 463). By contrast, enriched urban middle classes can all the more easily shift to animal protein diets as the cost of feed is artificially low. In Nigeria, for example, because of a huge overvaluation of the national currency, the prices of US imported maize and wheat—both of which can be fed to animals (particularly to chickens)—were much lower than local costs at the mill gate during the early 1980s. Thus, in 1983, the price of imported maize was about $315 per ton compared with $1,200 for local maize delivered in Lagos (Giri 1986: 76–7; Andrae and Beckman 1986; FAO 1986: Main Report, ch. 1, para. 1.6).

If there is a crowding-out effect arising from food–feed competition in Africa, it is definitely not a market-engineered effect operating through a price increase, but rather a government-engineered effect operating through a price decrease. Indeed, in the face of the mounting craze of urban middle-income classes for livestock products, the government would be impelled to cheapen the foodgrains—for example, by letting the national currency appreciate in real terms—to the detriment of domestic producers who thereby get impoverished.

Now, it is important to realize that so far the bulk of African imports of cereals are intended for direct consumption. The fast-growing food import bills of many African states are less the outcome of increasing adoption of animal protein diets in the cities than of massive displacement of local staples or local food grades by foreign foods or grades. This substitution effect is partly the result of the low prices of imported foods (thanks to foreign food aid or export subsidies granted to foreign food producers, at least for some products during some periods), currency overvaluation, and depressed world prices following overproduction in developed countries and of blatant distortions in the marketing and transport systems, and partly the outcome of radical changes in consumer preferences.

Concerning the price effect, it is interesting to note that in 1982 'while the international price of rice was three times that of sorghum, in West Africa it was rarely more than twice as much and sometimes only the same' (World Bank 1986b: 92). As for the price of wheat flour, it was about the same as that of maize in Nigeria and the Ivory Coast while the ratio of the former to the latter was much higher in the international market (ibid.). But the macroeconomic and price policies of African governments are not always responsible for odd price ratios between 'superior' imported foods and traditional staples. Thus, during the years 1983–4, the retail price of millet grown locally exceeded that of rice (mostly imported) in the free market of Dakar (Berg et al. 1986: fig. 9, p. 55), as a result of a marked fall in the international price of rice in the world market. Turning to the marketing and transport systems, the main point to emphasize is that these systems have been built up during the colonial period to facilitate the export–import trade rather than to move local produce from the countryside to the urban markets. Finally, changes in consumer tastes have been induced by various forces among which we may note: rapid rates of urbanization; the international demonstration effect of what many urban dwellers in Africa consider as superior goods (US quality maize in Nigeria, short broken rice in Sahelian countries, white bread and skimmed milk all over large parts of the continent, Italian tomato sauce with chemical ingredients in Senegal, etc.); the aggressive advertising campaigns of transnational food corporations; and, last but not least, the existence of various intrinsic advantages of foreign over local foods (low perishability, low time-intensiveness of the required culinary preparations, especially so when foreign foods can be consumed in attractive and convenient processed forms, like wheat in the form of bread).

The importance of trend changes in African food consumption patterns and their dramatic impact on food imports can be illustrated with reference to West Africa. Here, per capita consumption of wheat products and rice grew at an average annual rate of 8.5 and 2.8 per cent, respectively, between 1966–70 and 1976–80. By contrast, consumption of traditional foods locally grown either barely increased (by 0.27 per cent for maize) or declined (by 1.5 per cent for millet and 1.7 per cent for sorghum) (World Bank 1986b: 92). In the Sahelian region only, demand for rice increased by more than 8 per cent a year during the period 1976–82 whereas domestic production hardly expanded. As a consequence, Sahelian countries today produce only half of the quantities of rice they consume. The situation is worse still with regard to wheat and wheat products. Consumption has grown at the high rate of 11 per cent per year, although local wheat production is practically non-existent. No wonder then that these countries produce only 5 per cent of the wheat they consume (Giri 1983: 77–8). Moreover, Giri noted that 'the demand for bread does not spring any more only from the urban classes which have more or less adopted European modes of consumption, but also from low-income urban classes and even from rural populations . . . Thus, in the valley of the Senegal river, the traditional breakfast composed of millet couscous and vegetables has largely given way to a "Europeanized" meal with soluble coffee, concentrated milk or milk powder, and bread' (ibid., 78). This is confirmed by a consumption survey conducted during the late 1970s in Dakar (the capital city of Senegal) and in two small towns of the interior of the country (Louga and Linguère). Indeed, this study has come to the conclusion that (1) rice and bread absorbed almost 90 per cent of the total household budget devoted to cereal consumption, and (2) this proportion did not vary significantly across various income classes (CILSS 1979: 245).[4]

In the Ivory Coast—one of the few sub-Saharan countries which recorded a rise in its per capita food output during the last decades—around 15 per cent of the total import bill is spent on food items. The import content of domestic cereal consumption exceeds one-third while that of consumption on meat, fish, and milk products is higher than one-half. On the whole, food imports have grown at a much higher rate than domestic food production, per capita food imports have increased rapidly, and the import content of aggregate food consumption has risen significantly. Cereals and cereal-based products (almost exclusively wheat and rice) represented 27 per cent of the country's food imports on average for the years 1978–80, which was much less than the share of meat and milk products (38 per cent), but much more than the share of other product categories (12.5 per cent for fish and fish derivates and 10 per cent for beverages and tobacco). Finally, it has been estimated that half the food expenditures by urban dwellers were spent on imported items in the early 1980s (Haubert and Frelin 1985: 21–2).

Table 10.1 compares the respective rates of increase in the imports of various food products during the 1960s and 1970s for the whole of sub-Saharan Africa.

The following trends emerge from an analysis of food imports into Africa during the last decades:

- rising per capita food imports;
- preponderant share of cereals in total food imports (contrary to what was observed in the particular case of the Ivory Coast);

[4] However, expenditures on cereal consumption represented only 30% of total food expenditures. Note also that, for the whole of Africa, per capita production (and consumption) of traditional staples has increased at the following negative rates during the period 1970/1–1983/4: millet: −3.9%; sorghum: −3.2%; roots and tubers: −1.3%; cassava: −1.6%; pulses: −2.0% (FAO, *Production Yearbook, 1975, 1985*).

Table 10.1 Average annual rates of growth of imports of various food products in sub-Saharan Africa, 1961–1984 (in volume)

	1961–3 to 1969–71 (%)	1970–1 to 1983–4 (%)
Cereals	9.0	9.7
Wheat	12.9	9.6
Rice	4.9	10.4
Maize	8.7	12.6
Milk products	7.2	7.9
Sugar	2.5	5.0
Meat	1.3	11.1
Animal and vegetable oil	11.5	13.0[a]

[a] This estimate is for the period 1969–71 to 1977–9.

Source: Adapted from World Bank (1981: table 5.3) and FAO, *Production Yearbook and Trade Yearbook, 1975, 1985*.

- near-complete dominance of grain imports by three cereals (wheat —almost 50 per cent; rice—almost 30 per cent; and maize—almost 20 per cent);
- rising import content of domestic food consumption, particularly so in the case of grain, milk products, meat, and edible oils;[5]
- heavy concentration of consumption of imported foods in urban areas: thus, in 1980, 90 per cent of imported cereals were consumed in the cities (FAO 1986: Main Report, ch. 4, para. 16).

To sum up, many African countries have been subject to profound changes in their food consumption patterns during the last two decades. As could be expected, these changes have been especially rapid and marked in big cities: it is probably not fortuitous that by and large countries which have recorded the highest growth rates of food imports during the 1970s are also those which urbanized at the fastest pace (see FAO 1985: 109). However, the new consumption patterns are gradually spreading to small towns and to rural areas. Therefore, low production performances, and even declining yields per

[5] Between 1969–71 and 1979–81, for example, the share of rice and wheat in total grain consumption increased from 18% to 25% (FAO 1986: Main Report, ch. 2, para. 43). In 1982–4, the import content of domestic consumption of milk and milk products exceeded 50% in 15 out of 43 African countries for which data are available (FAO 1986: Annex I, ch. 3, para. 20). Note also that the cereal deficit in Africa amounted to about 25 million tonnes on average during the years 1982–4 (15.7 million for North Africa and 9.1 million for sub-Saharan Africa). This figure compares rather well with the grain deficit of the USSR during the 1980s (more than 30 million tonnes per year). However, what is really alarming in the case of Africa is the prospect for the future: thus, according to FAO projections, Africa's grain deficit would reach 70 million tonnes in the year 2010 (43.5 million for North Africa and 26.6 million for sub-Saharan Africa). See Giri (1986: 48) and FAO (1986: Main Report, ch. 2, Fig. 16).

unit area, in the case of traditional staples (millet, sorghum, yams, cassava, white maize, beans, plantain bananas, etc.) are not necessarily due entirely to supply factors, but may also arise partly from increasingly demand-constrained markets. It is no doubt true that these consumption shifts have been induced, at least in part, by policy-determined factors—like the price policies and the outward-looking strategy of economic development pursued by many African states. But the real question lies in whether they are or have become irreversible, in the sense that they have led African consumers to modify their taste configurations for good.

In other words, can one reasonably expect that drastic measures aimed at reversing the 'faulty' policies—like heavy taxation or strict rationing of 'superior' imported foods—will bring consumer preferences back to their initial position? I think we must realistically assume that changes in consumer tastes such as have occurred in Africa are not easily reversible, especially so for urban dwellers who have been accustomed to the new foods for rather long periods of time. As a consequence, in the numerous African countries where foreign foods cannot be produced locally, or could be produced only at prohibitively high costs, the governments will continue to be under heavy pressure to subsidize their production or their consumption. Evidently, such subsidies are an intolerable drain on these countries' limited resources and their rates of economic growth thereby get reduced. In fact, even if the governments could withstand the pressures from the urban consumers, economic growth performances could still be impaired. This would occur if the demand for 'superior' foods is price inelastic so that it would be maintained at the cost of depressed rates of household savings, were the government to raise food prices drastically.

In these circumstances, reduction of rural poverty and improvement of food security would be best attained through measures of agricultural self-reliance aiming concurrently at protecting traditional local food producers from cheap imports and enhancing the attractiveness of traditional staples. The latter could be achieved through a variety of measures, like the development of more efficient transport and marketing systems; improvements in the quality of traditional foods (better packing, easier storage, new and faster methods of preparation); and the enlargement of their possible uses (e.g. the use of cassava as animal feed; the production of bread from a mixture of wheat and millet or even from millet alone; the invention of new food items using root and tuber crops as ingredients; use of sorghum, maize, or millet together with wheat to make pasta; production of couscous from pre-cooked millet; production of sorghum or millet semolina).[6]

---

[6] Certain attempts have already been embarked upon, like the experimental production of bread from wheat and millet in the Sahelian region (Berg et al. 1986: 10). In its recent and comprehensive study of African agriculture, FAO also emphasized the need to improve traditional staples (FAO 1986: Main Report, ch. 4, para. 25).

(b)   Fast population growth

Even assuming a constant pattern of food consumption with no marked shift towards foreign foodstuffs, African agriculture would still be confronted with the dramatic challenge arising from historically unprecedented rates of population growth. Africa is in fact the only region of the world where population growth actually accelerated during the 1970s and the early 1980s. The annual population growth rate in Africa was 2.1 per cent in the mid-1950s, 2.7 per cent in the late 1970s, and as much as 3 per cent during the years 1980–5 (as against 2.2 per cent in Asia and 2.3 per cent in Latin America). Moreover, Africa's population growth rate is projected to continue to increase throughout the late 1980s and the early 1990s until it levels off at about 3.1 per cent by 1995. By that time, population will be growing at 1.9 and 2 per cent per year in Asia and in Latin America, respectively (FAO 1986: annex I, ch. 2, para. 2.5; Eicher 1984: 457).

What is particularly alarming in the case of Africa's demographic trends is precisely that her population growth will level off at an astronomically high rate (more than 3 per cent), and that this levelling off process will itself last during a rather long period of time. Indeed, for a variety of complex factors which have made for a pro-fertility cultural environment and have created a kind of political indifference to population growth problems (due to a myth of Africa as being a land-surplus continent), there is not much hope that fertility levels will be reduced in the coming years (Eicher 1984: 458, 1986c: 244–5). The situation is especially confounding for more than one-third of African people living in nine countries where population will grow at an average yearly rate equal to or higher than 3.5 per cent during the years 1980–2000 (Kenya, Tanzania, Zimbabwe, Botswana, Rwanda, Libya, Uganda, Nigeria, and Zambia). A number of African countries will reach or have already reached a maximum rate of population growth exceeding the 4 per cent threshold (Kenya—4.3 per cent; Zimbabwe and the Ivory Coast—4.2 per cent; Uganda and Libya—4.1 per cent). Most African countries, however, will have annual population growth rates in the range 2.5–3.5 per cent up to the year 2000. Their maximum rate of growth will typically oscillate around 3.1–3.3 per cent, with the exceptions of the Ivory Coast (see above), Senegal (3.6 per cent), and Malawi (3.5 per cent) (FAO 1986: Annex I, table 2.1).

Whatever the reasons accounting for these almost incredible trends, the point is that for several decades to come Africa's land, pasture, and forestry resources will be subjected to heavy pressure and the well-known threats to her ecological equilibria will go on increasing. Just to give an example, the aggregate population of Sahelian countries is expected to increase from 31 to 120 million inhabitants between 1985 and 2025 (Pennisi 1986: 55). Only to feed her growing population at the present level of per capita food consumption, Africa would thus need to increase her food production at a rate of, say, 3.2 per cent per year for several decades in succession. This is of course an impossible challenge for her to meet. It is therefore not surprising that in order to reach the conclusion that more than half the African countries could increase or stabilize their rates of food self-sufficiency during the next 25 years, FAO had to make extremely strong assumptions (FAO 1986: Main Report ch. 2). Now, if we leave aside the problem of food self-reliance to focus our attention on the issue of poverty alleviation, the following must be said: even assuming a high rate of job creation in (import-substituting) non-agricultural activities (which will not go without profound reforms in the management of African economies, and in the way they are exposed to international market forces), Africa will need to step up food production, at least in the short and medium term, in order to provide her fast-growing workforce with new incomes and more rewarding employment opportunities. Given that world markets for non-food agricultural products are much depressed, too much hope should not be placed on the expansion of exportable non-food production.

There is yet another demographic trend that must be borne in mind while analysing the agricultural situation in Africa: this is the steady decline in the share of total labour force engaged in agricultural activities. Thus, between 1960 and 1984, the farm labour force has increased at an annual rate much lower than the rate of population growth and the rate of growth of the total labour force (Johnston 1986: 156; Paulino 1987: 25–6). By contrast, the percentage of the population living in urban areas increased from 18.4 to 28.9 per cent between 1960 and 1980 (FAO 1985: 86). In Sudano-Sahelian Africa, urban population has expanded 3.5 times as fast as rural population and, in humid Central Africa, 5.5 times as fast (FAO 1986: Main Report, ch. 1, para. 1.15).

In so far as it helps to mitigate the absolute increase of the farming population and, thereby, to bring down the population pressure on land, the declining share of agriculture in the total labour force might seem to be a welcome trend. However, per capita domestic food supplies will be maintained only if there is a sufficient increase in (per capita) agricultural labour productivity to make up for the relative decline of the farm labour force. In quite a number of African countries, however, this condition is not likely to be satisfied and high rates of urbanization may well result in diminishing per capita food output. The reason for this becomes apparent when it is realized that farm labour is not homogeneous and that rural outmigration modifies the characteristics of the average worker remaining in agriculture. Indeed, it is a common feature of many African countries that internal migration streams are overwhelmingly dominated by single (young) men. Stories of entire villages deserted by their most productive male members are not rare in Africa, particularly so in countries where hard conditions prevail in the countryside (as in arid or semi-arid areas) or where attractive employment opportunities exist outside the agricultural sector (as in the oil-producing countries during the

1970s).[7] That the departure of many young male adult members from the village workforce—where and when it occurs—may seriously hinder agricultural growth is evident from the fact that heavy agricultural tasks are consequently neglected, which is bound to affect the productivity of both the land and labour efforts by the remaining workers. Of course, ordinary effects of labour shortages are also to be feared. Since in Africa demand for agricultural labour is highly seasonal due to single-season rainfall patterns, a labour force mainly composed of women, children, and aged men and sufficient to carry out the ordinary farm works throughout the year will be inadequate for the peak season (Mellor and Delgado 1987: 2; Delgado and Ranade 1987: 124–8). Moreover, 'in the African farming systems seasonal labour shortages are a far more limiting factor in increasing productivity than in Asia, especially in view of the low level of African agricultural technology' (Lele 1984: 445).

It is true that the above effects could be offset or neutralized if, as suggested by some authors (e.g. Collier and Lal 1981; Hyden 1986: 57), migrant workers choose to invest part of their non-agricultural incomes in their home village with a view to introducing new technical configurations (of a labour-saving and/or land-augmenting type) in the family farm. But this poses the problem of the availability of new proven technical packages adapted to the needs of African smallholders. Since these new packages do not generally exist, remittances tend to be spent on consumption purposes, with priority being often given to the purchase of imported foods (Mathieu 1987: i. 33–9).

There are in fact two conditions under which the afore-described situation would probably not be a cause of great concern for many African countries: (1) a sufficient number of sustainable income-earning opportunities exist outside the agricultural sector to absorb the rural migrants productively, and (2) the intersectoral transfer of labour does not result in a tightening of the balance-of-payments constraint (which supposes that increased food imports are offset by new export proceeds). The situation of oil-exporting countries during the 1970s came close to satisfying these conditions but, unfortunately, the world economic crisis put an abrupt end to their growing prosperity. Income-earning opportunities in the oil-producing sector did not turn out to be sustainable and countries like Nigeria, Gabon, and the Ivory Coast were precipitated into a deadlock characterized by a sudden drop of their oil export receipts and by a rapid increase in their food import bill.

---

[7] In African countries which experienced an oil boom during the 1970s (like Nigeria and Gabon), the dearth of young male labour in the countryside created huge problems in the smallholder food-producing sector and was mainly responsible for its bad performance (see Monferrer 1985 for Gabon; Andrae and Beckman 1986; and Aboyade 1987: 246 for Nigeria).

10.3. *The role of supply factors: price- versus structure-focused analysis*

(a) *The dominant view*

Since the early 1980s and the publication of the famous Berg report (World Bank 1981), it has become fashionable to locate the most important impediment to agricultural growth in sub-Saharan Africa in 'the nature of incentives offered to producers' and in 'the actions of those who distort the operations of the market' (Bates 1981: 1–2). Crucial determinants of the present food crisis in Africa are seen to be lying in inefficient marketing state monopolies, inadequate distribution of modern agricultural inputs, neglect of agricultural investment in smallholder production, and misguided pricing policies. Yet it is clearly the latter problem—often seen in conjunction with the first one —which has been given most emphasis in many recent publications, particularly those issued by international organizations (CILSS 1979; World Bank 1981, 1986*b*; IFRI 1986; Berg *et al.* 1986 (on behalf of CILSS and OECD)). For example, the World Bank has estimated that in a number of African countries effective tax rates—representing the combined effects of currency overvaluation, formal taxation, official pricing policies, and inefficient marketing arrangements—have been such as to reduce the real incomes of agricultural producers below half of the real value of their production as measured by world market prices (World Bank 1981: 55–6; see also World Bank 1986*b*: ch. 4, pp. 61–84; Giri 1986: 68–9; Lele 1984: 441; Coquery-Vidrovitch 1985: 162–3; Bates 1981; FAO 1986: annex I, ch. 3, paras 3.4–3.7; Aboyade 1987: 241–52; Oyejide 1987: 257–73).

Heavy effective taxation of agricultural producers is not confined to export crops only, but is also found to be largely prevalent in the case of staple foods. In Mali, for example, an in-depth study of a large irrigated rice production scheme in 1979/80 has revealed that it cost farmers 83 Malian francs to produce a kilo of rice, but that the government paid them only 60 Malian francs (study quoted by Eicher 1984: 463). Another study conducted in the same country reached the conclusion that unit production costs of the two main traditional staples, millet and sorghum, were also higher than official producer prices (Kébé 1982).

Another way of assessing the underpricing of agricultural commodities in many African countries is to compare real official producer prices not with international prices or unit production costs but with current prices ruling in local parallel markets or in neighbouring countries. To refer again to the case of Mali, unofficial market prices for millet, sorghum, maize, and rice were three to five times as high as official prices in the late 1970s (Coquery-Vidrovitch 1985: 162–3; Gueymard 1985: 226 n. 6; Berg *et al.* 1986: 57).[8] The World Bank

---

[8] Thus, in Sept. 1981, the average unofficial price for 3 cereals (millet, sorghum, and maize) in 13 market-places of Bamako was 218 Malian francs per kilo while the average official price was only 85 francs (Gueymard 1985: 226 n. 6).

arrived at similar price discrepancies for Tanzania during the same period (World Bank 1986*b*: 75). Even if Mali and Tanzania are extreme cases, there is enough empirical evidence to show that there are often substantial differences —from 100 to 200 per cent according to FAO (1986: Main Report, ch. 4, para. 4.8; see also Anson-Meyer 1985: 277 and Pottier 1986: 51)—between official and unofficial or black market prices.

Two central ideas actually emerge from the dominant price-focused analysis of Africa's food crisis. The first idea follows from a rather straightforward interpretation of the above facts: African small farmers are subject to genuine extortion on the part of the state. This extortion reflects itself in negative pricing and taxation policies devised 'to pump the economic surplus out of agriculture' (Eicher 1984: 463; see also Bienen 1987). The outcome of these exploitative state interferences with market forces is alarming since low food crop prices have discouraged expansion of production for the market and have acted as a disincentive for investment in agriculture. By imposing heavy effective tax rates on export crops, African states have deprived many farmers —who constitute the bulk of Africa's poor—of an important complementary source of monetary income while at the same time denying themselves the possibility of earning scarce foreign exchange. Note incidentally that the tradition of placing relentless fiscal pressure upon the peasant sector was firmly established from the beginning of the colonial state when it was said to produce the same kind of 'demoralization, disaffection and disengagement' as is currently deplored nowadays (Young 1986: 44).

Some authors, rejecting the idea that state agents act irrationally, have tried to explain why African states follow such suicidal or self-defeating strategies of blatant discrimination against farmers (Bates 1981; Hart 1982; Commins *et al.* 1986). Robert Bates has grounded his attempt at understanding African political economy on the assumption that the state essentially tries 'to respond to the political demands it perceives to be important to satisfy in order to retain power' (Colclough 1985: 35). Basically, his socio-political theorization belongs to the 'rural–urban divide' or 'urban-bias' paradigm explored by Michael Lipton with special reference to India (Lipton 1977). The main clientele of most African states are considered to be urban residents (state employees, capitalist employers, merchants, members of the army, organized workers) who operate effectively as an interest group to influence state policies in urban-biased directions. Although Bates's analysis commends itself for its rigour and clarity, and although it offers numerous useful insights into the mechanisms of political patronage in Africa, it can be criticized on several grounds. First, it takes too much for granted that African state policies are systematically and unambiguously biased against agriculturists, a point to which I shall soon return. Second, it often seems to imply that the urban bias is engineered exclusively through state intervention in otherwise unbiased market processes (Toye 1987: 129). Third, the whole demonstration of Bates rests primarily on the assumption that the policy choices made by African governments are relatively unaffected by external factors, like the current world economic crisis, the role of foreign investors, of aid donors, and of international agencies (Bienefeld 1986: 7–9). This assumption is all the more unsatisfactory as growing public deficits in many African countries are to a significant extent the outcome of external forces, a situation which is not likely to change so long as a substantial part of the governments' revenues comes from import and export taxes. Last but not least, Bates' rational choice/public choice framework is questionable and inherently limited in so far as it assumes (a) that individuals implicitly apply a material benefit-cost calculus to their involvement in politics and (b) that policies are the outcome of the competition and interaction of organized social groups. The former assumption rules out any possibility of symbolic and affective actions in politics while the latter implies that 'the state can exist only as a neutral arena or, in the form of the state bureaucracy, as a specially-privileged social group' (Moore 1987: 9–11).

Keith Hart has taken a somewhat different approach to the problem. His pivotal hypothesis is that modern states in Africa cannot be viable and achieve their historical objective of transforming the economy unless they can assure that reliable revenues flow into their treasury. As a result, most of their efforts tend to concentrate on undertaking large-scale projects orientated towards cash crops (state farms, irrigation schemes, settlement, and land reclamation projects), and on controlling agricultural trade through parastatals or publicly sponsored co-operatives which are able to provide the public exchequer with regular and sizeable proceeds for the least administrative cost.[9] And there is a priori no reason to expect that undertakings which are most profitable from the treasury's standpoint (allowing for administrative costs and political feasibility considerations) are also the most socially efficient (Hart 1982, mainly ch. 4). Given that 'the State is not monolithic and does not form a homogeneous bloc directed principally towards exploiting the peasants' (Gentil 1986: 212), perhaps one of the greatest advantages of Keith Hart's hypothesis is that it does not simplistically assume that all state actions are by necessity anti-rural or anti-agriculture. His main point is indeed that treasury considerations can prompt African states to encourage projects or to take steps—including easy acceptance of unscreened foreign aid—that can inhibit agricultural growth. Nowhere does he suggest that governments in Africa consciously neglect or purposefully and systematically exploit the agricultural sector.

This being said, one can rather easily agree with both Robert Bates and Keith Hart that it is not satisfactory to treat all state actions as 'bad' policies, obvious mistakes, or irrational interventions. However, it is no doubt as simplistic an attitude to take the opposite extreme view and to assume that they all form parts of a coherent strategy which would obey the functional exigencies of a rational, single-minded administration or government. In many instances, it is as fruitful a hypothesis to consider that state policies can be

[9] For a similar, albeit less articulated, analysis, see Dupriez (1980: 149–58).

unpredictably inconsistent or badly planned[10] for various reasons such as imperfect information, misperception about state interests, or inner conflicts between the government and the state bureaucracy, between different Ministries or departments, etc. As Sara Berry has aptly noted, it is only when Ministries of agriculture, rural development agencies, parastatals, and so forth are assumed to 'act consistently and cooperatively in pursuit of single, well-defined sets of goals' that a theory of the state of the type proposed by Bates (and Hart) can be taken seriously (Berry 1984: 65–6; see also Gephart 1986: 57–9; Bienen 1987: 298).

The second central idea underlying the price-focused analysis of the 1980s is that Africa's agricultural woes are essentially due to misguided, although possibly explainable, government policies. This is taken to imply that Africa's agricultural and other problems could largely be resolved by a domestic realignment of policy measures. Basically, the policy changes advocated are all measures aimed at privatizing the economy, 'getting prices right', and facilitating responsiveness to market signals. It is explicitly assumed that African farmers are highly price-responsive and that a decrease in the effective tax rates they face will pay high dividends in terms of enhanced agricultural production and investment.

To amend the 'faulty' or inadequate pricing policies by eliminating the most glaring price distortions, and to call into question many of the anti-market prejudices which are so common in Africa, are certainly necessary steps to be taken in many countries of the continent. To that extent, the price-focused analysis of the African food crisis has undoubtedly done a good job. In fact, during the last few years, and often under the combined pressures of the International Monetary Fund and the World Bank, many African governments have adopted corrective measures aimed at liberalizing agricultural trade and granting more remunerative prices to agricultural producers, particularly in the case of food crops (see e.g. CILSS 1979: 147; Gueymard 1985: 228–35; Berg et al. 1986; FAO 1986: Main Report, ch. 4, para. 3 and ch. 5, para. 39; Giri 1986: 74–5; Mellor and Delgado 1987: 4; Colclough 1985: 32).[11] Nevertheless, the above interpretation of Africa's predicament is also dangerously misleading in so far as it conveys the idea that food imbalances will be essentially redressed and much rural poverty will be alleviated simply by restoring the market signals and giving the farmers their dues. As one author aptly remarked: 'whilst prices are important, they are only *one* element in the process of eliciting a desirable pattern of production and distribution'

---

[10] This is clearly the path followed by M. Anson-Meyer in her analysis of Benin, Ghana, Nigeria, and Togo (Anson-Meyer 1985: 276–84) and by R. Galli in her case-study of Guinea-Bissau (Galli 1987).

[11] On the whole, it is probably correct to say that real agricultural prices for many food crops have risen since the late 1970s. An outstanding exception is rice in most Sahelian countries where it is mainly produced in governmental irrigation schemes. The situation has been less satisfactory for many export crops, however, and this is in spite of the substantial currency devaluations that occurred in a good number of African countries.

(Colclough 1985: 30). More pointedly, what needs to be emphasized is that 'the lack of technology, not the lack of farmer motivation, is the major brake on expanded food, livestock and export crop production' (Eicher 1986a: 26). Hard realities must be faced squarely: 'Africa's agrarian crisis is complex and it has been building up for several decades. Neither simplistic statements about external forces nor calls for open market, export-led growth, and increased foreign aid are the answers' (Eicher 1985: 98).

(b) The deficiencies of a price-focused approach

The dominant, price-focused, thesis on the African food crisis must therefore be seriously qualified and placed in a different and much larger perspective if it is to play a useful role. In the present section, without getting involved in a detailed argument which would take us too far, I would like to make a number of specific points and to give a few warnings which are important in the context of our whole discussion.

Empirical doubts From an empirical viewpoint, the price-focused approach to the African food crisis suffers from several weaknesses which may undermine its credibility. First, it is in fact not quite clear whether the prices of staples have been too low during, say, the last fifteen years. As has been pointed out above, significant price adjustments took place in many African countries during the 1970s which seem to have substantially helped to correct past distortions and to alleviate the tax burden on food producers. Thus, in a report published by CILSS (Comité permanent inter-états de lutte contre la sécheresse dans le Sahel), Elliot Berg himself, the main author of the famous World Bank report on sub-Saharan Africa (1981), confessed that: '. . . up to a certain point, "distortions" prevail that lower the prices [of cereals], and international aid seems to bear heavy responsibility in this situation. But, according to other criteria, it is not clear that official cereal prices ruling [in Sahelian countries] in 1977 were too low' (CILSS 1979: 147; in the same vein, see Colclough 1985: 32). Empirical evidence therefore appears to be much more mixed than is suggested or asserted by many statements or writings on 'peasants' exploitation' in Africa. The truth is that the implicit taxation of African smallholders varies significantly by country, by crop, and by period, so that broad generalizations must always be received with a good dose of scepticism.

Second, it must be realized that there are simply no satisfactory reference prices against which African domestic food prices can be measured to test whether they are 'too low' and to what extent. In particular, there is no way in which we can contend that exchange rates (whether official, or 'black', or 'grey') and world food prices are equilibrium prices. Regarding the latter, what must be emphasized is that international food prices are determined in residual markets, the demand and supply of which may represent only a minor share of world total supply and demand. World prices could only become reliable efficiency signals if agricultural markets in the developed countries were no longer sheltered *vis-à-vis* the international forces of competition, a situation which is not likely to arise, and perhaps rightly so.

Third, even admitting that important price distortions continue to prevail which get reflected in significant differences between official and black market prices, a basic difficulty remains which emerges from the following well-documented fact: in many cases the major part of staple food smallholder production is not actually disposed of through the official channel. Thus, FAO has estimated that only 5–25 per cent of domestic cereal output in most African countries is marketed via state trade organizations, the remainder being sold off in parallel markets (FAO 1986: Main Report, ch. 4, para. 4.8; see also Gueymard 1985: 226). The latter markets are not necessarily illegal since it may be a lack of circulating capital in the hands of the official marketing boards that prevents them from purchasing all the output offered for sale by the farmers. In other words, due to a shortage of liquidity, and to various transport and other logistic problems, many such boards operating in the field of staple food production are unable to exercise effectively the monopsonistic power granted them by the state. As shown by Johan Pottier (1986), government officials are so aware of the difficulties inherent in state marketing boards that they may actively encourage the peasantry to use private channels instead (at least when they are 'off duty'). This being said, it must be admitted that, more generally, 'it is extremely difficult to enforce monopsony for commodities that are primarily consumed in mass domestic markets' (Leonard 1986: 187). But, then, if this is so, one cannot expect that an upward adjustment in official producer prices will enhance total production. The only result it can yield is an increase in the quantities brought for sale in the open, official markets to the detriment of sales in parallel trade networks.[12] As has been actually observed in a number of cases, a rise of official food prices may thus create acute shortages in local or domestic markets (Berry 1984: 72).

Fourth, while insisting on the price-responsiveness of African farmers, too many authors do not carefully distinguish between aggregate supply response on the one hand, and supply response to changes in the prices of particular commodities on the other hand. In fact, they often provide evidence of high price elasticities of output for specific, single crops and then jump to the conclusion that more appropriate pricing policies will automatically boost overall production. This conceptual confusion is all the more serious as

---

[12] For obvious reasons, farmers are more dependent on state marketing channels in the case of export crops than in that of food crops. Yet, even in the case of export agricultural goods, possibilities of smuggling across borders often exist in Africa as borders are not well guarded and people have a long historical tradition of interregional trade. Thus, to quote an extreme example, the Secretariat for Planning of the Republic of Guinea-Bissau estimated that it lost as much in clandestine trade as it gained in official trade between the year of national independence and 1983 (Galli 1987: 94). In the circumstances a nation state has an obvious interest in raising the official purchase price of the contraband goods in order to avoid regular and important losses of scarce revenue and foreign exchange.

empirical findings concerning supply responses to price changes are not likely to converge whether we consider total production or production of particular commodities. While there is, for Africa as for other developing regions, a good deal of evidence pointing to elastic supply functions for a wide variety of smallholder cash crops, much less is known about aggregate food supply responses to movements in intersectoral terms of trade (Helleiner 1975: 36–41). However, recent evidence available for Asia (Herdt 1970; Krishna 1984), for a large sample of fifty-eight Third World countries (Binswanger *et al*. 1985), and for a small sample of nine African countries (Bond 1983), all converge to show that under conditions of technologically unchanging traditional agriculture aggregate short-term supply elasticities tend to be positive but low—in the range of 0.0 to 0.2 (see also Askari and Cummings 1977; Scandizzo and Bruce 1980).

According to John Mellor, if aggregate supply responses are low in modern agricultures, they are likely to be even lower in traditional agricultures 'because of the lesser use of purchased inputs and the lesser opportunity for transfer of labour resources to and from productive use in other sectors of the economy' (Mellor 1968: 24). There is thus good reason to believe that the same situation obtains presently in African smallholder agriculture, especially in view of its low level of technical sophistication (many African peasants have still only a hand-hoe as agricultural implement). Moreover, given the absence of specialized capital in African smallholder agriculture as well as the above-noted lack of alternative opportunities for land and labour use, long-term supply elasticities are not likely to be significantly higher than short-term elasticities. It is noticeable that the results obtained by Bond (1983)—although they must admittedly be treated with caution due to the low reliability of the statistical material used—do not show significant differences between these two elasticities for all but one country in the sample. In the case of Africa, therefore, little weight ought to be attached to the World Bank's argument according to which 'estimates of aggregate farm output responses have typically been of a short-term nature and have failed to reflect the fact that changes in prices have a long-term effect on the intersectoral flow of resources' (World Bank 1986*b*: 69).

Fifth, in many cases it is not clear from the evidence adduced in support of the price-focused thesis to what extent an expansion (depression) of production is due to an increase (decrease) in the price of output. Thus, Eicher has drawn our attention to the fact that the decline in agricultural exports from numerous African countries over the past 15–20 years is not necessarily or entirely to be attributed to misguided pricing policies as is commonly suggested. It increasingly appears that 'some of this decline might be a function of the deteriorating genetic resource base for perennial crops such as coffee, cocoa, coconut palm and oil palm' (Eicher 1986*a*: 13). Similarly, it would be a mistake to give the entire credit of output growth to rising producer prices when the latter have obviously been only a part of a whole package of reforms including technology, institutions, and agricultural policies. For example, in the case of Zimbabwe—often presented as a perfect illustration of the adequacy of price policy to stimulate agricultural production—we are warned that 'the favourable production response is more complex than higher prices and good weather . . . farmers were able to respond to higher prices because they had access to well-functioning input and output markets, an extension system that has given increasing attention to smallholders in recent years, and one of the strongest agricultural research services in Africa' (Eicher 1985: 92–3, 1986c: 261).

As Helleiner has rightly emphasized, 'what one seeks to understand is the effect of alterations in various packages of influences'. As a consequence, efforts at establishing the price responsiveness of smallholders in African agriculture—that is efforts which consist of selecting only one out of a myriad of influences and of measuring its separate impact on output with the help of the *ceteris paribus* assumption—are bound to be rather sterile and have 'probably already reached a point of rapidly diminishing returns' (Helleiner 1975: 43–4). As for Schäfer, who can certainly not be accused of underrating the role of prices, he admits that 'agricultural production evidently reacts more strongly to certain types of government activity in rural areas (road building, establishment of markets, degree of literacy) than to price increases' (Schäfer 1987: 132).

Theoretical caveats   The price-focused doctrine is not exempt from theoretical weaknesses either. In the first place, the presumption that African governments are to be held responsible for a wrong setting of the prices is hardly satisfactory. Indeed, as Sara Berry has pointed out, 'in criticizing African governments for reducing incentives to agricultural producers, economists often implicitly compare the existing situation to one in which state intervention is non-existent' (Berry 1984: 73). To the extent that agricultural markets are not reasonably competitive and can never be so—because a competitive environment is essentially hazardous and therefore tends to breed market controls—such an assumption is unrealistic. In other words, 'the choice facing African governments is often not one of controlled prices versus competitive ones, but of trying to regulate prices themselves or letting someone else take control' (ibid.). In this respect, it is interesting to note that when West African markets work well it is apparently more because they are controlled by well-organized kinship or community-based networks than because they are 'reasonably competitive' (ibid. 72).

Second, the analytical basis from which positive aggregate supply responses to price changes can be derived is far from being as strong as one would wish. In actual fact, it is only in the simple case of complete specialization or pure commercial farming—the entire output of the peasant family is marketed at a given exchange ratio to buy an outside consumer good—that positive price elasticities of agricultural supply can be obtained with unambiguous and rather plausible analytical conditions (Agarwal 1983 49–50 and appendix I). In the case of partial specialization or semisubsistence family farming—when only a part of the produce is marketed, the rest being consumed by the peasant family itself—no such clear-cut results can be arrived at, unless we are ready to make very special assumptions (ibid. 50–1; Sen 1966: 436–7; Nakajima 1970). This theoretical indeterminacy obtains whether we consider a model with a single product or with two products (plus leisure), and whether supply refers to output or to marketable surplus. In fact, as soon as we leave the standard and convenient world of pure commercial farms or agricultural *firms*, we are confronted with quite complex income and substitution effects. Take the income effect: an increase in the real income of a peasant family following a rise in the output price may induce it not only to consume more leisure (and, therefore, to work less), but also to consume more of the good produced and, other things being equal, to reduce its marketed surplus. Substitution effects go of course in the opposite direction: at a given real income, the peasant family would respond to a rise in the output price by increasing its work efforts, and by modifying its consumption basket so as to substitute the outside consumer good for the self-produced one (if they are at all substitutable, which is not to be taken for granted). From these considerations, it is apparent that the marketable food surplus will increase as a result of a favourable movement of the intersectoral terms of trade only if the structure of the peasant's preference between leisure, the agricultural self-produced good, and the manufactured outside good is sufficiently skewed in favour of the latter. Note also that because of the role played by leisure the price elasticity of the food market supply might be negative even in the case where food is an inferior good.

Economic theory does not therefore provide the upholders of the price-focused doctrine with the kind of decisive analytical proof they often give the impression of having in the back of their minds. Indeed, there can be no doubt that the situation of most African smallholders is much closer to the model of the semisubsistence farm—that is the model which leads to the most ambiguous analytical results—than to the model of complete specialization. This caveat should not be dismissed lightly on the ground that, since theory does not offer precise guidelines, we can forget about it. As a matter of fact, a good observer of the African scene has recently noted that a rise of income or output may prompt the smallholder in Africa not to increase his marketed surplus and to accelerate his capital accumulation, but to set apart for his own consumption a larger part of his produce and perhaps to shift to the production and consumption of a 'superior' crop (e.g. rice instead of millet) (Coquery-Vidrovitch 1985: 158). Specific evidence confirming the possibility of atypical supply reactions is actually available: for example, Malawian smallholders have responded to a deterioration in their terms of trade by increasing their output (Ghai and Radwan, 1983; Harvey, 1983), while Nigerian food producers have apparently not reacted to a dramatic improvement of their terms of trade in the years 1968–77 (Collier, 1983: 208). For another thing, historical accounts of the experiences of both USSR and China teach us that raising food producer prices may be a counter-productive strategy. This happens because peasants, when they start from a very low level of living, tend to respond to an increase in their real income by retaining a larger proportion of what they produce. Attempts at bettering the standard of living of the mass of individual peasant families may thus result in a decrease in the marketed food surplus, a difficulty which does not arise with estate capitalist or collective farming. Here is a very vexed dilemma of which the Communist leaders of the USSR and China were well aware and which gave rise to heated debates within the Communist Party's structures (Kemp 1983: chs. 3, 5). Conversely, as the experience of the Soviet Union during the 1922–3 'scissors crisis' has revealed, peasants do not necessarily withdraw from the market when the terms of trade are turned against them. This phenomenon, we are told, follows from the attempt of peasant families to maintain their standard of living in the face of a general adverse economic change (Millar 1976: 52–3).

The experiences of the USSR and China apparently also confirm the hypothesis advanced by Thomas Robert Malthus and John Stuart Mill (see Platteau 1978: ii. 431–40, and 1987) according to which the best way to induce the peasants to part with more of their produce lies in increasing the output and the range of consumer goods at prices which they are willing to pay (Kemp 1983: 55). In this case, note that dynamic changes usually occur in the preference functions of the peasants and that a comparative-static framework of analysis is no longer adequate to analyse the effects of changes in output prices. However, by deciding to step up the output of consumer goods or to allocate more foreign exchange to the import of such goods, the government is only replacing one development dilemma by another. In fact, it chooses to slow down the pace of capital accumulation and economic growth in order to increase food market deliveries.

Finally, reverting to a comparative-static framework, it is worth stressing that the impact of agricultural price increases on agricultural production and market sales may be seriously affected by shortages of consumption 'incentive goods'. In the extreme case where the shortage of these goods is so acute that the marginal utility of money is zero, agricultural market supply would be completely price inelastic even if farmers have a strong aversion to leisure. In the context of some poor countries of sub-Saharan Africa, this assumption is not as implausible as it might appear at first sight. In Guinea-Bissau, for example, the dramatic collapse of agricultural exports (mainly oilseeds) and marketed surplus of food crops (mainly rice) in the late 1970s and the early 1980s was to a large extent the result of the reluctance of the peasantry to produce any surplus for the market in a context of severe scarcity of consumption goods.[13] The only regions in which Guinean farmers or fishermen continued to produce marketed surpluses were located along the northern

---

[13] Consumption and other goods were allocated by priority to the capital city of Bissau.

border and off the Atlantic coast, that is in areas where a contraband trade had developed with the Senegalese which was difficult for the Guinean authorities to check. The same kind of acute scarcity of consumption goods prevails, or at times prevailed, in other African countries as well (Ghana, Mozambique, Sierra Leone, Chad, Benin, Tanzania, Zaïre, etc.). In Mozambique, it resulted in food marketed surpluses being so low at the beginning of the 1980s that many state employees had to take to part-time agricultural occupations to be able to meet their subsistence needs. In countries which have no domestic industrial base and where most consumer goods must therefore be imported, a vicious circle is at work when they are subject to tight balance-of-payments constraints. Indeed, since there is not enough foreign exchange and not enough consumer goods offered for sale in the local markets, peasants are not interested in producing export crops or food crops above their own subsistence needs. As a consequence, the government has to import more food to feed the urban dwellers at a time when its export revenues are at a low level. Its foreign exchange deficit deepens and the macroeconomic situation continues to deteriorate. The above process is a rather accurate description of what actually happened in countries like Guinea-Bissau and Mozambique in the late 1970s and the early 1980s.

The real African challenge and the role of technical change   To put the price-focused doctrine in the right critical perspective, one has only to remember the real challenge that Africa will have to face up to during the coming decades. In the words of Carl Eicher: 'Agricultural production must be doubled from the 1970–84 average of 1.8 per cent to the 3.6 to 4.0 range in order to match the annual growth in food demand arising from population growth (3.2 per cent) and increase in per capita incomes' (Eicher 1986b: 36). Even if we make the absurd assumption that a price hike can succeed in doubling the rate of growth of agricultural output in the short term, it is plainly evident that no amount of price policy will ever succeed in sustaining such a high rate of agricultural growth over a period of several decades. On the best assumptions, raising real prices of agricultural goods may enhance their output and, hopefully, their marketed surplus, but this will be essentially a once-for-all effect which is not likely to lead to the continuous increases Africa desperately requires for a long time to come. Mellor and Delgado have actually warned that, in most African countries, such once-for-all effects have already been largely exhausted: 'further increases in food prices where they have been already rising rapidly are less critical than often is supposed' (Mellor and Delgado 1987: 4). And another author has emphasized that 'if there is no modernisation policy making it possible to increase yields, supply can be relatively inelastic in spite of an increase in real prices' (Morrisson 1985: 71).

It can even be argued that, in the absence of technical change, increased real prices could cause a decline of agricultural production in the long run. In the circumstances negative long-term price elasticities of agricultural supplies would result from an overexploitation of fixed land resources. In the short term, the cultivators would assumedly respond to a price rise by putting more land into cultivation. If this extension takes place through a shortening of the fallow period, the fertility of the land would gradually decline and, after a certain time, the initial increase of output on the fallow lands would be erased by a fall in the average land productivity in the surrounding area.

To get out of this trap, either large investments beyond the scope of smallholders will have to be undertaken to reclaim or rehabilitate uncultivated lands, or land-augmenting technical progress will be needed. If labour is scarce, and/or if rural standards of living are to be improved, technical change will also have to enhance labour productivity. Continuous upward shifts of agricultural production functions must therefore be generated in Africa for her agriculture to be able to meet the challenge before her: price policy considerations will be secondary to this crucial requirement. In fact, as the experience of India during the period 1975–6 to 1983–4 shows, agricultural production and investment may well increase rapidly *in spite of* internal terms of trade turning against the agricultural sector (Tyagi 1987: 30–6). For this situation to occur, all that is needed is that 'productivity rises at a rate faster than the rate by which the terms of trade move against the agricultural sector' (ibid. 34). This can happen when rapid technical advances are being made, or when past progress is spreading out to new areas.[14] Neither of these two conditions was satisfied in India between 1952–3 and 1963–4 and, as a consequence, adverse movements of net barter terms of trade during this period resulted in slow growth of agricultural production and investment.

Now, to contend that agricultural production may increase despite adverse movements of intersectoral terms of trade does not imply that agricultural prices should not be raised. A reasonable position would apparently be to argue that, in order to ensure adequate food supplies under conditions of rapid population growth, what is needed is a balanced package of technical change and incentive prices (Krishna 1984; Timmer 1986). There are two serious arguments in favour of policy interventions to raise food prices. First, higher prices may be expected to accelerate agricultural growth by facilitating investment and setting in motion autonomous processes of change. Second, higher prices can be defended on equity grounds since they would have the effect of increasing the real incomes of the smallholder producers from whom most poor people in Africa are drawn. However, there are problems with both arguments which tend to make them much less effective than they appear at first sight. For one thing, because of the relatively egalitarian structure of agricultural holdings in Africa (compared to Asia and Latin America), returns to agriculture are generally low and 'accumulation is difficult in the absence of specific policy

---

[14] The experience of developed countries tells the same story: 'There are many episodes in the record of advanced countries in which the (lagged) terms of trade facing agriculture have stagnated, and yet farm productivity has grown 2–3 percent a year for considerable periods' (Krishna 1984: 170).

interventions to this end' (Delgado *et al.* 1987: 6). For another thing, it must be borne in mind that the effect of agricultural price increases on the producers' real incomes is proportional to their net sales. As a consequence, a price reform is likely to favour comparatively rich farmers while leaving the real situation of poor, quasi-subsistence smallholders almost unaffected. Note that these two objections are to some extent exclusive in so far as an egalitarian agrarian structure tends to entail an egalitarian distribution of rural incomes. There is yet another consideration that may run against raising food prices. This is the classical argument of David Ricardo according to which rising prices for wage goods tend to slow down non-agricultural growth by causing upward pressure on money wages. Because of the (presumed) ensuing erosion of industrial profit margins, both the incentive and the ability to invest would be dampened, the former because the returns on industrial investments are reduced and the latter because the pool of profits is narrowed (Mellor 1968: 27).

A few queries about the presumed fiscal oppression of agriculture   It is a proposition currently encountered in both the orthodox and the Marxian literature that African farmers are squeezed by the state. All the blame for the stagnation of agricultural production is then laid upon the price and fiscal policies pursued by most African governments. What deserves to be pointed out, however, is that the evidence adduced in support of this thesis is usually far from satisfactory. In particular, evidence of a heavy tax burden on agriculture is no convincing proof that this sector is discriminated against. Indeed, as Uma Lele has reminded us, 'given agriculture's importance in the GNP, it is natural that the agricultural sector should constitute the major source of government revenues and that governments should control internal agricultural trade to generate revenues' (Lele 1985: 164). A balanced picture of the fiscal treatment of agriculture can be obtained only if we have a rather precise idea of the direction of the intersectoral public capital flows.

In actual fact, when we look at the overall balance between receipts from direct and indirect taxes and government expenditures in agriculture, we do not find that the agricultural sector has been systematically overtaxed in Africa (Faucher and Schneider 1985: 61; Morrisson 1985: 72). Sara Berry probably comes close to the truth when she writes that 'postcolonial governments have vacillated between extracting surplus from farmers and subsidizing them' (Berry 1984: 80). Nevertheless, it must be admitted that, in the above judgements or calculations, no account has been taken of invisible resource transfers, particularly those which are achieved through movements of the internal terms of trade. Furthermore, estimates of total intersectoral capital flows (whether on public or private account, or both) are not available for Africa. Now, even if reliable estimates existed pointing to systematic net resource transfers from agriculture to the other sectors of the economy, there would still remain the problem of determining the normative criterion on the basis of which such transfers could be regarded as inappropriate or socially inefficient. The question cannot be avoided since 'surplus extraction from agriculture is clearly not always contrary to the interests of the society, nor even to the long-term interests of the peasantry' (Bienefeld 1986: 7).

To discuss this issue is clearly beyond the scope of this chapter. Suffice it to say here that a more or less general feeling is that 'far fewer resources are plowed back into agriculture by most African countries than would seem justified' (Lele 1984: 440). Such a feeling is usually grounded on comparisons of the shares of agriculture in the national budgets as between Africa and Asia. Thus, for example, it appears that independent African states have commonly invested only 5 to 12 per cent of their public development expenditure in agriculture while India's public sector expenditures on agriculture ranged from 23 to 27 per cent over a considerable span of thirty-two years (1951 to 1983). Estimates of roughly the same order obtain for Malaysia over the years 1971–85 (Eicher 1986b: 38–9; see also Eicher and Mangwiro 1986: 17–21; Lele 1984: 440; FAO 1986: Appendix I, ch. 3, para. 10–13; Lipton 1987: table 16.1, pp. 214–16). In fact, increasing the net flow of resources to agriculture can be justified on the grounds that, for reasons that will be explained later, agricultural technology development in Africa will be a costly process. Moreover, such an increase could help build up the basis from which sizeable net transfers of resources from agriculture to other sectors will be possible in the future (see Mellor 1984). In the short and medium run, however, it will prove very difficult to give effect to this policy reorientation because the international environment is highly detrimental to the interests of Africa (Colclough 1985: 32). A situation of falling agricultural prices, rising public sector deficits, mounting debt repayment obligations, and flagging commitments of foreign aid is hardly one in which substantial reductions of tax rates on agriculture (particularly on export crops) or significant increases in public expenditures on food production are easy to enforce politically and economically.

A final remark is in order. If sufficient attention is not paid to considerations of allocative efficiency in the process of planning public expenditures for agriculture, net intersectoral resource transfers in favour of this sector will not succeed in ensuring its long-term self-sustainability. This issue is especially relevant in sub-Saharan Africa where there are at least three important ways in which public resources for agricultural development have been inefficiently allocated under the joint responsibility of local governments, bilateral donors, and international aid agencies. First, following the colonial pattern of priorities, a disproportionate share of the agricultural national budgets has been devoted to promoting a few export crops. As will be explained later, food crops have been correspondingly neglected in terms of extension, research, market-ing arrangements, and public investments.[15] Second, a large part of these

---

[15] A good illustration of this export bias is provided by the striking contrast, in Mali and Burkina Faso, between the neglect of staple food crops and the privileged access of cotton growers to public resources (Morrisson 1985: 70).

budgets in many countries has been spent on subsidies (e.g. subsidies on the price of fertilizers), presumably to compensate for high rates of taxation. As a result, investment expenditures have been kept at a rather low level.[16] Third, government resources have been excessively concentrated 'on a subsector of relatively large-scale farmers' (Johnston 1986: 163), as well as on large-scale, capital-intensive, enclaved, and mostly unprofitable ventures, such as state farms, big land settlement schemes, large-scale and ill-conceived irrigation projects, public co-operatives, agro-business corporations, large-scale ranches equipped with sophisticated infrastructure, etc.[17] Incidentally, this shows that it is not very meaningful to talk about *general* exploitation of agriculturalists in Africa. A small number of large private farms—owned by privileged farmers, wealthy businessmen, or state employees—have often been provided with generous loans, subsidies, infrastructure, and technical assistance (Berry 1984: 80).

(c) *Conclusion*

To sum up, the real challenge confronting African agriculture today is not so much that of finding new political coalitions prepared to reverse 'faulty' pricing policies. It is much more to solve the problem of how to generate technological improvements on an endogenous basis and how to spread them out as quickly as possible to large areas of the continent. This is not to say that a congenial price environment is unnecessary for that purpose: low prices for agricultural goods can indeed hamper agricultural growth by diverting resources to other sectors, by inducing the farmers to consume more leisure, and by discouraging investment in agriculture and the adoption of technical innovations (since real returns are low and the savings pool is restricted). But it must be clearly realized that a technological breakthrough of the kind needed in Africa today will not be price induced. As Raj Krishna has put it, the price regime 'cannot by itself explain the evolution of basic scientific knowledge and the level and growth of public investment in research, extension, infrastructure, and human capital . . .' (Krishna 1984: 170). Therefore, 'the task of accelerating agricultural growth is primarily techno-organizational' and the main aim of price policies should be to avoid retarding or frustrating the main techno-organizational effort (Krishna 1970: 190).

Technological change, up to a certain point, can arise from the initiative of the farmers themselves. Yet the cultivators' dynamism alone obviously cannot be expected to produce agricultural innovations at the pace required. If increasing pressure on land resources can lead to adaptive technical changes when the rate of population growth is moderate, population-led agricultural growth of the type analysed by Ester Boserup (1965 and 1981) is not a reliable

[16] In Zambia, the percentage of the agricultural budget spent on subsidies exceeds 70% (Lele 1984: 442).

[17] For a case-study of Gabon, see Monferrer (1985).

mechanism when population expands rapidly, say, at more than 2 per cent per year (Eicher 1986a: 15; Delor-Vandueren 1988: ch. 4). In the same way, even though we know that peasants are able to respond positively to profit opportunities when the latter are not too risky, there is far less evidence that they can take appropriate decisions when their environment begins to change dramatically and quick responses are called for (Mellor 1970: 217).

In view of the above, the new technology and the institutional innovations that go hand in hand with it will have to be produced by the state as public goods (Lele 1985: 161–2), and as part of a science-based agricultural development strategy. It is in this perspective that the problem of the African state must be looked at and that the urgent need to develop efficient bureaucracies must be assessed. The removal of technological, institutional, and internal market constraints is the primary objective that should serve as a guideline for identifying the reforms required in the organizational structure of the African countries. The main problem with a doctrine concentrating on short-term pricing policy considerations is precisely that organizational and structural issues tend to be neglected (Brett 1986: 22).

10.4. *The role of supply factors: structural constraints and handicaps*

When attention is excessively focused on issues of short-term pricing policy, there is an almost inevitable proclivity to ascribe the present difficulties of African agriculture to 'mistakes' or errors currently made by the local governments. By the same token, the natural constraints Africa is ridden with and the structural problems she has inherited from her historical past tend to be neglected or downplayed. This is particularly evident among orthodox or neo-classical economists who feel more at ease with short-term macroeconomic problems than with long-term issues which often involve many non-economic aspects. Such a neglect is especially regrettable since, as we shall see below, Africa is confronted with structural constraints and handicaps—i.e. growth-inhibiting factors or barriers which cannot be easily removed or will never be eliminated at all—that put her at a clear disadvantage compared to other regions in the Third World. Therefore, whenever comparisons are attempted between Africa and these other regions—e.g. when one contemplates the transfer to Africa of the Green Revolution technology applied in Asia and Latin America—it is absolutely essential that these structural differences be borne in mind. Any strategy of agricultural development which does not take them into account is doomed to failure.

On the other hand, the fact must be reckoned that Africa has little prospect of succeeding in developing non-agricultural production on a large scale, even less in penetrating foreign markets for manufactured products. Structural constraints on agricultural production ought therefore not to be construed as insuperable obstacles to agricultural growth but, rather, as sensitive points on which local governments and foreign actors must concentrate their efforts in the future.

In the remaining part of the chapter, attention will be restricted to such structural constraints and handicaps as appear to have an important bearing on the present food situation in Africa. They involve quite varied aspects which go from soil conditions and water accessibility to land tenure systems and political dysfunctioning, through population densities, technological and infrastructural factors. Wherever possible, explicit comparisons with other Third World regions, particularly with Asia, will be made.

(a) The effects of a wide dispersal of the population

Comparative evidence on population sparsity A striking demographic feature of Africa is her combination of low population densities and low urbanization rates which make for a very scattered population. This is at variance with the situation observed in Asia where the density of population is very high in most areas; and with that observed in Latin America where comparatively low population densities are counterbalanced by a well-concentrated pattern of population settlement (particularly in the coastal areas).

In the middle of 1984, the density of population was around 110 persons per square kilometre in Asia (excluding the Arab oil-exporting countries except Iran and Iraq); 19 persons in Latin America; and 18 persons in Africa, the latter figure being a weighted average of a density of 24 in sub-Saharan Africa and a density of only 15 in North Africa. In Africa, population densities ranged from 8 persons per square kilometre in Somalia and Sudan to 104 in Nigeria, which is in sharp contrast to densities of 178 in the Philippines, 228 in India, and 681 in Bangladesh.[18] On the other hand, the percentage of total population living in cities was 28 per cent in sub-Saharan Africa in 1984 (as against only 16 per cent in 1965) while it exceeded 40 per cent in all Latin American countries and worked out to as much as 83 per cent in Chile, 72 per cent in Brazil, 85 per cent in Uruguay, and 84 per cent in Argentina (World Bank 1986b: table 31, pp. 240–1). Finally, it is important to bear in mind that most African countries are small from the standpoint of their population base: more than half of them had actually fewer than 5 million people in the beginning of the 1980s (Eicher 1984: 454).

An immediate and obvious implication of the scattered pattern of population settlement in Africa is the high per capita cost of providing roads, railways, health, schools, agricultural, and other services to the population. Since this issue is quite important and often neglected in the literature on the African food crisis I will look at it a little more closely, trying to highlight several ways in which it affected the history of Africa and determined certain policy choices made by modern African governments.

---

[18] All the figures have been calculated from World Bank (1986b: table 1, pp. 180–1).

Looking back into history   When populations are much scattered, as in Africa, there is little scope for labour specialization and market development: rural families tend to produce themselves all or most of the products which they need, roads or waterways remain undeveloped, and large amounts of natural resources remain out of reach of an existing transport infrastructure. Ester Boserup has reminded us that before the arrival of the Europeans there was practically no labour specialization in the sparsely populated areas of Africa. North Africa and parts of West Africa (most notably, the medieval empires of the Niger bend) seemed to be the only important exception with their long experience of trade (including long-distance trade) in agricultural and non-agricultural goods (Boserup 1981: 146; see also Giri 1983: 15–41 and Bates 1984: 240–1). On the whole, it can therefore be said that, in contrast to the situation observed in Asia and Latin America, large parts of Africa entered the nineteenth century with no transport infrastructure worth the name, with no indigenous merchant classes accustomed to money transactions and urban life, and with no ancient traditions of bazaar trade, 'preindustrial urbanization', and specialized craftsmen. Also, as a result of lack of product specialization and limited exchange of goods, agricultural technologies remained rudimentary, socio-economic differentiation or stratification failed to develop to any significant extent, and the dominant culture tended to reflect peasant values rather than forming a distinct 'élite culture' (Fallers 1961: 110; Hyden 1986: 54–5, 57, 78 n. 10). Moreover, in a number of areas politically structured in empires or kingdoms, Africa's failure to acquire technological advances was reinforced by the fact that the rulers sustained their regimes by appropriating surpluses from long-distance trade and not by promoting agricultural development. In consequence, 'African societies south of the Sahara never developed the institutional mechanisms that tied rulers to a system based on the exploitation of land' as happened in Europe and Asia and, in particular, African pre-colonial cities 'were not productively linked to their rural hinterlands' (Hyden 1986: 54, 69).

The colonial episode has further reinforced the above handicaps of Africa. For one thing, the sparsely populated colonies got very few railways: 'only the Union of South Africa with mass immigration of Europeans had more than six meters of railways per square kilometer in 1970, and six countries had no railways at all' (Boserup 1981: 148). Moreover, 'two-thirds of the African railways built in the colonial period connected mines to a coastal harbour' (ibid.). This was the natural outcome of a colonial policy grounded upon criteria of short- or medium-term economic profitability since railway building was usually uneconomic in the sparsely populated areas of Africa except when it could be justified by the existence of rich mineral deposits. Therefore, 'in most of the African continent, cultivable land, forests, and mineral deposits were not utilized. The sparse population outside the small enclaves of colonial development had the choice of remaining subsistence producers or migrating, assuming that they were not removed by force or prevented from migration by police measures, as often happened' (ibid. 148–9). With the truck revolution a cumulative bias actually developed in large parts of the continent. Areas with small and sparse populations were bypassed by road building because it was not profitable to transform them into areas of cash cropping and there was little incentive to construct roads in regions without railways with which to connect them. To sum up, 'the skewing of the transport system in favour of the enclaves continued to be an important feature in the sparsely populated hot colonies' of Africa (ibid. 150).[19]

For another thing, the policies pursued by most colonial governments and administrations did not encourage the formation of an indigenous merchant class nor that of indigenous skilled craftsmen. In fact, if we except North Africa, coastal West Africa (where mercantile communities were established for a long time), and parts of coastal East Africa (where Zanzibari and Swahili planters were involved in economic intermediation), virtually all the petty trading in urban and rural areas was handled by immigrant communities coming from regions with urban and commercial traditions (Lebanese, Indians, Greeks, Portuguese, Syrians, etc.). And all the other skilled oc-cupations which the indigenous population lacked abilities to fill were equally exercised by foreigners and 'ethnic entrepreneurs' (Boserup 1981: 152; Young 1986: 28). In many instances, however, the colonial governments positively prevented the spontaneous emergence or development of private traders and small entrepreneurs by contracting directly with indigenous village chiefs for the recruitment of labour and the procurement of cash crops, possibly through co-operatives effectively controlled by the colonial governors. These indigen-ous chiefs were usually made a more or less explicit link in the colonial administrative structure (see below, Section 10.4(f)). Therefore, when the trade functions were not performed by foreigners or exercised by inter-mediaries subjugated to foreign interests, they were often bureaucratized and placed under the strict control of the colonial authorities.

Thus, Catherine Coquery-Vidrovitch has noted that in equatorial Africa 'capitalism intruded at one go, under the then relatively completed form of colonial capitalism, and it did not at all try to strike a bargain; during the years 1885–1910, there was no attempt on the part of the Western countries to raise up, encourage or utilize an indigenous "middle class", quite the contrary' (Coquery-Vidrovitch 1985: 130). In the case of the British colonies in Africa, we are told that 'the eschewing of private enterprise, and the promotion of state agencies to expand colonial production, provoked little or no antagonism from within the British state apparatuses', and one reason advanced by the Colonial Office towards vindicating this policy was that 'colonies ought not to be exploited by private enterprise' (Cowen 1982: 150; see also Bézy et al. 1981, 9–47 for the case of the Belgian Congo and Gentil 1986: 35–6 for that of

---

[19] The situation was altogether different in the few African countries endowed with climatic conditions close to those obtaining in the temperate zone (Maghreban countries, Zimbabwe, South Africa), since those regions received massive inflows of European immigrants.

Western Africa). For Crawford Young, it is clear that 'Generally, the new colonial economy required destruction of intra-African trading systems which were not Europe-oriented and the capture of their resources' (Young 1986: 28).

There is also much evidence to show that in commercial and other matters the policies followed by the colonial states were strongly influenced by the interests of the dominant European companies. As a matter of fact, it was usually when those interests became threatened by the active competition arising from the petty trading sector of ethnic immigrants (and, more rarely, of small indigenous merchants) that the colonial administration extended its control over the sphere of circulation (marketing, banking, services). It was at the behest of a foreign merchant class with which it often colluded that the colonial state initiated mercantilist policies designed to control competition and to give monopoly powers to a small class of vested economic interests from the West. Even the creation of state marketing boards was sometimes used to maintain very high profits for the expatriate marketing sector, thus destroying the bargaining power of the independent local small-scale traders (Brett 1973, 1986: 23–4; Bézy et al. 1981: 23–6; Berry 1984: 79–80). Sometimes also, marketing board monopolies were conceived by colonial authorities as fiscal devices intended for taxing profits from price booms (notably during the prolonged commodity boom of the 1950s). Thus, in a number of countries, the surpluses earned by those boards were automatically transferred to the state capital account (Giri 1986: 67–8; Young 1986: 33).

It is clear that independent African states have inherited a number of problems which have their roots in the considerable scattering of their populations over huge land areas and which were only exacerbated during the colonial period. First, there is the problem of the racial tensions and latent or open rivalry between the indigenous communities and the immigrant middle classes. By monopolizing the access to all jobs requiring a minimum amount of skill, the latter have prevented the former from entering into contact with modern technology and from experimenting with new ways of thinking and calculating in an environment increasingly dominated by market forces. A considerable gap, both technological and educational, thereby developed between the two groups, undermining the social cohesion of the whole societal fabric (Boserup 1981: 152). Furthermore, it is against this background of sharp ethnic division of labour that the hostility of many African governments towards private trading (easily equated with speculative, exploitative, and antisocial practices) and the free play of market forces can be properly understood (Lele 1976: 297; Johnston 1986: 174). The administrative approach of many colonial governments to trade and commerce is another powerful factor that helps explain the numerous attempts of modern African states at extending their control on domestic purchases and sales of both agricultural and non-agricultural goods. The influence of this historical ante-cedent was, however, greatly reinforced by another circumstance pinpointed by Sara Berry: 'The fact that most postcolonial regimes in Africa took office under pressure—from below, above, and within—to take responsibility for developing their economies meant that they were obliged to adopt an interventionist stance toward economic activities and institutions' (Berry 1984: 67; see also Young 1986: 32).

Second, post-colonial governments have inherited from the previous rulers a highly skewed, export-orientated transport network. Most of the population remained isolated from potential markets and sources of supplies 'by large empty spaces without infrastructure for modern transport'. In this context, many rural families continued 'to keep a low labour input in agriculture' and 'to have a high degree of self-sufficiency of both agricultural and nonagricultural products' (Boserup 1981: 150). Consequently, the emergence of specialized craftsmen at the village level was further delayed. In addition, no link was built up between urban and rural areas and 'the imports of European manufactured goods and of products from the lands of origin of the urban middle class acted as a formidable obstacle to development of urban crafts and industries' (ibid. 153). Rural areas devoted to cash cropping exported their surplus production instead of growing food to meet the demand of expanding cities.

A hard but inescapable dilemma   In actual fact, the above description fits in rather well with the present situation of many African countries. Rather than counteracting tendencies initiated in their past histories, independent governments have often followed in the footsteps of their colonial predecessors by reinforcing the 'enclave' character of their economies and by developing a host of 'urban biases'. Even today, most African countries have but a small fraction of the roads per square land area that are found in India and in so many other countries of Asia and Latin America (Mellor and Delgado 1987: 4). For another thing, Uma Lele has remarked that investments in the road system have been greater in countries like Kenya and Malawi than in many other African countries with lower population densities and more inadequate transport facilities: thus, road mileage per square mile of land area is only 0.02 in Sudan, 0.1 in Zambia, and 0.15 in Zaïre, compared with 0.23 in Kenya and 0.31 in Malawi (Lele 1984: 445). But Lele ought not to be surprised at this: African governments are only following the same logic—the logic of economic profitability—as the previous rulers of Africa. Indeed, sparser populations tend to make the building up of transport systems a more uneconomic proposition since the market potential and the frequency of exchange transactions are comparatively lower.

The fact that in Africa human settlements remain small and very much scattered in spite of a tremendous demographic acceleration during the last decades goes therefore a long way towards explaining the major infrastructure deficiencies and the profoundly unbalanced pattern of spatial development commonly observed in this continent. A vicious circle and an unequalizing process of cumulative causation of the type analysed by Myrdal (1963) are evidently at work:

- transport networks are comparatively expensive to build in sparsely populated areas;
- labour emigrates from these areas, sometimes along with their families, sometimes not, to improve their conditions of living and to find better work opportunities in more densely populated areas;
- as a result, the former regions are further depleted of their population and the per capita cost of constructing new lines of communication further rises;
- due to poor transport systems, the per capita cost of providing various services (health, school, agricultural extension, etc.) to the population is correspondingly enhanced.

Because of this process, entire rural regions are increasingly marginalized and vast amounts of potential food production possibly lost.

Many authors have pointed to inadequate rural infrastructures as a crucial factor responsible for the slow growth of food production in Africa, and they have underlined the consequent need to expand the transportation network to and from the isolated rural areas. Thus, Mellor and Delgado have recently expressed the opinion that 'improved rural roads are probably the single most important factor in transforming rural Africa' since 'more and better roads would improve the delivery of farm inputs to and farm products from the widely dispersed smallholder population' (Mellor and Delgado 1987: 4). The dominant literature of today, which emphasizes the commendability of 'small farm' or 'unimodal' strategies of agricultural development (Johnston 1986; Johnston and Kilby 1975; World Bank 1981, 1986b), takes a position very similar to that expressed above. What needs to be stressed here is the simple truism that, however commendable it may be on various theoretical grounds, such a strategy is especially costly and difficult to implement when rural populations are widely dispersed. It is true that village labour could be more intensely mobilized to build up feeder roads in rural areas. Yet, as long as the latter cannot be connected with a national all-weather transport network, their usefulness will remain quite limited (Lele 1984: 450).

There is a serious dilemma here and by bypassing it one runs the risk of indulging in wishful thinking, a luxury which African governments certainly cannot afford. In fact, a number of strategic orientations chosen by them and often regarded as irrational or absurd can be explained on reasonable grounds when the scattered pattern of human settlement in Africa is taken into consideration. The oft-noted preference of the African authorities (and, to a large extent, of the big donor agencies from the West) for large-scale agricultural projects is a case in point. Indeed, such projects allow for a heavy concentration and neat phasing of the government's efforts and avoid the wastes inherent in the sprinkling of these efforts over large, sparsely populated areas. Moreover, the wide dispersion of African smallholders makes for high risks of leakage of revenue and for heavy administrative costs of revenue collection per unit of money gathered by the taxation bureaucracy. In this context, centralized marketing boards are attractive since they enable the state bureaucracy to pass over to the peasants part of the administrative costs of revenue collection: indeed, peasants are forced to bring to some central point the produce upon which implicit or explicit taxes will be levied and to bear the corresponding costs of transportation. Likewise, large-scale agricultural projects and state farms offer the advantage of relatively easy taxability (see above, p. 461).

The above considerations are bound to play a crucial role when the state machineries are new, inexperienced, and short of skilled revenue officers, as is certainly the case in many countries of the African continent. The fact that numerous large-scale agricultural projects and parastatals turn out to be actually ineffective and wasteful of scarce resources only adds to the complexity of the African situation.[20] But it should not lead one to believe that the smallholder-focused strategy of agricultural development is automatically and unambiguously cost-effective as compared to other approaches which give more emphasis to economies of scale and concentration gains. There are clear cases where it would be more economical to reform large-scale projects or state integrating agencies than to wind them up altogether and to rely completely on private decentralized initiative. Thus, for instance, small irrigation schemes along the river Senegal are too dispersed to make private mechanical workshops for the maintenance of tubewells economically profitable. Services have therefore to be provided by the SAED, the parastatal entrusted with the task of organizing and running large-scale irrigation works in the area.

(b) Handicaps on the natural resources front

From her low population densities (at least when compared with Asia), can one infer that Africa is a land-abundant continent? After all, contrary to what was observed in Asia and Latin America, most of the output gains in Africa during the last decades resulted from an extension of the agricultural frontier.[21]

Today, however, there is enough evidence to show (1) that this frontier has been extended to its limits in a large number of countries or (2) that in many instances it would be more costly to bring new lands into cultivation than to intensify production on existing agricultural (or pasture) lands. Moreover, Africa is handicapped by difficult climatological and soil conditions, while with respect to water potential and scope for efficient water management she is

---

[20] Not all large-scale projects and state boards have been failures, however. Famous successes such as Ethiopia's CADU, Rwanda's Coffee Marketing Board, the Kenya Tea Development Authority, the Botswana Meat Commission, the CMDT in Mali, and the SOFITEX in Burkina Faso (both working in the field of cotton production and marketing) are worth bearing in mind (for more details, see Lele 1975 and 1976; Swainson 1986, Morrison 1986).

[21] In sub-Saharan Africa, output per hectare growth rate represented only 8% of the production growth rate during the 1970s, compared with 62% for the whole developing world. During the 1960s, it was −9% (Mellor and Johnston 1984: 536; see also Paulino 1987).

also at a clear disadvantage compared to Asia and Latin America. Let us now examine these various aspects of Africa's land and water resources in greater detail.[22]

Land reserves   An FAO study has reached the conclusion that, given the existing technology, Africa's base of cultivable land resources could enable her to feed her whole population in the year 2000 if massive population movements are allowed for (FAO 1986: Annex II, ch. 7). This is of course a completely unrealistic assumption. When attention is drawn to the situation of individual countries, the picture that emerges is quite different because land resources are inequitably distributed across the African continent. Thus, it appears that 21 countries are virtually unable to become food self-sufficient if no technological change is introduced in their agricultural sector. By the end of this century, their number will have risen to 28 even assuming that all their arable lands have been brought under cultivation (FAO 1984 and 1986: Annex II, ch. 7).

As Carl Eicher has remarked, it is time 'to shelve the misleading cliché that Africa is a land abundant continent' and 'to stop thinking of African countries as if they were all the same' (Eicher 1985: 94–5). In fact, only about one-third of the continent can be classified as land abundant (Sudan, Zaïre, Cameroon, Guinea, Sierra Leone, Zambia, Mozambique, and Angola), and in these countries, 'seasonal labor shortages, not land, will be the major constraint on expanding production' (ibid. 95). Of the total land reserve of Africa (estimated at 603 million ha), a large part (75 per cent) is located in two regions: humid Central Africa and sub-humid and semi-arid Southern Africa. It is also noteworthy that 75 per cent of the land reserves in the Sudano-Sahelian region are located in one country, Sudan (FAO 1986: Annex II, ch. 6, para. 6.13).

Another one-third of the African countries are in semi-arid areas where the land frontier is rapidly being exhausted (e.g. Senegal, Niger) and the remaining countries (again one-third of the total) are in a land-scarce environment where the frontier is already exhausted (e.g. Rwanda, Malawi, Burundi) (Eicher 1985: 95). In fact, Africa offers the contrasted picture of large, but very unequally distributed, land reserves coexisting with huge land masses that are and will always remain inhospitable to farming. Around one-third of Africa's soils are too arid to permit any kind of cultivation and 42 per cent of land surfaces are made of either desert or sandy soils (21.8 and 20.3 per cent, respectively). Furthermore, almost half of the African continent is completely unsuited to direct rainfed crop production because the lengths of growing periods are too short (less than 75 days), and only 30 per cent of it is well suited climatically to the rainfed production of millet, sorghum, and maize, the staple food crops (FAO 1986: Annex II, ch. 2, para. 2.7, and ch. 3, table 3.1).

The situation is made much worse still by the fact that in regions with significant land reserves—that is mainly in tropical humid Africa—there are very serious obstacles to the expansion of the agricultural frontier. These

---

[22] South Africa is always excluded when reference is made to the African continent.

obstacles may arise from problems of land fertility and soil conservation, from operational difficulties regarding the reclamation and the draining of the lands, and, above all, from health risks affecting both animals and human beings. In many parts of Africa animal trypanosomiasis is the most important constraint to livestock production and to the use of animal draught power in agriculture. The extent of the area affected, estimated at some 38 per cent of the total land area of Africa, covers 37 countries where some 55 million livestock units are at risk. Trypanosomiasis (sleeping sickness) also affects human beings, and since it virtually precludes human settlement on some of the best-watered and most fertile lands, it can really be considered as one of the major scourges of land development in Africa (FAO 1986: Annex II, ch. 6, paras. 29–30; World Bank 1984: 102–3; Eicher 1986*b*: 18). Unfortunately, the control of the vector —tsetse flies—is particularly difficult and, in any case, its success will depend on a high standard of management and follow-up monitoring, on effective public health research, on careful land use planning, and on the willingness of governments and aid donors to incur large expenditures.[23]

To take two other examples, fertile river valleys are closed to human settlement because of the large-scale prevalence of onchocerciasis (river blindness), and schistosomiasis badly affects most of the African continent, particularly the Nile Valley and the countries immediately south of the Sahara, and in East and Central Africa below the equator. As the experience of several water resource development projects has amply illustrated (Aswan Dam in Egypt, Gezira Scheme in Sudan, Volta Lake in Ghana, etc.), any change in the aquatic component of the vector habitat (irrigation, water diversion or impoundment, etc.) is likely to increase the prevalence of schistosomiasis drastically (FAO 1986: Annex II, ch. 6, para. 6.26–7, and Table 10.6).

Given the above constraints, it is not surprising that since the early 1960s, the amount of agricultural land per person in agriculture has gone down regularly in Africa (Cohen 1980: 358), and this despite rising rates of urbanization. The same constraints largely account for the fact that 'despite the abundance of land relative to population, the number of hectares of cropped area per farm worker is small compared with that in other developing areas' (Paulino 1987: 35). In the words of Michael Lipton, much of Africa outside the Nile Valley and Rwanda–Burundi 'contains few persons per acre, yet many persons per efficiency unit of land' (Lipton 1987: 213–17).

Soil structure Perhaps the most serious natural handicap of Africa lies in the highly fragile structure and poor physical characteristics of most of her soils. African tropical soils are often thin and depleted and, if they are easy to cultivate by hand (e.g. with a hand hoe), they are not very productive and they require long periods of time to recover after they have been farmed. These problems have to be traced back to the fact that a large part of the African

---

[23] Trypano-tolerant breeds of livestock exist (e.g. in West Africa) but they can only be used in particular ecological conditions.

continent is made of ancient geological strata which are strongly weathered. Soils are therefore easily degraded and washed away; they present serious deficiencies of mineral salts and they are all the lower in plant nutrients as surface temperatures are very high (FAO 1986: Annex II, ch. 3, para. 3.7, and Annex IV, ch. 2, para. 2.4). Lush vegetation conceals the low inherent fertility of much of the land in the humid tropics. On the other hand, Africa is also badly handicapped by her drought susceptibility: there is a high or very high expectation of drought over 60 per cent of the continent, a problem which was less serious when populations were smaller and unlimited space was available (ibid. Annex II, ch. 2, para. 2.21 and table 2.4).

In fact, out of the six climatic zones into which Africa can be subdivided (on the basis of temperature and moisture, mainly), only two are relatively well suited to rainfed agriculture: subhumid and mountain East Africa, and subhumid and semi-arid Southern Africa. In the other regions, rainfed agriculture is only possible on a limited percentage of total land area (ibid., Annex II, ch. 2). Moreover, according to FAO, as much as half of Africa's rainfed cultivable land is marginal in quality. Only in regions with a reasonably wide range of moisture conditions, namely Mediterranean and arid North Africa and the afore-mentioned two regions, do marginal lands constitute no more than about one-third the extent of the total potentially cultivable rainfed area (ibid. Annex II, ch. 6, para. 6.12).

As has already been noted, a very large part of the African continent is actually covered by sandy soils of various kinds, which are predominant in the semi-arid and subhumid climates and present the characteristics described above (low content in plant nutrients, fragile structure, high susceptibility to wind blowing). In the humid areas the soils of tropical lowlands predominate 'with their associated problems of acidity, low nutrient retention capacity, aluminium toxicity, low initial phosphate and potassium contents and a tendency to fix phosphate in forms unavailable to plants' (ibid. Annex II, ch. 3, para. 3.7 and 3.8). Even under high-level inputs, sandy soils and acid soils of tropical lowlands have low cultivation factors (corresponding to one or two years of cultivation in every five to seven years) as a result of low inherent fertility. Phosphorous and nitrogen are grossly deficient in many African soils while other nutrient deficiencies are also quite common, in particular potassium, sulphur, calcium, and microelements such as zinc and copper. In the fertile soils of tropical highlands weed growth is often more critical than nutrient constraints. As for dark clay soils, they are difficult to cultivate because they are hard when dry, sticky when wet and prone to waterlogging. Their tendency to compact and harden during the dry season results in high early season runoff and severely restricts pre-season and post-season cultivation (ibid. Annex II, ch. 3, para. 3.11–29; Collinson 1987: 80). Other physical limitations of African soils include: (1) very low structural porosity reducing root penetration and water circulation; and (2) generally poor infiltration (Matlon 1987: 61–2).

To sum up, 'there are practically no extensive areas or soils in Africa without limitations of one sort or another' (FAO 1986: Annex II, ch. 3, para. 3.34). Perhaps paradoxically, conditions for agricultural production tend to deteriorate rather than improve with the transition from dry to wet climate (ter Kuile 1987: 97). Some constraints are irremovable and must therefore be endured: thus, over the third of the continent covered by various soils of arid climates (including shallow soils, shifting dunes, saline, calcareous and gypsiferous soils), intensive development is generally not possible. However, in many cases constraints can be overcome through the farmers' own efforts, community development, or government intervention and, more likely, through a mixed use of these three levels of intervention. From a technical standpoint, success in overcoming or removing these constraints will not be achieved unless appropriate soil management techniques are used which are carefully tuned to the specific characteristics of the agroclimatic environment. Land development or reclamation schemes will have to be grounded on careful analysis of soil structures, moisture conditions, and temperatures (FAO 1986: Annex II, ch. 3, para. 3.9 and 3.34–8).

Land development in Africa is bound to be especially difficult not only because African populations are comparatively scattered (see above), but also because the physical environment for agriculture (and cattle-raising) in this continent is marked by an exceptional diversity of agroclimatic and soil characteristics, of farming systems and socio-economic conditions (Berry 1984: 60 and Johnston 1986: 159). These highly diverse ecological (and socio-economic) conditions are found even within individual countries and within small regions or subregions. Just to take one example, African soils have greatly varying abilities to supply and retain nutrients and to respond to fertilizer applications (be it through organic manures, mineral fertilizers, or biological nitrogen fixation by leguminous plants). Due to such heterogeneity of environmental conditions and wide variations in farming (and livestock) systems by agroecological zones, rigid technical packages have absolutely no chance to succeed. The fact that only highly differentiated strategies of soil management and land development can form a sound basis for agricultural development in Africa makes technological progress a comparatively costly process and, in particular, it compounds to a considerable degree the administrative difficulties created by low population densities. Note that the huge losses resulting from pests, plant diseases, rodents, grasshopper and bird attacks—the latter being an especially serious problem in Africa—can also be remedied only if they are dealt with in a selective way and at a much decentralized level.[24]

---

[24] A well-known parasite in Africa is the striga which attaches itself to the roots of millet and sorghum, two crops often cultivated in association. Quelea (weaver) birds are famous for the havoc they often play in the harvests of these two traditional subsistence crops. On the other hand, rice harvests are also highly susceptible to bird attacks as well as to rats and borers.

There are other sources of great variability which are typical of Africa, particularly of semi-arid areas. Thus, the crop-growing season is short compared to other semi-arid tropics with similar rainfall (Matlon 1987: 60). As a consequence, the seasonality of labour input to agriculture tends to be very high in Africa, 'not only absolutely but also compared to the semi-arid tropics of South Asia' (Delgado and Ranade 1987: 118). Moreover, interyear variability of rainfall is also very high in Africa and this has a considerable impact on agricultural activities in rainfed and traditional irrigation systems. A clear illustration of this is provided by the following example: in the Senegal river valley, the area cultivable under flood recession agriculture varies between 10,000 and 150,000 hectares depending upon the importance of the flood (Mathieu 1987: i. 22).

Irrigation potential   Lipton has recently expressed the opinion that 'over the next forty years, SSA [sub-Saharan Africa] cannot feed its people without massively expanding the irrigated portion of its cropland' (Lipton 1985: 75). Unfortunately, compared to other regions of the world Africa has a lesser quantity of surface waters per unit of land area while at the same time suffering from greater evaporation. Large rivers like the Nile and the Niger cross vast tracts of interior marshlands (the Sudd in Sudan and the Niger delta) where considerable quantities of water get lost. Several other basins (e.g. Lake Chad) are deprived of any outlet into the sea and lose the totality of their waters through evaporation or percolation (FAO 1986: Annex IV, ch. 2, para. 2.5). There now seems to be a growing consensus that the irrigation potential of Africa is quite limited, in any case much more limited than that of Asia, and that rainfed agriculture will remain the most important and most economical way to increase foodcrop production in most African countries (CILSS 1979: 162–7; Eicher and Baker 1982: 133–9; Lele 1984: 445; FAO 1986: Annex IV; Matlon 1987: 65–9). This is a clear handicap in so far as the potential yield increases that can be obtained from high yield varieties are in general considerably lower under rainfed agriculture than under irrigated agriculture with generous application of fertilizers.

In Africa surface waters are distributed in a very unequal way and most water resources are not located in areas where aridity seriously limits production.[25] Almost half of irrigable land areas are already abundantly watered by rainfall. Out of the remaining potential of 20–5 million hectares, 9.5 million have actually been put under irrigation (between 38–47 per cent), of which 6.1 million hectares represent modern irrigation, mainly under major government schemes (above all in the Maghreb countries, Egypt, and the

---

[25] Thus, the Zaïre basin which covers 16% of the total land area in sub-Saharan Africa carries as much as 55% of the average annual flows running in this region. Unfortunately, the river Zaïre does not flow through areas where low rainfall puts a serious drag on rainfed agriculture. However, some of the large rivers of the continent flow through extensive arid areas (Nile, Niger, and Senegal) (FAO 1986: Annex IV, ch. 2, para. 2.8).

Sudan), and 3.4 million hectares represent small-scale and traditional flood, swamp, surface, and low-lift irrigation developed at the village or household level (above all in Nigeria and Madagascar). Whereas in India and Indonesia about 25 per cent of the total arable land area is under irrigation, the corresponding proportion is less than 5 per cent in Africa and it will take much time and efforts to raise it to its likely maximum of 10–14 per cent. If in North Africa most of the irrigation potential is presently exploited, the same cannot be said of sub-Saharan Africa where as much as 88 per cent of the potentialities are still unused (FAO 1986: Main Report, ch. 2; Annex II, ch. 6, para. 16; Annex IV, i; Paulino 1987: table 2.8, 36). It is therefore with respect to the latter, yet untapped, potential that one can speak with Lipton about the necessity for Africa to expand massively her irrigated croplands.

Such expansion must actually take place mainly in a group of twelve countries, eight of which have seriously restricted rainfed opportunities (the six Sahelian countries plus Kenya and Botswana), and four of which have a rainfed growing period of less than 120 days on more than a quarter of their territory (Chad, Ethiopia, Sudan, and Tanzania). Other countries with a sizeable portion of their arable lands in the semi-arid zone (e.g. Guinea-Bissau, Nigeria, Cameroon, Angola) also need to develop irrigation in their high-risk tracts (FAO 1986: Annex IV, ch. 6, para. 6.5–6.7). Under all other conditions, according to FAO experts, first priority ought probably to be given to rainfed development because it 'demands fewer scarce government financial or managerial resources; less imported materials, fuel and equipment; does not require profound social change; and has a quicker impact'. However, these experts admit, 'irrigation may *eventually* become essential in these [remaining] countries, but in the short and medium term rainfed development is likely to be a better national strategy for food supply than large-scale modern irrigation' (ibid. ch. 6, para. 6.2; for a similar position, see Spencer 1986: 217).

It is an unmistakable fact that access to water is much costlier and more problematical in Africa than in Asia: thus, for example, the unit cost of water is between two and three times as high in Africa as in India (FAO 1986: Main Report, ch. 2). This is of course the basic reason why most irrigated lands are devoted to export crops (e.g. cotton, sugarcane, and sugar beets) and to 'superior' foodcrops (wheat—essentially in North Africa—and rice— essentially in sub-Saharan Africa). With their low unit values subsistence crops cannot be profitably raised under irrigated agriculture.[26] Note also that,

---

[26] Between 50 and 60% of the total irrigated land area is devoted to cereal crops. Nevertheless, by far the largest portion of lands under *modern* irrigation schemes is used for raising export crops (FAO 1986: Annex IV, ch. 2, para. 2.60–3). The question could be asked why traditional foodcrops are not displaced by high-value crops under dryland farming systems too. There are two main answers to this question. First, due to technical reasons, most crops with high unit values could not be profitably raised under rainfed agriculture. Second, the food diet in the African countryside still remains heavily biased in favour of traditional staple foods which the farmers are keen to produce themselves and to which they give absolute priority in their time allocation pattern.

institutional and administrative problems apart, traditional irrigation (including flood-recession farming systems, swamp drainage, and irrigation schemes under controlled submersion) is likely to be less cost-effective than modern irrigation with complete control of water. This is due to the fact that crop yields under traditional irrigation systems are generally much lower and much more subject to wild fluctuations arising from natural hazards. At this point, it is interesting to mention a number of technical reasons which tend to make irrigation much more costly and problematic in Africa than, say, in Asia (ibid., Annex IV, ch. 2, para. 2.6–8 and 2.37; ch. 5, para. 5.8–9):

1. High unit costs of imported capital and intermediate goods result from long distances and poor roads, particularly in land-locked countries.

2. Reservoirs and dams are often required to perform the essential function of stabilizing the erratic flows of many African rivers. Because of the central basement complex (shaped like a saucer) of the African continent, suitable dam locations will be found along the rim and these sites 'usually require either considerable lengths of canal to bring the water to the irrigable areas or pumping'.

3. 'Major flood protection dykes are often necessary for irrigation schemes. The lower costs encountered for irrigation in the flood plains in Asia are also due to the fact that such dykes already exist, having been built a long time ago.'

4. The distribution of irrigable soils 'is often patchy, calling for complex water distribution and drainage networks with considerable land levelling where surface irrigation is concerned'.

5. Sources of groundwater are rather few (compared to Asia). Moreover, they are usually scattered and difficult to locate, and they do not replenish themselves easily. They are frequently found at great depths (more than 100 metres), and, as such, they are not suitable for developing cheap small-scale irrigation. None the less, abundant shallow sources of underground water exist along the alluvial beds of some large rivers (like the Nile, Niger, and Senegal).

6. African rivers—except those having their source in the younger geological strata of North Africa or mountain East Africa[27]—carry fewer sedimental matters than rivers in other regions of the world, particularly in Asia. Such a deficiency accounts for the oft-noted fact that the fertility of irrigated fields begins to decline a few years after the completion of irrigation projects, thus making it necessary to apply significant doses of mineral fertilizers to restore economic profitability (see Mathieu 1985a, for irrigation schemes in the Senegal river basin, and 1985b, for schemes along the Niger in Mali). As hinted at above, Asia is in a much more favourable position since her great rivers 'get much of their water and alluvium from head-waters outside the tropics and

---

[27] Sedimental matters can also be locally abundant in the enlarging areas which have lost their plant cover following overgrazing or deforestation. In this instance, however, the nutrients are obtained at the cost of destroying land resources elsewhere in the region: think, for example, of the considerable quantities of sediments flowing away from the Abyssinian plateau as a result of huge deforestation to be eventually dispersed among the fields of Egyptian farmers along the Nile river.

carry a richer load of nutrient-bearing silt'. In addition, 'the permanent snow cover of the Himalayas also represents an enormous resource for recharging underground aquifers, whereas the high rates of evapotranspiration in sub-Saharan Africa reduce significantly available water surpluses' (Eicher and Baker 1982: 134).

7. Other problems arise from heavy clay soils which call for considerable mechanization, and from birds, grasshoppers, and rodents which can cause tremendous destruction by attacking irrigated rice crops in the process of ripening.

8. Finally, possibilities of multiple cropping are far more limited in Africa than in Asia because of the much poorer waterholding capacity of soils in the former than in the latter continent (Matlon 1987; Delgado and Ranade 1987: 126–8).

Conclusion The situation of Africa with respect to agricultural natural resources can be summarized in the following way:

1. Africa still possesses considerable land reserves and uncultivated lands are often of high fertility (particularly those located in deltas, swamps, and floodplains). However, these land reserves are very unequally distributed and they are largely inaccessible due to serious animal, plant, and human diseases. This is in contrast to what obtains in other parts of the world where great civilizations of past millennia tamed the infested river valleys and coastal swamps through long-sustained measures of land reclamation and sanitization (Hart 1982: 101 and Bray 1986: ch. 3).

2. A large part of the African continent (around one-third) is covered by various soils of arid climates. In these regions intensive development is usually impossible while prevention of degradation of the sparse vegetation is imperative on the desert margins.

3. African soils are often fragile, shallow, and depleted, and rainfed agriculture is only possible on a limited portion of the total land area which moreover comprises a good deal of marginal lands. In addition, soils in Africa have a very low waterholding capacity.

4. Africa is distinguished by an exceptional diversity of agroclimatic conditions, which further complicates the task of soil management. This is a crucial point since progressive intensification of use of land already cultivated will not be a viable strategy unless highly differentiated and very careful soil management techniques are applied under rainfed agriculture.

5. In semi-arid tropics the crop-growing season is very short and rainfall varies considerably on a year-to-year basis with dramatic effects on rainfed and traditional irrigation agricultural systems.

6. The irrigation potential of Africa is rather limited, especially so if considerations of economic profitability are added to those of technical feasibility. In many countries rainfed development will remain the most cost-effective

way to increase staple food production, at least in the short and medium term. It is mainly in the Sudano-Sahelian belt and in a few other countries— particularly so in deltaic plains and river valleys—that irrigation development will be an essential element of future food strategies.

7. For various technical reasons, the scope for comparatively cheap small- and medium-scale irrigation is much less extensive in Africa than in Asia.

8. Large tracts of Africa's land are drought prone, a problem which has become increasingly serious with the decline of the average annual rainfall observed in sub-Saharan Africa since the mid-1950s.

(c)   Retarded and biased process of technology generation

The lack of Green Revolution-type breakthroughs in African agriculture   In sharp contrast to other developing areas, sub-Saharan Africa has been characterized during recent decades by low and more or less stagnating per acre yields of many subsistence food crops. On average, the yields of cereals in Asia and Latin America are at present twice as high as they are in Africa (Giri 1986: 59). Worse still, in many African countries, yields of traditional foodgrain have declined, sometimes to a marked degree and for a large number of consecutive years. From Table 10.2 a rough idea can be obtained of the comparatively poor performance of sub-Saharan African agriculture with respect to growth of yields per land unit.

Furthermore, recent evidence has shown a picture of small or negative per capita productivity change in the agricultural sector of many parts of the African continent (Paulino 1987: 23–8). On an average (but not at the margin), productivity of agricultural labour seems to be significantly higher in Asia than in Africa in spite of much more acute land scarcity (Delgado and Ranade 1987: 122).

The factors responsible for such a disappointing performance are complex and not always easy to disentangle. There is no doubt, however, that an overwhelming cause lies in the absence of any significant dynamics of technical

Table 10.2 Average annual percentage change in yields of cereals, 1960–1984

	Wheat	Maize	Rice	Millet	Sorghum
Developing countries					
1960–70	3.54	2.47	2.20	3.19	3.53
1970–84	3.87	2.91	2.44	0.13	1.43
East Africa (south of Sahara)					
1960–70	2.28	0.96	1.10	1.11	0.68
1970–84	2.73	−0.58	−0.42	−1.00	−0.90
West Africa (south of Sahara)					
1960–70	1.10	1.76	0.15	−0.41	−2.87
1970–84	1.86	−0.26	1.55	0.03	2.31

Source: Adapted from World Bank (1986a: table B-3, p. 60).

change in African agriculture. It is often the lack of new, and adequately tested, technical packages geared towards the needs of small farmers which has prevented them from increasing the productivity of their land and which has led them, in areas subjected to heavy population pressure, to break the fundamental rules of agroecological balance in extensive agriculture, and to cause the land fertility to decrease inexorably. Thus, a group of FAO experts have recently come to the conclusion that there are practically no technical packages ready to be transferred to African farmers with respect to most food crops under rainfed conditions, particularly in the Sudano-Sahelian belt. This is especially disquieting since 'it is also in this belt that possibilities of extension of rainfed area under present practices are extremely limited' (FAO 1986: Annex IV, ch. 6, para. 6.3). Moreover, lack of technical advances in conditions of increasing land scarcity and poor off-farm work opportunities tends to lead to decreasing levels of rural welfare. Indeed, *when technology is held constant*, intensification of land use following a decline in the amount of agricultural land per person in agriculture (e.g. through a move from shifting to permanent cultivation practices) is generally associated with increased labour requirements per unit of land area and, therefore, with diminishing returns to labour.

It would be absurd to envisage the production of new food technology only in terms of the sacrosanct trinity 'seeds–fertilizers–pesticides'. There are apparently many ways in which African farming systems can be made more efficient, e.g. through rotational improvements (including tree crops, leguminous plants, and mixed farming), better integration of crop and livestock production, new crop management practices, improved methods of soil conservation, improvement of intercropping systems, introduction of animal draught power wherever feasible (possibly after controlling severe animal diseases), diffusion of more effective work tools, or of seeds more carefully disinfected and better sorted out. This being said, it cannot be denied that the production of new, high-yield varieties of seeds—and of new, more productive livestock breeds—forms an essential component of the technical revolution which has occurred in agriculture during the present century, and that it can probably not be bypassed by Africa without putting her food-producing capacity in serious jeopardy. It is basically a correct and appropriate attitude to emphasize the deep implicit knowledge which African farmers possess about their natural environment, and to point to the untapped or neglected potentialities which lie in the store of local traditional practices. Nevertheless, this should not mislead us into thinking that, contrary to what has happened in all other areas of the world, Africa does not need to shift gradually from traditional resource-based agriculture to a science-based agriculture in which the discovery of new genetic processes and new plants or breeds occupies a central position. This is all the more so as many African farmers are actually perplexed and even anxious before the new challenges confronting them.

That Africa is far from having completed—or even from having embarked upon—the above shift is plainly evident from the fact that no major breakthrough in high-yield varieties for most food crops has occurred there so far. This is exactly what Eicher means when he writes that 'in fact, the green revolution has barely touched Africa' (Eicher 1984: 464). Apparently, the only exception is maize for which East and Southern Africa have accumulated a backlog of new technology from the colonial period. In fact, Southern Rhodesia was the first country after the United States to release a hybrid variety of maize (the SRI) for commercial farmers and this success was achieved after seventeen years of continuous research efforts (from 1932 to 1949). The dominant variety today—the SR-52—was produced after eleven more years of research, but it is only since the early 1970s that it has been used at the smallholder level (Lipton 1985: 77; Eicher 1986a: 10 n.). In Kenya, research on hybrid maize started only in the mid-1950s and the Kenyan variety known as Kitale was released about ten years later (Lipton 1985: 77; Eicher 1985: 93, 1986a: 10–11). However, even with respect to maize, a lot remains to be done in Africa. For one thing, the new hybrid varieties such as the SR-52 and the Kitale have benefited only a few countries—Zimbabwe, Kenya, Malawi, Tanzania, and Zambia—and, within these pioneer countries, only some regions, while they could be used on an area roughly twice as large as that presently cultivated with them (FAO 1986: Main Report, ch. 2, para. 2.19). For another thing, serious amounts of adaptive research are needed to discover hybrid varieties of maize suited to other agroclimatic regions, particularly to West Africa where research on maize is still in its infancy.

No comparable breakthroughs have taken place for other food crops. As a matter of fact, there is today wide agreement among agricultural experts that, under actual farming conditions (as opposed to ideal conditions prevailing in experimental research stations), traditional local seed varieties remain superior to the new varieties developed through modern genetic research. Either the latter do not give better average yields than the former, or they appear to be much more sensitive to pests, drought, winds, etc., which makes them too risky for most farmers to adopt. Thus, for example, after ten years of research and trials on improved varieties of rice in West Africa, the conclusion has been reached that 'only 2 of over 2,000 imported varieties were yielding as well as the best local varieties' (Eicher 1986a: 9). With regard to sorghum and millet, two important staple foods in low rainfall areas in West Africa, the Sudan, Ethiopia, and Southern Africa, forty-four years of research started by the French during colonial times (1931 to 1975) did not lead to any noticeable improvement in yields. As a result, ICRISAT—an Indian research institute specialized in problems of arid and semi-arid agriculture—was invited to set up a sorghum and millet research programme in the Sahel in the mid-1970s. Today, however, the failure of this attempt at transferring hybrid varieties from India to West Africa is officially admitted (ibid. 9–10 and FAO 1986: Main Report, ch. 2). As a result, 'probably less than 2 per cent of total sorghum, millet, and upland rice area in West Africa is sown with cultivars developed through modern genetic research' (Spencer 1986: 224).

The situation for other African staple foods—like cassava, yams, and root crops—is basically similar to that described above. Again, the same conclusion can be extended to livestock production since the record of recent attempts to introduce new breeds is distressingly poor: local breeds remain superior to the so-called 'improved breeds' developed through scientific approaches, mainly because they turn out to be much more resistant to local diseases (Leonard 1986: 201 and FAO 1986: Annex III, ch. 3, para. 3.54–62).

It would be wrong and dangerous to infer from the afore-mentioned failures that in Africa traditional agricultural technologies and practices have a decisive and permanent advantage over modern technologies and practices derived from a science-based approach. Indeed, it will be argued in the following sections that underlying the bleak picture given above are structural factors, biases, and constraints that can be redressed or released to a significant extent provided drastic corrective measures are taken up. These obstacles and distortions often arise from policy trends that can be traced back to colonial times or to deeply engraved misconceptions about the nature or process of technical change on the part of African governments and international donor agencies. But they may also originate in special difficulties resulting from some structural characteristics of the African continent. The above two categories of technical change-impeding factors will now be analysed in succession with a view to identifying a new set of reasons why Africa is lagging so much behind Asia and Latin America with respect to food technology and production.

Misguided policy trends: the 'export bias'   A conspicuous feature of the agricultural strategies followed by most African governments lies in the modest investment in research on food crops compared to similar investments on export crops. Lipton has rightly noted that in Africa 'the lack of "congruence" between research effort and the importance of a crop' takes on extreme proportions and is in fact far more serious than in most of Asia (Lipton 1985: 70). Thus, for example, in 1976, sub-Saharan Africa spent almost twice as much money on national soybean research as on national cassava research, although the area covered by the former crop represented only 3 per cent of that covered by the latter (ibid. 70 n.)! In 1984, only 7 per cent of the agricultural scientists working in this region devoted all their research efforts to millet and sorghum while these two food crops accounted for as much as 41 per cent of total cereal production and almost 60 per cent of the total land area under cereal crops (FAO 1986: Main Report, ch. 1, para. 1.26 and Annex I, ch. 3, para. 3.29). This said, Table 10.3 shows that the discrimination in agricultural research efforts runs essentially against traditional staple foods while 'superior' food crops which are mainly consumed in urban areas (like wheat, rice, beef, pork, and vegetables) fare much better.

The biased allocation of research efforts between (traditional) food crops and export crops is in fact a direct legacy of colonial research systems. As a rule, the agricultural development strategies of colonial powers were 'geared almost

Table 10.3 Research as percentage of the value of
product, by commodity, average 1972–1979 period

Crop	Research (%)
Export crops	
Soybeans	23.59
Coffee	3.12
Cocoa	2.75
Sugar	1.06
Citrus	0.88
Groundnuts	0.57
Bananas	0.27
Cotton	0.23
Food crops	
Traditional staple foods	
Cassava	0.09
Coconuts	0.07
Sweet potatoes	0.06
Intermediate crops	
Maize	0.44
'Superior' food crops	
Pork	2.56
Poultry	1.99
Beef	1.82
Vegetables	1.56
Wheat	1.30
Rice	1.05

Source: Adapted from Judd *et al.* (1986: table 6, p. 92).

exclusively to the expansion of export crop production for the metropolitan
countries' and, therefore, their research efforts were largely concentrated on
export crops and on the needs of commercial farmers and managers of
plantations (Lele 1984: 447; Eicher 1984: 460; Giri 1983: 237–8; Spencer
1986: 220–1). Quite often, these efforts were highly productive and yielded
impressive results since in many cases new seed or plant varieties were
developed which were well adapted to African agroclimatic conditions. In this
sense, Hart is right in pointing out that 'the colonial period saw the ground-
work laid for the development of a scientific agriculture' (Hart 1982: 98).

Well-known examples of colonial, Green Revolution-type breakthroughs
are: the development of hybrid oil palm in Zaïre, Nigeria, and the Ivory
Coast (thanks to the pioneering research carried out in the INEAC—Institut
national pour l'étude agronomique du Congo—created in 1933 in the Belgian
Congo); of cotton plants adapted to Sahelian conditions in Mali and Burkina
Faso (under the aegis of the CFDT—Compagnie française pour le
développement des fibres textiles); of a new type of coffee—known as

Arabusta—obtained again in the INEAC by crossing Robusta and Arabica types; of varieties of cocoa suited to West African environmental conditions (under the impulse of the West African Cocoa Research Institute in Ghana); and of high-yielding groundnut varieties in Senegal and Gambia (through the efforts made at the research centre of Bambey which was created as early as 1913).

What all these examples converge to show is that a science-based agriculture is possible in Africa as elsewhere: local varieties can be surpassed by modern hybrid varieties, new plants can be adapted to her highly specific conditions, and plant-breeding materials can be successfully transferred from other regions of the world (as demonstrated in the case of imports of oil palm materials from Asia; of cotton and maize materials from the United States; and of coffee materials from South America). There are good reasons to believe that the same positive results could be obtained for food crops if only sufficient resources were devoted to developing an adequate research base and if the research efforts aimed at improving their yields were conducted with the same determination as was encountered in the case of export crops. The success story of hybrid maize in Zimbabwe and Kenya provides further support to this thesis. However, this should not be taken to mean that it is necessarily wise to devote large amounts of research efforts to the development and adaptation of alien plants (like wheat in drought-prone areas or rice in rainfed areas). Such efforts may well be wasteful of scarce research resources which would be better committed to traditional food crops with a long history of adaptation to the African soil. In this respect, the positive research discrimination which 'superior' food crops are presently enjoying in Africa is probably as disquieting as the longer-lived 'export research bias'.

A last remark is in order. Eicher has noted with apparent good sense that the low priority given to investment in research on food crops during the colonial period could be defended because population and demand for food were growing in a relatively slow fashion and surplus land was available which could easily be brought under cultivation by smallholders when the need arose (Eicher 1984: 460). After all, the only real breakthrough which took place in food crop technology was the afore-mentioned development of hybrid maize in Southern Rhodesia (and, later, in Kenya) where an important community of politically influential European farmers were engaged in production of both food and export crops (Johnston 1986: 166). It is also interesting to note that while developing their export-biased agricultural strategies colonial adminis-trators could take advantage of the strong division of work and leisure prevailing in sub-Saharan Africa where most agricultural tasks were per-formed by women (Boserup 1981: 147). Underemployed men were thus induced or forced to work in the new money economy either as wage labourers on plantations or as peasant producers of export crops. As a result, the new cash crops became 'men's crops', although women often helped to produce them, and the food crops remained 'women's crops' considered as a part of women's traditional obligations to provide for the family consumption (ibid.). Therefore, a kind of collusion was created between colonial administrators and leading male villagers in so far as the latter had no interest in improving the food crops and their whole attention was concentrated on enlarging the scope and increasing the yields of export cash crops.

As is evident from the above discussion, several powerful forces converged during the colonial period to produce an 'export bias' in agricultural development strategies. However, the agricultural research policy followed by the Belgians in Zaïre shows that another approach was possible which gave more weight to long-term considerations and to the well-being of the masses (including women). As a matter of fact, the agricultural research system which was established in 1933 (the INEAC) was not only a strong organization which eventually became the largest of its type in Africa and obtained impressive results (see above), but it also devoted a significant part of its resources to research on food crops. In this respect, it is noteworthy that the INEAC was independent of the colonial administration and that its financing was rather diversified (Eicher 1986a: 13, 1986b: 10).

Misguided policy trends: the 'technological dependence bias'   With respect to agricultural technology development and diffusion, the experience of the last decades has taught us a very important lesson: the model of direct 'material' technological transfer does not work because agricultural technology is highly 'location-specific' (Hayami and Ruttan 1985: 271). It is true that the development and rapid diffusion since the Second World War of modern high-yielding varieties of rice, wheat, and maize in Asia and Latin America has followed a dramatic process of agricultural technology transfer. Yet what deserves to be emphasized is the following: if the new seed varieties propagated during the 1960s and the early 1970s were those developed by international agricultural research centres (such as the IRRI for rice and the CIMMYT for wheat and maize), they have been gradually replaced by crosses of the international centre varieties with *local* varieties developed by national research and experiment institutions so as better to suit local environmental conditions (Hayami and Kikuchi 1981: 44–5). This creative process of adaptation of prototype high-yielding varieties (or of other prototypes of genetic material and equipment) developed in temperate zone countries has been made possible 'by a series of institutional innovations in the organization, management, and financing of agricultural research' in the receiving countries themselves. More than the direct transfer of materials and designs, it implied the international migration of scientific manpower and the development of indigenous research capability (Hayami and Ruttan 1985: 264; Johnston 1986: 165). It can therefore be concluded that from a technical standpoint the success of the Green Revolution in Asia and Latin America was due to two main factors: (1) the existence of a large store of scientific and technical knowledge in advanced countries which could be used in tropical countries through the mediation of highly performing international research centres; and (2) a considerable strengthening in the latter countries of capabilities for research, experimentation, and administration of agricultural programmes, through the building up of new institutions (including agricultural universities), a marked increase in the supply of well-trained scientists, engineers, and administrators, and a rapid accumulation of on-the-spot practical knowledge and learning by doing.

In actual fact, the experience of Africa with agricultural technological change during the twentieth century largely bears out the above diagnosis. It does so in both a positive and a negative way. The positive test is provided by the history of technical change during the colonial period. Indeed, it is evident from this history that technical breakthroughs were always the outcome of well-focused and long-sustained adaptive research and experimentation carried out in locally established research-experimentation networks. The story of oil palm technology development, as reported by Eicher, is particularly illustrative in this regard:

INEAC's pioneering research on hybrid oil palms [in the Belgian Congo] laid the foundation for the modern oil palm industry in West Africa. Basic information on oil palm genetics was transferred to Nigeria and after a decade of adaptive research in the 1950s, Nigerian hybrid varieties became the centerpiece of the eastern region's smallholder oil palm scheme in the early 1960s. The Nigerian hybrids yielded 300 per cent more than local (wild) varieties under farm conditions. (Eicher 1986a: 13)

As for the negative test, it is supplied by the numerous cases of failure in international direct transfers of agricultural technology to Africa during the last decades. Such failures even occurred when foodgrain varieties were transferred from other tropical developing areas (like Mexico and India) with apparently similar agroclimatic characteristics. The disappointing results obtained by ICRISAT—a renowned and competent Indian agricultural research centre—when it tried to transfer hybrid sorghum and millet varieties from semi-arid India to Sahelian countries in the late 1970s have already been mentioned. Causes of this failure were located in 'unforeseen problems with disease, variability of rainfall and poor soils' (Eicher 1984: 464), and in 'the difficulty of transferring, crossing or adapting exotic varieties so that they suit local conditions especially regarding striga weeds and quelea (weaver) birds' (Lipton 1985: 78). Other experiences of direct international transfers of agricultural technology in general, and of genetic material in particular, do not tell a different story. After more than two decades of experimentation, optimism about the possibility of transferring the Green Revolution technology to Africa has faded away. FAO experts refer to the 'excessive confidence' which has been put in transfers of imported technologies from other continents (FAO 1986: Main Report, ch. 4, para. 4.75). The US Department of Agriculture considers that high-yielding varieties have distressingly failed to spread to Africa (quoted by Lipton 1985: 77). Bruce Johnston writes that among the factors responsible for inadequate rates of technological progress in

African agriculture are 'overly optimistic expectations about the availability of profitable technical innovations adapted to Africa's diverse environmental conditions and impatience for quick results'. According to him, 'this over-optimism about the potential for direct technological transfer' partly resulted from a misinterpretation of Asia's experience with the Green Revolution (Johnston 1986: 164–5). Finally, Eicher reached the conclusion that 'international technology transfer of plant varieties has been constrained by differences in soil conditions, pest regimes, farming practices' (Eicher 1986b: 24), and, one could add, by differences in rainfall patterns and moisture conditions, in access to water and water quality, and in a host of varied socio-economic conditions. His judgement can be extended to livestock technology and animal genetic material, as is evident from the following excerpt:

Starting with great confidence in the early sixties, western donors imported western models of ranches, capital intensive abattoirs and planeloads of exotic cattle in an attempt to 'bring development' to Africa. But in practice, these livestock improvement programs failed under institutional and environmental conditions that were sharply different from those in North America, Europe and Australia. (ibid. 18; see also Leonard 1986: 201)

In the light of the above analysis, the low pace of technical change in African agriculture must be attributed to an 'absence of effective local scientific capacity to screen, borrow, modify and adapt the most promising technology to local conditions' (Eicher 1986b: 24); to sheer neglect of the potential contribution of local materials (seeds, forest, fish, and livestock species) in development of new varieties or of local systems in development of new technologies (thus, serious research on intercropping started only in the 1970s although in most countries intercropping occupies over 90 per cent of cropped area—Spencer 1986: 224); and to a lack of genuine commitment to, or investment in, improving food crop technology, particularly at the smallholder level. While the latter factor—low priority to investment in food crop research —was at work both during the colonial period and the post-independence era, the other factor—inadequate adaptive agricultural research capacity—is characteristic of post-independence Africa. However, this should not be taken to mean that African governments only are to be held responsible for this dramatic underinvestment in research-building capacity. As a matter of fact, the responsibility of the international aid community is also heavily involved and, moreover, the dearth of trained African scientists and administrators can undoubtedly be traced back to colonial times.[28]

While many Asian countries benefited from sizeable foreign aid programmes with a high priority on long-term objectives of institution-building

---

[28] Carl Eicher has reminded us that, by the time of independence in the early 1960s, there was only one faculty of agriculture in French-speaking tropical Africa. Furthermore, between 1952 and 1963, only 4 university graduates in agriculture were trained in Francophone Africa, and 150 in English-speaking Africa (Eicher 1984: 459).

and development of graduate training in science and agriculture, Africa had curiously to be content with programmes of more limited size and shorter duration (Johnston 1986: 165). Data compiled by FAO for the period 1974–83 clearly illustrate this distortion: only 3 per cent of donor contributions to agriculture in Africa were used to develop national research systems and training, compared to 5.4 per cent in Asia. Furthermore, during 1974–9, 22 per cent of donor assistance to agriculture went into direct support of crop production in Africa, compared to only 5 per cent in Asia (Mellor and Delgado 1987: 3). Some authors have explained this differential treatment of Asia and Africa in terms of an all-pervasive 'extension bias' in the analysis of the needs of the African continent. Thus, Eicher has noted that after independence, 'donors assumed that inexpensive extension workers (mainly Africans) were a substitute for relatively expensive agricultural research scientists (mainly Europeans)' (Eicher 1986b: 8; see also Evenson 1978 and Johnston 1986: 166). Lagging agricultural development in Africa was seen primarily as the consequence of a failure to make effective use of available technology due to various reasons among which lack of knowledge and motivation among farmers stood foremost. Technical assistance and community development programmes therefore appeared as the best strategy to generate rapid modernization of African agriculture. In varietal research, all that was thought to be needed was 'importing varieties from other parts of the world, testing them for adaptability, and selecting the suitable ones' (Spencer 1986: 225).

To a large extent, however, this 'extension and community development bias' (Eicher) was also at work in Asia, especially during the 1950s (Hayami and Ruttan 1985: 264). It is in fact the availability of *new* technologies tuned to Asia's ecological conditions but requiring on-the-spot adaptation which largely imposed, during the late 1960s, a major revision of past conceptions and strategies. Whatever the reasons may be, there is a clear contrast between Asia and Africa: while in Asia foreign aid has been used to strengthen indigenous scientific capacity to carry out research and field experiments as well as to generate new technologies adapted to local circumstances, in Africa it went mostly into direct assistance projects, thus preventing Africans from developing their expertise and skills. Africa has remained a big builder and receiver of agricultural extension programmes 'which have generally been quite ineffective because they have had so little to extend' (Johnston 1986: 166), and of complex integrated rural development projects which cannot be properly handled due to an evident lack of trained manpower. In this respect, it is probably revealing that in 1980, the ratio of agricultural extension workers to research workers was more than three times as high in Africa (9.9) as in Asia (3.2) and Latin America (2.7) (computed from Judd *et al.* 1986: tables 1 and 2, pp. 82–5). Also telling and typical of so many African countries is the case of Senegal where the National School of Agriculture—the first establishment to offer an undergraduate training in agriculture in the country—was not created until nineteen years after national independence (in 1979) (Eicher 1984: 471).

English-speaking countries did not fare much better since in the mid-1960s there were only three African scientists working in research stations in Kenya, Uganda, and Tanzania (Eicher 1986a: 19).

Obviously, Africa will not be in a position to master her long-term process of agricultural development if she does not call radically into question the present human capital model grounded on 'overseas training and the provision of expatriate experts to Africa' (Eicher 1986b: 35). Indeed, the current situation under which the number of African scientists, technicians, and administrators capable of dealing with Africa's agricultural problems is too low and too slowly growing involves many long-term social costs. It cannot be otherwise when national development plans are designed by foreign agencies (often donor agencies), when research priorities are decided by foreign directors or scientists, and, most importantly, when the learning by doing is appropriated by an ever-growing and continuously changing community of expatriate technical experts whose central commitment is elsewhere. Such a deep and chronic dependence on foreign aid and expertise can only alienate and frustrate all the Africans who work—whether formally or not—under the orders of foreigners and, moreover, it is bound to undermine the authority and prestige of national governments (Helleiner 1979; Lele 1984: 450; Lipton 1985: 72; Eicher 1986c: 264; Mellor and Delgado 1987: 3). This is all the more so as foreign technical assistance is very costly, often of mediocre quality, and 'tackled in an *ad hoc* and half-hearted manner' (Eicher 1986b: 41).

Therefore, if Africa is to acquire the capacity to adapt and generate new technologies targeted to her specific conditions—particularly with a view to intensifying agriculture on dryland farming systems—she must increase her education and training programmes for high-level agricultural personnel (biologists, agronomists, irrigation engineers, agricultural economists, rural sociologists, etc.) and change her graduate education priorities by downgrading studies in law, medicine, arts, and social studies. The well-conceived role of the international community would be to encourage this reshuffling of priorities and to support the process of institution-building as it has done with apparent success in Asia.[29]

As a matter of fact, it is not only the level but also the orientation of investment in agricultural research which has been inadequate during the last decades in Africa. Three important sources of misallocation of research resources will be briefly mentioned here. First, instead of pursuing the colonial tradition of strong national or regional research services, donor agencies chose to invest heavily in the establishment of big international research centres (IRC) located in Africa but staffed with expatriates. This decision turned out to be 'a major research policy mistake' since it meant (1) that the building of indigenous scientific capacity got only casual and slight support and (2) that priority was given to international technology transfers over local generation of

---

[29] For more concrete proposals, see Eicher (1984: 472).

new technologies and development of local materials directly relevant to the targeted areas (Eicher 1986*b*: 9–12; Spencer 1986: 225).

Second, too many resources (whether in the IRCs or in national research services) have been committed to applied research at the expense of basic science (soil science, plant physiology and pathology, etc.) (Lipton 1985: 71; Eicher 1986*a*: 11–12; Mellor and Delgado 1987: 4). This bias is obviously the reflection of the 'extension' or 'technological dependence bias' according to which international diffusion of available technologies can be the engine of technical change in African agriculture.

Third, research efforts have been dispersed over too many crops or commodity programmes and over too large a geographical area. Experience in Africa (during the colonial period) and elsewhere has shown that successes have usually been achieved by long-term, highly focused research on one single commodity (Eicher 1984: 470, 1986*b*: 11–13). Lipton has aptly remarked that 'dispersion prevents any one group of scientists from applying, to any agricultural research challenge, the "critical mass" of time and interdisciplinary cooperation needed for progress' (Lipton 1985: 72). This certainly applies to Africa where difficult problems such as low soil fertility, serious livestock diseases, and destructive pest attacks cannot be resolved unless long-sustained research efforts (extending to ten or even twenty years) are devoted to them. In addition, African agricultural research centres have been seriously handicapped by numerous inefficiencies originating in poor personnel management and work discipline, lack of performance incentives and professional advancement, inadequate operating funds, high rates of staff turnover, untimely budgetary allocations, poor financial management and planning of resources (Spencer 1986: 222–3).

Structural disadvantages: limited size of nation states and traditional consumption patterns   Two structural disadvantages of Africa deserve to be pointed out in the context of the present discussion. The first one follows from the already noted smallness of many African nation states (see above, p. 475), a feature which was imposed on Africa by the old colonial powers at the time of independence. Indeed, the above argument about the negative effects of dispersion of research efforts on the rate of technical progress in agriculture takes on added significance if the absolute size of the research services or centres is small. Unfortunately, considerations of national prestige and autonomy have led the newly independent African states to dismantle the highly efficient regional research institutes which had been built during the colonial period, and to convert them into national institutes with much more limited resources at their disposal. Thus, for example, the famous EAAFRO (the East African Agriculture, Livestock and Forestry Research Organization) was dismantled after the breakup of the East African Community in 1974 so that 'the scientists in the 94 research stations in the EAAFRO network had to discontinue their cooperative research programs on common problems in Kenya, Tanzania and Uganda' (Eicher 1986*b*: 13–14).

The outcome of this parcelling out of the research set-up inherited from the colonial powers is truly alarming: only one-third of the African countries today have an agricultural research establishment above the critical size—about 100 scientists—required to run and test three adequate commodity programmes. To make matters worse, research workers are usually dispersed into many tiny stations which are supposed to cater to the differentiated needs of various agroclimatic zones and/or farming systems (Lipton 1985: 71–2; Spencer 1986: 233; Mellor and Delgado 1987: 3). Edjem Kodjo is therefore right to call on all African governments to create larger political spaces or entities because only they would allow for more systematic regional co-operation and enable the member-states to meet Africa's present and future challenges in a satisfactory way (Kodjo 1985). Such a move would actually mean a return to a long-established historical tradition in Africa, a tradition which was largely broken down by the colonial powers for political and administrative reasons (Coquery-Vidrovitch 1985: 127–35).

There is a second structural handicap which limits the possibilities of agricultural technical change open to Africa. This handicap arises from traditional consumption patterns that prevent Africa from benefiting from the international pool of scientific and technical knowledge to the same extent as Asia and Latin America. A striking feature about Asia's Green Revolution is that comparatively rapid advances could be made, from a relatively modest research investment, in the development of modern hybrid varieties of wheat and rice (wheat and maize for Latin America) transferable to tropical areas. We know today that such impressive results could not have been obtained if the prototype high-yielding varieties had not already been in existence in advanced, temperate zone countries (Japan, the United States, and Europe). In other words, modern biogenetic research targeted to the needs of Asian (and Latin American) tropical countries was 'able to draw on a large backlog of past research accomplishments on wheat and rice [and maize] in the temperate regions' (Hayami and Ruttan 1985: 270, 279). This is an important feature as it is increasingly recognized today that breakthroughs in agricultural research 'are often a result of past research in which a great deal of work has already been done' (Spencer 1986: 231).

In Africa, however, wheat and rice are not part of the traditional food diet and, even though we have noted that their consumption has risen quickly during the last decades, especially in urban areas, the main African staple foods still remain, with the exception of maize, traditional cereals (sorghum and millet), a variety of root and tuber crops (notably cassava, yams, and sweet potatoes), and pulses. In Central Africa, roots and tubers account for as much as 50 to 65 per cent of calorie intake and the proportion is still higher—from 65 to 80 per cent—in humid West, East, and Southern Africa (Spencer 1986: 232). Since such commodities are not consumed in the temperate regions, there was no backlog of readily available knowledge which African countries could draw upon. As a result, wrote Hayami and Ruttan in a cautious style, 'the flow of new technology from the newer [international research] institutes, and its impact on agricultural production, has proceeded more slowly. Accomplishments have taken the form of incremental gains rather than revolutionary breakthroughs' (1985: 270).

(d) The problematic shift to intensive agriculture: the issue of labour availability

The urgent need for intensification   Our analysis of Africa's natural resources and constraints has made it clear that the exhaustion of the land frontier in some countries and the high marginal cost of opening new land for cultivation in other countries have led to declining land–labour ratios in response to rising population pressure. It is in fact because land farming systems have remained basically extensive that Africa is characterized simultaneously by relatively low population densities and relatively high land pressure. A shift from extensive to intensive farming and livestock systems has therefore become inevitable if African agriculture is to avoid falling into a deepening crisis of sustainability. This is especially so as 'African soils tend to deteriorate quickly under conditions of increasingly regular or intense exploitation' (Berry 1984: 68; see also Delgado *et al.* 1987: 11). Note, however, that intensification is not an altogether new phenomenon in Africa since high population densities and intensive systems of cultivation were well established in areas of urban growth (e.g. Hausaland) or in areas subject to chronic insecurity (as in northern Cameroon, central Nigeria, and northern Tanzania where slave raiding prevented mountain-dwellers from moving freely into the plains), long before European incursions of the late nineteenth and early twentieth centuries (Berry 1984: 69, 87–8; see also Pingali *et al.* 1987: 49–50).

Intensification of agriculture will not always take the form of irrigation development—particularly that of modern irrigation systems with complete control of water—because, as we saw, Africa's irrigation potential is rather limited and many African irrigation projects are costly in economic terms (see above, pp. 486–8). In many cases, at least for a long time to come, it will have to take place under rainfed conditions within the framework of dryland farming systems. In consequence, most land productivity increases will arise from higher crop yields and better crop mixes rather than from enhanced cropping intensity. This will hold especially true in arid and semi-arid areas where the rainy season is short and access to water difficult or costly.

Now, whatever the circumstances in which it occurs and whatever the exact forms it takes, intensification of land use generally requires the application of increasing amounts of labour (and other inputs) to a given cultivated area. This is so not only because current productive operations (such as land preparation, fertilizing, weeding, harvesting, and animal husbandry) require comparatively large doses of labour when the productivity of the land is increased, but also because many labour investment activities associated with land (such as levelling, destumping, terracing, draining, bunding, and irrigating) are an indispensable component of agricultural intensification. Strictly speaking, the agricultural soil must be gradually 'constructed' (Giri 1983: 222, 1986: 64), as is clearly evident from the history of agricultural development in Europe, Asia, and pre-Columbian Latin America. In these continents, vast amounts of family and village labour have been used to build fences, pick stones, remove stumps, construct flood embankments, level and terrace land, drain water, and so forth, all labour-intensive and hard works which have mobilized many generations of farmers (Boserup 1965; Ishikawa 1981; Bray 1983, 1986; Eicher 1985: 88). Equally important is the fact that investment labour is also required on a recurrent basis in order to maintain the land infrastructures once they have been built. Indeed, if the soil can be 'constructed', it can also be destroyed, and the process of soil destruction is especially rapid in countries—like those of Africa—where problems such as leaching, wind or water erosion, and flooding are permanent threats.

The problem of labour shortage   It is, therefore, an inescapable reality that, in Africa as elsewhere, increasing and stabilizing agricultural yields will take time and require enormous inputs of labour. For technical and economic reasons, the use of mechanical devices—assuming that African countries can afford them and have the capacity to service them properly—and of other labour-saving technologies will substitute only partially for labour. As pointed out above, there are historical antecedents of intensive agriculture in Africa. Some areas have overtly stridden along the road to intensification, like the Dogon area in Mali and the Kirdi area in Cameroon (Giri 1986: 64). None the less, the general picture gives much less support for optimism regarding the pace at which Africa will be able to make her transition from extensive to intensive agriculture. Evidence of this is provided by the disappointing performance of irrigated farming, various schemes for intensive culture (including fish culture), and many soil conservation or land improvement programs during the last twenty or thirty years. Moreover, many observers of the African scene would agree with Goran Hyden that 'more labor-intensive husbandry is a necessary corollary to the adoption of yield-increasing technologies. Yet, this is not happening on the average peasant farm in Africa' (Hyden 1986: 60). Since it would be simplistic to assume that this failure can be attributed solely to state mismanagement or corruption, we must look for other factors or constraints operating in the African countryside. In this respect, the increasingly oft-cited evidence of labour shortage (Berry 1984: 86; Lele 1984: 445; Mathieu 1985a; FAO 1986: Main Report, ch. 4; Delgado and Ranade 1987: 124–30) appears to be a central and perhaps paradoxical cause of retarded—or blocked—intensification of agriculture in Africa. What is not clear, however, is the exact nature of this labour scarcity and the factors which account for its emergence.

A first possibility, or a partial explanation of the afore-mentioned phenomenon, is that labour shortages are largely seasonal. In the circumstances, acute dearths of labour during the short peak season—the rainy season in rainfed agriculture—can be reconciled with the fact that 'unemployment and underemployment of rural labor are also increasing, particularly where population pressure on land is rising rapidly' (Lele 1984: 445). The question then is: why do African farmers not make better use of the time available during the off season, as their Asian counterparts did, to build up, consolidate, restore, maintain, and repair rural infrastructures which can improve the land and ensure a better spread of agricultural activities across the year? Another possibility is that labour shortages result largely from rural outmigration (of a transitory, circulatory or permanent kind), or from the development of off-farm work opportunities. This fact is as well documented as that of marked seasonal variations in agricultural demand for labour in dryland farming systems. Thus, it has been found that rural poverty often forces people to seek off-farm employment to supplement meagre income from agricultural activities, and that smallholding households (in countries like Kenya, Lesotho, Tanzania, Burundi, Senegal, Burkina Faso, Zambia, Niger) may derive a substantial part of their annual income from such off-farm sources (Berry 1984: 81–3; Hyden 1986: 55–7; Mathieu 1987: i, ch. 2; FACAGRO and ISA 1989).

A straightforward interpretation of the increasing commitment of African smallholders to non-agricultural activities is that the expected income from these activities is higher than the implicit returns to their on-farm labour (Delgado and Ranade 1987: 129), and/or that vulnerability to risk of falling into distress is thereby reduced thanks to diversification of their activity portfolio. From there, it would be tempting to conclude that intensification of agricultural production is not justifiable on the grounds of allocative efficiency considerations and that African countries would do better to develop by diversifying their production into non-food activities. Even though the necessity of economic diversification in Africa is indisputable, it does not follow from this that agricultural intensification should be eschewed. Indeed, the above conclusion can be criticized from several angles. First, since intensification of agriculture involves the production of capital goods (including land improvements) and since there are obviously no futures' markets where anticipations about future returns could be taken into account, maximizing behaviour on the part of private agents is not conducive to intertemporal social optimality. Of course, uncertainty regarding future returns is not restricted to the agricultural sector and, as such, it cannot be considered as a conclusive argument in favour of encouraging agricultural production. Rather, the point it serves to emphasize is that the existence of comparatively low returns in agriculture is not a sufficient reason for giving up agricultural production if technical changes can be introduced in this sector and if a long-term perspective is adopted (as it should always be when development strategies are discussed). The fact that investments associated with these technical changes require comparatively low amounts of foreign exchange is an important consideration. It should prompt African states to incite their farmers—through education, material incentives, or more direct support—to undertake works and to make technological shifts that are or could be socially profitable in the longer run. Note incidentally that there is a comparatively great role for public sector investments in technological change in Africa since in many parts of the continent the resource base for rural capital accumulation is rather narrow due to low average labour productivity (Delgado and Ranade 1987: 124, 134).

Second, alternative incomes obtained outside the agricultural sector may have a non-productive origin in the sense that they do not result from the creation of new value added but from simple income transfers. Not infrequently, these transfers have a more or less forced character as witnessed by the spawning of thiefs and crooks of all hues in many African big cities.

Third, important externalities are involved in the individual decisions taken by African farmers so that, on this ground also, the market cannot be expected to perform efficiently. For instance, by neglecting to take soil conservation measures on his own plot of land for the sake of increasing his short-term private income, a farmer may cause a decrease in the productive capacity of his neighbours' lands. Therefore, low agricultural incomes obtained in an environment dominated by unhampered competitive market forces (or by inefficient institutional arrangements) do not give a correct idea of the potential incomes which could be earned under a more congenial system of economic regulation.

Finally, it is too simple to assume that migration decisions are exclusively influenced by economic considerations. Thus, the desire to escape from the hierarchical social structure of many African village societies may be an important determinant of migratory moves by young male villagers. Indeed, it is a well-known feature of traditional lineage societies in Africa that social relations are strongly differentiated on the basis of age (and sex).

There is yet another possible cause of labour shortage in intensive farming activities. It deserves to be dealt with at some length not only because, for reasons that will soon become apparent, it is largely ignored or underplayed in the specialized literature, but also because it is capable of resolving questions that are left unanswered by the above two lines of argument. Two such questions arise from facts commonly observed in areas where modern irrigation facilities are available:

- Why is it that, during the peak agricultural season, African cultivators often appear to give preference to traditional rainfed farming over irrigated farming, even though the latter could afford them higher and more reliable incomes than the former?
- How can we account for the fact that, even during the off season, farmers working in modern irrigation schemes tend to treat maintenance and repair works in a rather casual way? And, more generally, how can we

explain that African farmers are 'often more concerned with saving labor than conserving cultivated area' (Berry 1984: 86), even where there is an acute shortage of land?

Related to the latter observation is the well-documented and sobering experience that in the Sahelian states of West Africa, 'the amount of new land being brought under irrigation each year (around 5,000 hectares) is roughly equal to the amount being abandoned each year *because of neglect and lack of maintenance*' (Eicher 1986*a*: 4; see also Johnston 1986: 170). The situation was somewhat better in Senegal between 1982 and 1983, since the SAED came very close to achieving the ambitious objective set out for it by the government: to bring 2,575 hectares of new land under irrigation in the Senegal river valley. However, half of the tremendous effort made by the SAED (construction of new facilities over 2,400 ha) was lost because 1,200 hectares of irrigated land were in the meantime abandoned following degradation of the infrastructure (Mathieu 1985*a*: 655).

As for the former observation, a recent FAO in-depth study of African agriculture has reported that:

Modern irrigation schemes have commonly suffered from the farmers' insistence on maintaining the traditional diversity of their rural activities. On projects in Sierra Leone, the Gambia and Madagascar, planting of wet season irrigated rice was delayed until labour was released from work on rainfed crops elsewhere, thus reducing potential yields and overall irrigation intensity. Destitute pastoral nomads settled on small-scale government irrigation schemes in Northern Kenya remained only until they had accumulated enough money to re-establish their herds and resume a nomadic life; plots were then left with women or sharecroppers. (FAO 1986: Annex IV, ch. 5, para. 5.24)

It is worth noticing that the observation that 'priority is given to the rainfed area as soon as the rains arrive' (ibid. para. 5.23) applies not only where the irrigated crop is a cash (export) crop such as cotton or sugarcane, but also where it is an (admittedly unfamiliar) foodcrop such as rice grown in modern irrigation schemes or even a traditional staple food grown in traditional flood irrigation systems (see, for example, Engelhard and Ben Abdallah 1986; Diemer and Van der Laan 1987).

Aversion to intensive work A partial clue to the afore-mentioned relative neglect of intensive farming in Africa lies in the existence of a cultural bias against the type of work implied in intensive farming practices. This bias follows from the fact that Africa has a millenary tradition of extensive agricultural and pastoral activities which get inevitably reflected in her cultural patterns and values. One could therefore argue that Africa is not only characterized by an extensive *agriculture* but also by an extensive *culture*, that is by a culture whose world-view is rooted in the idea of an infinite or boundless space. On the level of labour requirements, extensive agriculture and stock-farming present two noteworthy features. First, the productive tasks involved can be performed with a relatively light work burden because the favourable man–land ratio makes long-fallow agriculture (or pastoral nomadism) possible. Boserup has gathered data showing that labour input is relatively low in different parts of Africa where both subsistence food crops and export crops are being produced: average weekly work hours in agriculture turned out to be fourteen hours for men and boys and fifteen hours for women and girls. The work burden carried by women is of course much larger since they have to perform domestic chores in addition to their agricultural duties. However, for the family as a whole, and for men in particular, the total work burden is no doubt lighter than that of smallholding families in more densely populated areas with more intensive agricultural systems (Boserup 1981: 147–8). Just to take one example, under intensive farming practices, natural processes can no more be relied upon to restore the fertility of the land. Fertilizer must be applied by man and this operation takes time in so far as long walks are needed to collect the required manure, or manure crops have to be grown in some of the fields. Since these operations have to be repeated, off-season periods of leisure or non-agricultural work are bound to be reduced (ibid. 46). This is in stark contrast to the situation obtaining in African dryland systems. Indeed, if African farmers perform long and intense work hours during the relatively short agricultural season (since good soils are rock hard at the end of the dry season farmers cannot prepare the land before the onset of the rains), there is typically little work to be done during the following long dry season (Pacey and Payne 1985: 27–8; Delgado and Ranade 1987: 128). In fact, labour inputs per hectare in most of Africa are reported to be 'very low' (Delgado and Ranade 1987: 122).

A second essential feature of labour performances under extensive farming systems is that productive tasks involve much less drudgery than those required by intensive farming systems. Thus, it is certainly easier to sow broadcast in an open field than to transplant rice seedlings in an irrigation scheme: while the cultivator can almost stand up while accomplishing the former agricultural operation, he (or she) must break his (or her) back and sink into mud to perform the latter. Also, it is apparently a more comfortable task to open a new field through the slash-and-burn technique when the existing land has become exhausted, than to take constant care of the same piece of land (or animals) in order to ensure that its long-term productivity is not impaired. Indeed, the latter strategy involves considerable 'husbandry skill', continuous and painstaking efforts to build up and maintain protective dikes, flood embankments, draining canals, conservation ditches, and so forth.

Intensive farming systems thus involve far more complicated, labour-consuming, and toilsome processes than extensive systems. Therefore, it should not come as a surprise that people who have been accustomed for millennia to extensive (agricultural and stock) farming practices look at the prospect of intensifying production with some strong reluctance and distrust. This attitude is especially noticeable among the old-age classes whose values and beliefs crystallize the history of the society's past practices. As always, young farmers display more enterprise and resilience in the face of new challenges. Consequently, the relative position of the young-age classes in village relations of power is bound to play a determining role in the rate of adoption of intensive farming practices. Opposition of the elders to their aspirations for change—on the basis of traditional authority patterns—can only prompt them to escape from rural poverty through migration, a decision which has long-run adverse effects on the economic future of the villages as well as on the future ability of the domestic food supply systems to feed growing populations.

Several writers have noticed the strong aversion which African village elders may display for the type of work required by agricultural intensification, and many field-observers of African rural realities could join them on this point. Intensive practices are often considered as debasing and status-lowering, just good to be performed by slaves, subordinates, or women. Thus, Catherine Coquery-Vidrovitch has reported that the Zarma peasants in Niger have strong cultural prejudices against the growing of rice in modern irrigation schemes:

Walking backwards for the transplantation of rice is traditionally considered by old people as 'slave's labour' which 'brings misfortunes'. It is for this reason that such people have refused to adopt the work cadences which the Chinese have introduced in the Kolo irrigation scheme at the door of Niamey. The Chinese have since turned to the young . . . and, in spite of the difficulties encountered, the results appear promising. (Coquery-Vidrovitch 1985: 187; my translation)

Another author has pointed out that among the Mandingues rice-growing activities have been entrusted to women (Singleton 1983: 7), which reveals the low status of this occupation since in Africa women are often treated as beasts of burden (Coquery-Vidrovitch 1985: 151). In Zambia, weeding is considered too degrading for men and has remained a typically female activity (Pausewang 1987: 8). In the same vein, it is not uncommon to see old farmers who have taken to irrigated farming entrusting the actual work to share-croppers of inferior socio-economic status (Mathieu 1985b, 1987: i. 148; Engelhard and Abdallah 1986: 141). More generally, Keith Hart has remarked that 'the social and material conditions that would compel a laborer to work like an Asian peasant, up to his knees in paddy water . . . do not yet exist in West Africa' (Hart 1982: 88–9). An FAO study came to a similar conclusion when it emphasized recently that under the present circumstances 'labour availability for intensive production under irrigation is likely to remain a serious concern for some time to come in parts of sub-Saharan Africa with little tradition of intensive irrigation' (FAO 1986: Annex IV, ch. 5, para. 5.23). One of the main barriers to the spread of intensive systems of production would lie in the fact that they demand 'more time and cash' than the African farmers have been accustomed to commit to traditional agriculture (ibid. ch. 3, para. 3.8).

A clear indication of the unwillingness of many African farmers to adopt intensive farming practices—as illustrated again by the case of irrigated farming—is provided by the well-documented fact that acceptable commitment of the irrigators has usually been obtained only where few other options existed for them. For example, small- and medium-scale village irrigation schemes in Senegal (along the river Senegal), Mali (along the river Niger), and Burkina Faso (using small dams) have been successful whenever smallholders could no more satisfy their food consumption needs from rainfed or flood-recession farming due to severe drought conditions (ibid. ch. 2, para. 2.40, and ch. 5, para. 5.30; Boutillier 1980: Hart 1982: 89; Mathieu 1983a, 1983b, 1987). In the Soninké villages of Senegal, it has been observed that the cultivators who have shifted most resolutely to irrigated farming are people from lower socio-economic strata (descendants of slaves, sons of artisans, or outsiders) who do not possess any land of their own and can have access to flood-recession lands only on costly terms (Weigel 1982a: 321–3). Revealingly, however, when some alternative opportunities exist to work outside the village, outmigration is often preferred to intensive farming. Thus, the Sarakollé from the Senegal river valley have migrated almost everywhere in West Africa and, not infrequently, they have travelled much longer distances (up to France) to find work. In the same way, many young Mossi (from Burkina Faso) have settled in Ghana and the Ivory Coast. By contrast, the Mafas of northern Cameroon, blocked in their mountains, first by the persecutions of the empires of the Chadian Basin and thereafter by those of the Foulbé sultans, had no other alternative than to intensify their system of production at the cost of tremendous efforts (Giri 1983: 222).

To sum up, in the many parts of Africa where there is practically no tradition of intensive farming (notable exceptions are Northern Africa, Madagascar, Nigeria, and Guinea-Bissau), villagers usually have a strong aversion to the kind of work required by the intensification of agriculture (and stock farming). Cultural prejudices against intensive work—particularly among the elder male members of the village communities—reveal the profound dislike of African farmers for long work hours and toilsome productive tasks carried out on a continuous basis. Therefore, intensive farming tends to be taken up as a last resort when all other income-earning possibilities have been exhausted or have vanished. And, even then, there is a tendency to entrust the 'dirty' work to low-status people, including women. If intensive farming is not perceived as a survival necessity, villagers are likely to prefer more leisure to more income, so high is the disutility associated with intensive work. Young farmers, none the less, do not necessarily react in this way, especially so if the elder members of the village community allow them a sufficient margin of freedom and if the income prospects afforded by intensive farming are reasonably good.

Perverse effects, self-defeating strategies or self-fulfilling prophecies   The above-described situation is typical of a transition period and, as such, it is basically unstable. It is unstable because it is fraught with inner contradictions which

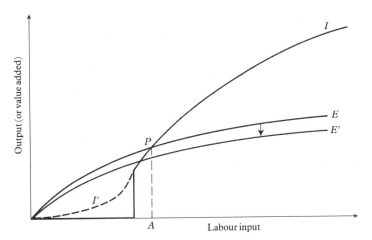

Fig. 10.1 Hypothetical relations between 'extensive' and 'intensive' production curves with certain outcomes

render the results of many intensive enterprises or projects rather unpredictable. As a matter of fact, intensive agriculture is characterized by 'threshold-effects', meaning that if minimum amounts of labour input are not applied (e.g. for gathering and application of fertilizers, for maintenance of land infrastructure), its productive performance is likely to be inferior to that of current extensive farming practices.[30]

This situation is depicted in Fig. 10.1, where labour input is measured along the horizontal axis and agricultural output along the vertical axis. Curve *E* is a production curve which shows the maximum amount of produce that, say, a village can get for each amount of labour input through an expansion in cultivated land area (whether this is achieved via additional deforestation, shortening of the fallow period, or otherwise): following Hayami and Ruttan (1985: 310), we may call this strategy 'external land augmentation'. This curve has a conventional Ricardian shape since its slope is continuously decreasing to reflect diminishing returns to labour as lands of lower fertility are brought under cultivation. As for curve *I*, it is supposed to describe an 'internal land augmentation' strategy in which labour efforts are applied to improved land

[30] Thus, in a modern irrigation scheme (with complete control of water) in Timbuktu (Mali), it was found that in the plots where the technique of broadcast sowing (without recourse to fertilizer) was used, the average yield per hectare was not much higher than that obtained under more traditional farming systems (including flood irrigation systems). But it was much lower than the average yield obtained by those irrigators who applied fertilizers and used the technique of transplantation. Moreover, the variability of yields was much lower in the latter than in the former case in spite of the fact that the control of water was good in both cases. Calculations of net monetary returns per labour input unit confirmed the above differentials (Islands of Peace 1984, 1985, 1986). The lesson to be drawn from this example is straightforward: there is no sense in applying extensive farming practices (broadcast sowing and no application of fertilizer) to land improvement infrastructures designed for intensive farming.

infrastructure and farmers use land-augmenting technologies. Curve I exhibits a discontinuity to reflect the indivisibility referred to above. Or, alternatively, a curve I' may be constructed which is comprised of two phases: a first phase during which output is low but increases quickly as additional labour inputs are applied, and a second, more conventional phase, during which returns to labour are declining. Because of the pressure of population on land, curves I and I' rise above curve E beyond the crossover point P, but if farmers put in less than OA units of labour efforts, the 'internal land augmentation' strategy will be less productive than that of 'external land augmentation'. However, in so far as the latter strategy causes a gradual decline in the fertility of all the existing village lands (e.g. because of increased soil erosion following new encroachments upon the forest lands), the production curve E will shift downward from E to E', thus increasing in due time the relative advantage of intensification for a given amount of labour input and lowering the crossover point beyond which curve I rises above curve E.

From the above conceptualization or 'stylization' of the relations between 'internal' and 'external' land augmentation strategies, it is easy to understand how the transition from extensive to intensive agriculture can be arrested due to the operation of 'perverse' effects. Indeed, if African smallholders are reluctant to devote enough time and efforts to intensive agriculture—because of their perception of the risks and costs of adoption of intensive farming practices (including the disutility associated with toilsome intensive work)[31] —a vicious circle 'low returns—insufficient application of inputs—low returns' may easily develop (Platteau 1985: 96–7). This will result in a kind of 'self-fulfilling prophecy', since the farmers will be able to mention the disappointing results obtained from intensification to vindicate and strengthen their belief that it is not worth the trouble and the drudgery it requires.

The problem is in fact more complicated than is suggested by Fig. 10.1, because outcomes are not certain. It could be argued, therefore, that the reluctance of African smallholders to adopt intensive farming practices arises from the fact that these practices are not only perceived as costly in terms of utility, but also considered to increase vulnerability to risk irrespective of their being new and unfamiliar. In this context, the oft-noted observation that African farmers are unwilling 'to abandon the traditional risk-spreading strategy of a mix of agricultural activities in favour of full-time work on the irrigated plot provided by the government' (FAO 1986: Annex IV, ch. 3, para. 3.8) would appear revealing. Yet, this is not an entirely convincing argument since some intensive agricultural technologies are ostensibly designed to reduce risk (Ghatak and Ingersent 1984: 15). Improved water management in drought- and flood-prone areas is a case in point. In the circumstances, risk aversion on the part of smallholders may not be a valid—or complete

---

[31] Bear in mind that labour input units measured along the horizontal axis in Fig. 10.1 are not 'utility-wise' homogeneous since the disutility associated with 'intensive' labour efforts is much higher than that associated with 'extensive' efforts.

—explanation for their reluctance to shift to intensive farming practices on a full-time basis. Once again, it would appear difficult to account satisfactorily for such behaviour without bringing cultural or non-economic factors into the picture.

It has already been noted (1) that African smallholders often have recourse to full-time irrigated farming only when no other alternative is available, and (2) that they tend to return (or give renewed priority) to rainfed farming as soon as the rain comes back in sufficient quantities, be it within the season itself or during a forthcoming agricultural year. The latter phenomenon has been widely observed in West Africa in the years 1985–6, when Sahelian farmers responded to the return of abundant rains by abandoning the modern irrigation schemes in which they had taken refuge during the drought years. What deserves to be stressed in the context of the present discussion is that this kind of unstable attitude on the part of the producers is likely to reinforce the afore-mentioned 'perverse' effect. Indeed, continuous and unpredictable shifts between rainfed extensive farming and intensive agriculture tend inevitably to thwart labour and other investments in land improvements. Unless public agencies are ready to maintain the new land infrastructures when the peasants are not forthcoming to do the job themselves, or to impose upon the latter a minimum of discipline, the capital which these infrastructures represent will be degraded and its future productive capacity will be inexorably impaired. As a consequence of their self-defeating strategies, farmers will thus be caught in a basically precarious situation since their livelihood will no more be guaranteed in times of unfavourable weather.

In Fig. 10.2, a situation has been described in which intensive farming eventually becomes almost technically inferior to extensive agriculture due to

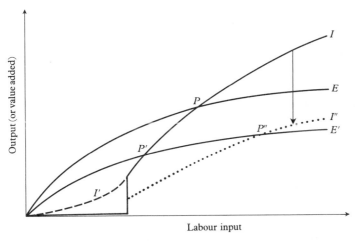

Fig. 10.2 Hypothetical relations between 'extensive' and 'intensive' production curves with uncertain outcomes

severe neglect and lack of maintenance of land improvement infrastructures. Curve E is the production function which obtains under rainfed farming when rainfall is reasonably adequate in terms of both quantity and timing pattern. Curve E' is also a rainfed farming production curve but it is observed when drought conditions prevail. A single intensive farming production function is assumed to obtain under both 'states of the world', reflecting the fact that intensive agriculture is supposed to be potentially both yield-increasing and yield-stabilizing or risk-reducing. The relative advantage of technology I over technology E is therefore greater when drought conditions occur, not only because the distance between the two curves is then larger, but also because the crossover point shifts leftwards (from P to P'). Provided that the disutility associated with intensive work is not too high and that individual preferences are not too skewed in favour of leisure (the marginal rate of substitution of leisure for income is not too high), the farmers would maximize their inter-temporal utility by making a complete shift to intensive agriculture. If this is not the case, however, the risk is high that land improvement infrastructures will not be properly maintained. In Fig. 10.2, such a neglect would be reflected in a downward shift of the intensive production curve from I to I'' and there would be a real possibility that intensive farming practices become less profitable than extensive practices, even under conditions of poor weather (curve I'' is below curve E' over most of the relevant range). Eventually, the interest of the farmers would lie in sticking to their traditional agricultural system!

It is worth noticing, incidentally, that in conditions such as those analysed above, it is very difficult to assess the comparative profitability of intensive and extensive farming practices. In particular, conclusions that irrigation schemes are unprofitable in many parts of Africa ought to be qualified or stated in a less peremptory way than they often are.[32] It is a lesson to be learned that such comparative exercises or cost–benefit analyses are extremely delicate and difficult to interpret in conditions of agricultural transition or rapid technical change.

The myth of the good peasant   The kind of analysis that has been offered here is not much in vogue among development specialists nowadays. Many social scientists consider that one cannot really talk about 'a general cultural bias against labor intensive practices' without implying the 'pejorative view' that

---

[32] It is often suggested that village irrigated agriculture is not (very) rewarding because net monetary income is negative, after having deducted rice for family consumption from the gross produce (Coquery-Vidrovitch 1985: 177; Haubert and Frelin 1985: 27; Mathieu 1985b: 55). But this is no convincing evidence since there is no economic sense in effecting this subtraction to arrive at conclusions about the profitability of this technique. However, what the above evidence shows unambiguously is that the irrigated plots are too narrow to provide for the irrigator's family livelihood and that they are just a supplementary source of income and consumption. In fact, such plots are also a narrow basis for employment as it appears that average weekly work hours on them do not usually exceed a few hours.

African farmers are lazy (see e.g. Berry 1984: 69, 97 n. 4). This is of course a *non sequitur* as all economists acquainted with the subjective theories of peasant equilibrium know very well. However, by insisting that farmers in Third World countries behave so as to maximize their (expected) incomes or profits (after allowing for risk considerations and, possibly, for transaction costs), economists have actually lent credence to the view that values play no role in the choices made by agricultural producers. Moreover, this restricted type of peasant rationality is supposed to hold not only with respect to static allocative decisions but also with respect to innovation and change: farmers are receptive to innovation provided that the changes contemplated are 'appropriate', that is low cost, low risk, and fitting well into the traditional agricultural cycle. This myth of the 'good peasant' which emerged as a (rather healthy) reaction against the long-lived prejudiced view of the irrational peasant is also a reflection, in the field of agrarian economics, of the proclivity of the economic profession to produce complete explanations of individual behaviours on the basis of economic variables alone.

In fact, recognition that peasants may have a strong aversion to labour-intensive practices does not imply that they behave irrationally in the economic sense. This is evident from the fact that such an assumption can be easily accommodated into the neo-classical framework by entering two distinct types of labour (extensive and intensive), in addition to income and leisure, into the peasant's utility function, and by assuming that each type of labour is associated with a different production technique. The disutility of intensive labour may then be so high as to exceed the utility increments associated with the extra incomes resulting from application of intensive technologies (assuming constant leisure).

This said, the central problem is not whether agricultural producers behave rationally when considered individually (according to economic theory, they are rational by assumption), but whether the social outcomes they produce together are desirable when assessed in a long-term perspective. The foregoing analysis purported to show that, if sufficient attention is paid to cultural factors such as the norms, values, and beliefs which shape the individuals' preference orderings or limit the range of feasible strategies, there is a real possibility of rational farmers producing socially disastrous long-term results. To understand this, it must be borne in mind that individual behaviours are influenced by collectively produced cultural patterns that reflect past experiences of people's adaptation to their environment as well as the customary ways in which they have been interpreted and evaluated by the society concerned. In most parts of Africa, these experiences are clearly tied to a long tradition of land-extensive agricultural practices. It is therefore no wonder that local cultures have tended to emphasize the merits of the way of life implied by land-extensive farming systems and to underplay or even deride alternative systems of production and social life.

The problem arises because cultural systems do not adjust instantaneously to marked changes in environmental parameters, in particular to rising pressure of population on land resources. To say this is not to contend that African meaning and agrarian systems are fundamentally conservative or rigid. They are bound to change and they have already started to evolve, particularly under the pressure of new dramatic challenges and under the aegis of young age-classes (for evidence of this, see Pingali and Binswanger 1986). But a transitory period cannot be escaped during which Africa will be relatively handicapped because she is equipped with an *extensive culture* at a time when she must shift to *intensive agriculture*. Such a contradiction underlies the observation made by FAO experts that 'only in a relatively few cases has the fundamental conflict between traditional sub-Saharan attitudes to agriculture and the intensive demands of modern irrigation been satisfactorily resolved' (FAO 1986: Annex IV, ch. 5, para. 5.30). Policy makers as well as intellectuals would do well to reflect on this a little more than they usually do. Indeed, the length of the transition period is not a priori determined and, depending upon the approach to rural education and agricultural extension, this period may be rather short or become dangerously long.

It may also be noted that the so-called common property resource problem, to which economists usually refer to explain why individually rational actions sometimes produce socially harmful effects, cannot be analysed without mentioning cultural factors at some point. Thus, a crucial question which suggests itself is why the traditional modes of resource management and of control of access have ceased to play their customary regulatory role.

Towards a more balanced assessment   Now, much in the same way as it is simplistic to attribute all the woes of Africa to policy mistakes committed by local governments, it would be absurd to ascribe the rigidity of agrarian systems, to the extent that it exists, solely to inappropriate—even though understandable—attitudes on the part of smallholder producers. Cultural factors in general must also be considered to shed only partial light on the problematic shift of Africa from extensive to intensive agriculture. If they were largely brought into focus in the above discussion, it is only because they are systematically downplayed in most analyses of Africa's current food crisis. In such complex matters, single-factor explanations cannot be trustworthy. It is nevertheless evident that a number of causes which are commonly pointed at in the specialized literature can be roughly summarized under one heading: *organizational problems*. These problems usually originate in both the state and the rural communities:

Group action by farmers or public investment by the government is required and in turn demands both leadership and discipline. These qualities cannot be developed immediately as the need arises; such organizational capacity and habit grow in a rural society only over time, perhaps several generations. (Hayami and Ruttan 1985: 312).

With particular reference to irrigation, one can agree with Uma Lele that 'in most of Africa there is not the complex institutional and managerial capacity to operate irrigation systems indigenously' (Lele 1984: 441). Perhaps the most commonly cited problems of organization are those linked with the rationing or the delayed distribution of crucial inputs, such as fertilizers, new seed varieties, credit, or spare parts for transport, irrigation, and production equipment. Difficulties at the level of national economic management and balance-of-payments deficits, absence or imperfection of essential markets (most notably, capital and insurance markets), and inopportune interferences of the state with the development of local markets are all factors to which such deficiencies may be traced back.

The technical challenge posed by the required technological shift must not be underestimated either. For farmers accustomed to extensive farming practices, intensification of agricultural production represents a complete departure from the past:

It is not only a question of mastering the complexities of the numerous cultural operations involved in the new technology: think of the need for a right spacing of the seedlings in the nursery when the transplanting technique is used for rice cultivation; or of the split application of fertilizers at various stages of the vegetative cycle of the plant; or of the need for an adequate drainage in order to prevent salinity. It is also a question of performing efficiently the mechanical tasks (lest the motor pumps would break down or wear out quickly) as well as the management tasks (if the gasoil is not available in the right quantities in the right time, the whole system is disrupted) which are an essential component of the new technologies. (Platteau 1985: 97)

In the case of irrigated farming again, major problems often arise from structural defects in irrigation systems which are clearly the responsibility of state agencies or foreign contractors and consulting bureaux. When systems of water control are not adequate, farmers lose confidence in timely and adequate water arrivals, and they justifiably tend to run away from irrigation schemes.

It is not difficult to understand how the above mishaps, deficiencies, and dysfunctionings can significantly increase the riskiness of—and reduce the motivation for—adoption of intensive farming practices, thus postponing further the time at which Africa will be able to meet adequately her food challenge. But the fundamental fact must be accepted that it will take time to resolve all these problems. An essential lesson from the Asian experience is precisely that considerable periods of social adjustment and institutional development are needed before intensive agriculture (as well as intensive stock-raising and fish farming) can be made to work satisfactorily. The experience of North Africa points to the same conclusion (FAO 1986: Annex IV, ch. 3). It is no doubt true that sub-Saharan Africa can learn and take inspiration from solutions evolved in Asia (see Lipton 1985) and North Africa. Yet, as in the case of new seed varieties, Africa cannot escape the need to go through the lengthy and painful process of learning by doing which solutions suit best her own environmental and social conditions. In the words of Goran Hyden:

governments and donors alike have ignored the narrow margins of survival that
characterize African countries at all levels. Above all, they have failed to adequately
look for African solutions to African problems . . . It is high time, therefore, that the
present crisis in Africa is recognized to a very large extent as the product of human
arrogance and impatience in years past. Africa's problems are not primarily its
backwardness and poverty, but rather the unwillingness of those concerned to accept
that the continent is caught in its own historical process of development . . . They
[African governments] have almost totally ignored the fact that development is a
do-it-yourself process. (Hyden 1986: 53, 65)

(e)   The problematic shift to intensive agriculture: the issue of property rights

The presumed inadequacy of existing land tenure systems   Traditional land tenure
systems are often regarded as a major impediment to the growth of agricultural
output and productivity in Africa. Only a few authors would probably go as far
as Jacques Giri when he says that Africa is in need of a genuine land reform
(Giri 1983: 271).[33] But it may be taken for granted that most of them would
agree with Eicher that 'land tenure and land use policy issues will be of strategic
importance in the 1980s and 1990s as the frontier phase is exhausted, land
markets emerge, irrigation is expanded, and herders shift from nomadic to
seminomadic herding and sedentary farming systems that integrate crops and
livestock' (Eicher 1984: 455-6).

   The main thrust of the argument could be formulated as follows: there is a
fundamental disequilibrium or misfit between existing land arrangements that
reflect a long tradition of extensive farming practices and the requirements of
growth in the context of intensive agriculture. More precisely, communal
control over access to land and the absence of active rural land markets are
supposed to discourage investment in land improvements, careful soil husbandry practices, and intense and continuous labour efforts. As a matter of
fact, there appear to be two rather distinct theses in this argument which are
not always clearly distinguished by their proponents. Both are nevertheless
well-known views commonly expounded in the literature about contractual
choice, property rights, and transaction costs (see e.g. Demsetz 1967; Williamson 1985; Binswanger and Rosenzweig 1986).

   The first thesis assumes the existence of communal tenure (or arrangements
allowing multiple interests in a given piece of land) and considers it to be a
major disincentive to labour and investment efforts and to conservation
practices because decision-making is diffused among many persons (management problem); because the risk of labour-shirking or asset mismanagement is
comparatively high while the cost of controlling it is also substantial (transaction cost problem); and because the effectiveness of sharing incentives is low,
especially if the produce has to be distributed in accordance with social rules or
norms (incentive problem). Of course, all these difficulties are assumed to be

---

[33] Thus, for example, Keith Hart wrote that 'land reform is not a significant issue in West
Africa, but reform of the land law is' (Hart 1982: 92).

greater as the size of the social unit in which land rights are vested increases.

Thus, attention has often been drawn to serious deficiencies in land husbandry and conservation measures that result from the open access nature of many African lands:

Communal and allocated lands are frequently abused because neither farmers nor graziers feel any responsibility for their conservation. To the farmer there is little to be gained from constructing conservation ditches if they are to be trampled by another's cattle when farms are open to communal grazing after harvest. In some rangeland areas it often pays the herder to over-use the forage; if he does not, someone else will and he will be the loser. (FAO 1986: Annex II, ch. 9, para. 9.22; see also Platteau 1985: 98; FAO 1986: Main Report, ch. 4, para. 4.89)

It is interesting to note that the above problem—usually referred to as the 'common-property resource problem' or 'the tragedy of the commons'—would not arise if land was available in plenty and/or if the internal solidarity or the authority structure in the group controlling the land was strong enough to enforce adequate management rules. As we know, the first condition ceased to characterize most parts of Africa only recently due to increasing pressure of population on land resources. Violation of the second condition—i.e. the existence of effective social structures that discourage opportunistic behaviour on the part of their members—is the result of several complex factors such as commercialization of agriculture, large incidence of migration, interventions from state systems of bureaucratic control, redefinition of social rules of access to productive resources under the impact of colonialism and post-independence national policies, and so forth. It is also true, however, that the two conditions are narrowly interrelated since opportunities of conflicts over land-use rights increase considerably when land becomes scarce, and they may thereby undermine or thwart the conflict-management capacity of traditional social systems.

The second and main criticism of communal tenure clearly assumes a system of individualized occupancy: land is held and controlled by a social group which allocates it to individual households for their personal use. Here, the crux of the argument is that traditional systems of communal tenure in Africa do not provide security of tenure. As a result of this insecurity, farmers are reluctant to invest in physical capital and to adopt innovations that would increase the value of their land for fear that the benefits would be appropriated by other persons and would not accrue to their own children (see e.g. Christodoulu 1966; Dorner 1972; Cohen 1980: 353–5; Giri 1983: 270–1; Bachelet 1986: 154). Without ensuring the security of smallholders' rights of access to land, the 'accretionary type of capital formation whereby family labor improves land productivity and the productivity of livestock herds over generations' will not occur in Africa as it did in other parts of the world (Eicher 1985: 88). Moreover, under communal tenure systems, land cannot be used as a collateral to raise credit and the occupier's ability to invest is correspondingly restricted (Cohen 1980: 354–5; Noronha 1985: 189–90; FAO 1986: Main Report, ch. 4, para. 4.90). Communal control over access to land is therefore seen as a factor that limits both the willingness and the ability of smallholders to undertake long-term investments in physical equipment and land improvements. Finally, corporate tenure is held to block the flexibility in land use that is considered essential for a dynamic farming sector. In a nutshell, the idea is that land cannot be efficiently used unless it is 'commoditized', that is unless it is transformed into a fully marketable asset (Cohen 1980: 354–5).

The view that existing arrangements with respect to control of, and access to, land resources in Africa are a major factor inhibiting the growth of agricultural output and land productivity is very appealing because it appears to be grounded on commonsense arguments. In fact, as we shall see below, the criticism of communal tenure systems can offer fruitful insights into Africa's disappointing performance of food production only if it is qualified and amended in several important senses. In substance, the main idea that will be developed below is that in many African countries today, the debate over whether to grant formal or customary land titles has become much more critical than the assessment of the relative merits of communal and individual tenure systems.[34]

Inadequacy of African agrarian systems: a critique of the conventional view   To start with, there are three important facts that are clearly neglected by the critics of traditional communal tenure in Africa. First, these critics have partly misunderstood the systems of land-use rights they were evaluating. In effect, security of tenure under such systems is often greater than they seem to believe (Cohen 1980: 360; Noronha 1985: 181–95; FAO 1986: Main Report, ch. 4, para. 4.87). It is no doubt true that possession of land under communal tenure is neither exclusive nor definite. Possession of land is personal and statutory, since only someone considered to be a member of the relevant social group is entitled to a portion of the communal resources. However, except in extreme circumstances (as in the case of open conflict with customary chiefs or headmen), the allottee's right of access is safeguarded as long as he keeps cultivating the land.[35] Moreover, the heirs would normally be given the lands that were cultivated at the time of the death of the allottee, even though their rights do not generally extend to lands which had been cultivated by the same but were under fallow when he died. Finally, land can be exchanged, loaned, or gifted (or even pledged) among members of the same landholding group, whereas transfers of land outside the group are subject to strict approval of the

---

[34] While writing this section, I drew much inspiration from a long review paper by Raymond Noronha (1985). Since then, however, I have elaborated the ideas presented here in a more original fashion (see Platteau forthcoming).

[35] This has two obvious implications: (1) the allottee does not have the freedom or the right to decide whether or not to use the land allocated to him; and (2) land in surplus of his requirements can be taken away from him by the customary land authorities.

village chief or the earth priest. In the light of the above, the right of a cultivator under traditional African communal systems cannot be termed a usufructuary right: the scope of the former is obviously larger than that of the latter (Noronha 1985: 195).

It is also evident that when the critics of communal tenure consider that the practice of shifting cultivation leads to insecurity of possession, they are guilty of confusing a system of land usage with title. Indeed, what is then being criticized 'is not so much land law as a form of land usage' since shifting cultivation 'reflects a relative abundance of land and a relative poverty of soils as well as minimal use of other inputs' (ibid. 192). Of course, the point remains essentially correct that land laws corresponding to extensive land usage are not appropriate for the kind of intensive farming practices that are so urgently required in Africa today. It must however be admitted that, contrary to what is suggested by the critics of communal tenure, individual tenures can exist under a system of communal tenure. Garden lands offer a good illustration of this possibility since they 'were always deemed to belong to the family that cultivated them' and did not fall under the scope of the general rules of land allotment and control (ibid. 186–7, 193). Interestingly, especially in areas of high population densities, these lands were usually well settled (possibly terraced or even irrigated) and subject to continuous cultivation thanks to regular application of vegetal manure and careful soil husbandry practices (see e.g. Raynaut 1976: 287–8 and Dupriez 1980: ch. 9).

This takes me to the second, and more important, weakness of the conventional view that communal tenure is a barrier to agricultural growth and investment in Africa. This weakness originates in a clear underestimation of the flexibility and adaptation capacity of traditional African land arrangements. As a matter of fact, there is much evidence to show that the mounting pressure of population and the increasing commercialization of agriculture, particularly since colonial times, have given rise to gradual but meaningful changes in land tenure arrangements in the direction of increased individualization of tenure and growing incidence of land transactions. As noted by John Cohen, 'corporate-tenure land is much less static and inalienable than the ideal model and Western logic lead one to believe' (Cohen 1980: 361).

Apparently, even before the advent of colonialism, exclusive appropriation of land and land sales did occur in some places even though they were strongly prohibited by customary law. What is worth noting, in this respect, is the fact that those 'illegal' practices seem to have mainly taken place in areas where land was becoming increasingly scarce (Boutillier 1963: 116–18; Raynaut 1976). Thus, we are told that, among the Hausas of Niger,

There is no doubt that, even before the arrival of the Europeans, private appropriation and sales of land parcels could occur in areas where population was heavily concentrated, and where land was scarce and subject to intensive farming practices. However, during the expansion period, when large areas of cultivable lands became available again, less clear-cut and more unstable land relations re-emerged. Those fluctuations were more the effect of pragmatic adjustments to evolving environmental conditions than manifestations of profound changes in the people's cultural patterns. (Raynaut 1976: 288—my translation)

The process of individualization of tenure titles has received a decisive impetus—or, in most cases, has been initiated—under the combined effect of population growth, the development of communications, the rise of markets, the adoption of new plants, and the increasing incidence of taxes[36] which characterized the colonial period. From his detailed survey of the existing literature on the subject, Raymond Noronha has concluded that 'the history of tenure during the colonial regime shows a gradual emphasis on individual (or family) appropriation of land for its own use', as well as a growing potential for land sales to non-members of the group following marked increases in land values (Noronha 1985: 105; see also Berry 1980; Pingali and Binswanger 1986). The traditional image of Africa as a 'seemingly changeless society ruled by legislation that only countenanced "communal" tenure' now appears to be a stereotype that cannot even stand the facts pertaining to colonial times (Noronha 1985: 78). The results of the pioneering study of Ghanaian cocoa-farmers by Poly Hill have thus been amply confirmed (Hill 1963). In particular, it is interesting to note that many cash crop growers opted for migration with the main purpose of escaping from the social control of their native village and from their social duty to share the newly earned income. In the new area, on the other hand, the rules of communal tenure could not be applied since there was no group to enforce them (ibid. and Noronha 1985: 79). When the growing of new tree crops was undertaken in the native area itself, customary principles of access to land were adjusted to allow for the new circumstances. As explained by Noronha: 'Now the customary rules of tenure provide that the field is "occupied" when crops are grown', and since trees are crops, as long as they are standing on the field, the field is considered to be 'occupied' (Noronha 1985: 78).

Land sales increased during the colonial period. However, as they were in open violation of customary land laws, they were often disguised under the form of traditional land exchanges or gifts. Moreover, the practice of land pledging began to spread and, apparently, not a few lands changed hands through land foreclosure (Raynaut 1976: 284–5; Coquery-Vidrovitch 1982: 66–71). Finally, it is worth remarking that adaptations of land tenure arrangements were not the only changes generated by the newly emerging socio-economic conditions. Indeed, changes in the patterns of inheritance also

---

[36] Thus, in the already quoted study of a Hausa community in Niger, Claude Raynaut has shown how the increasing burden of taxes led household heads to abdicate their fiscal responsibility for the entire group of their dependants. As a result, junior members of the extended family system began to neglect work on the collective fields and to devote more time to their own, individually controlled, fields (or to wage employment). The collective fields were then subdivided among them and they became personally entitled to the whole produce obtained from these 'individualized' plots of land (Raynaut 1976: 282–3).

occurred (as in Ghana between the two world wars) which usually consisted of a shift from matrilineal to patrilineal inheritance. This shift can be easily understood once it is realized that matrilineal succession loosens the nuclear family solidarity (since property is inherited by persons outside the nuclear family) while, on the contrary, patrilineal succession ensures that the fruits of family labour, investment, and risk-taking will accrue to the children of the deceased father (Noronha 1985: 98–9 and Coquery-Vidrovitch 1985: 155).

It seems ironic that in some cases resistance to change in the traditional system of land rights was offered by the government of the colonial power (that is the 'putative agency of capitalist expansion') against the pressures from members of the indigenous agrarian societies (Coquery-Vidrovitch 1982: 71–80; Bates 1984: 242–8). Thus, in parts of West Africa, in Zambia, and in Kenya, the policy of the colonial government actually promoted tribalism by forbidding any registering of individual titles of land ownership and sale transactions of land. According to Bates, the form of property law encouraged by the colonial powers 'was shaped by the desire of the colonial state for political domination of an agrarian population and by the nature of the political accommodations it had to make in order to secure its hegemony' (Bates 1984: 248). In Kenya and Zambia, two territories where the institution of chieftaincy was non-existent, the British colonial authorities promoted the establishment or the preservation of communal property rights as part of their effort 'to elaborate systems of rural political control over an agrarian population'. This was done by (creating and) empowering local chiefs loyal to the colonial power to allocate the key resource in an agrarian economy according to their own will. In Kenya, interestingly, the demand for enforcement of private rights to land was pressed all the more urgently by the Kikuyu as they felt increasingly insecure 'in the face of the uncompensated seizure of lands by the colonialists'. None the less, in other areas where the colonial authority was not reliant upon the creation of rural élites, the situation was different and the agrarian policies it followed often tilted towards commercialization of land rights or extreme forms of 'Junkerization' of landed relations (ibid. 244–7).

Post-independence Africa has been characterized by the many attempts of national states to pass land laws that would be in accordance with the socio-political philosophy of the ruling regimes. In this respect, Africa has shown considerable diversity and the only common denominator behind all these attempts is the apparent difficulty 'to categorize any nation as falling entirely into the "individual tenure" or "communal tenure" camp' (Noronha 1985: 107). Revealingly, however, the trends initiated during the colonial period—individualization of tenure and increased land transactions—continued unabated in most countries 'despite legislative intervention generally, though at times taking advantage of legislative enactments' (ibid. 108). In the words of John Harbeson: 'patterns of land tenure, insofar as they have changed markedly, appear to have evolved less in response to specific governmental policy initiatives than as a result of, and in conjunction with broader patterns of socio-economic change' (quoted from Noronha 1985: 135; see also Cohen 1980: 356; Mathieu 1985a; Hesseling and Mathieu 1986: 317).

In fact, the movement towards increasing individualization of land tenure, increasing freedom from interference by customary land authorities (as attested by the growing number of sales without permission), and increasing incidence of patrilineal modes of land transmission has accelerated during the last decades as land availability became a more and more acute problem and as opportunities of market involvement multiplied in many African countries. A gradual process of 'wresting of lands from lineage, to sub-lineage, then to extended family, and, finally, to the nuclear family' (Noronha 1985: 184; see also Raynaut 1983: 92) is under way almost everywhere, even though the methods through which it works itself out may vary significantly from country to country depending upon the state laws, the posture of the administration, and other exogenous factors. What Raynaut has said about Niger could be easily extended to most other areas where land has become a scarce factor:

Land possession takes on an increasingly private character, the sharing of family property between the sons becomes the rule, the land is increasingly parcelled out, and land use rights as well as the control of the land are increasingly transferred through other methods than inheritance. (Raynaut 1976: 284—my translation)

A third source of dissatisfaction with current criticism of communal tenure in Africa lies in the fact that group titles to land or communal resource exploitation are deemed to be a priori, and sometimes dogmatically, less efficient—that is, apparently, less conducive to growth of land productivity —than private property rights and family management. To enter into a detailed discussion of this problem is clearly beyond the scope of this chapter. But two points are worth making with a view to calling into question drastic statements of the above kind.[37] First, as has already been pointed out with respect to the 'tragedy of the commons' (see above, p. 519), inefficient collective management of productive resources may arise not only from maladjustment to changing environmental conditions (declining land–population ratios), but also from dissolution of solidarity structure or erosion of authority patterns in traditional landholding groups. Clearly, there are activities subject to externalities, indivisibilities, and scale economies, such as livestock management and irrigated farming in modern irrigation schemes. And the experience of Africa so far does not show unambiguously that private or state management is systematically superior to traditional forms of group management. Thus, for instance, management of watering points has probably never been as efficient—in a long-run perspective—than when these points were the property and the responsibility of well-defined social groups (Leonard 1986: 202). In some cases, it may therefore be wiser to revive or to support such groups than to interfere with their normal functioning by superimposing new structures upon them (Putterman 1985).

[37] For a more theoretical discussion, see in particular Bonin and Putterman (1987).

Second, success stories of communal property and collective management are not rare in Africa, but the informal character of the social group and its relative freedom from inopportune state interventions seem to be important conditions of success. An illustration is provided by the case of Serahuli kinsmen who 'pool their savings to purchase heavy agricultural equipment from the state and have recently begun to grow rice on large, mechanized, irrigated farms worked by labor mobilized within corporate kin groups of up to one hundred or more persons' (Berry 1984: 84; for other examples, see Robertson 1987: 62–63; Diemer and van der Laan 1987; von Braun and Webb 1989). Note in passing that such forms of traditional partnership are not necessarily democratic, since they are bound to reflect the internal inequalities of African village societies.[38] In the light of such experiences, it is difficult to accept uncritically the view that the emergence of innovators and progressive rural entrepreneurs is hampered by corporate patterns of land use.

Land tenure systems as impediment to agricultural growth: the real issue   From the above discussion, the impression could be gathered that existing land tenure systems do not pose major problems in Africa since, thanks to their inner flexibility, they gradually adapt to the changing circumstances. To rising land pressure and increasing commercialization of agriculture, African land tenure systems respond by shifting from communal to individual tenure arrangements in which farmers have more incentive to intensify their labour efforts and to undertake investments in land improvement. This is however a grossly simplified view of the process of agrarian evolution at present under way in Africa. An analysis which is so obviously grounded on a mechanicist evolutionist interpretation of human and societal processes can hardly be convincing. Land systems cannot be expected to adjust automatically and harmoniously to satisfy the evolving functional needs of agricultural development and population growth. Historical processes of transition are always characterized by tensions arising from the clashing of contradictory forces. The outcome is necessarily influenced by the way in which the political power—crystallizing the existing class structure of the society—has decided to deal (or to refrain from dealing) with the newly emerging situation, and by the relative bargaining power of the social groups/classes that have an interest in maintaining or breaking the status quo. That agrarian systems can resist pressure for change is evident from the afore-mentioned and currently observed fact that farmers may have to leave their native village and escape from the indigenous system of socio-political control to be able to respond to new challenges and opportunities as they like (see e.g. Geschiere 1984: 18). How far the established power structure will go to meet the new demands will depend upon numerous factors—among which its own interest in the change always comes foremost —and cannot be predicted a priori and mechanically. The following example

---

[38] These inequalities are inherited from the long pre-colonial history of African village settlements and/or they have developed or have been accentuated during the colonial period.

shows clearly that, as in the case of attitudes *vis-à-vis* new agricultural technologies and farming practices, adjustments in land tenure arrangements can never be considered to proceed smoothly and instantaneously:

In sub-Saharan Africa much land for traditional uncontrolled flood irrigation is still allocated on a seasonal basis by community leaders according to ancient custom. Land access for fixed, more intensive forms of irrigation, especially vegetables production, has however been subject to the same trends which have affected land access for the rainfed cultivator. Due to population pressure and commercialization of agriculture, individuals have increasingly *attempted* to claim long-term rights of occupation or personal ownership. (FAO 1986: Annex IV, ch. 4, para. 4.55)

The transition process will be all the more unstable if the new *de facto* emerging rights of access to land are not properly guaranteed, say, because there is a clash or a discrepancy between formal legislation and customary land rights. We have seen how a system of individual property tends to develop over a factor when this factor becomes scarce. But this is not the whole story since, concomitantly, there are likely to be numerous conflicts—actual or potential —with respect to the control and the use of the scarce factor. If such conflicts are not settled in a clear-cut and definite fashion, insecurity over land rights develops which is highly detrimental to investment efforts and, as will be explained below, wasteful of non-land resources as well. In extreme cases, a situation in which communal tenure rights are well established could be more conducive to agricultural growth and investment than another in which individual tenure expands in a quick and anarchic way.

In Africa, unfortunately, many insecurities presently exist because the land laws passed by many governments are ambivalent, confusing, inconsistent, inapplicable, or badly applied. As a result, access to and control of the lands take place 'within a framework of conflicting legal and political principles and practices' (Berry 1984: 92). As Hart noted with respect to West Africa, 'a confusing and conflict-ridden situation has been loosely organized through the erection of a dual system of "traditional" chiefs and law courts' (Hart 1982: 91; see also Mathieu 1983a, 1985a). After a detailed survey of national land policies in a large number of African countries since independence, Noronha has reached a similar conclusion: the insecurity of possession and use of the land 'arises when the "law" is in a state of transition and the individual can then take advantage of two systems: the customary rule that recognizes the right to possession so long as land is being cultivated, and the formal law which will grant individual tenure' (Noronha 1985: 207; see also Marty 1985: ii. 794).

Of course, as the same study shows (Noronha 1985: 107–50), the situation varies a lot from one country to another. There are countries—such as Rwanda, Swaziland, and Tanzania—where confusion about use and possession of land is almost total due to the 'provisional' character of land laws enacted by the state, to frequent legislative changes, to non-implementation of stated policies or legislation, to inconsistent official statements, etc. In numerous countries—such as Nigeria, Uganda, Zaïre, Kenya, Zambia, and Liberia —long delays are needed until land titles are established, a result which must be attributed to complex procedures of bureaucratic control that tend to breed fraudulent practices. In Liberia, Zambia, and Zaïre, access to land and land transactions are subject to the approval of numerous layers of the administration and the government before the decision is confirmed or denied by the President himself (Hart 1982: 91; Masaki 1987: 93–7). In still other countries —such as Senegal, the Ivory Coast, Lesotho, Cameroon, and Zaïre again—the main insecurity lies in the power of the state to requisition lands for public purposes, to acquire lands with a view to leasing them to agribusiness firms, or to seize them 'in order to fight speculation'. For another thing, there are numerous countries—such as Malawi, Botswana, Kenya, Zaïre, Sudan, Lesotho, Burkina Faso—in which powers of land allocation have been formally transferred from customary authorities to the administration, but where earth priests, headmen, and other traditional land allocators remain in fact powerful. Conversely, some countries have opted for vesting customary village authorities (Ghana, Mauritania, Mali, Guinea-Bissau, Sierra Leone), or Rural Councils representative of both the traditional and the modern worlds (Senegal, Mali), with considerable prerogatives in land matters. There, the main risk is that continuous interferences by state officials or managers of parastatals (like those of the SAED in Senegal) deprive the local bodies or authorities from any genuine autonomy (Mathieu 1985a, 1987).

The costs of uncertainties of land rights   In spite of all the above variations, the general picture remains that of countries in which 'formal law has penetrated the rural areas only partially' (Noronha 1985: 143), and the superimposition of a new system of land rights has created serious uncertainties about the application of indigenous rules. The indigenous system of land tenure, despite all its flexibility, loses its effectiveness, particularly in those areas where competition for land is stiff and land has gained commercial value. As a consequence, land disputes have become more and more frequent. The pattern they follow appears 'fairly consistent': first, they arise about 'tribal' boundaries and, somewhat later, about intervillage boundaries; thereafter, they are increasingly concerned with family land boundaries and, finally, they tend to multiply within the (extended) families themselves (ibid. 212). Now, a situation characterized by continuing uncertainty about the effectiveness of land titles and the validity of land claims is bound to inhibit agricultural growth (and even general economic growth). The first way in which this can happen has already been pointed out: since their ability to forecast is greatly impaired by current insecurities regarding the exact nature of their rights, landholders are deterred from making decisions about long-term investments in land improvements. Accumulation of productive capital for development of intensive agriculture is therefore held in check.

Transaction costs are a second kind of social cost arising from ambivalent situations with respect to land titles. They are *ex post costs* when claimants have to waste time and money in long litigation procedures.[39] And they are *ex ante costs* when, through a variety of strategies, people try to insure themselves against the risks generated by the existence of a dual system of land laws.[40] Such strategies may be very costly indeed, from an individual as well as from a social standpoint. Moreover, the greater the insecurities, the higher the premiums people are willing to pay in order to control the above risks. Thus, for example,

It is the fear of expropriation by Government that makes the cultivator in Ivory Coast plant more coffee and cocoa, with very wide spacing, so that the returns are 'inefficient' and the ten hectares planted produce what could have been obtained from three hectares of close-spaced trees. The cultivator is afraid of the lands being acquired and future generations suffering from land shortages (Noronha 1985: 208).

Likewise, it is only for the sake of protecting their customary rights of access to the river Senegal that Peul herders have taken to irrigated farming in the valley near St Louis. In a revealing way, the work on small-scale irrigation schemes has been entrusted to old members of the community who do not take this occupation very seriously. By contrast, the young Peuls continue to devote all their time and efforts to traditional pastoral activities to which they attach overriding importance in spite of low returns (Mathieu 1987: i. 200; see also Le Bris *et al.* 1982: 193).

There are also countless cases where absentee owners living in cities cling to their rural lands in the expectation that they will turn into a useful productive asset, or that land transactions will become (or remain) difficult or costly in the future (or that land value will increase). Such a strategy entails *private* costs: the owners see to it that their lands appear to yield something—even if it is at a loss—lest the rightfulness of their claims to them should be questioned by the land authorities. But *social* costs are also clearly involved in so far as a scarce resource is used in a wasteful way.

Substantial costs—for both the individual and the society—may arise from more 'political' strategies too. Although costly, these strategies may be effective when property rights are 'politicized rather than privatized' (Berry 1984: 92) and when, through the newly established land control system, politicians and bureaucrats are given considerable power of patronage. The latter possibility is all the more easily encountered as, in Africa, there is no respect of 'universalistic civil service norms' within the bureaucracy. According to Brett, the African civil servant cannot be expected to act as a disinterested servant of the state since, being confronted with numerous and urgent demands for assistance, it is inevitable that his decisions come to be powerfully influenced

[39] Note that, almost everywhere in Africa, customary land tribunals have lost the right to settle land disputes (at least in theory).

[40] The distinction between *ex ante* and *ex post* transaction costs was first introduced by Oliver Williamson (1985).

by personal and other sectional interests, as well as by particular considerations and material advantages (Brett 1986: 26–7). In Africa, moreover, there are narrow links between the state bureaucracy and the rural élites—whether old or new—if only because African civil servants were typically recruited from a society of rural small-scale producers and retained their control over productive resources in their native village. 'Being placed in direct control of the resources to be provided by the state to direct producers,' writes Brett, 'it was inevitable that these should be used to extend their own private economic power and that of their kinship network' (ibid. 26; see also Hyden 1986: 57; Bienen 1987: 300–2).

It is in the above context that the strategies of 'politicized but unproductive accumulation' highlighted by Berry, and called 'politics of affection' by Hyden, must be understood (Berry 1984: 89–96; Hyden 1986: 57–63). In substance, the idea is that people have to invest heavily in loyalty and patronage relations in order to gain access to—and retain control of—productive resources, land in particular. The acquisition of resources and the defence of property rights are therefore largely pre-conditioned on 'membership in various social groups or institutions, ranging from the family to the state' (Berry 1984: 91; see also Putterman 1985: 185; Hyden 1986: 62; Mathieu 1987; Bayart 1989). In many countries (e.g. Senegal and the Ivory Coast), the ruling party is actually tied to rural areas 'through a client system that operates via ethnic and factional channels' (Bienen 1987: 302). Group-based modes of access to land and other productive resources thus prevent the farmers from becoming too independent from rural networks of social relations and political power. This is all the more so as loyalty and patronage are 'often associated with ascriptive forms of status or social identity', even though they 'do not flow automatically from them' (Berry 1984: 91). Bear in mind, however, that 'groups of access' are not, strictly speaking, traditional structures or institutions. Most of them, like the Rural Councils in Senegal or the village 'tons' in Mali, are mixed institutions in which elements of the old élites (headmen, councils of 'notables', earth priests, etc.) sit side by side with members of the new élite (members of the trading, business, professional, or military classes) and representatives of the administration and the government.

It is true, as has already been mentioned, that villagers always have the possibility of cutting off their costly socio-political ties with their native area through permanent outmigration. Nevertheless, for the reasons explained above, this is a very risky strategy which may work only under special sets of circumstances (e.g. when freely accessible land does still exist in other, land-abundant, areas). In this respect, it is revealing (1) that most migratory movements in Africa are apparently 'tied migrations' which have been decided or approved by the (extended) family or the kin-group; and (2) that most individual migrants are young people, that is persons belonging to a dependent and low-status social group in the traditional village communities of Africa.

The need for formal registration of land rights   From the foregoing analysis, it is evident that large amounts of resources are spent in gaining and protecting access to land. The mechanisms of access which have been outlined are socially wasteful since these resources are no more available for investment in increasing land productivity. Berry is therefore right when she says that 'more stable or less contentious conditions of access and adjudication of rights to productive resources' must be established to ensure future growth of agricultural production capacity in Africa (1984: 96). National and formal registration of land titles—which need not necessarily be private titles—is clearly a step in that direction. The case for introduction of such a system has been cogently argued by Noronha:

The need for land titling (and registration) arises when there are growing uncertainties about the application and effectiveness of indigenous systems to control land transactions. This takes place most often when there are dual systems of control both of which cover land transactions, areas of uncertainty between the two systems, growing land values and pressures on land, and the potential use of land for commercial gain. (Noronha 1985: 220)

This said, an important problem arises from the fact that adjudication and registration of land rights are complex and expensive operations for which many African states are ill prepared or ill equipped. As a matter of principle, they should not be undertaken when the expected social benefits (or reduction in social costs) are smaller than the likely administrative costs. Thus, it may be taken for granted that nation-wide registration and formalization of land titles are not justified in areas where land is abundant and/or has no commercial value, where land transactions and land disputes are few or non-existent, and where other markets are absent or poorly developed (ibid. 215–17, 220).

In a context of stiff competition for land, the security afforded by the traditional system of land control can no longer be relied upon to allocate land and to settle land disputes. A modern system of nation-wide registration and land-titling ought therefore to be substituted for the customary laws and practices. Such a conclusion might be strongly opposed by some authors on the ground that the latter system is more conducive to equality than the former, and that considerations of equity should have precedence over those of efficiency. Unfortunately, even if we agree with the second part of the statement, there is no sufficient reason to change the above-reached conclusion because the first part is seriously open to doubt. We know today that pre-colonial village communities of Africa were not exempt from various sources of socio-economic differentiation (see e.g. Boutillier 1963; Minvielle 1977; Coquery-Vidrovitch 1982; Weigel 1982b; Raynaut 1983; Robertson 1987; Bayart 1989: 159–73). What needs to be especially emphasized here is that, under the combined effect of increasing land pressure and commercialization of agriculture, traditional inequalities have been exacerbated, even in areas where customary rules of communal tenure still apply. Landlessness has increased because ancient village communities have tried to protect their rights of access to available land by imposing more and more stringent conditions of membership upon 'outsiders' (in order to deny them such access, or to drive them into marginal land areas). And processes of socio-economic differentiation have started off or accelerated precisely because customary authorities, like village chiefs and earth priests, have often exploited their privileged position of land-controller to promote their own interests whenever opportunities existed to do so. There is in fact considerable evidence to show that, thanks to their association with members of the new élite, the modern bureaucratic state, the international business community, and foreign aid projects, they have been able to confirm their élite status and to increase their material wealth (Cohen 1980: 357; Mathieu 1985a, 1987; Noronha 1985: 143–4, 203–6; Pingali and Binswanger 1986: 26; Hesseling and Mathieu 1986: 315).

Analysis of income distribution effects of politicized accumulation strategies has led Berry to a similar conclusion: group-based modes of access to productive resources 'have not necessarily served to redistribute income in an egalitarian manner, nor to provide security to the venturesome or to the poor and dependent' (Berry 1984: 94). In view of the above facts, one can strongly doubt that the interests of the poor and the weak would be better protected by divesting the state of all land allocation and adjudication prerogatives and by entrusting them to customary institutions dominated by members of both the old and the new élites.

A final remark is in order if we are to avoid a confusion of issues. To say that property or possession rights in land must be made secure and registered through formal/legal procedures is not at all equivalent to saying that a land market in which private titles to land are freely exchanged ought to be established. In fact, a good case can be made that, given the crucial importance of land assets in countries where most people depend on land for their livelihood, any private land market should be strongly regulated by the state. In the circumstances, indeed, free market transactions can easily lead to processes of land concentration in the hands of the élite and to the concomitant rise of a class of landless people. The important point is, however, that the same undesirable effects are likely to result from the free operation of customary systems of land tenure. As has been contended above, observation of current land situations in many parts of Africa suggests that this perversion of traditional land practices is a possibility that has to be considered very seriously. Therefore, in a context of increasing land scarcity, it is essential that the state takes upon itself the task of regulating the access to available lands and guaranteeing land titles with a view to avoiding all the efficiency and equity costs of non-intervention. Experiences of countries like Taiwan and South Korea show that regulation of the land market so as to protect the rights of smallholders can be effective in holding disequalizing tendencies in check (see e.g. Lee 1979). Moreover, in the case of these two countries, this result does not appear to have entailed substantial efficiency costs compared with a free land market situation.

As I have dealt at great length with this issue elsewhere (Platteau forthcoming), I will not probe further into it here. Suffice it to add that a strategy of control of land market forces does not necessarily imply that customary authorities ought to be divested of all their traditional prerogatives. As has been rightly emphasized by Coquery-Vidrovitch (1982: 83), any African state will be well advised to use the flexibility and adaptive power of indigenous land laws or practices in the design of its 'modern' land policy.

(f) Political instability and authoritarianism in the approach to rural development

The fragility of African states   In section 10.4*d* above, attention was drawn to some institutional or organizational barriers to agricultural growth in Africa. Probably one of the main lessons which can be learned from the Asian and the Western experiences is that intensive agriculture and rural infrastructures (technical, economic, social, and cultural) cannot be developed very far unless local farmer organizations and decentralized forms of peoples' associations emerge to mobilize communal labour and to take on-the-spot initiatives. Asian experience also teaches us that when the structure of the government is too centralized and too despotic (as in Korea during the Yi dynasty), or when the political situation is too unstable (as in north China when village communities were invaded by the northern tribes), the afore-mentioned developments are dangerously slowed down or blocked altogether. These two kinds of adverse circumstances are frequently encountered in Africa, and this helps explain why rural development and agricultural growth do not proceed at the pace desired.

Political instability, to begin with, is a recurrent feature of the African scene. In most countries, indeed, the state is a relatively new and fragile institution which is continuously threatened with military coups, social turmoils, and ethnic secessions (Hart 1982: 102–5; Leonard 1986: 205). Theodore Mars goes as far as saying that in Africa 'power when examined turns out to be a description of the lack of the existence of an institutional framework for political relationships' (Mars 1986: 17). This is not, however, a correct appreciation of the nature of the state in Africa. Jean-François Bayart (1989) has recently offered us a much more subtle analysis of the African state. According to him, African political systems are in the process of being made: it is even a striking feature of the societies in the south of Sahara that they are able to produce important institutional or administrative innovations which are described as processes of 'creolization' or 'political interbreeding'. The fact that the political construct resulting from these innovations looks very different from the classic Weberian state explains why so many Western observers are misled into thinking that African societies are undergoing a process of political decay or that Africa is a political vacuum (Bayart 1989: 296–300).

This said, it is hard to deny that most sub-Saharan African countries still have a long way to go before achieving a reasonable degree of national integration (see, e.g. Sandbrook 1986). It is therefore no wonder that 'obedience has to be extracted by the threat of force or the inducement of personal advantage', instead of being 'unproblematically extended' because those who obey feel morally inclined to do so (Mars 1986: 17). It is thus revealing that 'only thrice in post-colonial African history has a change of incumbents come about through the electoral processes'. Moreover, 'since 1966, 40 to 50 per cent of the regimes in the continent have been military in origin and in states not under military rule, intervention by the security forces remains a tangible threat' (Young 1986: 37, 41). In Africa, the military coup has become an institutionalized 'vehicle for ruler displacement', a feature which came to dominate the African political scene when it became clear that 'political monopolies guaranteeing incumbents indefinite prolongation of their mandates were becoming the rule' (ibid. 37).

There are of course many complex factors accounting for the volatile political situation of most African countries, and it is increasingly being acknowledged that they can be properly understood only if they are put in the right historical perspective. Three important points will be briefly mentioned here. First, many African states have inherited from the colonial period arbitrary and absurd boundaries which tend to make the objective of national unity comparatively difficult to achieve. What Hart has said about West Africa could easily be extended to other areas as well: 'The further balkanization of West Africa as the price of independence has only increased the problem of borders by multiplying them' (Hart 1982: 103). This is especially distressing in view of the long tradition of continuous flows of goods and people across large parts of Africa.

Second, historical studies have shown that the ethnic problem—which is an important destabilizing factor in post-independence Africa—has been largely 'fabricated' by the colonial powers in order to increase their administrative, political, and even religious control over the people subjected to their rule. Thus, Noronha considers that 'ethnic consciousness, if not born through colonialism, was reaffirmed and strengthened' (Noronha 1985: 65), while, for Coquery-Vidrovitch, the impact of colonialism has been to cause a shift from 'ethnic' to 'tribalist' identity feeling among African people (Coquery-Vidrovitch 1985: 127–35; see also Bayart 1989: 65–86).[41] Unfortunately, the

---

[41] By 'tribalisme', Coquery-Vidrovitch apparently means 'the manipulation of ethnic feeling' in order to further particularistic interests on the basis of race criteria. Such manipulation could be driven very far indeed. In Zambia, in order to avoid the costs of large-scale unemployment in the copper mines during cyclical downturns, the colonial government instituted an administrative procedure of purely artificial 'tribalization'. To retain rural land rights, urban dwellers (like factory workers) had to be 'tribalized', that is they had to affiliate with the political officials of a rural community and establish membership in a kin group belonging to that community. In times of crisis, laid-off workers could thus reincorporate themselves into the rural economy 'quickly and peacefully', with no cost for the colonial Treasury (Bates 1984: 249).

policy of granting concessions and privileges on the basis of tribal affiliations has not been discontinued by independent African states. On the contrary, ethnic identity has become an important criterion for rationing access to scarce government or administrative posts as well as to the monopoly rents allocated by the state bureaucracy (Platteau 1984: 78–83). As aptly noted by Young, 'The politically ambitious had discovered that crystallizing ethnic conscious-ness was the swiftest and surest way to attract a political clientele' (Young 1986: 36).

Nevertheless, it would be wrong to infer from the above that ethnic affiliations are always an essential dimension of the African state. In fact, the common denominator of African political systems is that they are all structured by rival networks of political factions articulated around individuals, families, religious, socio-cultural, and economic groups, subgroups, sects, castes, etc. These factions are often engaged in merciless struggles for access to power and to the wealth and material privileges which automatically reward the power-holders (Bayart 1989: 261–80). And it is precisely because these struggles are so fierce (since the stakes are so big) that the state in Africa 'is being imposed in the most elementary sense of the term' (ibid. 300).

Third, the political project of many African states at the time of independ-ence was to follow a 'socialist/populist strategy', that is a strategy directed towards instituting 'a rational and non-conflictual development process' by giving a central role to the state 'in relation to both overall regulation and direct intervention in the production process itself' (Brett 1986: 24). It was grounded on a domestic class alliance made of disparate elements which were supposed to transcend their own particularistic interests in the name of nationalist eman-cipation and progress. Such a project was bound to fail and to weaken the state structure not only because the responsibilities entrusted to the state clearly exceeded its capabilities, but also because it eschewed the crucial question of how and among whom to allocate the scarce resources available. In a rather paradoxical way, African countries have often attempted to escape or postpone the inevitable setting of priorities and to alleviate the accompanying class, regional, or ethnic tensions by increasing their dependence on foreign capital (both public and private), thus thwarting their initial plan of national emancipation.

Paternalistic and instrumentalist biases in the institutional approach to rural development Political instability tends to discourage investments and risk-taking in agriculture, and to jeopardize long-term efforts to reduce population pressure on limited land resources. Similar adverse effects result from the 'control orientation' (Leonard) or the 'top-down bias' of the institutional approach to rural development followed by many African governments. The latter have usually ignored the important lesson that self-sustaining growth of the rural economy cannot occur 'without a policy designed to make positive use of indigenous community institutions and organizational principles as a basis for modern rural development institutions' (Hayami and Kikuchi 1981: 225). Instead of building up on indigenous village-community organizations and mechanisms of decentralized decision-making—that is, instead of starting with what already exists and encouraging local associations or voluntary agencies to promote organizational development from below and to diversify institutional responsibilities (what Hyden has called the 'greenhouse' approach—1986: 71–6)—they have almost systematically preferred to establish highly centralized and bureaucratized institutions, often entrusted with monopoly or monopsonistic powers.

Thus, for example, Africa is well known for her long tradition of informal savings clubs—known as 'tontines' in West Africa—which in many cases are run by women on the basis of extremely sound principles of savings management. As has been pointed out, these clubs could well have been developed into small credit unions with a view to providing 'the base for small, cost-effective credit operations through links with more formal banking institutions' (Leonard 1986: 194). Instead, most African governments opted for setting up from the top complex multifunctional co-operatives one function of which is to provide credit to their members according to rather rigid administrative procedures. Tragically enough, women are normally deprived of access to membership on the ground that households are adequately represented by their male head. To take another example, instead of supporting traditional rural artisans by helping them to acquire better tools, learn new techniques, and adapt to new market opportunities (intensive agriculture requires better agricultural implements), many African governments have preferred to follow a largely inefficient and expensive top-down approach. As described by Michael Lipton, this approach involves 'the training of largely unskilled and inexperienced would-be entrepreneurs, mollycoddled in subsidised and capital-intensive "industrial estates" for a few years of market-unrelated "training", and then either sent out to sink (or, rarely, swim) alone, or permitted to pressurise their way to endlessly prolonged "estate" cocooning' (Lipton 1985: 80; see also Please and Amoako 1984: 57).

More generally, in a world dominated by pervasive production externalities and by high information and transaction costs, local associations—that is, typically, non-market institutions grounded upon tight social interactions —must develop to undertake collective actions and to create public goods, particularly around resources that are becoming increasingly scarce (Hayami and Kikuchi 1981: 11–23). If large-scale organizations cannot be dispensed with in some specific circumstances (e.g. in the cases where construction of dams or large canals is required to ensure adequate distribution of water), they ought to be avoided whenever and wherever possible, because they tend to encourage free-riding and to give rise to all sorts of incentive problems.

Two central considerations seem to have led African leaders to believe that agricultural institutions subsumed under central government control are more appropriate and more reliable than private voluntary organizations, possibly based on lineage and extended family connections. For one thing, rural masses were regarded as too amorphous and too exposed to merchants' exploitation to be capable of raising their standard of living without the constant protection and support of the state (*the paternalistic bias*). For another thing, public institutions were considered as the best way to make small-scale rural producers efficient instruments of government policies and programs, particularly those geared towards increasing agricultural exports and public revenues (*the instrumentalist bias*). At a more general level, the notion largely prevailed that 'economies can be developed like armies under a single command' (Hyden 1986: 65).

In many countries, the main rural institutions set up by the administration and the political system have taken the form of co-operative structures. As a rule, two chief tasks were assigned to them, both of which are revealing of the instrumental role reserved for the peasantry in most African strategies of national development. First, on the political plane, rural co-operatives were supposed to organize the villagers with a view to facilitating the transmission, towards the rural masses, of political orientations and instructions decided at the top. Second, at the economic level, their planned function was to serve as a relay between state societies, parastatals, and government departments on the one hand, and the mass of petty rural producers on the other hand. In more concrete terms, they were conceived as a kind of channel through which the state would distribute modern agricultural inputs and credit, convey market information, and collect the agricultural produce (mainly export products). It is no exaggeration to say that rural co-operatives, far from being partners or pressure groups with which the government has to negotiate, are in fact 'the lower element of state apparatuses' (Gentil 1986: 75).

In so far as co-operatives are considered and organized as a simple extension of the administration and the government, it is not surprising that the latter feel perfectly entitled continuously to intervene in the affairs of the former, by deciding and formalizing their rules of functioning (including the conditions of membership, the size of the co-operative, etc.), by appointing the chairman, by imposing certain activities (such as the cultivation of some crops or the building up of certain social infrastructures), by exercising permanent financial control, and so forth. In some extreme cases, like that of rural state organizations in Mali (the 'Groupements ruraux de production et de secours mutuel'), the government had even dispensed with the co-operative façade to organize the peasantry in a more direct and ruthless fashion (1960–8). Adhesion was made compulsory to all villagers and the administration (then under the strong influence of the dominant political party, the US/RDA) was authorized to 'influence' the election of village chiefs and peasant delegates (Gentil 1986: 61–73). In the particular case of the Office du Niger, government irrigation schemes were run like military work camps and extension officers were acting both as technical advisers and as police guards (Coulibaly 1985: 218–22). The 'villagization' programme of Nyerere in Tanzania also suffered from continuous and demoralizing interferences from the state bureaucracy, thus preventing the emergence of self-determining and democratic collective groups (Kitching 1982: 104–24; Putterman 1985: 181–6; Swantz 1987). Unfortunately, examples of this kind could be multiplied *ad infinitum*.

Social costs of the 'control model' Given the above set-up, the attitude of African smallholders who regard the co-operatives as 'belonging to the government, and not to the peasants' (Gentil 1986: 202; see also Jacquemot 1981; Geschiere 1984; Marty 1985) is perfectly understandable. Many such reactions have been actually observed. Thus, Tanzanian peasants perceived the 'collective fields' instituted under the 'villagization' programme as 'farms of the government' (Putterman 1985: 184), while on government irrigation schemes it is not rare that tenants 'feel and behave as if they were government labourers' (FAO 1986: Annex IV, ch. 5, para. 5.28). In Senegal, for example, smallholders regard the irrigated fields of the SAED as the 'gardens of the state' and, accordingly, they consider that maintenance of the infrastructure is the exclusive responsibility of the state, which does not fail to engender serious tensions with the extension and supervision personnel (Matthieu 1983a, 291). Evidently, the latter participate in the process of peasant alienation since they tend to behave as state employees (which they often actually are) and not as agents of the agricultural communities which they are supposed to serve. Moreover, they frequently embitter the relations between the peasants and the agricultural state services because of their 'lack of interest in peasant cooperation, except insofar as it serves personal and government aims'; and because of their 'habits of authoritarianism and attitudes of disdain for peasants' by which they convince themselves that they have finally succeeded in rising over their own peasant roots (Putterman 1985: 185).[42]

As could also be expected, rural small-scale producers use all sorts of defensive strategies or evasive reactions to thwart—or to minimize the effects of—the government's attempts at enrolling them against their will. African peasantries excel in the 'art of runaway' and are prone to seize all 'exit options' open to them (Bayart 1989: 308–15). Some of their strategies have been depicted by Dominique Gentil: putting in a minimum amount of effort when the compulsion is too strong (in collective fields); simulating submission while abstaining from undertaking any concrete action; sending a few village leaders or dummies to meetings which they will attend passively without making any commitment on behalf of the village community; taking maximum advantage of what the state offers, for instance, borrowing as much as possible and repaying as little as possible; selling a few bags of agricultural produce to the marketing co-operative while disposing of the largest possible portion of the

---

[42] It is revealing that in an official document the government of Mali has criticized rural agents of the central administration for the 'omnipotent power they have vested themselves with' and for the way they have 'traumatized' the population during 18 years of national independence (Government of Mali 1984: 9).

harvest through illegal channels (Gentil 1986: 147–8). The main defect of the top-down control model is now evident: it lies in the serious incentive problems that it inevitably creates at the level of rural producers. In the absence of participatory decision-making, the latter tend to consider themselves not as genuine members of the institutions which are supposed to be run for their benefit, but as simple customers or hired labourers with all the attendant consequences in terms of risks of labour-shirking, asset mismanagement, output underreporting, and other 'moral hazard' problems. The fact that such problems involve large social costs is too well known to deserve further elaboration.

What needs to be borne in mind, however, is that advantages distributed by co-operative societies or other rural organizations are far from being equally shared among the members or other potential beneficiaries. As in the case of access to land rights (see above, pp. 530–2), the old (rural) élite and the new (urban/rural) élite have managed to secure a preferential access to state favours. In most cases, this has been done by using traditional networks of clientelist relations to get 'elected' to key positions in the above organizations; or by establishing privileged relations with influential bureaucrats, party leaders, and government representatives who are often keen to distribute patronage in return for personal advantages or party support. As a consequence, far from being eroded by the emergence of so-called 'democratic', 'co-operative', or 'people's' organizations in the countryside, the structure of vertical leadership within African villages has actually been strengthened by the convenient alliance of rural élites and the new bureaucratic class.

Inequitable mechanisms for distributing state-channelled resources (credit, subsidies, modern agricultural inputs or tools, irrigation equipment, etc.) are particularly important and self-reinforcing with respect to the development of intensive agriculture. Indeed, access to the best lands belonging to the public domain is normally pre-conditioned on access to modern inputs on the ground that land belongs to he who can till it properly. In a rather cynical way, a customary principle of land allocation is thus invoked to justify growing socio-economic differentiation in African agriculture. This is what happens, for example, in the Senegal river valley, where good irrigated lands are often allocated to rich urban dwellers and to traditional village leaders because only they possess the equipment required to exploit them according to the rules of the SAED (Mathieu 1985a: 658–62, 1987).[43]

Autocratic legacy of the colonial system   To some extent, the problems which have been highlighted above are typical of most Third World countries. Where

---

[43] The positive experience of Ronkh village (on the Senegal river), where a group of rural youth could get access to a portion of SAED-allocated irrigated lands, actually confirms this analysis. Indeed, it is mainly because this group was led by an educated person who decided to put an end to his teaching career but could still act as a 'broker' for the villagers *vis-à-vis* the urban authorities, and because the group was strongly motivated, courageous, but also full of political tact, that it could eventually succeed in obtaining support from the SAED (Gentil 1986: 206–16).

Africa distinguishes herself, however, is in the comparatively high degree of authoritarianism commonly displayed in her top-down approaches to rural development, and in the strong resistance that such authoritarian modes of conduct oppose to change. To understand these two characteristics, one does not have to go very far back into African history since it was mainly during the colonial period that the control orientation of many present African political systems was shaped. Young has thus pointedly remarked (1) that contemporary African states remain 'deeply marked by the hegemonial pretensions and authoritarian legacy of the colonial state' since 'in innumerable ways, the peremptory, prefectoral command style of the colonial state remains embedded in its successor'; and (2) that the colonial state was much more authoritarian in Africa than in Asia and Latin America, with the result that subjugation and exclusion of civil society was particularly thorough in the former continent (Young 1986: 33–4, 46). The second feature is ascribed to two facts. On the one hand, 'the African colonial state was implanted in a highly competitive environment where consolidation of its rule was an immediate requirement'. On the other hand, the colonial class in Africa 'had a more profound conviction of its cultural, biological, and technological superiority, and a more systematically negative view of its subject population than was the case elsewhere' (ibid. 34).

With particular respect to rural/local organizations, a fascinating study on co-operative movements in West Africa (Gentil 1986) has revealed that the co-operative societies at present existing in the countries concerned are an almost exact replica of the colonial SIP, SP, SMPR, and SMDR (sociétés indigènes de prévoyance; sociétés de prévoyance; sociétés mutuelles de production rurale; sociétés mutuelles de développement rural). It is particularly worth noting that the latter societies were all considered to be part of the French colonial administrative system—Gentil calls them 'structures of a para-administrative type' (ibid. 43). This implied (1) that the colonial bureaucracy always took the initiative of creating them; (2) that it could use them towards achieving official objectives (in particular, the development of export cash crops and the collection of government revenues under the guise of membership fees); and (3) that it was entitled to intervene at every stage of their functioning. This intervention could go very far indeed since (French) province governors were automatically appointed chairmen of the 'co-operative' societies situated in their administrative territory, and since membership was often made compulsory for all the villagers (women and young people excepted) living in the area (ibid. 27–57). Even the ill-famed Office du Niger was in fact created in 1932 by the French to succeed the STIN (Service temporaire d'irrigation du Niger) which was a para-military organization run by military officers and relying upon a system of forced labour (Coulibaly 1985: 220).

Interestingly, village chiefs and their clients—provided that they professed allegiance to the new ruling power—were incorporated into the governing bodies of the colonial 'co-operative' societies. They were thus given a preferential treatment in the access to the resources, goods, and services provided through them. In fact, the political strategy of colonial powers consisted of incorporating submissive chieftains into the entire administrative machinery and not only into rural 'co-operative' organizations (Noronha 1985: 61–5; Coquery-Vidrovitch 1985: 112–27). In this way, even though they were not very high in the colonial hierarchy,[44] village chiefs came to be vested with enormous power at the local level: the power to allocate tribal lands; to collect revenue on behalf of the colonial state; to raise compulsory labour and to fix the criteria for selection of individuals; to punish defaulters when cropping programmes were imposed by the administration; and so forth. The whole political fabric of pre-colonial African societies was therefore perverted, since in these societies the village political sphere was traditionally 'plural' and the chief was not allowed to concentrate powers (Bates 1984: 245–8; Coquery-Vidrovitch 1985: 113, 126; Bayart 1989: 99–103). The result has been a hybrid and 'monstrous' creature vividly depicted by Coquery-Vidrovitch:

The 'chief' of today—whether the so-called 'traditional' chief or the modern bureaucrat—appears, strictly speaking, as a 'monster', that is as the combination, still badly effected and poorly understood, of two power systems which had initially nothing in common. Being so, he represents, at the least, an attempt at fusion between the old dominant groups and the new élites born from the colonization and decolonization processes. (Coquery-Vidrovitch 1985: 126–7—my translation)

In today's Africa, this 'monstrous' creature remains incorporated in a global political system of vertical relationships of personal subordination but, what makes matters still worse as compared with the colonial period, this system is now characterized by an almost complete 'patrimonialization of the state' (Young) as well as by chronic instability following the demise of colonial tutelage. The logic of this macropolitical system has been adequately captured by Young:

Abstract bureaucratic jurisprudence no longer sufficed after independence. Hostile cliques and conspiracies had to be pre-empted by ensuring placement of personnel at critical points in the state apparatus whose fidelity to the ruler was not simply formal, but immediate and personal. Thus rulers constructed an inner layer of control—key political operatives, top elements in the security forces, top technocrats in the financial institutions—whose fidelity was guaranteed by personal fealty as well as by hierarchical subordination. The surest basis for such fidelity is affinity of community or kinship . . . Beyond and often in addition to affinity, personal interest is the most reliable collateral for loyalty. Accordingly, rulers must reward generously and impose severe sanctions for any weakening of zeal. Thus public resources become a pool of benefits and prebends, while dismissal from office, confiscation of goods, and prosecution face those who show slackness in their personal fidelity. Holders of high office individually tend to become clients of the ruler and collectively a service class. (Young 1986: 38)

[44] In French colonies, the village chief was a simple assistant to the Commandant and derived no authority independent of the administration (Noronha 1985: 63; Coquery-Vidrovitch 1985: 121).

As is evident from the foregoing analysis, the preference for state control and direction and the authoritarian modes of conduct of most African rulers are a structural feature of contemporary societies in Africa. They answer the need of social control in a fluid political set-up dominated by ethnic and interdistrict competition, factional struggles, religious ties, and complicated relations of affection and patronage that cannot be encompassed by class analysis (Hyden 1986: 66; Bienen 1987: 298–300; Bayart 1989: 261–93). That the political economy of Africa described above is uncongenial to rural development hardly needs emphasis. It is sufficient to stress that villagers have many ways of expressing their resentment against a village chief who is not 'customary' but a creation of the colonial order. If they usually comply with his orders so long as he acts as a representative of the government (especially if these orders are backed up by administrative sanctions of superior links in the hierarchy), they are often found to hinder and to oppose him in his performance as a (pseudo-) traditional leader in the village (Geschiere 1984: 16–17). The ensuing cost in terms of lost opportunities of rural progress may be tremendous, since many African villages thus lack the minimum social cohesion and the leadership dynamics that are so badly needed to carry out communal projects of rural development, whether in the productive or in the social sphere.

10.5. *Conclusion*

African agriculture is confronted today with a dramatic challenge arising from both demand and supply factors. On the demand side, the picture is twofold: on the one hand, food consumption increases quickly, mainly as a result of very high rates of population growth, and, on the other hand, consumption patterns undergo drastic changes for a variety of reasons among which rapid rates of urbanization stand foremost. On the supply side, disappointing performances —although difficult to measure precisely due to the paucity and low reliability of the data available (see Berry 1984: 61–4)—can obviously not be attributed to a single factor or even to a small number of causes. While both supply and demand factors are responsible for the growing dependence of Africa on food imports and for the ensuing tightening of the continent's foreign exchange constraints, the poor performances of the agricultural sector and the gradual shift of consumption patterns towards import-intensive foods have combined to reduce the incomes of the majority of rural people.

In much of the specialized economic literature, attention has been essentially drawn to policy 'mistakes' currently made by African governments, either out of sheer ignorance of sound economic logic and unawareness of macroeconomic constraints, or because of considerations related to the 'political economy' of Africa understood in a narrow neoclassical sense (policies are the outcome of competition and interaction of organized groups made of rational individuals). The dominant image emerging from many such analyses is that of misguided, incompetent, exploitative, and corrupt states that are actually killing the peasantry from which they draw their living. Overvaluation of national currencies, urban food subsidies, and excessive reliance on foreign food aid programmes (all these policies having the effect of cheapening foreign foods artificially), high rates of effective taxation of agricultural production, inefficient distribution of agricultural inputs and food output, are considered to be the main factors acting as a brake on the expansion of domestic food supply. The main policy conclusion that seems to follow from such a diagnosis is that by just reversing the present policies and by redressing the existing economic distortions agricultural growth could be considerably stimulated. Admittedly, such reversals of economic policies will not be easily achieved since they require new political coalitions ready to call the 'old order' into question. Yet such a view has apparently been confirmed by policy changes in favour of agricultural producers during the last 10–15 years, usually imposed upon many African states by the world economic crisis and the 'instructions' issued by powerful international organizations (especially the IMF and the World Bank).

It would be absurd to pretend that the above school of thought is completely off the mark, since it has brought into focus a number of important problems that bear upon the agricultural situation in Africa. Moreover, bumper food harvests and grain surpluses recently recorded in several African countries (most notably in Mali and Sudan) seem to have partly resulted from policy reforms suggested by the price-focused doctrine, even though it is impossible to separate the influence of these reforms from the effect of exceptionally good climatic conditions. This said, the dominant view must be criticized, not only on its own ground because of internal weaknesses (both empirical and theoretical), but also and mainly because it has the effect of diverting attention from the most crucial issues confronting African agriculture today. Indeed, Africa will not be able to raise the incomes of the mass of rural smallholders on a sustainable basis, nor to reduce her food dependence with a view to sparing scarce foreign exchange for her industrialization, if rapid technical advances do not take place in the agricultural sector. More precisely, Africa has no choice but to generate and diffuse technological progress at a rate sufficiently rapid to cause regular increases in land productivity (so as to expand food supply despite the exhaustion of the 'land frontier'), and in labour productivity (so as to increase the real incomes of the farmers), probably at the cost of increased labour efforts. In the present context of Africa, the afore-mentioned challenge amounts to finding how African countries (particularly those below the Sahara desert) could make a significant shift from extensive to intensive farming and stock-raising practices.

When the question is posed in these terms, growth-inhibiting factors of a more structural type than those underlined in the 'price-focused' approach come to the foreground of analysis. More concretely, Africa appears to suffer from several serious handicaps which can be traced back to her colonial and pre-colonial history, or which result from specific characteristics of her physical environment. In many instances, she turns out to be at a disadvantage *vis-à-vis* other continents, Asia and Latin America in particular. This is not to say that such structural deficiencies and handicaps cannot or will not be overcome. But attempts at overcoming them will take considerable time, much energy, and large amounts of resources, while time runs against Africa and some badly needed resources (such as agricultural research personnel) are awfully scarce.

Six 'constraint areas' have been investigated in this paper. The underlying theses can be schematically formulated as follows:

1. In Africa, human settlements remain small and very scattered, with the result that the development of markets is slowed down and the per capita cost of providing numerous services to the rural population is quite high.

2. On the natural resources front, Africa is handicapped by the extraordinary diversity of her agroclimatic conditions; by the low quality and high fragility of her soils; by difficult and costly access to water; and by the inaccessibility of some of her best lands.

3. So far, African staple foods have not benefited from any technological breakthrough in high-yield varieties, a situation which must be ascribed to a variety of factors among which are: the structure of traditional consumption patterns; the small size of many African states; a large dispersion and a biased allocation of agricultural research efforts under the joint influence of 'export' and 'technological dependence' biases.

4. The transition from extensive to intensive agriculture and stock-raising is made more difficult because Africa has inherited an 'extensive culture' from her long history of long-fallow agriculture and pastoral nomadism.

5. Because land laws in Africa are at present in a state of transition and a dual system of land titles often prevails in the countryside, access to land is not properly guaranteed. As a consequence, land investment is discouraged and valuable resources are wasted in costly strategies of acquisition and protection of land rights.

6. Many African states are characterized by a high degree of political instability and by the 'control orientation' of their institutional approach to rural development. The 'paternalistic' and the 'instrumentalist' biases implied in this approach create many incentive problems for the rural sector, which turn out to be very expensive in terms of transaction costs and lost opportunities of agricultural growth.

From the above list of factors, it is evident that the problems which Africa will have to solve in order to trigger off new growth and development impulses in her agricultural sector do not lie wholly in the technological sphere. Changes in institutions and in the cultural and political systems will also be required. Moreover, it is worth stressing that the levels of income and the food security of the smallholder majority in Africa will not be improved unless serious attention is paid to equity issues and distributive effects of agricultural growth-promoting strategies. This is one of the main lessons from the discussion of the last two afore-mentioned constraints. As a matter of fact, in Africa as in Asia and Latin America—and contrary to a popular picture of Africa as a relatively egalitarian society—there is a high risk that the growth of sustainable productive income-earning opportunities in the countryside will bypass the poorer and politically weaker segments of rural populations, while encouraging the emergence of a small group of progressive rich farmers with a privileged access to valuable resources.

It is equally important to note that in many African countries—particularly in the arid and semi-arid areas—removing or reducing the various constraints that hamper agricultural growth will not be sufficient to grant new purchasing power to small family-operated farms. Strategies promoting diversification of rural production and creation of new off-farm employment opportunities will be needed—mainly during the dry season in areas where the rainy season is very short—to supplement the farm incomes of African smallholders. Priority should of course be given to activities having potential linkages with agricultural production or producing simple consumption and capital goods demanded by—or of potential use to—rural dwellers.

It would however be a mistake to think that, in the near future, development of non-agricultural activities could make technical change in agriculture superfluous or even wasteful. Indeed, given that in many instances investments in non-agricultural activities are likely to be much more import-intensive than investments in agricultural intensification in which labour investments play a considerable role, a relative neglect of agriculture would have two adverse effects upon the balance of payments. First, there is the effect resulting from the rising food import bill and, second, increasing imports of intermediate and capital goods will be required to create and sustain employment opportunities outside the agricultural sector. The problem is further complicated by the fact that the prospects of non-agricultural exports are rather bleak for Africa today. Furthermore, if non-agricultural activities are developed in the countryside to the detriment of agricultural production, the cost of transporting food will be high given the low population densities in most African countries. If, on the contrary, these activities are spatially concentrated, the acceleration of already fast-rising urbanization rates will entail considerable social costs besides causing rapid population depletion in entire regions of the continent.

There is not doubt that the challenge facing African agriculture today is tremendous. For one thing, given that populations grow very rapidly, all the changes required in technology, institutions, and cultural systems to solve problems of declining labour productivity and environmental degradation must occur simultaneously and within a short span of time. There is thus a serious risk that these changes will 'fail to emerge at a sufficiently rapid pace to prevent decline in human welfare' (Pingali and Binswanger 1986: 27). For another thing, difficulties are compounded by the fact that Africa's food crisis has deep historical roots which can be traced back to pre-colonial times (e.g. the lack of tradition of productive links between African cities and the rural hinterland) and to the colonial era (e.g. the export bias in agricultural research and the role of the colonial legacy in shaping contemporary African states). When placed in its right historical perspective, this crisis therefore appears to be far more difficult to overcome than many current prescriptions for simple policy reforms tend to suggest.

This is perhaps a disappointing conclusion for those who expect scientists to prescribe clear recipes for helping Africa out of her awkward agricultural predicament. Yet, the role of any structural analysis is precisely to shake off naïve beliefs in the illusory power of short-term policy measures to solve long-term development problems. Besides—and in a more positive way— it points to the necessity of carrying out in-depth country case-studies before venturing to suggest measures or strategies for agricultural development that must inevitably, to a large extent, be country specific. In effect, the main purpose of this paper was to identify sensible 'problem areas' which should be carefully investigated in the case of each African country or region contemplating the redress of present imbalances. In the very process of this identification, some schematization was unavoidable and idiosyncrasies were left out of the picture so that the issues highlighted could be made relevant for a large number of countries belonging to the African continent.

References

ABOYADE, O. (1987), 'Growth Strategy and the Agricultural Sector', in Mellor *et al.* (1987).

AGARWAL, N. (1983), *The Development of a Dual Economy: A Theoretical Analysis* (Calcutta: K. P. Bagchi & Cy).

ANDRAE, G., and BECKMAN, B. (1986), *The Wheat Trap: Bread and Underdevelopment in Nigeria* (London: Zed).

ANSON-MEYER, M. (1985), 'Les illusions de l'autosuffisance alimentaire: Exemple du Bénin, du Ghana, du Nigéria et du Togo', in Gagey, F. (ed.), *Comprendre l'économie africaine* (Paris: Éditions L'Harmattan); repr. from *Mondes en développement*, 41–2 (1983).

ASKARI, H., and J. T. CUMMINGS (1977), 'Estimating the Agricultural Supply Response with the Nerlove Model: A Survey', *International Economic Review*, 18/2, June.

BACHELET, M. (1986), 'Réformes agro-foncières et développement', in Verdier, R., and Rochegude, A. (eds.), *Systèmes fonciers à la ville et au village* (Paris: L'Harmattan).

BATES, R. H. (1981), *Markets and States in Tropical Africa: The Political Basis of Agricultural Policies* (Berkeley, Calif.: University of California Press).

—— (1984), 'Some Conventional Orthodoxies in the Study of Agrarian Change', *World Politics*, 26/2.

—— and LOFCHIE, M. F. (eds.) (1980), *Agricultural Development in Africa: Issues of Public Policy* (New York: Praeger).

BAYART, J. F. (1989), *L'État en Afrique: La politique du ventre* (Paris: Fayard).

BERG, E., *et al.* (1986), 'La réforme de la politique céréalière dans le Sahel' (Paris: OCDE and CILSS (No. 38132)).

BERG, R. J., and WHITAKER, J. S. (eds.) (1986), *Strategies for African Development* (Berkeley, Calif.: University of California Press).

BERRY, S. (1980), 'Rural Class Formation in West Africa', in Bates and Lofchie (1980).

—— (1984), 'The Food Crisis and Agrarian Change in Africa: A Review Essay', *African Studies Review*, 27/2, June.

BÉZY, F., PEEMANS, J.-P., and WAUTELET, J.-M. (1981), *Accumulation et sous-développement au Zaïre 1960–1980* (Louvain-la-Neuve: Presses universitaires de Louvain).

BIENEFELD, M. (1986), 'Analysing the Politics of African State Policy: Some Thoughts on Robert Bates' Work', *IDS Bulletin*, 17/1, Jan.

BIENEN, H. (1987), 'Domestic Political Considerations for Food Policy', in Mellor *et al.* (1987).

BINSWANGER, H. P., *et al.* (1985), 'Estimates of Agricultural Supply Response from Time Series of Cross-Country Data', EPOLS Division Working Paper (Washington, DC: World Bank).

—— and ROSENZWEIG, M. R. (1986), 'Behavioural and Material Determinants of Production Relations in Agriculture', *Journal of Development Studies*, 22/3, Apr.

BOND, M. A. (1983), 'Agricultural Responses to Prices in Sub-Saharan African Countries', *IMF Staff Papers*, 30.

BONIN, J. P., and PUTTERMAN, L. (1987), *Economics of Cooperation and the Labor-Managed Economy* (London and New-York: Harwood Academic Publishers).

BOSERUP, E. (1965), *The Conditions of Agricultural Growth* (London: Allen & Unwin).

——(1981), *Population and Technology* (Oxford: Basil Blackwell).

BOUTILLIER, J. L. (1963), 'Les rapports du système foncier toucouleur et de l'organisation sociale et économique traditionnelle: Leur évolution actuelle', in Biebuyck, D. (ed.), *African Agrarian Systems* (London: Oxford University Press).

——(1980), 'Irrigated Farming in the Senegal River Valley' (Department of Agriculture Economics, Purdue University).

BRAY, F. (1983), 'Patterns of Evolution in Rice-Growing Societies', *Journal of Peasant Studies*, 11/1, Oct.

——(1986), *The Rice Economies: Technology and Development in Asian Societies* (Oxford: Basil Blackwell).

BRETT, E. A. (1973), *Colonialism and Underdevelopment in East Africa* (London: Heinemann).

——(1986), 'State Power and Economic Inefficiency: Explaining Political Failure in Africa', *IDS Bulletin*, 17/1, Jan.

CHRISTODOULU, D. (1966), *Basic Agrarian Structural Issues in the Adjustment of African Customary Tenures to the Needs of Agricultural Development* (Rome: FAO).

CILSS (1979), *La politique céréalière dans les pays du Sahel: Actes du Colloque de Nouakchott* (Paris: Comité permanent inter-états de lutte contre la sécheresse dans le Sahel (CILSS)).

COHEN, J. (1980), 'Land Tenure and Rural Development in Africa', in Bates and Lofchie (1980).

COLCLOUGH, C. (1985), 'Competing Paradigms—and Lack of Evidence—in the Analysis of African Development', in Rose (1985).

COLLIER, P. (1983), 'Oil and Inequality in Nigeria', in Ghai and Radwan (eds.), 1983, 191–248.

——and LAL D. (1981), 'Poverty and Growth in Kenya', World Bank Staff Working Paper No. 389 (Washington, DC: World Bank).

COLLINSON, M. (1987), 'Potential and Practice in Food Production Technology Development: Eastern and Southern Africa', in Mellor *et al.* (1987).

COMMINS, S. K., LOFCHIE, M. F., and PAYNE, R. (eds.) (1986), *Africa's Agrarian Crisis: The Roots of Famine* (London: Frances Pinter).

COQUERY-VIDROVITCH, C. (1982), 'Le régime foncier rural en Afrique noire', in Le Bris *et al.* (1982).

——(1985), *Afrique noire: Permanences et ruptures* (Paris: Payot).

COULIBALY, C. (1985), 'Intérêts de classes, politique alimentaire et sujétion des producteurs: Le Cas de l'Office du Niger au Mali', in Haubert *et al.* (1985).

COWEN, M. (1982), 'The British State and Agrarian Accumulation in Kenya', in Fransman, M. (ed.), *Industry and Accumulation in Africa* (London: Heinemann).

DELGADO, C., MELLOR, J., and BLACKIE, M. (1987), 'Strategic Issues in Food Production in Sub-Saharan Africa', in Mellor *et al.* (1987).

——and RANADE, C. (1987), 'Technological Change and Agricultural Labor Use', in Mellor *et al.* (1987).

DELOR-VANDUEREN, A. (1988), *Démographie, Agriculture et Environement—Le cas du Burundi*, Université Catholique de Louvain, mimeo.

DEMSETZ, H. (1967), 'Toward a Theory of Property Rights', *American Economic Review*, 57/2, May.

DIEMER, G., and VAN DER LAAN, E. (1987), *L'irrigation au Sahel—La crise des périmetres irrigués et la voie haalpulaar* (Paris and Wageningen: Karthala and CTA).

DORNER, P. (1972), *Land Reform and Economic Development* (Kingsport: Kingsport Press).

DUPRIEZ, H. (1980), *Paysans d'Afrique noire* (Nivelles: Terres et Vie).

EICHER, C. (1984), 'Facing Up to Africa's Food Crisis', in Eicher and Staatz (1984).

——(1985), 'Famine Prevention in Africa: The Long View', in *Food for the Future* (The Philadelphia Society).

——(1986a), 'Transforming African Agriculture', *Hunger Project Papers*, 4, Jan.

——(1986b), 'Western Science and African Hunger', Inaugural Lecture for the 1985/6 Foreign Francqui Lecture, the Catholic University of Leuven (Belgium).

——(1986c), 'Strategic Issues in Combating Hunger and Poverty in Africa', in Berg and Whitaker (1986).

——and BAKER, D. C. (1982), 'Research on Agricultural Development in Sub-Saharan Africa: A Critical Survey', MSU International Development Paper No. 1 (East Lansing, Mich.: Michigan State University, Department of Agricultural Economics).

——and MANGWIRO, F. (1986), 'A Critical Assessment of the FAO Report on SADCC Agriculture and Agricultural Sector Studies', background paper prepared for a SADCC Meeting, Harare, July (Rome: FAO).

——and STAATZ, J. M. (eds.) (1984), *Agricultural Development in the Third World* (Baltimore, Md. and London: Johns Hopkins).

ENGELHARD, P. and T. BEN ABDALLAH (1986), *Enjeux de l'aprés-barrage-vollée du Sénégal* (Dakar: ENDA et République Française, Ministère de la Coopération).

EVENSON, R. E. (1978), 'The Organization of Research to Improve Crops and Animals in Low Income Countries', in Schultz, T. W. (ed.), *Distortions in Agricultural Incentives* (Bloomington, Ind., and London: Indiana University Press).

FACAGRO and ISA (1989), *Séminaire sur l'étude des systèmes d'exploitation agricole au Burundi* (Bujumbura: Faculté des Sciences Agronomiques and Institut des Sciences Agronomiques).

FALLERS, L. A. (1961), 'Are African Cultivators to be called "Peasants"?', *Current Anthropology*, 2/2.

FAO (1984), *Capacité potentielle de charge démographique des terres du monde en développement*, Technical Report FPA/INT/513 (Rome: FAO).

——(1985), *The State of Food and Agriculture 1984* (Rome: FAO).

——(1986), *African Agriculture: The Next 25 Years* (Rome: FAO (Main Report + 5 Appendices)).

——(various years), *Production Yearbook and Trade Yearbook* (Rome: FAO)

FAUCHER, J. J., and SCHNEIDER, H. (1985), 'Agricultural Crisis: Structural Constraints, Prices and Other Policy Issues', in Rose (1985).

GALLI, R. E. (1987), 'On Peasant Productivity: The Case of Guinea-Bissau', *Development and Change*, 18/1, Jan.

GENTIL, D. (1986), *Les mouvements coopératifs en Afrique de l'Ouest* (Paris: L'Harmattan).

GEPHART, M. (1986), 'African States and Agriculture: Issues for Research', *IDS Bulletin*, 17/1, Jan.

GESCHIERE, P. (1984), 'Segmentary Societies and the Authority of the State: Problems in Implementing Rural Development in the Maka Villages of Southeastern Cameroon', *Sociologia ruralis*, 24/1.

GHAI, D., and RADWAN, S. (eds.) (1983), *Agrarian Policies and Rural Poverty in Africa* (Geneva: ILO).

——(1983), 'Growth and Inequality: Rural Development in Malawi, 1964–78', in Ghai and Radwan (eds.), 1983.

GHATAK, S., and INGERSENT, K. (1984), *Agriculture and Economic Development* (Brighton: Harvester).

GIRI, J. (1983), *Le Sahel demain* (Paris: Karthala).

——(1986), *L'Afrique en panne* (Paris: Karthala).

Government of Mali (1984), *Recueil de documents sur les tons villageois* (Bamako: Ministère du développement rural).

GUEYMARD, Y. (1985), 'L'évolution de la politique de commercialisation des céréales au Mali', in Haubert *et al.* (1985).

HART, K. (1982), *The Political Economy of West African Agriculture* (Cambridge: Cambridge University Press).

HARVEY, C. (1983), 'The Case of Malawi', *IDS Bulletin*, 14/1, Jan.

HAUBERT, M., and FRELIN, C. (1985), 'Quelle autosuffisance?', in Haubert et al. (1985).

——and TRONG NAM TRAN, N. (eds.), *Politiques alimentaires et structures sociales en Afrique noire* (Paris: Presses universitaires de France).

HAYAMI, Y., and KIKUCHI, M. (1981), *Asian Village Economy at the Crossroads: An Economic Approach to Institutional Change* (Tokyo: University of Tokyo Press).

——and RUTTAN, V. (1985), *Agricultural Development: An International Perspective* (Baltimore, Md., and London: Johns Hopkins).

HELLEINER, G. (1975), 'Smallholder Decision Making: Tropical African Evidence', in Reynolds, L. (ed.), *Agriculture in Development Theory* (New Haven, Conn., and London: Yale University Press).

——(1979), 'Aid and Dependence in Africa: Issues for Recipients', in Shaw, T. M., and Heard, K. A. (eds.), *The Politics of Africa: Dependence and Development* (New York: Africana Pub. Co.).

HERDT, R. (1970), 'A Disaggregate Approach to Aggregate Supply', *American Journal of Agricultural Economics*, 52/4, Nov.

HESSELING, G., and MATHIEU, P. (1986), 'Stratégies de l'État et des populations par rapport à l'espace', in Crousse, B., Le Bris, E., and Le Roy, E. (eds.), *Espaces disputés en Afrique noire: Pratiques foncières locales* (Paris: Karthala).

HILL, P. (1963), *The Migrant Cocoa-Farmers of Southern Ghana* (Cambridge: Cambridge University Press).

HYDEN, G. (1986), 'African Social Structure and Economic Development', in Berg and Whitaker (1986).

IFPRI (1986), 'Food in the Third World: Past Trends and Projections to 2000', Research Report No. 52 (Washington, DC: IFPRI).

IFRI (1986), *RAMSES 86/87: Rapport annuel mondial sur le système économique et les stratégies* (Paris: éditions Atlas economica pour l'Institut français des relations internationales).

ISHIKAWA, S. (1981), *Essays on Technology, Employment and Institutions in Economic Development* (Tokyo: Kinokuniya Cy.).

Islands of Peace (1984, 1985, 1986), *Annual Reports on the Timbuktu Project* (Huy).

JACQUEMOT, P. (ed.) (1981), *Mali: Le paysan et l'Etat* (Paris: L'Harmattan).

JOHNSTON, B. F. (1986), 'Governmental Strategies for Agricultural Development', in Berg and Whitaker (1986).

——and KILBY, P. (1975), *Agriculture and Structural Transformation: Economic Strategies in Late-Developing Countries* (London: Oxford University Press).

JUDD, M. A., BOYCE, J. K., and EVENSON, R. E. (1986), 'Investing in Agricultural Supply: The Determinants of Agricultural Research and Extension Investment', *Economic Development and Cultural Change*, 35/1, Oct.

KÉBÉ, Y. (1981), 'L'agriculture malienne, le paysan, sa terre et l'État', in Jacquemot (1981).

KEMP, T. (1983), *Industrialization in the Non-Western World* (London and New York: Longman).

KITCHING, G. (1982), *Development and Underdevelopment in Historical Perspective* (London and New York: Methuen).

KODJO, E. (1985), *Et demain l'Afrique* (Paris: Stock).

KRISHNA, RAJ (1970), 'Models of the Family Farm', in Wharton, C. R. (ed.), *Subsistence Agriculture and Economic Development* (London: Frank Cass).

——(1984), 'Price and Technology Policies', in Eicher and Staatz (1984).

LE BRIS, E., LE ROY, E., and LEIMDORFER, F. (eds.) (1982), *Enjeux fonciers en Afrique noire* (Paris: Karthala).

LEE, E. (1979), 'Egalitarian Peasant Farming and Rural Development: The Case of South Korea', in Ghai, D., Khan, A. R., Lee, E., and Radwan, S. (eds.), *Agrarian Systems and Rural Development* (London: Macmillan).

LELE, U. (1975), *The Design of Rural Development: Lessons from Africa* (Baltimore, Md.: Johns Hopkins).

——(1976), 'Designing Rural Development Programs: Lessons from Past Experience in Africa', *Economic Development and Cultural Change*, 24/2, Jan.

——(1984), 'Rural Africa: Modernization, Equity, and Long-Term Development', in Eicher and Staatz (1984).

——(1985), 'Terms of Trade, Agricultural Growth, and Rural Poverty in Africa', in Mellor and Desai (1985).

LEONARD, D. K. (1986), 'Putting the Farmer in Control: Building Agricultural Institutions', in Berg and Whitaker (1986).

LIPTON, M. (1977), *Why the Poor Stay Poor* (London: Maurice Temple Smith).

——(1985), 'Indian Agricultural Development and African Food Strategies: A Role for EC?', in Callewaert, W. M., and Kumar, R. (eds.), *EEC—India: Towards a Common Perspective* (Leuven: Peeters).

——(1987), 'Agriculture and Central Physical Grid Infrastructure', in Mellor *et al.* (1987).

MAROT, E. (1987), *Autosuffisance alimentaire: Une stratégie pour le développement économique et la sécurité alimentaire?* (Namur: Faculté des sciences économiques et sociales).

MARS, T. (1986), 'State and Agriculture in Africa: A Case of Means and Ends', *IDS Bulletin*, 17/1, Jan.

MARTY, A. (1985), 'Crise rurale en milieu nord-sahélien et recherche coopérative', unpublished Ph.D. thesis, Université François Rabelais, Tours.

MASAKI, N. (1987), 'Élevage bovin chez les Suku de Feshi' (Zaïre), unpublished Ph.D. thesis, Fondation universitaire luxembourgeoise, Arlon.

MATHIEU, P. (1983a), 'Agriculture irriguée et cultures traditionnelles de décrue dans la zone du lac de Guiers', in *Le Lac de Guiers: Problématique de l'environnement et de développement* (Institut des sciences de l'environnement, Université de Dakar).

——(1983b), 'Présence ou absence des travailleurs et avenir du travail dans les aménagements hydro-agricoles', *Mondes en développement*, 11/43–4.

——(1985a), 'L'aménagement de la vallée du fleuve Sénégal: Transformations institutionnelles et objectifs coûteux de l'autosuffisance alimentaire', *Mondes en développement*, 13/52.

——(1985b), 'Évaluation du périmètre de Korioumé: Île de paix de Tombouctou' (Huy: ASBL 'Les Iles de paix').

——(1987), 'Agriculture irriguée, réforme foncière et stratégies paysannes dans la vallée du fleuve Sénégal, 1960–1985', unpublished Ph.D. thesis, Fondation universitaire luxembourgeoise, Arlon.

MATLON, P. (1987), 'Potential and Practice in Food Production Technology Development: The West African Semiarid Tropics', in Mellor *et al*. (1987).

MELLOR, J. (1968), 'The Functions of Agricultural Prices in Economic Development', *Indian Journal of Agricultural Economics*, 23/1.

——(1970), 'The Subsistence Farmer in Traditional Economies', in Wharton, C. (ed.), *Subsistence Agriculture and Economic Development* (London: Frank Cass).

——(1984), 'Agricultural Development and the Intersectoral Transfer of Resources', in Eicher and Staatz (1984).

——and DELGADO, C. (1987), 'Food Production in Sub-Saharan Africa', Food Policy Statement No. 7, Jan. (Washington, DC: IFPRI).

————and BLACKIE, M. (eds.) (1987), *Accelerating Food Production in Sub-Saharan Africa* (Baltimore, Md., and London: Johns Hopkins).

——and DESAI, G. (eds.) (1985), *Agricultural Change and Rural Poverty: Variations on a Theme by Dharm Narain* (Baltimore, Md., and London: Johns Hopkins).

——and JOHNSTON, B. F. (1984), 'The World Food Equation: Interrelations among Development, Employment, and Food Consumption', *Journal of Economic Literature*, 22, June.

MILLAR, J. R. (1976), 'What is Wrong with the "Standard Story"?', *Problems of Communism*, July–Aug.

MINVIELLE, J. P. (1977), *La structure foncière du Waalo Fuutanké* (Office de la recherche scientifique et technique d'outre-mer (ORSTOM), Dakar Centre).

MONFERRER, D. (1985), 'L'introduction de l'agriculture capitaliste en Afrique et ses conséquences: Le Cas du Gabon', in Haubert *et al*. (1985).

MOORE, M. (1987), 'Interpreting Africa's Crisis: Political Science versus Political Economy', *IDS Bulletin*, 18/4, Oct.

MORRISON, S. (1986), 'Dilemmas of Sustaining Parastatal Success: The Botswana Meat Commission', *IDS Bulletin*, 17/1, Jan.

MORRISSON, C. (1985), 'Agricultural Production and Government Policy in Burkina Faso and Mali', in Rose (1985).

MYRDAL, G. (1963), *Economic Theory and Underdeveloped Regions* (London: Methuen & Co Ltd.).

NAKAJIMA, C. (1970), 'Subsistence and Commercial Family Farms: Some Theoretical Models of Subjective Equilibrium', in Wharton, C. R. (ed.), *Subsistence Agriculture and Economic Development* (London: Frank Cass).

NORONHA, R. (1985), 'A Review of the Literature on Land Tenure Systems in

Sub-Saharan Africa', Research Unit of The Agriculture and Rural Development Department, Report No. ARU 43 (Washington, DC: World Bank).

OYEJIDE, T. A. (1987), 'Food Policy and the Choice of Trade Regime', in Mellor *et al.* (1987).

PACEY, A., and PAYNE, P. (eds.) (1985), *Agricultural Development and Nutrition* (London: Hutchinson).

PAULINO, L. (1987), 'The Evolving Food Situation', in Mellor *et al.* (1987).

PAUSEWANG, S. (1987), 'Who is the Peasant? Experience with Rural Development in Zambia', Derap Working Papers, No. A 371 (Bergen: Chr. Michelsen Institute).

PENNISI, G. (1986), 'Le Sahel cherche de nouveaux équilibres', *Cooperazione*, 60 (French edn.).

PINGALI, P. L., BIGOT, Y., and BINSWANGER, H. P. (1987), *Agricultural Mechanization and the Evolution of Farming Systems in Sub-Saharan Africa* (Baltimore, Md., and London: Johns Hopkins).

——and BINSWANGER, H. P. (1986), 'Population Density, Market Access and Farmer-Generated Technical Change in Sub-Saharan Africa', Agriculture and Rural Development Department, Report No. ARU 58 (Washington, DC: World Bank).

PLATTEAU, J.-P. (1978), *Les économistes classiques et le sous-développement* (Paris: Presses universitaires de France).

——(1984), 'Das Paradoxon des Staates in wirtschaftlich rückständigen Ländern', *Osterreichische Zeitschrift für Soziologie*, 4/9.

——(1985), 'India as an Engine of Green Revolution in Africa?', in Callewaert, W. M., and Kumar, R. (eds.), *EEC—India: Towards a Common Perspective* (Leuven: Peeters).

——(1987), 'The Problems of Consistency and Relevance in Malthus's Analysis of Underdevelopment', Cahier de recherche de la faculté des sciences économiques et sociales (Namur).

PLATTEAU, J.-P. (forthcoming), *Land reform and Structural Adjustment in SubSaharan Africa: Controversies and Guidelines* (Rome: FAO).

PLEASE, S., and AMOAKO, K. Y. (1984), 'The World Bank's Report on Accelerated Development in Sub-Saharan Africa: A Critique of Some of the Criticism', *African Studies Review*, 27/4, Dec.

POTTIER, J. (1986), 'Village Responses to Food Marketing Alternatives in Northern Zambia: The Case of the Mambwe Economy', *IDS Bulletin*, 17/1, Jan.

PUTTERMAN, L. (1985), 'Extrinsic versus Intrinsic Problems of Agricultural Co-operation: Anti-incentivism in Tanzania and China', *Journal of Development Studies*, 21/2, Jan.

RAYNAUT, C. (1976), 'Transformation du système de production et inégalité économique: Le Cas d'un village haoussa (Niger)', *Revue canadienne des études africaines*, 10/2.

——(1983), 'La crise des systèmes de production agro-pastorale au Niger et en Mauritanie', in Raynaut, C. (ed.), *Milieu naturel, techniques, rapports sociaux* (Paris: Éditions du Centre national de la recherche scientifique).

ROBERTSON, A. F. (1987), *The Dynamics of Productive Relationships: African Share Contracts in Comparative Perspective* (Cambridge: Cambridge University Press).

ROSE, T. (1985), *Crisis and Recovery in Sub-Saharan Africa* (Paris: OECD).

SANDBROOK, R. (1986), 'The State and Economic Stagnation in Tropical Africa', *World Development*, 14/3.

SCANDIZZO, P. L., and C. BRUCE (1980), 'Methodology for Measuring Agricultural Price Incentive Effects', *World Bank Staff Working Papers*, No. 394, June.

SCHÄFER, H. B. (1987), 'Farm Prices and Agricultural Production in Developing Countries', *Intereconomics*, 22/3, May/June.

SEN, A. K. (1966), 'Peasants and Dualism, with or without Surplus Labour', *Journal of Political Economy*, 74/5, Oct.

——(1981), *Poverty and Famines: An Essay on Entitlement and Deprivation* (Oxford: Oxford University Press).

SINGLETON, M. (1983), 'Présence et absence de barrages en Afrique', paper given at the international conference 'Barrages en terre et développement des zones rurales en Afrique', École polytechnique de Thiès et AUPELF, Senegal.

SPENCER, D. S. C. (1986), 'Agricultural Research: Lessons of the Past, Strategies for the Future', in Berg and Whitaker (1986).

SWAINSON, N. (1986), 'Public Policy in the Development of Export Crops: Pineapples and Tea in Kenya', *IDS Bulletin*, 17/1, Jan.

SWANTZ, M.-L. (1987), 'Development: From Bottom to Top or Top to Bottom? Grassroots Dynamics and Directed Development—The Case of Tanzania', Paper 87/106 (Centre for Development Studies, Universiteit Antwerpen).

TER KUILE, C. (1987), 'Potential and Practice in Food Production Technology Development: The Humid and Subhumid Tropics', in Mellor *et al.* (1987).

TIMMER, C. P. (1986), *Getting Prices Right: The Scope and Limits of Agricultural Price Policy* (Ithaca, NY: Cornell University Press).

TOYE, J. (1987), *Dilemmas of Development* (Oxford: Basil Blackwell).

TYAGI, D. S. (1987), 'Domestic Terms of Trade and their Effect on Supply and Demand of Agricultural Sector', *Economic and Political Weekly*, 22/13, Mar. Review of Agriculture.

VON BRAUN, J., and WEBB, P. (1989), 'The Impact of New Crop Technology on the Agricultural Division of Labor in a West African Setting', *Economic Development and Cultural Change*, 37/3.

WEIGEL, J. Y. (1982a), 'Organisation foncière et opération de développement: Le Cas Soninke au Sénégal', in Le Bris *et al.* (1982).

——(1982b), *Migration et production domestique des Soninké du Sénégal* (Paris: Office de la recherche scientifique et technique d'outre-mer (ORSTOM)).

WILLIAMSON, O. (1985), *The Economic Institution of Capitalism* (New York: Free Press).

World Bank (1981), *Accelerated Development in Sub-Saharan Africa: An Agenda for Action* (Washington, DC: World Bank).

——(1984), *World Development Report: 1984* (Washington, DC: World Bank).

——(1986a), *Poverty and Hunger: Issues and Options for Food Security in Developing Countries* (Washington, DC: World Bank).

——(1986b), *World Development Report: 1986* (Washington, DC: World Bank).

YOTOPOULOS, P. (1985), 'Middle-Income Classes and Food Crises: The "New" Food–Feed Competition', *Economic Development and Cultural Change*, 33/3, Apr.

YOUNG, C. (1986), 'Africa's Colonial Legacy', in Berg and Whitaker (1986).

11

Famine Prevention in Africa: Some Experiences and Lessons

Jean Drèze

11.1. *Introduction*

Faith in the ability of public intervention to avert famines is a relatively new phenomenon. Not so long ago, even James Mill felt compelled to use the most fatalistic language to inform his friend David Ricardo of his apprehensions as to the consequences of a spell of adverse weather in England:

> Does not this weather frighten you? . . . There must now be of necessity a very deficient crop, and very high prices—and these with an unexampled scarcity of work will produce a degree of misery, the thought of which makes the flesh creep on ones bones—one third of the people must die—it would be a blessing to take them into the streets and high ways, and cut their throats as we do with pigs.[1]

Ricardo had full sympathy for Mill's feelings, and assured him that he was 'sorry to see a disposition to inflame the minds of the lower orders by persuading them that legislation can afford them any relief'.

Fatalism to such a degree would be extremely hard to defend today. An enormous amount of evidence now bears testimony to the potential effectiveness of concerted action for famine prevention.[2] More than ever, the occurrence of a famine in the modern world is an incontrovertible sign of some massive failure of public intervention—often originating in war situations.

This observation applies as much to sub-Saharan Africa as to the rest of the world. At the risk of some oversimplification, it could be argued that even in this region the phenomenon of large-scale famine is now mainly confined to war situations. Contrary to popular belief, there is considerable evidence that famine vulnerability in sub-Saharan Africa has significantly decreased this

This chapter is an outgrowth of collaborative work with Amartya Sen, published in our book *Hunger and Public Action* (Drèze and Sen, 1989). I am most grateful to John Borton, Diana Callear, Jane Corbett, Rob Davies, Thomas Downing, Carl Eicher, Jim Gordon, Roger Hay, Judith Heyer, Renée Loewenson, Siddhartha Mitter, S. T. W. Mhiribidi, Richard Morgan, David Sanders, Lucy Spyckerelle, and Daniel Weiner for many helpful comments, suggestions, and personal communications relating to the case-studies appearing in section 2.4. I have also greatly benefited from extensive comments by Robin Burgess on an earlier draft of this chapter.

[1] Letter of Mill to Ricardo, 14 Aug. 1816. Quoted in Jacqemin (1985: Annexe historique, p. 18), where Ricardo's reply is also quoted.

[2] For a few examples of the ability of public intervention to prevent or contain famine mortality in the most diverse historical and socio-economic contexts, see Valaoras (1946), Binns (1976), Smout (1978), Will (1980), Kiljunen (1984), Otten (1986), and Drèze (1988), among many other studies.

century, and also that this reduced vulnerability is partly attributable to the improved quality of public intervention.[3] African countries, however, receive little credit for this achievement. The disasters that periodically visit (usually war-torn) countries such as Ethiopia, Sudan, or Mozambique tend to over-shadow the more positive experiences that have taken place elsewhere.

This chapter investigates some of these experiences. It will be argued that a number of impressive examples of successful famine prevention can be found in contemporary Africa, from which there is a great deal to learn. To start with, Section 11.2 provides some elementary observations on the strategy of famine prevention. Section 11.3 brings out some of the perception biases which divert attention away from positive experiences of famine prevention in contemporary Africa. Section 11.4 is devoted to selected case-studies of such experiences. The last section offers some concluding remarks.

11.2. *Famine prevention and entitlement protection*

It is now well understood that famines can be fruitfully analysed as 'entitlement failures' suffered by a large section of the population.[4] Those who cannot establish command over an adequate amount of food have to perish from starvation. Famine prevention is essentially concerned, therefore, with the *protection of entitlements*. That much might be obvious enough, but a few interpretational issues should be addressed straightaway to avoid misunderstanding the content of that superficially simple message.

First, while famines involve—and are typically initiated by—starvation, many of the people who die from a famine die in fact not from starvation as such, but from various epidemic diseases unleashed by the famine. This happens primarily through the spread of infectious diseases helped by debilitation, attempts to eat whatever looks eatable, breakdown of sanitary arrangements, and massive population movements in search of food.[5] Famine prevention is, in fact, intimately connected with the avoidance of epidemics, even though the first and basic culprit may be the failure of food entitlements.

---

[3] On this see e.g. Wrigley (1976), Caldwell (1977, 1984), Bryceson (1981a, 1981b), Kates (1981), Herlehy (1984), Hugo (1984), Bernus (1986), Borton and Clay (1986), Downing (1986), Wood et al. (1986), World Food Programme (1986a), Caldwell and Caldwell (1987), de Waal (1987), Hill (1987), Iliffe (1987), Vaughan (1987), and Kates et al. (1988). Of course, it is arguable that this record of reduction in famine vulnerability remains shamefully poor when viewed against a background of rapidly increasing opulence at the world level over the same period.

[4] On the 'entitlement approach' to famine analysis, see Sen (1981). For various critiques of this approach, see Rangasami (1985), Bowbrick (1986), Devereux (1988), de Waal (1988b), Eicher (1988), and Kula (1989).

[5] This emerges clearly from a large number of empirical studies of famine mortality, including those of Foege (1971), Stein et al. (1975), Sen (1981), de Waal (1987), Dyson (1988), and O'Grada (1988), among others. Interestingly, it is also possible to find cases of famines where excess mortality has been attributed mainly to direct 'starvation deaths' (see Valaoras 1946, on the Greek famine of 1941–2, and Biellik and Henderson 1981, on the Karamoja famine of 1980). On related matters, see also Sorokin (1942), Rotberg and Rabb (1983), and Hugo (1984).

Thus, when acute deprivation has been allowed to develop, the task of containing famine mortality may require substantial attention to health care and epidemiological control. This consideration links with the general importance of seeing hunger and deprivation in terms of entitlement failures in a broader perspective than that of *food* entitlements only (see Drèze and Sen 1989). At the same time, it is important to bear in mind that in the case of famines the collapse of food entitlements is the initiating failure in which epidemics themselves originate, and that the protection of food entitlements at an early stage is often a more effective form of action than medical intervention at a later stage.[6]

Second, while the entitlement approach asserts the *inadequacy* of aggregate food availability as a focus for the analysis of famines, it does not assert its *irrelevance*. Aggregate food availability remains important, but its influence has to be seen only as an element of a more complex entitlement process. This general point is of obvious relevance in the context of analysing the causation of famines, but it also has to be borne in mind when the attention is turned to the *prevention* of famines. In particular it is important to see that (1) the improvement of food availability can play a helpful or even crucial role in preventing the development of a famine, whether or not the threat of famine is accompanied by a decline in food availability, and (2) at the same time, many other influences are at work, and a broad view should be taken of possible options for action—including that of protecting the food entitlements of vulnerable groups even when it is not possible to bring aggregate food availability to a particular level.

Third, the protection of entitlements in the short run has to be contrasted with the general promotion of entitlements in the long run. In the short run, famine prevention is essentially a question of countering an immediate threat of entitlement failure for vulnerable groups. In the long term, of course, a durable elimination of vulnerability involves more diverse areas of action, including the expansion of general prosperity, the reduction of insecurity through economic diversification, the prevention of armed conflicts, and the protection of the environment. However, even within a long-term perspective, the task of building up reliable entitlement protection systems remains quite crucial. Indeed, in most cases it would be rather naïve to expect that efforts at eliminating vulnerability could be so successful as to allow a country to dispense with distinct and specialized entitlement protection mechanisms. While famine prevention is not exclusively concerned with the protection of entitlements, much of the discussion in this chapter will concentrate on this elementary and urgent aspect of the problem.

---

[6] Empirical studies sharply bring out the effectiveness of famine prevention measures which concentrate on protecting entitlements to staple foods, supplemented with basic health care services such as vaccination, oral rehydration, and the provision of simple vitamins. See e.g. Swaminathan *et al.* (1969), Ramalingaswami *et al.* (1971), Berg (1973), Krishnamachari *et al.* (1974), Otten (1986), de Waal (1987) and Drèze (1988).

Fourth, the task of entitlement protection also has to be distinguished from a notion of 'famine relief' which conjures up the picture of a battle already half lost and focuses the attention on emergency operations narrowly aimed at containing large-scale mortality. Devising planned, coherent, effective, and durable entitlement protection mechanisms is a much broader enterprise. Entitlement crises have many repercussions on the rural economy and on the well-being of affected populations, and a comprehensive strategy for dealing with the scourge of famine must seek to ensure that human beings have both secure *lives* and secure *livelihoods*.

This is not just a question of immediate well-being, but also one of development prospects. Consider, for instance, the so-called 'food crisis in Africa', discussed in a number of contributions to this book (see especially Chapter 6 below). The current débâcle of agricultural production in much of sub-Saharan Africa has, not without reason, been held partly responsible for this region's continued vulnerability to famine. But one is also entitled to wonder how farmers who are condemned every so often to eat up their productive capital in a desperate struggle for survival can possibly be expected to save, innovate, and prosper. There is indeed considerable evidence of the lasting adverse effects of famine on productive potential as well as on the distribution of assets.[7] It is reasonable to think that improved entitlement protection systems in Africa would not only save lives, but also contribute to preserving and rejuvenating the rural economy. The alleged dilemma between 'relief' and 'development' is a much exaggerated one, and greater attention needs to be paid to the *positive* links between famine prevention and development prospects.

Finally, seeing famine prevention as an entitlement protection problem draws our attention to the plurality of strategies available for dealing with it. Just as entitlements can be threatened in a number of different ways, there are also typically a number of feasible routes for restoring them. Importing food and handing it over to the destitutes is one of the more obvious options. The overwhelming preoccupation of the journalistic and institutional literature on African famine relief has been with the logistics of food aid and distribution, reflecting the continued popularity of this approach. But there is a good case for taking a broader view of the possible forms of intervention, and indeed the rich history of famine prevention over the world reveals a great variety of possible strategies for the protection of entitlements.

In this respect, the sort of relief methods commonly employed in many parts of Africa today are bound to look somewhat unimaginative and unambitious. Particularly problematic are intervention strategies that are contingent on the

---

[7] See e.g. Swanberg and Hogan (1981), Chastanet (1983), de Waal (1987), Glantz (1987b), McCann (1987), and Hay (1988). Numerous reports on the 1983–5 famines in sub-Saharan Africa also emphasize the acute problems caused (*inter alia*) by shortages of seeds, oxen, or human labour during the recovery period, often resulting in a shrinkage of sown area and other forms of production losses.

rapid arrival of food aid from the other side of the globe.[8] While effective action is undoubtedly first and foremost a question of political motivation and pressure, it also requires a sound choice of intervention strategy. Both problems plague famine-prone countries in Africa and both need to be urgently addressed.

11.3. *African challenge and international perception*

It is widely believed that most African countries lack the political structure (perhaps even the commitment) for successful pursuit of comprehensive strategies of entitlement protection. There may be truth in this in some cases. The inaction and confusion of some governments in the face of crises have been striking. The role of war in exacerbating food crises in Africa also needs persistent emphasis. Nevertheless, an excessive concentration on failure stories has probably given an exaggerated impression of the apathy, incompetence, and corruption of African governments in the context of famine prevention. As was mentioned earlier, there is some evidence that the willingness and ability of many African countries to respond to crises have been improving over time, in some cases to a very considerable degree.

Furthermore, state action is not immune to the influence of political ideology, public pressure, and popular protest, and there is nothing immutable in the nature of contemporary African politics. It is, of course, true that the development of a workable system of famine prevention calls for political as well as economic restructuring, but political changes—no less than economic transformations—are responsive to determined action and popular movements.

While examining experiences of success and failure in famine prevention, it has to be recognized that international perceptions of these past experiences are often seriously distorted. In particular, for reasons of journalistic motivation (which has its positive side as well, on which more presently), the media tend to overconcentrate on stories of failure and disaster. To the extent that successes do get reported, the balance of credit is heavily tilted in favour of international relief agencies, which enjoy—and need—the sympathy of a large section of the public.

This phenomenon is well illustrated by an episode of successful famine prevention in the State of Maharashtra in India in 1972–3. The impressive success achieved at the time by the government of Maharashtra in preventing a severe drought from developing into a famine by organizing massive public works programmes (at one point employing as many as five million men and women) has been described in some detail elsewhere.[9] This event, however,

---

[8] The mode of operation of international agencies bears some responsibility for the perpetuation of these intervention strategies. See McLean (1988) for a perceptive discussion of this issue.

[9] See Ch. 3 in this volume.

caused very few ripples in the Western press, and received extraordinarily little attention from social scientists outside India until recently.[10]

While the government of Maharashtra was employing millions of people on relief works, various international agencies were involved in feeding programmes on a relatively tiny scale—often importing modest amounts of wheat, biscuits, and milk powder from the other side of the globe. However, the role of the latter appeared to be oddly exaggerated. One of the relief organizations —indeed one that has altogether distinguished itself for many years by its far-sighted initiatives and actions—had no hesitation in reporting in its *Bulletin* how a poor peasant sighed that the drought 'may be too big a problem for God; but perhaps OXFAM can do something'. There are other self-congratulatory snippets in the same vein about OXFAM's heroic deeds in Maharasthra and other drought-affected parts of India at that time:

I suddenly realised that, driving 20 miles out of Ajmer on the road to Udaipur, all the scattered green patches I saw in the brown desert were in some way or another due to OXFAM.

In spite of the feeding programme the children have not gained weight. Stina at first thought her scale was wrong, but she discovered that the children now get almost nothing to eat at home. One shudders to think what would have happened to them without the feeding scheme. What's happening in other villages, where we aren't feeding?[11]

The donor's exaggerated perception of its achievements is coupled with a somewhat astonishing lack of information about what the government was doing on an enormously larger scale. As late as December 1972, by which time the government-led relief programme was in full swing, the same *Bulletin* reports: 'we have no information as yet of the extent of the Indian government's programme'. The fact that an organization with as remarkable a record of helpful action and leadership as OXFAM could fall into this trap of making mountains out of molehills and molehills out of mountains shows the difficulties of objective perception and reporting on the part of an institution directly involved in the act of relief and dependent on the preservation of a particular public image.

The highly selective focus of public discussions on famine is also evident in the case of Africa. For instance, until recently Botswana's remarkable record of famine prevention had received very little recognition, to the point that a

---

[10] The first in-depth analysis of the Maharashtra drought published in an international professional journal outside India is that of Oughton (1982), who focuses, however, more on the crisis of entitlements than on the success of public response. On the latter, see Ch. 3, and the further contributions cited there.

[11] These citations are from OXFAM (1972, 1973) and Hall (1973). It must be emphasized that it is not the intention here to blame OXFAM in particular for sharing in a form of disaster reporting that seems to be, in fact, common to the publications of many relief agencies when these are addressed to the wider public. The point is simply to illustrate certain biases which an institution of this kind seems to find it hard to resist, for understandable reasons.

leading expert on Africa described it as 'Africa's best kept secret'.[12] Examples of underreported successes in famine prevention in Africa, most of them involving large-scale government intervention, can also be found in countries as varied as Burkina Faso, Cape Verde, Kenya, Lesotho, Mali, Mauritania, Niger, Tanzania, Uganda, Zimbabwe, and even to some extent Chad and Ethiopia.[13]

It is arguable that popular interpretations of the recent 'African famine' of 1983–5 have themselves involved important misperceptions. Though drought threatened a large number of African countries at that time, only some of them—notably war-torn ones—actually experienced large-scale famine. There was no uniform disaster of the kind that has often been suggested. In fact, a probing interpretation of the mounting evidence on this tragedy could well uncover many more reasons for hope than for despair.[14]

It is, moreover, far from clear that those countries where large-scale famine did occur were the ones most affected by drought. Such an impression is certainly *not* borne out by available food and agricultural production indices (see Table 11.1).[15] I shall argue, in fact, that the sharp contrasts which can be observed in the relationship between drought and famine in different countries have a lot to do with the contrasting quality of public action in various parts of Africa. In particular, a number of countries where drought was extremely severe in 1983–4 (indeed often more severe than in the much-discussed cases of Ethiopia or Sudan, in terms of declines in food and agricultural production indices) met with notable success in averting large-scale famine. Vivid illustrations of this fact are found in the experiences of Botswana, Cape Verde, Kenya, and Zimbabwe (see Table 11.2).[16] There is as much to learn from these 'quiet successes' as from the attention-catching failures that can also be observed elsewhere in Africa. Some of these success stories are further examined in the next section.

---

[12] Eicher (1986: 5). The experience of this country will be further discussed in Section 11.4.

[13] See e.g. Kelly (1987) on Burkina Faso; Freeman *et al.* (1978) and van Binsbergen (1986) on Cape Verde; Borton and Clay (1986), Cohen and Lewis (1987), and Downing *et al.* (1989) on Kenya; Bryson (1986) on Lesotho; Steele (1985) on Mali; UNDRO (1986) on Mauritania; de Ville de Goyet (1978), CILSS (1986), and World Food Programme (1986c) on Niger; Mwaluko (1962) on Tanzania; Brennan *et al.* (1984) and Dodge and Alnwick (1986) on Uganda; Bratton (1986) on Zimbabwe; Holt (1983), Nelson (1983), Firebrace and Holland (1984), Peberdy (1985), Grannell (1986), and World Food Programme (1986b) on Ethiopia (including Tigrai and Eritrea); and Autier and d'Altilia (1985), Brown *et al.* (1986), and World Food Programme (1986a) on Chad.

[14] A large number of the references cited in the previous footnote deal with the 1983–5 crisis.

[15] Nor is this impression confirmed by meteorological information—see J. Downing *et al.* (1987).

[16] Table 11.2 includes four of the five countries appearing at the top of Table 11.1. The fifth (Niger) is not included for lack of detailed and reliable information on the experience of that country. It is, however, interesting to note that, according to at least one authoritative study, 'Niger is probably one of the few African countries where the government has, for more than a decade, proclaimed and shown a strong commitment to guarantee the subsistence of the population' (CILSS 1986; my translation).

Table 11.1 Food and agricultural production in sub-Saharan Africa, 1983–1984

Country	Per capita food production 1983–4		Per capita agricultural production 1983–4	Growth rate of agricultural production per capita 1970–84
	(1979–81 = 100) (1)	(1976–8 = 100) (2)	(1979–81 = 100) (3)	(% per year) (4)
Cape Verde	62	n/a	n/a	n/a
Zimbabwe	73	68	82	−1.4
Niger	83	78	83	0.7
Botswana	83	n/a	84	−3.8
Kenya	87	82	93	−1.3
Senegal	88	70	89	−2.1
Mozambique	88	75	87	−4.3
Ethiopia	88	94	88	−0.6
Sudan	89	72	93	−0.5
Togo	90	93	90	−1.1
Zambia	92	89	93	−1.1
Angola	93	81	91	−5.6
Guinea	93	92	94	−1.0
Malawi	93	100	96	0.1
Tanzania	95	91	93	−0.6
Burundi	95	87	95	0.5
Ivory Coast	95	111	90	0.5
Cameroon	96	83	95	−0.8
Burkina Faso	98	90	99	−0.2
Uganda	98	96	100	−1.7
Ghana	98	80	98	−3.9
Nigeria	98	88	98	−1.0
Zaïre	101	97	102	−0.6
Liberia	102	100	99	−1.4
Benin	103	85	104	−0.3
Sierra Leone	104	84	101	−0.5
Mali	106	90	105	0.8
Guinea-Bissau	114	92	114	−0.9

Note: The countries included in this table are all those for which data are available from each of the three sources; Cape Verde has been added using van Binsbergen (1986: table 3). Figures for 1983–4 have been calculated as an unweighted average of 1983 and 1984.

Sources: (1) and (3): Calculated from FAO, *Monthly Bulletin of Statistics*, Nov. 1987. (2): Figures given by the United States Department of Agriculture, reproduced in J. Downing *et al.* (1987: table 1.1). (4): Food and Agriculture Organization (1986: annex I, table 1.2).

11.4. *Famine prevention in Africa: selected case-studies*

Declines in food or agricultural production are not, by themselves, reliable indicators of threats of large-scale entitlement failures. The fact that countries such as Botswana or Cape Verde have suffered very sharp production declines in recent years (without experiencing famine) hardly establishes the existence of a serious threat of famine in these countries. Nor does it tell us a great deal about how this threat—if real—was averted. These issues are taken up here for further scrutiny, for each of the four 'successful' countries appearing in Table 11.2. On closer examination it will clearly emerge that, in each case, a serious threat of famine *was* averted through determined public intervention.

Cape Verde

In his distinguished history of the Cape Verde Islands, Antonio Carreira wrote that 'everything in these islands combines to impose on man a hard, difficult and wretched way of life'.[17] A prominent aspect of the harshness of life in Cape Verde is the recurrence of devastating droughts, which have regularly affected the islands ever since their 'discovery' in the middle of the fifteenth century by the Portuguese. Many of these droughts have been associated with large-scale famine.[18]

In fact, it is hard to think of many famines in history that have taken a toll in human life proportionately as high as those which have periodically decimated Cape Verde in the last few centuries. Some of these famines are believed to have killed nearly half of the population (see Table 11.3). Even allowing for some exaggeration in these estimates, there are very few parallels of such wholesale mortality even in the long and terrible history of famines in the world.

These historical famines went almost entirely unrelieved. When one of the very few exceptions to this pattern occurred in 1825, the Governor of the islands was sacked for using Crown taxes to feed the people.[19] Left to its own devices, the population had little other refuge than the attempt to emigrate —often encouraged by the colonial authorities. Cape Verde's history of persistent migration is indeed intimately connected with the succession of famines on the islands. However, for most people this option remained a severely limited one, and as recently as the 1940s large-scale mortality was a predictable feature of prolonged drought.

[17] Carreira (1982: 15). According to several analysts, the climate of Cape Verde is even harsher, and the droughts visiting it more frequent and severe, than those of other Sahelian countries. See e.g. Meintel (1984: 56).

[18] For a chronology of droughts and famines in Cape Verde, see Freeman *et al.* (1978). For further discussion of famines in the history of Cape Verde, see Cabral (1980), Carreira (1982), Moran (1982), Meintel (1983, 1984), and Legal (1984).

[19] Freeman *et al.* (1978: 18). A strikingly similar incident occurred during the famine of the early 1940s (Cabral 1980: 150–1). A significant attempt at providing relief was however made during the famine of 1862–5, when employment was provided (with cash wage payments) on road-building works (see Meintel 1984).

Table 11.2 Drought and famine in Africa, 1983–1984: contrasting experiences

Country	Decline of production since 1979–81 (%)		Growth rate of per capita total gross agricultural production (1970–84)	Outcome
	Food	Agriculture		
Cape Verde	38.5	n/a	n/a	Mortality *decline*; nutritional *improvement*
Zimbabwe	37.5	18.5	−1.4	Mortality *decline*; no sustained nutritional deterioration
Botswana	17.0	16.5	−3.8	Normal nutritional situation; no starvation deaths
Kenya	13.5	7.5	−1.3	No starvation deaths reported; possibility of nutritional deterioration
Ethiopia	12.5	12.5	−0.6	Large-scale famine
Sudan	11.0	7.0	−0.5	Large-scale famine

Sources: The figures on food and agricultural production performance are from the same sources as Table 11.1. The assessment of 'outcome' in Botswana, Cape Verde, Kenya, and Zimbabwe is discussed further in this chapter. For estimates of excess mortality in Sudan and Ethiopia during the 1983–5 famines, see e.g. Otten (1986), de Waal (1987), Jansson *et al.* (1987), and Seaman (1987).

In recent years, Cape Verde may well have been the worst drought-affected of all African countries. Indeed, uninterrupted drought crippled the country's economy for almost twenty years between 1968 and 1986—leading to a virtual extinction of domestic food supplies and a near standstill of rural activity.[20] Half-way through this prolonged drought in the middle 1970s, the event was already described as 'the longest and most severe [drought] on record' for the country.[21] In this case, however, not only was famine averted but, even more

[20] In 1970, 70% of agricultural products consumed in Cape Verde were produced in the country (CILSS 1976: 8). This ratio had fallen to 1.5% by 1973 (CILSS 1976: 8), and only rose marginally thereafter (van Binsbergen 1986). According to one study, 'during the drought over 70% of the agricultural labour force has been unemployed' (Economist Intelligence Unit 1984: 38). It is not clear, however, how this calculation treats labour employed on public works programmes (on which more below). [21] Freeman *et al.* (1978: 98).

Table 11.3 History of famine mortality in Cape
Verde, 1750–1950

	Mortality attributed to famine (% of total population)
1773–6	44
1830–3	42
1863–6	40
1900–3	15
1920–2	16
1940–3	15
1946–8	18

Source: Moran (1982: table 1). The famines indicated here are only those for which an estimate of famine mortality is provided in that table. For the same period, the author mentions 22 further large-scale famines for which no mortality estimates are available.

strikingly, significant *improvements* in living conditions took place during the drought period.

It is convenient to divide the drought period into two parts, separated by the independence of Cape Verde from Portugal in 1975. The first part of the drought period is marked by an untypical attempt on the part of the Portuguese rulers at providing large-scale relief.[22] Relief was provided almost exclusively in the form of employment for cash wages in makeshift work (the adequacy of food supplies being ensured separately by food imports). According to one study, 55.5 per cent of the labour force was unemployed in 1970, but as much as 84 per cent of total employment was provided by drought relief programmes.[23]

These preventive measures succeeded to a great extent in averting a severe famine. There were no reports of large-scale starvation deaths, and the overall increase in mortality seems to have been moderate. The estimated infant mortality rate, for instance, which had shot up to more than 500 per thousand during the famine of 1947–8, was only a little above the 1962–7 average of 93.5 per thousand in the period 1968–75 (Table 11.4). On the other hand, a significant intensification of undernutrition during the same period has been reported in several studies.[24]

---

[22] Several commentators have argued that, in this case, action was motivated by the concern of the Portuguese government for its international image. See e.g. Meintel (1984: 68), CILSS (1976: 4), Davidson (1977: 394), and Cabral (1980: 134).

[23] Calculated from CILSS (1976: 3–4). This was the policy of *apoio* or 'support', which was later criticized by the government of independent Cape Verde for the unproductive nature of the works undertaken (see CILSS 1976, Legal 1984, and Meintel 1983, 1984).

[24] See e.g. Meintel (1984: 68–9), CILSS (1976: 14), and Freeman *et al.* (1978: 149, 203).

Table 11.4 Infant mortality in Cape Verde, 1912–1986

Year	Estimated infant mortality rate (deaths per 1,000)	
	(1)	(2)
1912	220.6	
1913	174.2	
1915	117.9	
1920	155.0	
1927	217.6	
1931	206.7	
1937	223.4	
1943	317.9	
1946	268.7	
1947[a]	542.9	
1948[a]	428.6	
1949	203.9	
1950	130.7	
1962	106.1	
1963	109.7	
1964	85.3	
1965	76.7	
1966	83.6	
1967	99.9	
1968	91.7	
1969	123.1	
1970	95.0	
1971	130.9	
1972	90.9	
1973	110.6	
1974	78.9	
1975	103.9	104.9
1980–5		77.0
1985		70.0
1986		65.0

[a] Famine years.

Sources: For the period 1912–75 (col. 1), Freeman *et al.* (1978: table V.26) (very close estimates are also reported for the 1969–74 period in CILSS 1976: table VI). For 1975–86 (col. 2), *World Health Statistics Annual 1985* and UNICEF (1987, 1988).

Since independence in 1975, Cape Verde has been ruled by a single party with a socialist orientation, namely the Partido Africano da Independencia da Cabo Verde (PAICV).[25] This party, described by the current Prime Minister as 'reformist, progressist and nationalist',[26] is flanked by the Popular National Assembly, which is elected every five years by popular ballot (on the basis of a single-party system). The government of independent Cape Verde has been consistently credited with progressive social reforms and development programmes. Notable areas of improvement have been those of education and health. Drought relief has been among the top political priorities.

Cape Verde's entitlement protection system since independence has consisted of three integrated components.[27] First, a competent and planned use of food aid has ensured an adequate and predictable food supply in spite of the nearly total collapse of domestic production. Food aid is legally bound to be *sold* wholesale in the open market, and the proceeds accrue to the National Development Fund.[28]

Second, the resources of the National Development Fund are used for labour intensive public works programmes with a 'development' orientation. In 1983, 29.2 per cent of the labour force was employed in such programmes.[29] The works undertaken include afforestation, soil conservation, irrigation, and road building, and according to a recent evaluation 'the results of these projects are positive, even on the basis of high standards'.[30]

Third, unconditional relief is provided to selected vulnerable groups such as pregnant women, undernourished children, the elderly, and the invalid. This part of the entitlement protection system includes both nutritional intervention (such as school feeding) and cash transfers, and is integrated with related aspects of social security measures. In 1983, direct food assistance covered 14 per cent of the population.[31]

The effectiveness of this fairly comprehensive and well-integrated entitlement protection system is visible from the impact of the drought after 1975.[32]

---

[25] In fact, until 1981, Guinea-Bissau and Cape Verde were jointly ruled by the binational Partido Africano da Independencia da Guine e Cabo Verde, which led the independence struggle against the Portuguese rulers.   [26] *Courier* (1988: 27).

[27] For further details, see CILSS (1976), Freeman *et al.* (1978), USAID (1982), Meintel (1983), Legal (1984), and particularly van Binsbergen (1986).

[28] This rule does not apply when the sale of food aid violates the conditions of delivery, e.g., in the case of the comparatively small quantities of food donated to Cape Verde under the World Food Programme. These are used for supplementary feeding.

[29] Economist Intelligence Unit (1984: 38).

[30] van Binsbergen (1986: 9). See also *Courier* (1988).   [31] van Binsbergen (1986: 10).

[32] In both the pre-independence and the post-independence periods, remittances from abroad also played an important role in mitigating the effects of the drought. Note, on the other hand, that remittances would not seem to explain the better record of famine prevention in the post-independence period, during which the world economic conditions were less favourable and emigration from Cape Verde considerably less common than during the first period (see e.g. Freeman *et al.* 1978: 139–40).

Table 11.5 Child undernutrition in Cape Verde, 1977 and 1984

District	School children suffering from undernutrition (moderate to serious) (%)	
	1977[a]	1984[b]
Boa Vista	41.8	7.8
Porto Novo	49.2	9.2
Ribeira Grande	54.3	5.8
São Vicente	38.1	10.7
Tarrafal	n/a	7.8
TOTAL	46.4	8.8

[a] Children aged 7–15 years.
[b] Children aged 6–18 years.

Source: van Vinsbergen (1986: table 2). According to the author, the two studies on which this table is based are 'reasonably comparable', and 'although the methodologies used by the different studies were not identical, it is safe to conclude that the nutritional status of school age children has significantly improved since 1977' (van Binsbergen 1986: 3–4). An independent study carried out in 1973 estimated that 38% of children aged 7–14 suffered from 'moderate protein-calorie malnutrition' (Freeman *et al.* 1978: table V.24).

Indeed, the adverse effects of the drought on the living conditions of human beings seem to have been remarkably small.[33] In addition to the successful prevention of famine, there are indications that the post-1975 part of the drought period has witnessed: (1) a *decline* in the infant mortality rate (see Table 11.4); (2) a significant *increase* in food intake;[34] and (3) a significant *improvement* in the nutritional status of children (see Table 11.5).[35] By any criterion, the success achieved by the government of independent Cape Verde in protecting the population from the adverse effects of a drought of un-precedented magnitude must be seen as an exemplary one.

Kenya

The history of Kenya, like that of Cape Verde, has been repeatedly marked by grim episodes of drought and famine.[36] As recently as 1980–1, famine struck

[33] There is a revealing contrast between this observation and the fact of huge livestock losses, which provide another measure of the intensity of the drought and of the threat of famine. The decline in livestock between 1968 and 1980 has been estimated at 12% for goats, 30% for pigs, 50% for sheep, and 72% for cows (calculated from Economist Intelligence Unit 1983: 43).

[34] On this, see Legal (1984: 12–16), who notes large increases in the consumption of maize, wheat, and rice in the post-independence period compared to the pre-drought period. The average consumption of calories, which 'for the vast majority of the population did not exceed 1500 calories per day' at the time of independence (CILSS 1976: 8; my translation), is now believed to have 'moved closer to the required level of 2800 calories per day' (van Binsbergen 1986: 3).

[35] A USAID study dated 1982 also mentions, without explicitly providing supporting figures, that 'by providing employment, the Government of Cape Verde's rural work program has had an acknowledged major effect on improving nutritional status' (USAID 1982: 15).

[36] See e.g. Wisner (1977), O'Leary (1980), Herlehy (1984), and Ambler (1988).

substantial parts of the population in the wake of a drought of moderate intensity. The government of Kenya has been widely praised, however, for preventing a much more widespread and intense drought from developing into a famine in 1984. This event has been extensively studied elsewhere.[37] I shall only recall here the main features of this successful response, and comment briefly on some of its neglected aspects.

Like Cape Verde, Kenya has a single-party system and an elected parliament. Since independence in 1963, the country has enjoyed a degree of political stability which compares favourably with many other parts of Africa. The freedom of the national media is somewhat limited but nevertheless far more extensive than in most African countries. The country also has a high degree of visibility in the international press.

More than 80 per cent of Kenya's population (around 19 million in 1984) is rural, and derives its livelihood largely from agriculture and livestock. The rural economy is more diversified, and has experienced more rapid growth since the early 1960s, than in most other parts of Africa. However, large parts of the country remain vulnerable to climatic and economic instability, particularly in the largely semi-arid areas of the Eastern and North-eastern Provinces (and parts of the Rift Valley).

The strategies adopted by rural households in Kenya to cope with drought or the threat of famine appear to be increasingly geared to the acquisition of food on the market and the diversification of economic activities (partly through wage employment).[38] The importance of off-farm activities in the rural household economy can be seen from the fact that, according to a survey carried out in six districts of the Central and Eastern Provinces in 1985, more than half of smallholder households had at least one member in long-term wage employment (see Table 11.6 below).

The 1984 crisis followed a massive failure of the 'long rains' in March and April 1984. According to Cohen and Lewis:

it was the worst shortage of rains in the last 100 years. Production of maize, the nation's principal food crop, was approximately 50% below that normally expected for the main rains of March–May. Wheat, the second most important grain, was nearly 70% below normal. Potato production was down by more than 70%. Pastoralists reported losing up to 70% of their stock. The situation had the potential for a famine of major proportions.[39]

---

[37] For in-depth analyses of the 1984 drought and the government's response, see Ray (1984), Deloitte et al. (1986), Cohen and Lewis (1987), Corbett (1987), J. Downing et al. (1987), and Downing et al. (1989). A particularly thoughtful and well-documented account of this event can be found in Borton (1988).

[38] For insightful studies of coping strategies in Kenya, see Wisner (1977), Bertlin (1980), Campbell (1984), Swift (1985), Downing (1986), Akong'a and Downing (1987), Sperling (1987a, 1987b), Anyango et al. (1989), and Kamau et al. (1989).

[39] Cohen and Lewis (1987: 274). The existence of a serious threat of large-scale famine in this event is also argued in detail in Corbett (1987). For statistical information on rainfall patterns and crop production during the drought, see Downing et al. (1989).

Regional disparities accentuate the alarming nature of these aggregate statistics. In the Central and Eastern Provinces, food production for the agricultural year 1984–5 was estimated by the FAO at 14 per cent and 26 per cent (respectively) of the average for the previous six years. In districts such as Kitui and Machakos, maize production was virtually nil both in 1983 and in 1984.[40]

While in specific areas the drought of 1984 meant the second or even third consecutive crop failure, for most areas the crisis was one of limited duration. The 'short rains' of October to December 1984 were above average. However, in terms of intensity and geographical coverage the drought of 1984 was certainly an exceptional one, and distress continued until the harvest of mid-1985.

The use of formal 'early warning' techniques apparently played little role in precipitating action. The need for action seems to have been detected partly from the visible failure of rains in early 1984 (followed by evident crop failures), and partly from the unusual increase in food purchases from the National Cereals and Produce Board later in the year.[41] While Cohen and Lewis stress the role of 'political commitment' in ensuring an early and adequate response, others comment that 'the government felt the need to forestall political instability that would result in the event of a widespread famine'.[42] The threat of political unrest seems to have been exacerbated by the fact that, somewhat unusually, the drought of 1984 strongly affected a number of politically important and influential areas of the Central Provinces as well as Nairobi.

Active public response to the crisis began in April 1984.[43] The first step taken by the government to deal with the threat of famine was to import large amounts of food on a commercial basis. The initial availability of substantial food stocks ensured that the lags involved in the importation of food did not have disastrous consequences. Additional food aid pledges were also obtained, but with a few minor exceptions their fulfilment occurred only in 1985, several months after the arrival of commercial food imports. The ability of the government to buy large amounts of food on the international market was

[40] See Borton (1988: table 3), and Maganda (1989: table 9.4).

[41] Cohen and Lewis describe the symptoms of an impending crisis as follows: 'By April 1984, the situation was obvious. The sun was shining beautifully, when it should have been raining; no early warning system was required' (Cohen and Lewis 1987: 276). Other authors, however, have stressed the role of rapidly increasing purchases from the National Cereals and Produce Board in arousing concern for the possibility of a crisis (see e.g. Corbett 1987, and Downing 1988).

[42] J. Downing et al. (1987: 266). It appears that the drought enjoyed only limited coverage in the local media, but attracted considerable international attention and concern (Downing 1988).

[43] For detailed accounts of the famine prevention measures, the reader is referred to Cohen and Lewis (1987), J. Downing et al. (1987), Borton (1988, 1989), and Downing et al. (1989). This case-study concentrates mainly on the government response, which represents the greater part of these measures, though the involvement of non-government agencies was not insignificant.

greatly helped by the availability of foreign exchange reserves and the peak in export earnings resulting largely from high world prices for tea and coffee.

Entitlement protection measures took two different forms. First, the government used food imports to ensure the continued availability of food at reasonable prices through normal commercial channels. In ordinary times, interdistrict food movements are exclusively organized by the National Cereals and Produce Board, which subcontracts the transport and distribution of food to licensed private traders. This arrangement was preserved and intensified during the drought, and most of the food imported was sold through the intermediation of private traders at 'gazetted' prices fixed by the government.

Second, direct support was provided to vulnerable households in affected areas. Initially, the government intended to provide such support mainly in the form of employment for cash wages.[44] In practice, however, the generation of employment fell far short of target, due to a lack of preparedness and supervisory capacity. On the other hand, the provision of unconditional relief in the form of free food rations (mainly from food aid) assumed considerable importance. In August 1984, nearly 1.4 million people, or 7 per cent of the total population, were estimated to be in receipt of free food distribution, and in January 1985 a very similar estimate was reported.[45] In drought-affected areas, the proportion of the population receiving food rations was much larger, and the survey of smallholders in Central and Eastern Kenya mentioned earlier found that over the same period the proportion of households receiving food assistance in the surveyed districts was as high as 45 per cent (see Table 11.6). The size of the rations distributed, however, appears to have been very small before the large-scale arrival of food aid in 1985.[46]

The allocation of relief to the needy was the responsibility of the provincial administration, which itself relied on famine relief committees and local 'chiefs' to identify those in need of support. The precise way in which this system actually worked is far from clear. According to Cohen and Lewis, the local chiefs 'knew the needs of their people, and by most reports did an effective, equitable job of distributing the government-supplied grain'.[47]

---

[44] The two slogans propounded by the government early on during the crisis were 'planning, not panic' and 'food imports and employment generation' (J. Downing et al. 1987: 265).

[45] Deloitte et al. (1986: 12). In 1985, the numbers in receipt of unconditional relief gradually decreased, though the amount of food distributed increased with the enlarged flow of food aid.

[46] The same survey reveals that, between July and Dec. 1984, the median food ration per recipient household varied between 197 and 633 calories per day in different regions (Downing 1988: table 4.19). For the same period, Anyango et al. (1989) estimate that 'the food relief averaged 5–10 per cent of individual requirements' for the recipients (see also Kamau et al. 1989). In 1985, the size of food rations was much larger, and did not in fact differ very much on average from the 'target' of 10 kgs of maize per person per month (Borton 1988, 1989).

[47] Cohen and Lewis (1987: 281). The authors had an active personal involvement in the government relief programmes, and provide a somewhat uncritical account of their implementation.

Another account, however, states that 'moving in the path of least resistance, the GOK [government of Kenya] would seem to rather divide the available food equally among recipients at the distributions thus defusing potentially uncomfortable situations'.[48]

It is not implausible that the allocation of food within specific communities was largely indiscriminate, and that 'targeting' operated mainly between different villages or regions (the impact of the drought was highly uneven geographically). On the other hand, an important factor facilitating the fair allocation of free food was the fact that most of it consisted of *yellow* maize, which is generally considered an inferior commodity in Kenya. The element of 'self-selection' involved in distributing a commodity that is somewhat disliked has been said by a number of commentators to have contributed to an allocation more geared to the most desperate.

Some indicators of the impact of the drought on the rural population in different ecological zones of Central and Eastern Kenya appear in Table 11.6. They reveal, *inter alia*, the importance of wage employment and remittances in sustaining affected households, and the broad coverage of food distribution in these districts at that time. The large cattle losses also confirm the exceptional severity of the drought.[49]

The precise impact of the drought on the well-being of the affected populations is hard to ascertain. Most commentators consider that 'famine was averted'. The apparent absence of confirmed reports of 'starvation deaths', as well as of distress migration on the part of entire families, lend some support to this view. On the other hand, there is clear evidence of widespread hunger as well as rising malnutrition in 1984.[50] Available data do not, unfortunately, seem to allow a detailed and reliable analysis of the demographic and nutritional impact of the drought.

While the credit which the Kenyan government has been given for averting a severe famine in 1984 appears to be largely deserved, an important query can nevertheless be raised as to whether the strategy it adopted made good use of available opportunities. A particularly compelling query, which seems to have escaped the attention of most commentators, concerns the balance between income support and price stabilization measures. Considering the small size of food distribution to vulnerable households in per capita terms (at least until

[48] Ray (1984: 2). Independent personal communications from two persons who were involved in the 1984 relief efforts confirm that food distribution centres typically did not discriminate between different groups of people, and provided identical rations to all recipients.

[49] For further details of livestock losses, see Borton (1988), Downing *et al.* (1989: ch. 1), Kamau *et al.* (1989), Anyango *et al* (1989), and Mwendwa (1989). The picture presented in other surveys is, if anything, grimmer than that offered by Table 11.6. According to Borton (1988), the 1984 drought may have depleted the *national* cattle herd by as much as 50% (p. vii).

[50] See the surveys of Anyango *et al.* (1989), Neumann *et al.* (1989), and Kamau *et al.* (1989). The relative absence of distress migration is discussed in Anyango *et al.* (1989).

Table 11.6 The 1984 drought and smallholder households in Central and Eastern Kenya

Characteristic	Households with the specified characteristic, by ecological zone (%)					
	1	2	3	4	5	All zones
Household member moved during 1984	23	7	21	26	38	25
Has a member in permanent employment	58	47	61	54	54	56
Received cash remittances from relatives or friends during drought	34	28	40	57	46	43
Major food changed during 1984	84	78	76	67	67	73
Received famine relief (from govt. or NGOs)	14	35	25	67	77	45
Slaughtered, sold, lost, or consumed cattle[a]	41(26)	45(35)	33(29)	44(46)	32(51)	38(58)

[a] In brackets, the percentage decrease in cattle holding, averaged over all households surveyed in the respective zone.

Source: Anyango *et al.* (1989: tables 13.6, 13.9). Based on survey data collected in Jan. 1985 by the Central Bureau of Statistics on behalf of the National Environment Secretariat. In Kenya, a smallholder is 'typically defined as a rural landowner with less than 22 hectares' (Akong'a and Downing 1987: 92). Ecological zones appear in increasing order of drought-proneness, based on rainfall data.

1985), it appears that famine prevention measures attempted to operate mainly through the level of food prices rather than through the generation of compensating incomes.[51] In turn, the stability of prices was pursued through a policy of commercial imports from abroad into the worst-affected districts. At the same time, however, government regulations prevented private traders from moving food from surplus to deficit areas within Kenya.

As was mentioned earlier, interdistrict food movements in Kenya are tightly regulated by the National Cereals and Produce Board, which subcontracts food transport to licensed private traders. Several studies have shown that restrictions on interregional movements have the effect of exacerbating the intensity of local shortages and the disparity of retail prices between regions.[52]

[51] According to Borton (1988), free distribution of food accounted for only 15% of the cereals imported between Sept. 1984 and June 1985 (p. 19).

[52] On this, see particularly Olsen (1984). See also Akong'a and Downing (1987) and Sperling (1987a). Note that the volatility of retail prices is compatible with the control of 'gazetted prices' mentioned earlier.

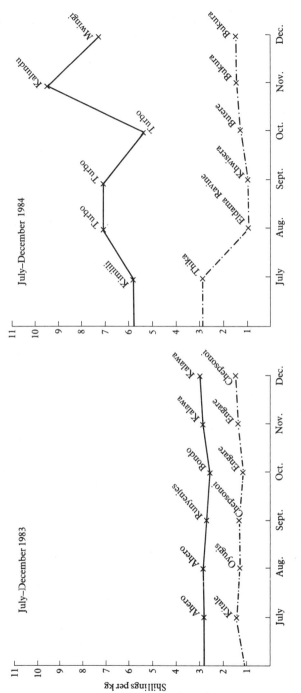

Note: The upper line indicates the retail price of maize in the market where it was the highest in the corresponding month. The lower line indicates the retail price where it was the lowest.

Source: As in Table 11.7.

Fig. 11.1 Minimum and maximum retail price of maize in Kenya, 1983 and 1984

Table 11.7 Retail prices of maize in Kenya, 1984

Market	Jan. 1984 (Kshs/kg)	Nov. 1984 (Kshs/kg)	Increase (%)	Province
Kalundu	2.50	9.31	272	Eastern
Mwingi	2.50	9.00	260	Eastern
Kiambu	2.14	5.30	148	Central
Machakos	2.40	5.76	140	Eastern
Iciara	2.53	5.94	135	Eastern
Limuru	2.02	4.19	107	Central
Runyenjes	2.57	4.70	83	Eastern
Thika	2.86	4.91	72	Central
Kandara	2.84	4.76	68	Central
Embu Town	2.92	4.89	67	Eastern
Eldoret	2.00	2.92	46	Rift Valley
Kitale	1.51	2.11	40	Rift Valley
Bondo	2.50	3.33	33	Nyanza
Ahero	2.51	3.19	27	Nyanza
Sondu	2.31	2.73	18	Nyanza
Mumias	2.35	2.69	14	Western
Luanda	2.71	2.57	−5	Western

Source: Republic of Kenya, Central Bureau of Statistics, Ministry of Finance and Planning, *Market Information Bulletin* (Jan.–June 1984 and July–Dec. 1984 issues). The markets in the table are all those for which data are provided in the *Bulletin* for both months.

This phenomenon was clearly visible during the drought year itself: while food prices were sharply rising in drought-affected districts, they were only sluggishly rising or even *falling* in many others (see Fig. 11.1 and Table 11.7). Maize prices in different markets varied, at one point, by a factor of nearly *ten*.[53] Even between adjacent districts, price disparities seem to have been exceptionally large (Table 11.8).

The detrimental effects of this policy of trade restrictions on the entitlements of vulnerable groups in drought-affected areas are not difficult to guess. For instance, after stressing the role of food shortages and high prices in undermining the entitlements of poor households in the Samburu district of northern Kenya, Louise Sperling comments:

[The] problem of local distribution was sufficiently severe to result in the convening of a district-level meeting as early as 14th June 1984. The District Commissioner called together the eleven or twelve wholesalers to discuss 'the erratic supply of commodities'. Maize prices are strictly controlled by the state, and the local traders claimed they were losing money on maize sales. The allowed mark-up could not cover the costs of

[53] For details of food price patterns during the drought, see the government of Kenya's *Market Information Bulletin*, and also Maganda (1989). Careful econometric analysis of time-series data on food prices in Kenya confirms that the interregional disparity of prices sharply increased in 1984 (Jane Corbett, Food Studies Group, Oxford, personal communication).

Table 11.8 Maize prices in Central and Eastern Kenya, 1984

Zone	Price of white maize (Kshs/kg)		Increase (Jan.–Dec.) (%)
	Jan.–Mar.	Oct.–Dec.	
1	3.98	5.94	49
2	3.25	5.50	69
3	2.80	6.20	121
4	2.94	7.22	146
5	3.49	10.24	193

Note: The ecological zones are the same as in Table 2.6.

Source: Anyango *et al.* (1989: table 13.10).

transport and loading to these more remote areas. Even considerable government pressure to encourage traders to keep their shelves full did not result in an increase in the local availability of maize . . . Again, the poor disproportionately suffered from these shortages. They could not afford to buy grain in bulk when it did arrive. Equally, they did not have the means to purchase alternative, more costly foodstuffs.[54]

It is not completely surprising, then, if the 1984 drought is remembered by some of the affected populations as *Ni Kwa Ngweta*, or 'I could die with cash'.[55] The strangulated flow of food through different parts of the country must have accounted for much of this paradoxical perception.

To conclude, while the efforts made by the government of Kenya in 1984 to import food and distribute it in drought-affected areas well ahead of large-scale famine were no doubt remarkable, it may be that certain aspects of the relief programme have not received adequately critical scrutiny. To some extent, the acute need to rush food from abroad into the worst-affected regions was a result of the parallel efforts that were made, partly for political reasons, to prevent food exports from surplus areas (or to direct such exports towards Nairobi). It appears that, in some respects, government intervention during the drought was undoing with one hand the harm it had done with the other.

Zimbabwe

The so-called 'Zimbabwean miracle' in food production has received wide attention recently. By contrast, the impressive programmes of direct entitlement protection adopted by the Zimbabwean government to prevent the prolonged drought of 1982–4 from precipitating a major famine seem to have been relatively neglected.[56] The assumption, presumably, is that a country

---

[54] Sperling (1987a: 269).   [55] Downing (1986: 7).

[56] To the best of my knowledge an in-depth analysis of these events has not been published to this day. However, see Government of Zimbabwe (1986a, 1986b), Gaidzanwa (1986), Leys (1986), Bratton (1987), Davies and Sanders (1987a, 1987b), Loewenson (1986), Loewenson and Sanders (1988), Mitter (1988), Tagwireyi (1988), and Weiner (1988), for many valuable insights.

with growing food supplies cannot possibly know the threat of famine. The experience of famines all over the world, however, shows how misleading and dangerous this assumption can be. In the case of Zimbabwe too, a closer examination of the facts reveals that the prevention of a famine in 1982–4 must be attributed as much to far-reaching measures of public support in favour of affected populations as to the abundance of food supplies.

Since independence in 1980, Zimbabwe has been ruled by the elected and re-elected ZANU (Zimbabwe African National Union) party led by Robert Mugabe, though the political system involves a multi-party structure. A notable feature of ZANU is its very wide and largely rural support base, inherited from the independence struggle. Political debate is intense in Zimbabwe, and the press is one of the most active and unconstrained in Africa. The press played, in fact, a conspicuous role in keeping the government on its toes throughout the drought period.[57]

In spite of the socialist aims of the government, the economy has retained private ownership and market incentives. On the other hand, the government of independent Zimbabwe has carried out a major revolution in the area of social services. The great strides made since 1980 in the areas of health and nutrition have, in particular, received wide recognition.[58]

In comparison with most other African countries, Zimbabwe's economy (including the agricultural sector) is relatively prosperous and diversified. However, the heritage of the colonial period also includes massive economic and social inequalities. The agricultural sector is highly dualistic, the larger part of the more fertile land being cultivated by a small number of commercial farms while peasant production remains the dominant feature of 'communal areas'. Even within the communal areas, sharp regional contrasts exist both in productive potential and in access to infrastructural support.[59] Further divisions exist between racial and class groups as well as between rural and urban areas. As a result, large sections of the population live in acute poverty in spite

[57] On the extensive coverage of the drought in the Zimbabwean press, see the accounts of Leys (1986), Bratton (1987), and Mitter (1988). Some of the more widely circulated newspapers, such as the *Herald*, did not always take a sharply adversarial stance given their generally supportive attitude *vis-à-vis* the ZANU government. However, even they played a role in maintaining a strong sense of urgency by constantly reporting on the prevalence of undernutrition and hardship in the countryside, echoing parliamentary debates on the subject of drought, calling for action against profiteering, and exposing the 'scandal' of rural women driven to prostitution by hunger (on the latter see the *Herald* 1983).

[58] See e.g. Donelan (1983), Government of Zimbabwe (1984), Waterson and Sanders (1984), Mandaza (1986), Davies and Sanders (1987a, 1987b), Loewenson and Sanders (1988), and Tagwireyi (1988). To mention only two important areas of rapid advance, the percentage of children fully immunized in Zimbabwe increased from 27% in 1982 to 85% in 1988 (Tagwireyi 1988: 8), and school enrolment increased at an annual rate of 20% between 1979 and 1985 (Davies and Sanders 1987b: 297).

[59] This point is stressed in Weiner (1987) and Weiner and Moyo (1988). For further discussion of production relations in Zimbabwe's rural economy and their implications for living standards and famine vulnerability, see also Bratton (1987), Rukuni and Eicher (1987), Rukuni (1988), and Weiner (1988).

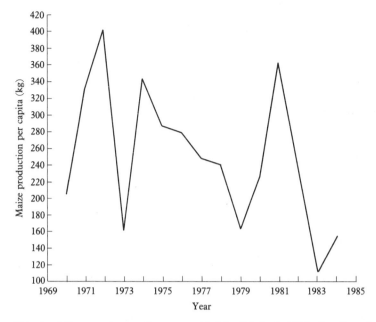

Source: Calculated from production figures provided in Rohrbach (1988: fig. 1), and from population data given in UNICEF (1988: tables 1 and 5).

Fig. 11.2 Maize production per capita in Zimbabwe, 1970–1984

of the relative prosperity of the economy as a whole. At the time of independence, health and nutrition problems in Zimbabwe were extremely serious, even in comparison with other African countries.[60]

The 'production miracle' in Zimbabwe is of relatively recent origin. In fact, from the early 1970s until after the drought period, there was—to say the least—little evidence of any upward trend in food production per capita (see Fig. 11.2). On the other hand, it must be remembered that, over the same period, Zimbabwe remained a net *exporter* of food in most years. The plentiful harvest which immediately preceded the drought ensured that large stocks of maize were available when the country faced the threat of famine.[61]

---

[60] See e.g. Sanders (1982), World Bank (1983), Loewenson (1984), and Government of Zimbabwe (1984). These studies give a clear picture of the connections between this poor record and the massive inequalities in economic opportunities and access to public services of the colonial period. In the early 1970s, for instance, the life expectancy of a European female was more than twenty years longer than that of an African female (Agere 1986: 359).

[61] It is worth noting that while the Zimbabwean 'miracle' has often been attributed to the astonishing power of price incentives (see e.g. *The Economist* 1985 and Park and Jackson 1985), the expansion of the rural economy since independence has in fact involved a great deal more than a simple 'price fix'. On the extensive and fruitful involvement of the government of independent Zimbabwe in infrastructural support, agricultural extension, credit provision, support of co-operatives, etc., see Bratton (1986, 1987), Eicher and Staatz (1986), Eicher (1988), Rohrbach (1988), and Weiner (1988).

The drought lasted three years, and was of highest intensity in agroclimatic terms during the second year (i.e. 1983). In the drier parts of the country, the maize crop (Zimbabwe's principal staple crop) was 'a total failure throughout the drought years'.[62] Maize sales to the Grain Marketing Board fell by more than two-thirds between 1980–1 and 1982–3. Livestock losses between 1978 and 1983 have been estimated at 36 per cent of the communal herd.[63]

For many rural dwellers, remittances from relatives involved in regular employment or migrant labour were a crucial source of support during the drought. As in the case of Kenya (discussed earlier), it was found in Zimbabwe that 'the households most engaged in selling labour to the wider economy . . . are the least susceptible to drought'.[64] Many households, however, did not have access to this source of sustenance, and for them government relief was often the main or even the only source of food.

The drought relief programme of the government was an ambitious and far-reaching one. Famine prevention measures were taken early in 1982, and given a high political and financial priority throughout the drought. The main entitlement protection measures were large-scale distribution of take-home food rations to the adult population, and supplementary feeding for children under 5. Commenting on the importance of free food distribution for the survival of the poor, one study of drought relief in southern Zimbabwe comments that 'for those without access to cash and other entitlements it was their only food intake'.[65]

It is not easy to assess how large a part of the population benefited from free food distribution. Estimates of 2 to 3 million people being fed in rural areas at the peak of the programme, as against a total rural population of 5.7 million in 1982, have been cited in various studies.[66] A survey of 464 households carried

[62] Bratton (1987: 224). This statement, more precisely, refers to the two least fertile among Zimbabwe's five agroecological regions. These two regions account for 64% of Zimbabwe's land, 74% of the 'communal lands', and about two-thirds of the communal area population.

[63] Bratton (1987: 223–5). Weiner (1988) reports declines in draught stock during the drought period of 47% and 21% respectively in the two agroecological regions mentioned in the previous footnote.

[64] Leys (1986: 262). On the importance of wage labour and remittances for the rural economy of Zimbabwe in general, and for mitigating the impact of the drought on the rural population in particular, see also Bratton (1987) and Weiner (1987).

[65] Leys (1986: 270). Similarly, Weiner (1988) states that 'during the 1982–4 period the government drought relief programme became the primary means of survival for about 2.5 million people' (p. 71). While the present discussion focuses largely on the food distribution component of the drought relief programme, it is worth noting that (1) policy developments during the drought included an increasingly marked preference for public works programmes (supplemented by unconditional relief for the destitute) as opposed to large-scale distribution of free food, and (2) the drought relief programme had a number of other important components, such as water supply schemes, cattle protection measures, and inputs provision. On both points, see Government of Zimbabwe (1986a).

[66] See e.g. Government of Zimbabwe (1983: 21), Bratton (1987: 237), and Mitter (1988: 4). The official version seems to be that 'at the height of the drought about 2.1 million people had to be fed every month' (Government of Zimbabwe 1986a).

Table 11.9 Drought and drought relief in Chibi District, Zimbabwe, 1983–1984

Village	No. of households	% of cattle which died in previous twelve months	% of population receiving food rations[a]
A	52	28	62
B	36	34	64
C	44	32	68
D	39	47	54

[a] Per capita rations of 20 kg per month.

Source: Constructed from Leys (1986). According to the author, Chibi was one of the worst affected districts.

out in four communal areas selected for their environmental diversity found that more than 50 per cent of the surveyed households were receiving free maize in 1982–3 and 1983–4.[67] Another study, focusing on four villages in one of the most affected districts, reveals a proportion of population in receipt of free food rations ranging from 54 to 68 per cent (see Table 11.9). Very similar findings are reported in a number of further household surveys.[68] While the precise extent of food distribution is difficult to ascertain, its scale was undoubtedly impressive. The size of individual food rations—officially 20 kg of maize per head per month—was also astonishingly large.

Of course, the task of organizing food distribution on such a gigantic scale was by no means an easy one. The implementation of relief measures, much helped by the popular mobilization, the administrative dynamism, and the political stability associated with the post-independence reconstruction efforts, has attracted favourable comments from many observers. But frequent complaints on the part of recipients about the delays, uncertainties, and frauds involved in food distribution have also been reported.[69] In relieving logistic constraints, the subcontracting of food delivery to the private sector played a major role. However, the aberrations involved in organizing complex procurement operations from rural areas to central government depots before hauling food back to the countryside for free distribution have been pointed out.[70] And disruptions in food deliveries seem to have intensified after the attempt was made (in September 1983) to substitute government transport for private transport.[71]

[67] Bratton (1987: table 10.8(b)).

[68] See especially Weiner (1988: table 6.4), and Matiza et al. (1988).

[69] On both of these viewpoints, see e.g. USAID (1983), Leys (1986), Bratton (1987), Davies and Sanders (1987b), and Mitter (1988).

[70] Bratton (1987: 238).   [71] Leys (1986: 270).

The free distribution of food raised its own problems. The population eligible for food rations seems to have been considered, in practice, as that of households without a member in regular employment.[72] How fairly this criterion was actually applied is not easy to ascertain, and conflicting views have been expressed on this question. For instance, one author reports on the basis of extensive field work in southern Zimbabwe that 'as far as I could assess, these criteria were applied fairly and, at the sub-district level, were felt to be fair', and the evidence presented from four village studies in one of the worst-affected districts broadly supports this assessment.[73] But another author suggests the possibility that 'in practice, the distribution pattern was indiscriminate; those who were ineligible received relief food, while those who were truly needy may have gone short'.[74]

The politicization of food distribution during the drought was also apparent in a number of ways (with both negative and positive implications). First, party cadres have played a major role in many places in implementing the distribution of food, and this seems to have led to some favouritism along party lines.[75] Second, the coverage of the drought relief programme in Matabeleland, the stronghold of political dissidents, has been described as 'exceedingly patchy'.[76] Third, food distribution was restricted to rural areas—a highly interesting feature of the relief programme given the frequent bias of public distribution systems in favour of urban classes. It is tempting to interpret this 'rural bias' as a reflection of the politics of ZANU and the predominantly rural character of its support base.

In spite of these reservations, the overall effectiveness of entitlement protection measures during the drought is beyond question. It is not only that 'starvation deaths' have been largely and perhaps even entirely prevented.[77] A

[72] Bratton (1987) describes the eligible population as 'the "needy" . . . defined as those with insufficient grain in the home granary and without a close family member working for a wage' (p. 238). Leys (1986), on the other hand, states that free food distribution was intended for 'the members of households in which the head of the household earned an income under the statutory minimum wage' (p. 269), but later adds that this involved 'distinguishing between those households where the head of household held a formal sector job' and others (p. 270). In practice it is likely that the two sets of criteria described by these authors did not diverge substantially.

[73] Leys (1986: 270). Mitter (1988) also gives credit to the ZANU government for 'the smooth running of the relief committees' (p. 5).

[74] Bratton (1987: 238). The viewpoint expressed by Bratton is based on a personal communication from a colleague at the University of Zimbabwe and would seem to be less robustly founded than that of Leys.

[75] Daniel Weiner (University of Toledo), personal communication. See also Leys (1986).

[76] Leys (1986: 271). The government put the blame on dissidents for disrupting relief efforts, and even at one stage held them 'responsible for the drought' (see Mitter 1988 for further discussion).

[77] According to Bratton, 'it is safe to say that no person in Zimbabwe died as a direct result of starvation' (Bratton 1987: 225). According to Leys, 'one consequence of the drought for some of the rural African population was hunger, and on occasion and specific places, deaths from starvation' (Leys 1986: 258).

Table 11.10 Nutritional status of children in Zimbabwe, 1981–2 and 1983

Area	% of children (aged 0 to 5) suffering from second or third degree malnutrition			
	Weight for age		Weight for height	
	1981–2	1983	1981–2	1983
Commercial farming area	42	14, 20[a]	16	8, 7[a]
Communal area[b]	20	11	13	3
Mine area	22	9	6	4
Urban area	6	4	6	2

[a] These figures refer respectively to (1) farms benefiting from a health project initiated in 1981–2, and (2) farms excluded from the health project.

[b] Resurvey (1983) area adjacent to that of baseline survey (1981–2) area.

Source: Loewenson (1986: table 3). Based on a sample survey of nearly 2,000 children in Mashonaland Central. For further details and discussion, see also Loewenson (1984).

further achievement of the government's ambitious relief programme, in combination with the general expansion of health and education facilities since independence, has been a noticeable improvement in the health status of the population of rural Zimbabwe in spite of the severe drought. An important indication of this improvement is the substantial reduction of infant mortality during the drought period.[78] A significant decline in child morbidity, at least in relation to immunizable diseases, has also been reported, and related to the government's vigorous immunization campaigns.[79]

The evidence on the nutritional status of the population during the drought is mixed. There was concern, with good reason, about sharply rising levels of undernutrition in the early phase of the drought, and these were expressed in many informal reports.[80] There is, however, some evidence of declining undernutrition after the relief programme expanded on a large scale in 1983 (see Table 11.10).[81] Taking the drought period as a whole, the available evidence suggests the absence of marked change in the nutritional status of the Zimbabwean population.[82] This is remarkable enough, given the severity of the initial threat.

[78] For detailed discussions of mortality decline in Zimbabwe since independence, see Davies and Sanders (1987a, 1987b), Loewenson and Sanders (1988), and Sanders and Davies (1988). It has been claimed that the extent of mortality reduction in Zimbabwe between 1980 and 1985 was as large as 50% (The Times 1985; Bratton 1987: 238).

[79] See Loewenson and Sanders (1988).

[80] See e.g. Bratton (1987: 224), Mitter (1988: 3–4), and Moto (1983).

[81] See Loewenson (1984, 1986) for further discussion of these findings.

[82] See Davies and Sanders (1987a, 1987b), Loewenson and Sanders (1988), and Sanders and Davies (1988) for detailed reviews of the evidence. See also the results of regular surveys (carried out by the government of Zimbabwe) presented in Tagwireyi (1988).

Botswana

As a land-locked, sparsely populated, and drought-prone country experiencing rapid population growth, massive ecological deterioration, and shrinking food production, Botswana possesses many of the features that are thought to make the Sahelian countries highly vulnerable to famine. There are, of course, also important contrasts between the two regions. One of them arises from the highly democratic nature of Botswana's political regime, and—relatedly perhaps—the comparative efficiency of its administration. Also, while many Sahelian countries have suffered from declining or stagnating per capita incomes in recent decades, Botswana has enjoyed a growth rate which is estimated as one of the highest in the world.

Economic growth in Botswana has, however, followed a highly uneven pattern. In fact, much of this rapid growth has to do with the recent expansion of diamond mining, a productive sector of little direct relevance to the rural poor. Against a background of booming earnings in industry, there is some evidence of increasing rural unemployment and falling rural incomes since the early 1970s. One study goes so far as suggesting that rural incomes in Botswana (inclusive of transfers and remittances) have been *declining* in real terms at the rate of 5 per cent per year during the period 1974–81.[83] The year 1981–2 marked the beginning of a prolonged and severe drought which lasted until 1986–7, and which would certainly have been accompanied by an even sharper deterioration of income and employment opportunities in the absence of vigorous public support measures. Fast overall economic growth is no guarantee of protection against famine.

The rural economy, mostly based on livestock, crop production, and derived activities, suffered a predictable recession during the drought. The output of food crops fell to negligible levels (Table 11.11). Cattle mortality increased substantially, and the decline of employment opportunities further aggravated the deterioration of rural livelihoods.[84] In a socio-economic survey of 284 rural households carried out in 1984, more than half of the respondents reported 'having no cash income' (other than relief income).[85]

By 1981–2, however, Botswana had set up an entitlement protection system

---

[83] See Hay *et al.* (1986), especially table 2. A published summary of the main results of this major study of drought relief in Botswana can be found in Hay (1988). On the rural economy of Botswana, see Chernichovsky *et al.* (1985).

[84] For details, see Hay *et al.* (1986) and Quinn *et al.* (1987). It should be mentioned that while livestock losses during the drought were perhaps not dramatic in *aggregate* terms (according to Morgan 1986, the size of the national cattle herd declined by 22% between 1982 and 1986), it has been frequently noted that these losses disproportionately hit small herds. Cattle deaths in small herds have been estimated at 'more than 40% for several years' (Diana Callear, National Food Strategy Coordinator, personal communication). Also, poor households in rural Botswana derive a greater than average part of their total incomes from crops (even harder hit by the drought than livestock). The threat which the drought represented to the entitlements of vulnerable groups was therefore much more serious than aggregate figures about livestock mortality and the importance of livestock in the rural economy would tend to suggest.   [85] Hay *et al.* (1986: 85).

Table 11.11 Food crop performance in Botswana, 1968–1984

Year	Area planted (000 ha)	Yield (kg/ha)	Output (000 tonnes)
1968	200	180	36
1969	240	258	62
1970	202	69	14
1971	246	293	72
1972	251	343	86
1973	139	101	14
1974	255	290	74
1975	250	284	71
1976	261	295	77
1977	255	290	74
1978	260	192	50
1979	160	62	10
1980	268	172	46
1981	274	201	55
1982	193	89	17
1983	226	63	14
1984	197	36	7

Source: Hay *et al.* (1986: tables 5, 6).

exemplary in its scope and integration. This system was, in fact, the outcome of a long process of experimentation, evaluation, and learning. Moderately successful but instructive experiments with famine relief in the 1960s and early 1970s were later followed by a series of evaluations and debates which provided the crucial foundation of Botswana's outstanding relief system.[86] The drought of 1979–80 played a particularly important role in this respect.

Famine relief during the 1979–80 drought was essentially an experiment in what may be called the 'strategy of direct delivery', based on the transportation of food into famine affected areas and its distribution to the destitute.[87] The operation was considerably hampered by logistic difficulties connected with the transportation and distribution of food, though a noticeable improvement occurred after the adoption of extensive subcontracting to private truckers.

[86] The Sandford Report (Sandford 1977) provided a useful background investigation of drought in Botswana. The Symposium on Drought in Botswana (Botswana Society 1979) which was convened, quite remarkably, in spite of the then prosperity of agriculture and the economy, was an invaluable forum of discussion on numerous aspects of the problem. Gooch and MacDonald (1981a, 1981b) provided an illuminating evaluation of relief efforts during the 1979–80 drought and far-reaching recommendations for improvement. For an excellent analysis of the development of Botswana's entitlement protection system, see Borton (1984, 1986).

[87] See Drèze and Sen (1989) for further discussion of this approach to famine prevention. The following details are based on Relief and Development Institute (1985), Morgan (1985), and especially Gooch and MacDonald (1981a, 1981b).

Food deliveries in different parts of the country matched poorly with the extent of distress. The allocation of food within the rural population was largely indiscriminate, partly because the selective distribution of food was found to be 'socially divisive'.[88] While a large-scale famine was averted, the relief operations did not succeed in preventing increased malnutrition, excess mortality, or even starvation deaths.[89]

The lessons of this experiment were not lost, however. In fact, the detailed evaluation carried out by Gooch and MacDonald made a crucial contribution to the design of Botswana's entitlement protection system as it exists today. Their recommendations included: (1) the issue of a Relief Manual providing clear and coherent advance guidelines to the administration about the provision of drought relief; (2) the adoption of a famine prevention strategy based on the unlimited provision of employment to the able-bodied (for a subsistence wage paid in cash), supplemented by unconditional relief for vulnerable groups. These recommendations, while not literally implemented to this day, have provided the basis for a sustained improvement in famine prevention measures.[90]

Careful planning (and buoyant government revenue) would not have gone far enough in the absence of a strong motivation on the part of the government to respond to the threat of famine. Drought relief, however, has consistently been a high political priority in Botswana, and an object of rival promises and actions on the part of competing political parties. It is also revealing that, when drought struck the country again in 1981–2, early action was forthcoming in spite of the absence of a formal early warning system.[91] As in India, the politics of famine prevention in Botswana are intimately linked with the accountability of the ruling party to the electorate, the activism of opposition parties, the vigilance of the press, and—last but not least—the rising demands for public support on the part of the affected populations.[92]

The drought of 1982–7 provided a severe test of the country's growing

---

[88] Gooch and MacDonald (1981b: 11). In other cases, the distribution of food was vulnerable to frank abuses.

[89] On this, see Gooch and MacDonald (1981b: 12–13).

[90] In the absence of an explicit Relief Manual, the Gooch–MacDonald Report itself has served as a surrogate contingency plan during the recent drought (Holm and Morgan 1985), and the associated measures have gradually 'sunk into' the administrative routine (Richard Morgan, personal communication).

[91] Botswana does have a well-developed 'nutrition surveillance' system, but this is used mainly for the purposes of monitoring and targeting rather than as a warning device, and the decision to launch a major relief operation in 1982 was taken long before the system detected a significant increase in undernutrition. Nor do other components of Botswana's evolving early warning system seem to have played a major role in triggering the government's response in 1982 (see e.g. Relief and Development Institute 1985).

[92] For a detailed discussion of this issue, and of 'the political value of drought relief' in Botswana, see Holm and Morgan (1985) and Holm and Cohen (1988). On the politics of famine prevention in India, see Sen (1982), Ram (1986), and ch. 3 in this volume.

ability to prevent famines. The entitlement protection measures invoked to avert the threat of famine in Botswana in this event involved three areas of action: (1) the restoration of adequate food availability, (2) the large-scale provision of employment for cash wages, and (3) direct food distribution to selected groups.[93]

Unlike in 1979–80, the restoration of food adequacy in 1982–7 relied on a more varied and discerning strategy than that of 'direct delivery'. While Botswana did receive large amounts of food aid during the drought, the support of incomes through employment generation (financed out of general government revenue) was not *tied* to the receipt of food aid. Moreover, food aid was substantially complemented by private imports of food from abroad, and it is plausible that had food aid been interrupted or delayed this alternative source of food supply would have enabled the relief system to operate with no major loss of effectiveness.[94]

Trade and distribution within the country has been largely ensured by Botswana's 'widespread and highly competitive retail network operating in all but the remoter areas'.[95] The effectiveness of this system, and of the process of spatial arbitrage, is visible from the remarkable degree of uniformity in the level of food prices in different parts of the country during the drought (Table 11.12). The contrast with our earlier findings on Kenya is striking.

Another important contrast between drought relief in 1982–7 and in 1979–80 has been the much greater reliance, in the former case, on cash-based employment generation as a vehicle of income generation. The provision of employment has, in fact, fallen short of the vision of 'employment guarantee' contemplated by Gooch and MacDonald, and it has been repeatedly observed that the demand for employment has exceeded the number of jobs available.[96] Nevertheless, the extent of income support provided to vulnerable households by 'Labour-Based Relief Programmes' has been considerable. In 1985–6 they provided around 3 million person-days of employment to 74,000 labourers. It

---

[93] It should be mentioned that the drought relief programme as a whole went far beyond these measures of short-term entitlement protection. Public intervention was also very significant in areas such as the provision of water and the promotion of agricultural recovery. For comprehensive analyses of the drought relief programme, see Tabor (1983), Borton (1984, 1986), Holm and Morgan (1985), Relief and Development Institute (1985), Morgan (1985, 1986, 1988), Hay *et al.* (1986), Quinn *et al.* (1987), Hay (1988), and Holm and Cohen (1988). See also Government of Botswana (1980, 1985*a*, 1985*b*, 1987, 1988).

[94] Botswana belongs to the South African Customs Union (SACU), which *inter alia* allows the free movement of food between South Africa, Botswana, Lesotho, and Swaziland. According to Tabor (1983: 71), 'in 1981, 89% of Botswana's imports came from South Africa or through South African borders'. See Cathie and Herrmann (1988) for an econometric analysis of the effect of SACU membership on food prices and food security in Botswana.

[95] Morgan (1985: 49).

[96] See e.g. Hay *et al.* (1986) and Quinn *et al.* (1987). This finding must be interpreted bearing in mind that the level of wages paid was 'roughly equivalent to the salary earned by maids and security guards in urban areas and considerably more than cattle herders earned on cattle-posts' (Quinn *et al.* 1987: 18).

Table 11.12 Price of maize meal in different regions, Botswana, 1980–1983

Region	Price in August 1980 (Pula/bag)	Price in April 1983 (Pula/bag)	Increase (%)
Ramotswa	3.84	4.73	23
Francistown	3.56	4.41	24
Mmadinare	3.73	4.70	26
Maun	4.22	5.38	27
Tonota	3.59	4.68	30
Molepolole	3.70	4.81	30
Mochudi	3.41	4.55	33
Gaborone	3.39	4.51	33
Lobatse	3.34	4.48	34
Kanye	3.41	4.58	34
Serowe	3.56	4.80	35
Palapye	3.36	4.54	35
Mahalapye	3.48	4.86	40
Selibe-Pikwe	3.33	4.71	41
Shoshong	3.38	4.82	43
Thamaga	3.35	4.97	48
Moshupa	3.38	5.02	49
All regions, unweighted average	3.53	4.74	34

Source: Tabor (1983: table 4.5).

has also been estimated that Labour-Based Relief Programmes 'replaced' almost one-third of rural incomes lost from crop failures between 1983 and 1985.[97] Informal evaluations of the productive value of the works undertaken suggest that the contribution of these programmes to national investment has been far from negligible.[98]

Along with this strategy of employment generation, free food has been distributed on a large scale, mainly in the form of 'take-home' rations. The eligibility conditions for food distribution in rural areas are very broad, and include not only the destitute but also other categories such as all preschool children, all children in primary school, all children aged 6–10 not attending school, and all pregnant or lactating women. As a result, the proportion of Botswana's population in receipt of free food rations was as high as two-thirds in 1985.[99] It has been argued, moreover, that 'this food is taken home, mixed in

[97] Quinn *et al.* (1987: 18, 21). The population of Botswana was a little over one million at the time.

[98] See Hay *et al.* (1986) for a detailed discussion.

[99] Calculated from Hay *et al.* (1986: tables 10, 11). According to the same source, yearly rations amounted to nearly 60 kg of food (mainly cereals) per recipient. For a succinct account of the various components of Botswana's food distribution programme, see Hay (1988).

the family pot and distributed as usual among the family members'.[100] Thus, in practice the distribution of food rations is largely indiscriminate.

A number of commentators have suggested that Botswana's entitlement protection system could be considerably improved by a better 'targeting' of resources towards vulnerable individuals or households.[101] Indeed, the rural society in Botswana is a highly inegalitarian one, with more than half of rural incomes accruing to the wealthiest decile of the rural population.[102] The indiscriminate distribution of food can be a rewarding form of political patronage, but it does not necessarily work to the greatest advantage of vulnerable groups.

How better targeting could be achieved, however, is not altogether clear. An adjustment in the balance between food distribution and employment generation in favour of the latter is an obvious option, which has indeed been advocated. Its attractiveness depends on how need-orientated the distribution of employment really is. In this case the answer to the latter question is far from clear, given that the conditions of employment seem to attract large numbers and that the available work is often divided equally among applicants.[103]

Be that as it may, the experience of drought relief in Botswana in 1982–7 amply demonstrates the effectiveness of a famine prevention system based on the combination of adequate political incentives and insightful administrative guidelines. While the drought of 1982–7 was far more prolonged and severe than that of 1979–80, and led to a much greater disruption of the rural economy, the extent of human suffering was comparatively small. There is no evidence of starvation deaths or of distress migration on any significant scale.[104] The nutritional status of children only deteriorated marginally and temporarily (Fig. 11.3). One study also reports that 'those who have experienced previous droughts say that the decline in suffering among the disadvantaged is dramatic'.[105] Further, drought relief measures in Botswana seem to

---

[100] Tabor (1983: 37). On this see also Hay et al. (1986).

[101] See e.g. Gooch and MacDonald (1981a, 1981b), Tabor (1983), Borton (1984), Relief and Development Institute (1985), Hay et al. (1986), and Holm and Cohen (1988).

[102] Chernichovsky et al. (1985: table 1.2), based on the 1974–5 Rural Income Distribution Survey. The same survey reveals that 5% of the rural population owns 50% of the national herd (Quinn et al. 1987: 5).

[103] See Hay et al. (1986). Note that, according to first-hand observations, about 80% of labourers are women (Tabor 1983; Morgan 1988).

[104] According to Morgan (1988), 'starvation, even among extremely isolated communities, was entirely averted during the droughts' (p. 37).

[105] Holm and Morgan (1985: 469). None of the studies cited in this section provide estimates of excess mortality during the drought. According to Borton, 'mortality estimates are poor in Botswana so it is not possible to estimate whether there has been a significant increase in the death rate' (Borton 1984: 92). Against the initial increase in undernutrition among children, it must be noted that (1) the incidence of severe undernutrition has been very small (Hay et al. 1986; Holm and Morgan 1985), and (2) seasonal fluctuations in nutritional status have virtually disappeared during the drought (Government of Botswana 1985a: table 5).

Note: The broken line shows the estimated incidence of undernutrition, taking into account changes in the recording system in 1985. The figures are derived from Botswana's Nutrition Surveillance System, which covered about 60% of all under-5s in Botswana in 1984 (Morgan 1985: 45). The increase in observed undernutrition in the early years of the drought may partly reflect the large increase in the coverage of the surveillance system that took place during those years (Hay 1988: 1125).

Source: Morgan (1988: fig. 5).

Fig. 11.3 Incidence of child undernutrition in Botswana, 1980–1986

have met with an impressive measure of success not only in preventing human suffering but also in preserving the productive potential of the rural economy.[106]

There is another aspect of Botswana's experience which deserves special mention here. A number of components of the drought relief programme, such as the distribution of food to certain vulnerable groups, the rehabilitation of malnourished children, and the provision of financial assistance to the destitute, have acquired a permanent status and are now an integral part of Botswana's social security system.[107] In the future, therefore, it can be expected that famine prevention measures will perhaps take the form of an *intensification* of social security measures applying in ordinary times. Such a policy development would be a natural extension of the current reliance on existing infrastructural and institutional arrangements for drought relief

[106] On this, see Morgan (1986). The preservation of the productive potential of the rural economy is related partly to the entitlement protection measures discussed here, but also partly to a wide array of explicit rehabilitation and recovery programmes. Though they are not the focus of our attention in this chapter, the importance of these programmes should not be underestimated.

[107] See Morgan (1986, 1988) and Holm and Cohen (1988) for further discussion of the interplay between drought relief and social security in Botswana in the last few decades.

purposes. This approach to the protection of entitlements during crises has, in general, much to commend it, in terms of administrative flexibility, likelihood of early response, simplification of logistic requirements, and ability to elicit broad political support.

11.5. *Concluding observations*

The African experiences reviewed in the previous section illustrate the challenging variety of political, social, and economic problems involved in the protection of entitlements in a crisis situation. It would be pointless, indeed inappropriate, to attempt to derive from these case-studies a blueprint for famine prevention in Africa. However, a number of commonalities involved in the recent experiences of famine prevention in Botswana, Cape Verde, Kenya, and Zimbabwe seem to provide the basis of some useful lessons.[108]

The importance of entitlement protection systems

There is a tendency, once the dust of an emergency has settled down, to seek the reduction of famine vulnerability primarily in enhanced economic growth, or the revival of the rural economy, or the diversification of economic activities. The potential contribution of greater prosperity, if it involves vulnerable groups, cannot be denied. At the same time, it is important to recognize that, no matter how fast they grow, countries where a large part of the population derive their livelihood from uncertain sources cannot hope to avert famines without specialized entitlement protection mechanisms involving direct public intervention. Rapid growth of the economy in Botswana, or of the agricultural sector in Kenya, or of food production in Zimbabwe, explain at best only a small part of their success in averting recurrent threats of famine. The distinguishing achievements of these countries (as well as of Cape Verde) really lie in their having provided direct public support to their populations in times of crisis.

This is an elementary point, and it is worth stressing only because it tends to be quickly forgotten after threats of famine have subsided. While entitlement protection is, intrinsically, a short-term task, building up flexible and effective response mechanisms is a long-term one. For most countries it involves a lengthy process of experimentation, evaluation, and learning. In countries such as Botswana and Cape Verde (or India for that matter), where a system of disaster response can be said to exist in a state of permanent preparedness, this process has taken several decades. It is encouraging that, after a long period of high exposure to contingencies and of reliance on international assistance, a number of countries in sub-Saharan Africa now attach increasing importance to the development of planned entitlement protection systems. These efforts need sustained attention and promotion.

---

[108] For a more general discussion of the issues considered in this concluding section, see Drèze and Sen (1989).

Initiative and agency

An important feature of recent famine prevention efforts in the four countries studied in this chapter is that, in each case, the initiative and conduct of emergency operations rested squarely with local or national institutions. This is not to say that international agencies played no positive part in such efforts. In fact, their contribution or partnership has, in each case, been helpful. But the essential tasks of co-ordination and leadership belonged primarily to the government and administration of the affected countries.

International perceptions of African governments are steeped in suspicion and sometimes even cynicism. It might be asked how this view squares with the positive involvement of national governments observed in the case-studies of the previous section. Part of the answer lies, undoubtedly, in the special features of the countries concerned. In particular, it is worth noting that the political systems of these countries involve greater pluralism and accountability than would apply in most other African countries.

It may be that, elsewhere in Africa, less confidence can be placed in the ability of national and local institutions to act as the prime agent in famine prevention. This pessimistic view needs, I believe, to be qualified in at least two ways.

First, it must be realized that, in spite of their frequently limited competence and motivation, local and national administrations often have, in many ways, an enormous 'comparative advantage' over international agencies when it comes to the implementation of entitlement protection measures. In particular, international relief agencies frequently find their operations encumbered by heavy and hasty investments in transport, storage, information, communications, administration, and the like when resources of this kind are, to some extent, readily available to the governments of affected countries.

Second, a notable pattern pervading many historical experiences of famine situations is that, when adequate incentives and pressure exist to elicit a response, the behaviour of the local administration is often characterized by an unusual degree of dynamism, initiative, and effectiveness.[109] The functioning of African administrations in ordinary times may therefore be a poor indication of their potential for response in crisis situations.

Early warning and early response

Formal 'early warning' techniques appear to have played only a minor role in the famine prevention experiences studied in this chapter.[110] Early response

---

[109] For further discussion of the possible motivations underlying the unexpected behaviour of administrations in crises situations, see Brennan *et al.* (1984) and Drèze (1988). See also the remarkable work of Pierre-Étienne Will (1980) on famine relief under the Qing dynasty in 18th-century China.

[110] This has been explicitly pointed out in the previous section in the cases of Botswana and Kenya. Cape Verde has no early warning system worth the name (CILSS 1986). There is no indication of Zimbabwe having a formal early warning system in any of the references cited earlier in relation to that country.

has been much more a matter of political incentives and motivation than one of informational or predictive wizardry.

As was mentioned earlier, the political systems of these countries are, by African standards, relatively open and pluralist (e.g. they all have an elected parliament). All except Cape Verde also have an active and largely uncensored press. The role of political opposition, parliamentary debate, public criticism, and adversarial journalism in galvanizing the national government into action has been central in Botswana as well as in Zimbabwe, and, to a lesser extent, in Kenya.

The general picture of public pressure that emerges in other African countries is admittedly not a very encouraging one. The opposition is often muzzled. Newspapers are rarely independent or free. The armed forces frequently suppress popular protest. To claim that there are clear signs of change in the direction of participatory politics and open journalism in Africa as a whole would undoubtedly be premature. But there is now much greater awareness of the problem and of the need for change. The long-term value of that creative dissatisfaction should not be underestimated.[111]

Moreover, it would be a mistake to regard sophisticated democratic institutions as indispensable to the existence of strong incentives for a government to respond to the threat of famine. It is true that the ability of a government to get away with letting a famine develop is much greater when there is no direct accountability to the public. But even fairly repressive governments should be—and have often been—wary of the prospects of popular discontent in such an event. Even where such prospects are remote, political ideology—if it takes the form of a commitment to the more deprived sections of the population —can be another creative force in motivating response. In the case of Cape Verde (and probably also Zimbabwe), this influence seems to have been important. As was pointed out in Section 11.2, the general attitude of African governments to the threat of famine is certainly not one of apathy and callousness (the main exception being, once again, related to war situations). There are good grounds for hoping that their commitment to famine prevention will receive further stimulation in the near future.

Food supply management

In each of the four countries studied in this chapter, the government took necessary steps to ensure an adequate availability of food. But the exact nature of these steps varied a great deal, and appealed to different strategic elements such as government purchases on international markets, private trade, food aid, and the depletion of public stocks.

This strategic diversity contrasts with the common belief that food aid is the only appropriate channel to enhance food availability in a famine-affected

---

[111] On the current role of the press in the context of African famines, and the emerging signs of positive change in some countries, see Yao and Kone (1986), Mitter (1987), and Reddy (1988).

country. It is true that three of these four countries (namely Botswana, Cape Verde, and Kenya) have *made use* of substantial quantities of food aid in their efforts to avert famine, but in no case have their entitlement protection measures been *contingent* on the timely arrival of such aid. In fact, entitlement protection policies have typically preceded the arrival of drought-related food aid commitments.

In this respect, entitlement protection measures in these countries have markedly departed from the strategy of 'direct delivery' commonly recommended or practised by international agencies such as the World Food Programme, which consists of dispatching food to affected countries, transporting it to vulnerable areas, and delivering it (in cooked form or otherwise) to famine victims. The case for exclusive reliance on the latter strategy rests implicitly on the combination of two assumptions: (1) that no effective entitlement protection is possible without a commensurate and simultaneous increase in food availability, and (2) that no reliable channel for increasing food availability exists other than the famine relief system itself. These assumptions appear to be highly questionable on both analytical and empirical grounds.

A particularly significant departure from the strategy of direct delivery is the use of cash support to protect the entitlements of vulnerable groups. This is not the place to assess the general merits and limitations of this approach.[112] But it is worth noting that reliance on cash support, which is sometimes thought to be highly unsuitable in the context of African famines, has been used with excellent effect in two of the four countries concerned (namely Botswana and Cape Verde).

Private trade and public distribution

Each of the four countries which have retained our attention has induced private trade to supplement the efforts of the public sector in moving food towards vulnerable areas. In Botswana and Cape Verde, this has taken the form of providing cash support on a large scale and leaving a substantial part of the task of food delivery to the market mechanism. In Kenya and Zimbabwe, it has taken the form of subcontracting to private traders the transport of food to specific destinations. In all cases, private trade could be confidently expected to move food in the right direction, i.e. towards (rather than out of) affected areas.

At the same time, the direct involvement of the public sector in food supply management has also been substantial in each country. The benefits of this involvement were visible not only in terms of its direct effects on the flow of food, but also in the noticeable absence of collusive practices or panic hoarding in the private sector itself. Further, the sharp contrast between the behaviour of food prices in Kenya and Botswana during recent droughts strongly suggests

---

[112] See Drèze and Sen (1989: ch. 6), for further discussion. It must be stressed that the success of a strategy of cash support can depend crucially on its integration with other policy decisions, e.g. those related to food supply management and the role of private trade.

that the positive involvement of the public sector in food supply management is often a far more creative form of intervention than the imposition of negative restrictions on the operation of private trade.

Aside from influencing market prices, public distribution can also perform the role of generating income for the recipients (when food is distributed at subsidized prices). The effectiveness of this particular mechanism of income redistribution depends, *inter alia*, on the extent to which it is possible to ensure that vulnerable groups have preferential access to the public distribution system. The experiences reviewed in this chapter indicate that the scope for redistribution can vary a great deal, depending *inter alia* on the nature of local institutions and politics. The advantages of food distribution *vis-à-vis* other forms of income generation, such as employment provision, depend quite crucially (though not exclusively) on these considerations.

Diversification and employment

As a final observation, we should note the prominent role played by the diversification of economic activities (especially through wage employment), and by the acquisition of food on the market, in the survival strategies of vulnerable groups during crises. This observation is, in fact, one of the most common findings of the now voluminous literature on survival strategies in different parts of Africa.[113] Two of its implications are worth stressing here.

First, while current food security problems in Africa clearly originate in part from the stagnation or decline of food production in that continent (leading to major losses of income for the rural population), it does not follow that the reduction of famine vulnerability must necessarily take the form of reversing that historical trend. Diversification and exchange have been an important part of the economic opportunities of rural populations in Africa for a long time, and open up alternative avenues of action that also need to be considered.[114]

Second, the potential of employment provision (e.g. in the form of public works programmes) as a tool of entitlement protection in some parts of Africa may be far from negligible. The strategy of employment provision has a number of distinct advantages (notably making possible the use of 'self-selection' and also the provision of cash relief) which cannot be neglected. The fact that affected populations positively look for work in crisis situations suggests this as a natural form of intervention. The scope for employment-based famine prevention strategies in different parts of Africa deserves further investigation.

---

[113] For a review of this literature, see Drèze and Sen (1989: ch. 5).

[114] For an illuminating discussion of the historical role of economic diversification and market exchange in East Africa and the Sahel, see Pankhurst (1985, 1986). For similar observations in West Africa, see Hill (1986).

References

AGERE, S. T. (1986), 'Progress and Problems in the Health Care Delivery System', in Mandaza (1986).

AHMAD, S. E., DRÈZE, J. P., HILLS, J., and SEN, A. K. (eds.) (1991), *Social Security in Developing Countries* (Oxford: Oxford University Press).

AKONG'A, J., and DOWNING, T. (1987), 'Smallholder Vulnerability and Response to Drought', in Akong'a *et al.* (1987).

————— KONIJN, N. T., MUNGAI, D. N., MUTURI, H. R., and POTTER, H. L. (1987), 'The Effects of Climatic Variations on Agriculture in Central and Eastern Kenya', mimeo (IIASA, Laxenburg); reprinted from Parry, M. L., *et al.* (eds.), *The Impact of Climatic Variations on Agriculture* (Dordrecht: Reidel).

AMBLER, C. H. (1988), *Kenyan Communities in the Age of Imperialism: The Central Region in the Late Nineteenth Century* (New Haven, Conn.: Yale University Press).

ANYANGO, G. J., *et al.* (1989), 'drought Vulnerability in Central and Eastern Kenya', in Downing *et al.* (1989).

AUTIER, P., and D'ALTILIA, J. P. (1985), 'Bilan de 6 mois d'activité des équipes mobiles médico-nutritionnelles de médecins sans frontières', mimeo (Médecins Sans Frontières, Brussels).

BERG, A. (1973), *The Nutrition Factor* (Washington, DC: Brookings Institution).

BERNUS, E. (1986), 'Mobilité et flexibilité pastorales face à la sécheresse', Bulletin de liaison No. 8 (Paris: ORSTOM).

BERTLIN, J. (1980), 'Adaptation and Response to Drought: Traditional Systems and the Impact of Change', a special study submitted in part fulfilment of the requirements for the M.Sc. in Agricultural Economics, Wye College, University of London.

BIELLIK, R. J., and HENDERSON, P. L. (1981), 'Mortality, Nutritional Status, and Diet during the Famine in Karamoja, Uganda, 1980', *Lancet*, 12 Dec.

BINNS, C. W. (1976), 'Famine and the Diet of the Enga', *Papua New Guinea Medical Journal*, 19/4.

BORTON, J. (1984), 'Disaster Preparedness and Response in Botswana', report prepared for the Ford Foundation by the Relief and Development Institute, London.

————(1986), 'Botswana Food Aid Management', paper presented at the WFP/ADB Conference on Food Aid for Development, Abijan, Sept.

————(1988), 'The 1984/85 Drought Relief Programme in Kenya: A Provisional Review', Discussion Paper No. 2 (London: Relief and Development Institute).

————(1989), 'Overview of the 1984/85 National Drought Relief Program', in Downing *et al.* (1989).

———— and CLAY, E. (1986), 'The African Food Crisis of 1982–1986', *Disasters*, 10.

Botswana Society (1979), *Symposium on Drought in Botswana* (Gaborone: Botswana Society).

BOWBRICK, P. (1986), 'The Causes of Famine: A Refutation of Professor Sen's Theory', *Food Policy*, 11.

BRATTON, M. (1986), 'Farmer Oganizations and Food Production in Zimbabwe', *World Development*, 14.

————(1987), 'Drought, Food and the Social Organization of Small Farmers in Zimbabwe', in Glantz (1987a).

BRENNAN, L., HEATHCOTE, R. L., and LUCAS, A. E. (1984), 'The Role of the Individual Administrator in Famine Relief: Three Case Studies', *Disasters*, 8.

BROWN, V. W., BROWN, E. P., ECKERSON, D., GILMORE, J., and SWARTZENDURBER, H. D. (1986), 'Evaluation of the African Emergency Food Assistance Program 1984–1985: Chad', report submitted to USAID, Washington, DC.

BRYCESON, D. (1981*a*), 'Colonial Famine Responses: The Bagamoyo District of Tanganyika, 1920–61', *Food Policy*, 6.

——(1981*b*), 'Changes in Peasant Food Production and Food Supply in Relation to the Historical Development of Commodity Production in Pre-colonial and Colonial Tanganyika', *Journal of Peasant Studies*, 7.

BRYSON, J. C. (1986), 'Case Study: The Lesotho Food for Work Programme of Catholic Relief Services', paper presented at the WFP/ADB Conference on Food Aid for Development, Abijan, Sept.

CABRAL, N. E. (1980), *Le Moulin et le pilon: Les Îles du Cap Vert* (Paris: L'Harmattan).

CALDWELL, J. C. (1977), 'Demographic Aspects of Drought: An Examination of the African Drought of 1970–74', in Dalby, D., *et al.* (eds.), *Drought in Africa*, ii (London: International Africa Institute).

——(1984), 'Desertification: Demographic Evidence, 1973–1983', Occasional Paper No. 37 (Development Studies Centre, Australian National University).

——and CALDWELL, P. (1987), 'Famine in Africa', paper presented at a IUSSP Seminar on Mortality and Society in Sub-Saharan Africa, Iford, Yaoundé, Cameroon, Oct.

CAMPBELL, D. J. (1984), 'Response to Drought among Farmers and Herders in Southern Kajiado District, Kenya', *Human Ecology*, 12.

CARREIRA, A. (1982), *The People of the Cape Verde Islands: Exploitation and Emigration* (London: Hurst & Co).

CATHIE, J., and HERRMANN, R. (1988), 'The Southern African Customs Union, Cereal Price Policy in South Africa, and Food Security in Botswana', *Journal of Development Studies*, 24.

CHASTANET, M. (1983), 'Les Crises de subsistances dans les villages Soninke du Cercle de Bakel de 1858 à 1945', *Cahiers d'études africaines*, 89–90, 23/1–2.

CHERNICHOVSKY, D., LUCAS, R. E. B., and MUELLER, E. (1985), 'The Household Economy of Rural Botswana: An African Case', World Bank Staff Working Paper No. 715 (World Bank, Washington, DC).

CILSS (1976), 'Aperçu sur la situation aux Îles du Cap Vert du fait de la continuation de la sécheresse', DPP/5-10-1976 (Comité permanent interétats de lutte contre la sécheresse dans le Sahel).

——(1986), *La Prévision de situations alimentaires critiques dans les pays du Sahel: Systèmes et moyens d'alerte précoce* (Paris: OECD).

COHEN, J., and LEWIS, D. (1987), 'Role of Government in Combatting Food Shortages: Lessons from Kenya 1984–85', in Glantz (1987*a*).

CORBETT, J. (1987), 'Drought and the Threat of Famine in Kenya in 1984', mimeo (Oxford: Food Studies Group).

CORNIA, G., JOLLY, R., and STEWART, F. (eds.) (1987), *Adjustment with a Human Face* (Oxford: Oxford University Press).

Courier (1988), 'Country Report: Cape Verde', *Courier*, 107.

DAVIDSON, B. (1977), 'Mass Mobilization for National Reconstruction in the Cape Verde Islands', *Economic Geography*, 53/4.

DAVIES, R., and SANDERS, D. (1987a), 'Stabilisation Policies and the Effects on Child Health in Zimbabwe', *Review of African Political Economy*, 38.

——— (1987b), 'Adjustment Policies and the Welfare of Children: Zimbabwe, 1980–1985', in Cornia *et al*. (1987), vol. ii.

DELOITTE, HASKINS, and SELLS (1986), 'Final Monitoring Report on the Drought Emergency Relief Program for USAID Mission to Kenya', report prepared for USAID.

DEVEREUX, S. (1988), 'Entitlements, Availability and Famine: A Revisionist View of Wollo, 1972–1974', *Food Policy*, 13.

DE VILLE DE GOYET, C. (1978), 'Disaster Relief in the Sahel: Letter to the Editor', *Disasters*, 2.

DE WAAL, A. (1987), 'Famine That Kills', mimeo (London: Save the Children Fund UK); to be published as a monograph by Oxford University Press.

——— (1988a), 'Famine Early Warning Systems and the Use of Socio-economic Data', *Disasters*, 12.

——— (1988b), 'A Re-assessment of Entitlement Theory in the Light of Recent Famines in Africa', Ld'A-QEH Development Studies Working Paper No. 4 (Oxford: Queen Elizabeth House).

DODGE, C. P., and ALNWICK, D. (1986), 'Karamoja: A Catastrophe Contained', *Disasters*, 10.

DONELAN, A. (1983), 'Zimbabwe: A Study of the New Nation's Attempts to Progress since Independence, with Particular Reference to Health and Nutrition', report submitted to the University of London in partial fulfilment of the requirements for the Diploma in Food Resources related to Community Development.

DOWNING, J., BERRY, L., DOWNING, L., DOWNING, T., and FORD, R. (1987), 'Drought and Famine in Africa, 1981–1986: The U.S. Response', report prepared for USAID, Settlement and Resources Systems Analysis, Clark University/Institute for Development Anthropology.

DOWNING, T. (1986), 'Smallholder Drought Coping Strategies in Central and Eastern Kenya', paper presented to the Annual Meeting of the Association of American Geographers, Minneapolis, 3–7 May.

——— (1988), 'Climatic Variability and Food Security among Smallholder Agriculturalists in Six Districts of Central and Eastern Kenya', unpublished Ph.D. dissertation, Clark University, Worcester, Mass.

——— AKONG'A, J., MUNGAI, D. N., MUTURI, H. R., and POTTER, H. L. (1987), 'Introduction to the Kenya Case Study', in Akong'a *et al*. (1987).

——— GITU, K., and KAMAU, C. (1989), *Coping with Drought in Kenya: National and Local Strategies* (Boulder, Colo.: Lynne Rienner).

DRÈZE, J. P. (1988), 'Famine Prevention in India', Discussion Paper No. 3 (Development Economics Research Programme, London School of Economics); published as ch. 1 above.

——— and SEN, A. K. (1988), 'Public Action for Social Security', paper presented at a Workshop on Social Security in Developing Countries held at the London School of Economics, July 1988; published in Ahmad *et al*. (1991).

——— (1989), *Hunger and Public Action* (Oxford: Oxford University Press).

DYSON, T. (1988), 'The Population History of Berar since 1881 and its Potential Wider Significance', mimeo (Department of Population Studies, London School of Economics).

The Economist (1985), 'Where Africans Feed Themselves', *The Economist*, 12 Jan.

Economist Intelligence Unit (1983), 'Quarterly Economic Review of Angola, Guinea Bissau, Cape Verde, Sao Tome, Principe: Annual Supplement 1983', The Economist Intelligence Unit.

——(1984), 'Quarterly Economic Review of Angola, Guinea Bissau, Cape Verde, Sao Tome, Principe: Annual Supplement 1984', The Economist Intelligence Unit.

EICHER, C. K. (1986), 'Food Security Research Priorities in Sub-Saharan Africa', keynote address presented at the OAU/STRC/SAFGRAD International Drought Symposium held at the Kenyatta International Center, Nairobi, May.

——(1988), 'Food Security Battles in Sub-Saharan Africa', paper presented at the VIIth World Congress for Rural Sociology, Bologna, 25 June–2 July.

——and STAATZ, J. M. (1986), 'Food Security Policy in Sub-Saharan Africa', in Maunder, A., and Renborg, U. (eds.), *Agriculture in a Turbulent World Economy* (London: Gower).

FIREBRACE, J., and HOLLAND, S. (1984), *Never Kneel Down: Drought, Development and Liberation in Eritrea* (London: Spokesman).

Food and Agriculture Organization (1984), *Assessment of the Agriculture, Food Supply and Livestock Situation: Kenya* (Rome: Office for Special Relief Operations, FAO).

——(1986), *African Agriculture: The Next 25 Years* (Rome: FAO).

FOEGE, W. H. (1971), 'Famine, Infections and Epidemics', in Blix, G., *et al.* (eds.), *Famine: Nutrition and Relief Operations* (Uppsala: Swedish Nutrition Foundation).

FREEMAN, P. H., GREEN, V. E., HICKOK, R. B., MORAN, E. F., and WHITAKER, M. D. (1978), 'Cape Verde: Assessment of the Agricultural Sector', report CR-A-219A submitted to the US Agency for International Development, General Research Corporation, McLean, Va.

GAIDZANWA, R. (1986), 'Drought and the Food Crisis in Zimbabwe', in Lawrence, P. (ed.), *World Recession and the Food Crisis in Africa* (London: James Currey).

GLANTZ, M. (1987a), *Drought and Hunger in Africa: Denying Famine a Future* (Cambridge: Cambridge University Press).

——(1987b), 'Drought and Economic Development in Sub-Saharan Africa', in Glantz (1987a).

GOOCH, T., and MACDONALD, J. (1981a), *Evaluation of 1979/80 Drought Relief Programme* (Republic of Botswana: Ministry of Finance and Development Planning).

————(1981b), *Evaluation of 1979/80 Drought Relief Programme: Synopsis* (Republic of Botswana: Ministry of Finance and Development Planning).

Government of Botswana (1980), *A Human Drought Relief Programme for Botswana* (Gaborone: Ministry of Local Government and Lands).

——(1985a), *The Drought Situation in Botswana* (Gaborone: Ministry of Finance and Development Planning).

——(1985b), *Report on the National Food Strategy* (Gaborone: Ministry of Finance and Development Planning).

——(1987), 'The Drought Situation in Botswana, March 1987, and Estimated Requirements for Relief and Recovery Measures', *aide-mémoire*, Ministry of Finance and Development Planning, Gaborone.

——(1988), 'The Drought Recovery Situation in Botswana, March 1988, and Estimated Requirements for Relief and Recovery Measures', *aide-mémoire*, Ministry of Finance and Development Planning, Gaborone.

Government of Kenya (1985), 'CBS/NES Survey of Drought Responses, Preliminary Findings', mimeo (National Environment Secretariat, Nairobi).

Government of Zimbabwe (1983), 'Development Policies and Programmes for Food and Nutrition in Zimbabwe', mimeo (Ministry of Finance, Economic Planning and Development, Harare).

——(1984), 'Planning for Equity in Health: A Sectoral Review and Policy Statement', mimeo (Ministry of Health, Harare).

——(1986a), 'Zimbabwe's Experience in Dealing with Drought 1982 to 1984', mimeo (Ministry of Labour, Manpower Planning and Social Welfare, Harare).

——(1986b), 'Memorandum on Drought Relief 1986', mimeo (Ministry of Labour, Manpower Planning and Social Welfare, Harare).

GRANNELL, T. F. (1986), 'Ethiopia: Food-for-Work for the Rehabilitation of Forest, Grazing and Agricultural Lands in Ethiopia', paper presented at the WFP/ADB Conference on Food Aid for Development, Abijan, Sept.

HALL, E. (1973), 'Diary of the Drought', Oxfam News, July.

HAY, R. (1988), 'Famine Incomes and Employment: Has Botswana Anything to Teach Africa?', World Development, 16.

——BURKE, S., and DAKO, D. Y. (1986), 'A Socio-economic Assessment of Drought Relief in Botswana', report prepared by UNICEF/UNDP/WHO for the Inter-ministerial Drought Committee, Government of Botswana, Gaborone.

Herald (1983), 'Hungry Buhera Women Search for Husbands', Herald, 16 Mar.

HERLEHY, T. J. (1984), 'Historical Dimensions of the Food Crisis in Africa: Surviving Famines along the Kenya Coast 1880–1980', Working Paper No. 87 (African Studies Center, Boston University).

HILL, A. (1987), 'Demographic Responses to Food Shortages in the Sahel', paper presented at the Expert Consultation on Population and Agricultural and Rural Development, FAO, Rome, June–July.

HILL, P. (1986), Development Economics on Trial: The Anthropological Case for a Prosecution (Cambridge: Cambridge University Press).

HOLLAND, P. (1987), 'Famine Responses in Colonial Zimbabwe: 1912–1947', mimeo (London School of Economics).

HOLM, J. D., and COHEN, M. S. (1988), 'Enhancing Equity in the Midst of Drought: The Botswana Approach', Ceres, 114.

——and MORGAN, R. (1985), 'Coping with Drought in Botswana: An African Success', Journal of Modern African Studies, 23.

HOLT, J. (1983), 'Ethiopia: Food for Work or Food for Relief', Food Policy, 8.

HUGO, G. J. (1984), 'The Demographic Impact of Famine: A Review', in Currey, B., and Hugo, G. (eds.), Famine as a Geographical Phenomenon (Dordrecht: Reidel).

ILIFFE, J. (1987), The African Poor: A History (Cambridge: Cambridge University Press).

JANSSON, K., HARRIS, M., and PENROSE, A. (1987), The Ethiopian Famine (London: Zed).

JACQUEMIN, J. C. (1985), 'Politiques de stabilisation par les investissements publics', unpublished Ph.D. thesis, Facultés des sciences économiques et sociales, University of Namur, Belgium.

KAMAU, C. M., GITAU, M., WAINAINA, M., ANYANGO, G. J., and DOWNING, T. (1989), 'Case Studies of Drought Impacts and Responses in Central and Eastern Kenya', in Downing et al. (1989).

KATES, R. W. (1981), 'Drought Impact in the Sahelian–Sudanic Zone of West Africa: A Comparative Analysis of 1910–1915 and 1968–1974', Environment and Development Background Paper No. 2 (Center for Technology IDS, Clark University).

——CHEN, R. S., DOWNING, T. E., KASPERSON, J. X., MESSER, E., and MILLMAN, S. R. (1988), 'The Hunger Report 1988' (Providence, RI: The Alan Shawn Feinstein World Hunger Program, Brown University).

KELLY, C. (1987), 'The Situation in Burkina Faso', Disasters, 11.

KILJUNEN, K. (ed.) (1984), Kampuchea: Decade of the Genocide (London: Zed).

KRISHNAMACHARI, K. A. V. R., RAO, N. P., and RAO, K. V. (1974), 'Food and Nutritional Situation in the Drought-Affected Areas of Maharashtra: A Survey and Recommendations', Indian Journal of Nutrition and Dietetics, 11.

KULA, E. (1989), 'Politics, Economics, Agriculture and Famines', Food Policy, 14.

LEGAL, P. Y. (1984), 'Alimentation et énergie dans le développement rural au Cabo Verde', Série énergie, alimentation et développement, No. 2 (Paris: Centre international de recherche sur l'environnement et le développement, école des hautes études en sciences sociales).

LEYS, R. (1986), 'Drought and Drought Relief in Southern Zimbabwe', in Lawrence, P. (ed.), World Recession and the Food Crisis in Africa (London: James Currey).

LOEWENSON, R. (1984), 'The Health Status of Labour Communities in Zimbabwe: An Argument for Equity', dissertation presented for the M.Sc. Degree in Community Health in Developing Countries, University of London.

——(1986), 'Farm Labour in Zimbabwe: A Comparative Study in Health Status', Health Policy and Planning, 1/1.

——and SANDERS, D. (1988), 'The Political Economy of Health and Nutrition', in Stoneman, C. (ed.), Zimbabwe's Prospects: Issues of Race, Class, State and Capital in Southern Africa (London: Macmillan).

McCANN, J. (1987), 'The Social Impact of Drought in Ethiopia: Oxen, Households, and Some Implications for Rehabilitation', in Glantz (1987a).

McLEAN, W. (1988), 'Intervention Systems in Food Crises: The Role of International Agencies', paper presented at the Seventh International Congress for Rural Sociology, Bologna, Italy, June.

MAGANDA, B. F. (1989), 'Surveys and Activities of the Central Bureau of Statistics Related to Food Monitoring', in Downing et al. (1989).

MANDAZA, I. (ed.) (1986), Zimbabwe: The Political Economy of Transition 1980–1986 (Dakar: CODESRIA).

MASON, J. B., HAAGA, J. G., MARKS, G., QUINN, V., TEST, K., and MARIBE, T. (1985), 'Using Agricultural Data for Timely Warning to Prevent the Effects of Drought on Child Nutrition: An Analysis of Historical Data from Botswana', mimeo (Cornell University Agricultural Experiment Station).

MATIZA, T., ZINYAMA, L. M., and CAMPBELL, D. J. (1988), 'Household Strategies for Coping with Food Insecurity in Low Rainfall Areas of Zimbabwe', paper presented at the Fourth Annual Conference on Food Security Research in Southern Africa, Oct.–Nov., Harare, Zimbabwe.

MBITHI, P., and WISNER, B. (1972), Drought and Famine in Kenya: Magnitude and Attempted Solutions (Nairobi: Institute for Development Studies).

MEINTEL, D. (1983), 'Cape Verde: Survival without Self-Sufficiency', in Cohen, R. (ed.), African Islands and Enclaves (Beverley Hills: Sage).

——(1984), Race, Culture and Portuguese Colonialism in Cabo Verde, Foreign and

Comparative Studies, African Series 41 (Maxwell School of Citizenship and Public Affairs, Syracuse University).

MITTER, S. (1988), 'Managing the Drought Crisis: The Zimbabwe Experience, 1982–83', undergraduate essay, Harvard University.

MORAN, E. (1982), 'The Evolution of Cape Verde's Agriculture', *African Economic History*, 11.

MORGAN, R. (1985), 'The Development and Applications of a Drought Early Warning System in Botswana', *Disasters*, 9.

—— (1986), 'From Drought Relief to Post-Disaster Recovery: The Case of Botswana', *Disasters*, 10.

—— (1988), 'Social Welfare Policies and Programmes and the Reduction of Household Vulnerability in the Post-Independence SADCC States of Southern Africa', paper presented at a Workshop on Social Security in Developing Countries held at the London School of Economics, 4–5 July; in Ahmad *et al.* (1991).

Moto (1983), 'Facing the Drought', *Moto* Magazine, Harare.

MWALUKO, E. P. (1962), 'Famine Relief in the Central Province of Tanganyika, 1961', *Tropical Agriculture*, 39/3.

MWENDWA, H. (1989), 'Agricultural and Livestock Monitoring Using Aerial Photography', in Downing *et al.* (1989).

NELSON, H. (1983), 'Report on the Situation in Tigray', mimeo (Manchester University).

NEUMANN, C. G., *et al.* (1989), 'Impact of the 1984 Drought on Food Intake, Nutritional Status and Household Response in Embu District', in Downing, T. E., *et al.* (1989), *Coping with Drought in Kenya: National and Local Strategies*.

O'GRADA, C. (1988), 'For Irishmen to Forget? Recent Research on the Great Irish Famine', Working Paper No. WP88/7 (Dublin: Centre for Economic Research, University College).

O'LEARY, M. (1980), 'Response to Drought in Kitui District, Kenya', *Disasters*, 4.

OLSEN, W. (1984), 'Kenya's Dual Grain Market: The Effects of State Intervention', mimeo (Oxford: Food Studies Group).

OTTEN, M. W. (1986), 'Nutritional and Mortality Aspects of the 1985 Famine in North Central Ethiopia', mimeo (Atlanta, Ga. Centre for Disease Control).

OUGHTON, E. (1982), 'The Maharashtra Droughts of 1970–73: An Analysis of Scarcity', *Oxford Bulletin of Economics and Statistics*, 44.

OXFAM (1972, 1973), Unpublished field reports.

PANKHURST, A. (1985), 'Social Consequences of Drought and Famine: An Anthropological Approach to Selected African Case Studies', unpublished MA dissertation, Department of Social Anthropology, University of Manchester.

—— (1986), 'Social Dimensions of Famine in Ethiopia: Exchange, Migration and Integration', paper presented to the 9th International Conference of Ethiopian Studies, Moscow.

PARK, P., and JACKSON, T. (1985), *Lands of Plenty, Lands of Scarcity: Agricultural Policy and Peasant Farmers in Zimbabwe and Tanzania* (Oxford: OXFAM).

PEBERDY, M. (1985), *Tigray: Ethiopia's Untold Story* (London: Relief Society of Tigray UK Support Committee).

QUINN, V., COHEN, M., MASON, J., and KGOSIDINTSI, B. N. (1987), 'Crisis Proofing the Economy: The Response of Botswana to Economic Recession and Drought', in Cornia *et al.* (1987).

RAM, N. (1986), 'An Independent Press and Anti-hunger Strategies', paper presented at a Conference on Food Strategies held at the World Institute for Development Economics Research, Helsinki, 21–5 July; published in *The Political Economy of Hunger*, vol. I,

RAMALINGASWAMI, V., DEO, M. G., GULERIA, J. S., MALHOTRA, K. K., SOOD, S. K., OM PRAKASH, and SINHA, R. V. N. (1971), 'Studies of the Bihar Famine of 1966–67', paper presented at a Symposium of the Swedish Nutrition Foundation.

RANGASAMI, A. (1985), '"Failure of Exchange Entitlements" Theory of Famine: A Response', *Economic and Political Weekly*, 20.

RAY, R. T. (1984), 'Drought Assessment: Kenya', mimeo (USAID/Kenya, Nairobi).

REDDY, S. (1988), 'An Independent Press Working Against Famine: The Nigerian Experience', *Journal of Modern African Studies*, 26.

Relief and Development Institute (1985), 'Strengthening Disaster Preparedness in Six African Countries', report prepared for the Ford Foundation, Relief and Development Institute, London.

ROHRBACH, D. D. (1988), 'The Growth of Smallholder Maize Production in Zimbabwe (1979–1985): Implications for Food Security', in Rukuni, M., and Bernsten, R. H. (eds.), *Southern Africa: Food Security Policy Options* (Harare: University of Zimbabwe).

ROTBERG, R. I., and RABB, T. K. (eds.) (1983), *Hunger and History: The Impact of Changing Food Production and Consumption Patterns on Society* (Cambridge: Cambridge University Press).

RUKUNI, M. (1988), 'The Evolution of Smallholder Irrigation Policy in Zimbabwe: 1982–1986', *Irrigation and Drainage Systems*, 2.

——and EICHER, C. K. (eds.) (1987), *Food Security for Southern Africa* (Harare: UZ/MSU Food Security Project, University of Zimbabwe).

SANDERS, D. (1982), 'Nutrition and the Use of Food as a Weapon in Zimbabwe and Southern Africa', *International Journal of Health Services*, 12/2.

——and DAVIES, R. (1988), 'Economic Adjustment and Current Trends in Child Survival: The Case of Zimbabwe', *Health Policy and Planning*, 3.

SANDFORD, S. (1977), 'Dealing with Drought and Livestock in Botswana', report to the Government of Botswana, Gaborone.

SEAMAN, J. (1987), 'Famine Mortality in Ethiopia and Sudan', paper presented at a IUSSP seminar on Mortality and Society in Sub-Saharan Africa, Yaoundé, Cameroon, Oct.

SEN, A. K. (1981), *Poverty and Famines* (Oxford: Oxford University Press).

——(1982), 'How is India Doing', *New York Review of Books*, 29.

SMOUT, T. C. (1978), 'Famine and Famine-Relief in Scotland', in Cullen, L. M., and Smout, T. C. (eds.), *Comparative Aspects of Scottish and Irish Economic History 1600–1900* (Edinburgh: Donald).

SOROKIN, P. A. (1942), *Man and Society in Calamity: The Effects of War, Revolution, Famine and Pestilence upon Human Mind, Behaviour, Social Organization and Cultural Life* (New York: E. P. Dutton & Co.).

SPERLING, L. (1987a), 'Food Acquisition during the African Drought of 1983–1984: A Study of Kenyan Herders', *Disasters*, 11.

——(1987b), 'Wage Employment among Samburu Pastoralists of Northcentral Kenya', *Research in Economic Anthropology*, 9.

SRAFFA, P. (ed.) (1952), *The Works and Correspondence of David Ricardo* (Cambridge: Cambridge University Press).

STEELE, I. (1985), 'Mali Battles Drought', *Africa Emergency Report*, Apr.–May.

STEIN, Z., SUSSER, M., SAERGER, G., and MAROLLA, F. (1975), *Famine and Human Development: The Dutch Hunger Winter of 1944/45* (New York: Oxford University Press).

SWAMINATHAN, M. C., RAO, K. V., and RAO, D. H. (1969), 'Food and Nutrition Situation in the Drought-Affected Areas of Bihar', *Journal of Nutrition and Dietetics*, 6.

SWANBERG, K. G., and HOGAN, E. (1981), 'Implications of the Drought Syndrome for Agricultural Planning in East Africa: The Case of Tanzania', Discussion Paper 120: 1–49 (Cambridge, Mass.: Harvard Institute for International Development).

SWIFT, J. (1985), 'Planning against Drought and Famine in Turkana, Northern Kenya', mimeo (Institute of Development Studies, University of Sussex).

TABOR, S. (1983), 'Drought Relief and Information Management: Coping Intelligently with Disaster', mimeo (Family Health Division, Ministry of Health, Government of Botswana).

TAGWIREYI, J. (1988), 'Experiences in Increasing Food Access and Nutrition in Zimbabwe', paper presented at the Fourth Annual Conference on Food Security Research in Southern Africa, Oct.–Nov., Harare, Zimbabwe.

The Times (1985), 'Harare Health Drive Cuts Infant Mortality', *The Times*, 4 Nov.

TORDOFF, W. (1988), 'Local Administration in Botswana', *Public Administration and Development*, 8.

UNDRO (1986), *UNDRO in Africa 1984–85* (Geneva: Office of the United Nations Disaster Relief Co-ordinator).

UNICEF (1987), *The State of the World's Children 1987* (Oxford: Oxford University Press).

——(1988), *The State of the World's Children 1988* (Oxford: Oxford University Press).

USAID (1982), 'Cape Verde: Food for Development Program', mimeo (Washington, DC: US Agency for International Development).

——(1983), 'U.S. Aid to Zimbabwe: An Evaluation', AID Program Evaluation Report No. 9 (Washington, DC: US Agency for International Development).

VALAORAS, V. G. (1946), 'Some Effects of Famine on the Population of Greece', *Milbank Memorial Fund Quarterly Bulletin*, 24.

VAN APPELDOORN, G. J. (1981), *Perspectives on Drought and Famine in Nigeria* (London: Allen & Unwin).

VAN BINSBERGEN, A. (1986), 'Cape Verde: Food Aid Resource Planning in Support of the National Food Strategy', paper presented at a WFP/ADB Seminar on Food Aid in Sub-Saharan Africa, Abijan, Sept.

VAUGHAN, M. (1987), *The Story of an African Famine: Hunger, Gender and Politics in Malawi* (Cambridge: Cambridge University Press).

WATERSON, T., and SANDERS, D. (1984), 'Zimbabwe: Health Care since Independence', *Lancet*, 18 Feb.

WEINER, D. (1987), 'Agricultural Transformation in Zimbabwe: Lessons for a Liberated South Africa', paper presented at the Annual Meeting of the Association of American Geographers, Portland, Oregon, 23–6 Apr.

——(1988), 'Land and Agricultural Development', in Stoneman, C. (ed.), *Zimbabwe's*

Prospects: Issues of Race, Class, State and Capital in Southern Africa (London: Macmillan).

——and MOYO, S. (1988), 'Wage Labor, Environment and Peasant Agriculture', mimeo (Harare: Zimbabwe Institute of Development Studies); in *Journal of African Studies*.

WILL, P. E. (1980), *Bureaucratie et famine en Chine au 18ᵉ siècle* (Paris: Mouton).

WISNER, B. G. (1977), 'The Human Ecology of Drought in Eastern Kenya', Ph.D. dissertation, Clark University, Worcester, Mass.

WOOD, D. H., BARON, A., and BROWN, V. W. (1986), *An Evaluation of the Emergency Food Assistance Program: Synthesis Report* (Washington, DC: USAID).

World Bank (1983), *Zimbabwe: Population, Health and Nutrition Sector Review* (Washington, DC: World Bank).

World Food Programme (1986*a*), 'Lessons Learned from the African Food Crisis: Evaluation of the WFP Emergency Response (Note by the Executive Director)', WFP/CFA: 22/7 (Rome: World Food Programme).

——(1986*b*), 'Interim Evaluation Summary Report on Project Ethiopia 2488', WFP/CFA: 21/14-A (WPME) Add. 1 (Rome: World Food Programme).

——(1986*c*), 'Aide alimentaire d'urgence fournie à la suite de la sécheresse 1984–85 au Niger', mimeo (Niamey: World Food Programme).

WRIGLEY, C. (1976), 'Changes in East African Society', in Low, D. A. and Smith, A. (eds.) (1976), *History of East Africa* (Oxford: Oxford University Press).

YAO, F. K., and KONE, H. (1986), 'The African Drought Reported by Six West African Newspapers', Discussion Paper No. 14 (African Studies Center, Boston University).

ZINYAMA, L. M., CAMPBELL, D., and MATIZA, T. (1987), 'Traditional Household Strategies to Cope with Food Insecurity in the SADCC Region', paper presented at the Third Annual Conference on Food Security Research in Southern Africa, 2–5 Nov., Harare.

INDEX OF NAMES

INDEX OF SUBJECTS

Note: Most references are to food e.g. *crisis* as a sub-entry refers to a *food crisis*; and *production* to *food production*

SOAS LIBRARY